Tucson

Tucson

A History of the Old Pueblo from the 1854 Gadsden Purchase

Second Edition

DAVID DEVINE

McFarland & Company, Inc., Publishers
Jefferson, North Carolina

LIBRARY OF CONGRESS CATALOGING-IN-PUBLICATION DATA

Names: Devine, David, 1949– author
Title: Tucson : a history of the old Pueblo from the 1854 Gadsden purchase / David Devine.
Description: Second edition. | Jefferson, North Carolina : McFarland & Company, Inc., Publishers, 2025 | Includes bibliographical references and index.
Identifiers: LCCN 2025019908 | ISBN 9781476695198 paperback ∞
 ISBN 9781476656052 ebook
Subjects: LCSH: Tucson (Ariz.)—History | BISAC: HISTORY / United States / State & Local / Southwest (AZ, NM, OK, TX)
Classification: LCC F819.T957 D48 2025 | DDC 979.1/776—dc23/eng/20250522
LC record available at https://lccn.loc.gov/2025019908

ISBN (print) 978-1-4766-9519-8
ISBN (ebook) 978-1-4766-5605-2

© 2025 David Devine. All rights reserved

No part of this book may be reproduced or transmitted in any form or by any means, electronic or mechanical, including photocopying or recording, or by any information storage and retrieval system, without permission in writing from the publisher.

Front cover image of Tucson, Arizona, courtesy of Tom Bergin.

Printed in the United States of America

McFarland & Company, Inc., Publishers
Box 611, Jefferson, North Carolina 28640
www.mcfarlandpub.com

For all those who
tirelessly and unselfishly
tried to save some
of Tucson's rich heritage

Table of Contents

Preface	1
One • Acquisition and Railroad Jubilation Followed by Economic Recession, 1854–1890	5
Two • A Diverse and Often Divided Community, 1890–1900	20
Three • Community Advancements and Tossing the Mayor, 1900–1910	36
Four • Statehood, the "White Plague," and a Serious Census Setback, 1910–1922	52
Five • Aviation and Athletic Accomplishments, 1920–1930	69
Six • Tough Times, Discrimination, and More Subways, 1930–1940	85
Seven • War, Growth, and Entertainment, 1940–1950	100
Eight • Ever Increasing Expansion, 1950–1960	114
Nine • Crime, Downtown Decline, and Urban Highways, 1960–1970	131
Ten • Social Change Mixed with Political Turmoil, 1970–1980	149
Eleven • TCE/AIDS/TEP, 1980–1990	175
Twelve • Sports Highlights and Water Lowlights, 1990–2000	200
Thirteen • Economic Decline but Transportation Improvements, 2000–2010	225
Fourteen • Shootings, Squabbles, and Much Slower Population Growth, 2010–2019	250
Fifteen • Approaching Tucson's August 20, 2025, Semiquincentennial, 2020–2024	275
Chapter Notes	299
Bibliography	325
Index	331

Preface

TEN YEARS AGO I WROTE THE FIRST EDITION of this book to spell out in a broad brushstroke fashion the who, what, when, where, and why of Tucson's history since the 1854 Gadsden Purchase brought Southern Arizona into the United States. This new version revises and updates the information contained in that book by including issues such as abortion, suffrage, and the 1918 Spanish influenza epidemic that weren't contained in the first edition. Additionally, some events and personalities from the past have been added along with extensive material on the years 2015 to 2024. This book also serves as a recognition of the community's semiquincentennial, the 250th anniversary of the August 20, 1775, date when the location of the Tucson presidio was initially selected.

The first book's preface included a brief review of the almost 50 years I've lived in Tucson and included a summary of my education at the University of Arizona, the local jobs I've held as well as my political involvement and other factors that influence how I perceive things and write about them. That book was mostly a decade-by-decade account from the late 1800s up until 2014, and its primary goal was to "trace some of the people and trends important in local history, hoping to provide the basis for more informed predictions about the community's near-term future."[1] This update hopefully will continue doing that.

Back in 2015, I defined Tucson as "a large college town with a major military base onto which a retirement community has been grafted."[2] In driving around much of the urbanized area in the spring of 2024, that split personality remained obvious. As a longtime midtown resident, I live with the convenience, clutter, culture, and sometime chaos of the central city. It amazes me how the suburbs are so dissimilar. Where the center of town has architectural diversity, the outlying areas display conformity. Where there is some charm and tradition in Tucson's older neighborhoods, the suburbs look like cookie-cutter replicas of Anywhere, USA.

Another difference between the central city and the suburbs is in their population makeups. According to the latest figures from the U.S. Census Bureau, the largest ethnic population of the city of Tucson is Hispanic at 44.8 percent. The suburban areas' percentages are much lower: Green Valley (5.4%), Catalina foothills (12.2%), Oro Valley (14.4%), Vail (22.6%), and Marana (28.3%). Only Sahuarita (39.2%) approaches Tucson's Hispanic percentage.[3]

Included in the preface to the original book was a series of questions. Ten years on, some of them have been answered, at least partially.

- Then: "Why do civic leaders and the general public seem to believe transportation is a higher priority than education?" Now: By their voting decisions, most people in Pima County continue to value transportation above education, and I believe that is one important reason the area's population growth basically stagnated following the 2008 national recession. As Tucson's economic leaders have repeatedly pointed out across the decades: "Businesses considering moving to Tucson place a high priority on the quality of a city's educational system," and if they don't find it, they may not come to town.[4]
- Then: "Was there ever an effort to restrict Tucson's sprawling character?" Now: There was an attempt in the 1970s that failed. The geographic expansion caused by sprawl has somewhat subsided in the last 15 years, however, because of two unusual occurrences—downtown and University area housing expansion along with a slower population growth rate. Since 2010, the number of people in Pima County went from about 980,300 to an estimated 1.06 million in 2023.[5] That is an annual growth rate of a little more than 6,000 a year, or approximately 0.6 percent. By traditional Tucson standards, that rate is extremely low and isn't all that much greater than the natural rate of growth calculated as births minus deaths. It is also considerably lower than the state of Arizona's population growth rate during the same period, but it is about equal to the national rate.[6] In other words, even though new homes are being built at a pace of a few thousand a year, mostly on the outskirts, Tucson isn't growing in population like it once did.
- Then: "Will the UA football team ever play in the Rose Bowl game?" Now: The University of Arizona will never play in the January 1st Rose Bowl game as it was traditionally staged between the winners of the Big Ten and Pac-10/12 conferences. The game is now part of the College Football Playoff system and thus has no conference affiliation. In addition, Arizona has joined the Big 12 conference.
- Then: How will the landlocked University of Arizona deal with its plans to increase enrollment to almost 50,000 students? Now: To house a growing enrollment, the UA relied on the private sector to build massive residential projects just west of campus as well as in the historic Fourth Avenue area.
- Then: "What are those large bodies of water in the middle of nowhere out by the Arizona–Sonora Desert Museum?" Now: They are Central Arizona Project recharge basins that resulted from the 1995 voter approval of the Water Consumer Protection Act and have been Tucson's lifeline to a somewhat secure water future.
- Then: "Why is Green Valley, with more than 21,000 people, not incorporated?" Now: Green Valley has about 23,000 residents, Vail around

the same number, and the remainder of unincorporated Pima County another 310,000 or so people. As demonstrated once again in the 2023 unsuccessful Vail incorporation drive, if the voters of an unincorporated area aren't given incentives—such as reduced services from Pima County—to become a municipality, they probably aren't going to support incorporating themselves. If they did, it would mean raising their own taxes to maintain the same level of government service they are currently receiving, and that is not a likely prospect.

- Then: "How did Tucson end up in the second decade of the 21st century as one of the poorest major metropolitan areas in the United States?" Now: Poverty remains a major problem but one that doesn't get much public attention anymore. Instead, symptoms of poverty such as housing affordability, low wage rates, homelessness, and the cost of rides on public transportation have more attention placed on them.
- Then: "Why was so much animosity created when the Tucson Unified School District was forced to cancel (for a time) its Mexican American studies program?" Now: While Republican Tom Horne returned to being Arizona's Superintendent of Public Instruction in 2023 and vowed once again to oppose what he labelled ethnic studies and "ethnic chauvinism in our schools," it is highly unlikely Arizona's governor and attorney general, both Democrats, will assist him in his crusade.[7]

Another question that must now be asked concerns the long-held belief by Tucson and Pima County's political and business leaders that a bigger Tucson community would, of course, be a better one. Has that philosophy recently been discarded in favor of another idea? Is that "bigger is better" belief really in the area's rearview mirror since environmental and social issues are now the major focus in many local 21st century political races? That change by local historic standards from a community focused on population growth to one where other, non-growth-related issues predominate would be truly radical. But it may be inevitable given the hurdles of uncertain long-term water availability, immense educational challenges, rapidly rising housing prices, low wage levels, limited major economic sectors, and other factors that Tucson and urbanized Pima County face.

There are certainly some things that haven't changed since the publication of the earlier edition. This book would not have been possible without the assistance of several people. As always, my wife, Susie Morris, has been very supportive. Alice Bowman provided both excellent editing expertise as well as outstanding technical knowledge. Tom Bergin again designed the graphics. Plus, the librarians at the Arizona Historical Society and Pima County Public Library gave outstanding help. Unfortunately, some of the people who assisted with the first edition are no longer with us—Bill Bowman, Mary Canavan, Jim Ayres, and Stan Benjamin—and their assistance and support are missed.

The first edition of this book relied heavily on the stories contained in both the *Tucson Citizen* and *Arizona Daily Star* newspapers, and exclusively the *Star* after the *Citizen* ceased publication in 2009. The average Sunday paid circulation of the *Star* in 2010 was about 144,000.[8] Today the *Star*'s weekday circulation is around 43,500. One fallout of the drastic decline in circulation is a lower newspaper budget resulting in a noticeable lack of local news coverage in the last few years. That has made my information collection process more difficult and meant it was sometimes reliant on other sources.

There are a lot of figures and percentages in the new parts of this edition, and I'm hoping they allow a comparison to how things once were, either for the better or worse. Sometimes the definitions of words have changed—such as the federal government's definition of homelessness—and I've attempted to point those out in the endnotes. I've tried to avoid making mistakes, but undoubtedly there are some and for that I accept full responsibility.

In conclusion, ten years ago I wrote: "Tucson is at its best when it stays true to its own identity, history, traditions, and cultures. On the other hand, it is weakest when it tries to copy or mimic other communities." I also observed: "Tucson's story, in my opinion, is much less about projects and buildings than about people—their accomplishments, failings, hopes, and problems."[9] I still believe those things. Tucson's American story is really about the people who have resided near the Santa Cruz River since the 1854 Gadsden Purchase. It is a story that I believe is worth knowing, and I hope the reader of this updated edition agrees.

• ONE •

Acquisition and Railroad Jubilation Followed by Economic Recession, 1854–1890

A short stretch of downtown street bears the name "Ochoa." The narrow passageway runs eastward along the north side of the St. Augustine Cathedral and its new Bishop Kicanas Pastoral Center. Across Stone Avenue is the recently opened multistory Hampton Inn/Home2 Suites. The street ends not far from the former site of Tucson's first publicly owned schoolhouse. More than one mile to the south, an elementary school with a colorful banner proclaiming its 100 years of service also carries the name "Ochoa."

WATER—IT WAS THE FIRST NECESSITY MENTIONED when Colonel Don Hugo O'Conor of the Royal Spanish Army on August 20, 1775, certified that he had found a suitable site to which the existing presidio at Tubac could be relocated. He noted the new location's advantages: "the requisite conditions of water, pasture, and wood occur, as well as a perfect closing of the Apache frontier." Borrowing from a name given to the Native village at the base of a nearby rocky hill, he called the place: "San Agustín de Toixon."[1]

One hundred years later, water was still a major topic for the isolated community of a few thousand people. The *Arizona Citizen* newspaper reported on August 21, 1875: "the heaviest rain fell in Tucson we have ever observed within a few hours. Every street was a river.... The dry arroyos all around were booming with water."[2]

That, of course, was common summer monsoon weather. What wasn't typical were the four earthquakes—one literal and three figurative—that rocked the small settlement of Tucson during the 1880s. The end of the protracted Indian Wars, the arrival of the Southern Pacific Railroad, and an extended economic downturn all significantly shook the community. These events also symbolized the other dramatic changes that were occurring in Tucson, a remote outpost in the vast Sonoran desert.

It was an actual earthquake in 1887, estimated up to 8.1 on the Richter scale and centered some 150 miles away in Mexico, that actually moved Tucson.[3] Young wagon maker Fred Ronstadt wrote succinctly in his ledger of the event: "May 3 a strong tremor lasted more than a minute at 2:15 in the afternoon."[4] While more than 50 people reportedly died in Mexico, the damage in Tucson was considerably less.

The *Arizona Daily Citizen* newspaper[5] reported adobe and brick buildings cracking, plaster and crockery falling, and dozens of clocks across town stopping.

The assumption was quickly made that an earthquake hadn't affected Tucson in at least 300 years. "Perhaps it is Geronimo's bad spirit that is shaking up his old haunts in Apacheland," speculated the *Citizen* about the quake.[6]

Geronimo by that time had surrendered. The end of decades of conflict between some of the Southwest's Native Americans and its early European settlers had basically concluded in 1886. The killing and brutality on both sides was finally over but would not be forgotten. For years afterward, White men would recount stories of numerous Indian atrocities, while Native Americans recalled the 144 Apaches, mostly women and children, murdered north of Tucson at the infamous 1871 Camp Grant massacre.

It was 15 years after that slaughter, in March 1886, when Geronimo, along with about 25 of his men, met south of the U.S.–Mexico border with General George Crook. According to newspaper accounts, Crook told the Apache leader that if he didn't surrender unconditionally, "he would hunt them and kill them all if it took 50 years."[7] In response, Geronimo reportedly said: "Once I moved about like the wind, but now I surrender to you and that is all."[8]

Word soon reached Tucson that Geronimo had agreed to end his many years of marauding ways and would proceed to Fort Bowie in Southeastern Arizona. Along their way to the fort, however, Geronimo and approximately 21 of his warriors had a change of heart and scampered back into Mexico.

That situation didn't last long. In early September 1886, the *Citizen* wrote that from his base in Mexico, Geronimo had declared: "[T]he Indians were out of provisions and ammunition, were faint and hungry, and would give up their arms and surrender unconditionally."[9]

The response to this outcome brought a joyous celebration to Tucson in September 1886. The end of the Indian Wars, the *Arizona Daily Star* believed, would bring about more than just peace. "The successful termination of the Apache troubles," the newspaper predicted, "will lift the cloud of distrust which has been suspended over us for many years, restore confidence and set free the wheels of industry within our midst."[10]

That was wishful thinking for a community already deep in financial doldrums. The economic downturn included the 1884 collapse of the Hudson & Company bank, Southern Arizona's "largest financial firm."[11] Established in 1879, the bank's general partner, Charles Hudson, according to a later analysis, "did not conduct business cautiously. He invested bank capital in mining stock and approved loans to mining companies, large and small, with questionable collateral."[12] Those risky investments would eventually contribute to the bank's failure.

Tucson's 1884 banking problems were exacerbated by drought and additional economic hardships. As a result, the community experienced a prolonged recession along with an actual decline in population: the 1890 census reported considerably fewer people living in Tucson and Pima County than in the previous decade. The

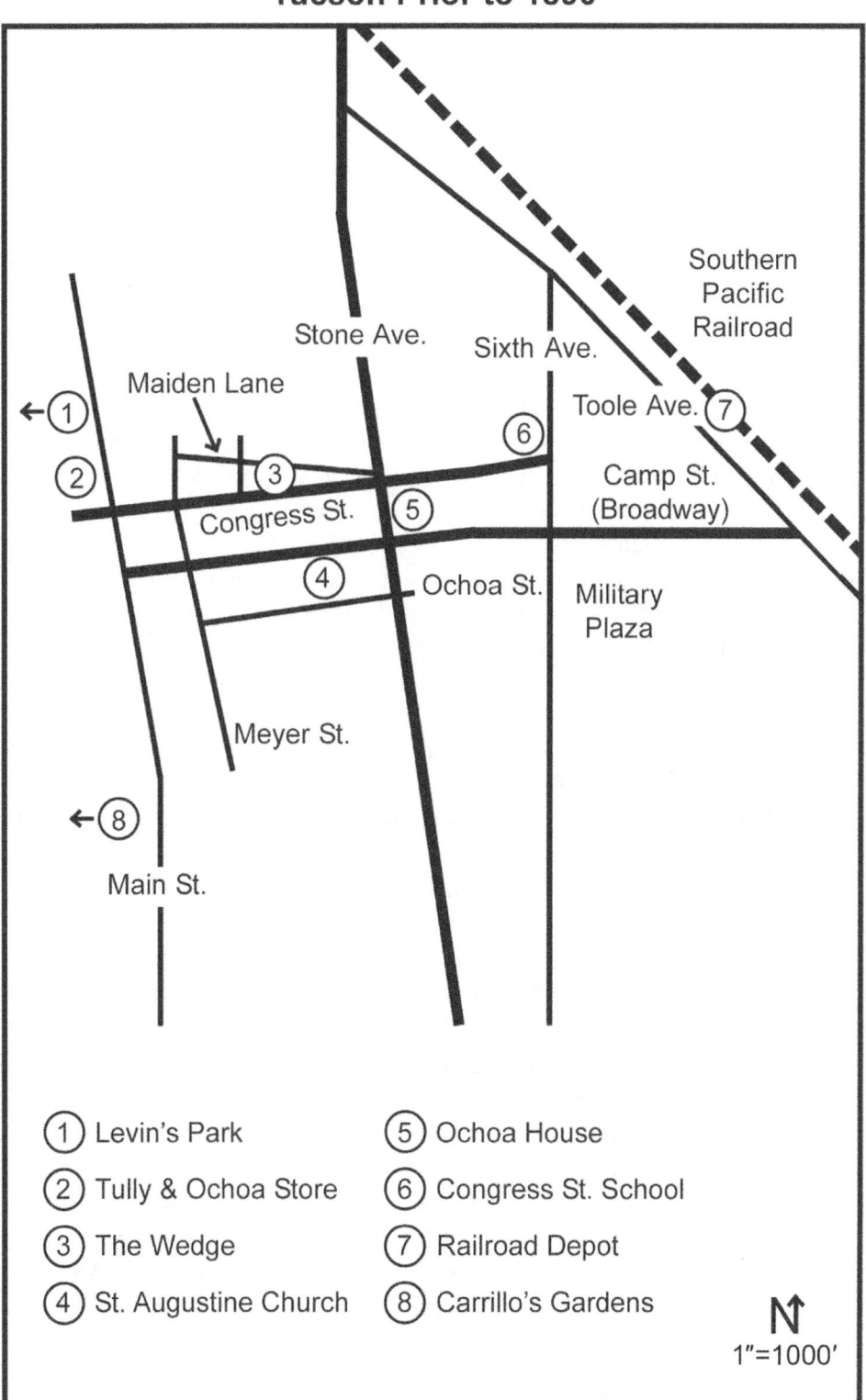

town dropped from 7,007 to 5,150 in population, while the county went from around 17,000 total residents in 1880 to less than 13,000 in 1890.

During that same period, Tucson lost one of its leading citizens, apparently because of his monetary troubles. James Toole was a former mayor, a prominent businessman, and the original treasurer of the "Society of Arizona Pioneers." That was an organization called together in early 1884 by Charles D. Poston when more than 100 men met in Tucson to discuss establishing an association of early settlers. Disagreement about what date a potential member must have moved to Arizona quickly erupted, with retailer Jacob Mansfeld suggesting April 30, 1871. That was the date of the Camp Grant massacre, and Mansfeld thought it fitting since "this was a time when the people of Arizona protected themselves from the Indians."[13] Eventually, though, a different date was selected.

Besides being a successful businessman, Toole was a partner in the Hudson & Company bank. Although he was exonerated of causing the bank's financial problems, many people in Tucson were left destitute by its collapse. After the bank failed, and obviously still distraught by its failure, Toole took his own life.

That wasn't the outcome that would have been predicted during the economic boom period five years earlier when Toole was Tucson's mayor. At that time, he had successfully negotiated an agreement with the Southern Pacific Company to bring the railroad to town. Not only was it anticipated that the trains would result in more people and prosperity for Tucson, but would also help conclude the seemingly endless Indian Wars.

It wasn't surprising, therefore, that on the morning of March 20, 1880, enormous excitement gripped Tucson as its residents awaited the appearance of the first ceremonial Southern Pacific passenger train and the dignitaries it was carrying. They would come to town, the largest settlement in the Arizona Territory, to mark a milestone in the construction effort to link Los Angeles with New Orleans, a task that would finally be completed in 1883.

Prior to the first train's arrival, however, the *Arizona Daily Star* had forecast possible dire consequences for Tucson because of the appearance of dozens of Chinese men, some of whom were laborers who had helped build the railroad line. The newspaper called these men "an ignorant, filthy, leprous horde of beings who may have the form of a human being but lack every element which enters into true American civilization—a horde of almost barbarians that have no higher aspirations than to eat, sleep, and consume opium."[14]

That venomous racism was the viewpoint of Lewis C. Hughes, publisher of the *Star*. He would spend many years attacking the Chinese in his newspaper, during 1879 even calling for the city "to establish at once such regulations as will locate the Chinese element in one section or location of the city … where they can be entirely separated from the remainder of the population."[15] Creating a Chinatown wasn't accomplished; instead, the few hundred Chinese men who settled in Tucson tended to congregate near Main Street north of Congress Street.

What was accomplished, however, were two issues—the vote for women and temperance laws—that Josephine Brawley Hughes, Lewis' wife, would spend decades striving to achieve. She was a founding member in 1883 of the Tucson chapter of the Women's Christian Temperance Union (WCTU) but soon came to realize that suffrage had to come first. Explaining this philosophy, she commented that after women had the right to vote: "then the victory for the protection of our homes and for the cause of temperance will follow."[16]

A small step for achieving the vote for women had come in the same year the WCTU chapter was established in Tucson. The 1883 Territorial Legislature approved women voting in school district trustee elections, just like men. As the *Weekly Citizen* informed its readers in the summer of 1883: "Ladies in Arizona can vote for School Trustees."[17]

The impact of this legislation was quickly felt in Tucson. In the summer of 1884, a mass meeting of almost all men was held to nominate three people to serve as school trustees for District #1. Among the handful of candidates was public school supporter, Maria Wakefield Fish, who thus apparently became the first woman to be considered for elected office in Pima County. While she wasn't selected, the precedent of women running for public office had been established.[18]

Successful Business Owner

The lengthy campaigns for total territorial suffrage and temperance would both succeed several decades after the effort to attract the Southern Pacific Railroad to lay tracks to Tucson had been accomplished. The rails arrived on March 17, 1880, and three days later, hundreds of Tucsonans rushed trackside to greet the initial railroad caravan. As they waited for the first passenger train, the crowd mingled together on a vacant dirt lot one-half mile east of town, kicking up dust as they moved around the future depot site.

Among this throng was five-foot, four-inch-tall Estevan Ochoa. Nervously pacing near him was Mayor R.N. Leatherwood, wondering what exactly he was going to say to Southern Pacific Company president Charles Crocker, one of the wealthiest and most powerful men in the nation. Ochoa also noticed Charles D. Poston shaking hands and patting people on the back, urging everyone to attend the grand banquet later in the day at Levin's Gardens down by the Santa Cruz River.

For his part, Ochoa had been honored with the distinguished responsibility of presenting Crocker with a silver spike to commemorate the momentous occasion of the railroad having finally reached Tucson. Somewhat surprisingly, given Tucson's racial divide at the time, the community's Anglo-American business and political leaders had selected Ochoa for the honor despite his Mexican heritage.

It was a fitting tribute since Ochoa had introduced the bill in the 1877 Territorial Legislature that provided the giant California railroad conglomerate with some legal authority to build west to east across the Arizona territory as it implemented the

Established in the 1870s, Levin's Park was a three-acre entertainment area near the Santa Cruz River. In addition to ramadas, pavilions, and liquid refreshments, it offered both bowling and roller skating opportunities (Arizona Historical Society, PC 1000, Tucson General Photo Collection, #25293).

nation's second transcontinental line. When he agreed to sponsor this legislation, Ochoa must have realized the negative impacts it might have on the large freighting company he co-owned with partner Pinckney Randolph Tully. The railroad could potentially ruin the business by dramatically undercutting its delivery prices for merchandise, but Ochoa sponsored the bill anyway.

That effort on behalf of Tucson was in keeping with Ochoa's character. Born to a well-placed family in Chihuahua, Mexico, on March 17, 1831, as a boy Ochoa had traveled to Missouri. Not only did he learn the English language there, but also the basics of the overland freighting business. Beginning in 1854, the people in Tucson and other isolated areas in the region had become part of the United States as a result of the $10 million Gadsden Purchase that transferred land south of the Gila River from Mexico to the U.S.[19]

The acquisition of this narrow horizontal swath of property was a focus of Jefferson Davis, former U.S Senator from Mississippi and current Secretary of War in the cabinet of President Franklin Pierce (1853–1857). He wanted the land transferred to the United States so the nation's first transcontinental railroad could be built near its southern border. He was seeking to implement this route, in part, so slavery could be exported from the Southern states to California.[20]

As a young man, Ochoa settled in New Mexico and went into business in Mesilla, a small community near the Rio Grande. Eventually moving to Tucson, Ochoa was in town in 1862 when it briefly fell under Confederate control. Ordered by the commanding officer to swear allegiance to the South, the lifelong Republican refused. Even though Ochoa knew it would cost him his property, he replied that he owed all he had in the world to the government of the United States and it would be impossible for him to take an oath of fidelity to any hostile power or party. Thus, he wanted to know, when should he leave town?[21] Ochoa's voluntary departure was short-lived, and after the Union army retook Tucson, he returned to his adopted home.

While Tucson's occupation by Confederate troops was relatively brief, most of the small town's White, male population's attachment to the South and the enslavement of Black people that it represented was longer lasting. Even after the Rebel soldiers had departed, many of the community's Anglo men were believed to retain their favorable views of the South. That sentiment had clearly been demonstrated earlier when, in 1861, a group of Tucson's White men petitioned for the region to become a territory of the Confederate States of America. That goal was accomplished in early 1862 after Jefferson Davis, President of the Confederate States of America, signed the legislation.[22]

For its part, the U.S. Congress in 1863 designated Arizona as a separate territory of the United States, apart from New Mexico, and in that same year Ochoa joined with the Mississippi-born Tully in a Tubac-based freighting company for Southern Arizona. Five years later, the partners moved their operation north to Tucson where goods were sometimes received from San Francisco via Guaymas, Mexico, or from Fort Yuma on the California side of the Colorado River. The firm of Tully & Ochoa would also freight much of its merchandise from the end of the railroad line in Missouri, an arduous and potentially dangerous journey that took three to four months. These risks included inclement weather, poor trails, and a lack of food and water for both the teamsters as well as the animals. There was also the constant threat of Indian attacks.

Even though freighting was difficult and sometimes hazardous, it could also be financially rewarding. The 1870 census showed Ochoa having property valued at $30,000, while most people in Tucson had only a few hundred dollars' worth. Eventually, the Tully & Ochoa Company had $100,000 invested in animals, equipment and property, and with those resources they brought commodities of all sorts to Arizona. In addition to securing general merchandise for its own large commercial store on Main Street in Tucson, the firm supplied other retailers with goods, and it also had military contracts to provision the forts of Southern Arizona.

The financial success of the business allowed Ochoa to travel extensively. In June 1874 he went on a buying trip that lasted several months and took in numerous cities around the nation. While in St. Louis, Ochoa was asked in a letter from a business associate to buy several specific items to be shipped west, including 50 sacks of coffee, 3,000 boxes of lard, plenty of candles, soap, and sugar along with one set of billiard balls and a pair of cues.[23]

Economic prosperity also permitted Ochoa to participate in politics. In 1866, two years after Pima County had been established, he took one of three seats on the county Board of Supervisors, where he was identified as "Stephen" in the minutes of his initial meeting.[24] Ochoa, called "Estevan" in subsequent meeting minutes, resigned his supervisor's office in November 1867. Seven months later, he was elected to the Territorial Legislature and won again two years after that.

During his second term as a legislator, working with his friend and ardent supporter of public education, Governor Anson P.K. Safford, Ochoa introduced Arizona's first meaningful public school law. In exchange for his political help, Ochoa's business received Safford's assistance in securing government freighting contracts.[25]

Previous attempts to establish public schools in Arizona had failed for several reasons. By 1870, excluding Indians, the huge territory had less than 10,000 total inhabitants and just over 1,500 children under the age of 18, so demand for public schools was low. Tucson, the largest community, had 3,200 people, only 724 of whom were under 18 years of age.

In addition to having a small, widely dispersed territorial population, Arizona had a Catholic Church that by 1870 was operating its own school in Tucson, and it didn't want any educational competition. One commentator noted of this religious opposition: "The priests were bitter in their denunciations, and were formidable antagonists, even going so far as to threaten parents if they allowed their children to attend the public school."[26]

While a Catholic himself, as well as a businessman who had refused to accept payment for transporting the materials needed to build the first Catholic school in Tucson,[27] Ochoa saw the need for public education in Arizona. His 1871 proposed territorial legislation initially had a lukewarm reception from his fellow lawmakers, but as chair of the Committee on Public Education, Ochoa managed to gather enough support for passage. While the bill had been whittled down during the adoption process, at least it set the stage for later implementation of Safford and Ochoa's public education goals.

School Builder and Politician

Within a few years of the education bill's passage, a public school with more than 100 students was operating in Tucson. There were also three Catholic schools and one other private institution in town by then. The public school building, though, was too small, and was rented by the school system, so Ochoa decided to do something about that sorry situation.

Having been elected to the Pima County school board in November 1874, Ochoa quickly went to work to erect a new schoolhouse. It would have three rooms and be large enough to accommodate 200 students. By April 1875, Ochoa had begun personally supervising construction of the adobe structure on the north side of Congress Street, just west of Sixth Avenue. As work continued on the new building, the public school year ended. At a celebration marking the occasion, 17-year-old student

Ignacio Bonillas told the audience: "Those friends who have so generously stood by us and aided us in our education, a life of gratitude will never repay."[28]

By October 1875, the narrow, 152-foot-long schoolhouse was completed. Built with 35,000 adobe bricks, the structure was complimented by a corral and outhouses. The school building, furnished at a cost of more than $1,000 with items transported from San Francisco, contributed to an outstanding unpaid debt of above $4,000, more than one-half of which was owed to Ochoa.

To reimburse Ochoa and the others to whom money was owed, the women of Tucson, along with Camp Lowell army officers and their wives, held a party in November 1875. In excess of $1,500 was raised, including more than $300 by auctioning off a gaily attired goat named "Mary's Little Lamb." The following month, Governor Safford, accompanied by Ochoa, visited the new schoolhouse that had 97 boys and 48 girls in attendance. The students put on a holiday show for their visitors after which each pupil was given a present picked from "a beautifully decorated Christmas tree."[29]

While construction of the schoolhouse project had generally gone smoothly, Ochoa's other 1875 civic endeavor was not nearly as successful. In early January he was elected mayor of Tucson by a wide margin in balloting which local saloonkeeper George Hand characterized simply as—"The election closed without a fight."[30] Ochoa was the third man to hold the office since the Pima County Board of Supervisors originally incorporated the two-square-mile Village of Tucson on April 24, 1871.[31] A business license fee, a tax on dogs, and the sale of vacant, municipally owned property primarily financed the village's $1,000 annual budget. Most of this money was spent for paying a marshal and a few police officers along with doing street work.

As one of his first mayoral acts, Ochoa pushed an ordinance through the five-member council outlawing gambling by minors, and he wanted it strictly enforced.[32] The council also decided that "all prostitutes and owners of homes of ill fame in Maiden Lane," located near Stone Avenue and Congress Street, be given three days to leave town or face the legal consequences.

As mayor, Ochoa left a distinct impression with some of his constituents. In June 1875 it was reported he had 11 vagrants arrested and put to work on projects. When the men complained, Ochoa replied: "[T]he road is open and free to Sonora [Mexico] for all those who will not work and have no visible means of support."[33]

The following month, Mayor Ochoa served as grand marshal for Tucson's 4th of July celebration. The assembled throngs watched a late afternoon procession around town that included 38 young women representing each state of the union and then enjoyed "refreshments consisting of various kinds of cake, candy, nuts, raisins, etc. Fireworks of varied character began [on July 3rd] and continued during the night and next day."[34] A profit of $19 was made, which was turned over to the schoolhouse fund.

While most people thanked Ochoa for his participation in marking the Fourth, bartender George Hand, who was often drunk, complained: "It was a very dull day for the 4th of July.... There were orations and the children had a fine time marching and singing in Levin's pavilion. There was a dance in the evening at the same place. Mayor Ochoa sent a constable to arrest me, for nothing, but he failed to accomplish his object. I left the dance at 12 o'clock and went to bed."[35]

For entertainment in 1875, residents of Tucson could visit Levin's Gardens, a three-acre amusement center near the Santa Cruz River operated by Alex Levin. It contained a dancing pavilion, brewery, soda and sarsaparilla factory along with a saloon. There were also gardens where hyacinths, tulips, and roses abounded, as did fruit trees and berry vines.

The two other options for outdoor entertainment in territorial Tucson would come later at Silver Lake and Carrillo's Gardens, both also near the river. The former was on the west bank of the Santa Cruz River, some distance south of town, and offered boat rentals for rides on a small, man-made lake along with bathhouses for swimmers and a hotel and pavilion.[36]

Carrillo's Gardens was established by Leopoldo Carrillo in 1885, around the time Alex Levin sold his outdoor recreational business. The garden was south of downtown and offered "ponds, grass and Arizona cottonwood and various palm trees. It featured beer gardens, picnic areas, shooting galleries, a zoo and dancing."[37]

Despite Mayor Ochoa's reputation for fiscal and social responsibility, by late 1875, the municipal government was $1,200 in debt and had to take out two, 2 percent loans totaling $305. As 1876 dawned, Ochoa didn't run for a second term. Charles Meyer, a 49-year-old native of Germany who operated a drug store while also serving as justice of the peace, was elected to replace him. Like Ochoa, Meyer in 1862 had departed town after the Confederate soldiers arrived, but unlike Ochoa, when he was elected mayor, Meyer refused the job. As a result, Ochoa unexpectedly remained mayor until another election could be held.

In the interim, the cash-strapped council unanimously decided to raise taxes. Pawn shops were assessed a $20 per month license fee, gambling establishments were charged $10, wholesale and retail liquor dealers had to pay $5 monthly, and those holding cockfights, $5. The new fees were to be paid within three days of the due date or penalties would be assessed.

Adopted on January 15, 1876, the new taxes drew a quick and harsh response from some quarters. In less than a month, 45 men, including businessmen John B. "Pie" Allen, Leopoldo Carrillo, and James Toole were petitioning for Tucson's disincorporation.[38]

Following territorial law, a disincorporation election was scheduled for March 20, but the attempt to dissolve the municipal government did miserably at the polls, going down 139 to 49. The next month, John B. Allen was chosen mayor at a special election. Thus, on May 1, 1876, Ochoa was finally able to step down from his role as mayor with the local government still almost $700 in debt.

Also during 1876, businessman Sam Hughes was building a new home on Main

Street. Ochoa was doing the same thing on a lot that comprised one-quarter of the block at the northeast corner of Camp Street (Broadway Boulevard) and Stone Avenue.

In November of that year, despite the political controversy that occurred while he was mayor, Ochoa was elected once again to the Territorial Legislature. As soon as the legislative session opened in Tucson in January 1877, Ochoa introduced a bill to allow the Southern Pacific Railroad Company of California to lay tracks across Arizona. In spite of serious legislative opposition—it was nearly defeated three times—the legislation finally managed to secure enough votes for passage. This was due, in part, to Ochoa's help; he served on a conference committee that amended the original proposal.

Governor Safford signed the railroad act into law on February 7, 1877, allowing Southern Pacific to build two lines across Arizona, one in the northern part of the territory, the other farther south near the 32nd parallel. It would be this second route, when completed, which would connect isolated Tucson by rail with the outside world.

This link, proclaimed the *Citizen* newspaper, meant enormous changes were coming for Arizona. "[T]his fair Territory has been helplessly lying on the mud-flats of misfortune," the paper observed in February 1877, "a prey to savage and murdering Indians. But now, since there surely is a prospect of having two railroads running through the country, will she not float off on the coming tide to a sea of universal prosperity?"[39]

Entrepreneur

Implementation of the railroad could obviously greatly impact Ochoa's freighting business. In 1875 the company was reported to have had $300,000 in annual sales, the second largest total in Pima County.[40] Throughout the 1870s, the firm of Tully & Ochoa was additionally investing in property and other ventures. They had two copper smelting furnaces in Tucson and owned more than 100 vacant lots in town. They were involved with copper mines, and Ochoa was even appointed temporary agent at the San Xavier Indian agency that served the 111-square-mile district created by the U.S. government in 1874. His company also owned a blacksmith shop, peach orchards, and two stage lines.[41]

Despite these secondary business ventures, Tully & Ochoa's primary commercial enterprises were freighting and retailing. In their Tucson store on Main Street, they offered a wide variety of merchandise including dry goods and hardware. In addition, everything needed by a rancher, or for a wagon train, from saddles to whips to wheel rims, could be purchased from the company.[42]

While passage of the railroad legislation might help some of Ochoa's secondary financial interests, it would almost certainly put his freighting company at great risk. Ignoring that potential, he had nonetheless pushed the legislative railroad act forward.

A few months after this bill was signed into law, a writer for the *Chicago Tribune* in May 1877 reported from Tucson, which was then experiencing an economic boom: "All eyes are turned toward Arizona and that capital and labor are making all haste to this new, and but little developed, but, unquestionably immensely rich mineral region."[43] The railroad legislation would greatly assist that transformation, and by the end of September 1877, Southern Pacific had completed a bridge across the Colorado River at Yuma on its way eastward.

Several weeks later, in a ceremony at Tucson's St. Augustine Catholic Church, the 46-year-old Ochoa married Altagracia Salazar, who was 24 years his junior. The bride wore a light blue silk gown along with a veil cascading down from a wreath of white flowers. Ochoa's business partner, P.R. Tully, served as best man.[44]

A son, Estevan II, and foster daughter, Juana, resulted from the Ochoa union. In later years, Juana said of her father: "Mr. Ochoa was a very fine man. He was interested in anything which would help the town and especially in the free public schools."[45]

In a 1940 interview, Ignacio Bonillas, the 1875 Tucson public school pupil who had spoken to an assembled group at the close of the term, recalled of Ochoa: "[He] was ... quiet, even-tempered, with low voice. I never saw him get excited.... He kept his charities to himself and was always very modest. He went more on doing good and helping others than on anything he would derive personal benefit from."[46]

On pleasant evenings, the Ochoas were often seen riding around town in a fine carriage. His personal wealth was increasing with each passing year, and the Tully & Ochoa company was taking on new responsibilities. In the summer of 1878, the couple departed for a trip of several months to New Mexico and Texas along the Rio Grande. Just as they were leaving town, the *Star* proclaimed: "The telephone is now in complete working order in Tucson.... Persons sit at each end of the line and converse freely.... It is attracting a great deal of attention, and hundreds of our citizens have tested its merits. It is a great invention, and one that will take the place of telegraphing."[47]

Things were also looking up in Tucson during the early months of 1880 as the railroad construction crew approached. To mark the arrival of the ceremonial first passenger train, a grand welcoming ceremony was planned for the community of 7,000, two-thirds of whom were Mexican Americans. Ochoa, however, was one of only seven Mexican Americans among the 105 men picked to serve on several committees selected to organize the event, his assignment being to help with invitations.

Much more importantly, Ochoa was chosen to present Charles Crocker of the Southern Pacific Railroad with a silver spike commemorating the momentous occasion. Thus, on the morning of March 20, 1880, after Crocker stepped down from his opulent train car and heard a welcoming speech, Ochoa handed him the spike while saying: "In testimony of the event due to your energy and perseverance, our wants as the second territory in the great confederation have been brought in contact with the civilized world. My fellow-citizens have conferred upon me the honor to present you with this silver spike, the production of the Tough Nut mine at Tombstone—one of the most important in the territory." Then, to loud applause, Ochoa concluded his brief remarks by imploring the people of Tucson: "Let us put our shoulders to the oars of progress until we become the bright star in the constellation of these United States of America."[48]

The enormous impact Southern Pacific trains were going to have on Tucson was quickly felt. Complementing its freight and passenger business, the company employed 220 men in town, paying them a substantial average wage of $90 per month.[49] In addition, implementation of the tracks meant that the president of the United States, Rutherford B. Hayes, could make a brief—but memorable—visit to the isolated community in October 1880.

Estevan Ochoa (center), his wife Altagracia Salazar, and their son Estevan II, were among Tucson's leading families when the railroad arrived on March 20, 1880, an event Ochoa was instrumental in making happen (courtesy the Ochoa family photograph collection).

After touring the dusty town of 7,000 people and attending a reception in his honor, Hayes spoke at the train depot, emphasizing the importance of public education. For his part, Civil War hero and current Commander of the Army, William T. Sherman, who was accompanying the president and who was not known as a fan of the Arizona territory, instructed the assembled crowd: "Straighten up the streets of the city and build the houses of bricks instead of adobes."[50]

Another major community event had occurred earlier in that same year with the opening of St. Mary's Hospital, west of the Santa Cruz River. A project of the Catholic Church, the building was funded by private contributions with two of the largest donors being freight company owners, Estevan Ochoa and P.R. Tully.

At the end of the next year, the *Star* in December of 1881 proclaimed, if with somewhat modest exaggeration: "Tucson has two banks, four churches, five schools, one kindergarten, one fire alarm bell, a volunteer fire department ... numbered houses and named streets, a fine climate, seven secret societies, three daily and four weekly newspapers, sixteen social clubs (including a coaching club), four places of public resort, 12,000 inhabitants, and the handsomest children in America."[51]

While that population figure was vastly inflated, Tucson was definitely the largest community in Arizona, a status local leaders repeatedly pointed to with enormous pride. As a result, boosters called Tucson the "Metropolis of Arizona," a title worthy of its premier population ranking.

Bankrupt Businessman

For a while after March 20, 1880, the arrival of the railroad even meant new business opportunities for the Tully & Ochoa freighting company. They opened a store near the rails at Pantano, 28 miles east of Tucson, from which they could supply miners in the area.

A railroad accident in late 1880, however, was an ominous harbinger of the firm's future. Six miles east of Benson, Arizona, two of their mule carts were struck by a moving train, destroying the wagons and killing some of the animals.[52] It was a sinister portent of things to come for the company. In spite of that, Tully & Ochoa continued to optimistically advertise in the city directory. "We were here first and intend to stay to the last," they stated in 1881. "We have helped to build up the country and have by fair dealing built up ourselves."[53]

Also building up the community around that time was an electric light company. In operation by 1882, the next year the *Citizen* was documenting the 32 customers of the system, proclaiming of Levin's Gardens at night: "the grove of cottonwoods looked as natural as in sunshine. One great curiosity here were the bugs, which surrounded the lights as if paralyzed by its overpowering rays. They were legion."[54] Things locally were beginning to change economically by then, however, and the nascent electric company wouldn't long survive.

Tragedy struck Tucson in 1883 when Andrew Holbrook, a 52-year-old Pima County guard, was murdered during a jailbreak attempt, becoming one of the first local law enforcement agents to die in the line of duty. In response to the killing, an unsuccessful attempt was made to lynch the culprit.[55]

By that time, numerous Tucson businesses were facing major financial difficulties. "Many of the old firms were already in trouble," concluded one analysis of this post-railroad arrival period. "Stock on hand had to be sold at a loss to compete with cheap new goods brought in by rail. Old customers failed to pay promptly when money was desperately needed, and some did not pay at all. Catastrophe followed."[56]

In addition, the silver mines of Tombstone, once thought to be the richest in the region, began playing out and then flooded. The result was an economic calamity for Tucson, with many of the community's long-established businesses being forced to shut their doors as the town's population began to diminish.

One • Acquisition and Railroad Jubilation Followed by Recession, 1854–1890

To save money, Tully and Ochoa relocated their retail store from its traditional headquarters on Main Street to a small space a few blocks away. Concurrently, the partners were offering a 40 percent stake in their Sonora, Mexico, silver mines for $20,000.

This and other efforts to cut expenses and raise capital proved insufficient and a series of legal judgments for nonpayment of bills were issued against the firm. Eventually, the 1884 foreclosure of Tully & Ochoa's business property brought in $150,000.

By 1885, P.R. Tully was looking for a new job and would eventually leave Southern Arizona before later returning. Ochoa, however, reportedly retired from business and lived a quiet life with his family. In May 1888, they went to visit his brother in El Paso and then proceeded to Las Cruces to see his elderly mother. While there, Ochoa died on October 27, at 58 years of age.

Ochoa's widow returned to Tucson but moved from the family's large Stone Avenue home into much smaller quarters. By 1899 the Ochoas' son was involved with a general merchandise business; sadly he would be brutally murdered by a disgruntled employee in 1902 when he was only 32 years old, leaving a widow and two babies behind. Ochoa's foster daughter, however, lived a long life in Tucson and his descendants would continue to play a prominent role in the community throughout the 20th century and to the present.

In its short obituary, the *Citizen* wrote of Estevan Ochoa: "That he was financially unfortunate detracts none from the good name he leaves behind. He was a courageous and enterprising citizen and will be long remembered for his good works."[57]

Ochoa accomplished many things—having a well-regarded family, operating a successful business for more than 20 years, being a prominent politician who achieved a great deal of good for his community, and personally financing and supervising the construction of Tucson's first publicly owned schoolhouse. By all accounts he was a humble man, but others considered him extraordinary.

During his lifetime, in 1870 Ochoa was honored to have a Tucson street named after him. His numerous good works were also aptly remembered in 1921 when a new southside Tucson school was named in his memory. In the motion to do so, it was simply stated that it was "in honor of a pioneer who was a friend and patron of the public schools."[58]

• Two •

A Diverse and Often Divided Community, 1890–1900

A little noticed small brick building, probably constructed early in the 20th century as part of a developing residential neighborhood, sits just north of the current Fourth Avenue underpass. Next to it rises 13-stories of the brand new Ari on 4th Avenue. The huge complex features 323 residential units with rents for a 400-square-foot studio apartment being $1,599/month.[1] A couple of blocks away along Herbert Avenue, a few adobe structures also are mostly hidden from public view. They are in the shadow of the Union on 6th development, another large mixed-use 21st century project.

LOOKED ON WITH DISDAIN BY MANY OF HIS FELLOW Tucson residents, while vehemently scorned by the *Arizona Daily Citizen*, was the man who in 1885 secured the University of Arizona for the community. The newspaper accused local attorney and Arizona territorial legislator C.C. Stephens of double-crossing his constituents by obtaining the school, and not the territorial capital, for Southern Arizona.

Concluding Tucson "does not care a fig" about a university, the morning newspaper also called it merely a "sop" for not getting the capital brought back to town. According to the *Citizen*, the 44-year-old Stephens was the dirtiest of dirty birds, morally depraved, and someone who should get out of town permanently.[2]

The saga of how the university ended up where it did began after the territorial capital in 1864 was placed in Prescott. Needing a set of laws with which to govern the vast territory, Governor John Goodwin requested William Howell, a federal judge based in the remote outpost of Tucson, to assemble a document. Utilizing existing state and territorial statutes, Howell did so, and his 400 page code, including a near total ban on abortions, was adopted by the territorial legislature in 1864.[3] Three years later, the capital was moved to Tucson, but elected officials from Yavapai County a decade later dominated the 1877 legislative session meeting in Tucson, the same one that had authorized the Southern Pacific Railroad to build across the territory. Being the most populous of Arizona's five counties, it had 40 percent of the seats in the legislature. Working with politicians from Maricopa County, the lawmakers from Prescott simply outvoted their Tucson counterparts and approved moving the capital northward.[4]

Two • *A Diverse and Often Divided Community, 1890–1900* 21

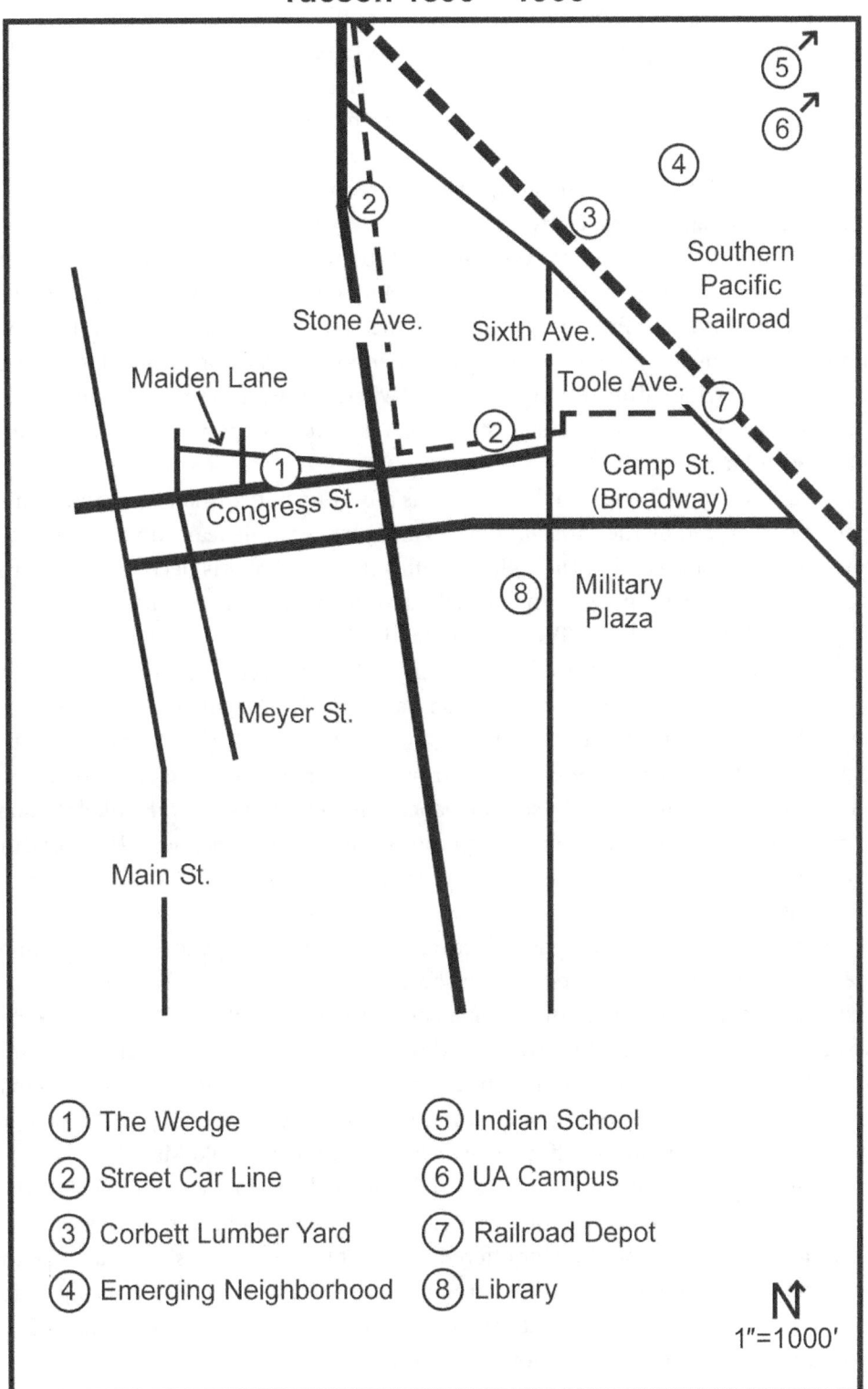

Tucson 1890 – 1900

① The Wedge
② Street Car Line
③ Corbett Lumber Yard
④ Emerging Neighborhood
⑤ Indian School
⑥ UA Campus
⑦ Railroad Depot
⑧ Library

N↑
1"=1000'

Since Tucson was the largest community in the territory, the "Metropolis of Arizona," the people of Southern Arizona forcefully demanded they get the capital back. For seven long years their elected officials tried diligently, but unsuccessfully, to accomplish that goal. Because of this impressive record of failure, Tucson's lawmakers prior to the 1885 legislative session met in the downtown stationery store of Jacob Mansfeld and decided they would focus their attention on having a university authorized for Tucson instead of trying to secure the capital.[5]

After the legislators left for Prescott, however, many Tucson residents got together and once more showed their support for bringing the capital back to town. To improve the chances of that happening, $4,000 in "sack" money was donated to distribute as needed in Prescott. By the time the Tucson bribe cash reached Prescott, though, Stephens had joined a majority of upper house legislators pledged to support certain policies, including leaving the capital where it was. As a result, he introduced the bill to establish the University of Arizona, and it was adopted and later signed into law on March 12, 1885.

The reaction in Tucson to this news was anything but cordial. At a community meeting organized by the *Citizen*, those in attendance wholeheartedly endorsed the condemnation of several of their elected officials. Based on his performance in the legislature, the newspaper specifically called for Stephens' immediate removal from office as well as an end to his Tucson law practice.[6]

For his part, Stephens tried to explain himself by declaring unapologetically: "[T]hat in getting the University, Tucson had something, which in time to come, would be infinitely more valuable than a dozen capitals."[7] Within 18 months of the legislative action, 40 acres of property far out of town had been donated for a campus by two local gamblers and a saloonkeeper. The *Arizona Daily Star* called the suburban site "magnificent" and wrote hopefully of the proposed school: "The founding of a territorial university in our midst is the most important step in the development of Arizona."[8]

On October 27, 1887, Stephens himself gave the opening address at a groundbreaking ceremony for the first campus building, but it wouldn't be until 1891 that instruction at the University of Arizona actually began. Part of the four-year delay was caused by a disagreement over the design of the first campus building. Some officials wanted it to be one-story while others thought it should be two. In a compromise, a tall, ground-floor basement was built under the one-story structure and, in time, this building would affectionately become known as Old Main.

When the University of Arizona officially opened on Monday, October 5, 1891, it was another momentous event in Tucson's history. The school's initial class had only a few dozen students, but the *Star* offered flowery phrases on the significance of the occasion. "Educational institutions are most desirable as a means of giving solidity, strength and tone to a community," the newspaper expectantly suggested. "They attract a most desirable class of young ladies and gentlemen."[9]

At the same time, 163 other students were attending an Indian school located about one-half mile west of the new and remote higher-education institution. Initially established in 1888 by the Presbyterian Church in downtown Tucson before it moved out near the new University of Arizona campus, the school's first superintendent was Howard Billman. Even though native people had been living in the Arizona desert for several millennium, the Reverend Billman wrote of them: "The children know nothing at all in the line of self-support. Nor do their parents for that matter. The boys can not handle a single tool. The girls are not capable of making a single garment."[10]

The school's Native American pupils were taught religion, living skills, farming techniques, and English. If they spoke their own language, they were disciplined. As Elsie P. Herndon, wife of the second school superintendent, commented: "We have never liked the custom of meting out punishment for talking in the Indian language, but it has always seemed the only means to promote the use of the English language."[11]

Some of these students were Papago (Tohono O'odham) Indians from the San Xavier reservation. Known for its mission church that was almost a century old by 1893, there were 427 people living on the relatively small reservation by then. In general, the residents of the reservation were "honest, industrious, and peaceable, self-supporting Indian[s]" according to someone who lived with them.[12] These people were, like their ancestors before them, mostly farmers growing wheat, barley and corn as well as raising cattle and horses along with chopping mesquite wood to be sold in town. However, their detractors, of whom there were many, labeled the Papagoes as lazy, lawless, and thieves.

Similar to these native people, the treatment of the Chinese in Tucson often included ridicule, belittlement, and threats. Plus, they were subject to the restrictions imposed by the 1882 federal Chinese Exclusion Act that outlawed new immigration. This legislation was extended in 1892 by the Geary Act that required all Chinese to register with a federal agent and carry a certificate of residency; if they didn't have it on them when questioned by authorities, they could face deportation.

Locally, despite an attempted economic boycott of Chinese businesses failing in the 1880s, in 1893 a petition was circulated asking for a separate Chinatown to be created. Similar to the proposal L.C. Hughes of the *Star* had made in 1879, this new effort sought to totally segregate the Chinese both residentially and commercially. More than 100 people signed the petition, but the city attorney ruled it unconstitutional, and the idea quietly disappeared.[13]

While the Chinese remained in the center of town, even as the university, the Indian school, and the San Xavier reservation were located on its outskirts, two events shook the central part of the community. The first was the brutal murder of a Tucson police officer in 1892. Under unknown circumstances, William Elliott was stabbed in the heart "on Meyer Street in Barrio Libre, the Mexican portion of the city."[14] Before dying, he fatally shot his assailant, thus the cause of the conflict would forever remain a mystery.

The other event that buffeted Tucson was the continuing economic downturn that followed the financial collapse of the early 1880s. With only a hint of exaggeration, longtime Tucsonan Mose Drachman lamented: "We practically stood still from 1884 [to] 1896—a period of twelve years. During that time, I don't believe there was a single house built in Tucson. Everybody was downhearted, discouraged and disgusted."[15]

Not everything in town came to a complete standstill, of course. Shortly before the university opened in 1891, local postmaster J. Knox Corbett moved his downtown lumberyard to a Sixth Avenue site that he had purchased for $475. He thus became one of the first businessmen to locate on the mostly virgin land north of the Southern Pacific railroad tracks.

Having arrived in Tucson in 1880 just before the railroad, the 18-year-old Corbett had been sent west from his South Carolina home to regain his health. From his new desert residence, Corbett wrote frequent letters to his parents and other relatives, offering tidbits of information about life in the isolated community. Unlike South Carolina, where he noted most meat was canned, Corbett indicated "plenty of fine beef, veal, deer and all kinds of fresh game," were available in Tucson, along with garden grown peas, beets, and other vegetables.[16] In the winter, Corbett stated in another letter, the afternoons were comfortable but the nights cool, while one June day he dryly commented: "It is a little warm here today. In our store it is only 112°, but they say here this is pleasant, [that] it will be hot in July and August."[17]

Marrying a daughter of Arizona pioneer Sam Hughes in 1885, Corbett eventually entered the cattle raising business and then became Tucson postmaster in 1890. By 1895 the Corbetts had two children, and he built a large wooden Victorian-style home on Eighth Street near his Sixth Avenue lumberyard. It would be their residence for several years until they moved back into town, occupying an imposing Main Street mansion that was surrounded by other large homes built by the community's elite.[18]

An Emerging Neighborhood and Other New Development

A block away from Corbett's Eighth Street home was a dwelling occupied by elderly Augustus Brichta, Arizona's first public school teacher. Born in New York City in 1821, he served in the Mexican-American War, came to Arizona in 1863, and finally settled in Tucson.[19] Several years before the Congress Street School was built by Estevan Ochoa, the community's first public school had been established by 1868 in a rented classroom, and Brichta was chosen to teach its 55 male students. Because of a lack of financial support from the government, however, the school lasted only one year.

By the late 1890s a small residential neighborhood containing both single-family units as well as diminutive apartment complexes was slowly emerging around the Corbett and Brichta homes. Occupied primarily by blue-collar families, many of the homes in this developing neighborhood were tiny adobe structures with dirt floors. The area also had a few commercial establishments to fill people's daily needs. Along with the Corbett Lumberyard, Tucson Sash, Door & Mill Company was located on Sixth Avenue in a large adobe building while three Chinese grocers and one Chinese laundry were found nearby.

According to the 1900 U.S. Census, this mixed-use neighborhood included more than 70 households containing a total of almost 350 people with diverse ethnic backgrounds. For example, living in a rental property located on Sixth Avenue between Seventh and Eighth streets, 51-year-old widow Refugia Byailis headed her household. Born in Mexico, she had lived in the United States for 20 years and had four sons ranging in age from 12 to 26, two of whom spoke English.

A few blocks away resided Chinese native, 41-year-old Sung Kei. He was a grocer who had been in the United States for almost three decades and spoke English as well as being literate. A renter like Byailis, he had three lodgers in his home, all Chinese men.

The Lorcuzu Franco family exemplified the most typical household in the neighborhood. He was 35 years old and his wife 10 years younger. They had been married for seven years and in that time had five children, four of whom survived. The couple were both natives of Mexico, and he earned a living as a day laborer.

Nearby resided a four-person household led by 50-year-old Pedro Aguirre. He had been born in New Mexico, and his 24-year-old son lived with him while working as a boilermaker helper for the Southern Pacific Railroad Company. Along with these two men, Aguirre's 18-year-old daughter and a 35-year-old boarder, who worked as a day laborer, also resided in the rented house on Sixth Avenue.

Mining prospector Robert Frazer was another resident of the neighborhood, and he headed a five-person household living in a home the family was purchasing. Frazer was originally from Maine, while his wife, Melinda, was an Arizona native. The couple had been married for 12 years and had had five children, three of whom survived.

Taken together, more than 60 percent of the households living in this small neighborhood contained someone who could speak English, but a literate person headed fewer of the families. Those living in this area also held a wide variety of occupations including washerwoman, carpenter, bartender, adobe brick maker, and a man who was employed at a lumberyard.

A few years after lumberyard owner J. Knox Corbett built his family home on Eighth Street in 1895, pressure began to mount on the municipal government to remove the "Wedge" from downtown Tucson. Named after a commercial triangular-shaped island, formed where Congress Street literally split apart into two roadways west of Stone Avenue, this area had long been Tucson's commercial hub.

The Drachman Cigar Store was at the eastern end of the Wedge for many years, and Herbert Drachman remembered that his father Sam's business had several folding chairs. Men, Drachman recalled, would often come by and literally take the chairs out into Stone Avenue where they could talk about sports and other current happenings. "It was a great gathering place for the baseball team, baseball fans and summer widowers," Drachman reminisced of those men whose families were fortunate enough to be able to leave town during the intense desert heat.[20]

By early 1896, the Tucson economy was finally beginning to recover from its extended downturn, and this created a minor building boom in town. The *Arizona Daily Star* modestly reported of this phenomenon: "If Tucson had built up as rapidly every six months from the date of its foundation as it has within the last six months it would be larger than London, Paris and New York combined."[21]

Some of the new construction included the development of retail establishments and commercial blocks stretching east from the Wedge out along Congress Street toward the train depot, passing the adobe public school house near Sixth Avenue. Looking to become part of this eastward business migration, wagon maker Fred Ronstadt was considering relocating his recently opened shop from west of Stone Avenue to a site two blocks to the east.

Ronstadt as a young man had come to Tucson from Mexico in 1882, and his parents, along with sister Emilia and brothers Richard and Jose Maria, soon joined him.[22] After working as a wagon maker for others for some time, as well as being employed by the railroad, Fred Ronstadt eventually went into business for himself. He also got involved with music and led the *Club Filarmonico Tucsonense* (Tucson Philharmonic Band) during the 1890s.

Since he was well liked, Ronstadt's fellow businessmen west of Stone Avenue didn't want to see him relocate his business from that area. One of them told him: "Fred, I hope you aren't going to move way out in the country, you have established a nice little business right here where you are, all your friends are bringing their work to you, but now that you are going way up to Scott [Avenue] and Broadway, no one will ever be able to find you."[23]

Ronstadt, however, did move a few blocks to the east, joining other businesses slowly migrating away from the Wedge and in the direction of the depot. Assisting this retail shift would be the 1898 inauguration of a mule-drawn streetcar system that ran west along Third Street from the university campus to Stone Avenue and then turned south to Congress Street. From there it went to the train station, thus making access easier to commercial establishments near the depot.

In 1894 three men—Carlos Velasco, Pedro C. Pellon, and Mariano Samaniego—called a gathering on the west side of town to organize the Alianza Hispano-Americana as a Mexican American political organization. Among the small group of men attending the initial meeting was retailer Carlos C. Jácome. Within a few years, the group's focus had shifted to a fraternal organization with lodges in several Arizona communities. At its first national convention held in 1897, Tucson was designated as the supreme lodge and headquarters with Samaniego elected as the first president.[24]

Suffrage and Utility Issues

Another person elected president of an organization was Josephine Brawley Hughes. In 1890 she was chosen to lead the territory's Women's Christian Temperance Union (WCTU) that had as its mission "total abstinence and national prohibition." The following year, Hughes was among a handful of leading women pushing for suffrage before the Territorial Legislature, and in March 1891 the Council (Senate) actually adopted a suffrage measure. Responding, Hughes immediately wrote the men who voted for granting women the right to vote: "please accept the thanks of the pioneer women of Arizona for championing their cause."[25] But the next day the majority of the legislators changed their minds, and the bill was defeated.

Undeterred, suffrage supporters turned their attention to an 1891 Constitutional Convention convened by the legislature in hopes of pressuring the U.S. Congress to grant Arizona statehood. While that idea was a political fantasy, 22 men were elected to serve as convention delegates, and they convened in Phoenix in September to draft a state constitution. One day during their deliberations, the men heard from a few women about suffrage, with Hughes reading from the Declaration of Independence and then pointing out "that all government should depend upon the consent of those governed, women as well as men."[26]

Tucson convention delegate, William H. Barnes, had a different opinion, saying: "Pima County [residents] ... were 75 percent against woman suffrage at this time. As many good women opposed the movement now as favored it. When all women wanted it, they would soon be granted the privilege."[27]

Irate, the *Arizona Daily Star* blasted Barnes in an editorial. "The Judge," the *Star* suggested of Barnes, "was evidently excited or had lost his balance. Try again Judge; it is doubtful if you have ever spoken to a dozen of women in the county on the subject."[28] But Barnes' viewpoint prevailed, and the convention didn't include suffrage in the draft document.

Continuing with her crusade while her husband L.C. Hughes served as territorial governor, in 1895 Josephine Brawley Hughes was elected president of Arizona's Woman's Suffrage Association. Two years later, the Territorial Legislature, in a surprising decision, expanded voting rights for women, granting them the privilege for city elections. But when Tucson held a water and sewer bond election in 1898, women weren't allowed to vote. After the bonds were overwhelmingly approved by men only, resident Andrew Cronly, once a water company employee, filed a lawsuit, claiming the vote was illegal, in part, because of the exclusion of women. In its ruling on the case, the territory's all male Supreme Court determined that the legislation authorizing women to vote in city elections was written with "ambiguity and uncertainty." Finding that portion of the law void, women were thus deprived of the right to vote in city elections.[29]

So, the decade of the 1890s closed with no additional progress on suffrage. What did change was that in 1899, with her husband no longer governor, the 59-year-old

Hughes was replaced as president of the Woman's Suffrage Association. The new leader was socially prominent Phoenix resident, Pauline Schindler O'Neill, who was 25-years Hughes' junior.

Another change pursued about the same time was Tucson's attempt to acquire the community's privately owned water company. When he became mayor in 1899, Gus Hoff earned $20 a month to oversee a municipality that had a $26,000 annual budget. A native of Germany, Hoff arrived in Tucson in 1881 and operated a successful wholesale grocery business. After the life-long Democrat was elected mayor, he worked diligently to facilitate the laying of sewer lines as well as acquiring the water company. The privately owned system had seven wells available for pumping and, to increase often low pressure, an 80-foot high, above ground storage standpipe holding one-half million gallons was available. Following the 1898 bond election, in July 1899, the city council authorized the purchase of the water system, and this step, according to the *Star*, was another example of how the community was progressing.

The water system, though, had serious maintenance issues. Broken pipes were frequent, and the *Citizen* reported the lines in the ground were "corroded and cracked." Observing that the men who sold the company had enriched themselves considerably by the sale, the newspaper concluded the city council had bought "a pig in [a] poke."[30]

While enough bond funds were available to purchase the water company, no money existed to install sewers. To cover this financial shortfall, in late 1899 the city council, at Mayor Hoff's urging, authorized selling off residential lots in four of the six blocks around the former Sixth Avenue Military Plaza. This was the property that had been transferred to the local government after the U.S. military abandoned it in 1873 when they relocated to Camp Lowell east of town. This new army facility, which would later be renamed Fort Lowell, was closed in 1891.[31]

Despite plans calling for two of the six Military Plaza blocks, all of which were simply vacant dirt parcels, to remain in public hands, selling lots for development from the other four blocks was hugely controversial because many people in town wanted all the land retained as open space. On the other hand, the *Star*, a strong supporter of selling the property, predicted that between $30,000 and $50,000 could be raised from the sale of the lots, with the proceeds being used to install sewers.[32]

To move matters along, the council by a four to two vote approved the sale of the first Military Plaza lot in early January 1900. Purchased for $500, this parcel was soon resold to a consortium of 34 local businessmen that included both J. Knox Corbett and Fred Ronstadt and this group intended to build a $3,000 home on the property.

Ignoring the intense public criticism leveled at them because of their breakup of the Military Plaza property, the city council then went ahead with subdividing additional land. They also left vacant a future library site on the west side of Sixth Avenue as well as a potential park site directly across the street to the east. (Today these two blocks are the home of the Tucson Children's Museum, located in the historic Carnegie Library building, and Armory Park, including a senior citizen center.)

Disregarding city hall's commitment to reserve two of the six Military Plaza blocks exclusively for non-residential uses, a serious challenge to this attempt to raise money to begin installing sewers by selling off the remaining land soon emerged. Local druggist George Martin, at the urging of several other businessmen, took matters into his own hands to try to thwart the sale of lots. Even though a city watchman was supposed to be guarding the site, very early on the morning of March 1, 1900, the 67-year-old Martin had a small shack with a corrugated metal roof erected on the Military Plaza land. After moving into his new abode, he offered to pay $40 for the piece of ground he was occupying plus transfer expenses, much less than the hundreds of dollars city hall wanted.

Martin's preemptive strike in the Military Plaza case infuriated Mayor Hoff. He told the druggist he had 10 hours to clear off the land while insisting the sale of the lots would proceed. Martin stayed put, and the native of Ireland who moved from Yuma to Tucson in 1884, soon became the community's center of attention, with hundreds of people visiting him to take his picture.

A decade before his involvement with the tragic/comical 1900 Military Plaza showdown, druggist George Martin is shown standing in his store with two unidentified men on the right (courtesy the UA College of Pharmacy Museum photograph collection).

With Martin still in place two days later, Hoff ordered the town marshal to evict him. The lawman asked the druggist to leave, a request that was refused, so the frustrated mayor fired the marshal. After an hour, however, Hoff's hot temper cooled down and he rescinded the marshal's termination.

After one week of the standoff, Tucson's city attorney finally weighed in with his opinion. He pointed out that the revenue from the lot sales would be used to finance the installation of a sewer system, but if Martin prevailed there would be very little revenue to collect. Based on that assumption, plus the attorney's belief that the town government was legally justified in selling the property, he thought a court of law would agree with him.

Ignoring Martin's unusual challenge to its power to sell the Military Plaza land to the highest bidder, the city government simultaneously continued to dispose of property, selling lots for prices ranging between $300 and $700. As the Military Plaza drama slowly played itself out, Tucson became the subject of ridicule by other Arizona communities for its handling of the ongoing episode. In response, the *Citizen* fired back: "Tucson moves along never wavering from the path of progress. Sensations are so common here that people don't allow such things to worry them."[33]

When Martin's court case was finally heard in May 1900, the judge ruled in favor of the city.[34] Even as the verdict was unsuccessfully appealed, the urgent need for a sewer system was dramatically displayed. Three workers cleaning out the cesspool in back of Martin's downtown drugstore were overcome by deadly fumes and perished. In response to this tragedy, the *Citizen* called the community apathetic concerning the installation of sewers and, siding with Mayor Hoff, the newspaper demanded: "What Tucson needs is a sewer system."[35]

What Tucson had already achieved by the end of the 19th century was a more reliable electrical system. Following the earlier demise of the first electric company, in October 1892 the Electric Light and Power Company was incorporated with $20,000 subscribed to operate the system and several prominent men, including retailer Albert Steinfeld, serving on the original board of directors.[36]

The new company may have provided more reliable service than its bankrupt predecessor, but it wasn't without its own problems. In 1893 it promised its customers that it would try to give them a 15-minute warning if service was to be cut off. Nature, however, wasn't so accommodating. In 1898 a summer monsoon caused havoc with the system by "breaking down poles, disarranging wires and burning fuses." The result was darkness around town for awhile and, as the *Star* observed, "candles became very much in demand."[37]

Other Improvements

A year after Tucson lost electrical power for a time, in 1899 local library supporter G.W. Pittock sent Andrew Carnegie a request concerning a possible donation to the community.[38] He emphasized to the well-known philanthropist that Tucson had 3,500 books and that 2,000 of them were checked out annually from its small library located on the second floor of city hall which was near Alameda and Court streets, not far from Maiden Lane.[39] To house its growing collection, the city needed a large new structure. In response to this plea, in November Carnegie offered a $25,000 construction grant if the city government would promise to allocate $2,000 a year in operating expenses along with providing a site for the new building.[40]

With great excitement the city council quickly responded to Carnegie's generous proposal. They pledged the operating money, which would be raised through a small property tax increase, and selected a Military Plaza site along the west side of Sixth Avenue for the library. Then Tucson waited for a reply ... and waited some more. It wasn't until three months later that Carnegie's representative contacted local officials, inquiring about what had happened concerning Carnegie's offer. At that point it was discovered that all the paperwork regarding the transaction had been lost in transit.

Upon learning of this mistake, the material was re-sent and soon accepted. After receiving word that the $25,000 would be available, a competition for the building's design was held with three local architects submitting ideas along with three from Phoenix and one from New York City. These concepts were put on display for the public to view and a committee selected to choose a winner. After suitable deliberation, and the not unexpected controversy about the selection process, the classical design of Tucson architect Henry Trost was picked. By August 1900, a low bid of $20,584 was accepted to construct the 4,200-square-foot building, the cornerstone was laid in November, and the library was opened for business the following year.

Not surprisingly, the choice of a Military Plaza location for the library had upset some people who thought the new building should be constructed closer to town on the Congress Street schoolhouse property. Others, though, wanted that prime piece of real estate sold for commercial purposes. That is exactly what was done when local businessman Levi H. Manning purchased the land for almost $26,000. "This property is considered very valuable," noted the *Citizen* at the time of the sale, "as the business center of the city is fast moving eastward."[41]

While this transaction meant demolition of the 25-year-old adobe brick Congress Street School, the proceeds of the sale would be used to pay most of the cost of three new schools. This construction took Tucson School District One from two to four facilities. The new schools would be named Davis, Drachman, and Holladay after the three sitting school board members—William C. Davis, Samuel H. Drachman, and Leonidas Holladay.[42]

At the same time, Mayor Gus Hoff wasn't the only one in his family who wanted Tucson to progress. His brother, Charles, ran both the streetcar system as well as Sunset Telephone. As the 19th century was nearing its end, the number of telephones in Tucson was expected to swell to 600, and since Phoenix had only half that total, the *Star* in 1899 suggested a reason for the difference: "Tucson folks are very social and visit as well as transact business by telephone."[43]

Retailer Albert Steinfeld had already seen numerous changes in the community since his 1872 arrival, and he firmly believed in the future of Tucson. After many years of economic problems, things were altering rapidly as the 1800s came to a close and Steinfeld was optimistic. "[H]e considers the outlook as very favorable," proclaimed the *Star* in 1899. "With our mining and cattle interests, there is every reason for expecting a prosperous era for Southern Arizona."[44]

Even though it had several signs of an economic recovery, along with the largest municipal population in the territory, Tucson still had only 7,500 residents in 1900, about 500 more than resided in the community 20 years earlier. The largest employer in town was the Southern Pacific Railroad, which paid out more than $60,000 in wages every month to its hundreds of employees.[45]

At that time, Tucson contained nine hotels that had room rates ranging from $1.50 to $5 per night. Forty miles north of town in Oracle, another tourist facility had opened in 1895. Built by William Neal and his wife, Annie Box Neal, the Mountain View Hotel had 12 rooms, each of which had hot and cold running water.

A friend of, and scout for, William F. "Buffalo Bill" Cody, Neal arrived in Tucson in the late 1870s. Over time he became a successful businessman owning thousands of cattle as well as transporting goods, gold, and the mail between Tucson and the mining town of Mammoth. Annie Neal as a child attended Catholic school in Tucson and was known for her "unusual charm and refinement."[46] The couple was married on January 4, 1892, at Tucson's old Saint Augustine Church.

Neal and his wife were both of mixed descent, including having black and Indian ancestors. That fact didn't seem to affect too much how they were treated in Tucson, but many other people were openly discriminated against because of their race or color. Upon her death in 1950, Annie Neal was remembered as "soft spoken and well educated."[47] Previously, the *Arizona Daily Citizen* had written in 1895 that her husband was "one of the foremost and most progressive citizens we have, true as steel, and a man whose word is as good as his bond."[48]

As the 19th century came to a close, the community had about 80 retail stores, many of them operated by Chinese men, along with two ice plants to manufacture 800-pound blocks of the important frozen commodity, and some small mineral ore processing facilities. There were also four Protestant churches as well as a new Catholic cathedral, but Tucson's first synagogue and an African American church were still a few years away from being built.[49]

With the growing number of places of worship, however, not everything in Tucson was spiritual in orientation. Around the dawn of the 20th century, the *Citizen* succinctly summarized the shadier parts of local society: "Tucson has six gambling halls, and about the same number of churches," it noted.[50]

At least by 1899 local economic growth was definitely increasing. The *Star* estimated $250,000 at a minimum had been spent during the year on major building improvements, including construction of the Eagle Flour Mill on Toole Avenue two blocks west of the train station. The Elks Club also had a new downtown home, as did the bachelor-only Owl's Club. Construction of 40 homes ranging in value from $800 to $8,000 had additionally taken place as Tucson, after many years of stagnation, began growing once again.[51]

Commenting on all this new development, the *Star* proudly proclaimed in April 1899: "Buildings are going up everywhere, and so many that it is hard to keep pace with them. Tucson has entered the Metropolitan class as a center of population. From now on the growth and expansion of Tucson will be very rapid as well as substantial."[52] Because of all these changes, Tucson remained the "Metropolis of Arizona," a population title local leaders considered rightfully deserved.

Not only did population growth rebound during the decade, but transportation methods also began to move away from the traditional horse and wagon. While a few bicycles had been seen on Tucson's dirt streets earlier, by 1893, following a national trend, their local use had exploded. There were so many bikes that the City Council had to adopt regulations requiring all bikes to have a bell and to ring it at every crossing, to limit their speed to six miles per hour, and to have a lamp for nighttime use. Violators of these rules faced a $7 fine.[53]

Despite the new laws, negative impacts occurred. One result of bicycling was the town's livery business that relied on horse and carriage was ruined. "The young men now do their courting," reported the *Arizona Weekly Citizen*, "on 'bikes' and excursions to the country are made on the same wheels."[54] Plus, some of the town's numerous dogs began chasing those on bikes and occasionally bit the riders. Even more significantly, accidents between bicycles and other conveyances began happening. In an 1895 incident, former recreational park owner, Alex Levin, was riding his bike on Congress Street when he collided with another bicyclist. Levin's leg was seriously lacerated while the other man "received a cut over the right eye and was temporarily unconscious."[55]

A few years later, by which time the biking fad was fading, a technical revolution that was even more dangerous appeared in town when the first locally owned automobile arrived on December 30, 1899. Brought to Tucson from Massachusetts by train, it was delivered to physician Dr. Hiram Fenner. The $600 steam-powered vehicle, or "Locomobile," was described as having one seat that accommodated two passengers. "Steam is generated by a gasoline tank of five gallons capacity," reported the *Star*, "and the water tank will hold sixteen gallons." Concerning its range, the newspaper remarked: "Fifty miles can be covered in five hours on a good road."[56]

While Dr. Fenner immediately test drove his new vehicle on the dirt streets of Tucson, and would sell it by the following August, there was intense disagreement at the end of 1899 about whether the 20th century was actually about to begin. The *Arizona Daily Citizen* ardently insisted the momentous occasion wouldn't take place for another 12 months—but many residents disagreed.

To celebrate the new century, assuming it started in January 1900, a dinner and dance were held by the Order of Railway Conductors. The water company brightly

The first University of Arizona football team in 1899 was vastly outweighed by their opponents from Tempe, and lost their initial game 11–2 despite the support of some 300 fans (courtesy the Patricia Stephenson photograph collection).

illuminated its eight-story tall storage standpipe to mark the holiday, while a special midnight mass was said at the new cathedral on Stone Avenue.

One month earlier, over the Thanksgiving holiday, the football team from the Arizona Territorial Normal School at Tempe journeyed south by train to take on the men of the University of Arizona. By that time, the Tucson campus had an enrollment of more than 150 students who paid a $5 matriculation fee, but nothing for tuition.

It was the Tucson team's first year of playing organized football, and their inexperience showed with the final score being 11–2 in favor of the visitors. The game was played at Carrillo's Gardens amusement center near the Santa Cruz River and was attended by 300 fans, including a contingent of University of Arizona women carrying canes wrapped in ribbons bearing the school colors of sage green and silver.

More than 12 months later, to usher in the 20th century, at least according to the *Tucson Daily Citizen*, the Elks Club on December 31, 1900, held a dance followed by a midnight dinner. A few days previously, younger people had gathered for a "hop" at the Hotel Hall on west Camp Street, that in 1902 would be renamed Broadway. "The music was a combination of instruments played by a colored musician," reported the *Citizen* of these festivities, "and was unusually good. The dancers were given the pleasure of dancing the two-step to 'Dixie,' and the waltz to other old-time southern airs, which was a treat for all."[57] At the end of the evening, the participants toasted the upcoming New Year. For its part, the *Citizen* simply asked its readers: "Have you made your new century resolutions?"[58]

• THREE •

Community Advancements and Tossing the Mayor, 1900–1910

On Fourth Avenue, one block south of Speedway Boulevard, a small city park provides an oasis of shady green in the West University neighborhood. Surrounded by imposing single-family historic homes built of brick, wood, or stone, Catalina Park with its splash pad and covered playground equipment attracts both local residents and homeless wanderers looking for a place to relax on a sunny afternoon.

THE FIRST 10 YEARS OF THE 20TH CENTURY saw significant growth and improvements in Tucson, which increased in population by 75 percent. The city went from having 7,531 people in 1900 to 13,191 by 1910, and in many ways it was a decade of progress. In 1902 the Desert Botanical Laboratory on Tumamoc Hill west of town was created "to investigate how plants manage to survive in hot, semi-desert environments."[1] That same year, Sabino Canyon, Bear Canyon, and Mount Lemmon were included in the Santa Catalina Forest Preserve designated by President Theodore Roosevelt, and they would later become a portion of the much larger Coronado National Forest.[2]

These environmental accomplishments were complemented by numerous physical changes to the community. New homes were constructed, such as Fred Ronstadt's imposing 1904 house on north Sixth Avenue that reflected his successful business, which by that time was shifting away from wagon making to more lucrative products. Sewers were also finally being laid, dirt streets graded, the streetcar system electrified, concrete sidewalks put in, water lines extended, and streetlights installed. To finance some of these capital improvements, voters in a March 1907 election overwhelmingly adopted three bond questions by a 10 to 1 margin. These measures meant $260,000 would be available for upgrading the water system, $15,000 to build a new city hall, and $25,000 to fight the constant possibility of fires.

Fire Threats and Suppression

Despite the regular newspaper reports of devastating blazes in Tucson—as well as nationally—it wasn't until the summer of 1908 that the city council actually

Three • Community Advancements and Tossing the Mayor, 1900–1910

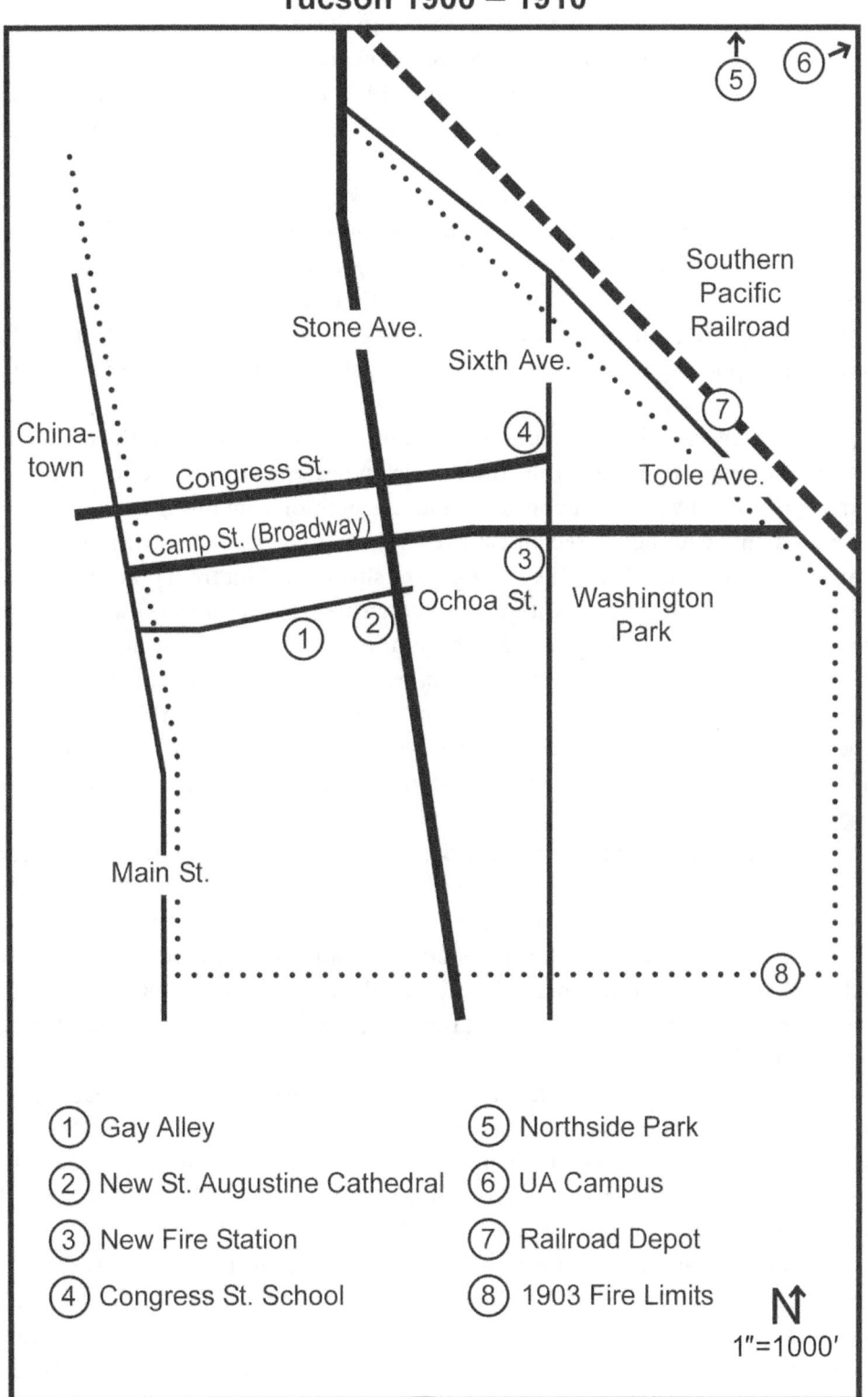

moved on spending some of the bond funds to construct a new fire station. Considering a site for the proposed building, the council sought to replace the cramped, out-of-date existing quarters on Church Street near Stone Avenue.

Reporting to the elected officials in June 1908, the council's Building and Land Committee recommended a new $7,500 station be built in Washington Park on 12th Street between Fifth and Sixth avenues.[3] Since the park was public property designated as open space after the controversial breakup of the Military Plaza property only eight years earlier, the idea was certain to cause controversy.

A lawsuit quickly threatened to stop the proposed fire station construction because some neighbors feared it would affect their quality of life while also potentially endangering school children that might cross the park. Concurrently, other residents responded to the idea with a petition asking that a combined city hall/fire house be built in the park.

Mayor Charles Slack introduced this joint building concept to the city council, and the majority backed him. Their decision brought strong reactions from the public. While some people supported the idea, a petition containing the names of 58 citizens demanded the elected officials reverse their vote to locate the city hall/fire station in Washington Park. They thought the site too distant from other downtown governmental facilities along with being inconvenient to the street railway line. This opposition was endorsed by both an editorial in the *Arizona Daily Star*[4] as well as the Chamber of Commerce. Department store owner Albert Steinfeld was president of the Chamber and succinct in his opinion on the controversy. "I think it would be a very great mistake," he said in summarizing his and many others' view of the community, "to put any buildings in Washington Park, if we expect to ever have any park system at all."[5]

L.J.F. Iaeger, Jr., proprietor of the Santa Rita Hotel located a few blocks from Washington Park, took the opposite perspective. "Every large city has its city hall in the center of a park," he declared. "[Tucson's] Carnegie Library stands in the center of a park and the location is a beautiful one. The same thing would be true of a city hall in Washington Park."[6] In a political quandary, at its August 1908 meeting the council sought a time delay by sending the matter to two subcommittees for further consideration.

Fire had been a major problem in Tucson since shortly after the railroad arrived in 1880. Prior to that, structures had been built almost exclusively of adobe mud brick. While fires in homes and businesses could cause death and destruction, the building material did limit spreading flames. That situation changed dramatically with the importation of lumber made possible by the railroad's arrival.

This movement toward the use of lumber began almost immediately after the railroad tracks touched town. One month after the train's arrival, the *Arizona Daily Star* was praising the architectural transformation which wood construction would bring. "How a frame house can be built in every way fitted for a warm climate is fully shown in the new railroad depot building," the newspaper wrote of the station being erected in Tucson. "It is a move that can be copied to advantage by those who desire frame instead of adobe for their future residences."[7]

The potential fire hazards of frame construction ignored by that endorsement were in addition to the existing threats posed by oil lamps, spontaneous combustion, plus mice and rats chewing on matches. The increased risk of fire soon led to the 1881 formation of a volunteer Tucson fire department that was originally equipped with only 22 rubber buckets, six axes, and nine shovels.[8] The volunteer firefighters were also aided by a 1,500-pound, centrally located bell along with an alarm system with 18 boxes scattered around town.

Complementing these early first steps, municipal fire regulations were adopted in 1883. These included the prohibition of man-made fires within 40 feet of buildings, along with requiring the enclosure of combustible materials such as hay or straw stored within 60 feet of structures.[9] By that same time, some fire plugs had also been installed, two hand carts with 1,000 feet of hose purchased, and a two-story fire station built on Church Street.[10] While Tucson's volunteer firefighters organized and disbanded a few times over the years, by 1886 the department had also acquired a hand-drawn hook and ladder truck.

To combat fires even further, in 1887 the city council adopted an ordinance restricting the erection of frame structures within the city's fire limits, defined as a small district centered on Stone Avenue and Congress Street. No wooden construction would be allowed in this area without prior permission from the council.[11]

The Tucson Fire Department finally moved away from hand-hauled equipment in 1900 when it acquired four horses to pull a chemical engine along with a hook and ladder truck.[12] By the following year, the municipality was also digging four new wells to provide more capacity and pressure to an expanding water system, finding an abundant supply at a depth of 40 feet.[13] The increased availability of water, though, did not necessarily mean greater firefighting protection, and the city council was still reluctant to allow frame construction. In 1903 the council went even further to control the fire threat. It outlawed almost all outdoor fires and purchased a horse-drawn wagon for the fire department that came equipped with two ladders and 1,500 feet of hose.

At about the same time, the council created the "Office of Inspector of Buildings" to regulate construction in Tucson. The ordinance that established this position contained language that mandated all buildings within the city fire limits be made of brick or stone walls.[14] Conversely, inside the city but outside the fire limits, generally defined at that time as Sixth Street and Toole Avenue on the north, Third Avenue on the east, 18th Street on the south, and Main Street on the west, any type of material could be used for construction.

One residential subdivision being developed outside the fire limits was located on municipally owned property just south of Feldman Street, a route that one day would become known as Speedway Boulevard. Centered around a block of land on Fourth Avenue that was set aside as a future park site, this 200-lot development had been subdivided in December 1902. Promising to install a water line to the area along with beautifying the park, which would initially be called Northside, in early 1903 the city government sponsored an auction of the lots. With prices as low as $200, on the first day of the auction 43 parcels were purchased, one for as much as $480, with a total of more than $10,000 being raised for local government coffers.[15]

Homebuyers in this subdivision could easily access the nearby University of Arizona. In 1903 the school had an annual budget of $40,000, a faculty of 20, and an enrollment of 175, many of whom were students in preparatory school, not college.

While enrollment was low, interest in sports on campus grew during the decade. In 1900 the school colors became blue and cardinal and the football team played four games and five in 1901. But one of those in the latter year was a walkover of the Phoenix Indian School because that team's coach alleged: "Arizona players punched and pulled Indians' hair," so he pulled the team off the field.[16]

In addition to football, the University had men's teams participating in baseball, basketball, and track and field. Scheduling was spotty during most of the period for all these sports, with only a few games and meets being contested each year.

Tennis was also played, and by 1907 women were on the team. The next year, women were also playing basketball but as the *Star* noted: "The girls have had some exciting games of basketball between themselves, and some time they hope to have teams from other schools to play against."[17] Those hopes were realized by 1910 when the University team took on high school students from Bisbee and Douglas, beating both.[18]

Transportation to the outlying campus from the center of town could be by foot, horse, carriage, streetcar, or for a few, by automobile. Because of the growing number of cars, in 1903 the city council adopted preliminary rules governing their use. Not only did the vehicles have to have a bell or horn, but also those driven at night had to be equipped with a lantern.[19] In addition, these strange mechanical contraptions were limited to speeds below seven miles per hour.

An even more revolutionary form of transportation appeared in town early in 1910. Having purchased Carrillo's Gardens in 1903, renaming it Elysian Grove, and adding a ball field and greyhound racing track, entrepreneur Emanuel Drachman was advised by his brother Mose to guarantee aviator Charles Hamilton $3,000 for an aerial performance. The money was quickly raised from leading businessmen, including Albert Steinfeld, and Hamilton, labeled a "man-bird" in publicity, was scheduled to become Tucson's first flyer the weekend of February 19 and 20.[20]

Utilizing a bi-plane that the *Citizen* characterized as looking "much like the old-fashioned 'box kite' with a lot of machinery attached," Hamilton's first flight covered 4½ miles at around 40 miles-per-hour and reached about 900 feet in height. The landing on the 200-foot-long runway especially graded for the event was a little rough with a wing of the plane being torn, but it wasn't anything serious.[21]

The next day Hamilton flew twice, both flights ending in crashes into a greyhound racetrack post. Aviator and bi-plane were OK, but local investors in the event were looking at a substantial loss. Because many spectators stood outside Elysian Grove's viewing area, thus avoiding the $1 price of admission, gate receipts only totaled $1,616, and one-half of that was owed to Hamilton. In the end, he received $2,800 for his daredevil performance and local backers were out $1,200 but thanked profusely by the *Citizen* for their generosity.[22]

New means of transportation, developing residential areas, an improving university, and an optimistic outlook had earlier led the *Arizona Daily Star* in 1903 to forecast marvelous things for the community, including a future population up to 50,000 people. There had been some setbacks, of course, including the 1902 premeditated murder of 34-year-old Tucson police officer William Katzenstein. The *Star*, however, was upbeat the following year when it glowingly predicted: "There is a great future in store for us, but to bring it on at once, we must cooperate."[23]

That spirit of cooperation extended to fighting fires. The Southern Pacific Railroad fire brigade helped combat blazes in Tucson, and by 1899 they had been designated a separate division of the municipal fire department. Both firefighting companies working together, though, couldn't save the San Xavier Hotel located next to the Southern Pacific train station on Toole Avenue. On Sunday morning, June 28, 1903, flames shot out of the hotel's kitchen and within 20 minutes the entire wooden structure was engulfed. An hour later, nothing was left of the two-story, 34-room building, but fortunately there was no loss of life.

In response to this and other fires, the city council quickly held a special session to discuss what to do. Deciding to replace some unusable hose and look into a new fire alarm system, the council also instructed the police to enforce the law concerning hay storage near buildings.[24]

The *Arizona Daily Star*, for its part, didn't think that was doing nearly enough. Pointing out that water pressure to fight the blaze at the depot hotel had been totally inadequate, the *Star* demanded the council take stronger steps. The newspaper wanted a halt in running new water lines to outlying housing developments being built on the city's periphery, a practice that decreased water pressure to existing portions of the city.[25]

While that building development restriction was apparently never imposed, some physical changes were being made to enhance the city's general appearance. Downtown's "Wedge," the commercial development west of Stone Avenue, had been almost totally removed by 1904; six years later the extension of Congress Street eastward between Fifth and Toole avenues was also approved.

Taking another legislative step, in 1905 the city council placed additional limitations on automobiles, requiring their registration and license numbering. Fees for this service would be $2.50, with at least a $10 fine or 10 days in jail imposed on violators. "The members of the council adopted the ordinance in rush time," observed the *Tucson Citizen* of the new automobile law, "in order that it might be easier for the [police] officers to identify scorchers [speeders] and to learn the name of the chauffeurs in case of accidents. It frequently happens that an auto scorcher runs down a pedestrian or collides with a [horse-drawn] rig and never stops to see whether death or merely a few broken bones is the result."[26]

At the same time, the Southern Pacific Railroad Company had decided by October 1905 to replace Tucson's original station with a new depot. It was to be constructed just south of the existing building, and the plans called for it to be considerably larger. Heralded as "the finest structure in the city" when it was finished by the summer of 1907, the new depot served seven passenger trains a day.

During that same year, the four blocks of property formerly occupied by the Tucson Indian School close to the University of Arizona were subdivided and sold. Because of the city's growing population, the land near the campus had become more valuable for residential development, so the school moved to a new location on 160 acres of vacant land adjacent to the Santa Cruz River and along the road to the mining camp of Ajo.

Albert Steinfeld was expanding his downtown retail business at about the same time. To stock his thriving department store, Steinfeld opened a large brick warehouse along the railroad tracks west of Stone Avenue, a structure valued at $60,000. This building, combined with the new depot and many other projects completed during the year, brought the total valuation of construction for 1907 to $700,000. "No other city in the southwest enjoys greater prosperity or has richer promise for the future," the *Arizona Daily Star* jubilantly proclaimed, "and there is no good reason why Tucson should not boast a population of at least 50,000 within the next five years."[27] (In reality, Pima County wouldn't reach that total until about 20 years later, and it would be the 1950s before the city of Tucson finally had 50,000 residents.)

Red Light Ladies and Politician Ben Heney

Throughout 1907, additional attention was being paid by the city council to the threat from fire, but controlling blazes, of course, wasn't the only thing on their agenda that year. In August, the elected officials became concerned about expansion of Tucson's red-light district away from Gay Alley, a short, narrow street south of downtown. This district had previously replaced Maiden Lane—that had been located in the Wedge—as Tucson's center of prostitution.[28] In response to the Gay Alley issue, the council was considering a measure to restrict houses of ill fame to a specific geographic location.

Before the council could act on an ordinance, however, 25 residents petitioned for the brothels of Gay Alley to be permanently closed. Citing a territorial law that prohibited operating a house of ill repute within 400 yards of a school, these citizens wanted both the Pima County district attorney and sheriff to act immediately.

Tucson's Engineering Department quickly surveyed Gay Alley and apparently determined all of it to be within 1,200 feet of the San Augustine School, a parochial institution located next to the cathedral. Based on that result, Pima County's district attorney, Benton Dick, declared, "If the figures of the city engineering department are correct, as is stated, every house of ill fame now being run in Gay Alley will be closed before the week is over."29

Following up on his pledge, Dick had one madam arrested and she was found guilty and ordered to pay $100 or serve 100 days in jail. An appeal of this verdict was filed, and the judge decided the territorial law didn't apply to parochial schools, so the brothels of Gay Alley continued to operate openly.

Not to be deterred, the city council looked for other methods to at least control the spread of houses of prostitution. Late in 1907, a special meeting was held to discuss the issue. Unable to attend because of personal business that required him to be out of town, Councilman George Benjamin "Ben" Heney laid out his views in a letter. Believing it was impossible to eradicate the red-light district simply by passing laws, Heney instead favored limitations on the women's behavior.30

Raised in San Francisco, Heney arrived in Tucson in 1880 at the age of 18 and eventually became a successful businessman with 10 general merchandise stores from Texas to California. He also served for eight years as Pima County treasurer, and while the *Star* criticized his performance in office, the *Citizen* called him: "the personification of honesty and integrity."31

In January 1907, Republican Heney was appointed to the Tucson City Council. Labeled "one of the leading business men of the city" by the *Citizen*, the newspaper also concluded of the new councilman: "He is fearless and progressive and is firm in his opinions."32

In late 1908, Heney sought the city's top elected position, joining a nonpartisan ticket of council candidates, and he was elected to a two-year term as mayor in December with 53 percent of the votes. In his inaugural address the following month, Heney said Tucson was heading toward a population of 50,000 and offered several recommendations for improving the community. One was to limit or prohibit the sale of alcohol in the red light district, while another was to "make immediate preparations for housing under its

Ben Heney may have been a highly successful businessman, but after months of bitter conflict with the city council, he was unceremoniously removed as mayor in 1909 (Arizona Historical Society, PC 162-#132).

own roof its fire apparatus—chemical and fire engines, hook and ladder rig, horses, etc."[33]

Two major fires around that time showed the need for improved firefighting capabilities. In December 1908, fire had destroyed the northside Whitwell Hospital, a tubercular institution at First Avenue and Adams Street. A few months later, a blaze gutted several buildings, including two grocery stores as well as a historic Chinese joss house located near Main and Pennington streets.[34] If it hadn't been for a persistent cat warning of the danger, that 4 a.m. fire may have done even greater damage.[35]

Ignoring continual hazards like those, a decision had been put off since the previous August on the location of a new central fire station, and Mayor Heney wanted to quickly resolve the controversial issue. Because of limited financial resources to build a combined city hall/fire station, and with some public opposition to locating the fire department in Washington Park, the council solicited offers for sale from private property owners for a fire house site. Four proposals were received, and the council chose a $6,500 lot on the west side of Sixth Avenue just north of the park.[36]

The local architectural firm of Holmes & Holmes quickly drew up plans for the new building, and construction of the brick and stone, two-story structure soon began; the building would be finished by June 1909. Once it opened, the fire department had a new station to house its equipment: a horse-drawn steam engine, a chemical engine, hose cart and wagon, and about 5,000 feet of hose. While construction of the new building was underway, the proposal was made and accepted to name the station after D.J. "Jack" Boleyn, Tucson's first fire chief. Having served in that capacity between 1881 and 1886 and then again from 1890 until 1898, Boleyn was reportedly killed while fighting a fire in 1910.

The 1909 city council additionally granted amnesty to the fire department's mascot, a dog named "Jack." Being unlicensed, Jack was in violation of long-standing municipal law, but after hearing that the dog accompanied the department's men on all their runs, the council voted to issue Jack a free license.

Meanwhile, a few California Bungalow–style residences were to be built around Northside Park on Fourth Avenue south of Speedway. While most of the homes adjacent to this park, renamed "Catalina" in 1915, were made of brick, some would be built of lumber. The wood construction proposal was from W.T. Wheatley, president of the Arizona Mill & Lumber Company. He suggested the frame homes he was building near Northside Park, combined with all the other economic activity going on in town, was good news for the community. This was especially true, he thought, because more luxury homes in town would help to decrease the traditional summer exodus of well-off families from Tucson.[37]

Two of Wheatley's homes adjoining Northside Park on Fifth Avenue were designed by a California architect. Despite their innovative appearance, however, the wooden building materials would add to the city's fire worries.

Considerable controversy surrounded the location of a new fire station that was finally settled during the 1909 administration of Mayor Ben Heney with the selection of this Sixth Avenue site (Arizona Historical Society, PC1000, Tucson General Photo Collection, #42889).

Political Controversies

Near the end of the decade, though, the municipal government had considerably larger problems. In February 1909, Mayor Heney demanded the resignation of the water department superintendent, a move that prompted that official to observe: "[T]he trouble with the water department seemed to be that 'a Democrat was at the head of it.'"[38]

After succeeding with that staffing change, Heney was dissatisfied with the man's replacement, even though Heney had appointed him. Thus in June 1909, Heney nominated a third man for the position, a step that infuriated all but one of the council members, or the "Solid Five" as the *Tucson Citizen* labeled them. Explaining the mayor's attempt to name another water superintendent, the *Star* observed that the new man Heney wanted was someone who had helped him win his election.[39]

In response to Heney's staffing change attempt, the "Solid Five" successfully fought to block it, and they were able to retain the previous water superintendent. As a result, less than six months after becoming mayor, Heney summarized the political situation by saying: "It is apparent to the dullest that the best interests of this community can no longer be subserved by the present make-up of the governing body of this city. Either I must resign as Mayor, or five men must resign as Councilmen."[40]

Neither of those steps was taken, of course, so within weeks of the water superintendent brouhaha, Heney dropped another bombshell. He publicly demanded the resignation of Councilman John B. Martin, one of the "Solid Five." Accusing Martin of graft for taking a bribe in a liquor license transfer case as well as seeking payoffs from the J. Knox Corbett Lumberyard, Heney's charges were quickly heard by the council.

Once the testimony was concluded, the "Solid Four" stood behind their compatriot Martin in a report exonerating him. A front page *Citizen* headline screamed of the outcome: "Councilman Martin Is Whitewashed,"[41] even as the *Star* calmly concluded: "Evidence submitted during the graft hearing does not substantiate the charges of Mayor Heney."[42]

Although defeated in that case, Heney wouldn't let the matter lie. He called a public meeting at the Congress Street Opera House to discuss his charges and urged everyone interested to attend. "Seats will be reserved for ladies," a large newspaper ad for the gathering announced. "Nothing in the evidence will be discussed that any sensible woman can not listen to with propriety."[43]

That night, the mayor once again presented his case against the councilman. What the *Citizen* saw as an appreciative, standing-room-only audience, the *Star* characterized as a "roaring farce comedy" performed in front of "many empty chairs."[44] Whatever the reality, Heney again explained his evidence against Martin. The only thing new in the talk, the *Star* stated, was that after 180 days on the job, Heney wanted out as mayor of Tucson. "The five of them can do whatever they please with me, and I hope they do it," the morning paper quoted Heney as saying. "I don't want the office. I can't work under these conditions. I can do this city no good."[45]

Not surprisingly, the *Citizen* saw and reported things about the gathering totally differently. According to it, during his oration, Heney predicted, "he had no doubt that the 'Solid Five' is framing a plan for his impeachment."[46]

Ignoring that possibility, Heney quickly turned his attention to seemingly more important civic matters. At the end of July 1909, he personally led a police raid that netted the arrest of 26 Chinese men for betting on dominoes. "Mayor Heney claims that in connection with the gambling joints," wrote the *Citizen* after its reporter went along on the raid, "lotteries and opium rooms have [also] been conducted. It is said that white men and even white women have been among the patrons of the opium rooms. Mayor Heney is determined to stamp out these yellow dens of vice."[47]

From their perspective, the *Star* was completely dismissive of Heney's actions. "[H]is honor got wise to the playing of dominoes down in Chinkville," the newspaper wrote derogatorily, "and a raid was framed up."[48] Within a few weeks, the first of the Chinese gamblers had been fined $100 and sentenced to serve 10 days in jail.

Turmoil on the city council and social vices weren't the only items grabbing newspaper headlines during the hot summer of 1909. On a more positive note, it was announced that a local group called the Tucson Boosters Club would be formed to promote the community. With a motto exclaiming "Tucson: The Best City in

Arizona," the mission statement of the organization proudly stated, somewhat ironically under the political circumstances: "We believe in Tucson and that its future prosperity is assured by its natural advantages and progressive citizenship."[49]

Some physical improvements were being made in town around the same time, including the grading of Fourth Avenue northward from the railroad tracks all the way past Northside Park to Speedway. To further enhance motoring opportunities in town, since Tucson, or the Old Pueblo as it was often referred to, had about 135 automobiles,[50] it was announced that a new road would be developed. Extending "The Speedway" eastward by seven miles to what would eventually be called Wilmot Road, the dirt route would then turn south for one mile before returning to the city along a path that would later be named Broadway Boulevard.[51]

Funds to pay for this grading project were solicited from automobile owners. Within three weeks $320 had been raised, including contributions from Postmaster J. Knox Corbett and Tucson's first car owner, Dr. Hiram Fenner. Work was soon underway and by early September 1909, the unpaved route was almost finished.

Mayor Heney, naturally, had other things on his mind. In mid–August 1909, the mayor suspended Marshal Nabor Pacheco, accusing him of neglecting his duties. Even though Heney had appointed Pacheco to fill a vacancy, the mayor said he had informed the marshal of the Chinese gambling scourge, but nothing had been done. Heney also alleged Pacheco had turned a blind eye to the selling of alcohol to prostitutes in Gay Alley as well as to the existence of other houses of ill fame in violation of Territorial law.[52]

In response, Pacheco immediately denied all the charges. "Heney tells an untruth when he says he notified me that gambling was going on," Pacheco insisted. "I never received such notification."[53]

To replace Pacheco, at least while the charges against him were being investigated by the city council, Heney nominated legendary Arizona Ranger Harry Wheeler. The *Star* declared Heney's action in seeking to appoint Wheeler, a Cochise County resident, a discredit to Tucson. "Couldn't the mayor find an honest man in Tucson to take the job?" they asked sarcastically.[54]

Wheeler didn't get a chance to serve, however. Even though he would literally be riding to the rescue, since he wanted to bring his beloved horse with him, Wheeler couldn't take the position because he wasn't a Pima County resident, and the law required a marshal to have lived in the community they were to serve for at least 30 days.

More importantly, after hearing the charges against Pacheco along with his defense, the city council soon exonerated the marshal. While one councilman had publicly predicted this outcome well before it actually occurred, the elected body heard testimony from numerous witnesses, including Heney, prior to rendering its verdict.

At the same time as backing Pacheco, the now "Solid Six" men of the city council publicly called for Heney to step down from his post. Citing the detrimental effects his continuous accusations were bringing to both the marshal and the community, the council adopted a motion that stated: "[I]t is the unanimous opinion of the councilmen that the best interests of the said city will be subserved by the immediate resignation of Ben Heney as mayor thereof."[55]

Heney quickly rebuffed the request so the *Star* pointed out: "[T]he question of how the council or anyone else will set about to remove him from office is being freely propounded."[56] Not giving up, Heney quickly picked another fight with the council, this time over Tucson's street commissioner.

Ousted from Office

After an automobile accident on Sixth Avenue between 18th and 19th streets resulted in injuries, including a broken collarbone for one of the victims, members of the council blamed Street Commissioner Nat Fulmer. They charged he hadn't had proper barricades installed along the street. In protest, Fulmer handed in his letter of resignation to the city clerk, but before it took effect, he changed his mind and asked Mayor Heney for his letter back. Heney complied by retrieving the letter from the clerk's office.

However, upon advice from the city attorney, the council accepted Fulmer's resignation and named a replacement. Thus, in October 1909, two men held the post of Tucson Street Commissioner, one performing the duties while the other was still reporting for work and planning to sue the city for his salary.

This relatively minor municipal dispute was the rationale behind the council's allegation that Heney had violated Arizona territorial law by taking Fulmer's resignation letter from the clerk's office. As punishment, they charged the mayor should be removed from his elected position. The *Star* labeled the accusation "Disorderly Conduct," but a *Citizen* headline declared: "Joke Charge Used for Serious Purpose."[57]

The council obviously wanted Heney's political head and a November 4, 1909, meeting was set to hear the charges. "Mayor Heney has worked honestly, conscientiously and in many ways well for the interests of Tucson," proclaimed the *Citizen* before this meeting. "Look at the Fire Department."[58] The extent of the changes for the volunteer firefighters were impressive, including the completion of a new, up-to-date central station.

The *Star*, though, gave credit for these firefighting improvements to the council's Building and Land Committee. They also said of the office of mayor: "It is already a huge joke—at least the man occupying it is something on that order."[59]

With the outcome of the council's removal hearing of the mayor never in doubt, the *Citizen* was forecasting dire consequences. "The expulsion of Mayor Heney from office on a trivial pretext merely because he does not agree with the City Council," the afternoon newspaper stated, "will only serve to make the fight more bitter, only serve to work injury to Tucson."[60]

Reportedly attended by hundreds of citizens, the "trial" of the mayor was political theater at its finest. He defended himself by admitting to the charge of removing the street commissioner's letter from the city clerk's office, but stated the document was Fulmer's property.[61]

Fulmer tried to accept blame for the entire episode by stating he had removed the resignation letter himself. That admission, however, proved to be false when Fulmer conceded he retrieved the letter from Heney.

After the mayor, to loud applause according to the *Citizen* but support from only one person as reported in the *Star*, made a final statement blasting the council for ignoring the moral ills of the community, the "Solid Six" unanimously voted him out of office. "Hoots and hisses interfered with the proceedings for several moments," commented the *Citizen*.[62]

Thus, Ben Heney was expelled from his elected position in November 1909, having served just 10 months of his two-year term. The *Star* saw only positives from this change. "[I]t is believed that under the new regime," the newspaper stated, "Tucson will enjoy an unprecedented period of prosperity."[63]

Republican Councilman Preston Jacobus was appointed to fill out the remainder of Heney's term and promised: "It will be the mayor and the council from now on."[64] That lofty sentiment, of course, didn't include Tucson residents, and within a year of Heney's ouster, a fist fight broke out at a Council meeting. Councilmember Mose Drachman, one of the "Solid Six," objected to being called a liar by a speaker and, according to the *Daily Star*, "rushed around the railing which divided the two men and they were soon at it." A few blows were thrown before others intervened and split the pair up.[65]

For his part, history would record that the impeachment of Ben Heney was based on a legal "technicality," but Tucson residents of 1909 knew differently. The *Citizen* had reminded its readers before Mayor Heney's last council meeting that the voters of Tucson would actually have the final say in the matter, declaring: "Tonight the Council are the judges. In December [elections], the people will be the judges."[66]

Voting and Other Restrictions

Two laws of the Arizona territorial government in Phoenix, where the capital had been moved from Prescott in 1889, would impact who could vote in those elections. First, only men would be able to participate. It wouldn't have been that way except Arizona Governor Alexander O. Brodie vetoed a total suffrage bill in 1903. After twenty years of trying, the women of the territory had finally convinced a majority of both houses of the legislature to adopt the measure. The *Arizona Daily Star* supported the proposal, but wanted educational qualifications placed upon all voters, which would eliminate the franchise, the newspaper wrote: "[for] the ignorant, both men and women."[67]

Instead, in March 1903, a strong majority of the legislature had simply adopted a law allowing women to vote, and the *Star* gleefully predicted: "There is no doubt the governor will approve the bill."[68] But then rumors started, indicating Brodie was being pressured by his wife, who was opposed to the theory of equal suffrage, or by saloon and gambling interests, who feared losing business, or by politicians who had voted against the bill and were afraid of the political consequences of their opposition. The excuse Brodie would use, it was speculated, was that granting suffrage to women was in violation of the 1863 Congressional organic act creating the Arizona territory. Trying to counter this argument, Tucson lawyer, and former territorial Attorney General, William Herring, telegraphed the governor, stating: "I am convinced that the validity of the [legislative] act in question cannot be successfully attacked in court."[69] Ignoring that opinion, Brodie vetoed the suffrage measure, and all the *Star* could write of the governor was that "he has committed an unpardonable and inexcusable blunder."[70]

On the other hand, six years later the Democrat-controlled territorial legislature did adopt a requirement mandating all voters be able to read and write English, and it went into effect. Directed in part at reducing the number of Mexican American voters because they were presumed to be Republican-leaning,[71] the *Tucson Citizen* editorialized of this law: "A man who cannot even read or write the English language is not of sufficient mental attainment to be any judge of either men or politics."[72] As a result, only literate men would be able to choose Tucson's elected officials in 1909.

Attempts to diminish the role of Mexican Americans in Tucson weren't only political. In 1908, as president of the Chamber of Commerce, Albert Steinfeld named 14 men to several committees. All of them were Anglo.[73]

Another discriminatory measure that impacted some Tucson residents had also been adopted by the territorial legislature in 1909. This law stated: "they [local school boards] may segregate pupils of the African from pupils of the White races, and to that end are empowered to provide all accommodations made necessary by such segregation."[74] At that time, Tucson schools had about 40 Black students out of a total enrollment of 2,300, but the district board did not move to establish a segregated school, so the Black pupils remained where they were.

While local public-school discrimination was held in abeyance, at least for a few years, around the same time the Black residents of Tucson were experiencing other forms of blatant racism. Despite that, in 1910 they celebrated the Emancipation Proclamation at a June event held at the Elysian Grove amusement center.[75] Earlier in the decade, though, the Pima County Board of Supervisors had made their views plain about employing a Black janitor. "We want no Negroes about the court house" was their straightforward 1906 opinion.[76]

A few years later, 1909 municipal balloting was held at which time two incumbent councilmen, as well as Marshal Pacheco, sought new terms. With many Tucson residents disgusted by the city council, with the *Star* not supporting the incumbents, and with the *Citizen* basically sitting out the campaign, all three office holders lost their elections. The *Citizen* listed five reasons for this outcome, including:

"Dissatisfaction by the men who honestly believed that the principles advocated by Mayor Ben Heney were right."[77]

For his part, Heney had predicted this political revolt the day after he was removed from office. "Only wait," he said then, "new hopes will be born, new aspirations will embolden the citizenry, and we will win. Good government—clean government—is bound to prevail as surely as truth, righteousness and morality are bound to prevail."[78]

• FOUR •

Statehood, the "White Plague," and a Serious Census Setback, 1910–1922

Near the southeast corner of Speedway Boulevard and Wilmot Road, tiny signs announce "Harold Bell Wright Estates." Throughout the subdivision, streets are named after characters from Wright's best-selling novels from the early years of the 20th century. Atop a prominent high point in the area, and with a Little Free Library kiosk now in front of it, the author's 1922 home still looks down on the community spreading around it for many miles in every direction.

"CHANGE" WAS THE WORD THAT BEST characterized Tucson during the second decade of the 20th century. The community was growing in population, statehood for Arizona became a reality, human rights were somewhat improving, at least for women, and remarkable new forms of transportation were emerging.

Even though motorized vehicles had been around for a while, a 1911 headline in the *Arizona Daily Star* informed its readers: "First Arrest for Speeding Made to Stick." Jack Martin had been apprehended exceeding the 10 mph speed limit on his motorcycle and had to pay a fine of $10.[1]

Preliminary strides were being undertaken at about the same time to link at least a portion of Arizona together by highway, while other efforts were directed at including Southern Arizona on a transcontinental road route. According to its backers, the advantages of this cross-country highway running through Tucson were enormous, including, as one Tucson supporter pointed out: "As conditions are now … we get none of the tourist business to which the winter climate here entitles us. Eastern owners of machines [automobiles] either ship their machines to the [west] coast or leave them behind. All this would be done away with if we had a system of good roads."[2]

A local roadway improvement was actually implemented when the $70,000 Fourth Avenue underpass beneath the Southern Pacific Railroad tracks was opened in June 1916. Car salesman Monte Mansfeld, son of pioneer Jacob Mansfeld, was one of several auto dealers clamoring to be the first to drive through the new underpass.[3]

Work was also progressing on improving Tucson's street system. Beginning in

Four • Statehood, the "White Plague," and a Census Setback, 1910–1922

Tucson 1910 – 1922

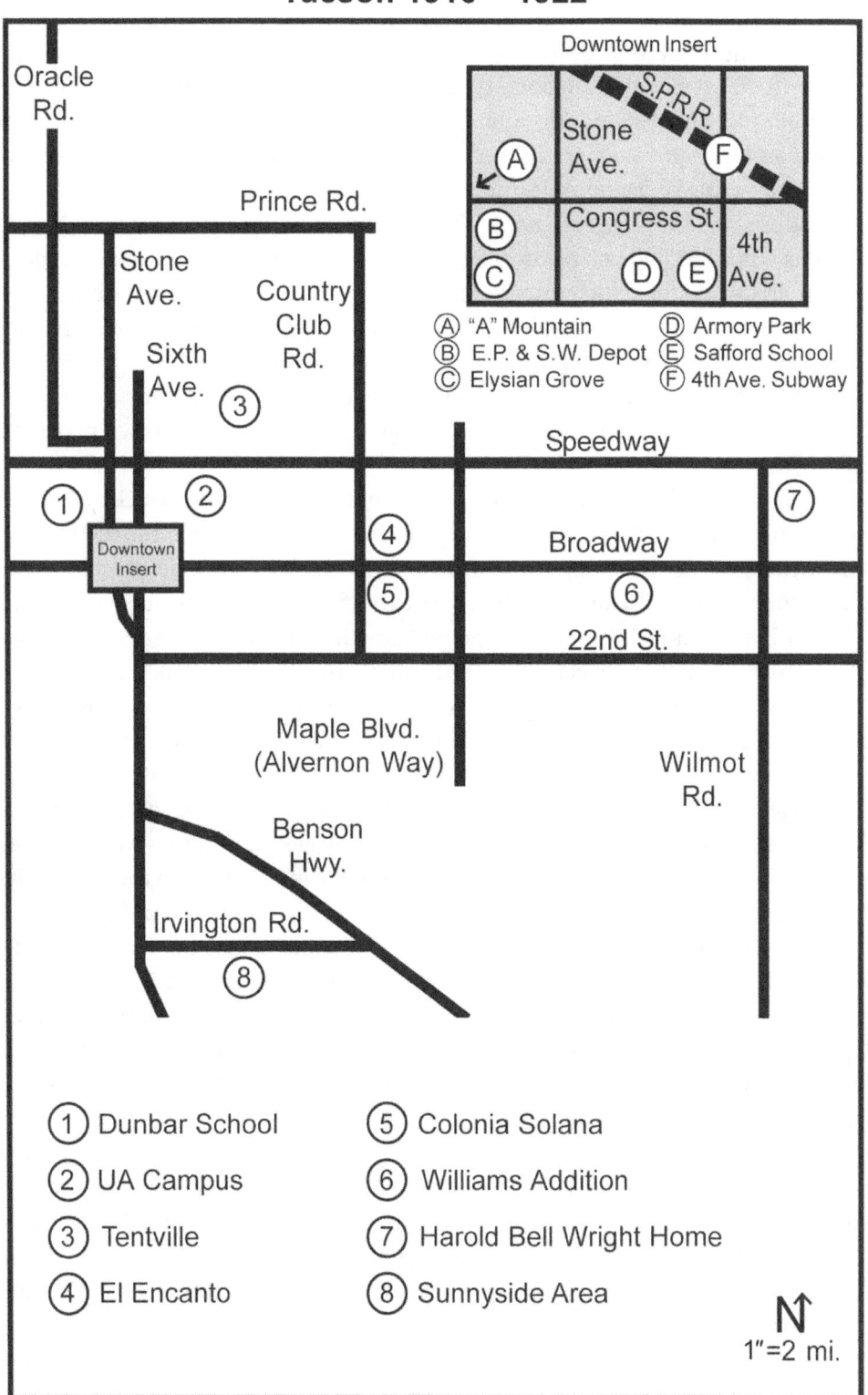

1910, the municipal government had begun a program of "macadamizing," or gravelling, dirt roadways.

If dealing with automobiles was becoming somewhat more commonplace, another form of novel transportation brought great excitement to Tucson. In November 1911, some 20 months after Tucson residents had seen their first airplane flight, pilot Calbraith Rodgers arrived in Tucson from Willcox, Arizona, spent two hours with a crowd of thousands, then flew off toward Phoenix.[4]

Rodgers had left New York hoping to fly across the country in less than 30 days, and thus win a $50,000 prize posted by wealthy newspaperman William Randolph Hearst. Frequent stops, including 16 crash landings, slowed the novice pilot down considerably and he averaged 56 miles per hour. When he finally arrived in Long Beach, California, he had spent almost seven weeks hopping across the nation.

Earlier in 1911, Tucson's first long distance telephone call had been made. Rancher Banning Vail called Los Angeles, and operator Gradye Drown placed the call for him.[5]

A few months later, Pima County held its first fair at the Elysian Grove amusement center near the Santa Cruz River. The site was transformed for the fair, and those attending the four-day event were offered displays on agriculture, mining, home economics, and school exhibits. Six years after that, local residents were provided with new natural wonders by the 1917 opening of Colossal Cave east of town. "To reveal its splendors," exclaimed the *Tucson Citizen* of the cavern, "calcium lights in colors will be burned in the halls and chambers."[6] Also during the decade, Tucson families continued the tradition of visiting nearby Sabino Canyon recreational area to enjoy the riparian scenery while picnicking next to the flowing water.

Tragedies and controversy continued to confront Tucson around the same time. Two Pima County law enforcement officers—Joe Meeks and James Mercer—were killed in the line of duty early in the decade. In 1910 a massive fire in the Santa Catalina Mountains burned for ten days before it was put out by valiant firefighters.[7]

The following year, University of Arizona president Arthur H. Wilde came under scathing criticism from the *Citizen* for not sufficiently backing the school's athletic program. "Athletics must not only be approved by a university," the newspaper editorialized, "they must be advocated, encouraged and supported by the authorities from the president down to the newest student, if the institution is to be benefited."[8]

The student council on campus quickly responded to that complaint by pointing out that 20 percent of the male students, out of a total enrollment of 500, practiced with the football team. It would be this squad, while losing to Occidental College in a 1914 game, that impressed a newspaper reporter so much with its dogged tenacity that he exclaimed: "the Arizona men showed the fight of wildcats."[9] The "Wildcats" label stuck and the school had earned a nickname.

Another university tradition established during the decade took place on Sentinel Peak west of downtown. In March 1916, using $250 in funds donated by local

To escape the desert heat and enjoy the abundant attractions of nearby riparian nature, Tucsonans, like this unidentified group in 1911, have long journeyed to Sabino Canyon to play and picnic by the water (Arizona Historical Society, PC 142–#92902).

businessmen to buy supplies, many students whitewashed a previously installed letter "A" on the hillside and since then it has been called "A" Mountain.[10]

Becoming a State

It would be primarily on the university campus that Tucson celebrated the momentous occasion of statehood. Southern Arizona in 1862 had been designated a territory by the Confederate States of America, and the following year the entirety of Arizona became a territory of the United States. For decades after that, however, territorial officials repeatedly failed to gain statehood from Washington, D.C. This perceived stigma cast a long shadow over Arizona that was only lengthened in 1906 when Arizona voters overwhelmingly rejected joint statehood with New Mexico. Finally the shadow began to lift in November 1908 with the election of Ralph Cameron from Northern Arizona as the territory's representative to the U.S. Congress.

Being a Republican, and thus a member of President William Howard Taft's political party, may have helped Cameron in his quest. On June 20, 1910, Congress authorized Arizona to develop a constitution in anticipation of acceptance as a new state of the union. In response, three months later, the all-male, mostly Anglo voters of Arizona selected 52 men to draft a state constitution. The group was overwhelmingly Democratic; among the eleven Republicans elected were five Pima County representatives, including retailer Carlos Jácome.[11]

Woman suffrage supporters pushed to include the measure in the draft constitution, but they were rebuffed. That snub, however, wasn't the reason, when the proposed constitution came before Arizona's electorate for approval in February 1911, both the *Citizen* and the *Arizona Daily Star* implored Tucson voters to reject the measure. They feared Taft wouldn't accept the document because of his opposition to the prospect of voters recalling judges. Labeling the constitution's provision allowing the recall of judges as "socialistic and un-American," the *Star* summarized: "Instead of bringing us statehood, [passage] most unfortunately will close the door against us."[12] Ignoring the newspapers' pleas, more than 70 percent of Tucson voters ratified the constitution, as did an even larger majority across the territory.

This enormous public support, though, didn't dissuade Taft from his philosophical opposition to the judicial recall. Based on that opinion, the president vetoed the Congressional statehood measure for Arizona.

In Tucson, the *Star* and *Citizen* both hoped for immediate passage of new legislation that would satisfy the president. This was quickly accomplished when Congress approved a measure requiring the removal of the judicial recall, and Taft signed it on August 21, 1911.

As the statehood dispute was playing itself out, Tucson businessman Fred Ronstadt had his own say about the matter. In a large newspaper ad he proclaimed: "Statehood or No Statehood, Say to the Outside World, 'I Live in Tucson' and I'm Glad of It."[13] At the same time, Tucson's afternoon newspaper, the *Citizen*, predicted statehood would bring the community neither greener grass nor more rainfall, but would result in more people.

Around that time, Businessman J. Knox Corbett wired Ralph Cameron: "all true Arizonans extend to you their hearty congratulations and appreciation for your efforts toward the successful termination of the statehood struggle."[14] Corbett also noted that he was 50 years old, had been a resident of Tucson for more than 30 of those years, spanning his entire adult life, and yet had never voted for president of the United States. Statehood, he knew, would change that.

The revised legislation approved by Taft mandated Arizona voters remove the judicial recall from the draft constitution before the territory could become a state. A vote on that proposal was scheduled for December 1911 and the *Star* left nothing to chance in its endorsement. The ballot question had two choices—for or against the amendment—and the newspaper showed which box to check along with admonishing its readers: "If you don't want statehood; if you want to be bound, hand and foot; if you want to be a puppet, with the owner of the Punch and Judy show in Washington pulling the string that makes dependent mankind dance, vote against the amendment."[15] Conversely, the newspaper forecast: "But if you want to be one of God's creatures, with all the rights of manhood and independence; if you want to be a free American citizen, vote for the constitutional amendment." Based on sentiments like that, the voters passed the required measure in resounding fashion.

As a result, at 10 a.m. on February 14, 1912, Valentine's Day—and for the first time in front of motion picture cameras—the president autographed the important piece of legislation making Arizona the 48th state of the Union. "'To My Valentine'—Statehood" screamed a bold headline in the *Star*. (In November 1912, Arizona voters reinserted the judicial recall into the new state's constitution.)

While there were huge celebrations across Arizona, the response in Tucson to statehood was rather subdued. There was a ringing of bells and whistles when Taft signed the proclamation but the only other event of note was a gathering at the University of Arizona. As part of a campus holiday, a parade by military cadets was followed by several speeches, with one orator proclaiming excitedly of the newest state: "It will be inhabited by the happiest, prosperous and most contented citizenship of any commonwealth in the union."[16]

Economic and Suffrage Gains but School Segregation

A trend in that more prosperous direction was already being seen in Tucson. Several months before statehood, the announcement had been made that three "skyscrapers" of up to five stories in height were planned for the downtown area. One of these new buildings would be the three-story future home of Albert Steinfeld's department store on Stone Avenue at Pennington Street. Several months later, plans were also being drawn up for a new armory to be built on the east side of Washington Park, the site of so much earlier controversy.

An enormous boost to the local economy was concurrently anticipated because of the decision by officials with the El Paso & Southwestern Railroad (EP&SW) to extend their tracks 67 miles into Tucson from Fairbank south of Benson, Arizona. The arrival in town of this line, which ran from El Paso, Texas, through Douglas, Arizona, and then on to Fairbank, was expected to bring hundreds of railroad maintenance jobs with it. Because of that, the 20 acres of land along Main Street south of Congress Street, which was needed by the company for a passenger depot as well as freight and shop yards, was purchased for $75,000 by a group of local citizens and donated to the railroad. The company later repaid that investment in full.

"It is far and away the most important, the most welcome, and most longed-for item of news which this city has received for more than a decade," glowingly proclaimed the *Citizen* in an August 1911 editorial.[17] The coming of the new railroad, a local business leader added, "will stimulate the growth of the city, develop undeveloped areas around us, give us greater population, and increase our prosperity."[18]

In anticipation of the new railroad's arrival, Emanuel Drachman closed the Elysian Grove recreation area in 1911. The 14-acres of land not far from the EP&SW depot site would be subdivided into residential lots for new homes. Since the Silver Lake recreation area had been shut down years earlier, the *Tucson Citizen* summarized of Elysian Grove's closure: "Tucson will be left without an amusement park of its character."[19]

By the end of 1912, and after a welcoming ceremony attended by 3,000 joyous residents, the trains of the E.P.&S.W. were actually arriving in Tucson. The railroad, however, only served Tucson for a little more than a decade. In 1924 the Southern Pacific Company purchased the line and moved all Tucson rail operations to its Toole Avenue station.

Among the immediate repercussions of the E.P.&S.W.'s decision to come to Tucson was a boost in land prices. "Real Estate is going up—going up to heights that will reap a golden harvest of dollars to the man who gets in on the ground floor," speculated one local company.[20] A group of Chicago entrepreneurs certainly believed in that future and plunked down $350,000 to buy 2,700 acres of land near Tucson. Their plans were to subdivide the property into 40-acre farms.

In addition to securing a second railroad for Tucson, the year 1912 also proved to be extremely important for the women of the new state. When the first Arizona legislature refused to approve a measure allowing women to vote in state elections, suffrage supporters used the citizen initiative process authorized by the Arizona constitution to place the question directly on the ballot.

Leading the local 1912 effort in support of suffrage was Dr. Rosa Goodrich Boido. Having first moved to Tucson in 1900 with her husband and two children, she established a medical practice on west Pennington Street that focused on serving women and children. She also soon became the first licensed physician in Pima County.[21]

The family departed Tucson in 1903 but returned eight years later and Dr. Boido was soon running unsuccessfully for a trustee position of School District One while being elected president of the Equal Suffrage Club. Not only did she host meetings of this group at her medical office and organize rallies to support suffrage, but she also personally gathered signatures to place the suffrage measure on the November 1912 ballot.[22]

Just before the general election on women's right to vote, Arizona pioneer and longtime Tucson resident, Josephine Brawley Hughes, implored the men of the state to approve the idea. "For more than thirty-five years," she wrote, "a loyal band of Arizona's women have been appealing for equality before the law and it is with a heart full of gratitude that I rejoice over the fact that all of Arizona's political parties have, in their platform of principles, endorsed women's suffrage."[23]

On election day, Hughes and Dr. Boido were at different polling places, urging passage of the suffrage measure. They distributed campaign materials, handed out water, and offered chairs to men needing a rest.[24] As a result of this effort, Arizona's male voters strongly endorsed the suffrage idea. Those in Tucson agreed, approving the proposal by a two to one margin, meaning women began registering to vote in 1913. (At the national level, women did not gaining voting rights until the adoption of the 19th amendment to the U.S. Constitution on August 26, 1920.)

Saloon owners and their patrons had feared passage of the Arizona suffrage measure could lead to a ban on alcohol, thus they opposed the ballot item. Since 1883, on the other hand, Tucson's chapter of the Women's Christian Temperance Union (WCTU) had been pushing for the right of women to vote because, in part, they thought it would allow women to influence the outcome of a vote on prohibition. That measure, these women believed, would lead to less drunkenness among men, fewer domestic violence cases, and reduce squandering of money at bars.

The saloon owners' concerns turned out to be justified when Arizona voters, led by women, adopted a statewide temperance measure in 1914. In anticipation of the January 1, 1915, introduction of this alcohol ban, the Steinfeld Department Store had a clearance sale on wine and liquor, with a bottle of Dewar's Special dropping from $1.50 to $1.15.[25]

Loopholes in the prohibition law, however, meant that personal consumption of alcohol in public places would continue. Responding, proponents sponsored a tougher prohibition measure on the 1916 ballot, and it also was approved.[26] But while saloons may have closed because of this law, the consumption of alcohol certainly didn't stop. As the *Tucson Citizen* reported in January 1917: "The bootleggers are abroad in the land plying their nefarious trade, apparently unmolested. It is as easy to get whiskey in Tucson as it was before the state went dry."[27]

Some people saw prohibition as socially progressive, but on the other hand, the territorial legislature had approved racial school segregation in 1909 without making it mandatory. Three years later, the *Arizona Daily Star* proudly proclaimed of the local district with six schools and 2,500 students: "Tucson has the best school system in Arizona, if not on the Pacific Coast."[28]

While Tucson schools were not segregated prior to statehood, a 1912 state law required that school board trustees "shall segregate pupils of the African race from pupils of the white races, and to that end are empowered to provide all accommodations made necessary by such segregation."[29] This law had been unsuccessfully protested by several Tucson African Americans, who called it needless since in their opinion there was "no friction between the blacks and whites anywhere in the west."[30]

Thus, in 1913 the first segregated school opened in Tucson in one room at Sixth Street and Sixth Avenue.[31] Taught by Cicero Simmons, who was paid $90 a month, 31 students were enrolled in nine grade levels. Five years later, Tucson School District One built a new segregated facility at 11th Avenue and Second Street, naming it Dunbar after nationally famous poet Paul Laurence Dunbar.

The Chinese had suffered discrimination since moving to Tucson before the Southern Pacific Railroad arrived in 1880. Many of them once lived near Main and Alameda streets in a tiny, unofficial Chinatown, but by 1911 the small residential area had disappeared to make way for new construction of homes for the wealthy. The relocation of these Chinese residents thus became one of the community's earliest urban renewal projects. Wanting to demolish many of the homes occupied by the Chinese, the city council in March 1910 notified the primary property owner, Dr. Hiram Fenner, of health and safety issues in the area. Responding, Dr. Fenner: "promised to cause the immediate removal of the tenants of the property."[32]

It took a while to accomplish this objective, but the Chinese men were all eventually displaced and the buildings leveled. Some of the men moved to a residential complex near the intersection of Congress and Meyer, where they and those following them would reside until relocated again by the Tucson Community Center urban renewal project some fifty years later.

West of town, on February 1, 1917, an executive order of President Woodrow Wilson created the Papago (Tohono O'odham) reservation. Cobbling together several smaller existing districts, including San Xavier, the presidential action meant the tribe officially had a home of its own.

More people in town at that time were putting strains on Tucson's water supply. Small pipes, low pressure, lack of meters, and an inexperienced staff led to continual problems with the system. "The sooner the people of this city wrestle with this water problem," extolled the *Citizen* in 1911, "and solve it for the present as well as the future Tucson, the better."[33]

To address the water shortage, the city government imposed limitations on summertime irrigation. In order to meet the long-term water needs for a future population of up to 75,000, a citizens committee was appointed by the city council to research the issue.

Combined with numerous physical improvements actually taking place on the ground, this was the kind of forward thinking that led both the *Star* and *Citizen* to forecast great things for the community. The city's afternoon paper predicted in January 1912: "With statehood, a new railroad, a customs smelter [a firm that processes not its own ore but that from customers], a good copper market, agricultural development and excellent prospects for many other good things, 1912 should be a banner year for Tucson."[34]

Harold Bell Wright and Oliver Comstock

While somewhat socially and racially divided, this growing community of Tucson was the one which popular author Harold Bell Wright decided to inhabit in 1912. Relocating his family from California, after spending only one week in town, Wright paid more than $5,000 for a Victorian-style home and its furnishings on Speedway near Fourth Avenue. "Mr. Wright has become so much attracted by the climate, the city, and the wealth of story-teller's material in Pima county," noted the *Tucson Citizen*, explaining the author's quick decision to reside in the community.[35] A national celebrity, he suffered from tuberculosis that led in part to his eventual long-term residence in Tucson.

Having the previous year published his first best seller—*The Winning of Barbara Worth*—Wright came to Tucson in 1912 to pen *Their Yesterdays*. The latter book contains contrasting viewpoints of the unnamed female and male characters and provides hints of Wright's love of nature and disdain for urban life. "And there was sunshine in her Yesterdays—bright sunshine—unclouded by city smoke," Wright wrote of his heroine, "and flowers unstained by city grime; and blue skies unmarred by city buildings; and there were beautiful trees and singing birds and broad fields in her Yesterdays."[36]

Despite its simplistic story, the book was another winner for Wright, who moved from Tucson after its publication but continued to visit on an annual basis. That changed abruptly in 1915 when a horse-riding accident in California inflamed Wright's tuberculosis. Retreating to an isolated camp in the foothills of the Santa Catalina Mountains outside Tucson to regain his health, Wright wrote another bestseller—*When a Man's a Man*. This book, according to *The American Magazine*, "had an advance sale of 600,000 copies: it took twenty-one railroad cars to ship the books!"[37]

When he first moved to Tucson in 1912, Wright lived a few blocks away from Oliver Comstock, and during the next 20 years the two men's lives often intertwined. Born in Indiana, Comstock moved west in 1907 because of the poor health of one of his nine children. He had been ordained a preacher in 1887 but gave it up to become a printer while also serving as a Tucson justice of the peace for two terms. In addition, Comstock would assist Tucson's unfortunate tubercular patients for a long time.

Popular author Harold Bell Wright not only wrote best-selling novels early in the 20th century, he also worked to help Tucson's less fortunate, and played a part in establishing the community's sprawling character (courtesy the Friedman photograph collection).

The city of 20,000 residents that Wright and Comstock inhabited included several thousand who suffered from tuberculosis, also known as "The White Plague." Nationwide, tens of thousands of people were dying from the disease each year. To try to avoid that fate, the sunshine of Southern Arizona had been prescribed for decades as a possible relief from the ravages of TB and other lung diseases.[38]

To take advantage of

To provide some relief to those suffering from tuberculosis, a circular 48-room sanatorium with shaded porches was designed by Dr. Hiram Fenner and opened at St. Mary's Hospital in 1900 (Arizona Historical Society, Buehman photo, #B38129).

that possible health-restoring climate, huge contingents of TB sufferers flocked to the warm Southwest. Some of these people lived in Tucson sanitariums, such as the two-story circular structure opened at St. Mary's Hospital in 1900, or as renters in small alley houses built behind the main residence. Those without sufficient financial resources, however, often ended up residing in hardship at "Tentville" that was located less than one mile north of Speedway between First and Campbell avenues. A ramshackle settlement of a place, it spread across almost one square mile of desert. "The nights were heartbreaking," a former resident of "Tentville" remembered years later, "and as one walked along the dark streets, he heard coughing from every tent. It was truly a place of lost souls and lingering death."[39]

Spurred into action by the suicide of a man suffering from TB, along with the suggestion that those inflicted with the disease should be sent off to more distant camps, Oliver Comstock helped poor tubercular sufferers in "Tentville" by distributing food and supplies. He was often seen carrying a pot of hot soup on the handlebars of his trusty bicycle. Using every means at his disposal to raise money to help the unfortunate victims, Comstock also began a small hospital that would eventually be named in his honor.

A few blocks west of this hospital were two other facilities for TB patients. The Whitwell Hospital, destroyed by fire in 1908, was rebuilt and renamed "Sanatorium for Diseases of the Lungs and Throat." Nearby, to serve men with tuberculosis, St. Luke's in the Desert was initially opened with seven living units by the Episcopal Church in 1918. Its founding was spurred when Arizona Bishop Julius Atwood, who had previously established a TB sanitarium in Phoenix, experienced the realities of tuberculosis in town. "[F]inding myself one day in Tucson," he recalled, "I was called to a house where a young man [with tuberculosis] was in hysterics because he was about to be turned out of his lodging house. It took almost the remainder of the day to find a place for him. The week previous, another poor fellow [with tuberculosis] had been found dead in a ditch near Tucson."[40]

To operate the small St. Luke's facility, which would later be enlarged, Bishop Atwood named a Board of Trustees consisting of four men, including himself. To raise the money needed to operate the non-profit sanitarium, he enlisted a number of socially prominent women, who called themselves the Board of Visitors.

The year 1918 also saw the worldwide Spanish Influenza epidemic strike in Tucson. By September, the disease had arrived, and as a result, the next month schools, churches and theaters were shuttered by public order. The University of Arizona also shut down while a temporary hospital was opened on campus to treat sick students.[41] The following month, 41 people were listed as dying from the flu or related diseases, and in November, with deaths exceeding 90 for the month, the city's Board of Health mandated the wearing of masks in public. Announcing this move, an *Arizona Daily Star* headline proclaimed: "Tucson Foils Flu Bug with Masks Today."[42]

Some members of the business community, religious institutions, and the general public objected to both the mask mandate and limitations on public activities, but Mayor O.C. Parker appointed 25 officials to enforce the edict. While many people flouted the mask law, several arrests were made. Limitations on public assemblies did not last long, but the masking requirement remained in effect until December 24 when a court order ended the mandate.

More than 300 people in Pima County outside the Papago (Tohono O'odham) reservation died from the disease in the seven months from September 1918 to April 1919. That represented almost one percent of the total population. "The hardest-hit age groups," reported an analysis of the epidemic, "were children under the age of 10 and young adults aged between 20 and 29."[43]

Earlier, after Oliver Comstock had personally managed the tuberculosis relief effort for several years, by 1917 its funding and administration were being directed by the community's Organized Charities. For his part, Comstock was extremely complimentary of the financial and other assistance provided by Tucsonans, once remarking: "I don't think there are any bigger hearted people than my friends in Tucson. I have never asked them for aid for my welfare work that I haven't received what I asked, and often more."[44]

This generosity was demonstrated by Harold Bell Wright who had moved back to Tucson by the end of the decade, intent on remaining permanently, because he believed the "climate was productive of clear thinking, the surroundings were ideal for writing." Seeking to help Oliver Comstock's efforts with tubercular patients, in 1920 Wright staged a production of his second book, *The Shepherd of the Hills*, at downtown's Safford School. Not only was Wright the play's author, but he also served as director and scene painter. The 800-seat school auditorium was packed for all three performances and the $3,000 raised from selling $1 and $1.50 tickets went to the Organized Charities. Following up on that success, Wright put on his play "Salt of the Earth" the next year to benefit Tucson's Tubercular Charity hospital and in 1922 spoke during a vaudeville show organized to support the Organized Charities.

World War I and a Sprawling Desert Community

While TB sufferers were flocking to town, Tucson simultaneously sent many of its own sons off to fight in World War I, even as the community was rocked by a war-related scandal. City engineer Charles F. von Petersdorff was a native of Germany, but an American citizen since 1887. When the United States entered the war in 1917, he tried repeatedly to enlist in the military to "have an opportunity of fighting for the country that has been his home the better part of his life."[45] His attempts, however, were denied. Then in early 1918, the federal government alleged von Petersdorff "[had] violate[d] the neutrality of the United States in 1915" by participating in a complex international oil and mining scheme with Germans residing in the United States. He denied the charges and immediately offered to resign his municipal position, but the city council unanimously rejected that offer. However, von Petersdorff did take a 60-day leave of absence, which did not suffice to exonerate him, and he eventually lost his job. It wasn't until August 1918, in San Francisco, that he was finally cleared of the charges, and by the following June he was in Los Angeles, hoping to be employed by the Southern Pacific Railroad as a watchman.

Back in Tucson, to provide men for the American war effort, a national registration program was being conducted for those between 18 and 45 years of age. More than 5,000 Southern Arizona men signed up, including 21-year-old Eleazar Herreras in August 1918. He was the son of Andres Herreras, a man who had been born in Mexico but became a U.S. citizen in 1902. The elder Herreras was a plastering contractor, miner, and rancher. Eleazar, who was born in downtown's barrio in 1897, began to help his father plaster adobe houses early in life, a skill that would benefit both him and his community in the decades to come.[46]

Like Herreras, most Tucson men willingly joined the military and were given a wristwatch by well-wishers as they left Tucson by train. Retailer Albert Steinfeld's son, Harold, however, attempted to avoid service and eventually an arrest warrant was issued for him. By April 1918, though, the young Steinfeld had changed his mind and enlisted.

Some of the Tucson men who fought, of course, didn't return—they died in service to their country. Twelve of these, all students at the University of Arizona, were recognized in early 1920 when U.S. General John J. Pershing dedicated the Berger Memorial Fountain next to Old Main on the campus in their honor.

For most other soldiers from Tucson, though, the war ended in November 1918, and they came home. The town they returned to was changing. Under the leadership of Andrew Ellicott Douglass, the Steward Observatory, funded by wealthy patron Lavinia Steward, had been established on the UA campus in 1916. Partially because of the war effort it wasn't until seven years later that the building would be dedicated and contain a 36-inch telescope.

Building permits for 1919 exceeded $1 million and were expected to increase by 50 percent in the next twelve months. Three annexations had also added to the city's physical size. At the same time, a new $125,000 downtown Opera House on Congress Street was completed, and the Overland Auto Company opened a large dealership on Sixth Avenue north of the railroad tracks.

Adding to these impressive accomplishments, in May 1920, the University of Arizona awarded degrees to 65 graduates, its largest senior class ever. A few years later, across Park Avenue west of the campus, real estate owner Louise Marshall and her husband Tom, a former UA football player, were planning to build a new $75,000 shopping center that would include a "handsome and well-equipped drug store."[47] Also, in 1920 Tucson voters approved $140,000 in water bonds to address pressure problems on the city's northside. Anticipating developments like those, the *Citizen* predicted at the beginning of the year: "1920 will be the best year in Tucson history, best in trade, best in population, best in expansion of business, best for the buyer and best for the seller."[48]

Apparently sharing those sentiments was Harold Bell Wright, and by that time his personal residential focus had turned to Tucson's remote desert. In 1920 he purchased almost 80 acres of land six miles out of town along Speedway, adding another 80 acres to the estate later. "Where else in Arizona or the world," Wright asked the *Tucson Citizen*, "could I find a site for this home of mine with eleven such ranges of mountains in the plainest view and in sight of the country which I love best?"[49] It wasn't until two years later that Wright and his second wife would occupy their new home, but the trend they established by moving far out of town into a lush desert surrounding was to have lasting impacts on the community.

Crediting Wright with initiating the push to sprawl Tucson into the unspoiled desert, one real estate executive concluded: "Wright started the urge to live out in the wilderness. Other wealthy men followed with similar fancy homes. This gave one real estate man an idea that if he could get the state to obtain a lot of the government-owned land around here and put it on the market, that land would be bought at high prices by newcomers longing for a home in the wilds."[50]

The possibility of a market of wealthy winter visitors, or possibly even permanent inhabitants, buying parcels of property far from Tucson's center soon caught on. In 1922 a few dozen residents of the Sunnyside area several miles south of town built a $2,000 one-room school and were planning to subdivide lots in order to attract homebuyers. Sometime later, the Williams Addition was developed along Broadway almost five miles east of the center of town, while closer in, both El Encanto Estates and the Colonia Solana subdivisions were planned.[51]

Population Problems and Solutions

The mostly wealthy people who lived in these outlying developments were exactly the type of people Tucson leaders were looking to attract; there just weren't enough of them to satisfy local dreams. Even though the Chamber of Commerce had adopted a campaign of "Bigger, Busier, Better Tucson or Bust," Tucson's population during the decade wasn't growing fast enough to satisfy the community's politicians and businessmen.

Before the 1920 census count began, estimates that up to 30,000 people, or possibly even 35,000, lived in the community were being confidently forecast, thus ensuring Tucson would remain the largest city in the state.[52] Despite that optimism, there were immediate problems for the 16 federal census enumerators who took to the streets to canvas Tucson. By late January, the Arizona director of the census, R.B. Leach, was citing difficulties with finding people at home and thought 5,000 people might go uncounted.[53]

"It will of course be a catastrophe if Tucson shows a population of 18,000 or 20,000," the *Citizen* editorialized, "…instead of 25,000, which is a conservative estimate of the actual number of people in the city limits."[54] Allegations were also later made that Phoenix officials were trying to manipulate their own census figures, and the *Citizen* stated of the state capital: "They sought a privilege given to no other city in the United States, that of holding their count open until they could rush in the names so as to overshadow Tucson, their old rival and always the metropolis of the state."[55]

Local boosters with enormous pride had pointed to that title—"Metropolis of Arizona"—for more than 50 years, but by 1920 that distinction was in danger of being lost because of alleged cheating up north. After the Phoenix scheme was publicly exposed, however, the idea of adding more people to their population was quickly dropped.

When the final census figures were released, they showed Tucson with only 20,292 residents. Even worse, the population of Phoenix had skyrocketed during the previous decade from 11,000 to almost 30,000, meaning for the first time the capital was the largest city in the state and that Tucson's reign as the "Metropolis of Arizona" was finished.

For the *Citizen*, the failure of Phoenix to have an even higher population was at least something to gloat about. "They are the metropolis of the state, all right," the newspaper sadly acknowledged, "but … to have less than 30,000—that is a catastrophe."[56]

Four • Statehood, the "White Plague," and a Census Setback, 1910–1922   67

Despite that snide comment, Phoenix had far outpaced Tucson's population growth during the preceding 10 years, and Southern Arizona business leaders weren't happy. "[I]t didn't set well with a lot of Tucson boosters when they found out that the 1920 Census showed that Phoenix had outgrown us by a considerable number of people, and it was a larger city," recalled Emanuel Drachman's son and local real estate legend Roy Drachman in a 1992 interview.[57] "So the people in Tucson decided—business people—what they should do. And they had meetings and decided to establish the Sunshine Climate Club."

By the fall of 1922, the local business community, including Tucson Sunshine Climate Club board member Hiram S. "Hi" Corbett, son of pioneer J. Knox Corbett, along with retailers Fred Ronstadt and Albert Steinfeld, galvanized the city around raising $50,000 to nationally advertise Tucson. The club's goal was to increase the population to 50,000 by 1930 or possibly even earlier, thus continuing the long-standing "Bigger is Better" philosophy of Tucson's leadership.[58]

According to a song entitled "Tucson Sunshine" written by a local minstrel, this goal could be accomplished if the community worked together.

> Now, Tucson's climate is a prize
> In all the world there is no better,
> And she would grow to mammoth size
> If we would only let her.[59]

On the morning of October 2, 1922, the Sunshine Climate Club dramatically launched its fund-raising campaign by awakening the community to the sound of 50 dynamite charges set off at Tucson High School on the north side of Sixth Street.[60] Tucsonans were soon receiving telephone solicitations from a "Miss Sunshine" asking them to participate, and in response, tens of thousands of dollars were quickly pledged.

At the same time, a Los Angeles marketing firm was preparing recommendations for how to spend the money. "Tucson from an advertising standpoint has two things to sell," the company concluded, "1. Climate [and] 2. Scenery."[61] In the latter category, the report called for highlighting the region's "wierd [sic], unusual" vegetation. The marketing firm further noted: "The giant Sahuara [sic], the yuyca [sic], the barrel cactus, and others have a peculiar fascination and appeal to those who are used to more conventional manifestations of plant life." Other ideas suggested for entertaining visitors included featuring Indian villages as tourist attractions as well as encouraging "the opening of a Mexican cafe for tourists" even though several small local Mexican restaurants already existed.

The dual attractions of climate and scenery, the report recommended, should be directed at health seekers and tourists alike, either of which could then become homebuyers. The report stressed, however, that businesses should not be targeted by the marketing campaign, perhaps to protect existing commercial establishments from competition.

Another group of people not to be encouraged to immigrate to town were impoverished victims of TB. "From the standpoint of numbers," the report stated, "the Tuberculosis sufferer is the best prospect." It then, however, continued: "We are very thoroughly aware of the danger to the community of bringing indigent tubercular cases here."[62] Although Tucson residents had taken several steps to help the poor who had tuberculosis, the report considered trying to encourage more of them to come to town as inappropriate.

While the Sunshine Climate Club's population-boosting effort was underway in 1922, the city government issued 150 building permits for both new residences and businesses, including three Chinese groceries. At the same time, "Tentville" was slowly disappearing. The demand for new housing in the area, combined with the provision of more health-care facilities for tubercular patients elsewhere, meant the slow demise of the poverty-ridden property.

Harold Bell Wright's new house east of Tucson was concurrently being completed.[63] The author would live in the house for almost a decade. During that time he continued to write while also being instrumental in the publication of *Long Ago Told*. This book, illustrated by Katherine Kitt, contained numerous legends of the Papago (Tohono O'odham) people. Wright commented of these stories: "They were to me so striking in the beauty of their conception and so significant in their relation to the character of these desert Indians that I was deeply impressed."[64]

His advancing age and other challenges eventually led Wright to return to California. Several years after the author's 1944 death, his 160-acre estate near Speedway Boulevard and Wilmot Road would be subdivided into one-half acre lots, the streets named after characters in his books. Before that happened, the best-selling author who loved the Arizona desert but who also helped initiate the residential sprawl which was to later characterize the community, wrote: "From every street and corner in Tucson, we see the mountains…. But of all the peaks and ranges that keep their sentinel posts around this old pueblo there are none so bold in the outlines of the granite heights and ragged can[y]ons, so exquisitely beautiful in their soft colors of red and blue and purple, or so luring in the call of their remote and hidden fastnesses as the Santa Catalinas."[65]

• FIVE •

Aviation and Athletic Accomplishments, 1920–1930

> *Chirping birds hidden in velvety palo verde trees and among the scraggly branches of creosote bushes offer peaceful harmony to visitors of a small desert cemetery on Alvernon Way just north of River Road. Among the hundreds of tombstones, a small rock monument holds a sign that states: "Established in 1899 by pioneer settlers of the community of Binghampton."*

A SLOWLY GROWING SILVER SPECK APPEARED above the horizon northwest of Tucson on September 23, 1927, and then circled the small but bustling city three times. Charles Lindbergh, piloting the *Spirit of St. Louis*, touched down at 2 p.m. following a five-hour flight from San Diego. As he taxied to a stop, Lindbergh was greeted by the cacophony produced by thousands of honking automobile horns.

Four months after making his historic solo journey across the Atlantic Ocean to Paris, Lindbergh came to Tucson to formally dedicate Davis-Monthan airfield. Among the welcoming gifts bestowed upon the 25-year-old aviator was a full-scale model of his airplane, made out of cactus and created by a local florist.[1] The famous pilot then rode in a motorcade along Tucson streets lined by thousands of cheering people. Before going to the University of Arizona, where thousands more awaited to hear him speak at the football stadium, the international celebrity was taken for a short visit with ex-servicemen who were patients at a government hospital in Pastime Park north of town.

That evening Lindbergh addressed a banquet crowd of more than 400 jammed into the university's dining hall for the formal dedication of Davis-Monthan. "The most important step now to be taken by aviation," Lindbergh told those in attendance, "is the construction and development of airports. It is a great pleasure to find a city with as good an airport as Tucson has."[2] Named after Samuel H. Davis and Oscar Monthan, two local military airmen killed in plane crashes, Davis-Monthan airfield would serve both municipal and military needs.

DM, as it was known, was not Tucson's first airplane strip. Earlier flights had landed downtown, and in 1917 property north of the community was set aside for aviation purposes and called "Oracle Road Landing Ground for Airplanes."[3] Then, in 1919, 80 acres of land along Sixth Avenue south of town was purchased at $30 an

Tucson 1920 – 1930

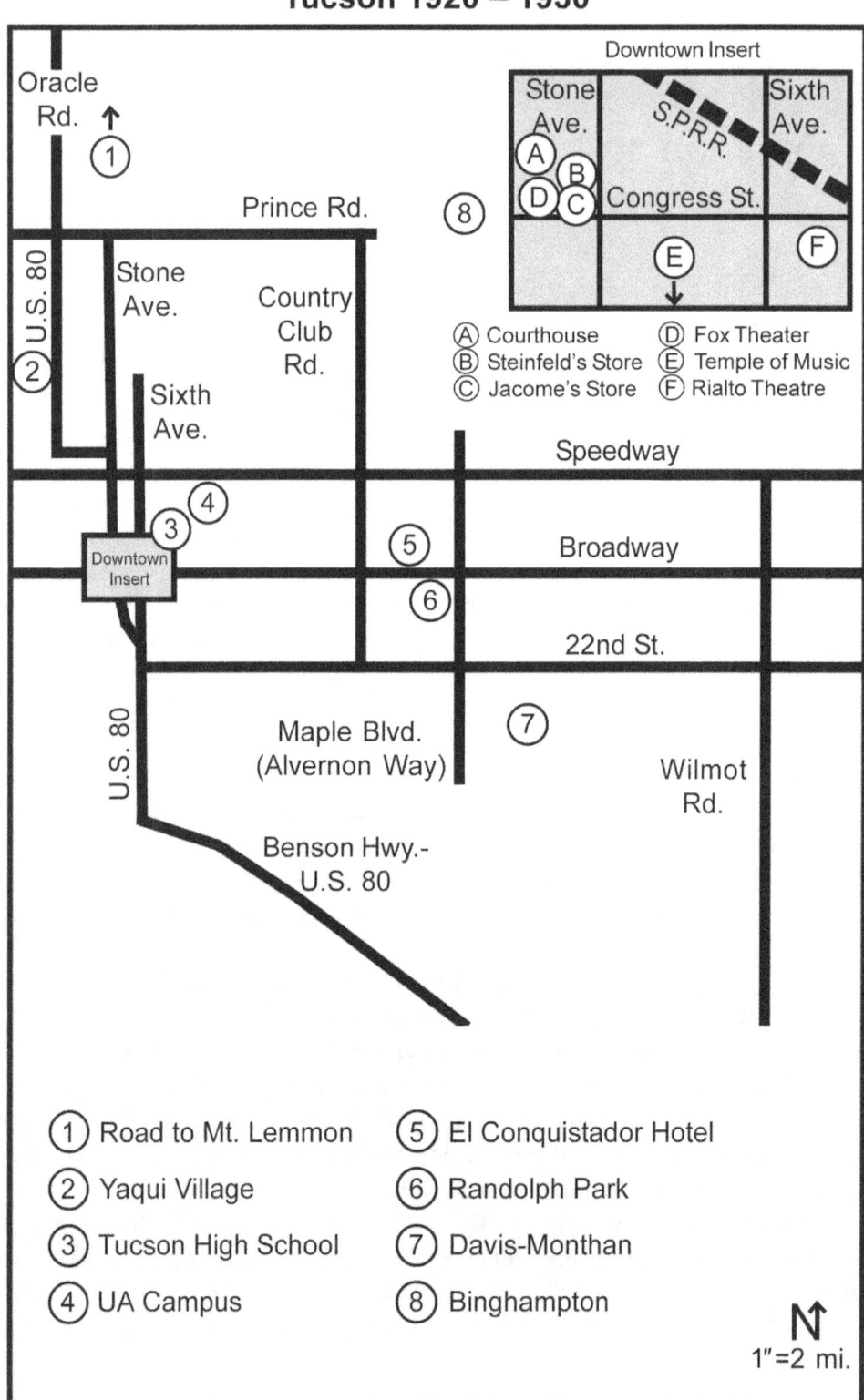

acre by the city of Tucson from businessman Levi H. Manning. It was to be used as a new air strip, making it the first municipal airport in the United States.[4] One of the early pilots to land at the new venue remarked: "We know from past experience that Tucson always welcomes aviators, and this is a reputation which it will be well for Tucson to continue."[5]

The U.S. Army soon stationed two men at the southside field, thus making it a combination municipal/military operation. With the introduction of larger planes into the military fleet, however, it became obvious by 1925 that Tucson needed a bigger airport. Therefore, after clearing 240 of the 1,280 total acres of desert land set aside southeast of the city for DM, a brick house was built for the soldiers stationed at the field, a 1,000-gallon gas tank erected, two hangars installed, and the new facility was ready for use.

More military planes weren't the only flights Tucson officials were hoping to attract to Davis-Monthan. As early as 1919, predictions had been made that the community would be on a great transcontinental route of commercial aviation. By the end of the following decade, three companies, including Southwest Air, were flying into Tucson, offering service to Los Angeles and El Paso. Two airplanes had also been used in the 1928 search for a teenager missing north of Tucson. One of the planes crashed near the Cañada del Oro riverbed, killing all four on board, among whom was Pima County sheriff's deputy Clifford Nelson.

New Residents, Luxury Living, and Sports

Several years before that tragic accident, many Yaqui Indian families were fleeing their Mexican homeland because of revolutionary fighting. Some of them settled in Tucson, and while most lived in a few downtown neighborhoods, others built very basic homes north of town near what later would be the intersection of Grant and Oracle roads. "[A]t the present writing [spring 1922]," one author noted, "there are about 30 families located here. They live in miserable shelters usually constructed of material gathered from the adjacent city garbage grounds or the mesas north of them.... [T]he head men assert that as soon as they may receive titles to the land, they will erect decent homes, plant gardens and live comfortably."[6]

Further east on the northside of town, 30-year-old builder John W. Murphey was using homesteading laws to acquire vacant land in the foothills of the Santa Catalina Mountains, intent on turning the gently rolling terrain into prestigious home sites. He would eventually purchase more than 8,000 acres, at an estimated cost of $15 per acre, and build hundreds of houses for affluent clients. Swiss-born architect Josias Joesler, whom Murphey had persuaded in 1927 to move to Tucson from Los Angeles, would design many of these homes.

After the federal government intervened, one parcel Murphey unsuccessfully sought to build on was a 40-acre plot just north of the Rillito Creek. Originally used as a desert cemetery by Mormon families who mostly lived and farmed along the riverbed, the first burial occurred in 1899 when 91-year-old John Harris was laid to rest in the graveyard.[7] Harris was related to Nephi and Elizabeth Bingham, the couple who, with their children, had first settled in the isolated area around 1898.

This land northeast of Tucson remained sparsely populated for a decade until revolutionary rumblings began rising in northern Mexico, and Nephi Bingham suggested Mormon families living there might want to relocate to Arizona. After a long covered-wagon trip, the first refugees in December 1909 arrived in Binghampton, called that since there was already a small settlement named Bingham elsewhere in Arizona. A feast which included both a freshly butchered pig and cow along with many other delicious treats welcomed the new arrivals.[8]

These people quadrupled Binghampton's population, and over time it would continue to grow. Sleeping on cornhusk mattresses and fighting constant battles with an endless supply of snakes, these pioneers were establishing a small settlement.

By 1910 a branch of the Church of Jesus Christ of Latter Day Saints (LDS) was organized in the area. Several years earlier, a schoolhouse had been built, eventually to be named after Alexander Davidson, the man who donated the land on which the building sat, and the school would also serve for a while as both a weekend dance hall as well as a LDS church.

At first raising crops such as sugar cane, the Binghampton farmers soon expanded agriculture in the area by installing handcrafted redwood flumes running from the Rillito Creek. These were used to transport intermittent water to irrigate adjacent fruit and pecan orchards and farm fields of alfalfa, wheat, barley, and oats. Huge holding ponds stored the unused water and these reservoirs were so large they attracted hundreds of ducks, which were hunted and sold to a meat market.[9]

Among his other agricultural endeavors, Nephi Bingham operated a dairy farm and grew milo and maize to feed the livestock. By 1926 his son Floyd was one of three dozen dairymen in Tucson who were joined in their farming pursuits by 30 poultry raisers and 15 beekeepers working on agricultural property scattered all across the north side of town.[10] A dropping water table, however, meant that farming in the area could not go on forever.

Despite that, a Mormon church eventually would be constructed near Binghampton, and the Davidson School became part of Tucson School District One in 1928. As the small community grew, the use of the settlement's cemetery also increased, including for Nephi Bingham himself in 1916 and his wife 36 years later.

Near the end of the century's third decade, homebuilder John W. Murphey also became involved with completing the El Conquistador Hotel. One of Tucson's first destination resorts, the hotel was located on Broadway three miles east of downtown. Financed in 1925 with $300,000 raised from more than 800 local subscribers, it was designed by Arizona's first resident female architect, MIT graduate Annie Graham Rockfellow, who worked for Henry O. Jaastad's firm.[11]

Hotel construction bills were mounting substantially beyond projections by July 1927, and the stockholders decided to lease out the El Conquistador and employed Murphey to oversee the massive building's completion. This was finally accomplished at a total cost of about $500,000, and on November 22, 1928, the palatial establishment was debuted at a formal dinner. Attended by 250 who paid $7.50, they dined on cream of celery soup followed by baked filet of sole and boneless squab chicken accompanied by potatoes chateau and alligator pear (avocado) salad with French dressing.[12]

Containing 70 rooms that started at $9 a night, including meals, the Mission Revival-style hotel had a staff of 36. It was fronted by an elaborately decorated porte-cochere that adjoined a copper-domed topped tower soaring 65 feet above the surrounding desert. The grounds of the hotel contained large lawns, 350 varieties of roses, and a magnificent cactus garden.

Just a few blocks west of the hotel was the Tucson Golf and Country Club that provided 18 holes of dirt play with greens oiled regularly to prevent their sand surfaces from blowing away in Tucson's frequent windstorms. A nearby 480 acres of land would eventually become a municipal park and golf facility. Purchased by the city of Tucson in 1925 for future development, the property was named after the late railroad baron and Tucson benefactor, Epes Randolph.[13]

Golf wasn't the only game making a splash in Tucson during the '20s. The University of Arizona football team had a successful campaign in 1921, compiling a 7–1 record while outscoring their opponents 418–30. As a result, at the end of the season they were invited to meet the Praying Colonels from Centre College of Danville, Kentucky, in the first Christmas Classic. Played in San Diego on a slippery field made worse by a driving rainstorm, Arizona lost 38–0 to a squad described as "the greatest football team in the United States."[14]

The following year, the University of Arizona band made its debut at a home football game. Founded in 1902 with 12 musicians, the group had a start and stop existence, but by 1922 it had 23 members and was solidly established.[15]

Having been introduced in 1922, polo was another sport being played by university students. By 1923 the club was the collegiate champion of the Southwest, and in 1924, when the school had an enrollment of around 1,600, they did even better—ending the season with their ponies on the east coast and playing Princeton in a two out of three series for the national title.

Tucsonans rallied around the polo club before the matches, and hundreds of them signed a telegram of encouragement urging: "Bring home that bacon, Wildcats."[16] A large crowd of enthusiasts gathered anxiously in front of the downtown Stone Avenue offices of the *Tucson Citizen* where the running score of the first match was posted. The western team lost 6–2 and dropped the next one by a score of 8–0, thus coming back without the championship.

Among those who had signed the telegram to the polo club were auto dealer Monte Mansfeld along with young businessman Roy Drachman. Also putting her name on the petition was Nora Nugent, owner of a downtown cafe—The Palms.[17]

Downtown and Other Happenings

Nora was born in 1883 into a military family living in Wyoming and her father, Patrick Sullivan, was assigned to Fort Lowell in Tucson soon after her birth. She later studied education and specialized police work at the University of Arizona and married Southern Pacific Railroad engineer William Nugent.[18]

The couple had three sons; after William Nugent died in 1918, his widow operated The Palms for a few years to provide the family with an income. Nora was eventually hired as Tucson's first policewoman, a job she would keep until her position was eliminated due to Depression-era budget cuts. (It wouldn't be until the early '50s before the department hired its next policewoman. In 1956, at age 73, Nora Nugent retired from Tucson School District One where she had worked mostly in the attendance office since the 1930s.)

Joining a police force of between 23 and 33 men, depending upon the time of year, in 1929 Nora Nugent was paid $1,500 annually. "In many instances," an *Arizona Daily Star* article reported, "[she acts] as foster mother to young women who are friendless and in trouble."[19]

"It is no wonder we have so many juvenile cases these days," Nugent told the *Star* in 1933. "We have few homes left. True, there are houses in which children eat and sleep, but home—no. I mean by homes a place such as I had as a child or as most of my generation had; a place where our friends gathered for happy evenings of games, dancing, songs."[20] Instead of that type of family life, Nugent was observing something different, including the attitude of children. "Even if their home conditions are fairly good," she explained to the *Star*, "their associates lead them away and they grow to feel that their parents are old-fashioned foggies." Based on that, Nugent concluded: "The whole trend today seems to be away from homes to public places— the movies, public dance halls, the open road in motor cars. Life itself is restive and young people respond to this speed-age."[21]

Tucson in the '20s certainly had a significant number of people interested in the speed provided by automobiles. To reduce this temptation, the city's first traffic light was installed at Congress Street and Sixth Avenue in 1927.

Near this intersection was where the community's new car dealerships initially congregated. One of those opening in the area was O'Rielly Chevrolet, founded in 1924 by 28-year-old Frank O'Rielly. Two years later, a new sedan could be purchased from him for $735, and other models were even cheaper. Within five years of going into business, O'Rielly's had outgrown its small space, so in 1929 the dealership moved a few blocks north of the railroad tracks. Relocating to a much larger Sixth Avenue building that had a vacant lot adjoining it—from which used cars could be sold—O'Rielly's joined two other new car showrooms already doing business across the street.

O'Rielly's was one of many businesses that was invading the territory south of Sixth Street between Fourth and Stone avenues, an area that was once the small, emerging residential neighborhood described earlier in Chapter Two. To facilitate business expansion like this, as well as supporting suburban residential development, the municipal government in 1920 asked for voter approval of $140,000 in bonds. The funds were to be used to add water storage capacity in order to extend the current system to the north side of town. At the same time, to supplement the existing Fourth Avenue subway, the city of Tucson also proposed spending bond funds to build two new $40,000 automobile underpasses beneath the Southern Pacific railroad tracks at both Stone and Sixth avenues. While the water bonds were overwhelmingly approved, voters handily turned down the underpass proposals.[22] One explanation for the defeat of the Stone Avenue subway project was "on the ground that it would benefit Albert Steinfeld, who has large holdings on that street."[23]

In 1925 Albert Steinfeld decided to retire from business and turned his commercial empire over to his son, Harold. Both men, however, would help welcome Santa Claus and his special train when it arrived at the Southern Pacific depot in December 1926.

Having come to town more than 50 years earlier, the elder Steinfeld had seen many significant changes in the community. "When I moved to Tucson," he told the *Arizona Daily Star* in 1927, "only candles were used for lighting. Then came coal oil, and everybody thought that was a big improvement. Then came gas, which was a revolutionary innovation. And finally the electric light, which had a hard time getting a foothold."[24]

Carlos Jácome had also seen many changes in Tucson since opening his La Bonanza store in 1896. First located on west Congress Street, the store moved a few blocks to the east during the 1920s and assumed the family name. At his store, Jácome believed in elaborate display windows to show off his merchandise and had a simple retail philosophy: "[T]here is always a customer for every item. We've just got to find that customer."[25] To assist these shoppers, all nine of Jácome's sons worked in the store.[26]

While the locally owned Steinfeld's and Jacome's, as well as their national chain competitor, J.C. Penney, offered a wide variety of shopping selections in the 1920s, much day-to-day retail business was still conducted in the dozens of Chinese groceries dotting the city. These were usually small, often very narrow, stores, stacked to the ceiling with merchandise which a grabber bar would be used to snag.

To obtain perishable goods, Chinese grocers daily visited commercial wholesalers located in warehouses next to the railroad tracks a few blocks west of the train station. Nearby was a dirt lot where a fresh produce market supplied fruits and vegetables.[27]

At that time, the pivotal role played in the community by the Southern Pacific Railroad remained extensive. The company continued to be the largest employer by far in town but periodically experienced labor-related work stoppages.

When Albert and Harold Steinfeld, shown standing next to the automobile, arranged for a "Santa Claus Special" train to arrive at the railroad depot on December 11, 1926, almost 2,000 Tucsonans of all ages joined them in welcoming the merry old bearded gentleman (Arizona Historical Society, PC 1000-#47308).

While SP stayed a constant in Tucson, one major educational shift that did occur during the decade was the 1924 completion of a new $750,000 high school on the south side of Sixth Street. When it opened in September of that year, the enrollment at the new Tucson High was 845 students. Unlike Tucson's primary school system, the high school was racially integrated. Thus, in 1925 Hayzel B. Daniels could be a star on the school's football team. An African American, Daniels was called the "Black [Red] Grange of Arizona" after he gained 301 rushing yards in a November victory over Bisbee. Earlier in the season, Daniels had to stay home while his teammates traveled to El Paso for a game. According to the *Arizona Daily Star*—which failed to elaborate on the openly racial segregation being practiced in Texas—Daniels didn't make the trip "because of Texas high school regulations."[28] In reality, of course, Daniels wouldn't have been allowed to play.

Unlike Red Grange at Illinois, Daniels would not be permitted to play collegiate football in his hometown after high school. Officials at the UA cited the Texas segregation issue as a problem. That snub didn't stop Daniels from attending the university. In the late 1940s he would become the law school's first Black graduate and would also later become Arizona's first Black judge.[29]

The Cultural and Social Scene Along with Auto Courts and Mountain Roads

In addition to the opening of the new Tucson High School, another major event occurring during the '20s was the Rialto Theatre premiering on east Congress Street with Emanuel Drachman being the majority owner. Using a banner headline reading: "Another Step in Progress of Tucson Marks Rialto Opening," the *Tucson Citizen* in 1920 described the special features of the new cinema and live-performance venue, including air-conditioned temperatures: "Thirty degrees below that of street if needed."[30]

Seven years later, the Temple of Music and Art on south Scott Avenue brought equal excitement when internationally renowned violin artist Jascha Heifetz played at the initial performance. Built at a cost of $175,000, among those who successfully pushed the Temple project were Mrs. Simon Heineman together with author Harold Bell Wright.

The Fox Theater made its debut in 1930 on west Congress Street to possibly the grandest pronouncements in Tucson's cultural history. Offering an even more elegant movie-going experience than the Rialto, the gala opening event was described as: "Music, color, light and gayety will dazzle thousands on the uptown streets."[31]

One other novel form of entertainment began in 1926. In the summer of that year, locally owned KGAR, later KTUC, started the first radio broadcasts from a downtown studio. Radio signals were also available to automobile drivers with a little ingenuity. In 1926 a Tucson man was taking a vacation and wanted some music to accompany him as he drove. "He has strung an aerial from the radiator cap on his car to the roof," reported the *Tucson Citizen*, "and just in back of the front seat he has placed a six-tube, one-dial Atwater Kent radio set. In this manner, while driving through the desert he may listen to any big city that he may care to tune in on."[32]

In addition to technological advancements like those, Tucson saw a shift in local government when voters in 1929 approved a new charter for the community. It established a council-manager form of municipal administration plus required council members be nominated by ward but elected citywide.

Another change related to local government also took place in 1929 when Pima County built a new courthouse on Church Avenue. Designed in the Spanish Colonial Revival–style by architect Roy Place, when trenches were dug for the building's foundation, the site revealed an interesting discovery. The *Tucson Citizen* explained of this finding: "Exposure by workmen engaged in excavating for the foundations of the new courthouse of the remains of the wall that enclosed Tucson when it was a Spanish outpost, has excited keen interest."[33]

Several miles east of downtown, the Desert Sanatorium and Institute of Research opened in November 1926.[34] Focused on helping people with "chronic pulmonary disease of many types" who could afford the luxury care, the 120-bed facility would become the Tucson Medical Center in 1944.

Also established during the '20s was a natural park west of the community. Agricultural agent and park supporter C.B. Brown had written romantically of this rugged territory: "Here are limitless views of desert vegetation, strange giant cacti forms, rock formations uprising sharply into forms and craggy peaks almost unreal to strangers, and ever fascinating in the changing flood of desert light."[35] To preserve at least some of this land from future homesteading and other development, the Pima County Board of Supervisors petitioned the federal government that owned it, and received 29,000 acres. As a result, on April 11, 1929, Tucson Mountain Park was dedicated.

One other significant shift occurring in Tucson during the 1920s was the advent of the auto court. Prior to the railroad's arrival in 1880, the few hotels in town were clustered downtown around Main and Pennington streets. When large numbers of passengers came by rail, however, the accommodation focus moved eastward to the area near the Toole Avenue depot.

By 1925 automobile ownership had skyrocketed in the United States to more than 10 million. To draw some of this potential rush of motorists, communities across the country established free campsites as tourist attractions. "The average expenditure daily of motorists in towns or cities in which they remain overnight is estimated at $7," stated a 1922 *Tucson Citizen* article. "Statistics just compiled ... reveal that a golden harvest follows in the wake of automobile tourists."[36] Believing these predictions, local governments nationwide subsidized campgrounds with taxpayer's money in order to draw traveling visitors.

Tucson's auto camp park was located on St. Mary's Road two blocks west of the railroad tracks and offered "brick club house and good store. Campers [are] supplied wood, water, use of phone, baths, etc."[37] Even though most cities quickly concluded that providing campers with free accommodations cost more than it was worth, Tucson continued to run its facility for several years. Despite that, privately owned, for-pay competition soon developed in town.

Since they no longer wanted to pitch a tent or haul around bulky sleeping and dining equipment, by 1927 many motorists were demanding more than just a free camping space. They were looking instead for a room for the night and were willing to pay for it. Thus, auto courts came into being that "had separate tent houses or one-room cottages that rented for about a dollar a night."[38]

At Tucson's Camp Dreamland, a mom-and-pop operation fronted by a service station on south Sixth Avenue, small cabins began to be built in 1927. The street was part of U.S. Highway 80, the mostly unpaved federal route going across Arizona from Douglas to Bisbee, then on to Tombstone, Benson, Tucson, Florence, and Phoenix before heading west toward Gila Bend and Yuma.

Prior to 1925 when the national system of identifying north-south highways with odd numbers and those going east-west with evens went into effect, business associations had collected donations to name and mark often unimproved cross-country routes. Snaking through Tucson during this era, Sixth and Stone avenues along with Drachman Street and Oracle Road became part of numerous named highways before they were designated as U.S. 80.[39] These named routes included the "Broadway of America," the "Old Spanish Trail," the "Bankhead Highway," along with several others.

In early 1922, a representative of the Bankhead Highway organization spoke to a local Rotary Club about his group and suggested there were two possible routes for the road through Southern Arizona, one that included Tucson and the other that did not. Named after John H. Bankhead, a United States Senator from Alabama between 1907 and 1920, the road was to run from the nation's capital to San Diego. Some Tucson supporters compared potential highway access like this as important as the arrival of the railroad. To help ensure that the Bankhead Highway went through town, a large contingent of businessmen, led by auto dealer Monte Mansfeld, journeyed to Phoenix in April 1922 to attend a highway convention.[40]

Monte Mansfeld had begun selling Ford automobiles on Broadway near Stone Avenue during the previous decade while also becoming actively involved in trying to improve the roads of both Tucson and Arizona. He eventually became chairman of the local Chamber of Commerce's Good Roads Committee for eight years, president of the Arizona Automobile Association for two years, and in 1929 was appointed to the State Highway Commission.[41] Even though Mansfeld was extremely influential, he couldn't get people to spell his last name correctly, so in 1929 he changed it to Mansfield.

While Mansfeld was making progress on improving some of the region's roadways, one proposed route wasn't going anywhere. The cool pine forests atop Mt. Lemmon in the Santa Catalina Mountains had been a lure to Tucson desert dwellers for decades, but access was limited to only the few who could afford to brave taking a mule train to the summit.

To change that torturous situation, in 1915 Pima County voters were asked to support spending $100,000 to build a road up to Mt. Lemmon. "The summers are hot here," observed the *Tucson Citizen* honestly. "Many people cannot afford to go to the coast, and a cool spot within two hours of the city would be a great boon to many."[42] After opposing campaigns ardently urging acceptance and rejection of the measure were waged, on Election Day the Mt. Lemmon road measure narrowly passed, but implementation wasn't to follow. Backers had pledged not to spend the money if the rough road couldn't be completed on budget. That proved impossible because of the daunting topography, so the road wasn't built.

Not to be deterred, by 1920 an extremely circuitous, bumpy, unpaved road up the north side of the mountain from the small community of Oracle had been opened. It required a drive from Tucson of 67 miles and about four and one-half hours over difficult terrain, but at least, within a few years, the road was graveled to cut down on the slick spots which developed after a rain.

In 1927, with no humor intended, the *Arizona Daily Star* suggested an aviation alternative to get up the mountain. "Why then spend half a million dollars or more," the paper editorially inquired of building a better, shorter road, "on a new route to Mt. Lemmon. For a fifth of that amount, a landing field could be built on top of the Catalina range, three or four planes could be purchased, and an airline established to Pima's Peerless Park—Mt. Lemmon."[43]

Suggesting that a downtown landing strip would be an ideal site for this airline to utilize, the *Star* opposed constructing a shorter road up the mountain's southeastern face. Spurred on by the *Tucson Citizen*, however, by 1928 the idea of spending $500,000 to build a new route to Mt. Lemmon was on the ballot again. Once more, both pro and con campaigns were launched, and this time voters handily defeated the measure. They did so again in 1930. (It wouldn't be until about 1950, after the toil of hundreds of prison laborers and $1 million spent, that the 25-mile short road up the Santa Catalina Mountains to Mt. Lemmon was finally finished.)

Problems with the Border and the Bottle

Many of the laborers who finally built this mountain road were Mexican nationals, incarcerated because of their illegal immigration into the United States. It had been Chinese workers, on the other hand, that had been the primary focus of early national anti-immigration legislation. That attention culminated in 1902 when the second Chinese Exclusion Act was adopted by Congress. This law completely eliminated legal Chinese immigration, a ban that was not lifted for more than four decades.

The impact of this and other immigration laws on the Arizona border south of Tucson slowly increased. Besides Chinese and Mexican nationals, European, Japanese, and Middle Eastern immigrants were also crossing the Mexican border into the U.S. and, as a result, Congress was told that more men and greater use of technology were needed to halt the human tide.[44] Mounted guards of the U.S. Immigration Service eventually replaced Custom Service line riders in patrolling the border. One of these men was Clifford Perkins, who inspected businesses, farms, and railroad trains for illegal entrants. He also went on horseback expeditions near the border and wrote of those he was searching for: "Entering the United States by wagon or on foot through that country was a hazardous, lonely proposition, and must have been a bewildering experience to the majority of Chinese who made the attempt."[45]

Law enforcement along the border for years remained directed at the Chinese but eventually began to include other illegal immigrants as well. This increased clampdown was mostly unsuccessful, while also being somewhat arbitrary. "Immigration Service employees, responding to growing labor demand in the Southwest," one historian noted, "selectively exempted Mexican migrants from the provisions of American immigration law through the 1900s and 1910s."[46]

By 1921 Congress had passed the Emergency Quota Act, which restricted legal immigration to three percent of the number of a specific nationality's population in the U.S. in 1910. Three years later it toughened that law further by reducing the figure to two percent of a nationality's population living in the U.S. in 1890. "In our opinion," the *Tucson Citizen* stated in 1924 of this revised statute, "it is the most important piece of legislation passed by [C]ongress in several decades."[47]

In that same year, the U.S. Border Patrol, then an agency of the U.S. Department of Labor, was created to try to seal the border against illegal immigration. That dream soon looked like a fairytale, however. "Not even a Chinese wall, nine thousand miles in length and built over rivers and deserts and mountains and along the seashores, would seem to permit a permanent solution," Secretary of Labor James Davis admitted in 1927.[48]

Even as some Chinese were being pursued along the border, Chinese Americans were financing a new Chinese Chamber of Commerce building in Tucson. In 1922 a 900-square-foot, $2,200 structure was erected on south Meyer Street to handle the business opportunities of the "rapidly growing" group.[49]

Tucson's African American community was also getting together. In August 1922, a meeting was called to organize a civic and political club that would inform all candidates for elected office of the "position and hopes and aspirations of the colored element of the population of Pima [C]ounty."[50]

These two racial groups joined the long established Alianza Hispano-Americana in representing the interests of some of Tucson's minority residents. By 1929, this fraternal/insurance society had 240 chapters with more than 14,000 members throughout the Southwest and Mexico. In addition, it occupied new headquarters on west Congress Street near Church Avenue.

During the '20s, Spanish-language newspapers continued to be published in Tucson, including the four-page, twice-weekly *El Mosquito*. Its major competitor was *El Tucsonense*, a more formal, six-page, thrice-weekly paper. Tucson's English-language newspapers, the *Star* and *Citizen*, also competed for advertisers and readers.

Years earlier, both English-language newspapers had given considerable coverage to the eventually successful effort to turn Arizona into a "dry" state. After the 1914 state prohibition initiative was adopted by voters, according to figures compiled by longtime Arizonan George Herbert Smalley, the positive social impacts of the ban on alcohol were dramatic. He found an almost 50 percent decrease in arrests across Arizona in the first six months of 1915 compared with 12 months earlier. In Tucson, however, the decline was only six percent. Based on his findings, Smalley naively suggested: "[T]he saloon has no chance of again opening for business in Arizona."[51]

In 1918 the Arizona legislature overwhelmingly endorsed the 18th Amendment to the United States Constitution, thus becoming the 18th state to ratify the National Prohibition Act, which eventually went into effect in January 1920.[52] Since they had had five years to live without legal liquor by that time, Tucsonans were well prepared. As a result, even though some illegal stills were shut down during the '20s, the federal liquor ban apparently wasn't very effective in town. "Bootleggers are said to be thicker in this section of the country than mosquitoes on the Jersey coast," declared the *Tucson Citizen* in 1921.[53] Yndia Smalley Moore, the daughter of George H. Smalley, added many years later: "[T]here were nightclubs here, speakeasies, not nightclubs. You had to ring a bell."[54]

George Smalley asked his daughter Yndia not to drink the liquor sold in the speakeasies since it could be poisonous. Somewhat hypocritically—because of his supportive stance on prohibition—he instead gave her a flask of whiskey she could take on dates. When Yndia was married in 1930, champagne flowed at the reception after she wed Capt. James P. Moore. For her wedding, she wore an elegant gown purchased at the recently opened downtown shop of Cele Peterson (née Fruitman).[55]

Also partaking of illegal alcohol during Prohibition was real estate investor, mining executive, and cattle rancher Levi H. Manning. While he had led an aggressive anti-gambling movement as mayor of Tucson in 1905, Manning apparently didn't mind ignoring liquor laws two decades later.

During the 1920s, Manning was having a large party at his downtown mansion located in an area of huge homes occupied by the city's elite. This section of Tucson had been referred to somewhat derogatorily since the previous decade as "Snob Hollow."[56] Manning needed some liquid refreshments for his guests and asked his friend Andres Herreras if he could supply him with 20 gallons of mescal. After some hesitation, Herreras agreed and had the illegal liquor delivered to his house by a supplier he knew.

One of Herreras' sons, though, wanted to keep some of the tasty liquid treat for himself. So he used a little water to dilute each gallon jug intended for Manning, who never suspected anything was amiss. "The darn thing was a hundred proof," Eleazar Herreras recalled many years later of his brother's ploy. "So what could happen? You could put [in] fifty percent water and you'd never know."[57]

Eleazar Herreras had learned some different lessons from his father, a plastering contractor. Helping out on construction jobs, he became familiar with designer and politician, Henry O. Jaastad, whom Herreras called his "second father."[58] Herreras would graduate from the University of Arizona in 1921 with a degree in mathematics and obtained an architect's license three years later, becoming one of the first Hispanics in Arizona to do so. He was later employed by the city of Tucson for decades as chief building inspector.

Among downtown projects being built during the 1920s were the 10-story Consolidated Bank at Stone and Congress and the even taller Pioneer Hotel at Stone and Pennington, the latter developed by Harold Steinfeld. Years later, Eleazar Herreras remembered the decade as an era of prosperity. "Mines were doing good business," he recalled of the '20s. "The price of copper was up, the price of cattle was up, and everybody that was in business was making money. And naturally, when you make money you start to improve."[59]

One of those who was investing in improvements was auto mechanic James Van Harlingen. Confident of the future, in 1928 he had a brick building constructed on Sixth Street east of Sixth Avenue to lease for ten years to a mattress manufacturing

Eleazar Herreras (pointing), shown in this 1932 photograph with two unidentified construction workers, was the city's chief building inspector for many years as well as being one of Arizona's first Hispanic registered architects and a dedicated volunteer for historic preservation (Arizona Historical Society, PC 1000-#73536).

company.[60] Located just north of Van Harlingen's garage, the façade of the $10,000 new building was crowned by the owner's name.

Regardless of economic optimism like that, the stock market crash of October 1929 threw the entire nation into severe financial turmoil. While headlines after the initial market downturn at first emphasized stock rallies among all the declines, an October 30 wire service story in the *Tucson Citizen* also acknowledged a "storm of hysterical selling which had been raging for nearly a week."[61]

That financial storm would consume the country, creating an economic Depression that would extend throughout the next decade. It would affect everyone, including the residents of Tucson, the small and slowly growing city in the Sonoran Desert.

• SIX •

Tough Times, Discrimination, and More Subways, 1930–1940

A large neon sign boldly announces the Arizona Motel on south Sixth Avenue north of I-10. This longtime establishment was recently purchased to eventually be converted into affordable housing and is located near other—more difficult-to-spot—remnants of 1930s era auto courts that still exist in South Tucson, the approximately one-square-mile municipality totally surrounded by the sprawling city of Tucson.

BY 1933, THE VAN HARLINGEN BUILDING on Sixth Street was vacant. It would remain that way almost continuously for the next five years until three governmental agencies, established to help combat impacts of the Depression, opened offices there.

Long before then, local charity groups combined to supply thousands of Tucson families with food baskets during the 1930 holiday season. The Christmas-time suicide of a 35-year-old father who was a new Tucson resident, on the other hand, summarized the desperate situation of many people in town. "I can not get any work," wrote Elmer Anderson in a farewell note, "and can not keep myself and boy so I will just get out of the way and this suffering. I will say goodbye.... I haven't worked in six months and can't stand this any longer. Goodbye."[1]

This World War I veteran's unfortunate employment situation wasn't unusual. The 1930 census showed that 14 percent of Tucson's 8,206 families had no one gainfully employed in the household.

Some residents later observed, however, that Tucson escaped the worst of the Depression. Major layoffs by the Southern Pacific Railroad Company, though, affected hundreds of families in town. Copper prices plummeted and many of the mines in Southern Arizona shut down, resulting in massive unemployment among miners. University of Arizona employees were forced to take cuts in salary. In addition, two of Tucson's four banks closed, and it was expected many of their depositors would lose most of their money.

The Depression also greatly affected one of Tucson's major economic engines—construction. As Eleazar Herreras recalled years later: "[T]here was no material

Tucson 1930 – 1940

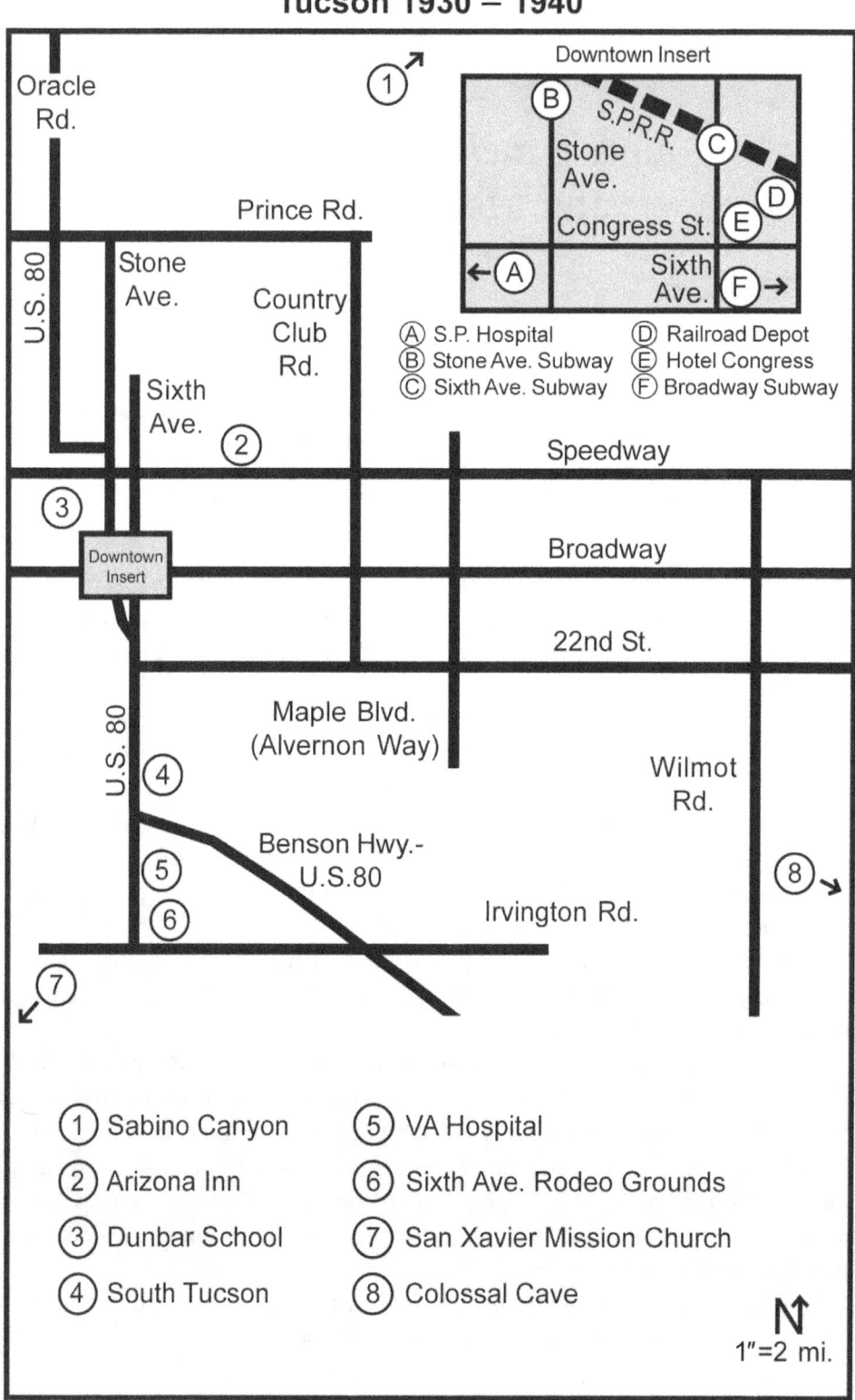

available. Certain material was available but it was extraordinarily high, very costly. Loans were curtailed, it was hard to get a loan.... Unemployment, lack of materials, high interest rate, the usual, one thing affected the other, the cost of living went up, and there was no income so we were in awful shape."[2]

While employed as the city's chief building inspector at that time, Herreras was also becoming a licensed civil engineer and helping to repair a Tucson historic icon. In 1937 lightning struck one of the towers at the San Xavier Mission, and he began to work on weekends to restore it, finally finishing the job in 1951. Also during the '30s, some work was being done to preserve the ruins of Fort Lowell on the community's eastside, but as Byron Cummings, director of the Arizona State Museum, noted in 1931: "[P]eople abuse the privilege of visiting the famous old historical settlement by digging under the walls for treasures and relics and otherwise damaging the premises."[3]

Overall during the decade, construction slowed dramatically. Statistics between 1929 and 1930 show a 40 percent drop in the value of building permits issued in Tucson. For his part, homebuilder John W. Murphey wrote simply in January 1933: "[B]usiness has been very, very dull and we have not built a house for over a year now."[4]

One result of the nationwide economic slowdown and subsequent loss of work was a move to force Mexican citizens living in the United States to return to their home country. Between 1930 and 1935, this effort resulted in the deportation of 500,000 people nationally,[5] with almost 19,000 of them leaving Arizona between 1930 and 1932.[6] While allegations were made that many Mexican nationals remaining in the U.S. were taking advantage of governmental assistance programs, one person working in that field didn't agree. "It has been found from experience...," a border patrol inspector reported, "an alien who is unlawfully in the United States does not apply for relief unless he finds it absolutely necessary, through fear that he will be found and deported."[7]

It wasn't only foreign nationals that faced difficulties with obtaining government assistance. Tucsonans registered their favoritism in 1934 by allegedly posting signs at the city limits proclaiming: "Warning to Transients. Relief for local residents only. Transients do not apply."[8]

At that time, at least in the opinion of longtime resident Melvin Hoefle, Tucson didn't exactly pull together during the Depression to help out its own less fortunate. "It was a case of dog eat dog," Hoefle suggested. "It's your fault that you lost your money, your fault that you don't have anything to eat. No, they didn't stick together."[9]

Attorney Harry O. Juliani, his wife, Lucille, and their children lived on Sixth Street near the University of Arizona, and she recalled the Depression much differently. "[N]early every day we had a few people knocking on the door.... I couldn't be feeding everyone who came, although I would have liked to, believe me, but I kept small cans of beans and always extra bread and if there was any fruit of any sort, so that at least I could give them something."[10]

To try to help out more, both private and public efforts were launched to create jobs in Tucson. In January 1931 the city council adopted a motion to require private property to be weeded and cleaned, hoping it would lead to some temporary employment opportunities.[11] At about the same time, the Steinfeld department store began paying two dollars for any pair of shoes that was brought in for donation to a needy person.

In late 1930 Isabella Greenway opened the Arizona Inn out in the desert on Elm Street, filling the charming $150,000 establishment with furniture made by disabled World War I veterans employed at the Arizona Hut, a rehabilitation center founded by Greenway and her husband a few years previously. Students at the Arizona School for the Deaf and Blind provided some finishing touches for the furniture. In August 1933 the 46-year-old Greenway would be nominated by Democratic voters to fill a U.S. Congressional seat left vacant when Lewis W. Douglas resigned to become director of the federal budget in the new Roosevelt administration. Greenway soon won the position, becoming the first woman in Arizona to do so, and then she was re-elected, serving until January 1937.

Another woman making an impact was Cele Fruitman. Despite the Depression, she came to Tucson in the early '30s to help her parents open and operate the downtown Co-Ed Shop. In 1939,

Cele Peterson, pictured here in 1934, built a highly successful retail business, and for decades was rightfully referred to as Tucson's "arbiter of fashion and grace" (courtesy the Tom Peterson, Jr., photograph collection).

having married Thomas H. Peterson several years earlier, she moved the store from Stone Avenue to Pennington Street and would eventually name it after herself.[12]

On the city's northwest side, the Amphitheater School District was constructing and opening a high school, the community's second after Tucson High. By 1939 it was predicted the new building, including middle school, would have about 350 students and 13 teachers.

One other change was implemented by the Southern Pacific Railroad Company at the site of the former El Paso and Southwestern Railroad freight depot near Congress Street. SP developed a hospital there for its employees, and, not unexpectedly in a community as racially divided as Tucson, this hospital included a separate, segregated ward for "Negroes."

Segregation, Repeal of Prohibition, and Federal Work Programs

Another segregated facility in Tucson was Dunbar School. Throughout the '30s, enrollment at Dunbar climbed from fewer than 200 students to almost 300. One of those teaching at the school was Elgie Batteau. Originally from Texas, she moved to Tucson in 1919 and recalled many years later: "I went to School District One to apply for a job shortly before I graduated [with a master's degree from the University of Arizona]; upon application I was told that the only school that Black teachers could teach at was Dunbar. I was upset because I wanted to be able to teach at any school in the district."[13] Not only did her race restrict her job opportunities, but Batteau found her gender did also. "Among all of the problems the Blacks had to incur," she observed, "the Black women had to incur more. A woman teacher could not be married; nor could she live alone. For young Black teachers it was pretty tough."[14]

Black students at the integrated Tucson High School also had it rough during the '30s. As classmate Richard Salvatierra remembered decades later: "[African Americans] were segregated in their own homerooms and, in effect, were treated more or less as second-class individuals."[15] It wasn't only Blacks, however, who were discriminated against at Tucson High. Salvatierra also recalled of his basketball coach: "When one of the players did something wrong during practice, the coach would yell across the court, 'Don't be a Mexican all your life.'"[16]

This type of treatment extended to public swimming facilities as well. "The pool [on 22nd Street near Fourth Avenue] was set aside for white people only on Mondays through Thursdays," Salvatierra remembered, "and for Hispanics on Fridays and [B]lacks on Saturdays. The pool was then cleaned and refilled on Sundays." Based on his experiences in 1930s Tucson, Salvatierra concluded: "I saw that discrimination against [B]lacks, Hispanics, Jews and Native Americans was common."[17]

The Chinese were another group facing continuing discrimination in Tucson. In a 1998 interview, 81-year-old Esther Don Tang vividly remembered one earlier incident of this happening. Her parents had placed an earnest down payment on a house in a Country Club Road subdivision, but before the family moved in "No chinks wanted" was scrawled on it. As a result, they didn't buy the house and lost $1,000 of their money.[18]

Esther was born in Tucson's downtown barrio in 1917. Her father ran a Chinese grocery store that would eventually blossom into a small local chain. Her mother, a native of China, wed her husband in Hong Kong in 1908, moved with him to the Arizona desert, and bore 10 children.

While Chinese groceries assisted the local economy, a simple method was proposed during the Depression for increasing tax revenues to help pay to expand government job programs—repeal of the prohibition on liquor sales. In the spring of 1932, an Arizona ballot initiative drive was launched to do away with the state's long-standing "dry" law and it was placed before the voters that November. By an almost two-to-one margin, Arizona's prohibition on liquor sales was thrown out, with 68 percent of Pima County voters supporting the repeal.

This move quickly resulted in both the suspension of local and state law enforcement efforts against alcohol production and sales, as well as the swift passage of a "wet" law by the Arizona legislature.[19] In August 1933 the state's voters also elected representatives to a convention that would establish Arizona's position on repeal of the 18th (Prohibition) Amendment to the United States Constitution. They exclusively chose "wet" candidates, even the one from Pima County who declared that he "never drank, but always voted wet."[20]

Given the convention's membership, it was no surprise that in early September 1933, the nation's newest state became the 21st to ratify the 21st amendment. "Arizona formally repealed the 18th [A]mendment today," proclaimed the *Phoenix Gazette*, "while delegates and visitors to a convention held at the statehouse drank beer and clanked the empty bottles to a merry tune."[21] It would be a few months later that enough states had ratified the constitutional amendment, and Prohibition was done away with nationally.

Arizona liquor sales would provide extra tax revenues to help the state fund needed projects, but there was also another way of creating employment opportunities during the Depression. It was through the work programs instituted by the Roosevelt administration including the Civilian Conservation Corps (CCC), the Federal Emergency Relief Administration (FERA), the Public Works Administration (PWA), and the Works Progress Administration (WPA).

Using more than $1 million in funds supplied by the PWA, the University of Arizona—with a full-time enrollment of about 2,400 students—embarked on an ambitious building program during the Depression. To address its space problems, in 1936 a wide variety of structures were added to the campus, including a science building, an auditorium, and a woman's gymnasium. The following year, the PWA supplied another $481,000 with which a dormitory and dining hall were built. Despite those available funds, the university's new Tree Ring Research lab was restricted to "four rooms and adjoining storage space on the second floor of the new

The Civilian Conservation Corps (CCC) crew at Colossal Cave, despite thinking it ate too many beans, was one of several across Tucson that helped build important projects for the community during the dark economic times of the Depression (courtesy the Colossal Cave Mountain Park photograph collection).

football stadium."[22] Led by Andrew Ellicott Douglass, the board of regents formally established the lab at the end of 1937.

The PWA also funded implementation of three reservoirs for the Tucson Water Department, one of which was installed near Randolph Park south of the El Conquistador Hotel.[23] Among other Depression-era construction projects, both the FERA and WPA helped build bridges and extend the road in Sabino Canyon northeast of Tucson.[24] The WPA also literally left its mark across the community on new sidewalks and curbs. It additionally built facilities for the Flowing Wells School District, paved the road to the top of "A" Mountain, and installed the swimming pool in Himmel Park east of the university campus.[25] Live concerts by the Old Pueblo Mexican Orchestra, as well as free adult education classes and a day nursery for Yaqui children, were also sponsored by the WPA.

Las Posadas, a Christmas-time parade of children from downtown's Carrillo School re-enacting the biblical journey of Mary and Joseph, was begun in 1937 but didn't utilize federal funds. Another project that did, however, was transforming the dirt golf course in Randolph Park into an amenity with grass.

Randolph Park in 1934 was the location of a CCC camp that housed young men who were working to improve Colossal Cave, almost 25 miles east of town. By 1935 a new camp was established near the cave; for the next few years, 200 men would labor to build walkways inside the cave and generally improve its facilities.[26]

Dinner at the camp was served to the workers in the early evening with frequent complaints about too many beans, although they apparently weren't actually that common on the menu. "There are three kinds of beans," one humorist wrote in a camp newsletter, "those we had yesterday, those we are having today, and those we will have tomorrow."[27] Continuing with his lament, he stated: "Beans may be served in seven ways: (1) plain beans, (2) fancy beans, (3) bean salad, (4) bean soup, (5) beans with chili, (6) beans without chili, and (7) bean sandwiches. We have yet to see them served with pancakes. We don't have beans for breakfast."

The CCC, which over time had nine camps around Tucson, also helped improve facilities at nearby Saguaro National Monument. The goal of protecting this immense forest of the giant cactus had been pursued by University President Homer L. Shantz, local scientists, and others for many years. It finally came to fruition in the waning days of the Hoover administration when the monument was created on March 1, 1933.

The CCC also did some work during the Depression at Tucson's rodeo grounds on south Sixth Avenue, formerly the site of the municipal airport before it was moved to Davis-Monthan. Established in 1925, the rodeo was initially held on vacant property east of town at an event sponsored by the Arizona Polo Association of Tucson. While participants informally rode through the city before the first two rodeos, by 1927 an organized downtown parade had been launched, and $20 was budgeted to support it.[28]

Organizational responsibilities for the rodeo had been transferred by 1932 to the Chamber of Commerce and Pima County Fair Commission. At around the same time, the rodeo grounds were moved to south Sixth Avenue where $18,000 was spent on improving facilities.

To raise much needed money for the university's polo club, a May 1931 appearance was made by Will Rogers at the Fox Theater. The famous humorist entertained a capacity crowd for almost three hours. Incorrectly predicting Republicans would continue to control the nation's politics after the November 1932 election, since he thought the economy would have turned around by then, Rogers remarked: "The Democrats only chance of winning is to have the people starve continuously until after the election and not just before. The Lord ... [is] apparently on the side of the Republicans, but [is] probably misinformed."[29]

New Subways

In part to help counteract the general economic slowdown, three major government-funded construction projects were planned in Tucson during the '30s. All of them were focused on accomplishing one thing—moving automobiles more easily into downtown via underpasses built beneath the Southern Pacific railroad tracks, just like the existing subway on Fourth Avenue already did.

By the middle of 1930, one underpass was being built along Sixth Avenue. Costing $219,000, this 147-foot-long subway required the removal of a building on the property of the J. Knox Corbett Lumberyard on the north side of the tracks. To replace this structure, and add space for a plumbing supply department, architect Roy Place was hired to plan a new building. He designed a structure at the corner of Sixth Avenue and Seventh Street and incorporated "Corbett" into its elaborate facade. (This building still stands and is now Corbett's, a restaurant with five pickleball courts.)

The Sixth Avenue underpass opened in November 1930 after a ceremony that included the Tucson High band marching through the subway followed by a parade of hundreds of cars. The contractor who built the subway unabashedly concluded the new underpass was more useful than the ancient pyramids of Egypt.

Six • Tough Times, Discrimination, and More Subways, 1930–1940 93

The other subway being built in 1930 was estimated to cost $330,000 and would be approximately, and impressively, more than 750-feet in length. Tunneling under 11 sets of S.P. tracks crossing Broadway, one of the distinctive features of this unusually long underpass was its sidewalk, which ran down the middle of the subway between the two lanes of automobile traffic.

Twenty men began work on the Broadway underpass in August 1930, and that number was soon doubled after businessmen in the area complained of the slow pace of construction. Local unemployed men were hired for the work, and this immediately caused friction with some of those who had moved to Tucson hoping to find jobs. "They [the newcomers] tell pitiful stories of families without food," it was reported, "without enough money to pay for their rent at local auto camps."[30] As a result of the preferential hiring practice, conflicts between men without jobs and those working on the Broadway underpass soon developed, and things became tense around the construction site for a while.

After a few delays, the Broadway underpass finally opened in June 1931 and was completed for $85,000 less than originally estimated. Considerably longer than two football fields, the dual-tubed subway quickly provided an opportunity for some joy-riding adventure.

"[E]very once in a while some darn fool would decide to drive through the wrong side as a thrill," businessman Roy Drachman clearly remembered years later of the Broadway underpass. "In fact, I was in a car twice when it did that. I don't know how I survived. But I was with somebody who had had too many drinks and it was on a Saturday night and we were driving downtown and [he] decided to give us a thrill and just veered over to the left side and went through the [subway]. Luckily, no one was coming in the opposite direction. It would have been a major tragedy."[31]

Tucson's fourth and final downtown underpass wouldn't be completed until the end of 1935. It was built along Stone Avenue, in part with $123,000 of federal funds that were supplied to allow the implementation of a subway allowing "big army guns" to pass through unimpeded.

Planning of this underpass was assisted by the 1930 abandonment of the trolley line that once ran along Stone Avenue.[32] For more than 30 years street cars crossed the railroad tracks at grade, but their gradual replacement in the 1920s by bus service made building the subway possible.

In December 1935 a crowd of 1,000 helped open the Stone Avenue subway in grand fashion. As a member of the Arizona Highway Commission, Tucson automobile dealer Monte Mansfield had been the primary advocate for the project, and he was to be the first to drive through the underpass. Some local prankster beat him to the punch, however.

The Stone Avenue underpass was different from the other three subways in several respects. First, to make it more convenient for motorists, it had four lanes for traffic instead of two. Second, to prevent trucks from getting stuck, the ceiling of the underpass was almost 14-feet high, not the approximately 11-foot height found in the other structures. Third, the architectural design of the Stone Avenue underpass was considered up-to-date. Finally, and most infamously, the subway retained storm water long after the other underpasses had drained.

Before its first birthday, a major problem with the Stone Avenue subway became very apparent. A huge nearby underground concrete box culvert had previously been installed to channelize the wide arroyo that ran just north of the railroad tracks. During a thunderstorm, water from the underpass had to be pumped uphill into this box culvert that could already be full of water. Thus, the Stone Avenue subway became a small lake until the level of water in the box culvert receded sufficiently to allow the entry of more water from the underpass.

In July 1936, a late-afternoon monsoon quickly filled the subway with water that didn't rapidly drain out. Two young men on their way to a friend's wedding were forced to swim the body of water that formed on Stone Avenue, damaging the presents they were carrying. "It is believed that this is the first case on record…" stated the *Arizona Daily Star*, "for the swimming of the [n]orth Stone Avenue subway."[33]

"Not so fast with bestowing that honor" was the theme declared by another story in the *Star*. Stating that Jack Doakes had submitted a petition to the city council signed by 125 residents, the article claimed his seven-year-old daughter, Elmira, held the distinction of being the first child to swim the subway. Based on that, Doakes believed she should have the Stone Avenue lake named after her.[34]

According to the same newspaper article, the council was also asked to grant a license to operate a ferry service across the ephemeral lake. They were additionally told that the U.S. War Department was looking into either erecting a pontoon or suspension bridge across the body of water to allow military vehicles to proceed unimpeded.

The entire story, however, was simply an elaborate hoax concocted by a comedic reporter.[35] Despite that, for decades afterwards, the embarrassing—and potentially dangerous—Stone Avenue body of water would be widely known as "Lake Elmira."

Cooling Off, Notorious Crimes, and an Incorporation Battle

The underpass, along with the remainder of Stone Avenue downtown, was part of U.S. Highway 80, the national road that wound its way from the Atlantic coast of Georgia all the way to San Diego. Along this route, as it wove through Tucson, dozens of auto courts had sprung up in the 1920s, and by the following decade some of these establishments had been transformed into cozy little motels.

Initially opened in 1930, the Arizona Tourist Court on south Sixth Avenue was an example of this commercial evolution. Originally having 10 units, the business was begun by Ruth and John Yunt. To attract customers to their rooms, which rented for $1.50 a night, they erected a large wooden billboard in front of the court. The sign would change over time, and by 1939 large neon letters proudly proclaimed "Arizona Court."[36] (Also evolving was the court, which by the 1950s had 32-units.)

Six • Tough Times, Discrimination, and More Subways, 1930–1940

Bud Yunt, who operated the business after his parents, recalled that a crude contraption once cooled each room. "It consisted of a towel being pulled through a pan of water by a roller," he said. "Behind the towel was a fan to blow the cool air into the room. When the towel was dry, it would be cranked forward."[37]

Trying to stay cool in Tucson's torturous summer heat had been a dilemma since humans first inhabited the area. By the early 1930s, Lucille Juliani was soaking bed sheets in cold water and rolling her three children up in them to take an afternoon nap in the hallway of their Sixth Street house.[38] Later they adjourned to camp cots set up in the back yard to sleep the night away.

As an alternative to this outdoor arrangement, some households had screened sleeping porches built on their homes to provide relief, but the desert heat was still extremely intense. The summer temperatures were so hot that by 1935 businessman Roy Drachman had decided to move to the cooler climate of Southern California. Before he did, a friend invited him over to see a new contraption.

"[H]e had taken one of these sixteen-inch oscillating fans that everybody owned..." Drachman remembered many years later, "and he'd taken that and had built a swamp cooler and put it on his window.... Well, before the day was over, I had two of them that I built myself. They were very simple to build."[39] Because of the rudimentary cooler, Drachman decided to stay in Tucson.

In the '30s, thanks to the swamp cooler, people in Tucson could finally cool off somewhat in the blazing summer heat; they also saw three headline-grabbing news stories. The first involved former UA professor and local real estate legend, Louise Foucar Marshall and her husband, Thomas. Married in 1904, by 1931 he was 60 years old and his wife four years his senior. They lived comfortably near the university campus—but on the night of April 27 she shot him several times as he slept.

From his hospital bed, Marshall blamed the shooting on his wife's suspicions that he was having an affair with their 53-year-old housekeeper, an allegation he labeled "unfounded." He also indicated Louise thought he was trying to poison her, another charge he denied. Despite the shooting, he refused to sign a legal complaint against his wife.[40]

Marshall was expected to recover, but a few weeks after the shooting he went to Los Angeles and died while there. Based on that, Louise was charged with first-degree murder, a capital offense.

Her 10-day trial was held in Nogales, Arizona, before a jury of twelve men, since women weren't allowed to sit on juries then, and generated banner headlines each day. Even though the prosecution argued it was a simple case of murder, the defense had witnesses who testified it was not the shooting that killed Tom Marshall but a botched operation in Tucson on his damaged hip that did.[41] It took the jury only 34 minutes to reach a verdict of not guilty.[42]

One of those testifying at the trial was James Revelle, a Black man who formerly worked as a masseur in Tucson, including for Tom Marshall. At the time of the trial, Revelle was serving a three-to-six-year sentence at the state prison in Florence for manslaughter. He pled guilty to the charge in the death of Olive Zeller, a woman on whom he had performed a botched abortion, and thus became the first Pima County resident to be sent to prison for violating the Arizona 1864 ban on almost all abortions.[43]

Much less violent than Tom Marshall being shot was the Tucson capture of Public Enemy No. 1—John Dillinger—and three of his gang members in January 1934. The relatively peaceful apprehensions began with clues obtained during a downtown fire at the Hotel Congress where two of the men were staying, and later involved investigative work by the Tucson Police Department.

Even with Dillinger's capture, the police weren't certain they had rounded up all the gang members, so to see if anyone would flag down Dillinger's large Hudson automobile, the department had it driven around town. As he motored about, officer Milo "Swede" Walker remembered: "I was going down Ninth Street and I had the radio turned on. I was listening to KSL, Salt Lake City, and thought to myself, 'What's happening to this world anyway? Here I am in Tucson, Arizona, listening to a beautiful orchestra playing in Salt Lake City, a thousand miles away from us down here.'"[44]

Walker soon had another surprise in store. "So all of a sudden," he recalled, "I hear a break in the program, and the announcer comes out and says, 'Flash! Flash! Flash! We just received word that John Dillinger, Public Enemy Number 1, and his gang have been caught in Tucson, Arizona,' and here I was driving John Dillinger's car down the street, listening to his radio, when this thing come in."[45]

After being put on public display for a day in the downtown county jail, the gang members were sent by train back to Ohio to stand trial for murder, while Dillinger was flown to Indiana to face similar charges. He escaped from jail there and eventually went to Chicago where he was killed outside a theater on July 22, 1934.

Dillinger's life may have ended violently, but the burning political struggle of the decade in Tucson began much more innocently. Built at a cost of $1.25 million, the four-story, Spanish-style Veterans Hospital on south Sixth Avenue had opened in October 1928 on almost 120 acres of land donated by businessman Albert Steinfeld. Intended to serve primarily tubercular patients, it replaced the rather rustic Pastime Park, a complex of wood-frame cottages on the north side of town which housed hundreds of sick veterans.

The new Veterans Hospital was a significant improvement. Unfortunately, the sewer line to the hospital ruptured in 1933, and the city of Tucson was responsible for maintaining it. Before repairing the break, the city attorney thought for legal reasons the municipality should annex an almost two-mile-long, three-block-wide strip of land which contained the sewer. That proposal to move the city limits from 25th Street south to the hospital, though, was opposed by many of the Anglo auto court owners along south Sixth Avenue, and the idea was quickly dropped.

Three years later, architectural designer and Tucson mayor, Henry Jaastad, recommended approximately the same area be annexed in order to expand the city's boundaries. Area auto court and other property owners again objected. They didn't want to pay the higher business taxes imposed by the city, nor be subject to Tucson's building codes. Some of them also feared that the illegal gambling they were conducting would be curtailed by the Tucson Police Department.

Ignoring that opposition, and wanting to continue its monopoly on municipal political power in Pima County, city officials took steps to annex the area anyway. As their only recourse to prevent the annexation, the Sixth Avenue property owners submitted a petition to the Pima County Board of Supervisors asking that an incorporation election be held for an approximately one-half-square-mile area south of Tucson. The board complied, and in balloting held on August 10, 1936, at the Yell-O-Inn auto court, the town of South Tucson was born by a 52 to 35 margin.[46]

Three Anglo auto court owners were among the five men appointed by the board of supervisors as the interim town council, and fighting fires was a major concern of the group. As South Tucson's fire chief later reported: "We had six fires in the past week.... The only way we have of putting them out is to use a garden hose and stomp with our feet, and that gets kind of tiresome, the stomping I mean."[47]

A few weeks before that, the Spanish-American Independent Club of South Tucson had leveled charges that the Anglo town clerk was never available to register Mexican American voters. That was especially important since the first municipal election for the new community was scheduled for April 1937, and the vote resulted in Sam Kipnis becoming mayor. Shortly after the new council took office, illegal slot machines suddenly appeared in six South Tucson businesses, including one operated by the mayor. For this and other shenanigans, the *Arizona Daily Star* wrote of the new community: "South Tucson is to be complimented for the consistently high quality, the ever-refreshing originality of the entertainment it dispenses so generously."[48]

The council also took some professional steps, of course. It hired as its attorney Harry O. Juliani, the man who had founded the Tucson Symphony Orchestra in 1928. The South Tucson council also adopted building codes similar to those in Tucson and employed inspectors to enforce these regulations.

The city of Tucson, however, was not satisfied with those administrative steps. It continued to require Tucson Water customers in South Tucson who were doing construction to obtain building permits from the larger municipality. If they didn't, their water would be shut off.

This double-permit stipulation infuriated South Tucson's elected officials, and in retaliation they imposed a $500 annual franchise fee on Tucson Water. The Tucson City Council announced in response that water service would be discontinued to the entire little community within 120 days.

Even though Mayor Kipnis resigned his position to try to curb the public uproar over the South Tucson council's actions, it was insufficient. On January 18, 1938, 258 petition signatures from South Tucson residents were turned in to the Pima County Board of Supervisors asking for dissolution of the 17-month-old municipality, and the board approved that proposal almost instantaneously.

Attorney Juliani tried diligently in court to overturn the dissolution action but lost a series of decisions. Afterwards, when he told the South Tucson council of the legal setbacks, he knowingly added—"Nothing in it, however, prevents a new start."[49]

Based on that insightful advice, another incorporation drive was launched and new petition signatures submitted to the board of supervisors. Eventually a second incorporation election was held, and on March 27, 1939, the former town was miraculously resurrected by a close vote of 70 to 63.

"There was great jollification among the townspeople as the word spread, a few minutes after the count was completed at 7 p.m." reported the *Arizona Daily Star*, "that the breath of life had been blown back into the corpse, and a number of the burghers took to their automobiles to execute an impromptu parade. After a few sashays up and down [s]outh Sixth [A]venue, main artery of the town, the celebrators descended on downtown Tucson, blaring their automobile horns and shouting jubilee."[50] On the other hand, as strong supporters of having only one municipal government which would have an aggressive annexation policy, both Tucson Mayor Jaastad and the editors of the *Arizona Daily Star* were terribly disappointed by the outcome of the South Tucson vote.

More People Need More Water

Around the same time, the *Star* was clamoring for Tucson to reach the long-coveted population milestone of 50,000 by the date of the 1940 census and saw annexations as one possible way to accomplish that cherished goal. The city's efforts proved futile, however, when only 36,763 people—an increase of about 4,000 from a decade earlier—were listed as Tucson residents by the census.

Despite that failure, local leaders had been thinking for years about much larger increases in population. As community promoter Monte Mansfield boldly predicted in 1935, Tucson could reach a population of 150,000 within fifteen years. (The actual population of Tucson in 1950 was 45,454 and for Pima County 141,216.) In response to that 150,000-person possibility, the *Star* surprisingly questioned the value of the "growth for growth's sake" philosophy. The newspaper editorialized: "Some of us have lived in bigger cities and have come to Tucson to live because we liked Tucson as she was and is and did not like the municipal monstrosities which we know too well."[51]

No matter what its future size, steps to ensure enough water was available for Arizona had begun at the regional level with the Colorado River compact of 1922. This agreement divided up the resources of the river among its seven bordering states. While a representative of Arizona had signed the deal, the state legislature refused to endorse it, arguing that Arizona was being shortchanged.

At the local level, in 1930 the city of Tucson paid $141,000 for 3,500 acres of land near Sahuarita, 18 miles to the south. The intention was to pump 20 million gallons of groundwater a day to Tucson. In response to this decision, the *Citizen* stated: "It

Six • Tough Times, Discrimination, and More Subways, 1930–1940

removes the greatest potential handicap on the city's growth.... Tucson may now build with complete confidence."[52]

A long-standing proposal that the city obtain additional water from the nearby Papago (Tohono O'odham) Reservation was also revived in front of a highly skeptical U.S. Senate subcommittee 1931 meeting in Tucson.[53] By 1937, decision-making about water on the reservation was further affected when the tribe's first voter-adopted constitution became effective.[54]

Earlier in the decade, the Tucson Chamber of Commerce had pushed a plan, originally suggested 30 years previously, to build a 250-foot-high dam across Sabino Creek northeast of the city. While the primary goal of the proposed dam and lake was to create tourism and recreational benefits for the community, it could also provide more water for a growing population.[55]

Local residents by 1934 were actually applying for permits to build cabins around the proposed lake, but planning for the Sabino Canyon dam project proceeded slowly. It wasn't until 1936 that the idea got a public hearing in Tucson, and a farmer from the Marana area northwest of Tucson stated all the water could be used there for agricultural purposes. For his part, homebuilder John W. Murphey stressed that the dam project would not only protect the foothills of the Santa Catalina Mountains from flooding, but would also supply a water source for future suburban subdivisions. Despite these positive arguments, the federal government's decision to require one-half of the dam's estimated $1 million construction cost be paid for from local funds quickly doomed the concept.[56]

In many respects, water had played an important role in Tucson throughout the 1930s. A raging flood on August 13, 1940, continued that trend. Thunderstorms dumped two inches of rain on southeast Tucson in a short span of time. As this water rushed toward downtown and then the Santa Cruz River, it brought destruction along with it. Flooding the basements of the new car dealerships on north Sixth Avenue near Sixth Street, the torrent pushed a parked car through one of the nearby showroom windows.

On Toole Avenue, the produce stored in the basements of grocery warehouses was soon floating on a sea of rainwater. As the water streamed forward along west Sixth Street, the flood shorted out the generating equipment of the Tucson Gas, Electric Light and Power Company. As a result, for the next 60 hours much of the community would be without electricity. Needless to say, stores selling candles were kept busy.

A city without power meant many people spent an uncomfortable few days in the summer heat. At the same time, a motorboat was spotted on "Lake Elmira" since the water had completely submerged the Stone Avenue underpass.

This monsoon storm foretold additional shocks and changes to come in the next decade. Like the earlier 1880s earthquakes that had shaken the community in so many ways, the 1940s would bring enormous changes to the desert community of Tucson.

• SEVEN •

War, Growth, and Entertainment, 1940–1950

In midtown Tucson sits a cozy baseball stadium. "No other Cactus League [spring training] ballpark is endowed with as rich a history as Tucson's Hi Corbett Field," was once written of this place.[1] Starting in 1928, baseball was first played here. The Cleveland Indians, beginning in 1947, followed by the Colorado Rockies in 1993, brought major leaguers to town each spring to train. That 64-year streak of professional big league March games ended after 2010. Hi Corbett Field then became the home of University of Arizona baseball in 2012, and in 2024 the home team won the last Pac-12 league championship there.

"BACK IN THE YEAR 1920," BEGAN AN EDITORIAL published in the *Arizona Daily Star* two decades after that date, "Tucson had a population of 20,000. Beyond the university there was scarcely a house. South of 22nd Street was open country as was that area north of Drachman [S]treet."[2]

Following 20 years of steady, if often sometimes slow, population increases, that open country was beginning to gradually disappear. Giving the Sunshine Climate Club major credit, the *Star* declared: "Tucson by its advertising has sold the desert to the nation and made it a great asset."[3]

By 1940, Roy Drachman was managing the club while his cousin Oliver was treasurer of a laundry and dry-cleaning business. Oliver and his wife Alice were among those moving out into the relatively pristine desert beyond the developed community. "We bought this lot, an acre lot [in El Encanto subdivision near Broadway and Country Club Road], in 1940," Drachman recalled many years later.[4] "Paid $2,300 for it which was a big sum, really. About a month after we bought it, we said we made a mistake…. It's too far out of town, we never should have bought it. So we tried to sell it, couldn't sell it, so the next year we went ahead and built. How lucky can you be?"

Hollywood Comes to Town

While that good luck was occurring east of downtown, on 320 acres of Pima County-owned land about 12 miles west of the city, another type of good fortune was

Seven • *War, Growth, and Entertainment, 1940–1950* 101

Tucson 1940 – 1950

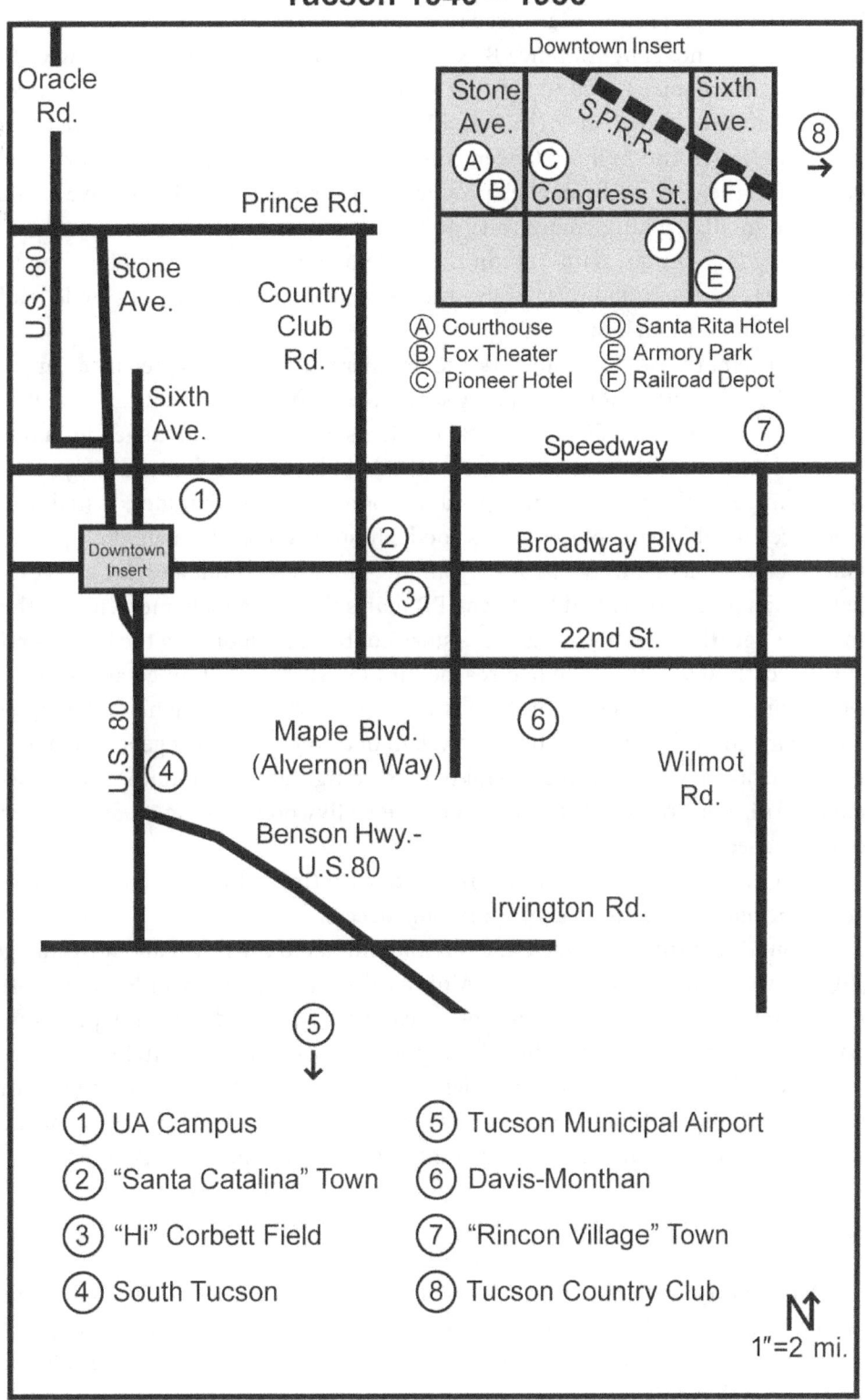

taking place. Hollywood and Columbia Pictures had arrived to film the movie *Arizona* and was constructing a sanitized re-creation of 1860s Tucson.

Based on a novel by Clarence B. Kelland, *Arizona*, had a set consisting of 150 buildings that required around 300,000 adobe bricks to construct. In addition to a cast that included stars Jean Arthur and William Holden, the movie utilized 1,400 cattle, 750 horses and mules, 80 oxen, and 20 buzzards. Filming would take three months and the price of the movie's production was pegged at an impressive $2 million.[5] The small, friendly community of Tucson impressed Holden, who told *The Cleveland Plain Dealer*: "[I]n Tucson … movie people were never mobbed on the street, where an autograph was never asked for, and where, by golly, you could really feel alive like a normal human being."[6]

By November 1940 the film was set to premiere in Tucson. To prepare an appropriate celebration, the movie company sent a west coast press agent to town. Considered an arrogant city slicker by local residents, the PR man arranged for a huge menudo luncheon to be one of the festivities held before the first showing of *Arizona*. "Gingerly the press agent dipped a spoon into [his menudo], tasted, then announced to all in earshot that it was good. He approved of the menudo," gleefully remembered someone who was at the banquet and knew about a secret ingredient that Tucson jokesters had added to the PR man's bowl as a little memento.[7] "Then [the press agent] dug in in earnest," the story continued, "spooning the broth for all he was worth. It was when he had reached midbowl that he stopped abruptly and peered into the milky depths of the dish…. Then, with a shaking hand, he dipped into the menudo and spooned out the eyeball of a cow. There was general laughter. In a moment, he was on his feet—napkin pressed tightly to his mouth—and in seconds had disappeared from the ballroom. The Hollywood press agent didn't return to the luncheon."

The film was much more warmly received. Debuting at five sold-out Tucson theaters, *Arizona* was proclaimed an enormous success.

Around that time the location of civilian flights to town was about to change. With growing military use of Davis-Monthan, including the installation of three new runways and the construction of housing for thousands of army personnel, space at the airfield became limited. In response, the city of Tucson in 1940 acquired an initial 360 acres of land seven miles south of downtown, and later more land would be bought. By 1941 the facility was being used by private planes, and the next year commercial aircraft joined them at the new "Tucson Municipal Airport."[8]

The Home Front

An event of much more obvious historic importance occurred on the first Sunday of December 1941. Alva Torres, who was nine years old at the time, had gone to the Fox Theater with her little sister, and many years later she sharply recalled the memories of that day.

"[W]e were watching a movie," Torres remembered, "and all of a sudden, the whole theater went dark. A manager came out on stage wearing black pants and a real white shirt and a tie. They put a spotlight on him, he walked across the stage, and he said, 'Ladies and gentlemen, the Japanese bombed Pearl Harbor this morning.'"[9]

World War II would bring immense changes to Tucson. Local residents from all walks of life voluntarily joined the military in large numbers. For those that didn't enlist, a draft board had been established as early as May 1941, with auto dealer Monte Mansfield serving as chair and Hiram S. "Hi" Corbett—politician, lumberyard owner, and baseball enthusiast—was also on the board. Estimates were that more than 60 percent of the men from the community eligible to serve, along with many women, did so.[10] Almost 400 of these people gave their lives for their country while another 15 were listed as missing in action.[11]

Among those from Tucson who were killed in action were five sets of brothers, including the Carrillos. Having been raised near the San Xavier Mission, 22-year-old Stephen Carrillo was a marine who died during the Naha campaign on Okinawa in 1945, three days before his army brother Raymond, 29, was killed during the same battle. The Carrillos were among an estimated two-thirds of the total population of Papago (Tohono O'odham) Indians who relocated from their Southern Arizona reservation after 1941 in order to join the war effort or to find employment.[12]

Another resident who left town during the war was Johnny Gibson. Back when he was 14, Gibson's family moved to Tucson for his brother's health; after the war, Gibson would return to become a barber and a nationally famous bodybuilder. In the service, Gibson was an army medic before being captured by the Germans and held for a while as a prisoner of war. He said of his military job: "The idea of war is to kill and destroy. Our idea was to keep everybody alive."[13]

While many Tucsonans served overseas during the war, on the University of Arizona campus thousands of sailors were going through a 60-day training course. In the middle of the Sonoran Desert, it covered such topics as "seamanship, navigation, ordnance, naval administration and naval regulations and customs."[14]

Large numbers of novice pilots were also receiving preliminary flight training near Tucson. A civilian-operated school used Ryan Field, located out on Ajo Road west of town, while the U.S. military was utilizing the newly established Marana Basic Flying School north of the city. Those getting instruction there included members of the Chinese Air Force. In 1943 the *Arizona Daily Star*—along with many others in Arizona and the United States who had once called the Chinese a subhuman form of being—now reported of these foreign trainees: "Their intelligence and discipline have received the highest of praise."[15]

Following the Japanese attack, the population of Davis-Monthan jumped from just over 2,000 to almost 10,000 within one year. At the same time, more than $3 million was spent to make needed improvements on the base.[16]

Almost 2,000 bomber crews, a total of approximately 20,000 people, were trained at DM during the war years, and life in Tucson for those in the military apparently wasn't considered too difficult. Serving at DM might have been relatively easy, but wartime flying was highly dangerous. During the war, more than two-dozen planes from the base were in accidents somewhere that resulted in almost 150 deaths.[17]

Many DM crews were being trained to operate the B-24, one of the nation's heavy bombardment aircraft. Manufactured in San Diego, Fort Worth, or Detroit, the B-24 was sent to Tucson to be modified by the Consolidated Vultee Aircraft Corporation for different theaters of war. Employing up to 4,000 people, the company established its facilities at the new southside municipal airport. Using round-the-clock shifts, Consolidated turned out more than 5,000 finished planes during the war.

Included among those working for the company was 72-year-old upholsterer Edward Menzies, whose son was in the army and grandson in the navy. Also at Consolidated was diminutive Molly Crouch, who did electrical wiring work on planes. Crouch had three sons in the Marine Corps and two daughters who worked for Consolidated in San Diego. Another employee of the company was William Hodgman. By September 1943, however, he left his job to join the merchant marine. "It will be sad to leave all my friends at C.V.A.C. [Consolidated Vultee Aircraft Corporation]," he wrote his mother shortly before his departure. "I have so many, but I must go… I can't sit when I *know* I can *help* in ways not many can."[18]

To keep absentee Tucson residents like Hodgman informed of what was going on in their hometown, as well as what was happening with local members of the military, Oliver Drachman began publishing and mailing out 3,000 weekly newsletters entitled "Letter from Home." Those who received these regular missives exuberantly expressed their appreciation to Drachman. "It means a lot to we fellows who are so far from home to know we are being remembered by the folks back home," wrote one soldier from an anonymous "Southwest Pacific Area."[19]

Tucson's Spanish-American Mothers and Wives Association conducted an effort somewhat similar to Drachman's. First produced in June 1944, the publication "Chatter" was provided to Mexican American families to send to those they knew in uniform. The 300-member Association also did other things to assist the war effort. "They would sell war bonds and help the Red Cross," summarized one account, along with supporting the families of those who had members serving in the military.[20] Comparable efforts were also conducted by other organizations, including a Jewish women's club.

For individual households in Tucson and across the nation, the war meant many items were in short supply because they were being rationed. Among these necessities were gasoline, sugar, meat, and shoes. As Alva Torres remembered, to get by her family occasionally drove to Nogales, Sonora, Mexico to buy sugar and meat while filling up their gas tank for the trip back to town.

Other people took a different approach to acquiring scarce commodities. Isabel Baffert Mikelatis' father operated a commercial grocery warehouse on Toole Avenue where she worked during the war. "Every once in awhile," she recalled, "somebody would cut a hole in the roof [of the warehouse], jump down on the flour that was there [in sacks] and go down into the basement and steal the cigarettes."[21]

Instead of being stolen, scrap metal was being collected in large quantities to be recycled and used in the war effort. By July 1942, the Pima County Salvage Committee had been formed to meet a federal quota, and within six months had overseen the collection of 3,300 tons of metal.[22]

Because rubber was also in short supply and vitally needed for military purposes, automobile tires were rationed. Ruben Moreno recalled years later that as a teenager during the war: "We were also involved in collecting rubber. We scoured the neighborhood for old tires, anything that was made of rubber, and brought it in for the war effort."[23]

In addition to rationed items, many other products were in short supply. Estella Jácome remembered that at the family's downtown department store enough jeans never seemed to be available. "[W]e used to keep the Levis for the ranchers," she said. "[I]nstead of giving them to the students, we used to keep them for the cowboys because we realized that they had to have the Levis for their work."[24]

The Southern Pacific train station was refurbished in 1941 and also played a role in the local war effort. To honor the tens of thousands of troops that would see it as they rode through town, boarded a train, or disembarked from one, the station displayed a large neon American flag, dedicated at a ceremony held in July 1942. Near this colorful flag was featured a sign proclaiming to all military personnel: "Thanks to you this will be flying when you get back."[25]

A USO (United Service Organizations) canteen was also installed for a while at the depot where thousands of traveling troops were given coffee and donuts. Another USO was established in Tucson but only after some racial hostility. The initial concept was for the second USO to cater to Black soldiers who were stationed at Fort Huachuca in Southeastern Arizona, the nearest military base with a segregated African American unit. After a vocal public outcry against this proposed USO, with fears expressed that Black soldiers could overrun Tucson and property values would fall, the original idea was withdrawn in January 1942. The plans for the Black USO were then changed to involve a much smaller space.

Explaining her support for this revised concept, Ada P. McCormick, a local "crusader for human rights and social justice issues," took out an almost half-page newspaper ad in early 1942. "It is such a tiny humble place for $40 a month where a black boy [sic] on leave can wash his hands and eat a sandwich and find a friendly face," she wrote of the USO idea. Concerning the racial situation in Tucson, she pointed out: "The colored boy [sic] can't use the comfort stations [toilets] of white people."[26] Eventually the small USO facility near the segregated Dunbar School was approved and opened.

Morgan Maxwell, Sr., became principal of Dunbar in 1940 and later remarked of the school: "The classrooms were crowded, poorly furnished and outmoded.

There was no cafeteria, no physical education department and an inadequate playground."[27] After he was appointed principal, Maxwell would successfully work to change that deplorable situation.

At the same time, of course, daily life continued in the bustling desert community. One of the major events was the preparation of Tucson's first comprehensive land-use plan. Having completed much of its work by 1943, the comprehensive regional planning program produced a number of documents, including a population forecast. "The population of Tucson and its immediate environs," this report suggested of a community that then had about 75,000 residents, "will likely approximate 100,000 by 1960."[28] (The city's actual population in 1960 was almost 213,000 and for all of Pima County more than 265,000.) Expecting much of this growth to occur outside the existing Tucson city limits, the plan's prediction was that the metropolitan region would more than double in area to become a sprawling 35 square miles in size.

More Racial Tensions but Also Celebration and Community Changes

Even as a relatively bigger Tucson was being contemplated during World War II, some local residents were raising objections about the community they then called home. Founded in 1943, the Tucson Committee for Interracial Understanding was a 125-member group that pointed out ethnic and racial tensions in town and sought to eliminate them. The committee quickly ran afoul of the editors of the *Arizona Daily Star* who labeled it a Communist front organization. This accusation was made after the group had an out-of-town speaker in 1944 that, according to the *Star*, declared: "Tucson is torn by disunity.... All of its racial groups are taught to hate and despise each other."[29]

While the *Star* admitted there was local discrimination against African Americans, the newspaper, ignoring lots of evidence to the contrary, also stated that no such bias was shown toward either Mexican Americans or Native Americans. Responding to that claim, the Committee for Interracial Understanding stressed that New Mexico and Arizona "are the only two states in the nation with an appreciable Indian population where Indians are not permitted to cast a vote."[30] They also emphasized that members of the Jewish faith were discriminated against in Tucson, with only two of the dozens of regional guest ranches accepting Jews as visitors.

It was bias against African Americans, however, that was the focus of much of the committee's work. That was due, in part, because Blacks were openly discriminated against, including at Tucson's theaters. "Whenever we attended the movies," remembered Pearlie Mae Purdie decades later, "we always had to sit in the balcony. The balcony was called 'the crow's nest,' because we were [B]lack. We weren't allowed to sit on the main floor."[31]

Native Tucsonan, Ruben Moreno, summarized the local situation simply: "There was," he said of his hometown, "quite a bit of racism."[32] A particular case cited by Moreno was the treatment of his boyhood friend, Henry Oyama, along with Oyama's sister and widowed mother. Even though Oyama's mother was from Mexico and spoke Spanish, because she had been born in Japan, following the Pearl Harbor attack the family was sent off to a federal internment camp in Arizona along the Colorado River where they were enclosed by a barb wire fence patrolled by armed guards. After 18 months there, Oyama and his mother took jobs in Kansas City, and he was eventually drafted into the U.S. Army.[33]

Nationwide, a minuscule percentage of the 117,000 Japanese Americans ordered to report to internment camps refused to comply. The few resisters were sent to prison instead, and one of those penal facilities was on Mount Lemmon. Gordon Hirabayashi of Seattle, a protestor of internment, hitchhiked to Arizona in 1943 in order to serve his 90-day jail sentence. He helped build the Catalina Highway while on Mount Lemmon.[34] Also imprisoned at this mountaintop camp were conscientious objectors to the war effort, among whom were Hopi Indians and members of the Jehovah's Witnesses.

While these American citizens were held in confinement, foreign prisoners of war were incarcerated at 23 other sites across the state. Of these, four were in Southern Arizona, including a camp in Sahuarita for 250 Germans.

In 1945 Tucson quietly marked the end of the war in Europe on May 8. Church services were held, stores and banks closed for the day, and at Tucson High the students sang "Onward Christian Soldiers" during an assembly.[35]

If Tucson had been quiet in May, it was a different story on August 14, 1945, when President Harry S. Truman proclaimed to the nation in a radio address that the Japanese had surrendered. By then, Tucson was really ready to party. "A very noisy but welcome siren began to screetch [sic] to all Tucsonians that it was time to close shop and begin the celebration," Oliver Drachman excitedly announced in "Letter from Home."[36]

Hearing the siren, people flocked downtown for an impromptu parade that included one car occupied by four teenagers. The coupe was dragging scrap metal and a washtub plus carrying a sign which proudly announced: "We dood it—again!" One of those watching the parade was an elderly man who was kissing every woman he saw. "I just love it," he told the *Arizona Daily Star*, "and you know there isn't one of them hardly that objected to it.... I'll be 80 in December and I like the gals just as well as I ever did. And they like me, too."[37]

The end of the war meant Consolidated Vultee Aircraft closed. About the same time, Davis-Monthan was deactivated with only a storage area for airplanes remaining. By early 1948, however, some military activity would return to the base.

That same type of resurgence after the war could not be said of the railroad. Beginning in 1946, Southern Pacific began replacing its high-maintenance steam engines with more efficient diesel-powered locomotives, and the company's local workforce started to steadily shrink. As one railroader recalled of this time: "When the modern equipment came in, it was different. You saw men going, jobs being abolished and lost."[38]

The number of auto courts in town also slowly began to decrease around the same time. As commercial airplane travel became more common, long-distance automobile driving easier, and chain-owned motels started to proliferate, the era of the "mom and pop" auto court was beginning to disappear.

While local jobs were being lost in the airplane maintenance, railroad, and auto court industries, Tucson's economy, nonetheless, was enjoying some new stimulus in the post-war era. One of those growth areas was moviemaking.

After sitting idle for several years after the completion of *Arizona*, with only one film during the war having been shot west of town at what was dubbed Old Tucson, by the end of 1945 the movie set was literally collapsing.[39] In 1946, thankfully, the location was leased to the Junior Chamber of Commerce. They made some much-needed improvements, and in just more than a decade after the Jaycees took over, 20 movies were filmed at Old Tucson including such popular Westerns as *Broken Arrow* (1950), *3:10 to Yuma* (1956–57), and *Gunfight at the OK Corral* (1957).[40]

Even as moviemaking occasionally brought celebrities to town, those seeking the pleasure of Tucson's climate and scenery impacted the community on a much larger scale. Thus, continuing the long-standing tradition of people moving to the Arizona desert for their health, during the war the Bonanno family had relocated from the east coast.

Joe Bonanno was involved with one of New York's five organized crime families, but came west in 1943 because his eldest son Salvatore, or Bill, had an ear infection for which the best treatment was thought to be sunshine. Once in Tucson, 33-year-old Joe Bonanno would continue with his New York criminal operations.[41]

Many law-abiding households also moved to Tucson around the same time, of course. As Gilbert Ronstadt, pioneer Fred's son, observed: "[T]he people who came here during the war to work for such firms as Consolidated [Vultee Aircraft] stayed. In other words, when the war was over you didn't have an exodus. These people stayed here and formed part of the core of our community."[42]

It wasn't only those who worked in Tucson during the war that helped expand the population. Helen Urech Shaffer recalled that her future husband from upstate New York had gone through town on a troop train one winter during the war. "He peeked out of the curtain," she said, "and saw there was no snow, and it was December."[43] Based on that, after serving in the South Pacific, "[h]e remembered Tucson, the place with no snow, and ended up down here."

Like Shaffer's husband, thousands of others came to Tucson after the war. In addition, many Tucson residents returned to their changing community. One of them was Lonnie B. Reed, who in 1948 became the first African American hired as a patrolman by the Tucson Police Department.

In addition, new entertainment came to the growing community. Tucson Greyhound Park opened in October 1944 for a 60-day season. In 1947 radio station

To improve conditions near the northside Pasqua Yaqui village, a recreation center was opened in 1942 where children living in the area could come to play (courtesy the Patricia Stephenson photograph collection).

KCNA was financed by well-known popular writer Erskine Caldwell, author of *Tobacco Road* published in 1932, and *God's Little Acre* the following year. Caldwell had moved to town early in the '40s,[44] and a few years later, retailer Cele Peterson was taking to the airways from her fashionable downtown shop for a daily radio program. Other entertainment additions to the community included the opening of a recreation hall near the Yaqui village on the northside of town and the 1945 establishment of a men's professional golf tournament. The El Casino Ballroom on 26th Street debuted a few years later in a building that would be called: "the social center for Tucson's Mexican-American community."[45]

Bringing entertainment of a different sort was Bill Veeck. Upon purchasing the Cleveland Indians major league baseball team in 1946, Veeck was intent on moving their spring training to the Southwestern desert where he owned a large ranch east of Tucson. The primary reason for the move, Veeck explained, was the blatant racism toward African American baseball fans that he had personally witnessed in Florida.[46]

Persuading the New York Giants to join his team in Arizona, Veeck's all–White roster trained at Randolph Municipal Baseball Park, a facility that opened almost two decades earlier to accommodate a team in the Arizona State League. (The stadium would be named in honor of Hiram "Hi" Corbett during 1951.) In early 1948, the Giants and Indians returned to Arizona for spring training, and by that time the Cleveland roster included Larry Doby, the first African American to play in the American League. Because of the color of his skin, Doby was excluded from staying at the Santa Rita Hotel where the rest of the team boarded. When his wife and infant daughter joined him in Tucson a few years later, they too weren't allowed in the hotel and wouldn't be for several more springs. Instead, Doby and other Black ballplayers had to stay at a small house located near the segregated Dunbar School. "The town and the weather were great; some of the people were and some weren't," Doby charitably recalled of his days in Tucson.[47]

Despite overt racial discrimination like that, the Southern Arizona tourism industry had generally benefited from World War II since overseas travel was obviously out of the question. "Tucson had 112 guest ranches within 50 miles and also eight important private schools that attracted youngsters from wealthy families from the Midwest and East Coast," observed Roy Drachman. "When the war ended," he continued about the local economy, "there was a pent-up demand for all kinds of buildings that could not be constructed during the war—especially homes."[48]

Despite experiencing overt racism in Tucson in the 1940s and '50s, Hall of Fame baseball player Larry Doby expressed thanks to some people in the community (National Baseball Hall of Fame Library, Cooperstown, New York).

The building boom that followed World War II began to transform the community as it spread out like no other time in its history. Concurrently, in 1948 tragedy struck when 33-year-old John Anderson, chief criminal investigator for the Pima County Sheriff's department, lost his life in Sabino Canyon.[49] A 15-year-old boy had climbed up one of the canyon's steep cliffs but couldn't make it to the top and had to spend the night on a narrow ledge. In the morning, Anderson was lowered from the top, dropped a rope to the boy, and then started back up. Losing his grip, he fell 500 feet to his death, a tragic scene captured by *Arizona Daily Star* photographer Sam Levitz.[50]

Two years earlier, in 1946, the Jácome's family-run downtown department store celebrated its 50th anniversary by holding a large banquet at the Pioneer Hotel on Stone Avenue. By following the advice of their father, Carlos C. Jácome, to

"Make your store a friendly one and you will live forever," six of his sons, three of whom had served in the military during the war, successfully carried on the retail business.[51]

The war and its aftermath brought many people to town, and to obtain enough water for all these new residents, while at the same time consolidating its utility empire, the Tucson City Council started to acquire water companies by annexing land into the city limits. By 1947 the city had purchased eight private water companies, one of the many legacies left behind by retiring mayor of Tucson, the 75-year-old native of Norway, Henry O. Jaastad. During Jaastad's 1933 to 1947 remarkable reign as mayor, water storage for the community went from 3.0 to 11.5 million gallons being pumped from 27 wells.[52] Other accomplishments during Jaastad's record-setting seven terms in office included the implementation of land-use zoning laws along with tripling the miles of paved streets to 90.

Incorporation and Other Battles

On the other hand, years before Jaastad's retirement, he and the city had lost the bitter South Tucson incorporation battle. During Jaastad's tenure, the city—in its continuing drive to be the sole municipal power in the county—helped defeat another incorporation effort. In 1938 the attempt to have "Santa Catalina" form a municipality from land that included El Encanto and several other subdivisions along Broadway was quashed.

Another incorporation effort came just after Jaastad left office. Desiring home rule, along with zoning laws that did not exist then in unincorporated Pima County, 251 residents of the proposed "Rincon Village" signed a petition seeking to live in the region's third municipality. Generally bounded by River Road on the north, Kolb/Sabino Canyon roads on the east, Davis-Monthan to the south, and Columbus Boulevard on the west, the community was 25 square miles in size, more than double that of the city of Tucson.

Less than 1,300 people lived within the sprawling boundaries of Rincon Village, and some of them didn't like the idea of being incorporated or of having zoning laws apply to their rural land. Despite that, the Pima County Board of Supervisors approved the incorporation petitions, and by May 1947, a five-member town council had been appointed and held its first meeting.[53] Spurred on by a disgruntled property owner who opposed the incorporation, Arizona's Attorney General John L. Sullivan sought to disband the municipality since he believed it didn't meet the legal definition of a city. After a two-year legal battle, the court system agreed and the town was dissolved.

At about the same time, the fate of Old Main on the University of Arizona campus was under consideration once again. Almost a decade earlier, in 1938 Tucson's chief building inspector, Eleazar Herreras, had declared the 47-year-old building "unsafe, dangerous and condemnable."[54] As a result, students on the campus wanted the building demolished so that a union could replace it, but a large number of alumni rallied around saving the historic structure.

Summarizing these preservationist sentiments, the *Arizona Daily Star* in 1938 editorially noted of Old Main: "[N]ow there is a possibility that it will be torn down and replaced by a modern structure similar to those ugly, coarse, factory-like oven-hot buildings which have recently been added to the campus."[55] Instead of that, the *Star* suggested Old Main could "stand to show how modern architecture in Tucson has degenerated into muddled conglomeration of aping of things far removed from Tucson."[56] At about the same time, though, the *Star* concluded of Old Main: "The chances are that whether it is repaired or not, its end is not far off."[57]

For his part, Old Main's architect, J.M. Creighton, knowingly wrote about the first structure on the UA campus: "The old building should never be wrecked. It can be used as a sign post pointing back to the men who blazed the trail in Arizona and laid the foundations for higher education on the burning sand of the desert."[58]

At the end of this 1938 dispute, Old Main remained standing since it would cost more to tear down than to leave alone, but the building was ignobly abandoned and boarded up. Four years later, in 1942, the shuttered structure was somewhat restored at a cost of $89,000 for use as the naval training center.

In 1947 there was another push by students to locate a union on the site. University president J. Bryan McCormick appointed a five-member committee to look into the issue and, while they did so, students spoke out about the building. "Take down Old Main and put the new union build[ing] in its site," one remarked. "Old Main can be preserved by a model replica in the new building."[59]

In May 1948, the Associated Students organization on campus formally petitioned the Arizona Board of Regents to replace Old Main with a union.[60] A few weeks later, President McCormick's committee recommended a different site for the new union, and it was this location that was eventually selected.[61] Thus, Old Main narrowly escaped demolition once again and would remain standing.

The university's treatment of African Americans was, on the other hand, undergoing a slow change. Prior to the mid-'40s, the UA's athletic department "was totally geared to all the blatant prejudices against [N]egroes," according to one later review.[62] That attitude finally began to change before the end of the decade when Fred Batiste was recruited out of Tucson High School by football coach Bob Winslow. He would go on to become the first African American to letter in both football and track at the university.

Batiste's older brother, Joe, had not been as fortunate. An exceptionally gifted athlete, he was an international track star while still attending Tucson High. For his athletic accomplishments, Joe Batiste was named to honorary United States Olympic teams in both 1940 and 1944. While Tucson gave Joe Batiste a downtown parade for his achievements, the University of Arizona refused to recruit him and he ended up attending Arizona State College at Tempe instead.

Another African American facing discrimination on the campus was Morgan

Maxwell, Jr. Because of the color of his skin, in 1947 he was not allowed to eat at the "Coop," a dining area in Old Main. With the assistance of student body leaders Stewart and Morris Udall, that segregation practice was changed.[63]

Also facing discrimination after the war was Tucson's Jewish population. In 1947, 28 prominent Tucsonans, including Frank O'Rielly, Oliver Drachman, Monte Mansfield, and Harold Steinfeld, had incorporated the Tucson Country Club some distance east of town. The following year the group opened a golf course on 20 acres of land which would be surrounded by a 375-acre upscale subdivision.[64] Jews and Blacks were prevented from joining the country club, a situation that would not change for about 25 more years.[65]

Thus, at the same time as Tucson was growing in population after the war, some of its citizens were being excluded from full participation in the community because of their race or religion. Despite that, local supporters were immensely proud of how far Tucson had come. "The Tucson of 1949," concluded one such booster, "is a city just coming into its own. The permanent population is now 126,850 with a winter influx of 150,000 tourists."[66]

Reflecting this population growth, a new retail center was developed by Roy Drachman in 1948. He had left the management of the Sunshine Climate Club for the much more financially lucrative field of real estate development and sales. His new center was located at 22nd Street and Cherry Avenue, called "Pueblo Plaza," and it was reportedly the first suburban strip-shopping center in town.

Another sign of change was the burgeoning home construction industry. A few years after he returned from military service in World War II, Frank E. Russell and his wife purchased a new $7,750 home near the intersection of what would later become Campbell Avenue and Grant Road, then a narrow, two-lane paved street.[67]

Russell recalled of his hometown when he left for the war: "It was a quiet, little place." After the conflict ended, he said, things were different. "Little subdivisions sprung up along with strip-shopping centers. There was rapid growth all over Southern Arizona."[68]

The 1940s, and especially World War II, were responsible for many dramatic changes in Tucson. These changes—rapid population growth, the sprawling nature of development, and a heavy reliance on government, tourism, and construction to provide jobs—would continue to influence Tucson in the decades ahead.

• EIGHT •

Ever Increasing Expansion, 1950–1960

> On Ellington Place south of 22nd Street once sat a large structure in the center of a residential neighborhood. The former Julia Keen School was closed by the Tucson Unified School District in 2004. In February 2023, a fire destroyed part of the building and a nonprofit group, Flowers and Bullets, purchased the property and demolished sections of the structure to help implement its mission to "reclaim our cultural roots and amplify them through sustainability, art, and rebellion to heal and empower our neighborhood."[1]

AN INCESSANTLY RINGING TELEPHONE JOLTED awake Pima County Assessor Leo Finch in the middle of a January 1951 night. He finally answered, and his response led to what Mayor Joseph Niemann would call the "'biggest thing' that ever happened to Tucson."[2] For its part, the *Tucson Citizen* labeled the announcement that Hughes Aircraft would be coming to town "the biggest economic windfall in Tucson's history."[3]

Real estate broker Roy Drachman was phoning Finch late on that winter's evening because he needed help in tracking down the owners of land adjacent to the Tucson Municipal Airport. Representatives of Hughes Aircraft had given Drachman less than 16 hours to acquire options on two enormous swaths of property in the area. If he could successfully complete that task, the company was committed to building a huge plant in Tucson.[4]

With Finch's assistance, Drachman succeeded with his assignment. Thus, early in February, construction on the massive 545,000-square-foot, $7.3 million plant began, but the negotiations which led up to that ultimate conclusion had begun many months earlier.

Officials from both Hughes and the United States Air Force had become concerned about the possibility of an enemy attack on the company's plant in Southern California. Based on that, a survey of several Southwestern cities, including Albuquerque, El Paso, and Phoenix was conducted by the firm looking for a relocation site, with Tucson finally being selected.

Many locals gave the cooperation displayed between Drachman and four other men—Mayor Niemann; Pima County Board of Supervisors chair J. Homer Boyd;

Eight • Ever Increasing Expansion, 1950–1960

Tucson 1950 – 1960

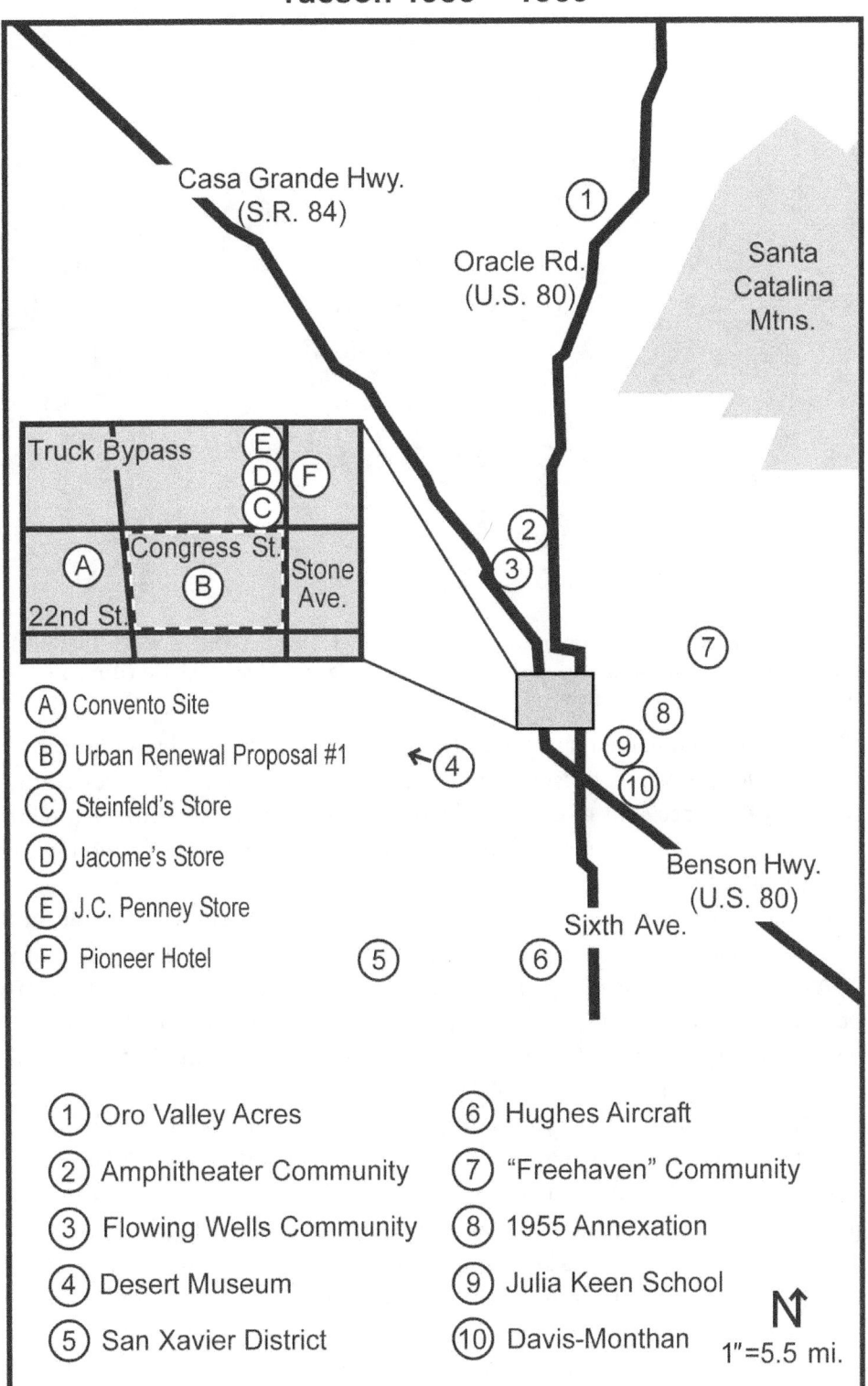

Roy Drachman, Oliver Drachman, and Monte Mansfield (left to right), three of Tucson's leading businessmen and longtime boosters, share a laugh at a 1957 appreciation dinner for Mansfield (Arizona Historical Society, PC 1000-#51932).

Chamber of Commerce manager C. Edgar Goyette; and auto dealer Monte Mansfield, president of the Tucson Airport Authority—the lion's share of credit for the company's decision to choose Tucson. "Cooperation," the *Citizen* glowingly declared, "meant everyone working together for the community's good, without thought of personal gain."[5] In addition to the property his company bought near the airport, however, reclusive Howard Hughes also wanted to acquire other vacant land in Tucson. He had Drachman round up numerous options and ended up buying 20,000 acres (31.25 square miles) scattered around the city, a process that eventually netted Drachman $95,000 in commissions. Mansfield owned one of these parcels, 640 acres in the Catalina foothills, for which he paid less than $2,000 many years earlier: he sold it to Hughes for $105,000.[6]

The decision by Hughes Aircraft to locate in Tucson was speculated to potentially turn the community into the "electronics capital of the industrial world."[7] Initially to produce the Falcon air-to-air missile, local idealistic dreams envisioned the plant becoming a "great, peacetime industry dedicated to the progress of mankind."[8] The total number of those to be employed was quickly predicted to be 10,000 within two years of opening. (It wasn't until 1956 that even one-half that number was actually achieved, and the 10,000 figure wasn't reached for 50 years.)

While the $35 million annual payroll at Hughes would dwarf every other Tucson private employer, its hiring practices were also receiving accolades. Not only was the company going to employ many people with disabilities, but it would also hire a lot of women. "We haven't had much work for women here," pointed out Eleanor Mansfield, wife of Monte. "I'm so glad the Hughes company is known for employing women in responsible jobs and at good wages."[9]

As Hughes made headlines with its hiring practices of women, a few years later one Tucson woman was named to the state legislature to fill a vacant seat. After her 1953 appointment, Democrat Etta Mae Hutcheson, better known as "Ma Hutch," was soon assigned to the labor committee and said proudly: "I have been connected with organized labor all of my life and can think of nothing in which I am more interested."[10]

Racial Harmony and Disharmony

Two years earlier, the African American children who attended the segregated Dunbar School had finally been allowed to somewhat enter the mainstream of Tucson community life. In March 1951, the Arizona legislature repealed the state's mandatory school segregation law, three years before the *Brown v. Board of Education* case did so at the national level. Once the legislature acted, Tucson School District One superintendent Robert Morrow quickly pushed to integrate Dunbar. The school board soon approved, and in May 1951, 57 pupils of Dunbar became the last graduates of the segregated institution.

To try to erase the memory of educational discrimination that had existed in the community since 1913, Morrow recommended the school be renamed John Spring after an early Tucson educator. "We have great respect for Dunbar as a great Negro poet," Morrow told the school board, "but the name connotes a Negro school, and we wish to eliminate all possible aspects of segregation from our school system."[11]

Despite the changes, Morgan Maxwell, Sr., remained principal of the rechristened school. During his time at Dunbar, Maxwell had improved the facility from its previous second-hand status by insisting it be treated the same as any other school in the district. While Maxwell would stay at John Spring, the 19 African American teachers who had previously been there were reassigned to other schools across Tucson. When students returned to their newly integrated schools in September 1951, there were no problems. That was such a noteworthy occurrence in a racially divided nation, it even received mention in the national publication, *Time* magazine.[12]

More common in the United States was the discrimination against African Americans as practiced by many of Tucson's hotels, including three of its leading establishments: the Santa Rita and Pioneer hotels downtown and El Conquistador on Broadway Boulevard. They simply didn't accept Black people as guests. To combat racial discrimination like that, in 1955 recently elected Democratic mayor Don Hummel created a Committee on Tolerance. Two years later a community survey on racial issues was completed and: "The mayor pointed out … that there is discrimination against colored peoples in 77 percent of Tucson's hotels, 67 percent of the motels, and in 33 percent of the city's restaurants."[13] In response, in 1958 it was proposed by Tucson officials that the state legislature ban discrimination in all Arizona places of public accommodation, but that wouldn't be done until 1965.[14]

Also, in 1958 balloting was taking place on the Papago (Tohono O'odham) reservation west of Tucson. The tribe's approximately 8,000 members would vote down a number of possible changes to their constitution, including having the tribal chairman elected directly by the members and not by the tribal council.[15]

The following year of 1959 saw a long-standing state misogyny bill, which forbade many interracial marriages, overturned in court. Japanese American Henry Oyama wanted to wed Mary Ann Jordan but Arizona law forbade it, so the couple legally challenged the measure and a Pima County Superior Court judge ruled it unconstitutional. After months of delay, the two were finally able to marry on December 28, 1959, at St. Augustine Cathedral. At the ceremony, between teardrops, Jordan joyfully observed: "We're finally here."[16]

At the same time, the once-despised Chinese American residents of Tucson were being accepted more into local society. Not only did a large Chinese cultural center open in the former Rainbo Bakery building near Sixth Street and Sixth Avenue in 1956, but the Tucson Advertising Club named businesswoman Esther Tang as its Woman of the Year for the previous year. Humbly accepting the honor, Tang wrote: "I share it with my people, the Chinese of this and other communities who have always been a source of encouragement and inspiration to me."[17]

Back in 1924, it was halting Chinese immigration into the United States that was a major factor in the creation of the U.S. Border Patrol. Three decades later, stopping Mexican crossers had become the agency's primary focus. In the Tucson area, fewer than 75 officers of the Border Patrol were apprehending about 250 illegal entrants each month.[18]

Growth Plans, the Aviation Industry, and Economic Diversification

At the same time, as ongoing racial disharmony confronted the community, a June 1955 strike shut down the service of the Tucson Rapid Transit (TRT) company. The privately owned firm provided service to 15,000 daily riders on much of the community's north and east sides while another privately owned company, Old Pueblo Transit, offered bus service to the primarily minority residents of the south and west sides of town.

Before striking, the 52 TRT bus drivers had rejected a 15-cent raise to their maximum $1.45 an hour salary, but after 34 days the strike ended without a wage resolution. In October, the drivers struck again. This time they were hoping for a 30-cent-an-hour increase, but prior to the second strike a company spokesman had warned: "If they strike this time, they'll think the last one was a vacation.... Don't think we can't sell our buses and close down the whole business, and we'll do it too."[19]

Instead of shutting down, the strike dragged on into early November, and downtown merchants reported their business was off by 40 percent due to the lack of bus service. One month later, the 43-day impasse was finally settled when 10 businesspeople agreed to put up the $3,000 difference between what the drivers demanded and the company was offering.[20] With the holiday shopping season approaching, downtown retailers didn't want a lack of transportation to cut into their sales any further.

While the bus strike had been traumatic, it was a much more genteel face that the local business community wanted to portray to potential Tucson visitors. In 1953 the Sunshine Climate Club reported an estimated 250,000 tourists had spent $30 million in Tucson.[21] Some people, though, weren't happy with this trend, and one critic went so far as to declare that the Sunshine Climate Club exclusively advertised in order to bring "canes, crutches, cripples and Cadillacs" to town.[22]

In response to that type of criticism, and to attract additional manufacturing firms like Hughes Aircraft, the Chamber of Commerce in 1953 got more involved with advertising Tucson's industrial advantages. The Chamber had already begun promoting the community to light industrial companies, and a 1952 brochure proclaimed that one of Tucson's attractions was "[a] highly favorable labor situation, with a relatively strike-free record."[23]

On top of this favorable labor situation, Tucson could offer an attractive quality of life. This amenity was greatly enhanced by the increasing use of refrigeration instead of swamp coolers to chill Tucson homes and businesses in the scorching and often muggy summer months. The use of refrigeration as air-conditioning became more common in the '50s and only grew with the passage of time. "The added comfort provided Arizona residents by the universal use of home refrigeration," Bert Fireman, historian at Arizona State University, noted in 1973, "contributed to the unprecedented housing boom and urbanization that has prevailed in Arizona since World War II."[24]

A trained labor force and an appealing quality of life were among the reasons that brought Douglas Aircraft to town in 1954, initially to work on B-47 jet bombers.[25] Modifying the B-47 had also been a major government contract for Grand Central Aircraft. That company had located in Tucson in 1950, occupying the giant hangars at the municipal airport which had been erected during World War II for Consolidated Vultee. Once having up to 4,700 employees, after finishing its government contracts and not being able to replace them, Grand Central quickly dwindled in size and finally closed, only to be replaced by Douglas Aircraft and its thousands of workers. In 1958, however, employment at Douglas Aircraft had fallen to 500 people and speculation about the plant's closing was a local topic of conversation. By 1959 those rumors became reality when the plant ceased operation.

Once Davis-Monthan Air Force Base had been reactivated after World War II, complaints about the noise produced by B-47s flying out of there were heard. DM officials sought to reduce the problem but the loud noise persisted, and in 1957 the lone Republican on the city council, Harlow Phelps, went so far as to propose moving the base's runway six miles out of town. Mayor Hummel blasted Phelps for making such a suggestion, saying he had done "immeasurable harm" to the community. Hummel pointed out: "[T]he airbase has a 50 million dollar annual payroll and that there would be a tremendous impact on our economic welfare and health if the facility were removed."[26]

In 1956 Hummel had also pulled city representatives from a joint governmental planning committee that was looking at the possibility of enacting zoning restrictions around DM in order to protect the base from land-use encroachment. "He opposed the proposed ordinance," the *Arizona Daily Star* reported some time later, "as 'too drastic' and one that would prohibit erection of schools, hospitals, movies and other places of public assembly in a vast area."[27]

While some Tucson residents complained about military aircraft noise, DM staff members were more concerned about the students at the new Julia Keen elementary school. Named after a local educator who served as a district principal for 32 years, in 1953 Tucson School District One located Julia Keen and its 345 students directly northwest of the DM runway.[28]

The potential hazards of both military and civilian airplane flights couldn't be underestimated. In January 1956 a small plane approaching the private Gilpin airport on the city's northwest side crashed on the playground of the Flowing Wells Elementary School, killing all four on board. Later that same year, DM commander Col. Louis Lamm commented: "I pray to God that no airplane ever goes into any of our schools or places of assemblage. It is very doubtful that anyone would survive."[29]

Having DM in Tucson also brought other potential dangers to the community. Because the base was home to Strategic Air Command bombers, predictions were made in 1957 that the city was Arizona's "prime target" for a potential H-bomb attack by the Soviet Union.[30] The following year, local civil defense officials were making plans to save as much of Tucson's population as possible from a potential conflagration. Anticipating a nuclear attack by plane, not by ICBMs in that mostly pre-missile era, those civil defense plans would provide three hours of evacuation time once the Soviet aircraft were spotted. "[T]here won't be much left of the city," it was dryly concluded in 1958, "but there's a good chance the people will escape with their lives."[31] By the following year, however, estimates were that 45,000 residents of Tucson would either be killed or injured in a nuclear blast.[32]

Another perceived threat developed in October 1957 when the Soviet Union launched the first space satellite. Sputnik caused an international sensation, and residents of Tucson even had the chance of seeing it in the night sky shortly after it went into orbit.[33]

There were much more specific threats to the Tucson soldiers who went to fight in Korea. On a warm July 1950 day, 237 Marines, seen off by hundreds of their relatives and friends, boarded a train at the Toole Avenue depot. These servicemen were members of Company E, 13th Infantry Battalion, known as "Easy Company," and by the end of the year they were fighting in bitter Korean cold near Chosin Reservoir. Several Tucsonans died there, including 21-year-old Manuel Moreno who left behind a pregnant wife. He was one of about 75 local residents killed in Korea during the war.[34] Fortunately, many others from the company survived, and after returning to Tucson, they formed a close-knit group of veterans.

While the Korean War was being fought an ocean away, many changes occurred in Tucson during the decade. By 1956 Gilpin airport was scheduled to close in order to use its 226 acres for industrial purposes, but that plan fell through so some of the land was sold. At about the same time, a new 11-story control tower adorned with a neon "TUCSON" in capital letters was installed at the municipal airport. Also, because of federal budget cuts, the U.S. government was ending its use of the Marana Air Base for training military pilots and, although some airplane maintenance work continued there, around 700 civilian jobs were eliminated.[35]

Despite this and other business events occasionally providing setbacks to the local economy, metropolitan Tucson kept growing rapidly in population. Copper mines at Silver Bell, San Manuel, and Twin Buttes brought hundreds of high-paying jobs to the region. Employment at the Pacific Fruit Express, which handled large volumes of produce brought in by train, increased. Cotton farming also aided the local economy, but pleas for volunteer pickers had to be issued once in a while.[36]

Disregarding the mostly positive economic signs, real estate mogul Roy Drachman insisted he wasn't satisfied. In 1958 he criticized the community's industrial development strategy, stating: "I shall continue to live in Tucson and be a chronic wailer until something is done to ensure a bigger and a better city."[37] Drachman believed Tucson's economy was not well balanced but, instead, was overly dependent on military and other governmental spending. As an alternative, he wanted to see more emphasis placed on attracting industries that used cotton or copper, both products of the area.

Diversification of the local economy wasn't the only concern of Roy Drachman in the late '50s. After watching an Arizona football team give a miserable performance of 27–0 against New Mexico on an October evening in 1957, Drachman wrote: "The UA should either get in or get out! We should either have a representative football team or else we should say we are giving up trying to compete with other state universities and colleges and from now on we will field teams to play schools such as LaVerne College, Pomona, Occidental and similar education institutions."[38]

This public outburst was penned only two years after star running back Art Lupino had thrilled UA fans with his football exploits, but by '57 Drachman wasn't alone in his beliefs about the pigskin program. He and many others blamed UA President Richard Harvill for the disastrous condition of the team. Finally yielding to the pressure, a change of UA head coach was made in February 1959. Later that fall, with a new coach on the job, school mascot Wilbur the Wildcat also made his debut at an extremely exciting football game against Texas Tech.

Athletics weren't the major focus of attention for some people on campus.

Instead, one accomplishment noted by the university was that enrollment finally exceeded 10,000 students. The future of astronomy at the UA also looked bright after the 1958 announcement that the National Science Foundation would locate the world's largest observatory complex on Kitt Peak, 40 miles west of Tucson.

Bigger Is Better Plus Downtown Development

Because of its rapid growth, the city of Tucson had reached the magical 50,000 mark in population by 1954. Having first been discussed as a critical target for the city almost half a century earlier, it was the annexation of 12 subdivisions over a four-year period that finally accomplished the goal. The immediate impact of this achievement was that the municipal government would collect more sales and gasoline taxes from the state of Arizona.

To serve a burgeoning population, local school districts went on a building spree. Not only were numerous elementary schools constructed, including one in the Pascua Yaqui village on the northwest side of town, but also within the span of a few years several new high schools opened. These included Pueblo ('56), Catalina ('57), Sunnyside ('57), Flowing Wells ('58), and Rincon ('58).

All of this school construction required raising property taxes substantially, and a 1957 taxpayer revolt led to two District One construction bond issues being rejected. Officials at city hall around the same time proposed capping the municipality's property tax rate in exchange for the imposition of a one-half percent sales tax. Voters overwhelmingly approved this idea, and Mayor Hummel enthusiastically called it "the first step toward a more glorious city."[39]

To provide sufficient water for all of Tucson's present and potential residents, municipal officials were making big plans. In 1958 they proposed a $20 million water expansion program that would allow the company to have 385,000 customers by 1970, about two and one-half times the number it then served. The city would use some of its revenues to continue acquiring privately owned companies, with the stated intention of basically becoming the region's monopoly water utility.

The need to diversify Tucson's water supply had become apparent earlier when an extended 1953 drought and over-pumping led to a substantial fall in the water table. By the end of the decade, the prediction was even made that a dropping groundwater table could endanger the area's economy.[40] In response, the Chamber of Commerce adopted a resolution that simply denied a shortage of water.[41]

To supplement existing groundwater resources, city of Tucson and state of Arizona officials were eyeing the Colorado River. While a lawsuit between California and Arizona over the amount of water from the river each could claim dragged on in court for years—and then decades—the state was making plans to eventually tap into the Colorado any way it could, including "without federal aid if necessary."[42]

With the apparently abundant and everlasting river water as a possible future supply, along with all the other supposedly positive local changes taking place,

Mayor Hummel was beaming with confidence about Tucson's future. To keep prospering, Hummel believed the municipality had to keep growing rapidly. In 1955 the city annexed a six-square-mile area on the eastside, increasing its geographic size by 50 percent and its population by 85,000. Hummel also went so far as to naively proclaim in 1956 that after many years in second place, Tucson was once again poised to become "the largest city in Arizona."[43] "Phoenix is surrounded by incorporated communities," Hummel explained of his bold and ultimately foolish prognostication, "which limit its growth. Tucson, with one exception, has no such handicap." (By 1960 Tucson had 213,000 residents while Phoenix had more than twice that number.)[44]

That one exception, of course, was South Tucson. In March 1956 Mayor Hummel, echoing the sentiments of Tucson officials from almost 20 years earlier, called for the little community to join its much larger neighbor. "I think the entire town would be better off under one roof," Hummel suggested.[45]

Shortly after that invitation went unanswered, the Tucson City Council held a surprise meeting. It annexed land all around the tiny town, thus theoretically cutting it off from any future expansion while leaving the city of Tucson seemingly unimpeded in its quest for new growth through development and annexations.[46]

After taking a couple of years off from major annexation efforts, in 1959 the city went after a huge amount of property along its eastern and northern borders. Successfully completing this attempt would basically double the city's geographic size while adding 70,000 more people to its population. Many of those Pima County residents didn't want to be annexed and one argued: "The city did not keep the promises it made to people annexed two years ago, and it can't be trusted now."[47]

To combat the city's annexation initiatives, and following the model established by South Tucson during the 1930s, three portions of the proposed massive annexation area sought instead to independently incorporate themselves. Residents of the Flowing Wells and Amphitheater districts, along with an eastside area labeled "Freehaven," all wanted self-government. Mayor Hummel in response asked for cooperation while also publicly wondering just what it was people objected to about being brought into the city.

When petitions from the three areas were submitted to the Pima County Board of Supervisors asking for incorporation elections to be called, it wasn't surprising, given legal and political history, when the requests were denied. Instead, the board decided the areas were "not communities under the law." Minutes after that action was taken, the Tucson City Council formally annexed 20 square miles of land that pushed its boundaries north to Roger Road and east to Kolb Road, with Mayor Hummel declaring: "Tucson's future has now been assured."[48]

As the city, along with the entire metropolitan area, was spreading out in all directions, much focus still remained on downtown. Pointing specifically to new construction there, the *Arizona Daily Star* proclaimed at the end of 1956: "At the corner of Alameda Street [and Stone Avenue], a new [nine-story] 'skyscraper' eased its way into the air ... for what will be the $1,000,000 Arizona Land Title and Trust Co. building."[49]

Numerous other changes were also appearing downtown. As early as 1950, Harold Steinfeld had worked with his retail competitors, the Jácome family, to move their store from Congress Street to the northwest corner of Stone Avenue and Pennington Street, right across from the Steinfeld Department Store. According to a newspaper article, Steinfeld had ideas that Pennington Street in Tucson could become a smaller version of Park Avenue in New York City. By 1957 a major addition was being made to Jacome's; at the same time J.C. Penney moved from its previous downtown location on Congress Street to a larger building right next to Jacome's on Stone Avenue. To mark its opening, 82-year-old J.C. Penney himself came to town and greeted more than 2,000 well-wishers.[50]

It was on Pennington Street in November 1956 that Cele Peterson's apparel shop burst into flames. Ignited by an accidental spark from a welder's torch, the inferno quickly consumed the contents and the building, but amazingly no one perished. In addition to swift work by firefighters, the existence of a sprinkler system was credited with saving several lives.[51] After the fire, Peterson would reopen her store and remain in business for years to come.

A concept that failed to materialize immediately was about 12 miles north of downtown. In 1958 a proposal was floated to build the $44 million Oro Valley Acres to include "a resort hotel, health spa, golf club, professional buildings, shopping center, a mile-long lake, and guest ranch."[52] There were also to be at least 600 one-acre housing lots, many of them surrounding the golf course. The idea, however, didn't go anywhere for quite a few years.

At about the same time, shopping centers with enormous free parking lots were actually springing up around the city and challenging downtown's retail dominance. One 1957 example was the Southgate Shopping Center at 44th Street and south Sixth Avenue. Covering 75,000-square-feet of space, the center included a market, a small department store, a drug store, and several other shops. Developed by Roy Drachman and former judge Evo DeConcini, the strip center was reportedly the first of its kind on Tucson's south side.

By far the biggest threat to downtown's supremacy of the retail sector, however, appeared in 1958. That year, Joseph Kivel announced plans for the "Elcon" regional shopping center, a north-south oriented outdoor pedestrian mall surrounded by 5,000 free parking spaces, an amenity in sharp contrast to the limited metered parking that predominated throughout the downtown area. The new shopping complex was to contain up to 100 stores, be anchored by a Montgomery Ward and a Levy's Department Store, and would be built east of El Conquistador Hotel along Broadway.

Facing paid parking and perceived traffic congestion problems, as well as increased competition from outlying retailers, downtown and civic leaders looked for solutions. On March 20, 1955—the 75th anniversary of the day the railroad arrived in town—the city of Tucson released a study that recommended removing the railroad tracks from the downtown core entirely. Intended to provide both expansion space for the central business district as well as a more coherent traffic pattern, the plan called for relocating the tracks southward. While many Tucsonans enthusiastically endorsed the idea, the Southern Pacific Company rejected it out of hand, saying it would cost them $20 million to implement. Thus, the tracks stayed put.

Another proposal that went nowhere began in 1953 when the Pima County Board of Supervisors suggested building a governmental complex to the north of the existing domed courthouse. Demolition of several historic homes, including the imposing house on Main Avenue built by J. Knox Corbett almost one-half century earlier, would be necessary. The project was to be financed by a bond issue, but voters overwhelmingly turned down the idea.

Still seeking major solutions to downtown's challenges, including the poor physical condition of some buildings, by 1957 Mayor Hummel was ardently preaching the need for a federally funded urban renewal program.[53] In 1958 the city obtained a $151,000 federal grant to begin surveying a proposed urban renewal area. It was bounded by Congress Street on the north, Stone Avenue on the east, 22nd Street to the south, and a new truck bypass on the west. Approximately 5,000 people, many of whom were longtime, mostly poor Mexican American residents, lived there. In the view of Mayor Hummel, redevelopment: "would wipe out an area that contributes greatly to the crime problem and would provide for off-street parking and for better circulation of traffic."[54]

A few years before this urban renewal push, the city council had authorized the appointment of a committee intended to "preserve and mark historical sites in Tucson."[55] Lamenting the past loss of many older buildings, the sponsor of the adopted motion, Councilman Richard Summers, stated: "Before certain individuals and interests perpetuate the materialistic doctrine that has pervaded Tucson since 1920—the doctrine of 'the bigger, the newer, the faster and the better,'—I would like a competent analysis of what little is left to us of our one priceless and irreplaceable asset, the Spanish atmosphere of the older portion of Tucson and our historical buildings and ruins."[56]

One place Summers may have been referring to were the remains of the 18th-century Mission San Agustín and Convento. Located south of Congress Street and west of the Santa Cruz River, the adobe buildings had long been neglected and were slowly melting away during rainstorms. The final, ignoble blow came when the city of Tucson bulldozed what was still standing and then installed a garbage dump on the site.

Goodbye to Some Existing Motels and Notable Personalities

Another area Summers may have thought worth saving was Tucson's historic barrio. Situated south of downtown, the barrio was also adjacent to where the community's first freeway was being built. Originally authorized by Tucson voters in a 1948 bond election, the proposed route for the roadway west of the central business district connected U.S. 80 (Benson Highway), with State Route 84 (Casa Grande Highway).

Promoted as a truck bypass around downtown prior to the '48 election, some of the backers of the bonds were retailers Alex Jácome and Harold Steinfeld; businessmen "Hi" Corbett and Monte Mansfield; and cousins Oliver and Roy Drachman. In contrast, the bond issue was vehemently opposed by several of the remaining auto court owners on Sixth Avenue and Oracle Road. Ignoring them, by a 2-1 margin Tucson voters approved $850,000 worth of financing to acquire needed right-of-way for the truck bypass roadwork.

The four-lane divided highway was estimated to cost $5 million to construct and would be paid for by the state of Arizona. As the project neared completion in 1955, the proposal was made to build a $1 million Sands Motel at Congress Street along the new truck route. Tucson motel owners who had supported the highway project seven years earlier loudly protested that if the state and city governments approved this request, they would break "promises [which] were made [that] there would be no business development along the thoroughfare."[57]

Opponents of the motel project went so far as to hire local attorney Stuart Udall, who had been elected to the U.S. House of Representatives in 1954, to argue their case. Mayor Hummel said the city council's only responsibility was to determine what the proper zoning was for the motel land. Udall's efforts thus proved futile when business zoning was granted to the property and construction of the new motel proceeded.

A couple of years later, plans for installing through town the national interstate highway system, that would be called I-10, rekindled the issue of zoning along new limited-access roadways. The federal highway would be built inside the divided lanes of the existing truck bypass. Members of the North Tucson Business Association sought an injunction to stop everything except industrial uses next to the new interstate, but the request was denied and commercial development began springing up as work on the interstate got underway.

That legal setback didn't deter existing motel and auto court owners with establishments on city streets from trying once again to protect their interests. Over the opposition of many of these accommodation business owners, in 1959 the city council, on a 4-3 party line vote with Democrats in the majority, approved another rezoning application for a motel along the interstate route on land owned by the Bricklayers, Masons and Plasterers' Union. As a result of new motels like this being approved near I-10, by the late '50s the once vibrant auto court and motel scene on south Sixth Avenue and Oracle Road was beginning to fade. (Fortunately, a few of these establishments, with their colorful neon signs, are still in business.)

In 1954 another high-profile story got Tucson's attention. The U.S. government was attempting to revoke Joe Bonanno's citizenship so he could be deported. Federal officials charged Bonanno had lied on mandatory paperwork when he denied being previously arrested or being "a member of the Grand Council of Sicilian underworld gang, located in Brooklyn, N.Y."[58] Lawyers for Bonanno refuted the allegations and offered local character witnesses, including former Arizona Supreme Court judge, Evo DeConcini, in Bonanno's defense. Agreeing with those arguments, federal judge James Walsh dismissed the charges.

Another notable person making the front page of Tucson newspapers was President Dwight D. Eisenhower. He came to Tucson in 1957 for an overnight stay as part of a survey he was making of drought damage in western states.

Senator John F. Kennedy visited during 1958 for a long weekend and stayed at the Arizona Inn. He addressed a $25 a plate fund-raising dinner crowd at the Pioneer Hotel downtown and also attended church. Stephen Ochoa, a former Tucson city councilmember, accompanied Kennedy to the service. Ochoa's grandfather was the man who, in 1877, had introduced the territorial legislation to allow the Southern Pacific Railroad Company to build across Arizona.

Someone else receiving public attention during the 1950s, although not necessarily on the front page of a newspaper, was architect Eleazar Herreras. After 23 years with the city of Tucson, most of it spent as the chief building inspector, he retired in 1953 to enter private practice.[59]

The 1954 death of 86-year-old pioneer Fred Ronstadt was given much more public attention. In a front page story, the *Arizona Daily Star* wrote of Ronstadt: "An energetic campaigner for civic improvements in Tucson from his arrival here in April 1882 ... Mr. Ronstadt was an ardent Tucson booster."[60] In addition, the newspaper also mentioned Ronstadt's many musical contributions to the community.

The 1959 passing of Monte Mansfield at age 75 was also given front-page coverage. The *Citizen* summed up Mansfield's life succinctly by stating: "[He was] generally acknowledged to be the man who played the greatest role in Tucson's growth."[61]

Another sad event had occurred the previous year. Three young Boy Scouts—Michael LaNoue, David Greenberg, and Mike Early—perished while trying to climb Mount Wrightson in the Santa Rita Mountains south of Tucson. A freak November snowstorm blanketed the mountain with several feet of snow and caught the Scouts in its frozen grip.[62]

One other person who died during the decade was 30-year-old deputy sheriff Jack Brierly. Rushing on his motorcycle to the scene of a fatal pedestrian accident, Brierly was killed when a car turned in front of him on Speedway Boulevard at Swan Road.

Famous local artist Ted DeGrazia received some attention in 1954 when he completed his nondenominational Chapel in the Sun in the foothills of the Santa Catalina Mountains. Three years later, the temperamental artist was threatening to permanently leave town because of zoning regulations adopted by Pima County for unincorporated areas.[63] Despite the complaints, he stayed put.

The mid–'50s also saw a number of important anniversaries. The centennial of the Gadsden Purchase, which brought Southern Arizona into the United States, was commemorated in December 1953 with the issuance of a postage stamp. The next year, Harold Steinfeld had the city's largest sign, ten tons of steel showing an illustration of covered wagons, erected on top of his downtown department store to celebrate the 100th anniversary of the business' founding in New Mexico. Along with the Southern Pacific Railroad, in 1955 Saint Mary's hospital was marking 75 years in Tucson. The next year, the Valley of the Moon, a whimsical attraction on the north side of town, noted a quarter century in the community.

That was only one of an expanding number of local entertainment opportunities. Television had been introduced to Tucson in February 1953 when, from its station on Drachman Street, KOPO Channel 13 was the first on the air. By the end of the year, it was estimated that 50 percent of Tucson households had televisions and viewers were given warnings about how to watch their sets. For example: "Night vision can be reduced sharply by those who view TV for a long period."[64]

During the previous year of 1952, the Arizona Desert Trailside Museum, which was later renamed the Arizona-Sonora Desert Museum, was established several miles west of town. It was the brainchild of Bill Carr and Arthur Pack who wanted a place devoted "to the plants and animals of the Sonoran Desert."[65] With a surprisingly large crowd of 1,000 in attendance on opening day, the museum had "the purpose of acquainting the public with their rich but vanishing heritage in wildlife, plant life, and scenic values, to the end that, through knowledge, will come appreciation and a better attitude toward all resource conservation."[66]

Back in town, drive-in theaters kept popping up during the decade. Memorable events for 1955 included golfer Tommy Bolt winning the annual Tucson Open for the second time; the Tucson Arizona Boys Chorus, 16 years after its founding, making its initial trip to Europe; and the first Tucson Gem and Mineral Society show being held at the Helen Keeling Elementary School along Glenn Street and attracting about 1,200 visitors. Then, in 1957, for $50,000 Pima County purchased 37 acres of the eastside military ruins at Fort Lowell from the Boy Scouts with the express purpose of preservation. Also, in 1957 the gym at the new Catalina High School was filled with 3,000 teenagers and their somewhat bewildered parents to see a string of musical stars including Chuck Berry, Paul Anka, Fats Domino, and a band called the Crickets with lead singer Buddy Holly. "It was the rock 'n' roll concert to end all rock 'n' roll concerts," remembered one-time teenager, attorney Bill Risner many years later.[67]

Annual events sponsored by the Tucson Festival Society were also attracting large audiences. In 1958 these included La Fiesta de la Placita, which drew 7,000 people downtown, as well as a pageant at San Xavier del Bac that brought 10,000 to the iconic mission.

A little more than a decade after attending as a high school student the 1957 "rock 'n' roll concert to end all rock 'n' roll concerts," Bill Risner was a practicing attorney and ardent opponent of a proposed urban freeway system (courtesy the Bill Risner photograph collection).

While family-oriented recreational opportunities were rapidly multiplying in Tucson during the 1950s, illegal activities were also on the rise. Drug usage was a growing problem, and gambling was still prevalent.

Despite problems like those, the 1950s was mostly a decade of dynamic transformation for the community. The population of the metropolitan region had almost doubled to 260,000. At the same time, due to numerous annexations, the number of city residents over that span of 10 years had grown by five-fold to 213,000 and accounted for almost 82 percent of the county's total population.

Highlighting many of the positive changes taking place in Tucson, in 1958 *Arizona Highways* magazine portrayed the community in the best possible light. "Tucson is a big modern city," it noted, "with the friendliness and easy informality of a small town."⁶⁸ As for the city's future, one commentator wrote in romantic terms: "Someday, the wide bowl rimmed by the rugged ranges of the Catalinas and the Santa Ritas, the Rincons and the Tucsons, will be filled from edge to edge with urban people—a half million of them at least…. That way the future lies. Who is to say the way is not good?"⁶⁹

• NINE •

Crime, Downtown Decline, and Urban Highways, 1960–1970

A few dozen cars on a Saturday morning are parked in front of the Casino of the Sun on Tucson's far southwest side. Just behind the attractive building are beige and brown stucco single-story homes. In a nod to Southwestern architectural tradition, some of the flat-roofed houses have artificial vigas protruding from their front facades. These homes were among the first to be built in the new Pascua Yaqui village once it was established in 1964.

A VERDICT IN 1966 WAS QUICKLY REACHED in one of Tucson's most notorious murder trials to date. After the jury of eight women and four men received the case, Charles "Smitty" Schmid was convicted within two hours and sentenced to death.

Schmid, the 23-year-old so-called "Pied Piper" of Tucson, was found guilty of strangling Gretchen Fritz, 17, and her 13-year-old sister, Wendy. The prosecution charged he killed the two girls to cover up his murder of another teenager, Alleen Rowe. (Before he could be executed, Schmid was stabbed numerous times by two other inmates and died of his wounds in 1975.)

During Schmid's trial, widely read national *Life* magazine wrote in a major article: "[W]hat disturbs them [local residents] far beyond the question of Smitty's guilt or innocence are the revelations about Tucson itself that have followed on the disclosure of the crimes. Starting with the bizarre circumstances of the killings and on through the ugly fragments of the plot—which in turn hint at other murders as yet undiscovered, at teenage sex, blackmail, even connections with the Cosa Nostra—they [Tucsonans] have had to view their city in a new and unpleasant light."[1]

How did *Life* see a community where for an amazing 45 weeks the *Sound of Music* would be shown at the Catalina Theater concurrent with Schmid's trial? "It [Tucson] is glass and chrome and well-weathered stucco," the magazine concluded, "[but] it is also gimcrack, ersatz and urban sprawl at its worst."[2]

Reflecting the emerging split personality of the formerly small Southwestern town, by the 1960s the rate of crime within the Tucson city limits was soaring. The

Tucson 1960 – 1970

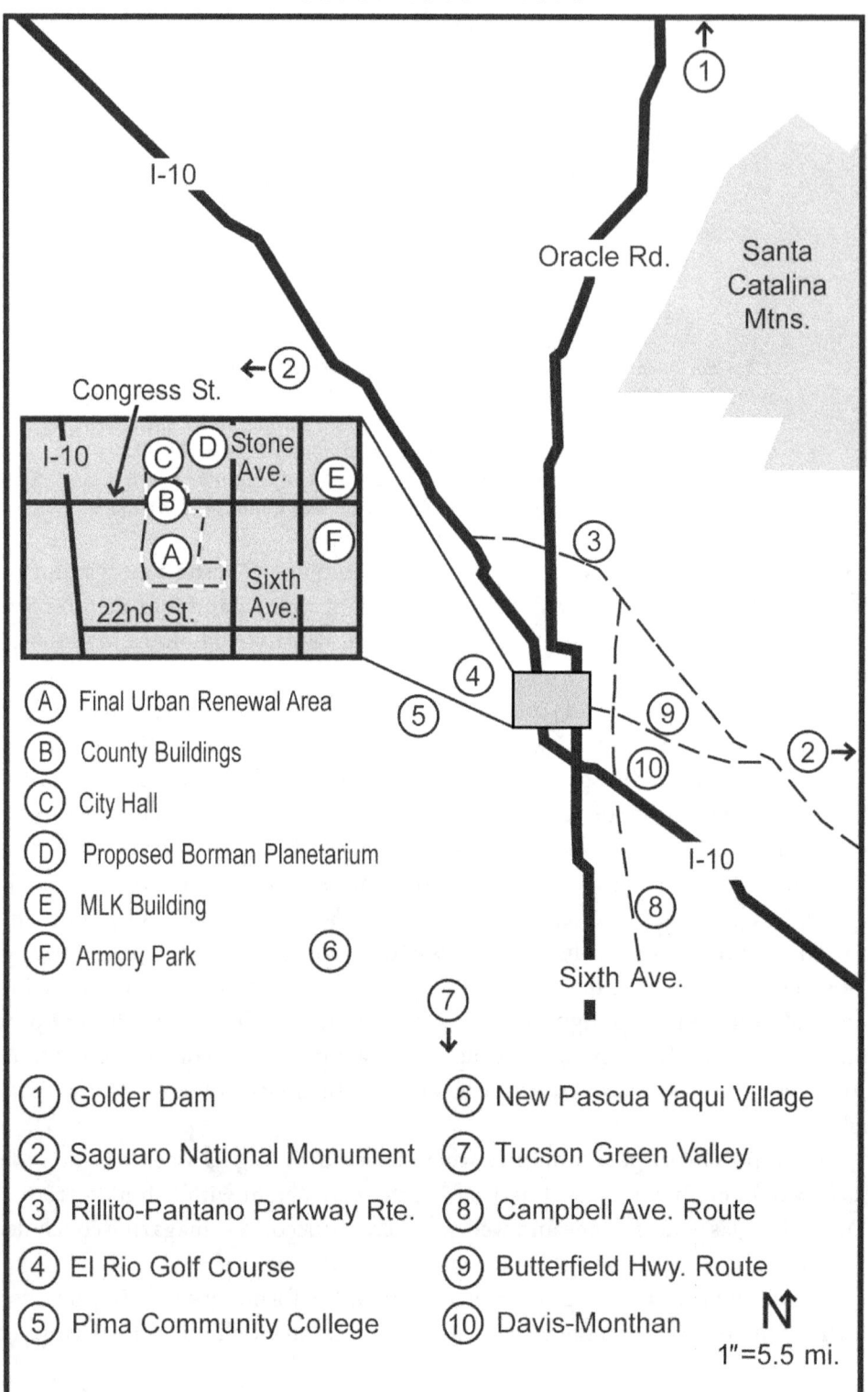

annual number of reported rapes rose to 114 in 1960, a 60 percent increase from the previous year.[3]

As the decade progressed, even bombings became somewhat regular occurrences in town. At first these explosions, which began with a 1962 car bombing, were blamed on underworld figures. This was especially true when, in July 1968, the patio of the Elm Street home of reputed Mafia kingpin, Joe Bonanno, was rocked by a blast.[4] A few months later, an explosive device went off at the home of former Arizona Supreme Court justice and Bonanno acquaintance, Evo DeConcini. Those were two of ten Tucson bombings in 1968 alone.

In March of the following year, jeweler Newton Pfeffer fell to his death from the 11th floor of downtown's Pioneer Hotel. His apparent suicide was reportedly the result of "Cosa Nostra pressure," which included gangsters swindling the jeweler out of $1.5 million worth of wholesale merchandise.[5] In response to this rampant rise in illegal activity, a countywide commission was formed in 1969 "to look into crime."[6] Shortly thereafter, arrests were made in some of the bombing cases. Instead of being associated with the Mafia, however, suspicions were cast upon a rogue FBI agent who was rumored to be using his criminal associates as vigilantes.

During the '60s, there were also numerous other challenges to traditional social mores, including long-held views on public gambling and nudity. In 1965 the Jewish War Veterans tried to hold bingo games in their hall, a practice considered illegal by the Tucson Police Department. By 1967, topless dancers in Tucson were being charged with indecent exposure. In 1969 the Marana School District even tried to regulate the length of a male student's hair, an attempt they lost in court.

Another perceived threat throughout the decade was from Communism. A 1961 state law was enacted that "outlaw[ed] the Communist party in Arizona and require[ed] public employees to take loyalty oaths."[7] Under the law, public school teachers who did not sign the oath could keep their jobs but wouldn't be paid.[8]

Considering the motive behind this legislation to be a signal that "people should fear social change," two Tucson schoolteachers refused to comply with the law.[9] Barbara Elfbrandt worked for the Amphitheater School District and her husband, Vernon, for Tucson School District One. After the Arizona Supreme Court found the law constitutional in 1964, and having already gone several years without pay while relying on financial assistance from others, Barbara Elfbrandt appealed this ruling to the United States Supreme Court. Two years later, the nation's highest court overturned the Arizona law. For her persistence in this case, Elfbrandt was selected as one of the community's "Outstanding Tucson Women of 1966" by the *Arizona Daily Star*.[10]

The Vietnam War also increased the perceived threat of Communism. During a time span of about four years ending in June 1969, 91 military personnel with Tucson connections would die there. One of those was 20-year-old former Sunnyside High School student Billy Lauffer who was an army private killed in combat. For his heroic actions, Lauffer was posthumously awarded the Medal of Honor.[11] (In 2005, a Sunnyside Unified School District middle school was named after Lauffer.)

Sparsely attended rallies opposing the Vietnam War were occasionally held in Tucson, often accompanied by small groups who supported the conflict. In October 1969, the largest protest occurred when up to 9,000 people gathered on the University of Arizona campus.

While the Vietnam War did not usually stir up a great deal of local emotion, the murders of John F. Kennedy and Martin Luther King, Jr., certainly did. After President Kennedy's 1963 assassination, the city basically shut down for several days of mourning. King's 1968 killing resulted in the establishment of a local scholarship fund.[12] His widow also visited Tucson a year after his death and spoke at the university to an overflow crowd of 3,400. At about the same time, a public housing project for senior citizens, under development in the downtown area, was named after the slain civil rights leader.

More Civil Rights Concerns

The drive for civil rights also stirred strongly held feelings. The need for change was expressed by a 1960 survey that showed that, despite some progress, almost 30 percent of the city's restaurants along with many of its hotels and motels continued to discriminate against African Americans.[13]

When the Arizona State Legislature failed to adopt regulations that would legally prohibit this type of racial segregation, in 1960 the Tucson City Council took up the idea of a public accommodation ordinance. After alarmist warnings from some in the business community that enacting such a law would be "tantamount to an admission that Tucson is a segregated city," the council delayed action for four months.[14] Using that time, local businessmen collected petition signatures from many establishments that promised they wouldn't discriminate, and the public accommodation legislation was then dropped from council consideration.

By September 1963, however, the local chapter of the NAACP began protesting at the Pickwick Inn on Benson Highway, claiming its owner was biased against African Americans. Once it quickly got that situation changed, the NAACP said it wanted the city council to adopt an ordinance banning segregation in accommodations.

Shortly after President Lyndon B. Johnson signed the Civil Rights Act of 1964, the council responded to the NAACP's request and considered an accommodation ordinance. Even though Tucson City Attorney Calvin Webster publicly declared local elected officials had no legal authority to do so since it was a state issue in his opinion, the council, by a 4–2 margin, adopted the ordinance anyway. In casting the deciding vote, Republican Mayor Lew Davis courageously stated, "I will vote in favor of this ordinance because it is good for Tucson, good for this council and good for everybody."[15]

Irrespective of the new law, occasional complaints of discrimination continued. In 1967 Black students leveled charges of racial hostility at the University of Arizona, claims backed up by a report from the federal Office of Civil Rights but refuted by University President Richard Harvill.[16]

On the other hand, another minority group saw a benefit from the federal government. At the urging of many local leaders, 200 acres of land far southwest of town was provided in 1964 to Pascua Yaqui Indians for a new community. The goal of this move was to improve on the deplorable conditions in which the Yaquis lived at their long-established Old Pascua Village near Grant Road.[17] Within a few years of the legislation's adoption, the first of 16 new homes was completed in the emerging Yaqui settlement. It was a three-bedroom house in which Mrs. Felipa Suarez and four of her adult children would reside, replacing a dilapidated structure she had occupied in Old Pascua Village.[18]

Demonstrating a less harmonious note, 250 Mexican American students walked out of Tucson High in 1969 claiming racial discrimination at the school. That same year, labor leader Cesar Chavez said in a local address that he planned to try and unionize farm laborers in Pima County.[19] Some observers considered his goal unlikely to be achieved, however, since there just weren't that many farm workers left around Tucson, and they proved to be correct.

A protracted work stoppage in the mining industry during the decade, though, did impact Tucson's economy significantly. In July 1967 a strike against several companies halted much of the copper mining in Arizona, and it wouldn't be settled until the spring of 1968.

The negative economic impact of that and other work stoppages in the industry demonstrated the importance of copper mining in Pima County. By 1964 several local mines employed more than 3,300 people and generally paid them high wages. The role of the industry grew even larger the next year when the Anaconda Mining Company began developing the Twin Buttes mine south of Tucson.

Another labor action, but one that lasted only a few hours, was the 1969 resignation of almost 200 city police officers, about two-thirds of the entire force. Demanding substantial pay hikes before returning to work, the officers didn't accomplish their goal but did receive the promise that city hall would "immediately undertake an evaluation of all positions in the city, and ... [t]he police department will be considered first in this evaluation."[20] Based on that pledge, the police resignations were rescinded.

During May of the previous year, the Tucson Transit Company, which had formerly been known as Tucson Rapid Transit, experienced another protracted bus driver strike, and by the end of the year it was planning to go out of business. In response, the city of Tucson started subsidizing the company, enabling bus service to continue.

City hall officials also got involved in another transportation issue when they objected to the 1968 proposal by the Southern Pacific Railroad Company to totally end its daily passenger service to Tucson. The Interstate Commerce Commission rejected that request, so the company planned to operate six passenger trains a week, three going in each direction. (Amtrak still operates six passenger trains a week to Tucson.)

Aviation Ups and Downs Plus Infrastructure for Growth

Just as passenger train service was declining, improvements in Tucson's aviation sector were occurring. Signaling the end of the propeller era, the first commercial jet flew into the southside municipal airport in September 1960. The following year, air connections with Mexico were inaugurated, meaning the airport was at that point technically an international facility, and it would assume that name in 1963.

The need for special land-use zoning around Tucson's two major airports—Davis-Monthan and Tucson International—was also a continuing topic of discussion. Despite some nearby landowners complaining about the possible loss of property value, height and use restrictions near the municipal airport were adopted in November 1962. Five years later, Davis-Monthan officials once more promoted the same type of regulations for land near the military base, but again local legislative action didn't follow. A string of fatal crashes involving DM pilots, the worst of which horrifically killed four people on the ground near south Alvernon Way and 29th Street in December 1967, intensified calls to adopt some land-use restrictions near the base. Ignoring those concerns, in 1969 the Pima County Board of Supervisors surprisingly approved the expansion of Julia Keen elementary school located off the northwest end of the DM runway.

In addition to safety issues, the arrival of the extremely loud F-4 Phantom jet-fighter at DM in 1964 resulted in noise complaints from across the city. In response, the Air Force changed flight patterns and took other measures to try and reduce the impact, but to little effect.

While its planes may have inflicted some problems, supporters of DM pointed out the enormous positive economic impact the base had on Tucson. These financial benefits from military expenditures were substantially increased in 1960 with the announcement that 18 Titan intercontinental ballistic missile (ICBM) silos would ring the city. This move meant hundreds of servicemen coming to the region to staff the ICBM facilities along with an estimated 2,000 construction jobs also being created. Thus, in December 1962, the first of the huge missiles was lowered into the ground in the Three Points area west of town.

Aside from the positive and negative effects of DM, there were other less perceived, but potentially deadly, hazards lurking. One became reality on March 29, 1963, when the Supreme Cleaners building at Grant Road and Stone Avenue exploded into a huge wall of flame, killing seven and injuring more than 30 people.[21]

Another, more constant, concern to the community came from the increasing amount of air pollution. While it was only a minor irritant at the beginning of the '60s, a UA professor warned then: "[I]n 10 years time we will have a real problem if we don't do something now."[22] Among the culprits pointed to as causing the dirty air were automobile exhaust, DM planes, and copper smelters in the region. By 1968 a UA study concluded air pollution in Tucson really was a serious problem. After that, the Pima County Board of Supervisors adopted air quality regulations, but exempted both smelters and automobiles, while the Tucson City Council appointed a committee to study the issue.

At that same time as they were half-heartedly addressing air pollution, local elected officials continued to work on expanding Tucson's street and highway system to accommodate a rapidly growing population. Construction of I-10 through the city crawled slowly along throughout the 1960s while work on I-19 southbound toward the Mexican border got underway. Also being implemented was a 1967 idea, nicknamed the suicide lane, to install a reversible lane on Broadway Boulevard that would have the center turn-lane carrying one-way through traffic during morning and afternoon rush hours.

The cause of considerable political controversy, but eventually winning voter approval in 1962, was the replacement of the unique downtown Broadway underpass. The new subway, a $2 million rendition, was a wider and much shorter tunnel than the original version. It opened in October 1963 to music played by the Tucson High marching band.[23]

Progress was also promised in correcting frequent flooding problems in the Stone Avenue underpass. The swiftly rising body of water that formed there during thunderstorms had affectionately been called "Lake Elmira" since the summer of '36. Thirty-one years later, the installation of new drains would theoretically fix the potentially deadly situation, but of course storm water continued to flood the underpass after they were installed.

Regardless of that obvious failure, planning for other transportation improvements continued. In 1961 proposals for two new major roadways were unveiled. One was the Butterfield Route running eastward from I-10 through downtown's historic barrio and then heading toward Davis-Monthan. The other was the Campbell Avenue Penetration Route that went all the way from the municipal airport to north of Prince Road. These ideas were followed in 1964 by plans calling for a freeway bypass across the northern edge of the city, generally following the Rillito and Pantano washes.

Even though plans for the entire Butterfield Route still lacked final acceptance, a short stretch of construction work did begin on it with the divided thoroughfare running about 1,000 feet eastward from I-10 before abruptly stopping. That, however, was all that was accomplished of the three proposed urban freeway projects during the entire decade.

Despite that lack of implementation, in 1968 a plan calling for a network of metropolitan limited-access highways was released by the Tucson Area Transportation Planning Agency. In response to this comprehensive roadway proposal, many people objected, among whom were young attorney Bill Risner and county planner Ron Asta, with Asta stating: "We have grave reservations about the need for a central expressway system at all."[24] Based on that type of opposition, a revised conceptual plan calling for only the Rillito-Pantano Parkway, along with one other urban highway, was recommended by the agency.

On the "future water supply" front linked to population growth, after more than four decades of discussion, disagreement, and debate, the Central Arizona Project (CAP) finally gained approval from the Congress of the United States. The 1960s had begun with findings that some land subsidence was occurring in Tucson due to groundwater depletion.[25] After Morris K. "Mo" Udall's brother, Stewart, became Secretary of the Interior in the new Kennedy administration in 1961, Morris narrowly won his brother's former seat in the U.S. House of Representatives. Mo thought additional CAP water was needed for the state and in 1963 observed: "Arizona's economic and population growth is one of the marvels of recent time.... But this growth must ultimately come to a halt in the next decade unless more water is obtained for the heavily populated areas of Maricopa, Pinal and Pima counties."[26]

Ignoring opposition to the CAP canal ranging from the Sierra Club to the popular national *Reader's Digest* magazine, five years later President Johnson included funds for the water project in his 1968 proposed budget. At the same time, Secretary Udall and his brother Mo, among many others from Arizona, lobbied hard for a CAP authorizing act in Congress. As a result, on September 30, 1968, Johnson signed such a bill into law. While Arizona leaders celebrated this momentous event, some of them continued to predict that much greater water supplies would be required.

Another '60s project intended to eventually increase the supply of water was an ongoing look at employing reclaimed sewage water for eventual public reuse. Based on the perceived need to develop all available sources of water, this difficult-to-sell approach was initially studied in 1963, and then again two years later.[27]

A different use of water was taking place several miles north of Tucson, just across the Pinal County line. Seeking to create an attraction that would draw up to 400,000 people annually by offering "a major resort hotel, convention center, exhibition hall, apartments, churches, shopping centers, schools, and single-family residential developments," these proposed improvements by Lloyd Golder III were to be built around the 260-acre "Lago del Oro."[28] This lake would be formed by impounding intermittent water from the Cañada del Oro wash behind the man-made earthen Golder Dam that was constructed in 1964. Even as water flowed into the lake, though, it leaked through the dam almost as quickly and by early 1968, Lago del Oro was being called "just a big mudhole."[29]

While that attempt at providing an enhanced desert lifestyle hit a major roadblock, some technological advancements were more successful. Direct dialing between telephones came to Tucson in 1961, and five years later touch-tone phones were available. Then in 1967 Pima County became the first government in Arizona to order IBM electronic voting machines to replace manually operated lever devices.

Entertainment, Personalities, and City Upgrades

Entertainment opportunities in Tucson were also blossoming during the '60s. The 50th anniversary of Arizona statehood in 1962 included a downtown parade of antique cars, and major improvements were made to the ski area on nearby Mount Lemmon the following year.³⁰ In Randolph Park, a small zoo opened in '66 to the delight of children and adults alike. Nearby at Hi Corbett field, the Toros, Tucson's 1969 entry into the AAA Pacific Coast League, began playing professional baseball in front of usually sparse crowds. Also opening in Randolph Park in 1969 was the Tucson Botanical Gardens, five years after its establishment at the home of founder Harrison Yocum, and five years before its move to a permanent location on Alvernon Way.

These new entertainment endeavors were combined with a host of continuing attractions. Expansion of the desert gem, Saguaro National Monument, was achieved early in the decade. Land west of Tucson in 1961 was designated part of the monument, resulting in both "east" and "west" districts. The annual downtown rodeo parade had an estimated 165,000 viewers in 1964, and by the end of the '60s, 150,000 people were attending the ninth annual Aerospace and Arizona Days at Davis-Monthan. Around the same time, the University of Arizona Press was about to celebrate the 10th anniversary of its founding. In January 1960 the press produced a new edition of *Arizona Place Names* by Will C. Barnes, first published in 1935 and later updated by Byrd Granger.

Three Tucson residents who obtained some acclaim during the decade were Francesca Jarvis, Raúl Castro, and Margaret Sanger. Jarvis was an actress appearing with Sidney Poitier in the 1963 locally filmed *The Lilies of the Field*. Not only did she travel to Europe to promote the movie, but when Poitier won the Best Actor Oscar for his performance, Jarvis was in the Los Angeles audience.

Pima County Superior Court Judge Castro was named U.S. ambassador to El Salvador in 1964. Four years later he was sent by President Johnson to Bolivia to be ambassador there.

In 1965 Planned Parenthood proclaimed Sanger its "Woman of the Century" at a conference held at the Pioneer Hotel. One speaker said of the 81-year-old Sanger, the organization's founder and longtime Tucson resident: "America is fortunate to have this little woman who has assured a healthy life to all mothers."³¹

Decades earlier in New York City, Sanger had begun promoting the use of birth control and was arrested eight times as a result. As she recalled in 1964: "Every time I was put in jail it was a mistake.... It was by somebody who didn't know anything and thought I was advocating abortion. Actually, I was trying to get people to give up abortion and use contraception."³²

In the century after the 1864 Arizona Territorial Legislature had adopted an anti-abortion statute, very few prosecutions for violating the law had occurred in Pima County. Regardless, by the 1960s many young women were travelling to Nogales, Sonora, for abortions, sometimes with tragic consequences.³³

By the early '60s, another Tucson woman, state representative Etta Mae "Ma Hutch" Hutcheson, was known for her unwavering support for the University of Arizona while also being called "one of the most influential members of the

Legislature."³⁴ A few years later, Hutcheson's downtown district would also be represented by Ethel Maynard, the first Black woman elected to serve in the legislature.

Much younger in age than either of those women was Linda Ronstadt, Gilbert's daughter and Fred's granddaughter. She left Tucson to pursue a music career in Los Angeles, had a hit single "Different Drum" with the Stone Poneys, and by 1968 *Billboard* magazine was writing of the 22-year-old: "Watch out for Linda Ronstadt."³⁵

Gaining even greater fame during the decade was Frank Borman, who was selected in 1962 to be a NASA astronaut. The 1946 Tucson High graduate blasted off in December 1965 for a two-week mission into space aboard Gemini 7. Following the successful flight, 75,000 people lined a Tucson parade route to honor Borman's triumphant return to town.³⁶

An earlier idea to build a downtown planetarium to be named after Borman quickly resurfaced following his memorable 1968 Christmas Eve flight around the moon as part of Apollo 8. Listed on a county bond package the following year, the $1 million planetarium was to include a 300-seat auditorium and a 16-inch telescope. In March 1969, however, county voters rejected the idea by a lopsided three-to-one margin.³⁷

Before his first flight into space, astronaut Frank Borman (center) spoke in 1964 to the Tucson Press Club Forum and was joined by his Tucson High classmate, Morgan Maxwell, Jr., and Mrs. Ruth S. Bugbee, his mother-in-law (courtesy the Morgan Maxwell, Jr., photograph collection).

Also experiencing difficulties was a suburban development south of town. Originally called Tucson Green Valley when it was proposed in 1961, construction on apartment units began in 1963, but rental interest was so low that within three years the entire development was on the auction block. By the end of the decade, though, building activity on single-family homes for retirees was picking up momentum.

Plans were made in 1964 to build the city's third public library on Wilmot Road to complement the existing, and historic, downtown Carnegie Library and the relatively new Himmel Park Library. Also, in 1964 Mayor Davis proposed the city buy the private, westside El Rio Country Club, an idea that was finally carried out four years later.

Some community improvement projects, on the other hand, never materialized. In 1962 Harold Steinfeld sold the Pioneer Hotel to local interests who said they planned to add a 23-story hotel/apartment tower on the site along with a convention center that would hold 3,000 people. Within months, however, those plans were sharply curtailed, and eventually the existing hotel was simply remodeled with a Spanish decor.[38]

Another proposal that never came to fruition was the 1969 plan to ask voters to approve $26 million in bonds to install streetlights along all Tucson roadways, a possibility that was dropped even before making it on the ballot. Another failure was the city council's 1966 ban on self-service gas stations. Because of safety concerns, the elected officials initially outlawed them but then almost immediately changed their minds.[39]

One other, somewhat controversial, idea that actually proceeded, if quite slowly, was establishment of a permanent home for the Tucson Art Center. In 1968 space in Randolph Park was proposed for a new building, but the city council suggested the block north of city hall instead. It wouldn't be until the next decade, though, that construction of a new facility actually took place at that location.

Tucson municipal officials also dealt successfully with other issues. The '60s began with voters approving a city charter amendment that lengthened the terms of office of city council members from two to four years. In 1964 Tucson voters also accepted doubling the city's half percent sales tax. Then, despite a survey that found local residents to be some of the highest taxed people in the western United States, in 1969 voters doubled the local sales tax again to two percent.[40] (The primary sales tax in 2024 was 2.6 percent.)

Land-use proposals, especially the contemplated construction of high-rise developments along major arterial streets, also confronted the community. In 1969 the city council looked favorably on a lonesome 22-story project on Broadway Boulevard at Rosemont Avenue.

Meanwhile, the city's attempt at continuing the aggressive annexation program that began in the 1950s was ebbing and flowing. After serving six years as mayor, Don Hummel stepped down in 1961 and, reflecting the city's long-standing drive for monopoly municipal political power in Pima County, he called the annexation effort the most important accomplishment of his tenure. That same year, a law adopted by the Arizona Legislature seemed certain to assist the city. The law prevented new towns from incorporating if they were within six miles of an existing municipality unless that established city supplied its endorsement of the incorporation.

Regardless of that law, intense opposition to Tucson's forceful annexation program still percolated in most of the areas city hall wanted to claim. Seeking population notoriety and for financial purposes, the city wanted to have 200,000 residents by the time 1960 census data were collected, and a proposal early that year sought to bring 26 square miles of land inside the city limits. This area was home to 22,000 people who lived to the south and west of Tucson, and many of them opposed the suggested annexation, even buying TV ads to explain their case. Ignoring that opposition, the city council annexed the property with the help of signatures of approval from two large utility companies as well as the Southern Pacific Railroad. (Tucson's population in 1960 was 229,000.)

A 1964 proposal to add 18½ square miles and 30,000 residents on the north and east sides also stirred up a lot of opposition. Responding to claims that additional people would result in extra tax dollars flowing into the city's coffers, the superintendent of the Flowing Wells Irrigation District wrote the Tucson city manager: "If we are forced into a city which seems to have as its chief goal enticing more people into its boundaries for money—then you will only be adding this many more dissident, grumbling voices to the already insufferable cacophony of bickering, squabbling and name calling that extend from your highest officials to the man on the street."[41] After the huge area was substantially reduced in size and broken up into nine separate sections, some of them on the eastside were annexed while others on the northside were not.

Because of its aggressive annexation and other policies, Tucson City Hall was the focus of most public attention during the '60s. The Pima County Board of Supervisors, of course, wasn't completely immune from controversy. Even though its chairman, Lambert Kautenburger, was found not guilty in a 1960 bribery trial, a newcomer upset him in a subsequent election.

Not to be outdone, in 1961 the city of South Tucson also had several public officials charged with bribery, and the city clerk was forced to resign the following year after being found guilty of "loaning public money and failing to advertise certain delinquent properties."[42] On the other hand, as the decade ended, the overwhelmingly Democratic community was even having Republicans run for its council, including 21-year-old Dan Eckstrom, who narrowly lost his first election bid.

At the same time, local governments were talking about several possible consolidation issues. South Tucson turned its water service over to the city of Tucson while Pima County and city hall were having ongoing discussions about merging their individual sewer systems.

Not only were local governments looking to make changes to meet evolving realities, but retailers were also. New neighborhood and regional shopping centers were springing up all around Tucson, mimicking the sprawling nature of the community. The El Con Mall on Broadway spearheaded this trend when Levy's Department Store opened in 1960. Also having a shop at El Con was Cele Peterson, who then proceeded to open her third ladies fashion store in 1963 in the Casas Adobes Shopping Plaza at Ina and Oracle roads on the community's far northwest side.[43]

El Con's obvious success put the fate of the historic El Conquistador Hotel next door in doubt. That uncertainty ended when the establishment closed in 1964, and then was demolished four years later to provide room for an even larger Levy's store. At the same time, J.C. Penney decided to build a big new store at El Con while keeping their downtown store open; by then Levy's had chosen to close their central city business.

Further east on Broadway near Wilmot Road, as the first phase of a planned shopping center, a new Sears store opened in 1965. It had 250,000-square-feet of space along with free parking for 1,650 cars. Those were amenities the Sears store downtown could not possibly offer, so it too closed.

The steady abandonment of downtown by retailers was a sign of the changing Tucson marketplace. It showed the central business district simply couldn't compete for retail and other customers with newly developing areas. Symbolizing this shift was the Paramount movie theater on east Congress Street. Long known as the Rialto after it opened in 1920, the cinema shut down in 1963 following more than four decades in business. "The entire downtown area was 'practically a ghost town,'" reflected the theater's manager at the time of its closing.[44] (The theater would reopen in 1971 as El Cine Plaza and show Spanish-language films before transforming into a pornographic cinema in 1973. After some start-and-stop uses by other movie ventures, by the mid-1990s a serious and eventually successful effort was being made to revitalize the space as a contemporary music venue to once again be called the Rialto.)

Urban Renewal

Responding to downtown's drastic decline—while attempting to dramatically change the future outlook for the area—a large 416-acre urban renewal program was proposed by city hall officials. Even though it initially received lackluster community support, in 1960 Mayor Hummel insisted the program was "the key to Tucson's future."

"This area," Hummel suggested of the expansive area bounded by Congress Street to the north, Stone and 6th avenues on the east, 22nd Street on the south, and the future route of I-10 on the west, "must be eradicated for a growing downtown!"[45] Along with the scores of property owners, UA professors, and historic preservationists who disagreed with Hummel was architect Eleazar Herreras, the city's former chief building inspector. He considered government involvement in the project inappropriate and would support it only if it was financed by the private sector.[46]

Disregarding that type of opposition, the city pressed ahead and hired attorney S.L. Schorr to coordinate its urban renewal program. "[T]he slum blight in the renewal area," Schorr observed during 1961 in almost biological terms, "is approaching dangerously near to the heart of the downtown business district."[47] A city study showed the proposed urban renewal area contained 850 families and that almost all of the buildings in the district were considered "substandard."

To change what they considered a totally unacceptable situation, Hummel and Schorr wanted to use federal urban renewal funds to demolish the existing structures and then redevelop the area using both public and private financing. A civic center would be built along with replacing existing businesses on Congress Street with a new shopping complex. Elsewhere within the vast urban renewal area, residential units as well as hotels and motels were proposed.

While Hummel aggressively pushed the project, after he stepped down from office and Republican Lew Davis became mayor in 1961, Schorr was forced out of his job. Eventually, a significantly scaled-down proposal was put forward that included a shopping village, convention center, and multi-family residential units. Even that modified plan was initially rejected by the city council. In May 1962, Tucson voters, by an almost 2–1 margin, also said no to a $4 million bond request to build a civic auditorium.[48]

Near the end of 1964, however, local political views concerning an urban renewal program radically shifted because Tucson's economy was in a serious downturn. With the urban renewal project seen as a job creator, real estate professional Roy Drachman was appointed to head a committee to establish a program. In February 1965, the city council gave tentative approval to a substantially scaled-back 79-acre plan that was less than one-fifth the size of the original 1960 proposal. Stretching from Washington Street on the north to 15th Street on the south, a community center and governmental building complex were recommended. They would replace the 263 structures housing 1,200 mostly Mexican Americans who lived in the area, along with 105 existing businesses.

Following a public hearing attended by 400 people, the city council unanimously backed the project in November 1965. A few months later, Tucson voters also endorsed the concept when they approved spending up to $14 million to get the project started.[49] The council then employed attorney Schorr, the city's former urban renewal director, as legal counsel for the program.

Loud cries of displeasure from affected property owners soon arose as city officials began buying up parcels of property in the urban renewal area. Claiming the city's low appraisals were "so ridiculous it's close to fraud," one of them charged: "[The city's] appraising the people and not the property."[50] City leaders denied those allegations, and in October 1967 bulldozers began leveling the first of the hundreds of buildings slated for demolition, a pivotal undertaking that would reverberate throughout the community for decades to come.

Redevelopment plans were prepared to build new county offices along with a community center in the urban renewal area. The county's governmental complex—three tall buildings housing a new courthouse, a health and welfare building, and administrative offices—required the demolition of the longtime headquarters of the Alianza Hispano-Americana fraternal insurance organization on west Congress Street. The group, though, had much larger problems to worry about around that time as its president was convicted of grand theft, and it eventually went out of business.

Once completed, the new county buildings would complement the nearby high-rise city hall. Originally built in 1961 as a one-story structure, a 10-story tower was later added next to the existing building. The new city hall was dedicated in October '67 to music played by the Tucson High band.[51]

Even as the urban renewal program swept away hundreds of families, old homes, and businesses from a large corner of downtown, preservationists were trying to save at least a few historic structures from demolition. They were successful with the Fish/Stevens House on Main Avenue and the nearby Cordova House. The Samaniego House and the so-called Fremont House near the community center site also avoided the wrecking ball. However, most of the old buildings in the path of urban renewal simply came tumbling down.

During the decade, other efforts were underway to preserve Fort Lowell on the city's eastside, and in 1968 the ruins came under the control of the Arizona Historical Society. Another preservation project was that of historic Locomotive #1673, which had been donated by Southern Pacific to the citizens of Tucson in 1955 to mark the 75th anniversary of the arrival of the railroad to town. To allow building expansion, the engine was moved in 1962 from in front of the Arizona Historical Society on Second Street to Himmel Park, east of the university campus. Believing even more should be done to retain the community's heritage, on April 12, 1965, the city council established a Historical Sites Committee.[52]

Educational Endeavors and a Manufacturing vs. Tourism Debate

While some people were trying to preserve at least a small part of the community's past, its current appearance was receiving loads of criticism. "This city is a signboard alley," declared artist Thomas Hart Benton during a 1962 visit. "It's like all other Western cities—ugly, like one big junk yard."[53] That same year, Mayor Davis labeled Speedway Boulevard east of Tucson Boulevard "the ugliest street in the U.S.," a sentiment famously spread nationwide by a *Life* magazine photograph in 1970.[54]

On a more positive note, St. Joseph's Hospital opened in 1961 on the city's eastside. Also during the decade, a medical school at the University of Arizona was finally in operation, but only after a long and often bitter struggle with opposition from the president of Arizona State University, the Maricopa County Board of Supervisors, and even Governor Paul Fannin. Ignoring these protests, the Arizona

Board of Regents approved Tucson as the site, and the community raised $2.8 million to help pay for the medical facility. In 1967 construction of the initial building was completed along Campbell Avenue, north of Speedway Boulevard, on property that included the university's former polo field.

While the university was gaining a medical school, in 1961 its athletic programs moved from the Border Conference to the newly formed Western Athletic Conference. The UA also had a two-time All-American baseball player in Eddie Leon, and its marching band performed at the first Super Bowl game that was played in Los Angeles. In 1968, UA track star, Ed Caruthers, won a silver medal in the high jump at the Olympics in Mexico City. Sometime earlier, the school had hired its first African American athletic coach. Willie Williams was employed to lead the track team and was reportedly the "first [B]lack head coach in any sport at an NCAA 1-A school."[55]

In 1962 the university community lost one of its most esteemed members when Andrew Ellicott Douglass died at the age of 94. "Few men in human history have started a new science," the *Tucson Daily Citizen* noted of the famed scholar. "As one of them, Douglass created dendrochronology—the study of the growth rings in trees."[56]

Longtime basketball coach Fred Enke retired from the university in 1967. A few months later, beloved coach and administrator, James Fred "Pop" McKale passed away, and the Arizona Board of Regents quickly endorsed naming the proposed campus indoor sports arena after him.

Enrollment at the university had reached 21,000 by 1966 and plans were adopted to expand the physical size of the campus. Another educational venue that would require a lot of land was Pima Community College. After county voters approved establishing the college by a 3–1 margin in 1966, a site selection process was undertaken. Attention in 1967 soon focused on land on the city's far westside, but the *Arizona Daily Star* editorially pushed instead for a downtown location in the urban renewal area. The cost of that proposal, however, was thought to be prohibitive, and the originally favored property on Anklam Road was selected.

At about the same time, Tucson School District One was seeking a new top administrator. Robert Morrow, superintendent for 27 memorable years, stepped down in 1968 after overseeing an incredible expansion in both the number of students as well as schools in the district. The next year, statistics revealed that Arizona was 10th in the country in its "estimated current expenditure per pupil in average daily attendance."[57]

Also retiring from his job in 1968 was Morgan Maxwell, Sr., longtime principal of the formerly segregated Dunbar/Spring School. Before departing the district, Maxwell stated: "The integration of schools in 1951 in Tucson is the greatest thing that has happened in education here."[58] In 1969, on the other hand, a report highlighted the continuing racial concentrations in district schools while an "open enrollment" policy was initiated to try and encourage greater ethnic balance.

In other educational news, after 72 years of service, the Tucson Indian School closed its west Ajo Road facility in 1960. Two years later, Tucson School District One opened Palo Verde, its fifth high school. At the same time, with an enrollment of more than 43,000, the district began using numerous portable classrooms at various elementary schools to accommodate its exploding student population. Compounding that space problem was the defeat by voters, twice, of bonds to pay for the proposed Sahuaro High School on the city's eastside. The issue was finally approved in 1965 after a business committee, headed by Oliver Drachman, made several recommendations about tax rates and other concerns to the school board. Also opening in the district during the decade, but with much less controversy, were Santa Rita and Cholla high schools in 1969. In other districts, Amphitheater opened Canyon del Oro High School on the far northside in 1964, and a few years later a new Sahuarita High School debuted several miles south of town.

The rapidly expanding number of high schools was one demonstration of Tucson's steadily growing population at the same time as the community's economy was diversifying. Helping to fuel the region's growth during the '60s was Burr-Brown Research Corporation. Cofounded in 1956 by Tom Brown in his garage, the company produced electronic instrument and control components, and by 1965 was building a new facility near the municipal airport for its 90 employees, a number that would grow to 400 within four years.

Also aiding the local economy was the 1966 announcement that Mount Hopkins, south of Tucson, had been selected for the Smithsonian Astrophysical Laboratory space observatory. Because of this and all the other space-related work going on in and around the city, including at the observatories on Kitt Peak some distance west of town, by the following year the community was being joyously labeled, at least by local journalists, as "the astronomy center of the world."[59]

Some other sectors of Tucson's economy also showed significant gains during the decade but, in general, manufacturing wasn't one of them. According to a report, the percentage of these usually high-paying jobs had fallen precipitously, going from 42 percent in 1954 to 15 percent by 1965.[60] As a result, several suggestions were made to address the shift away from manufacturing. Returning to the 1920s philosophy employed during the early days of the Sunshine Climate Club—which at the end of 1962 had merged with the Chamber of Commerce—one idea was to focus more attention on the health benefits of Tucson's climate.[61] Similar thoughts led Mayor Davis to proclaim in 1963: "More tourism could also replace a shortage of industry."[62] That approach, though, was belittled by a consultant in 1968 who observed: "Tucson's industry accounts for two or three times as much of the community's income than does the tourist trade, and that, for a community without seaside attractions too much emphasis is being placed on tourism."[63]

Another debatable issue was how the community should promote itself. Sticking to a long-established tradition, funds in 1961 were spent by the Tucson Industrial Development Board on out-of-town print advertising to attract new businesses. For his part, Roy Drachman mocked that approach as a foolish waste of money.

"Advertising in the *Wall Street Journal*," he suggested, "is worse than throwing money out the window…. At least if you throw it out the window, it will be spent here in Tucson."[64]

A final idea for attracting more jobs, this one from a 1967 *Arizona Daily Star* editorial, was to do something about the relatively high wages paid in Tucson. Pointing out that the typical factory worker in town made in excess of $7,000 a year (almost $65,000 in 2024 dollars), eighth highest in the nation and 12 percent more than the average paid in Phoenix, the *Star* said it wasn't surprising most manufacturing jobs coming to Arizona were going to the state's capital. "Tucson has found painfully out," the *Star* lamented, "how this high [pay] scale, largely made possible by the Hughes Aircraft, and the miners, keeps new industries out of Tucson."[65]

While the issue of high wages in Tucson, as they related to job creation and population growth, was being considered, there was an ongoing attempt throughout the decade to define what role city hall and other organizations should actually play in economic development activities. The Chamber of Commerce operated an industrial development department; in 1965 it also created the Tucson Industrial Development Enterprises Corporation (TIDE) to help pay for needed economic improvement projects. Regardless, the next year the city council established DATE—Development Authority for Tucson's Economy.

By 1969, while the local unemployment rate had fallen to 3.3 percent, the marketing philosophy of DATE was drawing intense criticism from some quarters. To attract new businesses to Tucson, DATE advertised that Mexican workers in Nogales, Sonora manufacturing plants, or *maquiladoras* associated with Tucson-based firms, produced goods for American markets and were available for "as low as 30 cents an hour in virtually inexhaustible numbers."[66] Not only would potential cross-border firms help increase the number of jobs in Tucson, they would also assist in keeping the rapid population growth rate going.

On the other hand, and as could be expected, utilizing low-wage jobs in Mexico as an attraction to locate a company in Tucson outraged local labor union members. DATE director, J. Karl Meyer, weighed in and staunchly defended the practice. "If Tucson is to remain competitive," Meyer suggested in 1969, "it must continue its twin-plant effort."[67]

• TEN •

Social Change Mixed with Political Turmoil, 1970–1980

Just north of the Pima/Pinal County line is the Saddlebrooke retirement community with thousands of natural-tone homes. During springtime, palo verde trees in magnificent yellow bloom highlight its roadways. Beneath nearby rolling scrub-covered hillsides lie the earthen remains of Golder Dam, its remnants near the Preserve Country Club golf course. A few golfers brave the 85° morning to play on the lush emerald fairways and greens.

SHOUTING "CHICANO POWER!," 250 PEOPLE stormed El Rio Golf Course on a sweltering August afternoon in 1970.[1] Driving the golfers away, the members of the El Rio Coalition demanded the 83 acres on west Speedway Boulevard be turned into "a city park for the low-income, largely Mexican American westsiders."

A few weeks later, another demonstration took place at El Rio, and sometime after that, seven protesters were arrested near the course. By that time, the El Rio Coalition had reportedly split into two factions—an older group that was negotiating with city officials about a park being developed in the vicinity of the golf course and a younger one that was less compromising. This second group included Salomón Baldenegro and Raúl Grijalva, the latter who said: "[W]e still maintain that the original goal is to turn ... El Rio park into a people's park."[2] Instead, City Hall eventually agreed to build a 38-acre park near the course, a decision blasted by the young activists.

That was just one example of the impact the 1970s would have on shaping modern Tucson. Driven by a skyrocketing population growth rate fueled in part by a booming economy—like the earthquake that shook Southern Arizona in 1887—social, economic, criminal, and political events of the '70s rocked the community.

So many people were moving to the Tucson region, home to around 370,000 people in 1970, that one 1979 study estimated that by 2012 the metropolitan area might total 1.5 million residents.[3] (The population in 2012 was actually estimated to be just less than one million.) The result of this exploding growth was an urban area spreading out seemingly at random across the desert landscape of Southern Arizona, and this sprawling character would be the focus of intense political and economic arguments.

Tucson 1970 – 1980

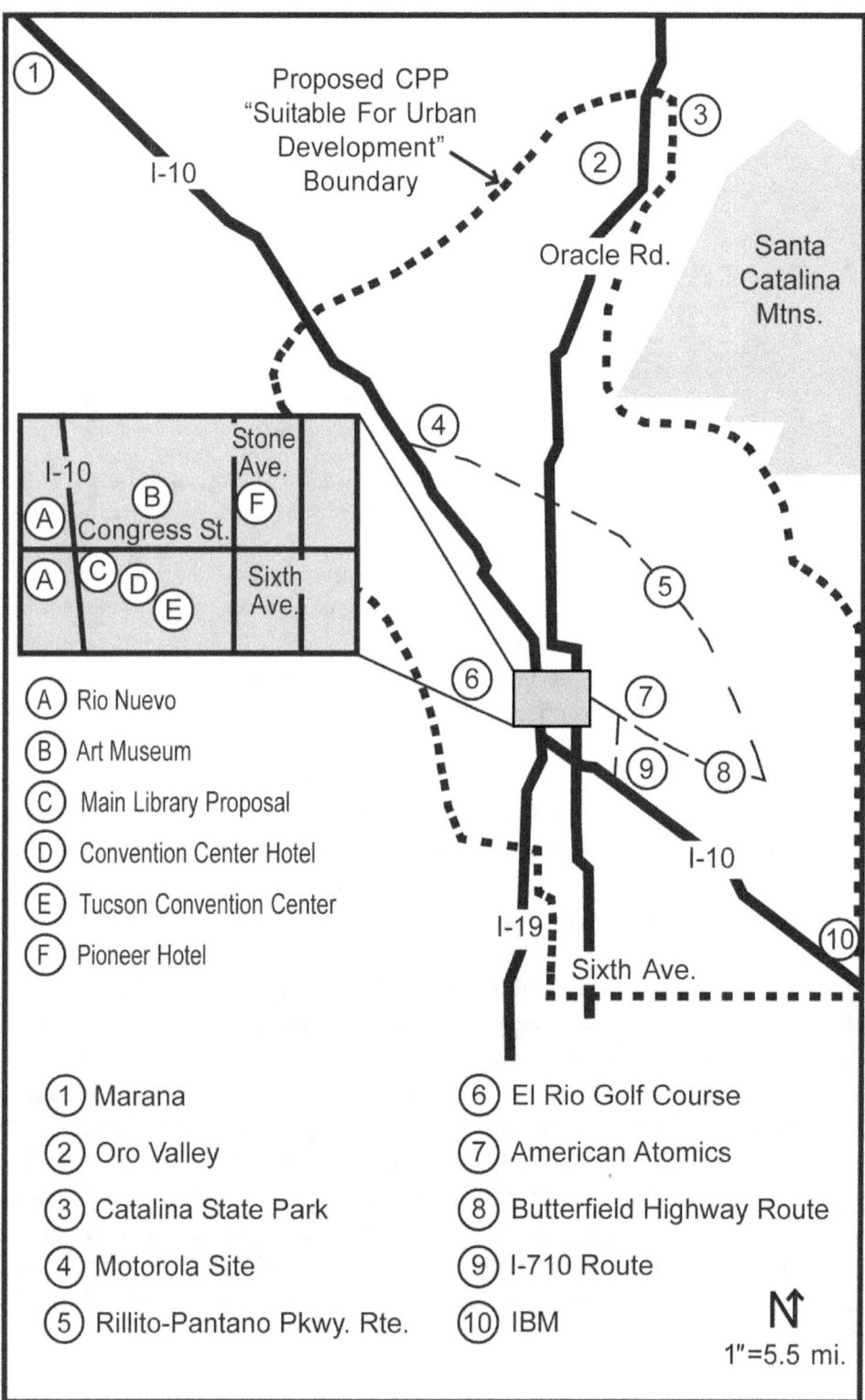

"Tucson's growth is good growth" declared the *Arizona Daily Star* in a 1979 editorial. "Not so many years ago," the newspaper proudly observed, "young people, especially those with technical skills, had to leave Tucson to find work that measured up to their educations. That is not the case anymore."[4]

To accommodate all this population growth, most new homes were constructed on the community's periphery. This scattered development covered an area of more than 550 square miles reaching south to Green Valley and all the way north to Oro Valley. This residential sprawl created some backlash, of course, and in 1973 a small group of young "eco-raiders" vandalized several subdivisions until caught and prosecuted. These and other objections to sprawl were mostly symbolic gestures thrown at the rapid physical changes occurring in Tucson. Much more serious were the political challenges to the community's long-standing growth philosophy of "the bigger the better" that played out during the decade.

By 1975, Tucson's traditional stance dating back to the 19th century that equated the number of residents with the quality of the community was under serious political assault. This conflict had been launched in earnest in 1972 when former Pima County land-use planner Ron Asta was elected to the board of supervisors. To reduce the negative impacts of rapid development, he initiated the "cactus power" crusade that "[challenged] the belief that endless growth is good."[5]

In 1973 Asta endorsed Barbara Weymann and Robert Cauthorn for the Tucson City Council and both won, making Weymann the first woman in Tucson history elected to the council. The cactus power movement continued to grow politically after that, and with Asta's help, by 1975 the Tucson City Council had a majority that supported growth views somewhat similar to his own.

Because of Asta's status, Tucson's business community focused their attention on defeating him in his 1976 re-election bid. Car dealer Jim Click—who had come to town in 1971 and within five years established himself as a major political player—said of the 1976 election decision: "This year you're going to see a lot of them (businessmen) getting off their butt and going to work."[6] That work would include not only political campaigning for, but also substantial financial contributions to, those who opposed the cactus power philosophy.

Republican Katie Dusenberry took on Democrat Asta in the supervisor's race and indicated she would bring balance and compromise to the board. The election was close with Dusenberry prevailing, thus becoming the first woman to serve on the board of supervisors. After taking office, Dusenberry's presence was quickly felt. During her first term in office there was an explosion in property rezonings, with more than 90 percent of the requests being granted.[7]

The cactus power philosophy was also under assault from another angle. While the average customer of Tucson Water was paying about $6 a month in 1973, substantially higher rates were looming. Instead of adopting across-the-board increases, in 1976 the city council approved a system of charges based on the actual cost of delivering water. Thus, non-city residents living at higher elevations in the Santa Catalina foothills, where water had to be pumped or lifted up more than for those at lower elevations, could see increases up to 85 percent. Meanwhile, many central Tucson households inside the city limits would have a 33 percent increase.

While the Chamber of Commerce supported increasing water rates, it opposed this differential pricing method. The chamber was also against what were called "system development charge[s] for new water connections," a type of impact fee passed on to new users in order to help finance water system expansion. This latter charge, according to the *Star*, was "what angered builders and others most" about the water rate increases approved by the city council.[8]

Adopted in June 1976 by a 4 to 3 council majority with Bob Cauthorn, Margot Garcia, Doug Kennedy, and Barbara Weymann—all Democratic allies of the "cactus power" movement—voting in favor, the water rate increases and lift-charge approach to pricing immediately caused massive public outrage. One Tucsonan went so far as to protest by halting the watering of his lawn and posting a sign that read "'I Am Dying—4 Councilmen Did It' [signed] Grass."[9] (In the following decades, dirt or decomposed granite yards would almost universally replace grass lawns.) Attempting to defuse the intense public anger, the four council members quickly rescinded the lift charges.

Despite that retreat, a recall campaign, led in part by Pima Community College instructor John Varga and television salesman John Fitzgerald, successfully collected enough signatures and a special election was scheduled for January 1977. Cauthorn resigned before that vote to take a job in Florida. Richard Amlee, who was opposing Kennedy in the recall election, said he wanted to roll back the water rate increases and then take another look at the situation. Two weeks after saying that, Republican Amlee, along with fellow party members Cheri Cross and Schuyler Lininger, were overwhelmingly elected to replace the three Democratic officeholders. Meanwhile, James Hooton, who sided with the Republicans on the water issue, was elected to replace Cauthorn.

The success of the recall, at least to the editors of the *Arizona Daily Star*, revealed a political shift in Tucson that had little to do with higher water rates. Instead, it showed the business establishment favoring unlimited and basically unrestricted growth had flexed its political muscle. As the newspaper stated: "The truth of the matter is that the former [city] council majority was recalled as a result of the effort and money expended by interests who opposed them for reasons other than water rates."[10]

Another irony of the recall was that the newly elected group didn't lower water rates back to where they had been. They decided instead to charge every residential customer of Tucson Water the same rate wherever they lived, while modifying the contentious system development charge.

The recall election was only one shift in the back and forth of local political winds that had begun in 1971 when former city attorney, Republican Lew Murphy, narrowly edged out incumbent Democrat Jim Corbett to become Tucson's mayor.

Corbett had severely hurt his chances for re-election by sometimes acting irrational or being intoxicated in public, and declaring he wouldn't seek another term, then doing so.[11]

There were accomplishments during the decade, of course, including the successful implementation of a federally funded Model Cities program of downtown area improvements. At the same time, there were also plenty of continuing setbacks. For example, to replace the tiny Carnegie Public Library on Sixth Avenue, in 1978 city voters were asked to approve bond money to build a new library on Congress Street near I-10, a request they denied. Also going nowhere was an attempt to pick a cable TV company to provide service inside the city limits. The council ended up stuck in a long-running quagmire about what to do with no decision being made.

The ongoing struggle about proposed incorporations also continued. Following in the tradition of their dealings with many other potential municipalities, Pima County Supervisors rejected a 1970 attempt by 650 residents of Oro Valley, north of Tucson, to incorporate. After years of legal wrangling, in January 1974 the Arizona Supreme Court ruled in the town's favor, and two months later Oro Valley finally became the third city in Pima County. The focus in Oro Valley quickly turned to the question of future growth with a 1977 survey of residents indicating that less than 10 percent of them wanted the town to exceed a population of 4,500.[12] (By 2023, the number of residents of Oro Valley was estimated to be more than 48,000.)

Being outside the six-mile boundary that granted the city of Tucson veto power, much less controversy was attached to the 1977 incorporation of Marana.[13] The 1,600 residents of the original 10-square-mile town north of Tucson got their wish in March 1977.

South of Tucson, however, incorporation wasn't favored in Green Valley. Almost 4,500 people called the community home early in the decade, and the sale of homes was brisk. The idea of incorporation was debated and finally put to a vote in 1977, with about 70 percent of those casting ballots rejecting the proposal.

Already long incorporated, South Tucson confronted a number of challenges during the '70s, the major one being an unfortunate 1978 incident that was to have major monetary repercussions. A gunman was holed up in his 31st Street home, and when the police tried to enter the house, 29-year-old Tucson Police Department patrolman Roy Garcia, who was assisting, was shot in the back and permanently disabled by a bullet fired by a South Tucson officer. Garcia's lawyers quickly filed a negligence lawsuit against both the policeman and the town; as the 1970s came to a close, South Tucson faced financial peril because of the case.

The Pima County Board of Supervisors, meanwhile, may have changed some faces and growth philosophies during the decade, but they still managed a few achievements, including being the first county in Arizona to adopt a building code. The county also had its share of problems, one of which was significant election issues invalidating 28,000 presidential ballots in 1972.

Political Back and Forth While Pursuing Equal Opportunity

During the decade, one major governmental agency was created and then disbanded. With both city and county governments providing sewer service to different customers, a 1973 proposal was made to consolidate the two agencies into one Municipal Utilities Management (MUM) Authority, a suggestion endorsed by both governmental bodies. Within one year of implementation, though, disagreements were surfacing about MUM, and the attempt at governmental cooperation died in November 1976. Next came arguments about who would operate the already consolidated sewer system. After much haggling, it was decided it would be controlled by Pima County, an idea endorsed by a 4–3 city council vote at the end of 1978, but only after intense pressure applied by the president of the Southern Arizona Homebuilders Association (SAHBA).

The six-year tussle over management of the sewer system was matched by an ongoing, lengthy argument concerning the entire consolidation of city and county government. In 1972 the Chamber of Commerce urged creation of a metropolitan form of government, and Tucson's Mayor Murphy talked about the city becoming the sole municipal government for much of Pima County by annexing the whole Tucson valley from "mountain to mountain."[14] This idea, if implemented, would theoretically achieve the monopoly form of government overseen by a seven-person council that Tucson city officials had sought for decades.[15]

Instead of that single-city approach, by the end of 1975 a citizens' committee was recommending that one newly established, metropolitan-wide government be created.[16] A 1976 opinion poll found support for the concept, and a public vote was urged to decide the issue. However, because the Arizona State Legislature was required to authorize the election—and was reluctant to do so—the vote never happened.

Another idea that basically evaporated after having been studied for several years was a detailed plan for eastern Pima County. Early in the decade, work on a comprehensive planning process, or CPP, for the region was launched and it identified four future development options: "peripheral growth, activity centers, satellite cities, and contained growth."[17]

A 1974 public opinion survey found that almost 70 percent of the respondents favored less, or even no, population growth. The next year, initial CPP recommendations in a wide variety of areas were made in a 561-page draft report prepared by the planning staffs of the city and county. Among the major proposals were:

1. The contained growth option, supplemented by activity centers, should be pursued.
2. Major freeway projects should be opposed in favor of more mass transit.
3. The community should not purchase Central Arizona Project water.
4. Instead of promoting tourism extensively, economic efforts should be directed at "optics, health, leisure and recreation."
5. "New residents should pay the full costs of sewers, water, power, roads, schools, and other public improvements."[18]

The reaction from the political and business establishment to these and other CPP recommendations was swift and furious. The Chamber of Commerce labeled the proposals "socialistic" while Republican City Councilman Emmett McLoughlin, citing the $1 million cost of preparing the CPP, sought unsuccessfully at a 1975 council meeting to fire the city's entire planning staff.

By early 1977, changes in the political makeup of the board of supervisors with Ron Asta's departure, and on the Tucson City Council because of the recall election, signaled the end of the CPP debate. The plan was eventually whittled down to a 50-page generic report that was called: "a shadow of its former self—chopped up, emasculated and drained of excitement."[19]

The early 1970s conflict over Tucson's development direction concluded with the triumph of those who favored minimal government involvement in the new development process, little or no meaningful land-use planning, and continued taxpayer subsidies of required infrastructure. One proponent of maintaining the home building status quo talked about the emerging "drive until you qualify [for an affordable mortgage]" philosophy of the buying public. This approach to growth favored commuting ever-longer distances to remote subdivisions with lower-priced homes instead of paying higher costs closer to the center of town. "I don't favor controls on urban growth," this real estate representative remarked. "Builders build where the people want to live."[20]

Despite that seemingly powerful political sentiment, by the fall of 1977 Tucson's electoral pendulum was swinging once again. Two of the recall winners lost their city council seats to Democrats that year, and after winning a place on the board of supervisors in 1976, Democrat David Yetman even began pushing for new development to pay part of its own way, a proposal strongly opposed by the building industry. Then in 1979 the remaining two council members put in office by the recall election lost their seats to Democrats. The decade thus closed with the death of "cactus power" and the emergence of a different breed of Democratic politician—typically one that would endorse Tucson's traditional population growth model but be more socially liberal than their Republican opponents.

In some respects, these officials reflected the social changes that occurred in Tucson throughout the decade. These shifts began to take place on that humid August afternoon in 1970 at El Rio Golf Course. The frustrations expressed by those demonstrators were reflected in the bleak employment situation in Tucson for members of several minority groups. In 1970 there was only one Black patrolman out of about 300 on the force at the Tucson Police Department (TPD), and the following year, TPD acknowledged it had only four female officers—two who checked parking meters, one juvenile officer, and a woman detective. When a woman attempted to become a patrol officer, she faced enormous obstacles, including this 1971 attitude from Police Chief William Gilkinson: "I might point out that the position calls for a patrolman—that's MAN."[21]

This under-representation of women and minority groups was also found at the University of Arizona. A 1977 report on students showed that only 7.8 percent were minorities. "Calling it a token effort would be dignifying it," Salomón Baldenegro sarcastically said of the university's attempts to encourage minority enrollment.[22]

Another local minority group confronting significant problems were Native Americans. In 1970, 27 percent of the residents of the San Xavier district of the Papago (Tohono O'odham) Nation were believed to be without a job.

Several years later, Pascua Yaqui Indians, on the other hand, had a major success story. In 1978 they obtained tribal status—a time-consuming process separate from the designation of a reservation that had previously been accomplished.[23]

In 1975 Tucson's Chinese community celebrated the 55th anniversary of its Chamber of Commerce, a group that had grown to 500 members. The long-established Jewish community four years earlier had focused its attention on Tucson Country Club's discriminatory practices in granting memberships. Club officials immediately denied the 1971 allegation, but admitted the club had "no Jewish or Negro members at this time but it does have several Mexican American members."[24] After public and economic pressures were placed on the club, it quickly dropped the use of religious affiliation as a membership criterion.

The summer of '71 also saw the city's first meeting of the Gay Liberation Front that intended to address "the persecution of homosexuals by heterosexuals."[25] Five years later, the murder of a gay man vividly demonstrated the extent of this hatred. Four teenagers wanting to "hassle queers" beat Richard J. Heakin, a visitor from Nebraska, to death outside the Stonewall Tavern on north First Avenue. They later received only probation for their murderous actions because of their young ages with the judge in the case stating the sentence was "not a slap on the wrist" and that the defendants "have been punished enough."[26]

By 1977, while a Gay Pride Day picnic was held at Himmel Park east of the university campus, the First Christian Church less than two miles away was denying a gay congregation use of its chapel. That anti-gay sentiment was heightened further before the decade ended when a Marine Corps Reserve unit collecting Christmas toys for needy children refused to take 200 of them from local gays.

To many people in Tucson, though, it was the illegal entry of Mexican and Central American nationals into the United States that was of increasing concern. Almost 45,000 people were apprehended in 1973 in Arizona, a number labeled a "flood tide" by a U.S. Border Patrol official.[27]

For women, while employment barriers still existed, there were several major accomplishments during the '70s. For the first time, 60 UA women in 1974 were awarded athletic scholarships. By the next year, because of federal Title IX legislation, much more money was being spent on women's sports on campus. Southern Pacific Railroad, once a bastion of all-male train crews, had three women engineers and two women brakemen working in its Tucson division during the '70s. On the other hand, while the small Flowing Wells Volunteer Fire District had two women firefighters by the end of the decade, the much larger Tucson Fire Department had none among its 140-member staff.

To address issues like that, the city council established the Tucson Commission on the Status of Women. By 1978 the group was embroiled in controversy of its own when Councilmember Amlee publicly opposed the appointment of a lesbian to the commission, but he received no support from others on the council.

Educational Conflicts, Crime, and Pornography

Social protest was also being pushed at all levels of education. The '70s began at the UA with an unruly demonstration during a basketball game against Brigham Young University "because of the Mormon university's alleged racial discrimination."[28] The campus had additional Vietnam War protests; in May 1970 about 1,000 people marched against the invasion of Cambodia and the killing of four students at an anti-war rally at Kent State University.

The decade also saw the return to town of several men held as prisoners of war by North Vietnam. The first of these, Air Force Lt. Col. Jack Van Loan, was given a festive homecoming when he arrived at Davis-Monthan Air Force Base in March 1973. By the war's end in 1975, about 125 people with ties to Tucson had been killed. The mother of the last local man who died in Vietnam sadly suggested that too many lives were lost for a cause that may not have been worth it.[29]

In 1971, 36-year-old John P. Schaefer replaced the retiring and long-serving Richard A. Harvill as president of the UA. With a growing campus enrollment, that by mid-decade was approaching 30,000, a new library was opened in 1977 and the old library became part of the Arizona State Museum. At the formal unveiling of the new, modern building, Schaefer remarked: "The dedication of a library ... is the most significant day in the life of a university after it opens its doors."[30]

The university purchased an Ansel Adams photo exhibit in 1974. This, along with collections from four other famous photographers—Wynn Bullock, Harry Callahan, Frederick Sommer, and Aaron Siskind—was the basis for the university's establishment of a Center for Creative Photography. It was a facility announced in 1975 by President Schaefer, himself an accomplished amateur photographer.

Also expanding in both physical size and enrollment was the new Pima Community College. From a 1970 start that had some classes being held in a hangar at Tucson International Airport and a total student population of 4,400, the number of students at Pima zoomed up to more than 21,000 by the end of the '70s.[31] To handle part of this growth, in addition to the main westside campus, a downtown branch opened in 1974 near Speedway Boulevard and Stone Avenue.

The elected board governing Pima was often embroiled in controversy throughout the decade. The divisiveness got to the point in 1978 that board member Esther Tang suggested the entire five-person body resign "in order that credible educational leadership can be re-established."[32] Not surprisingly, no one on the board stepped down.

The contentious issues at Pima Community College, however, seemed relatively small compared to the legal and social turmoil that engulfed Tucson School District One, which would become Tucson Unified School District (TUSD) on July 1, 1977, due to action taken by the Arizona Legislature. The district's problems began with the U.S. Department of Health, Education and Welfare (HEW) issuing a 1970 report that was highly critical of the district's treatment of minority students.[33]

HEW eventually gave the district about two years to integrate 26 primarily minority schools. Separate lawsuits were filed around the same time by the NAACP and a Mexican American group seeking to end the district's alleged segregation, but a majority of the school district's governing board argued that any educational segregation was unintentional and caused by housing patterns, not official policy. Rejecting that argument, at the end of 1976 the federal government joined the lawsuits against the district, and in January 1977 a trial before U.S. District Judge William Frey began. Eighteen months later, Frey ruled the district: "has segregated students since 1951, despite the district's contention that it desegregated completely in that year."[34]

Frey ordered that nine district schools be desegregated, a ruling much less severe than many observers had anticipated. In response, the school district agreed to consider closing three schools and reassigning some students from three others. In addition to these steps, instead of using mandatory busing as its primary tool to achieve racial integration, TUSD promoted magnet schools that would use special programs to attract district-wide attendance, an idea which showed early signs of success. Two of those participating in 1979 in the magnet school program were Adelita and Raquel Grijalva, daughters of activist and TUSD school board member, Raúl Grijalva. Having gone to school in Tucson himself, Grijalva remembered being embarrassed to be a Mexican American when he attended junior high. "I was actually made to feel I wanted to be an Anglo," he recalled years later.[35]

When elected to the Tucson School District One board in 1974 as its second Mexican American member ever, Grijalva joined a five-person group that faced teacher animosity because of budgetary problems, an issue that reflected a growing battle over educational funding in Arizona. In 1970 it had been reported: "Tucson schools spend $82 to $97 more a year for each student's education than the national average."[36] By the end of the decade, however, Arizona was near the national bottom in school funding.[37]

Other Tucson school districts had problems and progress of their own. In 1974 the Sunnyside School District began experimenting with a 12-month school calendar—due to a lack of space—but canceled it after three years and built two new schools instead. Earlier in the decade, Marana School District had begun construction on a new high school, and the voters of the Catalina Foothills School District approved forming a high school district of their own in 1974. School districts were also facing a changing social landscape; in 1979 the Flowing Wells Board of Education barred a male teacher from wearing an earring to school.

Change was also being experienced in Tucson's medical arena, with mixed local reaction to the U.S. Supreme Court's 1973 *Roe v. Wade* abortion ruling. Catholic bishop Francis J. Green commented: "I'm terribly disappointed and saddened at the decision," while attorney Heather Sigworth observed: "From a feminist's standpoint, the results will be desirable."[38]

Before that landmark decision, Tucson had seen only a few local prosecutions for violations of Arizona's 1864 anti-abortion law. In 1971, however, the community learned that abortions were relatively common on Davis-Monthan Air Force Base. In a six-month period, 16 of the procedures had been performed there because, as a federal facility, it was not regulated by state law.[39] When President Richard Nixon, an abortion opponent, learned of this, he directed it be stopped in order to comply with state law.[40]

By early 1972, Planned Parenthood, which traditionally encouraged the use of birth control as an alternative to abortions, was reporting that despite its illegality, at least 125 women had abortions in Tucson within a three-month period.[41] In 1971 the organization had filed a lawsuit challenging the constitutionality of the state's anti-abortion law, and in September 1972 it was struck down by Pima County Superior Court Judge Jack Marks.[42] That ruling was soon overturned by an appeals court, but shortly after that, the U.S. Supreme Court issued its *Roe v. Wade* decision so most abortions became legal throughout the United States.

A few years later, up to 600 abortions were being performed annually at Pima County's new Kino Hospital. The county's right to do so was upheld by a court in 1977, but later that year the board of supervisors halted funding for most of the procedures.

Kino Hospital, located on Ajo Way, was a medical facility dedicated in 1976 and, because the majority of patients were indigent, taxpayers had to cover their bills. Two other new hospitals opened during the decade: El Dorado, on the eastside in 1978, and seven years earlier the 300-bed University Medical Center (UMC) along north Campbell Avenue. A noteworthy contribution to the community from UMC was the initiation of heart transplants. In 1977 Dr. Jack C. Copeland joined the university's College of Medicine, and within two years had performed his first local heart transplant. That meant UMC was one of only two places in the western United States offering the operation.[43]

It was a downtown fire earlier in the '70s, however, that possibly had the most profound impact on the community of any event during the decade. An intense blaze at the Pioneer Hotel on the night of December 20, 1970, claimed 29 lives, including many people from Hermosillo, Mexico, among whom were almost two entire families. Also killed in the fire were Margaret and Harold Steinfeld, top-floor residents of the hotel. It was written of the 82-year-old Harold, who had promoted Tucson throughout his life, that he "always professed to have more interest in the growth of the city overall than in the growth of Steinfeld's [Department Store]."[44]

Sixteen-year-old African American Louis Taylor was quickly charged with setting the fire. He was subsequently tried and convicted by a jury in Phoenix, even though the judge in the case, who later regretted making the comment, said after the verdict: "The evidence supports a conviction, but I would not have convicted him myself."[45] (By 2002, questions were being raised about Taylor's guilt, and in 2013 while still professing his innocence, he pled no contest to the crime and was released from prison.)[46]

Also, in 1971 Pima County Sheriff Waldon Burr and seven of his assistants had been arrested and charged with "receiving bribes, selling jobs and perjury." They were accused of accepting payoffs from a well-known prostitute and madam in town, and Burr was forced to resign his elected office.

While the very old profession of prostitution continued to routinely be practiced in Tucson, newer moral issues also surfaced. At an eastside bar in 1970 the city saw its first "bottomless" act, which led the city council to adopt an ordinance against nude performances. It wasn't only on the stage that political leaders sought to clamp down on nudity. In 1971 the city launched an "anti-smut crusade" against films that officials considered pornographic. The question of what constituted obscenity was crucial in a local 1973 trial involving the adult movie *Deep Throat*. The film had been shown at El Cine Plaza (Rialto) Theater on Congress Street downtown to 54,000 customers during an incredible seven-month run. It was so popular that the first print of the film wore out, so another had to be ordered. After a trial, the theater owner was acquitted, but a jury convicted the theater manager of "transporting an obscene film." That ruling, though, was overturned on appeal.

Even as substantial public attention was placed on this and other morality issues, the metropolitan region steadily climbed in national rankings of overall crime. During the '70s, Tucson was labeled "the drug-smuggling capital of the United States."[47] Tucson additionally had the seventh highest overall crime rate in the nation by 1974, a ranking that rose to second in 1976, before hitting the top rung the following year.[48] Rampant burglaries were the primary cause of this dubious distinction, but there were other factors. The city in 1970 had only 1.17 police officers per 1,000 residents, one of the lowest ratios in the nation. Later in the decade, cocaine sales in the community were increasing, and earlier it had been stated: "Tucson leads the nation in the sale of imported marijuana."[49]

A portion of Tucson's role in the use and distribution of illegal drugs might have been controlled by organized crime. One ongoing investigation centered on Joseph C. Bonanno, Sr., and in 1977 a journalism reporting team called him "probably the most powerful Mafioso in America, the boss west of the Rocky Mountains."[50] The 72-year-old Bonanno denied all the insinuations made against him, challenged the police to either arrest him or leave him alone, and told people to just call him "Joe."

In 1975 members of the Tucson City Council had other things on their mind besides crime rates. That year most TPD officers joined many firefighters in walking off the job for a week, seeking raises up to 20 percent in those high inflationary times. The strike ended when pay raises approximating 12.5 percent for many city employees were promised.[51] Within weeks, however, the council majority backtracked, and the promised employee pay agreement was killed. In its place, raises of under 10 percent for all city workers were approved, an about-face that infuriated Tucson's police officers. To prevent a recurrence of their labor action, in 1976 Tucson voters narrowly approved a no-strike clause for city employees.

The decade also saw some changes in local law enforcement tactics. Ignoring widespread public opposition, a police helicopter became a permanent fixture of TPD in 1972. Four years later, the use of the telephone number 911 to call emergency services became possible. Following that, in 1978 the 88-CRIME telephone hotline program was established and quickly led to its first two arrests.

Also during the '70s, a Tucson firefighter died as a result of a blaze and two public safety officers were killed in the line of duty. Severely injured in a 1972 fire, Edward H. Bell lived another seven years before passing away. In 1974, 27-year-old TPD detective Barry Headricks was fatally shot in an operation targeting heroin. Then a few weeks before Christmas in 1979, John Walker, a 22-year law enforcement veteran working for the Arizona Department of Public Safety, was gunned down at Tucson International Airport during an undercover buy of cocaine.

Plane Peril, People, and a Pachyderm

Other news from Tucson's airports was often dominated by conflicts about noise and safety concerns. Shortly after the decade began, a U2 reconnaissance plane crashed at Davis-Monthan, killing the pilot. As a result, Tucson School District One considered closing Julia Keen elementary school located off the northwest end of the base's runway. After 90 percent of the parents of Julia Keen's almost 800 students expressed support for keeping the school open, the school board agreed.[52]

Then in 1973 the chairman of the Pima County Board of Supervisors, Joe Castillo, suggested the possibility of closing DM and relocating it west of town to Avra Valley, pointing out that the move would provide a lot of potential urban land for new housing development.[53] Tucson's Mayor Lew Murphy immediately called for Castillo to be censured for even mentioning the idea. While not implemented, Castillo's proposal did at least spark some local political debate.[54]

At about that same time, the need for enacting zoning regulations to protect DM from further land-use encroachment intensified. These restrictions, it was stated in a 1975 report, were "needed because of the danger of plane crashes."[55] With the gradual replacement during the decade of the F-4, the A-7D, and the U2 by the A-10 "tank killer" jet, confidence in the safety of the base's mission rose. This led one DM official to state in 1977: "As for another crash like the one in '67 [that killed four people on 29th Street]? Never."[56]

That prediction proved extremely shortsighted less than a year later. Narrowly missing Mansfeld Junior High on Sixth Street, an A-7D experiencing fuel filter problems came down on Highland Avenue just south of the UA campus and burst into an intense ball of flames. While the pilot survived by bailing out of the doomed plane at the last moment, 19-year-old Clarissa Felix and her 21-year-old sister, Leticia Felix Humphrey, were killed in their car by the raging inferno. Reaction to the crash was swift as Air Force officials promised to reduce landing approaches over the city by one-half.

Another, much less tragic type of conflict between military aircraft and residents was occurring around Tucson International Airport (TIA). The Sunnyside School District board contended early in the '70s "that Air National Guard jet flights over its airport area school [Sunnyside Junior High School on Valencia Road] endanger the children and cause major classroom disruption because of aircraft noise."[57] While several legal efforts by the school board to enforce that view proved unsuccessful, the possibility of relocating the school—which predated the airport by 17 years—was eventually suggested. By 1974 there was an agreement to accomplish that goal.

Other changes also came to TIA itself. To help prevent skyjackings, security screening of passengers began at the start of the decade and by 1974 had expanded to include carry-on bags.

The decade also saw the opening of the Grace H. Flandrau planetarium on the UA campus in December 1975. Besides the small telescope at the Flandrau, other much larger ones in the area made headlines. In addition to the multiple scopes already in place atop Kitt Peak west of Tucson, in 1970 a 60-inch telescope on Mount Hopkins south of town was dedicated, and in 1979 the Multiple Mirror Telescope joined it there. Steps like these led the *Arizona Daily Star* to gush in 1972: "Tucson has become the astronomy capital of the world, a fact that should bring a feeling of pride to the city and all of its residents."[58]

The community could also be proud of many of the people associated with these accomplishments. One of them was Dr. Bradford Smith, a UA astronomer who worked on NASA's Viking mission to Mars as well as the later Voyager missions to Jupiter and other planets.

Smith was just one of many Tucson residents in the public spotlight. Morgan Maxwell, Sr., had a junior high school named after him in 1972, the first such recognition of a Black educator by Tucson School District One. Two years later, Raúl Castro of Tucson became Arizona's first Mexican American governor. Carmen Cajero was the first Mexican American woman in the Arizona State House in 1973, and Chuck Ford was the first African American on the Tucson City Council in 1979.

One other successful politician from Pima County during the decade was Dennis DeConcini, Evo's son. He was elected Pima County Attorney in 1972 and won a seat in the U.S. Senate four years later. Not so successful was Morris Udall, Tucson's Congressman since the early '60s. In 1976 he campaigned for the presidency, but lost the Democratic nomination to Jimmy Carter.

About the same time, another community political leader was stepping aside. Having served 10 terms in the Arizona Legislature, 80-year-old Democrat Etta Mae

For his decades of service to education in Tucson, a middle school was named in honor of Morgan Maxwell, Sr., in the early '70s. Pictured at the dedication ceremony are (left to right) Kathryn (Maxwell) Dixon, Kathryn McGowan Maxwell, Morgan Maxwell, Sr., and Morgan Maxwell, Jr. (courtesy the Morgan Maxwell, Jr., photograph collection).

"Ma Hutch" Hutcheson retired in 1972. Known as a fierce fighter for Pima County interests, Hutcheson was also a battler for herself. When a Republican colleague once accused her of being a Communist, "she went after him with a [wooden] coat hanger."[59]

Etta Mae "Ma" Hutcheson, known for her strong support in the Arizona Legislature for Tucson and the UA, welcomes U.S. Congressman Morris "Mo" Udall to her 1972 retirement luncheon (courtesy the Beverly Brown photograph collection).

Also gaining some public attention was ceramicist and sculptor Barbara Grygutis. She had been identified by the end of the '70s as one of Tucson's "premier" artists, and she acknowledged that the community's desert setting was reflected in her work. "You can't help being influenced by the landscape here (in Tucson)," Grygutis admitted.[60]

Deputy director of Pima County's Highway Department, 28-year-old Chuck Huckelberry, received some media attention for another reason. He objected in 1978 to the way his county sewer bill was calculated, so stopped paying it for a while.

Called "a genuine musical superstar," by 1975 Tucson native Linda Ronstadt was keeping company with internationally known celebrities as well as being romantically linked with California's governor, Jerry Brown. Other singing stars also appeared in Tucson's orbit during the '70s. They included former UA student Linda McCartney who, along with her internationally famous husband Paul, performed in town as well as buying 151 acres of property on the far eastside. Then in 1979 rock musician Eric Clapton wed Pattie Harrison, former wife of another Beatle, George, in Tucson.

At the other end of the celebrity spectrum was 27-year-old Joe Cavaleri. In 1978, according to the *Arizona Daily Star*, "he suddenly rose out of the stands at a [UA] baseball game ... to produce an 'Ooh Aah' cheer."[61] Thus, another Tucson personality was born.

One of the largest local celebrities was lucky to survive. In November 1970, the Tucson Zoo Commission voted to kill elephant Sabu after he had injured three people. Determining that the zoo's small elephant enclosure couldn't be enlarged to improve the animal's habitat, the commission instead recommended destroying Sabu.[62]

That proposal brought immediate and strong reaction from both an outraged public as well as upset politicians. Not only did the city council issue Sabu a reprieve, but it also approved enlarging his pen by a factor of ten, and for good measure, the council abolished the Zoo Commission.

Since the 1970s, when this photograph was taken, artist Barbara Grygutis continues to produce nationally renowned sculptures and once stated that Tucson's desert setting and landscape influence her work (courtesy the Barbara Grygutis photograph collection).

Things to See and Do Along with Downtown Problems

In 1971 Pima County was given the 38-year-old Rillito horse track that had survived hit and miss racing for many years. Eventually the county leased the First Avenue facility to a private group to operate. By 1976, however, lack of attendance was making it difficult to keep the track in business.

The opposite was true for the University of Arizona baseball team, which in May 1978 drew more than 23,000 to a three-game series with Arizona State. Two years earlier, the Wildcats had won the national championship, the first NCAA athletic crown in the university's history.

That same year, 1976, saw the UA deciding to join what would become the Pac-10 athletic conference. Both the UA and Arizona State University were admitted in 1978; not everyone on campus supported the decision, however. A faculty committee pointed out that "big-time athletics, especially football, siphon off vast university resources for 'an activity that is essentially not educational.'"[63] University

President John Schaefer and many other sports fans in Tucson, though, didn't share that opinion.

Meanwhile, some long-standing Tucson events continued and were joined by several new activities. The Tucson Festival celebrated its 21st anniversary in 1971 by adding an international mariachi contest to its lineup of cultural attractions. In December of that same year, the retail merchants along downtown's Fourth Avenue, who had been labeled "young long-haired businessmen," sponsored a one-day "festival of harmony," an event that would evolve over time into an extremely popular twice-a-year weekend street fair.

Reviving a tradition begun in the early years of the 20th century, a "Juneteenth" celebration took place in 1972 to mark the day in 1865 when the abolition of slavery was announced in Texas. In December 1973 the Christmas lights of Winterhaven failed to shine for the first time in 23 years. Due to the nation's traumatic oil-embargo-induced energy crisis, the event was canceled but was resumed the following year.

For those who enjoyed being outdoors, the Southern Arizona Hiking Club marked its 15th year in 1973. Also in the desert environment, the city of Tucson opened the Silverbell Golf Course on the far westside in 1979. Three years before that, Pima County had celebrated the inauguration of the Arthur Pack Golf Course on the city's northwest side. Pack had been instrumental in establishing what became known as the Arizona–Sonora Desert Museum, and by 1974 it had welcomed its five millionth visitor, five-year-old Valerie Semien.

Indoor fun for Tucsonans ranged from concerts to theater to bingo. Having been legalized for charitable organizations in 1972, by the end of the decade about 70 large bingo games were being played across town on a regular basis.

During the 1972–73 music season, the Tucson Opera Company, which would later become the Arizona Opera Company, was founded. Led by Ruth Booth—who had launched opera in Tucson during the 1950s—and Jim Sullivan, the new, professional company opened with a production of Rossini's *The Barber of Seville*.

Live theater in Tucson was also alive and well. In 1975 the Invisible Theater was performing "Brick Burnside in the 23rd Century A.D." in the student union on the UA campus. Around that time, actor Susan Claassen joined the company. (She would retire as its longtime managing artistic director in 2024.) Also being produced was "Gold Fever or Danger at Bonanza Creek," the first show of the newly established Gaslight Theater. (At different locations, both companies are still presenting several shows a year.) On another stage, at the age of 81, musician and composer Camil Van Hulse had his newest work, "Sinfonia Maya," premiered by the Tucson Symphony in 1978 during its 50th season. Also by the end of the decade, a six-screen theater opened at the El Con shopping center, making it Tucson's largest movie complex.

While El Con and the community's suburban shopping areas were generally doing well, downtown Tucson was suffering. The area's decline included the venerable Temple of Music and Art. Because of a lack of maintenance it seemed headed toward a questionable future, and by 1978 was reduced to staging performances of the all-nude variety show, "Oh! Calcutta!"

A few blocks away, construction plans for the Tucson Art Center, across the street from city hall, were being prepared. Representatives of the center indicated that the Cordova House on Meyer Avenue, dating from around 1848, would be substantially impacted by the development. The architect for the project went so far as to suggest removing much of the structure, saying saving it could only be justified for "sentimental reasons." In response, Tom Peterson, Jr., Cele's son who worked for the Arizona Historical Society, pointed out the home was "almost the only existing possibility for restoration of a typical Mexican townhouse from the pre-territorial period."[64]

The decision was quickly made to save and rehabilitate the Cordova House, an effort assisted by elderly architect Eleazar Herreras. Three other homes on nearby Main Avenue—the Stevens house, the Fish house, and the home of J. Knox Corbett—would also be preserved as part of the art museum complex, with its new modernistic main building finally being completed in 1975.[65]

Five years earlier, emphasis had been placed on the importance of a hotel to accompany the nearby Tucson Convention Center, which was then still under construction. As Martha Vito, manager of the Tucson Convention Bureau, explained in 1970: "A large hotel with 300 to 400 rooms immediately adjacent to the [convention] center is an absolute must."[66]

Construction of a $7.5 million privately financed hotel was announced in June 1971, six months before the convention center opened in festive fashion, including the participation of Maestro Arthur Fiedler, conductor of the Boston Pops Orchestra. The center was an immediate public success with first-year attendance doubling expectations. By 1974, however, the center was losing more than $2 million annually, even though indications had been given before it was built that it would be financially self-supporting.[67]

In addition to the convention center, La Placita commercial development next door ran into even more serious financial difficulties. Originally conceived by city planners and then approved in 1971 as a "Spanish village," the project of shops, restaurants, and limited office space was to be built on the last vacant parcel that remained from the urban renewal demolitions of the 1960s. Even though it was seen as commercial "new blood" for the downtown area, the project was in foreclosure within six months of its June 1974 opening, and bankruptcy for La Placita followed. In the opinion of real estate legend Roy Drachman, the center was "ill conceived at the very beginning ... they spent way more money than they should have on it."[68]

Many other things did not go right for downtown in the '70s. As a sign of what was happening to the area, property taxes were generally cut by 20 percent in 1971 to reflect "local economic conditions including the relocation of businesses out of the downtown area."[69] Among these relocations and closures were both Tucson daily newspapers, deciding in 1971 to abandon downtown for new headquarters on south Park Avenue. Also leaving was the iconic Steinfeld's Department Store (1973) that would be replaced by a 16-story Arizona Bank building, the city's tallest structure at the time. Other downtown businesses shuttered during the decade included the Fox Theater (1974), Cele Peterson's shop on east Pennington Street (1979), and Myerson's White House Department Store that same year. As a representative of this last business declared as the decade came to a close: "I don't think the downtown area is very viable for a retail store today."[70]

While retailers were fleeing the area, many governmental and office users, along with some residential projects, started congregating downtown. In 1974 the Armory Park Apartments were finished, and nearby a new senior center was to be built in the similarly named city park. City officials also unveiled plans for the La Entrada housing project that would later be built on Granada Avenue. The project was focused at a "young, fun market," because, in the words of one city staff member: "The way to revitalize the city is to bring revitalized people to the city."[71]

Plans for even more downtown development were being proposed, and by the end of the decade the city council had approved using millions in federal funds to start a "Rio Nuevo" project. Initially this proposal was to encourage the construction of up to 1,200 residential units as well as business development west of the Santa Cruz River on either side of Congress Street.[72]

Historic Happenings and Environmental Issues

Just east of that site, the 1960s had seen downtown's barrios labeled blighted slums by many community leaders who wanted them demolished. By the 1970s, though, attitudes toward the barrios specifically, and historic preservation in general, began to shift somewhat. Speaking in favor of a zoning law that would discourage demolition of historic structures, newly elected mayor Lew Murphy commented in 1972: "We're on the threshold of one of the biggest decisions the community will ever have to make—preserve historic values or forever commit ourselves to being just another city."[73]

A historic zoning ordinance for the city was adopted, and during the 1970s four downtown areas—Armory Park, the barrios El Membrillo and Libre, and El Presidio neighborhood, along with the Fort Lowell district outside the city limits on the eastside—had been designated for protection. Other projects to save individual historic structures and sites included preservation of the inappropriately named Fremont House next to the convention center.[74] Also during the period, three notable structures—the downtown *El Tiradito* or Wishing Shrine,[75] Old Main on the UA campus, and the mostly green-tile domed Pima County Courthouse—were placed on the National Register of Historic Places. Then in 1978 six people, including UA anthropologist Bernard "Bunny" Fontana, established the Patronato San Xavier to raise funds to preserve the historic and beautiful mission church.

Despite this progress in saving parts of Tucson's past, some historic buildings were demolished, including the 1909 fire station on south Sixth Avenue that had caused so much consternation over its location earlier in the century. Another historic building was inadvertently lost in 1978. To widen Campbell Avenue north of Speedway Boulevard, the city of Tucson acquired several homes near Elm Street, including a 45-year-old adobe house designed by noted local architect, Josias T. Joesler. Declaring that the city and the University of Arizona "make me sick the way they tear those things down," the man who purchased the condemned structure planned to move it several miles north to a vacant lot.[76] Just as the home reached its new location, however, it slid off the moving trailer and collapsed into a pile of mud brick rubble.

A more fortunate event was Tucson's founding celebration. Mayor Jim Corbett in early 1971 requested that City Clerk W.J. DeLong determine what Tucson's "anniversary date" was. Delong replied with three days from the 1870s, all having to do with the village or city of Tucson. But he also suggested a citizen's committee be appointed "to decide the matter."[77]

Noted University of Arizona anthropology professor James Officer was chair of the citizen's group and wrote Corbett in October, proposing that August 20, 1975, be considered Tucson's bicentennial since that date was "the two-hundred year anniversary of the decision by the Spanish government to establish a fort at Tucson."[78] This recommendation was opposed by UA anthropologist Henry Dobyns because "[a]ll that [Colonel Hugo] O'Connor [sic] did on 20 August was to inspect the site where the post then located at Tubac was later to move."[79] But the city council eventually ignored that objection and in 1973 officially endorsed the August 20 date.

To mark its bicentennial, Tucson held a five-day celebration in 1975. Among the numerous festivities were different days honoring youth and women along with a day highlighting Mexican American and Chinese American cultures. There was also an All Faiths Day, and fireworks concluded the day's celebration on August 20. (Since then, the date has been commemorated in both large and small ways.)

While honoring its past, the community was also facing some new challenges in the 1970s. One of these dealt with environmental threats, including exposure to radiation. The American Atomics Corporation plant was located in a mixed-use neighborhood on Plumer Avenue just south of Broadway Boulevard and used tritium "to make light sources for digital watches and other low-level lighting devices."[80] Tests conducted in 1979 on items in the surrounding area, especially food stored at the nearby kitchen of the Tucson Unified School District, found extremely high levels of the material. One federal official commented about the kitchen and American Atomics being in such close proximity: "My gut feeling is that it's a dumb idea,"[81] and local concern about the plant quickly grew. The school district decided to dispose of all the food it had in its kitchen, and shortly after that the plant was closed.

Earlier in the decade, the Tucson Gas and Electric Company had looked at using nuclear energy to meet its customers' future needs. By 1973 it had agreed to take 16 percent ownership of a consortium-financed nuclear power plant to be built west of Phoenix. Two years later the local utility company dropped that idea, and in 1977 instead decided to build a coal-fired generating plant near Springerville, Arizona, in the east-central part of the state. The following year, the utility also sold off its gas distribution division to Southwest Gas Corporation of Las Vegas.

Other environmental issues focused on air pollution and floodplain development. Public concerns about air pollution were definitely growing as the years passed, and in 1974 the smog level in Tucson exceeded federal standards on 64 occasions. The 1975 introduction of auto emissions testing in Pima County, even though many cars initially failed the inspection, would help reduce that problem.

Permitting construction in floodplains was another issue confronted. After some controversy, Pima County finally adopted "lenient" floodplain regulations in late 1974, and the city did so the following year.

Around that same time, Tucson was experiencing long-term drought conditions, with the summer of 1977 being the hottest on record since 1891.[82] That wasn't the only unusual weather during the decade. In 1971 a record 6.8 inches of snow fell on the community; then in June 1974 a rare tornado struck within one mile of the San Xavier Mission church, killing one person, injuring 31, and causing almost $400,000 in damages.

Efforts were also launched in the '70s to aid the environment, including a short-lived campaign for development of a "greenbelt" around Tucson. Despite not being implemented, this effort did have one positive outcome. After the Pima County Board of Supervisors rejected a major development proposal on land near Oro Valley, the board sought funding to create Catalina State Park on the same property. In 1974 county voters approved $4.5 million in bond funds, with the proceeds to be used to buy the needed land. Following many starts and stops, by the end of the decade Catalina State Park was close to becoming a reality with one of its main goals being the protection of a herd of bighorn sheep numbering up to 50 found in the nearby Santa Catalina Mountains.[83]

Water Worries but Roadways to Growth

Not far from the site of the proposed park was a water project of dubious distinction. In 1972 the controversial and somewhat repaired Golder Dam, just north of the Pima/Pinal county line on the Cañada del Oro, had natural runoff filling a lake originally intended for recreational uses and future development. For public safety reasons, though, the Arizona Water Commission ordered that process be stopped, and the lake eventually mostly dried up. By 1979, however, runoff from the wash during winter storms had created a 26-acre lake behind the dam with depths up to 120 feet.[84] In that same year, the Water Commission and Lloyd Golder III couldn't reach a legal agreement about fixing his leaky dam. As a result, the dam would eventually be permanently breeched.

The 1970s also saw a much more important water choice for the community. This one was between contracting for imported Central Arizona Project (CAP) canal water or continuing to rely on groundwater pumping enhanced by greater conservation efforts in order to meet the future demand for water. To some people, Tucson's rapidly increasing population, along with projections of immense future growth, meant additional water supplies were obviously required. This need was reinforced by predictions that land subsidence caused by extensive groundwater pumping would become a major problem in the community in the not-too-distant future.

The primary method of addressing these two concerns for decades had been the anticipated implementation of the CAP. That reliance on imported water, according to some, was misplaced. In both 1970 and 1975, the United States Geological Survey released studies indicating the Tucson area had hundreds of years of groundwater supply available.[85] To prevent subsidence, the first report warned that water would have to be withdrawn evenly across the entire metropolitan basin, something that was not being done.

Supporters of the CAP, though, pointed out the vast difference between annual rainfall and the amount of pumped groundwater.[86] Disputing that argument, and believing there were realistic alternatives, a long list of Tucson politicians and others opposed implementing the CAP in Pima County. These opponents included three members of the board of supervisors as well as some of the Tucson delegation to the state legislature.[87]

With that history as background, 1,000 people attended a public hearing on the CAP in early 1975. Those speaking in support of the project included the Southern Arizona Homebuilders Association (SAHBA) and the Tucson Chamber of Commerce. Representatives of the League of Women Voters and the Tucson Audubon Society were among those in opposition. By a 5–2 margin, the "cactus power" city council approved contracting for 100,000 acre-feet of CAP water.[88]

Besides apparently securing a future water source, other changes had come to Tucson Water during the decade. By 1973 the utility had acquired most of the private water companies within its service area boundary. Because of the eventual availability of CAP water, the utility was thus seeking to become the sole "wholesaler" of all water being distributed in the metropolitan area. In essence, even if it weren't the only municipal government in Pima County, that step would allow the Tucson City Council to substantially control many decisions about future growth and development outside the city limits.

To meet the anticipated demand of a rapidly growing population, Tucson Water was also looking at other potential resources, including conservation. A "Waterless Wednesday" program, begun in 1976, was replaced the following year by "Beat the Peak," an effort to lower intense summertime pressure on the delivery system.

In addition to water, Tucson's growing population and sprawling land-use character also required an appropriate transportation system. Thus, the 1970s began with more than 1,000 people attending a downtown public hearing on the issue. While the majority of them opposed a proposed freeway plan, the Chamber of Commerce supported the idea.

The Pima County Board of Supervisors quickly rejected most of the suggested freeways. In March 1970, the Tucson City Council did give its approval to two controversial projects—I-710 that would run north from I-10 generally along Campbell Avenue to tie in with Broadway Boulevard, and the Butterfield Parkway that would connect Golf Links Road with Aviation Highway before cutting across the southern edge of downtown and ending at I-10.

Public criticism of the downtown portion of the Butterfield route was intense. Opponents indicated the road would destroy the historic Wishing Shrine on Main Avenue, while displacing about 1,200 people, many of whom, as with the earlier urban renewal program, were impoverished Mexican American families. One of those who was threatened by the highway said: "We're old and poor.... Where are we going if they take our houses that we sacrificed for? Where are they going to dump me?"[89] In response to pleas like that, the downtown leg of the proposed roadway eventually disappeared from consideration.

An identical fate awaited I-710. In early 1975 both the city council, by a 4–3 vote, and a 3–2 majority of the board of supervisors, supported the project. By the end of the same year, however, the board was discussing how the federal funds for the proposed highway could be used for other roadway work instead, and in 1976 the I-710 proposal was formally abandoned. About $40 million of the funds would eventually be used to construct the Kino Parkway from Broadway Boulevard and Campbell Avenue toward Tucson International Airport, along with improving Golf Links Road and tying it into Aviation Highway.

Another multi-lane project—the Rillito-Pantano Parkway—was suggested to run generally along the route of those natural watercourses with the west end of the proposed roadway connecting into I-10. By the summer of 1978, representatives of four of Tucson's major private employers were publicly lobbying for three cross-town freeways, including the Rillito-Pantano.[90] Less than a month after that appeal, and even though there were worries about its cost and impacts on flooding, the Rillito-Pantano project was included in the Pima Association of Government's (PAG) five-year plan.

While actual construction work on several roadway projects had either been abandoned or stalled during the decade, some transportation improvements were nonetheless made. The existing rush hour reversible lane on Fifth/Sixth Street was lengthened in 1971, and Interstate 19 was finished from Tucson to Green Valley that same year. Having previously taken over the Tucson Transit Company and renamed it Sun Tran in 1975, the city in 1978 purchased Old Pueblo Transit that primarily served the city's minority populations living on the south and west sides and wrapped its routes into its own bus service.

After having been studied for five consecutive decades, a solution to the flooding at "Lake Elmira," the body of water created by storm runoff in the downtown

Stone Avenue underpass, had not been achieved. Ignoring many earlier broken promises to permanently fix the potentially dangerous situation, in 1974 the *Arizona Daily Star* editorialized: "It has taken a long time—and many washouts—but Lake Elmira finally will be dried out before next summer's monsoon season."[91] That prediction, like so many before it concerning the lake, would prove foolish.

Flooding underpasses and other worries were generally minor concerns in a community that was economically growing by leaps and bounds by the end of the decade.[92] Things hadn't started out that rosy in 1970. The Motorola company at that time tentatively purchased almost 200 acres of land on the community's northwest side at Orange Grove and Mona Lisa roads. According to unofficial and wildly exaggerated estimates, up to 25,000 people could eventually be employed at the planned facility.[93] The land was zoned for residential use, however, and many residents of the area objected to the proposed zoning change. After the Pima County Planning and Zoning Commission recommended against the rezoning, Motorola pulled out of the deal.

A private company actually making an impact on the economy was Gates Learjet. When it opened in 1976 near Tucson International Airport, the firm had less than 400 employees, but it reached 1,000 by 1979. That made it only one of five local private employers at that time to achieve that milestone, and the company had hopes of adding another 500 jobs within a year.

The biggest economic news to hit Tucson during the decade, however, was generated by IBM. The company decided to construct an enormous plant near I-10 and south Kolb Road to produce "computer storage systems and associated products." Future employment projections for the facility rose from 1,000 around the time the company first announced it was coming to Tucson, to 2,000 by 1977, to a whopping 5,000 by 1978. Based on predictions like that, many people in Tucson were looking ahead with great anticipation. "There is an attitude of optimism in this community," gleefully declared the *Arizona Daily Star* at the end of 1978.[94]

The Development Authority for Tucson's Economy (DATE) had been coordinating Tucson's economic development activities through much of the decade but eventually a human rights controversy doomed it. A 1977 DATE pamphlet that contained the phrase "our Mexican Americans are easy to train, will follow instructions, are more loyal, and equal or exceed the productivity of workers in other parts of the country" outraged many people.[95] Within a few months the Tucson Economic Development Corporation (TEDC) had been created as an alternative, and DATE was dead.

By the end of the decade, the construction industry was providing 14,500 jobs in Pima County. At the same time, after experiencing a series of strikes throughout the '70s, the local mining industry was on the rebound, and by 1979 mining employment was around 6,000. Shoppers from Mexico were also important to Tucson's economy, which was highlighted by a 1978 report that stated they had spent $50 million locally.

The bright economic news in the '70s, combined with the community's sprawling growth, resulted in substantial changes in Tucson's retailing sector. Following up on the earlier development of El Con Mall, several other regional shopping centers were either developed or planned. These included the 1975 opening of Park Mall on Broadway Boulevard and an expansion and facelift at El Con itself in 1979.

Other significant changes in retailing also occurred. Kmart opened its first Tucson discount store in 1970, while in 1974 former *Arizona Daily Star* photographer Sam Levitz established a "Direct to You" furniture warehouse near the Palo Verde overpass. (The business, that once had three Tucson locations, closed in 2024.)

More innovations, these technological in nature, were also appearing in local businesses, as the introduction of modern electronics into everyday life became a common occurrence. For example, by the end of the '70s many items were marked with a universal product code which allowed the price at checkout to be automatically read and displayed. By 1977, nine Automatic Teller Machines (ATMs) had been placed at Valley National Bank locations.[96]

Despite these and other technological advancements, not everything was bright on Tucson's economic horizon as the '70s came to a close. Local wages had fallen well below the national average, in part because of the faster creation of lower-paying jobs in the service and tourism sectors than in the higher-paying manufacturing and related fields. Also, due to soaring inflation, the prime rate for home loans had risen above 15 percent, negatively impacting the local construction industry. Plus, a national gas shortage driving up prices at the pump threatened Tucson's tourism trade.

Besides these problems, there were other perceived issues, including the city's somewhat shabby appearance. A number of these obstacles to economic improvements were summarized in a CBS television program broadcast in 1977 that focused on Tucson's pollution, water shortages, urban sprawl, and traffic.[97] Tucson boosters, however, were having none of that type of criticism. In 1974 the Chamber of Commerce had even looked for the community to become "one of the truly great cities of the future."[98]

Tucson had changed dramatically in several ways during the '70s. The major problem it faced in 1979, according to the director of the Tucson Economic Development Corporation, was that some companies "are worried that there may not be an adequate supply of labor and water here."[99] Despite that concern, there was an air of extreme optimism in Tucson about the future, with many people in the community looking forward with great anticipation to the arrival of the next decade.

• ELEVEN •

TCE/AIDS/TEP, 1980–1990

Hidden behind acres of new commercial development on Irvington Road west of I-19 is Tucson Water's Advanced Oxidation Plant. Inside a concrete block wall, the property contains air-stripping towers and several tanks used to process both trichloroethylene (TCE) and 1,4-Dioxane contaminated groundwater. The treatment continues long after these problems were first discovered.

ON AN UNUSUALLY COOL JUNE 1985 EVENING, a standing-room-only audience squeezed into a library room on Valencia Road. They had come to find out about the possible health effects from drinking tap water containing high levels of TCE. It was a solvent used as a degreaser and, beginning in the early '50s, had been indiscriminately dumped for decades into unlined disposal pits by some southside industries, including Tucson's largest private employer, Hughes Aircraft.

Dr. Patricia Noland, director of Pima County's Health Department, tried to assure those in attendance they were in no danger. According to reports, she "questioned any link between TCE and health problems, saying the chemical has been found to be 'a very weak carcinogen' in studies involving animals."[1] Public concerns, though, had been escalating since TCE was initially discovered in public water wells in 1981. At that time, an unnamed federal official stated, "Anyone who has a sole-source aquifer [like Tucson] and dumps anything on top of it is a fool. Personally, I wouldn't like to drink it."[2]

As time progressed, and with TCE several years later being labeled a "probable human carcinogen" by the U.S. Environmental Protection Agency, the extent of the spreading contamination became known.[3] Seven public water wells plus four at Hughes and 11 other private wells were closed by 1984. They covered an area that stretched almost five miles from the Hughes plant all the way north to Irvington Road. Cleanup of the problem, however, was slow in coming. Government officials, perhaps not wanting to implicate Hughes Aircraft, seemingly ignored the potential health impacts on the thousands of people who had drunk the polluted water for many years.

Based on that apparent lack of concern, the *Arizona Daily Star* published its own award-winning investigation in the spring of 1985, explaining it did so "because

Tucson 1980 – 1990

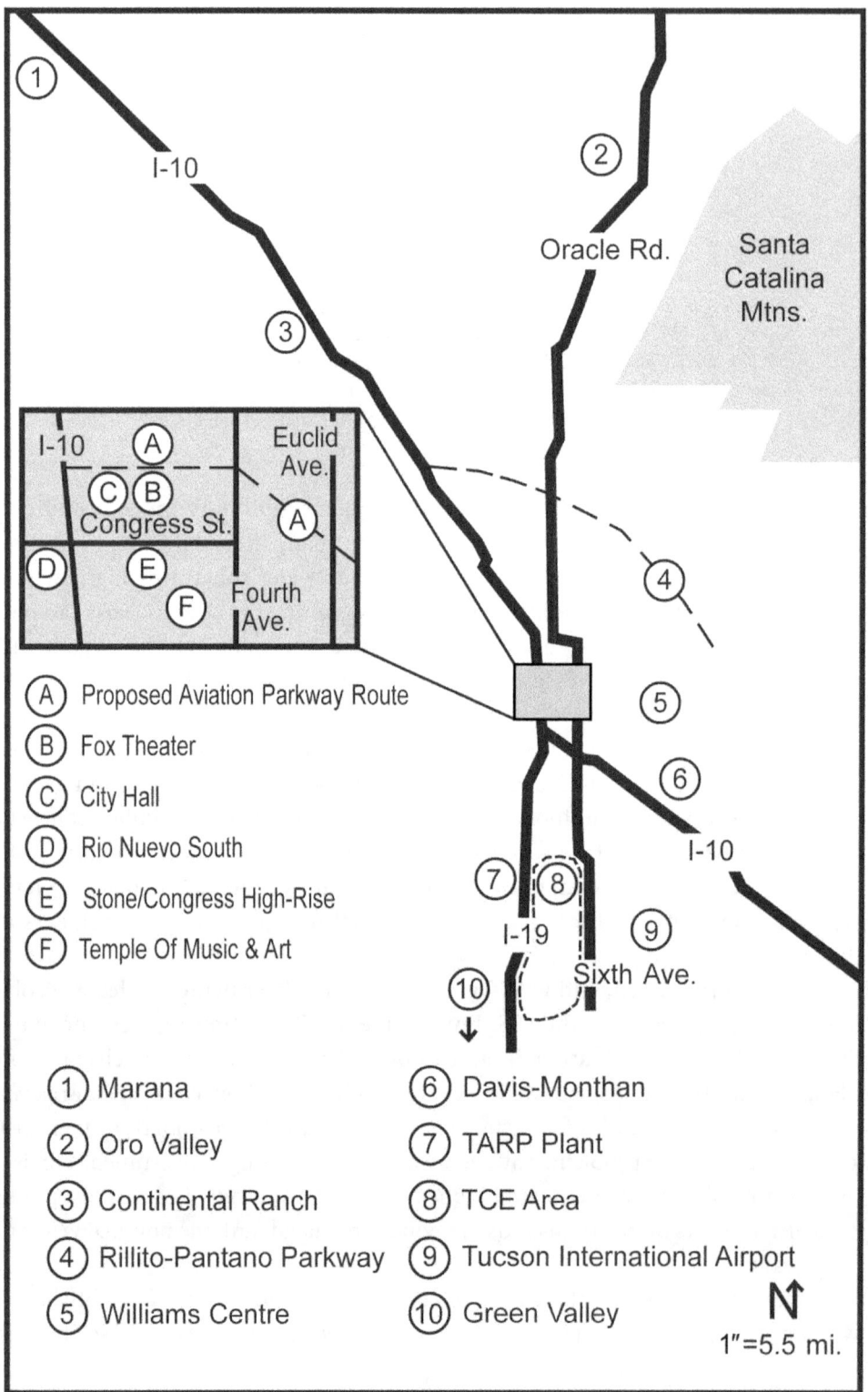

nobody else did."[4] The newspaper found "about 500 serious illnesses" in the affected area, including higher numbers than expected of several types of cancer as well as lupus. Thus, it wasn't surprising when hundreds of southside residents filed a lawsuit against Hughes and later the city of Tucson claiming both were negligent.

By 1987 Hughes and the U.S. Air Force finally began a TCE cleanup process that was expected to take decades to complete. As the 1980s came to a close, the city of Tucson had approved a $35 million partial settlement with the 1,600 claimants in their lawsuit, but due to an insurance company's reluctance to pay, that agreement wouldn't be fulfilled for 10 more years. (Hughes would settle with claimants in 1991.)

This wasn't the only major problem to confront the community during the '80s as Tucson was hit by a hard combination of economic and climatic punches. The decade, though, had begun on a somewhat more upbeat note when Tucson Water suggested installing a square-mile lake mostly in Pima County's westside Tucson Mountain Park. In addition to providing recreational opportunities, the purposed lake would be for "terminal storage" of some Central Arizona Project (CAP) water in case of emergencies with the canal. After criticism from environmentalists and county politicians, however, the city, at least temporarily, backed away from the idea.

As for the CAP in general, local battles concerning the project continued. "CAP water will be of a lower quality than [existing] groundwater," was acknowledged in 1981. "Its higher salt content gives the water a bad taste."[5] This prediction was in sharp contrast to the existing condition of water in Tucson. In 1987 the product coming out of local faucets was selected "the best tasting water in North America" by a panel of judges.[6]

Despite that anticipated decline in quality, the need to acquire large amounts of CAP water was driven by two major factors. First, the state's 1980 Groundwater Management Act mandated "Safe-Yield" be achieved by 2025, meaning groundwater pumping would have to balance natural replenishment. Second, the threat of local land subsidence due to over pumping was constantly looming.

To add needed chemicals to CAP water before it was delivered to customers, the Tucson City Council voted to build a large treatment plant west of town. That decision brought criticism since some people considered those chemicals potentially hazardous to health. Trying to prevent their introduction into the supply system, a ballot initiative was submitted to force Tucson Water to recharge the water into the area's dry riverbeds instead of chemically treating it. Following massive campaign spending by opponents, the initiative was voted down by a 2–1 margin in November 1987, and construction on the treatment plant soon began. (The plant has been mostly idle since the 1990s.)[7]

A proposal for installing inflatable dams in area streambeds was another idea for enhancing local water supplies.[8] That concept didn't go anywhere, but if the dams had been implemented, a few years later they would have been severely tested.

After several days of torrential rain beginning at the end of September 1983, Tucson and Southern Arizona were soaked, but the rain kept falling. It eventually totaled more than eight inches downtown, and the area's rivers and streams became raging torrents. As one eastside resident remarked, "I've been in Arizona since 1924 and I've never seen anything like it."[9]

Five local people died in the extended storm, and property and crop damage was estimated at more than $100 million. (In 2024 dollars this amount would be almost $314 million.) One of the most dramatic visual events was a new apartment building on north First Avenue being swept into the Rillito River as the earth beneath it was eaten away by the rushing water.[10]

Within 18 months of the '83 flood, Pima County was working on a linear park system along the Rillito River, and Chuck Huckelberry, the county's transportation director, foresaw much more than the original few miles that was then proposed. "[Huckelberry] envisions a fully integrated river park system threading through Tucson's urban area," the *Arizona Daily Star* observed in 1985.[11]

The Rillito River Park wasn't the only major recreational improvement being implemented during the decade. In 1983, after almost 10 years of effort, Catalina State Park near Oro Valley made its official debut and was called a "great urban park" by Governor Bruce Babbitt.[12] Existing recreational facilities also made news, sometimes for tragic reasons. In 1981 the Tanque Verde falls northeast of Tucson claimed eight people during a single flash flood, and by 1987 a total of 25 lives had been lost in the preceding 17 years at this dangerous spot.

Among others passing away during the decade was artist Ted DeGrazia, who died at the age of 73 in 1982. Five years later, educator and former principal of the once segregated Dunbar/Spring School, Morgan Maxwell, Sr., died. It had previously been noted of Maxwell: "He is worthy of the respect and gratitude of every Tucsonan who is concerned with the progress and future of our city."[13]

Tucson's self-proclaimed reputation as the Mexican Food Capital of the World also died during the '80s. It disappeared in an embarrassingly public fashion when Tucson's entry placed fourth—behind Santa Fe, Phoenix (ouch!), and Albuquerque—in a competition proposed by Mayor Lew Murphy.

At the same time, though, movies such as *Stir Crazy* and *Revenge of the Nerds* were being filmed in Tucson. On smaller screens, Tucson's public access TV station made its debut in 1983, and the next year the Tucson Catholic diocese launched KDTU, Channel 18, but after substantial financial losses it was sold in 1989. Also during the decade, adding to the radio airwaves, the homegrown KXCI community station founded in 1983 moved into a renovated house in downtown's Armory Park neighborhood.

Some cultural attractions in Tucson were also making changes. After 42 years of providing the community with first-class, thought-provoking speakers, the Sunday Evening Forum came to an end in 1984.[14] Other traditional activities in Tucson also experienced changes. In 1981, claiming roping events injured the animals, a small group out of an estimated 130,000 viewers protested at the annual rodeo parade. Parking and coordination problems often confronted the annual Gem &

Mineral Show, but at the end of the decade it was attracting approximately 50,000 people. In 1984 the Joe Garagiola Tucson Open golf tournament had a new name—the Seiko Tucson Match Play Championship—replacing an entertainer with a corporate sponsor who could supply major funding for the event.

Out in Space Along with Roads to Local Expansion

The community also had several space-related projects to point to with pride as one observer commented in 1981: "The Tucson area is often referred to as the capital of astronomy."[15] In 1982 the Mount Hopkins observatory, south of town, was renamed in honor of Fred Lawrence Whipple, who had led the effort to have it installed in 1968. Also, in 1982 the announcement was made that the University of Arizona would participate in the construction of a small telescope atop Mount Lemmon, and in 1985 astronomers on the UA campus were involved in the design of the Hubble Space Telescope.

The idea that produced the most astronomical headlines, however, was the university's proposal to place up to 18 telescopes and related facilities on Mount Graham in the Pinaleño Mountains east of Tucson. UA officials said the project was essential to maintain the area's lofty standing in the astronomy world, while critics vehemently decried the project's negative impacts on the environment, recreation use, and to a place considered sacred by the San Carlos Apache tribe. Following numerous and protracted legal battles, 1988 federal legislation, supported by Tucson Congressmen Jim Kolbe and Morris Udall, allowed for the construction of three telescopes.

Manufacturing mirrors for giant telescopes was also generating news. At a facility under the UA football stadium, casting, grinding, and polishing was taking place, leading professor of astronomy Roger Angel to comment in 1984: "At the moment, the UA is leading the world in learning how to make big mirrors."[16] Angel's idea for using spin casting for creating large mirrors would help revolutionize the telescope mirror-making process.

Another local sky-gazer getting attention was amateur astronomer David Levy. Using his own equipment in his Tucson-area backyard to locate new comets, Levy identified his first in 1984, and by the end of the decade had chalked up five. (By 2023, Levy had located a total of 23 comets, including Comet Shoemaker-Levy 9 in 1993.)

It was military aircraft flying every day above town that caught more people's attention, especially after the 1989 collision west of Tucson of two military helicopters that tragically cost 15 people their lives. Earlier in the decade, some military-related hardware began leaving the area. By October 1982 the first of 18 cold-war-era Titan missiles in the vicinity of Tucson was removed from its silo near Arivaca Junction, and within two years all of them were gone. The only thing that remained of their 20-year presence was a silo near Green Valley that opened in 1986 as "the only intercontinental ballistic missile museum in the world."[17]

Shown in this 2014 photograph, Roger Angel revolutionized the production of telescope mirrors decades ago when he introduced spin casting into the process (courtesy Roger Angel and Frank Gacon).

Land-use encroachment near Davis-Monthan Air Force Base, an on-and-off issue since the 1950s, continued to be discussed three decades later. The base commander warned in 1985 that the problem could eventually force DM to close, thus costing the community one of its leading economic engines. In response, local governments adopted some general zoning regulations that placed height and land-use restrictions on land near the base.

By 1983, two million passengers a year were using Tucson International Airport (TIA), and the next year the airport opened two enlarged concourses that included jet bridges to planes. Another addition to the airport during the middle of the decade was the introduction of F-16 flight training by the Arizona Air National Guard stationed at TIA to supplement the existing training being done with A-7 Corsairs.

One change that wouldn't happen at TIA during the '80s was the introduction of "Tucson Air." Responding to numerous complaints from area business people that the lack of direct airline service was a major impediment to the local economy, the proposal was made in 1989 to establish a Tucson-based service that would fly to both California and east coast cities. With investment interest lacking, however, the airline idea quickly faded, and one of the plan's backers said as a fitting eulogy: "'Tooth

Fairy Airlines' would be a more appropriate name for the proposed Tucson-based carrier 'because that, apparently, is where people think airlines come from.'"[18]

The tooth fairy didn't bring them, but by 1985 the city began replacing old-fashioned individual metal garbage cans with municipally owned plastic containers that a single driver of a garbage truck could automatically lift and empty. Some other environmental issues also made news. In 1989 there were 79 days when the temperature exceeded 100 degrees, a record-setting figure at the time. (The current record is 111 days set in 2024.) Air-quality was improving; annual local violations of carbon-monoxide standards fell from 64 recorded in 1974 to ten or less by the 1980s, primarily due to improvements in automobile engines. Despite that, the community still had occasional air quality issues, and former mayor Lew Murphy's 1988 solution to the problem was simple: build more roadways to reduce "stop and go traffic."[19]

To do that, the decade began with plans for the controversial Rillito-Pantano Parkway being supported by the Chamber of Commerce, the Southern Arizona Homebuilders Association (SAHBA), and other business groups. The Pima County Board of Supervisors then placed the parkway proposal on the November 1984 ballot for public endorsement, and by a large margin voters rejected the idea.

Another roadway idea that got shelved during the '80s was a city plan to reroute Mission Road south of Congress Street. Proposed to open up nearby vacant land for future commercial and residential development, the project was opposed by many people, including historians. They pointed out the importance of this area west of the Santa Cruz River because it once contained both Native American settlements as well as having been the site of the Spanish-era San Augustín del Tucson Mission and Convento. Anthropologist and field historian for the University of Arizona library, Bernard "Bunny" Fontana, proposed that instead of bulldozing the property for a roadway, it was: "ideal for an interpretive archeological exhibit, a cultural park and a museum, with reconstruction of former buildings."[20] Listening to pleas like that, the city council vetoed the Mission Road project in 1989.

Business organizations had earlier endorsed building a limited-access roadway that became known as Aviation Parkway. It would parallel the city's railroad tracks from Golf Links Road to downtown and then go on to intersect with I-10. Residents of central city neighborhoods, though, argued against the final section of the Aviation Parkway, its so-called "last mile," between Broadway Boulevard and I-10, instead favoring the widening of existing streets in the area. In December 1982, however, the Tucson City Council gave thumbs up to the Aviation Parkway proposal. In response to this type of major roadway decision, Tucson State Representative John Kromko began a ballot initiative drive to require a public vote on any limited access highway inside the city limits. Referred to as the Neighborhood Protection Amendment, the measure was narrowly adopted by voters in November 1985.

A much larger transportation-related issue was decided in December 1986. At a special election, Pima County voters were asked to approve a 20-year, $1.4

billion plan financed by a one-half-percent sales tax increase to fund transportation improvements heavily weighted toward new road construction. Ignoring dire predictions of what would happen if the measure were defeated, voters rejected it by a substantial margin. In response, real estate professional emeritus, Roy Drachman, warned after the sales tax defeat: "The impression is we aren't for growth. The word is out."[21]

A few years before then, and ignoring numerous ongoing land-use disputes, Drachman had declared Tucson's growth battles over. "People understand that growth is necessary for a vital local economy," he had optimistically suggested.[22] Architect Eleazar Herreras, on the other hand, saw the growth issue much differently. "It's a mess," he said of his hometown in 1986. "They call [growth] progress, but it has been progress for the worse, too much traffic, too much violence." Then, when asked what the future for the community might hold, the 89-year-old former city building inspector replied: "A bigger mess."[23]

Those were sentiments that noted local author Edward Abbey applauded. "Since the basic cause of traffic congestion (as well as of noise, smog, crime and other Tucson ills) is the sacrosanct and lunatic ideology of never-ending growth," Abbey wrote shortly after the defeat of the transportation tax, "let's adopt a policy of severely restricting and curtailing further urban expansion. With half a million people already living here, let's acknowledge the fact that Tucson is big enough."[24]

A serious attempt to accomplish that goal wasn't going to happen, of course, with Drachman and others like him who believed in the "bigger is better" philosophy guiding the community. Plus, several roadway improvements were actually completed during the decade. In addition, to handle rush-hour traffic, reversible lanes, like those already existing on Broadway Boulevard and on Fifth/Sixth streets, were installed on Speedway Boulevard and Grant Road in the early '80s.

Society Changes and Border Concerns

Getting around sprawling Tucson without a car became easier for some people; by the end of the decade the city council decided to have lifts installed on Sun Tran buses to accommodate people in wheelchairs. One Tucson resident in a wheelchair was Alamo "Bitsy" Reaves. She had started Handi-Dogs in 1974 to train dogs as service animals and by 1988 was named Tucson's Woman of the Year by the Chamber of Commerce.

In another sign of social change, Tucson became the first city in Arizona to adopt an anti-discrimination ordinance that included homosexuals. By 1988 Tucson's mayor, Tom Volgy, was also publicly reading a proclamation recognizing Gay Pride Week.

Tucson women, too, accomplished some of their goals during the '80s, with the first female firefighter, Deanna Lewis, going to work for the Tucson Fire Department. In 1984 there were more women admitted to the UA College of Medicine than men, and by the next year the same was true for the College of Law. Even so, problems for women persisted. In 1986 UA affirmative action officer, Doris Ford, stated that sexual harassment was an ongoing and under-reported problem on the campus.

One group concluding it was continuously being held back was Tucson's African American population of approximately 15,000 people. According to a 1980 representative of a Black police officers group, in the long history of the Tucson Police Department (TPD), "only one [B]lack has risen above the rank of officer."[25]

Several local governmental bodies, on the other hand, did take aggressive stands when Arizona's failure to enact a Martin Luther King (MLK) public holiday became a nationwide issue. The board of supervisors pressed for the holiday in 1986; the Pima Community College Board decided in 1987 to institute the holiday for its employees, and officials at the University of Arizona later expressed interest in following suit. (Arizona voters finally approved the holiday in 1992.)

Taking strides of a different sort was Tucson's Mexican American community. The Pima County Sheriff's Office agreed in a 1981 court settlement to push for more hiring and promotion of Mexican Americans, Blacks, and women. In that same year, Tucson Electric Power Company paid almost $900,000 to settle a discrimination lawsuit filed against the company by 340 of its Mexican American employees.

Overall, however, the lack of social progress was disappointing to many local Hispanic leaders. As local politician Raúl Grijalva summarized of the decade in 1989: "Collectively, our poverty rates went up, our levels of education achievements went down, and our political gains were minimal."[26] Reinforcing that viewpoint, in 1983 the chair of a UA subcommittee on the issue of hiring more minority faculty members acknowledged: "Affirmative action just hasn't taken place."[27]

Despite the extremely long history of racial subordination in Tucson, Mayor Lew Murphy somewhat surprisingly commented in 1986: "People tend to blend together here.... I do not sense a major [racial] problem in the community.... I suppose I get a different perspective being a middle-aged, Anglo-Saxon male."[28] Ignoring that Pollyannaish outlook, focus on the racial divide intensified in 1988 when an "English-only" public initiative appeared on the Arizona ballot. It was intended to "prohibit government agencies from printing material in any language other than English,"[29] and the initiative was narrowly approved by state voters in November 1988. One Mexican American leader reflected of the measure's passage: "It sent the message: 'You're not wanted—you and your kind aren't wanted.'"[30] (The law was ruled unconstitutional in 1998 by the Arizona Supreme Court.)

Conversely, there were some positive signs during the decade for the Mexican American community. In 1982 Manuel D. Moreno was appointed Bishop of the Tucson Catholic Diocese, and in 1988 a Hispanic Chamber of Commerce was formed.

Two other issues garnered a lot of headlines during the '80s, one that dealt with illegal immigration into the United States and the other with local efforts to assist people fleeing persecution and civil unrest in Central America. The decade began with the deaths in the western Pima County desert of 13 people from El Salvador.

They were attempting to enter the U.S. in July 1980, and, having little water, their fates were tragically preordained.

By 1981 an underground railroad, or sanctuary movement, was established in Tucson to assist "undocumented aliens seeking refuge" from military persecution in El Salvador, Guatemala, and Honduras. It was initially centered at the Southside Presbyterian Church whose pastor was John Fife.

The sanctuary effort soon began to grow rapidly across both Tucson and the nation. Thus it came as no surprise when the federal government—arguing that most of the refugees were simply seeking to improve their economic situation—indicted several sanctuary supporters for running an illegal alien smuggling ring. Eight of the 11 defendants, including Fife, were eventually found guilty of various charges and given suspended sentences and probation.

The sanctuary issue continued throughout the 1980s and so did growing worries about border security. In 1981 it was reported that 320 agents patrolled Arizona's border with Mexico and had apprehended almost 80,000 illegal crossers the previous year. Regardless, the retiring U.S. Border Patrol's chief of the Tucson sector observed in 1982: "I don't believe you can realistically control the border."[31]

Then in 1986 Congress passed, and President Ronald Reagan signed, an immigration law that allowed many illegal immigrants to remain in the United States under an amnesty provision. Almost 6,000 people in Tucson alone had applied as the 1988 program deadline neared and most would be granted amnesty.

Assistance of another type was provided in Tucson to the two local Native American tribes—Papago (Tohono O'odham) and Yaqui. In 1982 both announced plans to open high-stakes bingo games on their respective reservations, and the financial boost that would be supplied by these games was vitally important to both tribes. One need for these funds was demonstrated near west Grant Road at the Yaquis' Old Pascua Village; it was labeled "the uncontested worst pocket of poverty in Tucson" in 1980.[32]

Because of Congressional action in 1982, though, the small Pasqua Yaqui reservation southwest of Tucson was expanded in size to almost 900 acres. It was there that the tribe's large new bingo hall would open in early 1983. Given their high payouts, these games soon put many local charitable bingo operations out of business. The Yaquis, however, ran into frequent and recurring problems with their bingo enterprise, going through at least five different management companies and several extended closures of their bingo hall during the decade.

In addition to high-stakes bingo games, another type of major change was proposed for the San Xavier district of the Papago (Tohono O'odham) Nation. In May 1983 a California developer released plans to lease 15,000 acres "to build a huge commercial, residential and recreational development south of San Xavier del Bac Mission," but the tribal council and chairman rejected the idea.[33]

One other important change for the Nation did actually take place in 1986. It altered its name from Papago, a title meaning "bean eater" which had been bestowed by outsiders that some members thought was derogatory. The new name for the tribe was Tohono O'odham, or "Desert People."

Economic Issues

While local Indian tribes were banking on bingo to invigorate their economies, early in the decade Tucson in general continued to focus on electronic firms to boost the number of good-paying jobs. Based on some success stories, this strategy resulted in the word "boom" repeatedly being used in newspaper headlines concerning the local economy.

Because of the bright outlook for job creation, Tucson Tomorrow, a 1980s private group headed by Roy Drachman and initially dominated by homebuilders and land developers, sought to encourage local governments to begin planning for even more population growth.[34] Having grown by almost 50 percent during the 1970s to 531,000 people, metropolitan Tucson could reach 1.7 million people by 2012 according to one 1980 estimate.[35] (The 2012 population of Pima County was actually less than one million.)

Also during the '80s, another group of businessmen decided to form Tucson 30, an organization devoted to "bring 'good, solid growth to this town.'"[36] Among those involved at its 1983 beginning were auto dealer "Buck" O'Rielly, Tom Brown, the co-founder of manufacturer Burr-Brown Corporation, and property owner Humberto Lopez. After initially investing in Tucson in 1977, Lopez bought the downtown Santa Rita Hotel two years later and then purchased the hotel next to the convention center in 1984. Besides Tucson Tomorrow and the Tucson 30, the Tucson Economic Development Corporation (TEDC) was the publicly funded organization directly responsible for recruiting new firms and had nine Anglo men and one Mexican American man on its board in 1985.

Generally uplifting manufacturing news was common at the beginning of the '80s, and predictions were made in 1981 that Tucson would be among the top five fastest-growing cities for job creation in the United States over the next 10 years. That prognosis was issued even though the Tucson City Council, based on neighborhood opposition, had denied a 1980 request by General Instruments Corporation to buy a piece of municipally owned westside property for a plant that could provide up to 700 jobs. AiResearch Manufacturing Company, on the other hand, announced in 1983 it would build a facility near Oro Valley to produce electronic components for engines which could eventually employ 4,000 people. (In actuality, that number was never approached.) One TEDC official called the AiResearch announcement: "the best thing that has happened to this community."[37]

Other economic news from this period included mining, a foundation of the area's economy for decades, slowly losing importance while union membership and influence waned in Southern Arizona. Also during the '80s, Hughes Aircraft Company was sold to the General Motors Corporation. Shortly after that 1985 transaction, Hughes had more than 8,000 local employees, followed by 5,500 at IBM, and 1,100 at Burr-Brown, a company that had become publicly held by 1983. Altogether, the electronics industry accounted for more than 20,000 jobs in Tucson by that time.

Things began to change after that, and Tucson was rocked by a series of bad economic news stories. They began in February 1988 when Learjet tentatively decided to close its Tucson manufacturing facility, costing the community hundreds of jobs. A few weeks later, Hughes Aircraft announced it was laying off 600 employees. Then in June, IBM dropped a bombshell by saying it would end its Tucson manufacturing operations, eliminating 2,800 jobs. One elected official said of the IBM news: "That shoots the economy to hell."[38]

In response to this doom and gloom attitude—and citing other, more positive economic developments—Marshall Vest, an economist at the University of Arizona, observed of IBM's decision: "This is not a catastrophe."[39] Even before the IBM announcement, McCulloch Corporation that manufactured chain saws and other lawn and garden equipment planned to relocate to Tucson, and later Weiser Lock indicated it would open an assembly plant in town. Sears, Roebuck and Co. in 1989 decided to establish a "Telecatalog Center" in Tucson that would create 1,200 part-time jobs paying up to $6 an hour, while First Data Resources would employ 850 in similar occupations.

Many of the new jobs being created in Tucson, however, were not in manufacturing or other industrial sectors but were in tourism, construction, and government. A 1987 study showed the University of Arizona accounted for 22,200 jobs and poured almost $1 billion into the local economy. Davis-Monthan Air Force Base had 7,700 workers that same year with a total payroll of $318 million. An analysis indicated the U.S. Defense Department alone sent $1.4 billion to Pima County in 1988, and the federal government as a whole contributed a total of $3 billion to the local economy.[40]

The local tourism sector grew rapidly during the '80s. The number of hotel/motel/resort rooms more than doubled between 1981 and 1987 to exceed 12,000. By the next year almost 50,000 people in Tucson were reportedly employed in tourism-related businesses which generated close to $1.6 billion for the economy. Tucson Congressional representative Jim Kolbe, who had won his office in 1984, went so far as to declare in 1989 of its economic impacts: "Tourism IS the end of the rainbow."[41]

Aiding the tourism sector was the building of several luxury resorts. After receiving approval from a divided board of supervisors in 1982, Cottonwood Properties, headed by brothers George and David Mehl, developed La Paloma, a controversial 80-acre foothills area project that opened in 1986 and included a resort hotel with golf course and hundreds of residential units. Also debuting during the decade were the Sheraton El Conquistador resort (1982) in Oro Valley and Loews Ventana Canyon (1984) on the northeast side of town.

Conversely, distressing financial conditions sometimes exacerbated the local economic situation. Business and personal bankruptcies began to rise sharply in 1982 and set a record that year: it was broken in 1985 when almost 1,500 petitions were filed. After that the numbers just kept growing to more than 3,700 by 1989.

At the same time, wages in town were generally low, having completely reversed their 1950s position when pay in Tucson was higher than the national average. One job seeker observed of this situation at the end of 1984: "I know a lot of people [in Tucson] who used to work with me at the mines and now they're working at Circle K and gas stations and making next to nothing."[42] A 1988 report even concluded: "Tucson's standard of living is about 20 percent below the national average for mid-sized, urban areas."[43]

Tucson's low wages were sometimes actually used as a selling point to companies thinking about moving to town. As a result, one study early in the decade concluded: "Chiefly because wages here are lower, Tucson and Arizona will grow faster than the rest of the country during the next few years."[44] Thus, as Tucson grew bigger, it was also getting poorer.

City Hall Happenings Plus Continual Sprawl

The community's relative decline in wages and the growing dependence upon lower-paying economic sectors such as services, call centers, and tourism would also mean greater demands on local agencies trying to help the poor. The need for assistance from the Community Food Bank was rising rapidly early in the decade, and by 1982 it was estimated that 15 percent of families in the county lived on incomes below the federal poverty level.

Declining incomes also meant more homelessness for the truly destitute. To assist the city's burgeoning homeless population, estimated in 1986 to be between 2,000 and 3,000 people,[45] free, private feeding sites periodically popped up around Tucson but were then disbanded after complaints from neighbors. That was the pattern until the St. Martin's Center soup kitchen was established downtown in the Armory Park neighborhood and the Casa Maria Free Kitchen opened in South Tucson. Because of a lawsuit filed by the affected neighborhood association, however, St. Martin's was declared a nuisance and ordered closed by the Arizona Supreme Court in 1985.

Following that ruling, the Tucson City Council took up the unenviable task of trying to find another location to feed the homeless and decided on three public buildings, including City Hall itself. About the same time, poverty protestors set up a tent city at the nearby old Pima County courthouse and called it Murphyville. "It's named after Lew Murphy," declared homeless advocate, Brian Flagg of Casa Maria, "because the mayor is mean-spirited and has a callous attitude toward the homeless."[46] In response, Murphy sarcastically replied of Flagg: "It warms the cockles of my heart that the homeless in Tucson have a lobbyist."[47]

Besides its decision on a homeless feeding site, another initiative of the city council was a 1981 vote to finally select a cable TV company for city residents—Cox Cable Communications. Two years later the Tucson Public Library system celebrated its centennial, having grown to include 14 branches. Then, after years of debate, the city finally opened another public golf course—Fred Enke—on the southeast side of town. Based on the outcome of an advisory ballot measure, the city council also banned most new billboards in 1985. At the same time, voters approved a public campaign finance law for city elections.

Lew Murphy was re-elected to a fourth term in 1983 when he beat former Pima County Supervisor Ron Asta. Murphy would go on to become Tucson's longest-serving mayor, surpassing the previous mark of 14 years set by the legendary Henry O. Jaastad. In reviewing his time in office before retiring in 1987, and prior to the IBM downsizing announcement, Murphy stated: "The environment was preserved ... while the tax base was broadened and thousands of new manufacturing jobs were created."[48] He also mentioned some setbacks, including those on metropolitan government and regional transportation.

In 1983 Murphy had "resurrected the ghost of consolidating city and county governments, calling it 'an old idea whose time has come.'"[49] With the lack of state legislation allowing for this move to take place still standing in the way, a non-binding proposition concerning consolidation was placed on the city ballot. Almost two-thirds of voters supported the idea, but after that it basically dropped off the political radar for many years.

Around that time, the city of Tucson's aggressive annexation efforts were facing a substantial hurdle thrown up by the state legislature. Annexations for many years had required only that the owners of at least 50 percent of the total assessed property valuation of an annexation district sign in support. The legislature in the '80s added a new requirement that at least 50 percent of all property owners in the affected area also sign in favor. That radical change meant great difficulty in annexing any area with a sizable population. By 1988 Mayor Tom Volgy, a Democrat who followed Republican Murphy in office, was declaring the long-standing tradition of forced city annexations at an end.[50] Regardless, some property had been annexed earlier: the northside Tucson Mall in 1982; Midvale Farms on the southwest side the following year; the vacant but proposed Rita Ranch development on the southeast side; and Davis-Monthan Air Force Base in 1986.

One setback for the city council dealt with a new downtown main library. In 1986 the Mehl brothers of Cottonwood Properties proposed constructing a 22-story office building at the intersection of Stone and Pennington, the former site of Jacome's Department Store. A new library, to replace the cramped and outdated Carnegie building on Sixth Avenue, would be part of the complex, but within two years the proposal evaporated.

Other downtown efforts proved more successful. In the early years of the decade, a controversial, privately funded $1 million plan for the historic Temple of

Music and Art on Scott Avenue was unveiled. It involved constructing a five-story office tower on the west side of the building that would remove space in back of the existing stage, thus eliminating the possibility for most theatrical performances. In late 1984 the Tucson Artists' Coalition, aided by the new *Tucson Weekly* newspaper, mounted a drive to preserve the Temple as it was originally built in 1927, and City Council member Chuck Ford proposed that the municipality purchase the property. By 1987 the local government had acquired the Temple and then signed an agreement with the Arizona Theater Company to manage it once the building was restored.

The 1980s also saw a major proposal to erect two high-rise buildings at the southwest corner of Stone Avenue and Congress Street. Additionally included in this plan was a third proposed high-rise requiring the demolition of the nearby Fox Theater. In the end the Fox was saved because only one of the Stone/Congress towers would be built; when it opened in 1986 it became Tucson's tallest structure at 23 stories and it remains so.

Recognizing the importance of Tucson's historic theaters as well as other central-city assets, by 1988 a consultant group was recommending turning much of the downtown area into an arts district, including the old commercial warehouses along Toole Avenue. In anticipation of implementing the Aviation Parkway project, which would require demolishing many of these warehouses, the Arizona Department of Transportation (ADOT) had already purchased some of the buildings. Before the roadway construction began, however, the buildings were leased out by ADOT at affordable rates to dozens of artists, including sculptor Barbara Grygutis.

Changes were also happening at the Tucson Convention Center (TCC). To complement the existing adjacent hotel, city hall recommended building a large, high-rise luxury hotel.[51] A 1988 proposal, including $20 million in city subsidies, was made to encourage this idea, but it went nowhere. At about the same time, a major expansion of the TCC was begun. When it was completed in 1989, the $23 million project had more than tripled the floor space available at the center.

Further west, near Congress Street and the Santa Cruz River, plans for a "Rio Nuevo" effort to improve the area evolved throughout the decade. This redevelopment project had initially begun in the 1970s and was intended "to include about 1,200 apartments and supporting retail shops, offices and recreational areas," but it had become partially bogged down.[52] While hundreds of apartment units and some commercial establishments were built along or near St. Mary's Road, proposals to construct new housing and possibly two museums south of Congress Street and west of I-10 didn't materialize.

The perceived need to revitalize the greater downtown area was caused, in part, by the continuing exodus of traditional retailers. Alex Jácome, Sr., longtime president of the department store that bore his family name, died in 1980 at the age of 75. Within weeks the downtown establishment was closed after 84 years in business. That left J.C. Penney as the only major department store still remaining downtown.

After celebrating their 60th anniversary in the area in May 1981, by the end of the year the company had announced it would close its downtown store and establish a much larger one in the new and extremely popular Tucson Mall. In other retail news, Foothills Mall on the city's northwest side opened in 1982 and the decade concluded with the community's first two Walmarts opening in 1989.

Other new types of businesses were also emerging throughout the community. Established in 1969, by the 1980s locally owned AlphaGraphics was branching out with print shop franchises around the world. In 1971 eegee's opened to serve a popular frozen concoction, and by the end of the 1980s eegee's had 19 locations throughout Southern Arizona.[53] Also prospering was Pat's, the place for 76¢ chilidogs on Grande Avenue, as well as Lucky Wishbone, which had five stores selling a selection of fried foods. At the other end of the culinary spectrum, by the early '80s the Rancho del Rio Tack Room Restaurant on the city's eastside had earned a ranking of five stars from Mobil Travel Guide for five years in a row.

Also during the '80s, from Oro Valley to Green Valley, a series of technological and other changes were impacting the Tucson metropolitan area. In 1980 MCI Telecommunications Corporation appeared on the scene to challenge Mountain Bell for telephone service. By 1985 cellular phones, selling for up to $3,500, were being offered to Tucson customers, and that same year a signaling device replaced the caboose on Southern Pacific freight trains.

Gas stations across Tucson were transformed during the '80s from full-service operations to self-service franchises. In homes, to watch movies and other entertainment on television sets, the use of VCRs, costing no more than $270, was widespread by 1985. For those who wanted a good used book, there was Bookman's. It departed its small space on Broadway Boulevard in 1986 for the more spacious confines of a building on Grant Road. Another big change also came on west Grant Road: the Tucson Five Drive-In near I-10 was demolished in 1988 to make room for a 12-screen movie theater, the city's largest cineplex. Finally, by the early '80s retail stores selling home computers, priced between $700 and $3,000, appeared in Tucson, and they were very successful.

What didn't change during the '80s was the sprawling nature of the community. Resembling water spilled onto a dry desert floor, metropolitan Tucson was moving out in all directions, and instead of having "satellite cities" as proposed in the 1970s, it was developing some "satellite suburbs." These massive, master-planned developments, like Midvale Park on the southwest side, would include thousands of houses, extensive retail centers, and possibly other business uses. Large retiree communities, similar to bustling Green Valley, were also planned. One, Sun City–Vistoso, was near Catalina State Park while further north in Pinal County, Saddlebrooke was intended to contain more than 3,500 housing units for "active adults."

One rental project adjacent to the University of Arizona brought consternation to its central city neighbors and political controversy to the city council. The plan to build a high-rise private dormitory containing almost 1,500 bedrooms was vigorously opposed by residents of the West University neighborhood but approved near the end of 1987 as the last act of a Lew Murphy–led council. Despite that, the proposal was economically unfeasible and by 1988 had disappeared.

Homebuilding during the decade, on the other hand, continued to be a big part of Tucson's economy, but the '80s saw a noticeable change in the design of the standard single-family house. Many were two story and built on small lots in sharp contrast to the way things had traditionally been done in Tucson—single-story construction on a 7,000-square-foot or larger parcel.

After a few slow years, by 1983 boom times had returned to the homebuilding industry, and more than 11,000 housing permits were issued, including thousands for apartment units. Even though developers and homebuilders continued to pick political favorites at election time, new development and population growth by the late '80s had become almost a nonissue in local politics.[54]

The reality instead was that much of the region's projected population growth was to occur well outside the Tucson city limits. As the decade closed, the town of Marana—formerly 11 square miles in size—had grown to 65 square miles of mostly vacant land ripe for new development.

Also adding area during the '80s was Oro Valley. The original small town of 2.5 square miles and around 1,500 residents at first saw two annexations approved for large housing developments. After that the community continued to annex property and, following a legal fight, the town annexed the Rancho Vistoso development and increased its size to more than 17 square miles. Based on changes like that, one member of the town council reflected in 1988: "We're starting to lose the essence of Oro Valley."[55]

With more than 10,000 residents, Green Valley south of Tucson was still not a municipality. A 1985 study

For many years, Bernard "Bunny" Fontana, shown in this 2008 photograph, worked to preserve not only the San Xavier Mission but also the rich cultural history of Tucson and Southern Arizona (courtesy Vern Lamplot and the Patronato San Xavier photograph collection).

suggested the growing retirement community, if it didn't incorporate, could eventually lose political clout in Pima County to its northern neighbor of Sahuarita which was expected to grow rapidly. Taking that possibility into consideration, supporters of Green Valley incorporation tried again in 1989. They lost at the ballot box once more, this time by almost a 3 to 1 margin.

Along I-19 between Tucson and Green Valley, the "White Dove of the Desert" faced issues of another sort. "When you take a close look," observed Bernard "Bunny" Fontana in 1989 of Mission San Xavier del Bac, "you see we've already lost a lot and continue to lose more.... There are plaster and cement chunks falling, paint peeling off the frescoes, paintings and sculpture."[56] To rectify this deteriorating situation, a $1 million fundraising drive was launched by the Patronato San Xavier organization.

The 1980s saw the restoration of a few noteworthy historic structures. The original Temple Emanu-El on south Stone Avenue was dedicated as an historic site in 1982 and downtown's (Levi) Manning House was repaired and renovated into offices in 1984 after the expenditure of several million dollars. Much less money was spent by a new owner to rehabilitate the former Sixth Avenue home of Tucson pioneer, Fred Ronstadt.

By 1983, Ronstadt's granddaughter Linda, who still lived out-of-town, had been labeled "the reigning queen of contemporary music for the last decade."[57] After that she would go on to appear in *La Bohème* in New York and release the Grammy-award-winning *Canciones de Mi Padre* or *Songs of My Father*.

The decade also included two important anniversary celebrations. In 1980 Tucson marked the centennial of the arrival of the railroad to town. "I am working for the same company," ironically observed Southern Pacific Railroad conductor, Peter Ochoa, "that 100 years ago helped put my great-grandfather [Estevan Ochoa] out of business."[58] Four years later, the Arizona Historical Society commemorated its own centennial. It celebrated, in part, with an exhibit of nine women's dresses entitled: "Fashions at Our Founding."

At the same time, four noteworthy new books focusing on Tucson and Arizona's rich history were published. The first in 1982, with a paperback edition five years later, was *Tucson: The Life and Times of an American City* by C.L. Sonnichsen of the Arizona Historical Society. In 1986 *Los Tucsonenses, the Mexican Community in Tucson: 1854–1941* appeared. Tom Sheridan authored it with assistance from members of the Mexican Heritage Project, including writer Patricia Preciado Martin. "One of the primary purposes of 'Los Tucsonenses,'" Sheridan remarked, "was to document the systematic subordination over the years of Tucson's Mexican population."[59] The third book, by prolific writer and UA professor of anthropology, Jim Officer, was *Hispanic Arizona: 1536–1856* that was published in 1988. The next year, "Bunny" Fontana authored *Of Earth and Little Rain: The Papago Indians*.

Historic characters commemorated by two large statues brought completely different reactions when they were erected in Tucson during the 1980s. A 15-foot-tall likeness of missionary Father Eusebio Francisco Kino commissioned by the Arizona Historical Society was very warmly received when it went on display along Kino Boulevard late in the decade. The earlier installation of a statue of Mexican revolutionary Pancho Villa atop a horse in a small downtown park was looked at with disdain by at least one local historian. The piece, suggested the Rev. Charles Polzer, was "the flamboyant glorification of a murderer in our community [and] is inexcusable."[60]

Crime, Corruption, Athletics, and Education

Running into a variety of problems were two major land-use proposals. Developer Lew McGinnis received permission in 1981 to build the Williams Centre with offices and residences along Broadway Boulevard near Craycroft Road. He was also the developer of Peppertree Ranch, a satellite suburb eventually planned for 12,000 residential units north of Tucson. McGinnis was notorious for bouncing checks and by 1984 had sold both projects. In 1986 he was arrested and accused of stealing $1.6 million from his Williams Centre partners. McGinnis eventually entered a no-contest plea to that charge and was sentenced to pay back the money and serve five years of probation.

McGinnis sold Peppertree Ranch in 1984 to Lincoln American Savings owned by Phoenix businessman Charles H. Keating, Jr. The land was later renamed Continental Ranch with some of the property slated for development. As the 1980s came to a close, Keating was being accused of a "sham transaction" involving the Continental Ranch property in order to artificially inflate Lincoln's profits.

Other 1980s crimes, violent in nature and much more tragic in consequence, included the murder of several children. The first child killed was seven-year-old Cathy Fritz in 1982. Two years later, eight-year-old Vicki Lynn Hoskinson was murdered. That same year of 1984 saw the killing of twelve-year-old Michael Perry, and in 1986 two-year-old Zosha Lee Pickett was abducted from her home and murdered. While the killers of both Vicki Lynn Hoskinson and Michael Perry were quickly caught and convicted, the murders of Cathy Fritz and Zosha Lee Pickett went unsolved until 1992.[61]

By July 1986 the "Prime Time" rapist had been "striking for close to three years, terrorizing families, holding them hostage entire nights and taking 'most of their money.'"[62] For that, and the 30 rapes he reportedly committed, he was labeled the "most-wanted criminal in modern Tucson-area history." Eventually, after the community had been on edge for weeks, police confronted the perpetrator and he killed himself, ending the ordeal.

Additional major crime stories included a 1981 multimillion-dollar heist from a bank at Broadway Boulevard and Swan Road as well as the theft of a painting by Willem de Kooning valued at $400,000 being stolen from the UA Museum of Art in 1985.[63] Meanwhile, longtime Tucsonan Joe Bonanno continued to generate his own headlines. Convicted in California of trying to interfere with a grand jury investigation, he was sentenced to five years in prison but would serve only eight months before returning to town. Bonanno also wrote an autobiography in which he pointed out that former judge Evo DeConcini, father of U.S. Senator Dennis DeConcini, had been his friend until his son entered politics.[64]

The decade had begun with the unsurprising news that annually more than one in 10 local residents was the victim of a major crime. County Attorney Stephen Neely shockingly observed publicly in 1981: "Crime is out of control in Pima County."[65] To combat this ongoing onslaught of criminal activity, local law enforcement worked with the public to address the issue. Pima County also built a new jail to replace its existing "roach-infested semidungeon."[66] After Tucson's crime rate topped out at eighth in the nation in 1984, the annual increase in crime slowed somewhat. Even so, Tucson's reputation as a drug capital continued throughout the '80s, with a few new twists, including the 1984 synopsis by "local law-enforcement authorities and drug-rehabilitation experts" that a "snowstorm of cocaine [was] hitting" Tucson.[67]

Before the decade was over, five men were executed at a home on the community's southside and police, suggesting the obvious, stated: "The killings may be drug-related."[68] Peter Ronstadt, Tucson Police Chief and Fred's grandson, also observed that the murders could "foreshadow an increase in violence as drug-trafficking routes from Mexico into Southern Arizona grow more popular."[69]

In addition to a constant battle against crime, the decade also saw the deaths of several law enforcement agents in the line of duty. These included: Tucson Police Department narcotics officer Jeffery Ross, killed in a raid on a bar; TPD officer Ernest Calvillo, slain while trying to break up a fight; Oro Valley police officer Willis Henry "Bill" Gravell "killed while questioning a possible illegal immigrant from Mexico"[70]; and Department of Public Safety officer Ed Rebel, who was shot after a traffic stop. Also killed in traffic accidents while on duty were TPD officer James Smith and Pima County deputy Randall Graves.

Much less important, but gaining a lot more publicity, were two court cases involving the University of Arizona athletic department. First came football coach Tony Mason, who was fired in 1980. A series of stories in the *Arizona Daily Star* revealed Mason had allegedly committed numerous transgressions, including paying players, misusing travel money, and spending recruiting funds to bring non-recruits, including a massage club owner, to Tucson. Two *Star* reporters—Clark Hallas and Bob Lowe—were awarded a 1981 Pulitzer Prize for their work covering the story, and Mason was indicted on a series of charges but ultimately found not guilty. However, the UA football program still received sanctions from the NCAA.

The second case involved former UA basketball coach Ben Lindsey, who filed legal charges against the university. He accused the school of wrongfully firing him in 1983 after one season with a 4–24 record. Lindsey partially prevailed in court, winning a judgment of around $200,000.

Lute Olson came from the University of Iowa to replace Lindsey as basketball coach, and by 1988 the UA team made it to the Final Four of the NCAA basketball championships. A celebratory crowd of 20,000 welcomed the team home even though they didn't win the title. Tucson native, Sean Elliot, was on that team, and in 1989 he won the John Wooden Award as the nation's best college basketball player and was selected third in the NBA draft.

On the diamond, the UA baseball program won two more national championships during the decade. In addition, UA swimmer George DiCarlo won a gold medal at the 1984 Olympics, as did former UA students Tracie Ruiz and Candy Costie in synchronized swimming.

In other sports news, in 1986 a Tucson team of all-stars lost to a squad from Taiwan in the championship game of the Little League World Series, just as another local club had done in 1973. Also, even though the UA played North Carolina State at Arizona stadium in the inaugural Copper Bowl football game in 1989, community response before the contest was labeled "absolutely terrible" by one official.[71] Nonetheless, the final attendance was a somewhat respectable 37,000.

While these athletic diversions played out, total enrollment at the UA reached more than 30,000. To deal with an ever-expanding number of students, a 1980 committee of the Arizona Board of Regents recommended enacting a cap on enrollment of about that same number, an idea quickly dropped because of its possible impact on minority students. A tuition hike, however, was approved, raising the annual cost of an education to $650 for Arizona residents. In 1989 a new enrollment cap, this time at 38,000, was pushed before being rejected as "elitist."

Another issue confronting the UA during the decade was the 1981 resignation of John Schaefer as president. Henry Koffler from the University of Massachusetts at Amherst replaced him while Schaefer went on to lead the New York–based Research Corporation, whose headquarters moved to Tucson in 1983.

Also in campus news was the Schaefer-inspired Center for Creative Photography. Assisted by famous photographer Ansel Adams, in 1983 the center began a drive to secure financing for a new structure. When the building opened in 1989 on the UA campus, it was called "one of the most complete museums of photography in the world."[72]

A sculpture on the University mall along Campbell Avenue, on the other hand, met with considerable distain. Displaying the school's colors of red and blue, "Curving Arches" was a design labeled "clothespins," "tweezers," and "wishbones" by critics when it first appeared in 1981.[73]

One noteworthy 1965 UA graduate, Francis R. "Dick" Scobee, presented the school with some mementoes after his 1984 flight aboard the space shuttle Challenger. Tragically, in 1986 Scobee was the commander of the Challenger when it exploded just after launch in Florida. At a memorial service, Koffler said of Scobee: "He was a man who valued the [aerospace engineering] education which he received here."[74]

Like the research work in space Scobee had been doing, UA educational efforts continued at many levels. The Steward Observatory on campus was substantially expanded in 1983, and two years later the three millionth volume was placed into the university's library—a first edition of James Joyce's *Ulysses*.

Another change coming to the campus involved the increasing use of computers. One UA administrator in 1984 went so far as to boldly predict that he "can foresee a time when a personal computer will be as much a part of a college student's paraphernalia as notebooks and ballpoint pens are now."[75]

While attendance at the UA continued to grow, enrollment at Pima Community College was also climbing, reaching a record 23,176 in 1986. By 1988 the school's elected board of directors was in turmoil once again, and the extent of the dispute was especially deep.[76] Eventually, three members of the five-person board resigned, and a Superior Court judge removed one other because she didn't live in the district she was elected to represent. At about the same time, the school's president, Diego A. Navarrette, was removed from his position for falsifying his résumé. He was, however, given almost $100,000 as part of a legal settlement because, as one board member reflected: "the agreement would spare the college further legal and emotional costs."[77]

Other educational news in Tucson included the 1983 successful recall of the Vail school district board president. Also occurring during the decade was the opening of Desert View High School in the Sunnyside district and the completion of Mountain View as the Marana district's second high school. Also, the Arizona School for the Deaf and Blind marked its 75th anniversary in 1987, and the Tanque Verde School District its centennial two years earlier.

After surviving a decade of controversy in the 1970s, the following 10 years were relatively calm for the Tucson Unified School District (TUSD). Facing continuous declining enrollment because of urban sprawl, by 1984 TUSD also had a growing problem with dropouts, 28 percent from its high schools alone. This statistic was called "a community disgrace" by critics of the district.[78] At least the following year voters approved a spending override for TUSD. (That 1985 support would be the last TUSD operation and maintenance budget override district voters would approve.)

While voters in five Tucson area school districts, including Sunnyside and Amphitheater, approved budget overrides in 1987, TUSD voters in both 1988 and 1989 rejected further budget override requests. At least high school students by that time were receiving free textbooks thanks to the tireless political efforts of Tucson area legislator Bernardo Cajero, who had died in 1973, and his widow and legislative replacement, Carmen. At a ceremony held at Tucson High School in 1984, Governor Babbitt signed the textbook measure into law as Representative Cajero looked on.

Someone else who had died was an unidentified 28-year-old man. In March 1983 he became Tucson's first reported victim of AIDS, which at that time was described as: "a mysterious crippling of the body's immune system, [that] leaves its victims open to constant, often deadly infections."[79] By 1985 the Tucson AIDS Project had been established "to provide direct care and assistance to local victims,"[80]

Capping decades of effort by the Cajero family, 1985 state legislation provided free textbooks to Arizona's high school students. Shown at the signing ceremony held at Tucson High School are (left to right): Travis Bedford, Olivia Cajero Bedford, Governor Bruce Babbitt, and State Representative Carmen Cajero (courtesy the Cajero Bedford photograph collection).

and in 1986 the number of new AIDS cases in Pima County was 20; by 1987 that figure had jumped to 53.

Mental health was another medical issue receiving some attention throughout the decade. Arizona's services for the seriously mentally ill were labeled minimal in a 1986 national report,[81] while a study released two years later showed Arizona spent the least of any state on these services.[82] Trying to address deficiencies like those was a Tucson couple, attorney S.L. Schorr and his wife Eleanor, who in 1983 were among the founders of the Alliance for the Mentally Ill of Southern Arizona.

Other medical news included longtime Tucson Congressman Morris Udall revealing in 1980 that he had Parkinson's disease. In 1983 Roy Drachman donated $1 million for the new UA Cancer Center, a building that was under construction by 1985. Local hospitals garnered other 1980s headlines. After a sometimes-contentious process, Hospital Corporation of America (HCA) was chosen by the Arizona Department of Health Services to construct a 150-bed facility on North La Cholla Boulevard south of West Orange Grove Road that opened in September 1983 and was named Northwest Medical Center.

Politics and Electrical Power

Hospital Corporation of America was also managing county-owned Kino Hospital which continued to accumulate large annual debts, including almost $10 million in 1982 alone. That led to calls for the county to sell Kino, but in October 1984 an emotionally split Pima County Board of Supervisors decided to retain the facility.

It wasn't finances but heart transplants that made the most news at University Medical Center (UMC). By 1986 the 100th transplant had been performed, but it wasn't all good news for the UMC team led by Dr. Jack Copeland. In 1987 they inserted the wrong heart into a patient, a mistake that was rectified but which eventually led to a financial settlement in excess of $250,000.

Tucson Police Department officer Roy Garcia received a much larger settlement after having been shot accidentally by a South Tucson police officer in 1978. Two years later a jury awarded Garcia $3.6 million, but South Tucson only had $100,000 of insurance and $2.1 million in total assets. In 1984 a settlement was reached with Garcia receiving about $2 million in cash as well as a piece of South Tucson property valued at close to $1 million.

The ongoing financial difficulties facing South Tucson because of the Garcia case had prompted some residents to once again suggest the small municipality disband, and in 1985 an official disincorporation effort was launched. Pima County officials, however, eventually determined there weren't enough valid signatures to warrant an election. "You've heard Tombstone is the town too tough to die," remarked South Tucson Mayor Dan Eckstrom after this decision. "Well, South Tucson is the town that won't die."[83]

The town opened a new municipal complex on south Sixth Avenue in 1988 and named it after Eckstrom who, after re-registering as a Democrat many years earlier and winning election, had served as mayor for 15 years. He then resigned to take a seat on the Pima County Board of Supervisors, joining a political body that had seen a lot of changes during the decade.

In 1980 the supervisors supported by business and building interests—Conrad Joyner, Katie Dusenberry, and E.S. "Bud" Walker—had all been re-elected. Between 1980 and 1984, these three continued their "pro-growth" policies by approving almost every rezoning application they considered. Some of them had also supported the publicly despised Rillito-Pantano Parkway proposal. As a result, in the primary election of 1984, candidates opposed to the parkway challenged Dusenberry and Walker; in a reversal of past electoral power flexed by the development industry, both incumbents lost. Despite that, one homebuilder was philosophical about the defeat, pointing out those that were elected were not "no-growth."[84]

The Democrat who beat Walker, Ed Moore, agreed with that statement. He had been endorsed by the Neighborhood Coalition of Greater Tucson but stressed he wasn't "anti-growth." On the November night of his general election, Moore also said he saw his job as making "sure government has integrity, that it keeps its word."[85] Trying to implement that philosophy, by 1986 Moore's political tactics were being referred to as "Rambo-like" after the lone-wolf movie character. That same year, Moore called fellow Democrat, David Yetman, a "wimpy Mao Marxist" and Yetman responded by labeling Moore "a genuinely evil man."[86]

Meanwhile Yetman, borrowing an idea from local attorney Hugh Holub—while also taking a political jab at metropolitan Phoenix—talked semi-seriously about creating the new state of *Baja* (Lower) Arizona south of the Gila River. In a proclamation he had prepared, Yetman pontificated: "The people of Southern Arizona have developed a high degree of civilization and culture, which is lacking in the area north of the Gila River."[87]

After three terms, Yetman stepped down from the board in 1988. Raúl Grijalva, the former outspoken political activist and current member of the Tucson Unified School District board, decided to run for the seat as a Democrat and easily won.

The Tucson Electric Power (TEP) company was also undergoing major changes during the '80s, one of which would negatively impact thousands of shareholders, including many elderly investors. In late 1984 the decision was announced that TEP's wholly owned subsidiary, the Alamito Company, would be spun off. Alamito had been formed in 1977 to supply wholesale power to the utility from a distant generating plant at Springerville, Arizona, and one other facility. Theodore M. Welp, president, chief executive, and chairman of TEP, resigned in 1984 to assume control of Alamito. He and his associates at the new company then offered to buy it in 1985 but were outbid by others. As a consolation prize, Welp received approximately $5.5 million for his shares of Alamito.

While Welp made millions, the Alamito issue continued to haunt TEP because the utility company was "committed by contract to purchase all the Springerville power from Alamito through the year 2014."[88] In 1989 a complaint was filed "that rates charged by Alamito to Tucson Electric Power are 'far in excess of just and reasonable costs' for power from the Springerville" plant.[89] As one critic of the TEP/Alamito arrangement put it: "heads Alamito wins, tails TEP loses."[90]

The utility company was hit by another crisis in July 1989. Its chairman, president, and chief executive officer, Einar Greve, was forced to resign after it was disclosed he had sold almost 32,000 of his 36,000 company shares at $32 a piece.[91] Former University of Arizona president John Schaefer, a member of the board since 1983, was then named chair. Upon news of the management shakeup, TEP shares fell to less than $28.

As the decade wound down, a summary of the community's population growth showed that just fewer than 700,000 people lived in Pima County while the city of Tucson, because of annexations, had gone from 99 square miles in 1980 to 156 in 1989. Also that fall, the TEP stock price was under $21, and analysts were warning the company's "dark days might not be over."[92]

• TWELVE •

Sports Highlights and Water Lowlights, 1990–2000

Behind a security guardhouse at the Rita Road entrance to the southeast side UA Tech Park is a large directory sign. With 6,000 employees working for numerous firms at the park, four are listed on the marker: Citi Cards, Raytheon, IBM, and Café Zona. Originally built in the 1970s exclusively for IBM, the huge complex was impacted first by the company's 1988 local downsizing and second when the University of Arizona purchased the property in 1994.

RAUCOUSLY SCREAMING WHILE WAVING congratulatory signs—one of which simply read "R-E-S-P-E-C-T"—an estimated 50,000 people filled the University of Arizona football stadium in April 1997. They had come to welcome home the NCAA men's basketball champions from their triumph in Indianapolis. "When Tucsonans look in the mirror today," suggested the *Tucson Citizen*, "they see the face of a winner."[1]

The '97 basketball triumph was just one of several memorable moments in Tucson sports during the decade. The previous year, hometown heroine Kerri Strug thrilled the world with her courage while helping the United States women's gymnastics team win an Olympic gold medal. At those same games in Atlanta, former UA swimmer Amy Van Dyken took home four gold medals. In 1992 Tucson native Michael Bates had won an Olympic bronze medal on the track in the 200-meter race.

Other athletic accomplishments included: the UA women's softball team winning an impressive five NCAA titles during the decade; hundreds of cyclists annually riding in the El Tour de Tucson bike event; and the Tucson Toros claiming their first Pacific Coast League baseball title in nail-biting fashion in 1991, then repeating the feat two years later.

By 1998 Tucson had also become home to three spring training major league baseball teams. That came about because after 46 years in town, the Cleveland Indians departed for Florida in 1993 and were replaced at historic Hi Corbett field by the Major League's new expansion team, the Colorado Rockies. Even before then, the Southern Arizona Sports Development Corporation, a private group that included real estate

Twelve • Sports Highlights and Water Lowlights, 1990–2000

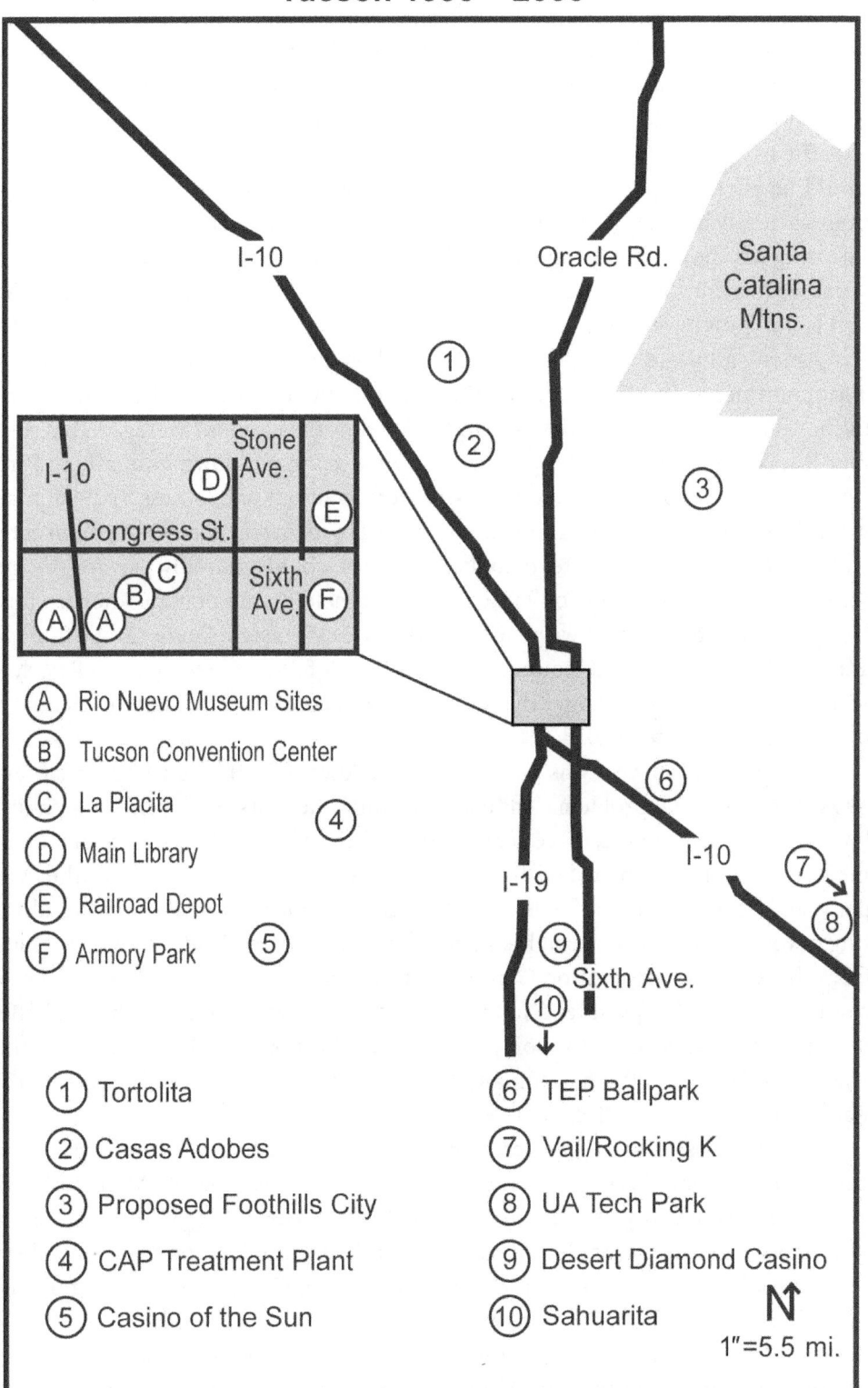

legend, Roy Drachman, was planning for a new spring training facility to accommodate two additional teams.[2] After both the newly established Arizona Diamondbacks as well as the existing Chicago White Sox expressed interest in training in Tucson, in 1996 the Pima County Board of Supervisors selected a site for the new ballpark near Ajo Way adjacent to Kino Hospital; it was controversial because it wasn't downtown.

The two teams signed 15-year contracts to use the $35 million facility, which would be partially paid for by a number of new or increased taxes. Springtime games actually began to be played there in 1998 with lifetime baseball fan Drachman throwing out the first pitch. The ballpark was labeled a "gem in the desert"[3] that was expected to attract additional adjacent investment, including a four-story hotel, but that facility was never built.

Among all these community points of athletic pride were some sports-related disappointments. In 1991 the graduation rate for UA athletes was shown to be near the bottom of the Pac-10 conference and well below the national average.[4] That same year it was reported that 1,000 greyhounds were being put down annually in Pima County. The pro hockey Tucson Gila Monsters went out of business by 1998, making it the seventh professional sports team to fail in town since the 1970s. Then at the end of 1998, the UA football team looked like they would assuredly play for the first time in the Rose Bowl game on January 1, a long-held dream of many diehard fans. "It's our ultimate goal and we're so close that we can taste it," one campus official admitted.[5] Fate intervened, however, and the team's failure to ever play in Pasadena on New Year's Day carried on. (That dubious streak continued through the demise of the Pac-12 conference in 2024.)

Having more success was Tucson Electric Power (TEP). The company's previous serious financial problems led to an ongoing slide in its stock price, which hit a low of less than $2 in 1992, three years after reaching a high of $50 a share in January 1989. In 1990 the TEP board of directors selected Charles Bayless to lead the company, and he intended to refocus on utility service almost exclusively, while admitting it would take years to straighten out the monetary mess. Under intense pressure from the Arizona Corporation Commission that regulated TEP, by late 1991 board chair and former UA president, John P. Schaefer, who was paid more than $108,000 per year for his services to the company, resigned his position along with two other board members. By 1994 the company was profitable once more, and its stock price was beginning to slowly rise.

As the TEP saga stretched across parts of two decades, numerous community cultural and social offerings continued while others came or went. After lasting 84 years, the once socially prominent Old Pueblo Club, consisting of important business and society figures, faded from view in 1992 having lost too many members. More successful was the less formal Mountain Oyster Club, comprised of ranchers and others, that celebrated its 50th anniversary in 1998.

The Tucson Folk Festival entered its second decade of providing a downtown weekend of music and fun by 1996, and on the stage in December of that same year the Borderlands Theater Company began the tradition of a Tucson Pastorela, "a form of Hispanic performance folk art with origins dating back to the early 1500s."[6] Other annual events included Cinco de Mayo festivities at Kennedy Park on the city's westside, a celebration that had been held at various locations around Tucson for well more than a century. A Norteño event in South Tucson featuring a unique blend of different border sounds and an annual Waila Festival of Tohono O'odham music and dance were also held. One music venue literally lost its roof during the decade when the El Casino Ballroom suffered severe damage during an October 1991 storm.

After 42 years, the San Xavier Festival at the Tohono O'odham mission ended in 1993. About the same time, to mark the centennial of the Arizona State Museum, a Southwest Indian Art Fair was begun on the UA campus as an annual event.

Early in 1995, a devastating fire struck the Old Tucson western theme park, destroying three-quarters of the facility. Damage from the apparently arson-caused blaze was estimated at $10 million, but by 1997 Old Tucson was back in business.

Location changes came to some well-established entertainment organizations. Safety concerns led the Tucson Rodeo parade committee in 1991 to move the parade from downtown, where it had been held since the 1920s, to a route on the city's south side. Also relocating in 1991 was the Loft Theater that left its initial UA area site for a closed movie house on Speedway Boulevard. Despite desperate attempts to keep them in town, the home-grown performing youth organization, "Up with People," moved to Denver in 1993.

Coming to a close in 1994 was original organizer Jim Griffith's 20 years of participation with Tucson Meet Yourself, an annual downtown gathering of cultural entertainment and food. Griffith may have stepped down from that event, but he was co-curator of a 1996 exhibit at the UA Museum of Art entitled "The Unbroken Chain: The Traditional Arts of Tucson's Mexican-American Community." Another landmark show entitled "Chicano Art: Resistance and Affirmation: 1965–1985" opened at the Tucson Museum of Art in January 1992 and included works by 90 Chicano artists from across the nation. One of those was Tucson photographer Louis Bernal who, before a bicycle accident led to years in a coma and his eventual death, had once suggested: "The responsibility of a Chicano artist is to feed the soul of his people."[7]

The 1994 edition of Tucson Meet Yourself featured hometown singer and songwriter, 77-year-old Lalo Guerrero. Having lived in Southern California most of his life, during the 1990s Guerrero would receive a National Medal of the Arts at the White House. He was also performing periodically in Tucson, and in 1996 Guerrero shared the stage with another Tucson native, Linda Ronstadt, at Tucson's annual *Mariachi Espectacular.*

People, a President, Crime, and Hospitals

The last year of the decade saw a presidential visit. In February 1999, Bill Clinton came for a talk about Social Security and was introduced by 81-year-old Tucson

A native of Tucson, famed musician Lalo Guerrero is shown in this 1985 photograph with his son, Mark, several years before Lalo received a National Medal of the Arts at the White House (courtesy the Mark Guerrero photograph archive).

native Esther Tang. While in town, Clinton dined at Mi Nidito restaurant in South Tucson and memorably ate "chips and salsa, a cheese crisp, tamales, a taco, a chicken enchilada, a chile relleno, a bean tostada, rice and a tortilla."[8] The presidential visit to the small enclave of South Tucson certainly impressed one resident who remarked: "He didn't go to the foothills, he didn't go over on Skyline (Drive).... He came here, where the real people are."[9]

Later in 1999 Clinton would honor two Tucsonans in Washington, D.C. In June he presented a President's Award to auto dealer Jim Click for his help in establishing a program to employ disabled people. Then in October, Betty Frey received the President's Service Award for her 38 years of effort in assisting Tucsonans to learn to read and write through the organization she established—Tucson Adult Literacy Volunteers.

Several local writers were prominent during the '90s including Barbara Kingsolver who, after her 1988 success with *The Bean Trees*, published *Pigs in Heaven* (1993), *High Tide in Tucson* (1995), and *The Poisonwood Bible* (1998). Two important books that focused on the past appeared during the '90s: Tom Sheridan's *Arizona: A History*; and *Whiskey, Six-Guns & Red-Light Ladies*, the 1875–1878 diary of Tucson saloonkeeper George Hand edited by Neil Carmony.

Added to the decade's list of authors was Roy Drachman, who in 1999 came out with *From Cowtown to Desert Metropolis*. The 93-year-old reflected on his

Honored for her many decades of community service, 81-year-old Esther Tang acknowledged she ad-libbed her 1999 introduction of President Bill Clinton, who stands in front of Congressman Jim Kolbe (courtesy the Tang family photograph collection).

community: "Tucson has developed with many good things about it, but it also has detriments, mostly in the failure to recognize that we are going to grow the way we have."[10]

As the 20th century ended, Tucson had evolved into a low-density, sprawling, amoeba-like mass that was almost completely automobile dependent. While some people called for more alternative forms of transportation, Drachman certainly wasn't among them. Writing in 1995, he commented on the idea of a light-rail system: "Tucson should completely forget about the possibility or advisability of building any kind of a rail line. It just won't work, and it will cost tons of money."[11]

Noteworthy from another perspective were two Tucson politicians. In 1991 State Senator Jesus "Chuy" Higuera was ousted from office and received a two-month jail sentence for his role in the AzScam casino gambling corruption scheme. Pima County Assessor Alan Lang won election in 1992, but by the summer of the following year his office was embroiled in controversy; he was bringing a gun to work as protection and was charged in a domestic violence case. The National Organization for Women launched a recall effort against him and voters threw Lang out of office in 1994.

Tucson during the '90s also lost several people that had made enormous contributions to the community. Don Bufkin, historian and cartographer extraordinaire, died in 1994. Two years later, Oliver Drachman, Roy's cousin, died at the age of 92 after a lifetime of service to his community in various civic capacities. Tony Zimmerman, the man most responsible for implementing the Summerhaven development on Mount Lemmon, passed away that same year. Yndia Smalley Moore, who did much to promote Tucson's rich history, died in 1997, and the next year Linda McCartney passed away in Tucson at the age of 56.

Someone who left a lasting political legacy, not only locally but nationally, also died. In 1991, because of his Parkinson's disease, Morris "Mo" Udall had resigned his long-held Congressional seat and was replaced by Ed Pastor of Phoenix after a special election. Udall received the Presidential Medal of Freedom in 1996, and when he eventually lost his battle with Parkinson's two years later, Udall was "remembered as a visionary statesman who won the hearts of Americans and colleagues on both sides of the political divide."[12]

Another Tucsonan who had been unselfishly devoted to his community died in 1992. Architect and former chief city building inspector, 95-year-old Eleazar Herreras had spent decades helping out on projects ranging from the San Xavier Mission renovation to preserving downtown adobe buildings. After passing away, he was remembered simply as "a Tucsonan we can all be proud of."[13]

Still alive as the decade came to an end was 94-year-old Joe Bonanno. A six-hour film about his life was produced in 1999 to be shown on the Showtime cable channel. Before its television premier, the first part was screened at the Loft Theater. One of those in attendance was actor Martin Landau, who portrayed Bonanno as a senior citizen in the film, and said of his subject: "The killing that Joe has done was always to protect the family."[14]

That type of sugar-coating of Bonanno's criminal career wouldn't decrease Tucson's overall crime statistics because, as a banner 1991 *Tucson Citizen* headline declared: "Tucson 12th in crime rate."[15] That nationwide ranking eventually receded somewhat, but by 1995 almost 100 homicides were recorded across Pima County, making it the deadliest year, by far, in Tucson's history. (The current Pima County record is 119 homicides committed in 2021.) Another crime with dramatic increases during the decade was auto thefts, with some of the thousands of vehicles stolen annually presumably being taken to Mexico.

Many crimes in Tucson were at least partially linked to drug trafficking, and that problem was only getting worse. One official characterized the situation in 1990 as Tucson being "among the top three or four wholesale drug markets (in the United States)."[16]

Horrific crimes also plagued the community. A murder that took a long time to solve was the 1996 car bombing death of businessman Gary Triano at the La Paloma foothills resort. (While the victim's shady business dealings led to public speculation about numerous suspects, eventually a hit man hired by Triano's ex-wife was arrested in 2008 and later convicted. She was finally apprehended in Europe in 2009 and found guilty of murder five years later.) Other notorious '90s crimes remain unsolved, however, including the 1994 murder of six-year-old Esther "Lizette" Galaz and the 1996 disappearance of seven-year-old Karen Grajeda.

There were also spurts of multiple violent murders throughout the decade. In 1992 three people died in a shooting at El Grande Market on 36th Street. Then in two related 1996 robberies, six people died, four of them at the Tucson Firefighters Association Union Hall on Benson Highway. Finally, the decade ended with three people shot to death at a Pizza Hut on the city's east side.

Several police officers also lost their lives in the line of duty during the '90s. These included UA officer Kevin Barleycorn in 1990 and Department of Public Safety officers David Gabrielli and John Blaser the same year. In 1993 South Tucson police officer John Valenzuela was slain, and six years later DPS officer Juan Cruz perished while on duty.

Also killed during the decade was Tucson Police Department detective Gabriel Abendano. While wearing a ski mask and trying to rob a man, he was shot in 1996. It turned out Abendano was a rogue cop within the department.

On the other hand, an honest and noble citizen who died in 1999 at the age of 63 was the man who founded the University Medical Center's (UMC) Arizona Cancer Center in 1976—Dr. Sydney Salmon. Not only had he been the center's only director, but he was also known as "one of the leading medical oncologists" in the nation.[17]

Making medical news for other reasons were two hospitals. Kino Community Hospital had run consistent annual deficits, in part because of its service to indigent patients, and by 1994 the long-discussed possibility of partnering the hospital with UMC resurfaced. That didn't take place, and by the end of the '90s Kino's total debt was $40 million—the future of the hospital was described as "bleak."[18] Then, near the end of 1999, it was announced that Tucson General, a 106-bed osteopathic hospital on north Campbell Avenue, would close. (A new UMC Cancer Treatment Center opened on the site in 2007 and would later expand to include other medical facilities.)

Social and Racial Issues

It was reported early in the '90s that some Tucson doctors were rejecting AIDS patients because they personally feared the disease that afflicted hundreds of county residents. In 1995 AIDS claimed 41-year-old Jerôme Beillard, one of the founders of the People with AIDS Coalition of Tucson. By 1996, almost 680 people in Pima County had died of AIDS since 1983, and in 1997 Tucson's three separate AIDS organizations merged to form the Southern Arizona AIDS Foundation.

The "Don't Ask, Don't Tell" policy concerning homosexuals had been implemented in 1993 for the U.S. military, a step Tucson Republican Congressman Jim Kolbe supported. "I don't like the idea of discrimination of people based on something other than performance," he stated.[19] Three years later, Kolbe acknowledged he was gay, an announcement that had little impact on his lengthy political career.

Women saw some occasional progress during the decade, including Capt. Ellen McKinnon becoming the first woman combat pilot to fly solo at Davis-Monthan in 1994, and in 1999 the Pima County Sheriff's Department having a woman, Martha Cramer, as its first female major. At the same time, Capt. Linda Burkett retired from the Tucson Police Department (TPD) after 28 years of service. "I think we are making progress," Burkett reflected on women at TPD. "There is a tremendous amount of acceptance in the [police] academy and a much greater acceptance in the department and in the community."[20]

Another woman, Elaine S. Hedtke, had spent 17 years working her way up through the ranks of TPD when she was appointed chief in early 1992. Within a year, however, she was receiving intense criticism from fellow officers for her management style, and she resigned in November 1993. "I have done my best, and I don't believe that I have shortchanged anyone along the way," Hedtke said in departing TPD.[21]

In 1998 Harold Copeland became the first African American to serve 25 years with TPD and then retire. When he left, Copeland was one of 28 Blacks in a department of almost 870 that also included 125 women and 169 Hispanics.[22]

During this same time there continued to be incidences of racial intolerance in Tucson. In 1995 an African American Pima County employee was awarded $250,000 because she was demoted by a supervisor who said a "token [B]lack" wasn't needed in her job anymore. Also during the decade, anti–Jewish literature was distributed in midtown neighborhoods. "Discrimination and hate issues are a big problem in Tucson," concluded a representative of the Jewish Communications Council in 1996.[23]

Some steps were taken to address these and related racial and social issues. In 1991 new University of Arizona President, Manuel Pacheco, made promoting ethnic diversity one of his top priorities. Pacheco's hiring earlier that year demonstrated how important achieving this goal could be. When the initial list of finalists for the president's job was announced, there were no Hispanics included. After loud protests from the community, Pacheco's name was added, and he was eventually hired, becoming "the highest ranking Hispanic in education in this country."[24]

Other news involving Mexican Americans included census statistics showing about 24 percent of 1990 Pima County residents were Hispanic. (By 2022 the racial makeup of Pima County was approximately 50 percent White, 39 percent Hispanic, and 5 percent Black, while within the city limits of Tucson, Hispanics outnumbered Whites.)[25]

The skyrocketing increase in the number of illegal crossers of the Mexican border was an ongoing issue. In 1992 almost 71,000 arrests in the Tucson sector by the U.S. Border Patrol set an annual record. By 1999, because of changes in the patrol's nationwide enforcement philosophy, that figure had amazingly increased almost seven-fold to reach more than 470,000 arrests, the highest total of any border sector in the United States.

Although annual deaths during the decade of those trying to enter the U.S. was

One of the founders of the People with AIDS Coalition of Tucson, Jerôme Beillard is shown at work on his computer before the disease claimed him in 1995 at the age of 41 (courtesy the Robert Markley photograph collection).

mostly in low double digits, the Border Patrol launched a public relations "Stay Out, Stay Alive" campaign in 1996 to warn people of the desert dangers.[26] That effort, however, didn't prevent nine Mexican men from trying to cross in June 1996, six of whom died in the intense heat. (A few years later, the number of annual documented crossing deaths in Southern Arizona exploded, exceeding 140 by 2002, remaining above that number until 2014, then exceeding it continuously starting in 2020.)[27]

There was also a dramatic rise in violence along the Mexican border, and allegations of abuse by some border patrol officials were heard throughout the decade. In 1998, though, 27-year-old border agent Alexander Kirpnick was killed in Nogales by a gunshot fired by marijuana smugglers.

To address these and other border issues, calls to build an impenetrable wall were heard as early as 1991, an idea opposed by many Arizona officials, including Governor Fife Symington. Some fencing was installed along the border anyway, and many more Border Patrol agents were added to the Tucson sector, exceeding 1,000 by the end of the decade. It was admitted in 1995, however, that these officers "can only try to slow the flow of illegal immigrants, not stop it."[28] In addition, the detrimental environmental impacts—including discarded trash and damage to desert vegetation—from the huge increase in crossers in the Tucson sector were becoming more noticeable, including on the Tohono O'odham reservation west of Tucson.

The Tohono O'odham, along with Yaqui Indians in town, also had other issues to address. The U.S. Attorney for Arizona in 1991 notified both tribes that the video poker and slot machines they installed in their high-stakes bingo halls were illegal, and in May 1992 federal officials seized 360 of the machines. While working relentlessly to retain the right of his people to offer gaming opportunities, 58-year-old Tohono O'odham chairman Josiah Moore died in April 1993. Less than two weeks later, an agreement between the two Tucson tribes and Governor Symington was announced that allowed for 2,000 slot machines. To house some of them, the Tohono O'odham opened its Desert Diamond Casino on Nogales Highway in October 1993, and the Pascua Yaqui the following March debuted its Casino of the Sun in an industrial-type building on its far southwest-side reservation.

The financial impact of tribal gambling was immediate. By 1995 projections were made that yearly profits of $50 million for the Tohono O'odham could be realized and the Yaquis estimated they might see $28 million.

The Tohono O'odham tribe was also involved with the revitalization of its historic San Xavier Mission. In 1992 an international team of experts began an extensive $1.7 million interior restoration effort. After six years of work, the project was completed in time to celebrate the church's 200th anniversary in 1997. Meanwhile, a vital piece of Tucson history went up for sale. In 1993 the Southern Pacific Railroad Company placed its 86-year-old Toole Avenue depot on the market. Five years later, the city of Tucson purchased it for $2.1 million with plans to restore the often-modified structure to its 1941 appearance.

Other noteworthy historic preservation activities included the 1994 sale by the Tucson Unified School District (TUSD) of the former Dunbar School to a group that planned to convert the building into "a museum and African American cultural center." The creation of a Jewish cultural center and museum in Tucson's first synagogue downtown on Stone Avenue was also warmly welcomed.

Downtown Doings Plus Roads and Water

Overall, the downtown area saw several highs as well as some lows during the decade. In 1990 the city's new main library on Stone Avenue opened while the Sixth Avenue Carnegie Library was converted into a children's museum. Called "Sonora," the blazing red sculpture in front of the new library drew howls of protest, with the *Tucson Citizen* newspaper commenting on the $150,000 piece: "[It] looks more like something from outer space than 'Sonora.'"[29]

Several other downtown improvements were seen more favorably, including the La Placita complex next to the Tucson Convention Center getting an exuberant multi-colored paint scheme in 1999. "Downtown was in such a near-death state," the paint project's coordinator suggested. "It took a shock treatment. That's what La Placita is. It's a wake-up call back to life."[30]

That had certainly not been the view of downtown at the beginning of the '90s. At that time thousands of people jammed its sidewalks for the twice-monthly

"Downtown Saturday Night" event, and the area's future appeared promising. By 1993, however, the president-elect of the Downtown Business Association said the area had an abandoned look with graffiti and boarded up buildings predominating. As a response, a downtown improvement district was created in 1998 that had property owners and Tucson taxpayers contributing funds to maintain the area.

Proposals were continuously made throughout the '90s to improve downtown's shifting situation. Many of these ideas focused on vacant land near Congress Street west of I-10 that had long been known as Rio Nuevo South. By 1993 the original Rio Nuevo effort—to install commercial and residential projects on both sides of Congress in this area—had been declared mostly a failure. Despite that, to supplement land it already owned, the city of Tucson began acquiring even more property with the goal being to develop "a one-of-a-kind cultural and historic park ... that would make it a 'must-see' tourist attraction."[31]

As chairman of the Tohono O'odham Nation, Josiah N. Moore worked tirelessly for tribal gaming rights until his untimely death in 1993, and thus would not live to see the benefits gaming brought to his people (courtesy the Jacob Moore collection).

Eventually some interesting project proposals popped up. One group was pushing a Sonoran Sea aquarium; another wanted to reconstruct the former Mission San Agustín and Convento buildings that had disappeared many years before. The Arizona Historical Society was also considering relocating its museum and headquarters to the Rio Nuevo South site while the University of Arizona proposed building a science center that would replace the financially struggling Flandrau Planetarium on campus.

Combining some of these ideas along with others proposed for the central city, in 1999 the city of Tucson put together a package of possible downtown improvements. To be funded primarily with $240 million in private sector money supplemented by $80 million in governmental assistance from state sales tax receipts, the Rio Nuevo proposal went before Tucson voters in November 1999, and one supporter commented before the election: "It seems inconceivable that this project could be anything but a smashing success."[32] With glowing prospects like that, voters by a wide margin approved the new Rio Nuevo plan and initial work was expected to begin quickly.[33]

Local malls and other retailers were making their own improvements. To attract more business, midtown's El Con Mall opened "The Pavilion" in 1993, but those small shops and booths failed to win the attention of many customers. As a result, in 1999 the space was converted into a megaplex theater with 20 screens, making it Tucson's largest movie house.

The Foothills Mall also searched for an identity. Having lost many tenants by 1994, the northwest side facility was struggling with a high vacancy rate. In response, the retail mall evolved into a "shopping-and-entertainment hot spot" featuring shops, restaurants, an expanded movie theater, and some discount stores. The transformation paid off, and by the end of 1998 the mall was completely occupied.

Tucson's two other major malls never faced occupancy problems. Park Mall increased its size by 50 percent late in the decade while Tucson Mall expanded to hold more than 200 stores, making it the area's largest shopping facility.

Also during the '90s, retailers began facing serious competition from on-line Internet sales. There were other technological advancements as well: cell phones began to proliferate, reaching a total of almost 250,000 users in Pima County by the end of the '90s; and the use of e-mail was rapidly increasing by 1995.

While technology was changing the way people shopped, worked, played, and lived, several ballot questions were voted on that helped determine major, long-term decisions for the community. One of those was a Pima County transportation election held in 1990. After the 1986 defeat of a similar measure that was heavy on road construction, proponents developed the $369 million Baja Plan that included more transit services. Despite that change, 61 percent of voters rejected the idea.

Regardless of that loss, several roads were widened or built. These included sections of I-10, and 40 years after it was conceptually proposed, Aviation Parkway from Golf Links Road to Broadway Boulevard was completed in 1996. This work replaced the second edition of the Broadway underpass with a larger, more modern looking third rendition. The entire new roadway was then renamed Barraza-Aviation Parkway to honor local Chicano activist Maclovio Barraza who was instrumental in founding the National Council of La Raza—"the most comprehensive Latino advocacy organization in the country."[34]

With some traffic finally using the parkway to access downtown, what to do about Barraza-Aviation's controversial last mile from Broadway to I-10 remained in flux. Estimates from 1994 were that it would cost as much as $94 million and might take 20 years to complete the required construction. (By 2014 projections were that the revised—and much reduced in size—last mile could be finished within four years at an estimated cost of $85 million. But while the roadway east of Stone Avenue was completed by early 2024, in October of that year construction work still continued west of that street.)

One other project that didn't get finished, even after more than 60 years of promises, was a solution to the flooding problems of the Stone Avenue underpass. During a 1996 monsoon storm, "Lake Elmira" almost claimed the life of a five-year-old boy whose mother drove into the flooded subway. Quick action by three men—Carlos Moreno, Carlos Razo, and Justin Coffman—saved the boy from the seven-foot-deep water. A solution to the underpass flooding problem, according to city officials, wouldn't be achieved until Aviation's last mile was finally fully implemented.

Much more tragic than the Stone Avenue incident were the deaths of eight people, including five children, in one horrific automobile crash in August 1997. The driver at fault ran a stop sign at 60 m.p.h. and may have been high on crack cocaine. That tragedy occurred in a residential area, and throughout the '90s neighborhoods across Tucson began implementing measures to try and slow cars down. Another transportation change took place when the Fifth/Sixth street traffic cones, a reversible-lane, rush-hour tradition since 1969, were removed for the last time in 1994.

Among non-automobile-oriented transportation improvements were the opening of the downtown Ronstadt Transit Center in 1991 and the northside Tohono Tadai (Desert Roadrunner) Transit Center three years later. The initiation of a volunteer operated historic trolley system along Fourth Avenue and University Boulevard occurred in 1993.

As transportation projects of various types were being implemented in the '90s, the long water saga of Tucson's Central Arizona Project (CAP) experience continued playing out. Construction work on the $110 million CAP treatment plant off of Ajo Way moved toward completion in the early '90s but consumers were warned the water could potentially be dangerous to kidney dialysis patients and tropical fish in tanks because of the chemical chloramine that was to be added as a safety precaution. The amount of total dissolved solids, tiny bits of corrosive particulate matter in the CAP water, was also expected to be triple the amount found in groundwater.

By October 1991 the CAP canal to Tucson was finished, and one year later the first of the community's treated Colorado River water started flowing to 84,000 homes.[35] Initially there were few complaints, but within months criticism of CAP water had become a tidal wave. First it was the yellowish color of the water, created in some older homes by the reaction of the treatment chemicals with galvanized pipes. Then pipes began to burst inside midtown homes as the chemicals, along with the newly reversed rotational flow of the water, sped up deterioration of the houses' old pipes. By the summer of 1993, a few local politicians were bravely calling for the CAP system to be shut off entirely. Given the severity of the problem, the Pima County Board of Supervisors, various state of Arizona officials, and even Governor Fife Symington tried to interject themselves into the controversy, with Symington asking that the CAP system be left on.

The Tucson City Council wavered for a while about shutting the system off, and eventually did so in 1994. They also created a CAP complaint office while being told at first that a fix of the problem would cost Tucson Water approximately $500,000, later raised to $73 million more in order to replace 200 miles of old main lines in the system. These continuing problems cost two Tucson Water directors their jobs, and the city council argued for years about what was the best option—trying to return to direct delivery of chemically treated CAP water to customers or recharging it into the ground before it was supplied to them.

At about the same time, and even though a plan to store CAP water in a man-made westside lake had apparently been dropped many years before, the drive by some local politicians to secure a lake for Tucson was resurrected. In June 1995, the *Tucson Citizen* was even editorializing: "Reservoir for CAP storage must be built."[36]

As all this was going on, a 1992 proposal that was adopted was important in terminating the long-held belief that Tucson Water should monopolize all water service in the urbanized area. That year the Tucson City Council decided not to take over the large Metropolitan Water District north of town, instead approving its sale to a group comprised of district customers.

That outcome, while historically noteworthy, was apparently insignificant in comparison to a move by a band of citizens who used the voter initiative process to place a proposal on the November 1995 city ballot. Referred to as Proposition 200, or the Water Consumer Protection Act, the question would let voters decide, among other things, whether to halt direct delivery of CAP water for five years while encouraging the water's use by farms and mines, not people. One of its strongest supporters was Jerry Juliani, the son of former South Tucson attorney, Harry Juliani, and his wife Lucille.[37]

From his perspective, Democrat Tucson Mayor George Miller stated: "The voters of this community should know that saying yes to [Proposition] 200 is saying no to the [CAP storage] lake."[38] Rejecting that and other arguments, 57 percent of Tucson voters approved Proposition 200. They had suffered enough from CAP, plus Tucson already had three small lakes in city parks that offered some limited recreational opportunities.

In response to the vote, the city council decided to establish large recharge basins costing an estimated $56 million on vacant land in Avra Valley within sight of the Arizona-Sonora Desert Museum. This was not a concept Proposition 200 backers endorsed because they thought the project was too expensive and that CAP water would eventually just replace the groundwater under the ponds. They instead favored recharging CAP water in area streambeds. That idea, though, was rejected by the city council in part because of the possible threat from old landfills along some of the waterways.

By the summer of 1997, opponents of Proposition 200 had filed enough signatures from registered voters to place its repeal on the ballot, in part to restore the storage lake as a possibility. That argument also failed when 59 percent of the voters rejected the measure. For its part, by early 1999 Tucson Water was beginning to test a blend of CAP and groundwater in a few neighborhoods.

Sometime later, Proposition 200 backers submitted petition signatures to place a new question on the November 1999 ballot. It would extend the proposition's provisions beyond five years while requiring CAP water be recharged in central Tucson streambeds, not in Avra Valley. Auto dealer Bob Beaudry had been instrumental in the passage of both Proposition 200 and the defeat of the 1997 attempt to repeal it. He again supplied hundreds of thousands of dollars to push the new proposal. Fellow car dealer, Jim Click, opposed the measure and indicated he and other business interests would spend up to $1 million to defeat it. That strategy worked, and the new proposition was rejected by 61 percent of the voters. Based on that outcome, recently elected Republican mayor, Bob Walkup, soon declared, "The [CAP] water war is over."[39]

In other water woes, the ongoing battle over trichloroethylene (TCE) tainted water continued throughout the decade. Hughes Aircraft Company agreed in 1991 to an $84.5 million settlement of TCE claims from about 2,000 individuals. Millions of dollars more in TCE payments were approved in 1997 for other people by the city of Tucson and the Tucson Airport Authority.

Another southside water pollution problem cost a Tucson city manager his job. In the summer of 1992, five members of the council dismissed Tom Wilson, who had replaced the long-serving Joel Valdez in 1990 after Valdez became a University of Arizona vice-president. Citing Wilson's lack of attention to leaking fuel tanks at a city service center near Ajo Way, the five also acted to protect a Tucson Fire Department whistleblower involved with the case.

Governmental Comings and Goings

Regardless of these numerous distractions, the Tucson city government did accomplish a few things. It created an Internet home page in 1996, placed some restrictions on "A" frame sandwich-board business signs, and after a 1997 election snafu, changed from a punch card to a "fill in the oval" voting system.

The related issues of annexations and incorporations also kept coming up throughout the '90s. Both Oro Valley and Marana continued pursuing their own aggressive annexation efforts, and the latter even got into an annexation duel with Tucson over two square miles of lucrative commercial property—a struggle the much smaller town finally won.

Almost all of the proposals to push the Tucson city limits north into the Catalina foothills, south along the industrial Palo Verde corridor, as well as further eastward went nowhere. As City Manager Luis Gutierrez admitted of annexation in 1996: "It's become a hard sell."[40] Some success in expanding the city limits did occur, especially when the city dealt with large parcels of mostly vacant land, such as the 1995 annexation of more than 16-square miles of property on the city's southeast side.[41]

Unlike annexations, an issue going before voters in 1995 was an incorporation effort by residents of Vail on the far southeast side. It went down to defeat by a tally of 281 to 223. The previous year, a third attempt at incorporating Green Valley also failed.

Controversially, in 1997 state legislators eased municipal incorporation rules in Pima County. For a two-year period, the legislature voided the 1961 law that gave existing cities, such as Tucson, veto power over incorporations within six miles of their boundaries. Based on that unique opportunity, voters in the Catalina foothills rejected incorporation while 3,000 people in Tortolita on the northside and 60,000 residents of nearby Casas Adobes decided to incorporate.

Mayor George Miller had aggressively, but unsuccessfully, argued against these two incorporations.[42] More effectively, the city of Tucson filed a lawsuit against the state's waiver of the six-mile rule, and that effort proved legally successful. Thus, as the decade neared an end, both Tortolita and Casas Adobes were on the road to legal extinction while their neighbors—Marana and Oro Valley—looked to carve them up through future annexations.

Oro Valley had a politically turbulent decade with several council members being recalled. The primary issue dividing the town was population growth and how to handle it, with one member of the council asserting in 1996: "developers run this town through other people."[43]

Despite that opinion, in 1994 Oro Valley adopted the first development impact fee in Pima County when it imposed a $1,035 tax on new home construction. This charge was labeled "inflated" by a representative of the Southern Arizona Home Builders Association (SAHBA) who believed it would just lead to higher home prices.[44]

Population growth was also booming in Marana as the town marked its 20th anniversary in 1997, and things were politically fairly quiet. The general philosophy of the community's governing body was to keep annexing vacant property while working to accommodate new development.

Also during the decade, Pima County's newest municipality—Sahuarita—was born. Supporters of incorporation in 1994 pushed the issue, and the election was extremely close. By a vote of 272 to 258, Sahuarita residents decided they wanted to incorporate.

Many of those people apparently wished to retain their rural lifestyle, but by 1996 a developer had announced plans for a 10,600-home project on 2,800 acres of land that would include a small lake. Thus, in 1999 the *Tucson Citizen* predicted: "If development goes as planned, the population of Sahuarita could jump nearly sevenfold in the next 20 years, from about 3,000 to more than 20,000."[45] (In actuality, by 2019 Sahuarita had approximately 31,500 residents.)

As Sahuarita was looking at rapid population growth, the landlocked city of South Tucson was actually about to grow a little in size as the 1990s came to a close. In an unusually friendly gesture, the city of Tucson was going to transfer to South Tucson a 25-acre slice of land between the tiny town's southern boundary and Interstate 10.

While rancorous political squabbling was historically common in South Tucson, generally it was unusual in the Pima County administration building, but that dramatically changed during the '90s. The decade began with contentious Supervisor Ed Moore winning a spirited 1992 re-election bid over political veteran John Kromko. Moore soon became chair of the board of supervisors, and as one of its first official acts, this board appointed Manoj Vyas as county administrator. After a few days, Vyas fired six top county officials, and within months at least four others would resign, including former county assistant manager, Chuck Huckelberry. By October 1993, though, Moore stepped down as chair, and the majority on the board soon shifted to his political opponents. By the end of 1993, Vyas had been demoted and replaced by Huckelberry. (Eventually the six administrators fired by Vyas sued the county and received a total of $3 million for their troubles, and some of them eventually even went back to work for the county.)

In 1996 voters tossed the volatile Moore out of office and replaced him with neighborhood activist Sharon Bronson. This was a result Supervisor Raúl Grijalva characterized as "a huge message for the home builders in Pima County. It says they can no longer buy elections in Pima County."[46] (Bronson would serve until 2023 when she resigned due to an injury.)

Spearheaded by land speculator Don Diamond and homebuilder William Estes, Jr., Rocking K was one huge development project Bronson had ardently opposed prior to her election. As the decade began, the concept for the far southeast side project had been downsized to include 10,000 homes and four resorts. Opponents of the proposal then collected 30,000 signatures in 1991 to place the issue before the voters, but for legally technical reasons, judges prevented that from happening. (Homes were finally being built in the first phase of the development by 2020.)

Two other controversial land-use proposals regulated by Pima County were Sabino Springs and Desert Springs. The former was a 476-home development adjacent to Sabino High School on the northeast side while the latter was a mixed-use project including a "village market and specialty boutique shops" close to Catalina State Park near Oro Valley. Attempts to refer both projects to the voters were tried—Desert Springs made it on the ballot in 1990 and was crushed at the polls by a four to one margin. Based on legal technicalities, judges kept Sabino Springs from being voted on and the development was implemented, again demonstrating the wisdom of land developers who used the court system to prevent public votes on their controversial projects.

In other development news, by 1996 the retirement community of Sun City Vistoso in Oro Valley had been built out quickly in only nine years, the last of almost 2,500 homes completed. Plans were soon unveiled to double the size of the existing Saddlebrooke "active adult" community in southern Pinal County to contain 4,000 homes. These developments reflected the increasing role those over 50 years of age were playing in home purchases, being the buyers in up to one-third of all new home sales.[47]

This home-buying trend was to be further enhanced when 6,000 houses were proposed for Canoa Ranch near Green Valley, an idea opposed by many people including astronomers at nearby Whipple Observatory on Mount Hopkins. The Pima County Board of Supervisors, after a public hearing that attracted 1,000 people, rejected the proposal in 1999, a vote that was called "the first defeat of a major local rezoning request in 25 years."[48] (Development of about 2,500 homes would later be approved for the area.)

Economy and Poverty Both Rising

Regardless of the Canoa Ranch decision, homebuilding for newcomers and retirees was booming. "Every day in Pima County, bulldozers and backhoes eat up 12 acres of desert. Every month, 580 homes get built and 1,400 newcomers arrive," was a 1999 summary regarding the impact of sprawl on Tucson's natural environment.[49]

Because of Tucson's generally low wages, however, many current residents simply could not afford a new or even an existing home. As a result, the community was consistently ranked in the bottom one-third on a national list of housing affordability. It was thus stated in 1995: "Fifty-one percent of [city of] Tucson households own[ed] their own homes during the most recent census in 1990. That was way below the national average of 65 percent."[50] (Home ownership in the city of Tucson was still 51 percent in the period 2018–2022.)[51]

Despite that, all the new residents flocking to Pima County were rapidly pushing up the total population, and projections for future growth reflected a belief that the trend would continue unabated. By 1990 Tucson was the 33rd largest city in the United States with a population of more than 405,000 people and Pima County in total was home to almost 667,000. Predictions were made that by 2050 between 1.7 and 2.75 million people might live in Pima County.[52] (The population of Pima County in 2024 was estimated to be about 1.07 million people.) To some residents, though, that was not necessarily good news. "The essence of Tucson is changing," one person lamented in 1994, "and the essence of what Tucson was is disappearing."[53]

It was people seeking jobs that was the biggest factor in driving up the Pima County population numbers. The '90s began with an unemployment rate around 3.5 percent, but then the nation as well as the local economy went through a short, but significant, downturn with unemployment in Tucson rising above 6 percent. One supposed cause of this uptick, the *Tucson Citizen* editorialized near the end of 1991, was: "Domination of City Hall by noisy no-growthers and NIMBYs [Not in My Back Yard] has damaged Tucson's economy and image. The message to business has been 'No Help Wanted.'"[54]

By 1993 the local economy had begun to strongly rebound, and Tucson was being called an economic "hot property." Even with that rapid local job growth, the occasional economic comparisons between Tucson and Phoenix were misplaced, at least in the view of Elliott Pollack, a Scottsdale, Arizona, economist. "Phoenix and Tucson aren't in the same league anymore," Pollack said in 1997, comments that would have been extremely painful to generations of earlier Tucson political and business leaders. "Tucson is a small town and Phoenix is a major metropolitan area."[55]

While the decade was mostly an economic boom period for Tucson, a shift in the job market that had previously begun was intensified. A 1992 *Tucson Citizen* headline inquired optimistically of the local economy, "Tucson Next Silicon Valley?,"[56] but in reality thousands of jobs in mining and manufacturing had been lost and replaced by lower-paying, service-sector positions. Leading this change was the emergence of telemarketing and teleservice jobs in Tucson, a field with approximately 2,000 total positions in 1990. These jobs paid around $6–$7/hour, and their total numbers increased rapidly. American Airlines opened a call center for up to 1,000 employees in 1991, and Sears, Roebuck added 1,200 part-time positions to its existing telecatalog center in 1992. As the decade came to a close, Tucson had more than 10,000 call-center workers, and wages at some of the companies had risen to between $8–$10/hour.

Other economic development news included Microsoft, to much fanfare, announcing in 1995 it would bring about 1,200 high-paying technical support jobs over five years to Tucson. "To have a company as well-known open up a location here is simply wonderful," gushed Mayor George Miller about the Microsoft news.[57] Less than a year after opening a small operation in Tucson, however, Microsoft decided to pull out of town due to low demand for its services, thus costing the community "bragging rights" that came with the company's brand.[58]

Additional industries and firms making news during the decade included Bombardier Inc. from Canada in 1990 buying Learjet, and it began increasing the number of its Tucson employees, reaching approximately 1,800 by 1999. Also, after almost 120 years of Southern Pacific serving Tucson's rail needs, in 1996 the Union Pacific Railroad Company bought out its longtime rival.

The U.S. led Operation Desert Storm against Iraq in early 1991 resulted in good economic news for Tucson because missiles produced at Hughes Aircraft were used in the military campaign. The short war, on the other hand, brought out hundreds of protestors downtown as well as many supporters on the UA campus. One student thought that if the U.S. hadn't taken on Iraq in 1991: "we'd be doing it 10 years from now—when they had nuclear arms."[59] A few people with Tucson connections were killed in the brief conflict, including Davis-Monthan pilot Lt. Patrick B. Olson. To welcome back those who fought, a parade was held in May and watched by about 6,500 people.

Around the same time as the war was coming to a conclusion, and with the concurrent collapse of the Soviet Union, defense industries across the nation and in Tucson were looking at converting away from exclusive military production. Then things quickly changed, and by 1993 Hughes Missile Systems, formerly Hughes Aircraft, was planning to add 2,000 local workers making on average more than $50,000 annually, thanks in part to a multimillion-dollar finanacial subsidy from the city of Tucson.[60] In 1997 Hughes was sold by General Motors Corporation to the Raytheon

Company. Two years later another 2,000 employees were added in Tucson, bringing the firm's total number of local jobs to almost 8,000 as the decade ended.

In other economic news, the 1990s began with fears that Davis-Monthan Air Force Base could be closed because of federal budget cutbacks, costing the community 5,400 military and 2,200 civilian jobs. Almost 2,900 people voiced support for keeping the base open at a public hearing in May of 1990 and 3,000 more did so in August. A few in the audience, however, backed closing the base and were "booed and insulted" for expressing their opinions.[61] By April 1991 the future of the base seemed secure—it would not close.

While DM looked safe, shutting down in 1994 was the Twin Buttes copper mine close to Green Valley. Starting in 1996, however, long-term plans southeast of town were being made by ASARCO to develop a new open-pit copper mine near Sonoita that would employ up to 600. (This proposal was tabled in 1998 and later replaced by the Rosemont Mine concept that continues to be fiercely debated.) North of Tucson, copper mining at Silver Bell was growing but it was announced in 1999 that the copper mine in San Manuel would be closed, throwing 2,200 people earning $16 to $20 an hour out of work.

Other job losses included the elimination of almost 400 jobs when Lockheed left in 1995 after only five years in town while McCulloch Corporation exited in 1999, after about a decade in Tucson. McCulloch relocated many of their manufacturing jobs to Mexico, a move that was enhanced by Congressional adoption of the North American Free Trade Agreement (NAFTA). When the arrangement had been reached between the U.S., Mexico, and Canada in 1992, local Congressman Jim Kolbe predicted: "What this means is more ... trade, commerce, jobs and economic activity for Tucson and Arizona."[62] In reality, by 1999, although some trade was increasing with Mexican businesses, more than 800 jobs in Tucson had supposedly been lost because of NAFTA.[63]

On a brighter economic note, there was a growing number of well-paying software jobs in the community, with average wages around $40,000 a year. Many more jobs, however, were found in lower-paying tourism and service positions that paid less than $20,000 annually, about $5,000 a year below the 1990 national average income. As a result of this dichotomy, Allan Beigel, a vice president at the University of Arizona, observed of Tucson as early as 1992: "This is a poor community that is rapidly becoming poorer."[64] Despite that view, as a Chamber of Commerce official happily observed in 1995: "People want to live here."[65]

Tucson's dubious distinction of being a poor community was certainly borne out by statistics as well as growing demands on social service agencies. Mayor Miller highlighted this problem in a 1994 speech by pointing out that 22 percent of city residents, and 32 percent of children, lived in households earning less than the federal poverty level. "That is unacceptable," Miller stressed.[66]

Ignoring those depressing poverty figures, a 1997 citizens' ballot effort to impose a $7/hour minimum wage within the Tucson city limits was soundly defeated by voters with the Chamber of Commerce leading the opposition.[67] (Nine years after that local election decision, Arizona voters adopted an escalating $6.75 minimum wage for the state that exceeded the federal figure of $5.15 an hour.)

Also during the '90s, the public's kindness toward the poor seemed to shift. Police broke up a traditional holiday season homeless encampment near downtown's federal building in 1993, and a few months later the same step was taken against a permanent homeless camp at the base of "A" Mountain. Mayor Miller observed by the end of 1998: "More recently, we've seen a generally intolerant attitude toward homeless people. A lot of people want to drive them off the streets."[68]

Educational Issues

In aviation news, space ventures involving the University of Arizona certainly took off. The major camera and the faint-object spectrograph, both developed at the UA, were aboard the Hubble Space Telescope launched in 1990. The Pathfinder craft landed on Mars in 1997 and sent back landscape photos taken with a UA designed camera. "Today is a glorious day," beamed research scientist Peter Smith. "Those are the rocks that may hold clues to the history of Mars."[69]

Most things happening on the campus were more earthbound. The Arizona Board of Regents raised annual tuition for in-state students to $1,478 in 1990. The next year Henry Koffler stepped down as UA president and was replaced by Manuel Pacheco, former leader of the University of Houston–Downtown.

Before departing, Koffler had pushed for a branch facility to be established, believing enrollment on the main campus should not exceed 38,000, only a few thousand more than then enrolled. After the university's 1994 purchase of the former IBM plant on the far southeast side to be used primarily as a research park, the huge complex was also suggested as the branch campus location. The new school, christened Arizona International Campus (AIC), was projected to have 500 students in its first year and eventually reach up to 10,000. When the school debuted in 1996 only 45 students had actually signed up, and after its second year of operation, and with only 105 students, AIC was moved from its remote eastside location into portable classrooms on the UA campus. (Enrollment never exceeded 417; the school was ordered closed in 2001 for budgetary reasons, and then permanently shut down in 2005 having graduated approximately 200 students.)

Generally praised for his time in office, Pacheco left in 1997 and was replaced by Peter Likins from Lehigh University. A few months later, the owners of Tucson's Canyon Ranch resort, Mel and Enid Zuckerman, donated $10 million to the UA College of Medicine's new Arizona Prevention Center, the largest gift in the school's history up to that point.[70] With additional financing like this, the last year of the decade saw the campus undergoing an extensive building program, including the start of a $26 million underground Integrated Learning Center built beneath the grassy mall, a facility that would later be named in honor of Pacheco.

After a tumultuous period during the '80s, Pima Community College regained its accreditation and had a rather quiet decade. It surpassed 30,000 enrolled students for the first time in 1992, with Hispanics accounting for 23 percent of that figure, and the next year Pima launched its Desert Vista campus on the city's southwest side, bringing the total number of campuses to five—West (main), Downtown, East, and Community being the other four.

While Pima had a subdued decade, the same wasn't true of the Tucson Unified School District (TUSD). The '90s started with two budget override questions being rejected by voters even as Tucson business leaders continually pointed out the importance of education in the community's economic development efforts. William Stephenson of the Tucson Economic Development Corporation, repeating a refrain stated previously by other economic development officials, observed in 1990: "Businesses considering moving to Tucson place a high priority on the quality of a city's educational system."[71]

In 1990 George Garcia, former chief of public schools in Kansas City, Missouri, became TUSD superintendent, and among his objectives for the district was "to commit [TUSD] to multicultural, non-sexist education."[72] As one step to help accomplish that goal, in 1996 activist Salomón Baldenegro again asked the district to establish a Mexican American studies (MAS) program, a request he initially made in 1969.[73] One reason for instituting the program was to address the wide dropout gap between Anglo (7.3 percent) and Hispanic (13.8 percent) high school students.[74] At first rejected by the TUSD board, implementing the Mexican American studies program idea became a rallying cry for many people. By 1998 the TUSD school board had approved the establishment of both Hispanic studies and an Asian American program, reflecting that TUSD was becoming a district with mostly minority population students.

School districts across town were in the news for various other reasons. Catalina Foothills voters finally approved bonds for a new high school in November 1990, and the $22.5 million facility opened in 1993. The next year voters in the fast-growing Vail School District turned down bonds to build their own high school. In 1998, however, the Sahuarita School District proudly debuted its new $11 million high school.

Offering alternatives to traditional public schools, the number of publicly funded charter schools in Tucson began to mushroom. In 1996 there were only 8 charters, but within three years that total had shot up to 36. They provided an education, however, to less than three percent of Tucson's 120,000 public school students.[75]

Like TUSD, also undergoing some turmoil in the '90s were both the Amphitheater and Tanque Verde school districts. The latter threw out four school board members in a 1992 recall election spurred by the board's failure to retain a popular principal. In 1997 the Amphitheater School District board was urged to allow unrestricted public comments at its meetings, a request finally granted two years later. (That move didn't stop critics of the district from successfully recalling three members of the school board in 2000.)

Environmental Debates

Amphitheater was also involved in one of the decade's longest-running environmental battles. In 1995 the 7-inch-tall cactus ferruginous pygmy owl, that was rare in Southern Arizona, became the focus of a heated public argument. Some environmentalists, including those from the Tucson-based Southwest Center for Biological Diversity, wanted the small bird listed as an endangered species and its habitat across northern Pima County protected by the federal government. Representatives of the development industry claimed that proposed step was an attempt "on stopping Tucson's growth."[76]

Prior to the tiny owl becoming a big issue, the Amphitheater School District had purchased property in northwest Tucson for a third high school. The location was in owl habitat area, and for a while it looked as if the district would have to abandon the site and build the school elsewhere. In 1998, however, a judge decided construction could proceed and Ironwood Ridge High School opened three years later.

The pygmy owl habitat issue may have been perceived as a public setback for local environmentalists, but they also gained a major victory. In 1998 a number of environmental groups called on the county to preserve ecologically important land. "We should have a regional conservation plan and it should be science-based," declared Carolyn Campbell of the Coalition for Sonoran Desert Protection.[77] Alan Lurie of the Southern Arizona Home Builders Association responded that "growth restrictions are unnecessary because builders have to work with the desert to sell their product."[78] Rejecting that point of view, within weeks the Pima County Board of Supervisors had adopted a concept plan developed by the environmental coalition, and by 1999 County Administrator Chuck Huckelberry and his staff had identified a draft list of properties for possible acquisition while a biological assessment of critical land was underway.

Environmental focus had been directed at a much different proposal at the beginning of the decade. In September 1991, eight people entered the Biosphere 2 built near Oracle north of Tucson, intent on living a self-sustained life for two years inside the three-acre enclosure; in part it was to test if it were possible to sustain life in outer space under similar conditions. Critics of the project questioned its scientific value while calling those involved with it cult members. Within a few months of the project's start, some outside air was being pumped into the structure, but oxygen levels continued to drop and additional oxygen was added.[79] Despite that setback, 2,000 people warmly welcomed the eight people when they emerged in September 1993.

Following that ceremony, the project devolved into an ongoing public spectacle. Once a second group was sealed inside the Biosphere in early 1994, Ed Bass, the Texas oilman financing the $150 million project, replaced the program's top managers. A disgruntled employee later opened doors on the sealed structure, and one of those inside left the project in solidarity with the ousted managers. The two sides ended up in a bitter court dispute.

After the Biosphere's second mission ended, Columbia University agreed to assume management responsibility. An article in the journal *Science,* however, pointed out that Biosphere 2 had "numerous unexpected problems and surprises.... The major retrospective conclusion that can be drawn is simple," the piece concluded. "At present there is no demonstrated alternative to maintaining the viability of Earth."[80]

Other environmental news included Saguaro National Monument becoming a National Park in 1994. Plus, the Tucson Audubon Society, an active participant in many local environmental issues, celebrated its 50th anniversary before the end of the decade.

The '90s had seen a lot of shifts in Tucson—economically, socially, politically, environmentally—and the perception of the community had changed for some people while others held on to their past beliefs. "I like Tucson," one 24-year-old commented in 1998. "There's nothing wrong with it and all my friends live here. I like that we're getting bigger."[81] Around the same time, though, an article in *The Atlantic Monthly* national magazine pointed out many of the community's faults, including that "Aside from the University of Arizona—somewhat of a social and economic island—and boom-and-bust military-aircraft industries, little is [in Tucson] except low-paying service jobs and a millionaire elite that acquired its wealth by sitting on real estate rather than producing anything."[82]

The decade, the century, and the millennium would come to an end on January 1 of 2000 as Tucson, along with much of the world, celebrated the beginning of the 21st century. They could do so locally at Downtown 2000 with music and "the largest laser show in the Southwest" or in more traditional fashion by listening to Rosemary Clooney and Michael Feinstein perform with the Tucson Symphony Orchestra. For their part, Native Americans from more than 100 tribes gathered at the Rillito horse racing track for a 10-day-long "Thunder in the Desert" that featured a sunrise blessing ceremony to welcome the new century. Then, at five seconds after midnight, Tucson's first baby of the dawning millennium, a seven-pound, eight-ounce girl, was welcomed into the rapidly changing world.

• THIRTEEN •

Economic Decline but Transportation Improvements, 2000–2010

At the School of Nursing in the Banner–University Medical Center complex is a serene patio centered around a small bubbling fountain. On a nearby red brick wall rises a mosaic-tiled piece of art in the shape of a beautiful mesquite. Entitled "The Tree of Life," it is dedicated to Cheryl McGaffic, Barbara Monroe, and Robin Rogers, instructors tragically gunned down at the school in 2003.

THE EUPHORIA AMONG COMMUNITY LEADERS following the positive outcome of the May 2006 Regional Transportation Authority (RTA) election was palpable. Why shouldn't it have been? After several earlier failed attempts to increase taxes to pay for transportation improvements, the fifth time proved successful.

"If the RTA, county and all our little governments can pull this one off," a newspaper commentator remarked shortly after the balloting on the proposed $2.1 billion, 20-year plan, "there's no telling where it might take us. Regional cooperation on water, perhaps? On land-use and zoning? Imagine the possibilities."[1]

That seemed like reasonable speculation. Since the beginning of the decade, Tucson and Pima County had seen amazing growth in population and jobs, with a banner 2006 headline in the *Arizona Daily Star* proudly proclaiming: "We Hit 1 Million Today."[2] (The 2010 census, with 982,000 residents in Pima County, showed that if that seemingly magic number had been reached in 2006, then some of them had left town.)

The lead up to the 2006 transportation balloting had seen a failed 2002 city of Tucson transportation vote. Following that, light rail supporters pushed their own concept, an idea Tucson Mayor Bob Walkup labeled a "fantasy."[3] Despite that opinion, by 2003 a proposal to vastly improve public transit service while also repairing deteriorated streets was on the city ballot. Opposed by both the Chamber of Commerce and the Southern Arizona Home Builders Association (SAHBA), the measure gained less than 40 percent backing.

Walkup, Oro Valley Mayor Paul Loomis, and attorney and former urban renewal director, S.L. Schorr, then advocated for the Pima Association of Governments

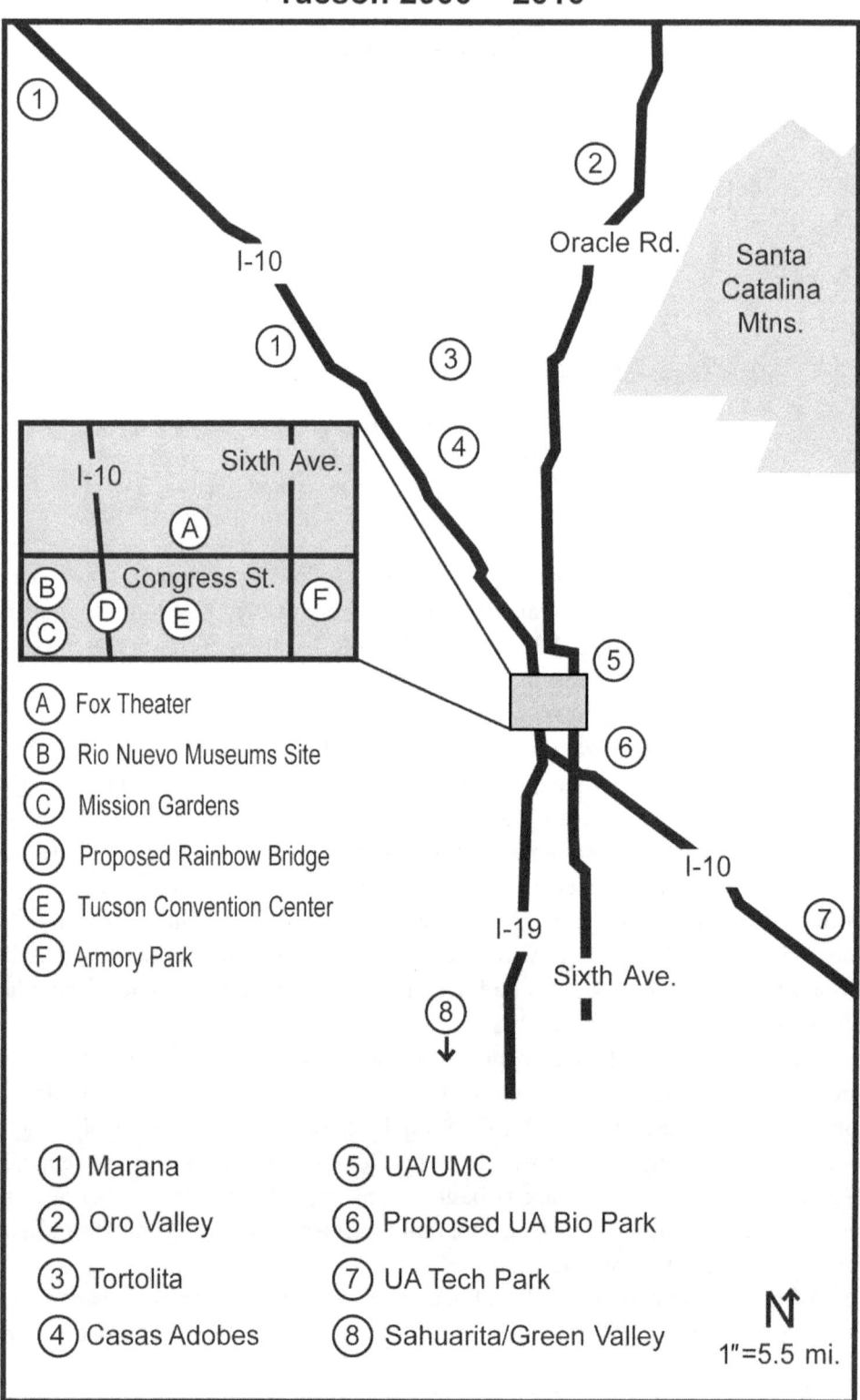

to prepare a new transportation plan and administer a one-half cent county-wide sales tax increase.[4] The plan ultimately proposed listed dozens of road projects, greater Sun Tran bus service, and 500 miles of new bike lanes and paths. It also contained a four-mile modern streetcar line running from the University Medical Center (UMC) to the anticipated main Rio Nuevo museum site on the west side of I-10—a concept called a "great people mover" by supporters but a "joke" by opponents.[5]

There was no money included in the plan for street maintenance even though the average motorist was paying an estimated $400 a year in auto repair costs due to poor road conditions.[6] Regardless, $1 million in campaign contributions backed the effort, and in May 2006 the measure was approved by a 3 to 2 margin, bringing broad smiles to the faces of local leaders who had suffered through two decades of transportation voter rejection.

The election issue didn't end there, however, since attorney Bill Risner was soon questioning the electronic voting process used to count ballots. This controversy resulted in the Arizona Attorney General's office getting involved, and it wasn't until the ballots were manually recounted in 2009 and the original results confirmed that the matter was finally resolved.

In other transportation news, some historic preservationists were upset by the loss of the 1916 Fourth Avenue underpass, sacrificed for a modern streetcar-friendly replacement. Plus, the "suicide lanes" on Broadway Boulevard (2001) and Grant Road (2004) were ended, bringing to a close Tucson's almost 37-year experiment with rush hour reversible traffic. Demanding higher wages, Sun Tran bus drivers struck once again in 2001 for 12 days.

RTA-funded projects started being implemented soon after the 2006 transportation election, elating many government officials and prominent businesspeople. Within a few years, however, discouragement and disappointment became the community's prevalent mood—with record numbers of home foreclosures and personal bankruptcies; a sharp rise in poverty; the loss of spring training baseball; and the mismanagement of the Rio Nuevo downtown improvement project, all of them glaring examples of Tucson's numerous shortcomings.

"Rio Never"

The Rio Nuevo 1999 voter-approved proposals were originally planned to feature a downtown aquarium along with an enormous Universe of Discovery, or science center, to replace the small Flandrau Planetarium on the University of Arizona campus. A westside complex including a new Arizona State Museum, the Arizona Historical Society Museum, a reconstructed Mission San Agustín and Convento, as well as the Mission Gardens project were also planned. When an initial layout for the entire concept was presented to the city council in 2001, project director John Jones remarked: "This is a vision to restore downtown Tucson as a public center for the entire community and at the same time put Tucson on the map as one of America's great cities."[7]

Doubts about the financial viability of the aquarium soon surfaced, and it was quickly dropped from consideration. University of Arizona officials then made the innovative suggestion to have the science center on both sides of I-10 and that concept evolved into a spectacular Rainbow Bridge suspending the science center from a gigantic arch above the Interstate highway. Estimated to cost $350 million, UA President Peter Likins in 2006 proclaimed of this proposal: "If the community has boldness, courage and imagination, we will have a transformed city. We will have put Tucson in a totally different space among American cities."[8]

Citing the project's costs, the university soon turned the lights off on the Rainbow Bridge. Instead, it proposed building a $130 million combination science center/Arizona State Museum on the main Rio Nuevo property west of I-10 and hoped to have both facilities open by the centennial of Arizona statehood—February 14, 2012. By early 2009, though, the university indefinitely suspended work on the project, referencing the severe economic downturn both locally and nationally.

As all this was going on, other portions of Rio Nuevo planned for west of I-10 were apparently moving forward. The Mission San Agustín and Convento reconstruction was scheduled to begin in 2007, and the Mission Gardens were slated for opening the next year. As Tucson City Manager Mike Hein proudly proclaimed in May 2007: "Tucson's time is now."[9] With nothing accomplished by the spring of 2008, and uncomfortable with the proposed construction phasing, Hein, however, put a halt to the entire westside process. Commenting on the apparently hopeless situation, an obviously frustrated *Tucson Citizen* staff penned an editorial entitled: "Let's call it 'Rio Never.'"[10]

At least stopping official government work on the Mission Gardens project didn't prevent a group of volunteers, including Tucson matriarch Cele Peterson who turned 100 years old in 2009, from pushing that idea forward. Other than their efforts, as the decade came to a close, about all that could be pointed to for years of Rio Nuevo work west of I-10 was a 15-minute, $820,000 video.

Not everything connected with Rio Nuevo was such a colossal failure, of course. Archaeological excavations near west Congress Street revealed settlement had taken place there as early as 2200 BC, meaning humans had lived at the base of "A" Mountain for more than 4,000 years. Combining millions of dollars of Rio Nuevo funding with other sources, the Fox Theater had been beautifully restored to its 1930 luster and had a dashing opening on New Year's Eve 2005. At the other end of Congress Street, the Rialto Theatre also used some Rio Nuevo money to help it reopen in early 2005, and it was an instant hit with young music fans.

Another successful use of Rio Nuevo funds was the partial recreation of El Presidio San Agustín del Tucson. This project at the corner of Church Avenue and Washington Street opened in 2007 and contained a small museum, a replica of a 20-foot high watchtower, and other items from around the time of Tucson's founding in 1775. Additionally, the Arizona Legislature in 2006 extended the length of Rio Nuevo funding for the entire project from 2013 to 2025.

While these were among Rio Nuevo's success stories, there were also plenty of other flops, including the demise of a complex of improvements adjacent to the Tucson Convention Center (TCC). Another highly visible failure of the Rio Nuevo process was the lack of follow-through on building a new, 12,500-seat arena to replace the dilapidated 9,300-seat existing facility. Also failing to materialize was a new, first-class TCC hotel. "Downtown revival and Rio Nuevo can't succeed without at least one such hotel," suggested the *Tucson Citizen* in 2006.[11] Following that advice, the city council eventually decided on a 30-story, 500-room Sheraton Hotel next to the TCC, and construction was expected to be completed by 2012. (Because of financing issues, both the hotel and arena projects were cancelled and renovations to the existing TCC delayed for several years.)

Having spent tens of millions of dollars of taxpayer's money and not having all that much to show for it, by 2008 Tucson politicians were publicly embarrassed and local residents perplexed at how much had gone wrong with Rio Nuevo. Since it was state sales tax receipts financing much of the project, members of the Arizona Legislature, on the other hand, were infuriated. As a result, in 2009 they took action to wrest control of the project away from the city of Tucson and give it to a nine-member board appointed by state leaders and with direction to focus primarily on the hotel and other TCC related issues.

As all that was occurring, other things were happening downtown. A new federal courthouse opened and was named after Evo DeConcini, the late jurist and reputed longtime friend of notorious Joe Bonanno. The Toole Avenue train depot was renovated in magnificent fashion in 2004, and not far away, some young entrepreneurs in 2007 were working to open the Sapphire Lounge, a relaxation spot for an "upscale crowd," a sure sign that things were beginning to change at least on the eastern end of downtown. In 2009, even Janos Wilder, who had moved his highly regarded restaurant at the Tucson Museum of Art to the Santa Catalina foothills many years previously, reported he would be opening a new establishment in the area. "[T]here are great things going on downtown…," Wilder suggested, "and we're really excited to be getting back there."[12]

Keep on Sprawling

Despite the overall upswing on the eastern end of downtown, one component mostly lacking from the area was the return of retail establishments. Instead, during the 2000s, many national retailers continued to move to the community's edges.

Among the chain stores dotting the Tucson landscape was Walgreen's with 33 local stores by 2001 and planning six more. (In 2024, there were approximately 36 Walgreen stores in Tucson.) The huge existing shopping center at I-19 and Irvington Road was doubled in size by the end of the decade to include J.C. Penney, Best

Buy, and an 18-screen movie theater. At El Con mall in 2007, an In-N-Out Burger debuted, and on its first day it was reported: "By 2 p.m. it was taking a good two hours for drivers to get their food, while walk-in customers were waiting about an hour and 15 minutes in line to order, then another 45 minutes to get their food."[13]

Several other changes had come to Tucson's original regional mall. At the beginning of the millennium's first decade, despite strong opposition from neighbors, the Tucson City Council authorized "Big Box" stores to locate at El Con, and Home Depot and Target opened there.

One new major shopping area—La Encantada on Campbell Avenue at Skyline Drive—got built. Controversial with its residential neighbors when first proposed, compromises were reached and the center debuted in 2003 with 22 stores, eventually expanding to almost three times that number.

Complementing these retail establishments, excitement gripped local homebuilders and homeowners early in the decade because record numbers of new homes were being constructed despite soaring real estate prices. In 1994 the median price of an existing home in Tucson had been $86,500 while a new home went for $132,300.[14] By the end of 2004, those prices had risen to $161,500 and almost $188,000, respectively.[15] Prices just kept going up from there because of the rapidly rising cost of land, higher prices for construction materials, and speculation being driven in part by investors from California.

Also increasing were government fees and taxes on new housing. Following other local governmental agencies, the city of Tucson finally adopted its own building impact fees in 2004 and increased them a few years later, adding about $9,000 to the cost of a new 2,000-square-foot home. In response, a representative of SAHBA critically remarked: "Impact fees are a real disincentive [to build].... More and more fees just push people further out, and quite frankly, it's government that's creating urban sprawl."[16]

On the other hand, Tucson's rapidly escalating home prices meant continuation of the long-standing tradition of huge numbers of households not being able to afford a home, but some steps were taken to address that issue. Since mortgage interest rates were low early in the decade, "no money down" and "adjustable rate" loans were used by financial institutions in many cases locally, as well as across the nation, to qualify potential homebuyers despite the potential risks involved.

As a record number of houses were being built year after year, according to University of Arizona economist Marshall Vest at the end of 2005: "Population growth is the engine of this [Tucson] economy.... It's a big black V-8 and it's getting a turbo charge from the real estate industry. The boom is still very much in place." Then Vest wondered: "The question is, when is the boom going to subside?"[17]

That seemed like a somewhat preposterous question with Pima County projected to more than double in population to 1.7 million people between 2000 and 2040.[18] (Current projections are by 2040 Pima County will have 1.2 million residents.) Much of this new growth was expected to occur in the suburban centers of

Vail, Sahuarita, Marana, and Oro Valley. One real estate agent even remarked of the latter community: "It's becoming a junior Scottsdale [Arizona]."[19]

With population growing at a steady clip and housing being built at a record rate, things looked bright as 2006 came to a close. "We are steaming," exclaimed one local commentator.[20] Then things began to rapidly change. Indications of a pending bust had been seen earlier when personal bankruptcies rose and the number of home foreclosures followed suit. At first these foreclosures were concentrated on Tucson's south and west sides of town where large numbers of minority and less-affluent people had subprime, or above market rate, mortgages they couldn't afford. Then the foreclosure problem spread like a wildfire across the entire community, fueled by increased unemployment and the resetting of many adjustable rate mortgages.

At the same time, the issuance of new home permits slowed from more than 11,000 county wide in 2005 to less than 5,000 two years later. Home prices were also sinking, in part because of the number of foreclosures flooding the market, often as "short" sales, or less than the mortgage amount. By the end of 2009, the median price of a new home was $182,000 and $158,000 for an existing house, both figures lower than they had been five years earlier.[21] Thus, as the decade came to a close, an estimated one-third of all homes in Pima County were "underwater," or worth less than the mortgage amount.

As a result of the slowdown, there was a drastic loss in the number of construction jobs—dropping from almost 30,000 in early 2006 to about one-half that number by the end of the decade. Growth and development had been major components of the Tucson economy for many years, along with government and military-related jobs, tourism, and service sector employment. In addition, the thousands of positions in the emerging call-center industry had seemingly positioned Tucson well economically. Vest had even stated at the end of 2006: "If you think we've seen a lot of growth in just the past few years, we ain't seen nothing yet…. Just wait."[22] Then the collapse of the local housing industry combined with a deep national recession quickly made that prognosis obsolete, and Tucson entered an extended period of slow or no economic and population growth as well as rapidly rising unemployment. "If you have a job, for heaven's sake, hold on to it," was the suggestion Vest gave to Tucson employees at the end of 2008.[23] That proved to be sage advice since by October 2009 the local unemployment rate had topped eight percent, lower than the national figure but still remarkably high based on Tucson's employment history.

Several traditional economic foundations of the community were substantially shrinking during the decade. These included filmmaking that brought only $2.5 million into the local economy in 2001 as compared to $28 million seven years earlier.[24] Cotton farming, with a mere 9,000 acres under cultivation in 2002, was down more than 30,000 acres from the mid-'80s,[25] while cattle ranching had dropped from 45,000 head in Pima County in 1999 to 15,000 eight years later.[26] Also on this list of traditional industries that were fading from view was copper mining that was at 1,700 workers in Pima County by 2001, down from about 9,000 in the mid-'70s.[27]

There were a few economic bright spots, of course. Because of the wars in Afghanistan and Iraq, U.S. Department of Defense expenditures in Pima County rose considerably. Shoppers coming from Mexico increased their spending to almost $1 billion in 2009, and tourism continued to bring in more than $2 billion to the local economy. Plus, a "conservative [2001] estimate" was that annually $350 million worth of marijuana was being distributed from Tucson. That meant the illegal activity had become a major local economic component and placed it "within [monetary] reach of some of Tucson's better known industries."[28]

Generally, however, the decade was more negative than positive for some specific companies. After only 11 years in Tucson, Weiser Lock in 2000 announced it was moving most of its manufacturing jobs to Mexico, then a few years later completely shut down its local operation.

Coming to the southeast side of town in 2002, however, was Slim Fast, which was labeled "the biggest catch by Tucson's economic boosters in the past five years."[29] Within two years, though, because of manufacturing process issues, the firm pulled its $20/hour jobs out of town and was later replaced by La Costeña, a Mexican-food company doing business as Arizona Canning.

Call centers, including Sprint, APAC, AOL, and GEICO, continued to hire so that by 2004 it was reported that the industry employed 16,000 people at 44 locations around town with an average wage of about $9/hour.[30] By 2006 the typical wage had risen to between $10 and $13/hour, but after the economic downturn, pay stagnated and the number of employees dropped to around 12,000.

The UA's Science and Technology Park on the southeast side was home to thousands of jobs, including IBM and Raytheon, and a new, park-owned 72,000 square-foot building opened there in 2003. The university's foray into developing a southside biotechnology center, however, was much less successful. In 2006, the UA unveiled plans to develop a bio park along Kino Boulevard south of 22nd Street on the former site of a small 1930s-era downtown airport. It was anticipated the location would "attract the best and brightest biotechnology minds in the world to Tucson."[31] By 2007 projections were that the park's first phase, including the construction of six buildings, could be completed within two years, and by the end of 2009 a ceremonial groundbreaking event was even held. (In actuality, the first building, at what was relabeled the UA Tech Park at The Bridges, opened in 2022 and was occupied mostly by university offices, technology firms associated with the university, or Raytheon. The second building also opened in 2022 and was built "to accommodate balloon-borne astronomy." A planned third building will be the new home of AZPM, the local public radio and television stations.)[32]

In other business news: locally founded Burr-Brown was sold to Texas Instruments for $7.6 billion in 2000, and two years later the company began laying people off from its Tucson plant, going from 1,250 employees down to approximately 300. In 2005, Tucson-based First Magnus Financial Corporation had been listed as one of the 500 fastest growing companies in the U.S., but two years later it was out of business, felled by the national mortgage crisis—its 800 local employees instantly unemployed.

Becoming Even Poorer

Those people joined a growing cadre without work and with little or no prospects for finding another decent-paying job. As a result, Pima County's poverty rate, which had actually lost a couple of points during the 1990s down to 15.2 percent, began rising steadily once again, and by 2006 Tucson was ranked the 33rd poorest major city in the United States.[33] (By 2022, poverty in Pima County was almost 15 percent, meaning its rate was 10th highest out of 12 major Southwestern cities.)[34]

As the decade began, in addition to rising poverty levels, local wages were only about 79 percent of the national average.[35] Thus, even though the cost of living in town was just slightly below the U.S. figure, because of lower wages, the number of people in Southern Arizona relying on some type of food assistance had exceeded an astonishing 300,000 by 2001.[36] Additionally, the number of homeless people living on the street in Tucson had reached an estimated 5,000 by 2004.[37] Another negative effect of the wage statistics was that many recent college graduates left town, some for Phoenix, seeking better pay. As one commentator noted of this long-term trend which for only a short period had been reversed several decades earlier: "Our best and brightest tend to go other places."[38]

It was the Greater Tucson Economic Council (GTEC) that was responsible for trying to overcome these daunting challenges and diversify the economy by bringing high-paying jobs to the community.[39] During the 2000s, however, GTEC had three directors, two transformations, and one seemingly unshakable reputation for not being very successful. By 2005, GTEC itself was gone, replaced eventually by TREO (Tucson Regional Economic Opportunities), the region's 12th economic development organization since 1950.

Warnings that Tucson was getting bigger but poorer were often issued. By 2007, reacting to the high rate of illiteracy in Tucson, one exasperated businessman stressed, "You have a very frustrated business community here that wants to compete globally and is not finding the quality of employees that they need."[40] In trying to explain this depressing economic situation, Vest from the UA reflected in 2009: "We haven't had much luck in recruiting [new industry] in the last decade.... We just have trouble getting quality jobs because of the quality of the work force, and that reflects the quality of education.... They've [Arizona state government] been doing it for the last couple of decades, shortchanging education in this state."[41]

The lack of financial investment in education was obvious with statistics continuing to show the state at or near the bottom for public school funding as well as for higher education. Plus, it wasn't only the state legislature that was withholding education money. Voters in Tucson on a regular basis refused to allow school districts to exceed their state spending maximums, defeats that included Pima

Community College (2002); Tucson Unified School District (2004, 2008, and 2009); Sahuarita (2009); Vail (2009); and Amphitheater (2009). Some spending override measures did pass, of course, including in the Sunnyside district in 2007. But possibly because of the generally poor personal economic situation combined with the chaotic performance of some school boards and administrators, many voters repeatedly decided not to support their local districts. Thus, in Pima County there was regular rejection of operational override requests, leading to a 2009 editorial headline in the *Arizona Daily Star* depressingly concluding: "Phoenix values education more than Tucson."[42]

In response to the deep cuts made in financial assistance to the University of Arizona by the state legislature, tuition began to skyrocket. Early in the 2000s, one year at the UA cost an Arizona resident $2,412, but by 2009 the price was $6,855. Even so, campus enrollment continued to grow, reaching almost 34,000 full-time equivalent students in 2009. Repeating a series of past failures, one change that didn't occur at the UA was planning to somehow cap the enrollment figure at around 40,000. President Peter Likins again pushed the idea in 2002, but the proposal went nowhere. In 2006, Likins stepped down as president after nine years and was replaced by Robert Shelton from the University of North Carolina. In 2008, Shelton interestingly insisted "We should focus on quality over quantity" even as campus enrollment continued to climb.[43]

Also with a new leader was Pima Community College. In 2003, Roy Flores replaced the retiring Robert Jensen and took over a growing institution. Other education changes in Tucson included new high schools opening in various districts: Ironwood Ridge (2001) in Amphitheater and both Cienega (2001) and Empire (2005 as an all-wireless laptop technology school) in Vail. In addition, the long-debated Tanque Verde High School finally opened in 2005.

In other education news, when school ended in May 2003, Tucson Unified School District (TUSD) had less than 59,000 students, a drop of more than 4,000 in five years.[44] During the same period, the Vail and Sahuarita school districts had grown rapidly. The number of charter schools was also expanding quickly, and by 2002 there were 5,000 students in these nontraditional public schools. Meanwhile, the Catholic diocese of Tucson opened two new parochial high schools—the eastside St. Augustine and Immaculate Heart on the northwest side—and the existing Salpointe Catholic High School marked its 50th anniversary in 2000. Then three years later, county voters approved the creation of the Joint Technological Education District (JTED) that would "finance new and existing career and technical education programs throughout Pima County."[45]

Rightfully or not, TUSD was the target of much public criticism, in part the result of continually shrinking enrollment. Blame was put on sprawl and charter schools, and TUSD officials promised to address the decline. The enrollment losses continued, however, and to help balance the district's budget, by 2008 Superintendent Roger Pfeuffer was proposing the closure of four elementary schools, including

Ochoa that was labeled a "treasure" by its supporters. After intense public opposition to Pfeuffer's recommendation, the TUSD board decided not to close any schools even though the steady drop in enrollment continued.

Another controversy flared up for TUSD in 2006 when Dolores Huerta, an associate of Cesar Chavez, spoke to an assembly at Tucson High School and proclaimed: "Republicans hate Latinos."[46] Outraged, Arizona's superintendent of public instruction, Republican Tom Horne, sent his deputy, Margaret Garcia-Dugan, from Phoenix to offer a counterpoint.

By the following year, Horne was pointing his political spotlight on the district's Mexican American Studies (MAS) program, calling the classes "ethnic chauvinism."[47] Although test scores showed students in these courses did better than their counterparts, at a news conference disturbed by hecklers, Horne insisted the students "should be taught that this is the land of opportunity and that, if they work hard, they can achieve their goals. They should not be taught that they are oppressed."[48] Working with members of the legislature, Horne then successfully pushed adoption of a state law that would mandate that public schools could not offer classes that "are designed primarily for pupils of a particular ethnic group [or] advocate ethnic solidarity instead of the treatment of pupils as individuals."[49]

The Border and Hard-Won Social Changes

Similar passions were displayed on both sides of the debate concerning people crossing the Mexican border. Proponents of greater security wanted more enforcement while others pointed out the immense toll being extracted in human lives. By October 1, 2000, more than 615,000 people had been apprehended trying to cross the Tucson sector's section of the border in the previous 12 months, an incredible increase of 145,000 in just one year. In May 2001, 14 crossers perished in the Southern Arizona desert heat in one day. Shortly after that, the Pima County Board of Supervisors designated $25,000 for water stations staffed by the Humane Borders group—but deaths kept climbing. By the end of 2002, a total of 145 deaths had occurred that year in Southern Arizona.

In response to the enormous number of desert deaths, several humanitarian groups emerged to try and stem the tide. The Rev. John Fife, who more than 20 years earlier had been involved with the Sanctuary movement, remarked: "It's not only legal to help provide aid to migrants, it's right, it's good and it's necessary."[50]

Opponents of illegal immigration, on the other hand, concentrated much of their criticism on the expense of providing American health care to foreigners along with the perceived threat of increased crime. In 2002, a Mexican criminal murdered Organ Pipe Cactus National Monument park ranger Kris Eggle. Assaults on other U.S. agents and unarmed crossers by criminals were escalating at the same time, and the environmental impact of the huge number of immigrants leaving trash and disturbing wildlife was becoming more acute.

On the border enforcement front, in May 2001, U.S. Attorney General John Ashcroft optimistically declared: "We believe we are beginning to get fundamental control of the situation."[51] Then 9/11 occurred and everything changed. Discussion of national immigration reform quickly vanished, and by 2005 the head of the Border Patrol's Tucson sector indicated his main job "is to watch out for terrorists and terrorist activity."[52] At the same time, the number of Border Patrol agents kept growing and reached 3,300 in the Tucson sector by 2009, almost tripling in number during the decade. After the economic slowdown occurred, a significant downturn in apprehensions took place, hitting a decade low at around 241,000 in 2009, or less than one-half the decade's high number mark.

Earlier, Arizona, voters had approved a ballot measure in 2000 that "would require that all public-school instruction be conducted in English."[53] Four years later, another proposition, this one entitled "Protect Arizona Now" by its supporters, was on the ballot. It was "aimed at keeping illegal immigrants from voting and receiving some government services" and passed by a 56–44 percent margin even though it was turned down in Pima County.[54]

Another group facing confrontation from the Arizona ballot box was homosexuals. In 2008, voters approved a constitutional amendment that defined marriage as between a woman and a man. (In October 2014, however, a federal court overturned this ban and gay marriages began in Arizona.) On the other hand, in 2000 a gay man had been stabbed outside a Fourth Avenue coffee shop by an assailant who declared: "Jesus hates fags, and this is what all fags deserve."[55] In response to this attack, 1,500 people held a march and Mayor Bob Walkup told the crowd: "We're not going to stand for this [hate] in Tucson."[56] Tragically, two years later Philip Walsted, a gay man, was beaten to death with a baseball bat near his university area home by a man who at his trial three years later exclaimed: "I have no remorse, no guilt, no regrets. I have and I will kill for my beliefs."[57]

At the beginning of the decade on the UA campus, a report showed that women were 27 percent of the university faculty, up from 17 percent in 1985, but still lagging behind the other two state universities. Women on campus also continued to be paid less than men—but by 2004 they did make up 53 percent of the students and received 55 percent of the awarded degrees.

In other parts of the community, prominent women in the labor force were becoming more visible. By 2006, Sharon McDonough had risen to the rank of battalion chief for the Tucson Fire Department and was named one of four working Mothers of the Year by a national publication. That type of change wasn't being shown at Tucson Country Club, however, where decades earlier there were problems because of the prohibition of Jews. In 2009, a civil rights complaint was filed: "saying the club discriminates against women by having a 'men's grill,' men-only tee times and membership policies that favor men."[58] Since the club was a private entity, the Arizona Attorney General's office dismissed the claim.

Significant population shifts were simultaneously taking place in Pima County.

The 2000 census revealed that Spanish was the sole language spoken in the homes of 180,000 people, up from 42,000 a decade earlier. There were also almost 5,000 Hispanic students on the university campus by 2002, a number that impressed longtime activist and UA employee, Salomón Baldenegro, because of its continued growth over the years.[59] That number, though, translated into only 13 percent of the students, slightly more than one percentage point higher than the 1994 figure. In response, local Chicana spokeswoman Lorraine Lee reflected: "For the last 30 years, the UA has done a very poor job of recruiting Hispanics."[60]

On the other hand, the new century had definitely brought substantial changes to Tucson's Native American communities. In 2003 the Tohono O'odham Nation elected their first woman—Vivian Juan-Saunders—as tribal chair. The following year, Herminia Frias became the first female chair of the Pascua Yaqui tribe, and also the first impeached from office when she was ousted in 2007.

At about the same time, revenues from their casinos were allowing the Tohono O'odham to distribute periodic checks to its membership. The nation in 2001 had opened a new casino south of town at I-19 and Pima Mine Road, then in 2007 replaced its casino on Old Nogales Highway with a much more elaborate $80 million complex that included a 150-room hotel. Meanwhile, at the Pascua Yaqui tribe's Casino of the Sun, around 75 percent of employees were tribal members, and by 2001 the tribe had opened a new facility—Casino Del Sol—that featured not only gambling but an outdoor concert venue seating 4,400.

Exclusive tribal gaming in Arizona was put to a statewide vote in 2002 by three competing ballot questions, one of which proposed also allowing slot machines at existing horse and dog racing tracks. After an expensive and bruising campaign, the single measure that barely passed did so only because of its large support in Pima County. This successful ballot initiative allowed only Native American casinos to install additional slot machines and for the first time to offer roulette and table games like poker, craps, and blackjack, thus becoming more like Las Vegas venues. In exchange the tribes would pay the state up to eight percent of their revenues.

Play Time Ups and Downs

Even as Tucson's casinos were expanding the types of gambling games they could offer, many other forms of entertainment, recreation, and culture were available. Marking important anniversaries during the decade were the Arizona International Film Festival (10th in 2001), the Arizona-Sonora Desert Museum (50th in 2002), and the International Mariachi Conference (20th in 2002). The following year saw the 20th anniversary of the Loft Theater's weekly showing of *The Rocky Horror Picture Show*. The Tucson Gem and Mineral Show, that attracted tens of thousands of visitors to town, marked its 50th anniversary in 2004. Other anniversaries included the Tucson Symphony (75th in 2003), the Tucson Pops Orchestra under Lazzlo Veres (50th in 2005), and an ever-larger All Souls' Procession (20th) in 2009.

In 2005, after many decades downtown, a new Chinese Cultural Center opened on River Road. Just getting started on the UA campus were two annual events: the Tucson Poetry Festival (2008) and the Festival of Books (2009)—the latter a springtime gathering that was to prove extremely popular.

Conversely, there were some entertainment losses. The eastside El Dorado, the midtown Catalina, and the drive-in DeAnza movie theaters all shut down, victims of ever-larger multiplexes and greater availability of in-home movies. Also closing after 38 years of providing fine-dining experiences was the upscale Tack Room restaurant, leaving only its iconic concrete boot sign on Sabino Canyon Road as a reminder.

From the world of sports there were also many stories of interest. Tucson's annual college football bowl game, the last incarnation of which was known as the Insight.com Bowl, departed for Phoenix in 2000. Two years later, three former UA golfers—Annika Sorenstam, Lorena Ochoa, and Don Pooley—all won professional tournaments on the same 2002 weekend. Then in 2004, after many years, the Ladies Professional Golf Tour stopped coming to Tucson because a corporate sponsor couldn't be secured. By 2007, however, the world's best male golfers were participating in a match play tournament at the Dove Mountain resort in Marana.

While the golf tournament was considered a major plus for the community, a huge blow was felt when Tucson lost its three spring training baseball teams. Even though Tucson Electric Park was a known money-losing operation for Pima County, estimates were that visiting fans annually contributed $30 million to the local economy. Nonetheless, first the Chicago White Sox broke their 15-year contract five years early and pulled out of town in 2008 for the financially greener pastures of Maricopa County; then the Colorado Rockies and Arizona Diamondbacks followed two years later. As the *Tucson Citizen* declared dejectedly when the White Sox announced they were leaving: "We're being stabbed in the back."[61]

Tucson's AAA minor league baseball team, the renamed but still poorly attended Sidewinders, won the Pacific Coast League and Triple-A championship in 2006. A couple of years later they also departed, leaving for Reno, Nevada, after being sold to new ownership. (While in 2011 AAA baseball returned to Tucson in the form of the Padres for three seasons, it was known from the beginning this was only a temporary arrangement while a new stadium was built for the team in downtown El Paso.)

Remaining in town and continuing to win on the diamond was the UA softball team. They won three NCAA championships during the decade, the 2007 triumph being called "Mowatt Miracle" after hurler Taryne Mowatt's unbelievable pitching performance.[62]

The UA football program wasn't nearly as successful and the team had a nine-year string of non-winning seasons until breaking that streak in 2008. Some UA athletes were also not very successful in the classroom. A 2002 report indicated only 44 percent of all campus athletes graduated within six years, compared to 60 percent nationwide at peer institutions. The men's basketball team had a zero percent rating in that survey.[63]

The basketball program faced many other serious challenges. In 2007, longtime Hall-of-Fame coach, Lute Olson, hired former assistant Kevin O'Neill, and then for personal reasons—a divorce—Olson took an extended leave of absence. O'Neill took charge for the season while being named successor-in-waiting. That arrangement collapsed after Olson returned to the program in April 2008—but he would never coach another game. Citing a stroke, Olson stepped down before the next season began, and the UA, after some intense drama, would eventually hire Sean Miller for $2 million a year as the new head coach, ending the Olson era.

However, it was the conclusion of the 2001 basketball season that some people would remember even more vividly. The team made it to the NCAA championship game before losing to Duke, and about 3,000 fans welcomed them home at a campus rally. The *Tucson Citizen* also reported that during a large, disruptive gathering along downtown's Fourth Avenue: "Police fired rubber bullets and pepper spray into crowds and arrested 17 people after cars were overturned and an RV set afire following Arizona's [82–72] loss in last night's NCAA basketball championship game."[64]

Civic leaders hoped the riot wouldn't damage the community's national image, but the fallout from that evening certainly proved detrimental to the reputation of the Tucson Police Department (TPD). A citizens' panel appointed to investigate the melee concluded that seven TPD officers should be punished for their actions, but no one was fired or demoted. In addition, an innocent bystander lost an eye after being hit by one of an estimated 450 beanbags and other projectiles used by the police, and the injured man was awarded $765,000. One unruly participant in the destructive melee was sentenced to a year in jail for his actions.

Crime, Medicine, Municipal Matters

Another crime-related story concerned the Tucson Catholic Church's attempt to deal with pedophile priests working in the diocese. In 2001, Bishop Manuel Moreno publicly and privately apologized for their disturbing crimes that had been committed over several decades. The diocese soon settled 11 lawsuits for a reported $14 million and the number of priests involved continued to rise, eventually reaching 28. By 2003, Moreno was replaced by Bishop Gerald Kicanas, and there were more legal settlements, including one for $1.8 million. These payouts helped drive the diocese into bankruptcy court in 2004. Later, even more abuse claims resulted in greater than $10 million in additional settlements before the diocese emerged from bankruptcy in 2005.

Throughout Tucson's past, much more common than basketball riots or pedophile priests was murder. In the 21st century, police attributed many of these slayings to "the bad killing the bad" with gang activity being a suspected prime cause.

Although the total number of homicides decreased after 2000 before spiking again later in the decade to record-setting numbers, some killings stood out. One horrible event was the 2002 shooting of three professors at the UA School of Nursing by a depressed 41-year-old student who then took his own life.[65]

Both the use and distribution of drugs also contributed to many murders in Tucson. By 2008 it was stated: "According to the [federal] Drug Enforcement Administration, 70 percent of the drugs that come into the country travel through Tucson."[66] One local police officer ominously added: "Drugs is [sic] an industry here."[67]

That industry resulted not only in many murders but also in the proliferation of numerous homes, or stash houses, used for drug drop-offs. In addition, there were high rates of other crimes, including property thefts, a category in which Tucson led the nation three times during the decade. Local police attributed these lofty rankings as much to record-keeping methodology as to actual crimes, but both the number of stolen cars in the community and thefts of things like bicycles at the University of Arizona were extraordinarily high. Additionally, the community had an inordinately large number of child abuse cases, most of which were related to illegal drug use.

Trying to combat all that crime was difficult because the city of Tucson had been habitually understaffed with police officers. In 2004, TPD had 1.8 officers per 1,000 people, well below the national average for major cities of 2.9. (By 2023, the number of TPD officers was 830, meaning the percentage of officers per 1,000 people had fallen to 1.6) That was one reason why a ballot proposition was promoted in 2009 to require the city to have 2.4 officers per 1,000 population within five years. In justifying their support for this measure, the presidents of the Tucson Police Officers Association and the Tucson Firefighters Association ominously stated: "The fact is, Tucson is not a safe place to live, work or play."[68] Opponents countered that the measure would strip elected officials of much of their budgetary decision-making capabilities, and the proposition was handily defeated.

Also during the decade, two TPD officers lost their lives in the line of duty. In 2003 Patrick Hardesty was shot pursing a violent criminal, and Erik Hite was gunned down five years later by a deranged man.

The 2005 death of another law enforcement officer—Timothy Graham—once again focused attention, at least for a little while, on Arizona's treatment of the mentally ill. Graham, a 30-year-old Pima County Sheriff's Department deputy, was trying to calm a bipolar and schizophrenic man who earlier that day had been released from a hospital's psychiatric unit. Assisting Graham was Good Samaritan cab driver Dawud Abusida. During the struggle, all three men tumbled into Ajo Way and were fatally run over by a truck. In response to this loss of life as well as to help the 6,000 seriously mentally ill people estimated to live in Pima County, voters in 2004 and again in 2006 approved bond funds to build a new psychiatric facility near Kino Hospital.

With Kino's mounting debts totaling at least $69 million accumulated during a nine-year period, in 2004 the hospital was finally turned over to University

Physicians Incorporated (UPI), the same group of doctors that operated University Medical Center.[69] To financially transition Kino out of debt, the Pima County Board of Supervisors agreed to subsidize it with a total of $127 million spread across a decade. Former state representative John Kromko argued this deal was using public funds to enrich a private corporation, but in 2005 County Administrator Chuck Huckelberry commented of the change in management: "They [University Physicians Healthcare—UPH] were the last chance for Kino and absent them we frankly would probably be shutting the facility down."[70]

Not surprisingly, the required county subsidies greatly exceeded the initial estimates. Instead of the projected $10 million for 2007, the facility, renamed UPH Hospital at Kino, was budgeted for $25 million. While huge county subsidies kept flowing, services and care at the hospital, at least in the opinion of some, were improving.

In other medical news, Pima County reported in 2001 that there had been more than 2,000 cases of AIDS or HIV identified since 1983, but the rate of new cases was falling substantially. In 2006, El Dorado Hospital along Wilmot Road on the eastside was in the process of closing just as a new 96-bed hospital—Northwest Medical Center Oro Valley—was opening

Other things occurring in Oro Valley included a commercial building boom early in the decade soon followed by an intense political debate over financial incentives the town was providing to attract even more sales-tax-generating establishments. Then, during the economic downturn, instead of firing employees, the town froze positions and asked volunteers to help out.

Nearby Marana took a different approach during the national recession including furloughs of municipal workers, voluntary employee payroll reductions, and most of its seven council members refusing to accept a pay raise. The once rural community of 1,600 people at the time of its founding in 1977 had exploded to about 35,000 residents by 2010.

Sahuarita south of Tucson was also growing explosively, and its signature element, a 10-acre lake stocked with fish, was completed early in 2002. Before then, a town mayor had resigned after "criticizing some council members as being too pro-development," and another council member was successfully recalled from office in 2001.[71]

Despite common municipal political squabbles like those, at least two other parts of Pima County wanted to incorporate, but not Green Valley. The voters of the retirement community south of Tucson turned down the idea for the fourth time in March 2001.

On the north side, though, the previous 12 months had seen a flurry of activity regarding the proposed Casas Adobes and Tortolita incorporations. Using the legal system, the city of Tucson had successfully foiled earlier attempts by the two communities to incorporate. Both fledgling cities thus sought to try again to form municipalities, but only Casas Adobes was given the go-ahead to vote by Tucson.

"The stooges for development want our vacant land," Tortolita attorney Bill Risner suggested of the opposition to incorporate the lush desert that made up that community. "So the neighbors [Tucson] would not give Tortolita the chance."[72]

Breaking with decades of opposition to just about every past attempt to form new municipalities in Pima County, the Tucson City Council in 2000 had, however, decided to stay out of a second Casas Adobes incorporation election. The campaigning was intense with the foes of incorporation prevailing by a 56 to 44 percent margin. As a result, in the spring of 2001, the former towns of Tortolita and Casas Adobes no longer existed.

Pima County's second municipality—South Tucson—was still around after more than 60 years. In 2000 it was reporting a dramatic drop in crime as well as an improving economy, and five years later, having served seven two-year terms as mayor, Shirley Villegas stepped down from the office.

In addition to its Rio Nuevo follies, the city of Tucson had a difficult decade in several other respects. It had four managers during the 2000s because one (Gutierrez) retired, one (James Keene) departed for another job, one (Hein) was fired, and the last one (Mike Letcher) was recently hired. (Letcher was fired in 2011 and replaced by Richard Miranda, who retired in the summer of 2014.) While this administrative shuffle was going on, Mayor Bob Walkup tried to resurrect the long-debated consolidated government concept. "If Tucson is to succeed in the 21st century," Walkup forecast in 2003 of the nearly 100-year-old idea, "we must consolidate two local governments [city and county] into one metropolitan government."[73] Just like the same suggestion that had been made so many times in the past, the idea went nowhere.

Some things were accomplished by the city, however. After years of haggling about the hundreds of huge billboards that still dotted the city, the issue was resolved with an agreement between city hall and Clear Channel Outdoor Inc. to remove more than 100 of the signs. Plus, after fighting over the measure years earlier, the city of Tucson smoothly transitioned from twice-weekly garbage service to once-a-week garbage and recycling pickups in 2002, and the latter program was instantly popular.

At least the city council, for a number of reasons, didn't have to deal with too many contentious water issues. Without major problems, Tucson Water began delivery of Central Arizona Project (CAP) water after it was recharged and blended with groundwater in Avra Valley. During the previous decade, however, thousands of claims had been filed against the city after its initial disastrous introduction of chemically treated CAP water, and they were finally settled for approximately $2 million. With much of Tucson Water's CAP allocation being recharged and then delivered to customers, the water table in central Tucson began rising. Concurrently, per capita use of water was falling rather dramatically, dropping by almost 20 percent between 1997 and 2007.[74]

At the same time, additional sources of water were being pursued, partially because of questions raised about the reliability of the CAP canal water during a period of higher temperatures and extended drought. One possible source of new water was using treated sewage for drinking purposes. First looked at four decades earlier, by 2005 a recommendation was made to begin using this source by 2014, but because of falling demand that hot-button decision was put off for an indefinite period.

Natural Wonders

In 2004 Pima County voters approved $732 million in bonds to pay for numerous improvement projects, including tens of millions of dollars for open-space acquisition. As one supporter of this proposal commented before the election: "By passing [the bonds], we protect what's best about Pima County for future generations—the Sonoran Desert and its unique wildlife, open spaces, and clean air and water."[75]

That type of land preservation was also a goal of Pima County's Sonoran Desert Conservation Plan that had been spurred, in part, by the legal battle over protections for the cactus ferruginous pygmy owl. Early in 2000, three homebuilding organizations, including the Southern Arizona Homebuilders Association (SAHBA), sued the federal government over its designation of 730,000 acres of land as critical owl habitat and they were eventually successful.

Despite that, by 2001 the Conservation Plan had moved from general concept to maps with designated boundaries—and SAHBA's opinion was not positive. "I think from first blush it's a growth boundary," commented spokesman Alan Lurie of the proposal.[76] Carolyn Campbell of the Coalition for Sonoran Desert Protection disagreed while County Administrator Chuck Huckelberry wrote: "Growth should be directed to areas with the least natural, historic and cultural resource values. The plan is not about *whether* the county continues to grow, it is about *where* the county grows."[77] Those lofty sentiments, however, didn't persuade the state of Arizona or the towns of Oro Valley and Marana to participate in the plan's preparation, with the latter working on its own document.

Seeking to preserve Tucson's natural environment as a leader of the Coalition for Sonoran Desert Protection, Carolyn Campbell speaks about achieving that goal in this picture from the late 1990s (courtesy the Carolyn Campbell photograph collection).

Other environmental changes

were also happening. President Bill Clinton in 2000 approved the Ironwood National Monument northwest of Tucson. A significant change to the landscape was later experienced at Sabino Canyon. A 2006 record flood altered its terrain substantially; the rushing water "destroyed portions of the [canyon] road, washed out trails and left a dangerous tangle of boulders, tree trunks and sand over long stretches of the pavement."[78] As a result, public access to parts of the canyon was limited for quite a while.

That inconvenience was minor compared to events on Mount Lemmon. The 2002 Bullock fire forced evacuation of cabins in and around the settlement of Summerhaven atop the mountain but did not destroy any of them. The next year's Aspen fire wasn't nearly so accommodating. By June 18, 2003, the fire was approaching Summerhaven and growing rapidly. Within two days it was six square miles in size and could easily be seen from Tucson far below as a long string of twinkling red lights. Eventually the fire would burn almost 130 square miles of forest before it was finally contained. When Summerhaven residents were allowed to return to their property in the middle of July, they found more than 300 homes destroyed. Less than twelve months later, however, they were in a celebratory mood as the rebuilding process was about to begin.[79]

Down in the Tucson valley, a number of historic buildings and objects were restored, relocated, or revived during the decade. These included improvements in 2000 to the El Casino Ballroom on 26th Street and the later major restoration of the structure. Locomotive #1673, dating from 1900, was moved from Himmel Park in 2000 to be put on display at the Toole Avenue train station. In 2007, for the 30th time, Maria Luisa Tena organized an 800-piece El Nacimiento nativity scene at the Tucson Museum of Art (TMA). Next to the museum's main building, in 2008 the TMA renovated the 1848-era Casa Cordova, one of Tucson's oldest structures.

Among many others, two ongoing programs aided the community. The first was "Youth on Their Own" that assisted teenagers living by themselves. The other was the Ben's Bells Project honoring the late Ben Maré Packard by weekly presenting small bells to those who through their actions "remind people to be kind, to help ease one another's pain."[80]

Star and Sky Writing

More good news for Tucson, according to Mayor Walkup in 2002, was that Davis-Monthan Air Force Base and its more than $1.5 billion in economic impact would be staying in town.[81] The following year, an estimated 350,000 people attended an "Aerospace and Arizona Days" at the base and a similar number did so four years later.

The size and enthusiasm of those crowds didn't stop public criticism from growing about both the volume of noise produced by DM planes as well as the risk from overflights. In response, the Air Force agreed to increase the altitude at which planes approached the base's runway. As the decade ended, reports that the new F-35 Joint Strike Fighter, a plane considerably louder than the A-10s based at DM, might come to Tucson raised new concerns in the community.

The Air Force, however, wasn't looking to locate the F-35 at Davis-Monthan. Instead it considered having them fly out of Tucson International Airport (TIA) as part of the Arizona Air National Guard training mission stationed there. In the end, the F-35 was sent instead to Luke Air Force Base in Glendale, Arizona, west of Phoenix.

Other news from TIA included continued improvements to its terminal, a record of more than four million passengers set in 2006, and the next year saw 25 nonstop flights from the airport. Then the economic downturn occurred, the number of flights dropped, travel counts fell significantly, and service to Mexico ceased.

When it faced competition from sites in Chile and Hawaii in the earth-based astronomy field, Tucson's designation as "Optics Valley" was experiencing challenges of another sort.[82] Part of the threat to that title came from urban light pollution from a growing community. On the positive side, Southern Arizona remained the location of dozens of telescopes, and many telescope mirrors were produced at the UA mirror lab. In addition, by 2000 a new Multiple Mirror Telescope Observatory had opened on Mount Hopkins south of town, and two years later a giant 8.4-meter mirror was shipped from the UA to the controversial observatory complex atop Mt. Graham east of Tucson. Not much later, a series of scopes—called VERITAS for Very Energetic Radiation Imaging Telescope Array System—was being built on Kitt Peak west of the city.

Tucson was simultaneously gaining status in outer space to the point that a 2005 *Tucson Citizen* editorial headline could *modestly* proclaim: "UA feats in space dazzle all the world."[83] Before that time, campus scientists were important participants in space efforts including the 2001 Mars Odyssey program, repairing the Hubble Space Telescope, and the 2004 Mars rover project. They also played a major role with the HiRISE (High-Resolution Imaging Science Experiment) photography mission of Mars.

It was a 2003 NASA decision that really set the University of Arizona apart, however. That year a UA team, led by Tucson High and UA graduate Peter H. Smith, was chosen to design, build, and operate the Phoenix Project. The mission was to land a craft on Mars in 2008, and it was to "seek evidence of water and elements of life on Mars by analyzing soil and ice samples scooped from the planet's northern arctic region."[84] Once the spacecraft successfully reached the planet, it began sending back valuable information and stunning pictures before it became a victim of the brutal Martian winter. As it died, looking ahead Smith exclaimed: "I think the future is very bright for the university to be involved in future space missions."[85]

While some people in the Tucson news were either famous media stars or worked among the stars, many others making impacts on the community were

Discussing an engineering model of the Phoenix Mars Lander with Arizona Governor Janet Napolitano, Peter Smith was one of the UA scientists who have helped put the university at the forefront of modern space exploration (courtesy the Peter Smith photograph collection).

simply local residents. One of those was writer Patricia Preciado Martin who in 2000 published *Amor Eterno: Eleven Lessons of Love*, her fifth book. The following year the Pima County Board of Supervisors approved a paid holiday for its employees in honor of farm-worker advocate, the late Cesar Chavez. (The Tucson City Council adopted a similar holiday in 2014.) Then in 2007, William D. Kalt III published *Tucson Was a Railroad Town*, an illuminating look at the community's illustrious rail history.

On the music scene, Mayor Walkup in 2002 presented nationally famous flutist R. Carlos Nakai with a special recognition award. In 2003, after 25 years at the helm of the Community Food Bank, Charles "Punch" Woods retired and was widely praised for his work. Also honored with a lifetime achievement award by the Society of Historical Archaeology in 2008 was Tucsonan Jim Ayres.

Around the same time, some notable people were departing town. Author Barbara Kingsolver moved to Virginia with her family in 2004, and longtime Urban League president, Ray Clarke, left for a similar job in Las Vegas two years later. By 2005, also leaving Tucson, once again, was singer and native, Linda Ronstadt, who continued to produce critically acclaimed albums.

War and Death

In 2001, uncertainty fell over the nation, and the city, on September 11th.[86] After the terrorist attacks in New York City, Washington, D.C., and Pennsylvania, more than 2,000 people quickly gathered on the UA mall to contemplate what had happened. Within days, another 2,500 attended a vigil at the Tucson Convention Center to remember the victims, and an estimated 15,000 people later formed a human U.S. flag at Tucson Electric Park. While about 40 Arab students at the university did depart the country out of fear of reprisals, the more typical local response was a "Vision of Peace" interfaith service held in December 2001 involving Muslims, Christians, and Jews.

President George W. Bush was a frequent Tucson visitor during the decade. In 2003, he spent a short time on Mount Lemmon surveying the damage caused by the Aspen fire. After being re-elected, he spoke in 2005 at the Tucson Convention Center about his proposed changes to the Social Security system. Later that same year he returned to Tucson to speak at Davis-Monthan about immigration policy. Then in 2008 he made his last visit as president to help raise funds for U.S. Congressional candidate, Tim Bee.

Protestors greeted Bush every time he came to Tucson, primarily objecting to his launching the 2003 war in Iraq. In contrast, those supporting the war waved American flags and carried signs with messages like: "Support our troops, screw France."[87]

Controversy also gripped the Tucson City Council when the Iraq war started. Protestors painted the huge "A" Mountain letter black, a city crew repainted it the traditional white, after which war backers, including four council members, colored it red, white, and blue. Following considerable political back and forth, the council decided to leave it the nation's colors until "the current conflict in the Middle East is resolved."[88] (Without fanfare, the "A" was quietly repainted white by the city in 2013.)

Local involvement in the Iraq conflict, as well as the war in Afghanistan, was extensive. By 2002, the A-10 "Warthog" based at DM had "become the mainstay of the U.S. ground war in Afghanistan," and it would also initially play a vital role in Iraq.[89] By late April 2003 some troops stationed at DM began returning safely home to the base from Iraq, but five months later the first Tucson native—Army Sgt. Sean Kelly Cataudella—was killed in the conflict. In December 2004, Staff Sgt. Tina Time died in Iraq, and the following April 18-year-old female Army Pfc. Sam Williams Huff was killed by a roadside bomb, thus becoming the first two women with Tucson connections to die in the ongoing war.

While those agonizing losses occurred far from home, there was also a 2000 accident in Marana that claimed 19 military lives. An MV-22 Osprey tilt-rotor aircraft on a rescue training mission crashed, killing all on board.

Others who died during the decade included longtime Tucsonan, 101-year-old

Lucile Budd Juliani (2000). Two businessmen who left indelible marks were engineer Tom Brown (2002) and famous furniture salesman, and former photographer for the *Arizona Daily Star*, Sam Levitz (2005). After publishing his memoirs in 2002 and continuing to perform beyond his 85th birthday, singer Lalo Guerrero passed away in 2005. Two years later, much admired civil-rights activist and vice-president of Chicanos Por La Causa, Lorraine Lee died of cancer at the age of 51. In 2004, Tohono O'odham artist Leonard Chana died and it was written of him: "his art always captured the subtle beauty, essence and joy of his people, their land and sacred traditions."[90] Craig Snow, who for a dozen years led the Tucson AIDS Project, died at 59 in 2006, as did 92-year-old Dr. Herbert Abrams, founder of the El Rio Health Center.

Out of town in 2000, University of Arizona baseball player Kelsey Osburn was killed by a batted ball as he practiced the game he loved. UA football recruit McCollins "MC" Umeh died on the UA practice field in 2004 of an enlarged heart. The next year, 22-year-old star basketball player Shawntinice Polk collapsed in McKale Center and died of a blood clot in her lungs.

A major UA supporter, local legend Roy Drachman died in 2002, but before his passing at the age of 95 he had a few final things to say about Tucson's growth. "We should have had more planning," Drachman insisted the year before his death. "Tucson 'is spread out more than it should be.'"[91] Death also took 97-year-old Joe

Lorraine Lee, much admired advocate and activist for Mexican Americans and the poor, celebrates a birthday with her husband, Alonzo G. Morado, and their daughters, Rita (standing) and Anisa (courtesy the Alonzo Morado photograph collection).

Bonanno in 2002, and it was fittingly observed of him: "[Bonanno] is probably the first Mafia godfather to die of natural causes."[92]

Also dying during the decade was the *Tucson Citizen*. Having been born in 1870, Arizona's longest continuously printed newspaper celebrated its 135th anniversary with a party in 2005, but by then its future looked shaky. The Internet had cut into ad revenues, afternoon papers were disappearing all across the county, and the *Citizen*'s circulation had dropped to a measly 17,000. On May 16, 2009, the *Tucson Citizen* published its last print issue.

A couple of stories the *Citizen* was able to cover before its demise were the U.S. Congressional elections of two very different types of Democratic politicians. After more than 30 years of both political activism and holding elected office, in 2002 Raúl Grijalva resigned his seat on the Pima County Board of Supervisors to run for Congress, a race he easily won.

A few years before, 30-year-old businesswoman Gabrielle Giffords had been elected to the Arizona House of Representatives, and in 2002 she captured a state senate seat. When longtime Tucson Congressman Jim Kolbe announced his 2006 political retirement, Democrat Giffords sought the hotly contested position. After raising large amounts of campaign contributions, Giffords prevailed even though Republican voters were the prevalent party in the district. In 2007, Giffords married NASA astronaut Mark Kelly and the following year she won re-election by beating George W. Bush-supported Tim Bee.

As the decade came to a close, Giffords held a town hall meeting in Tucson to discuss the proposed federal healthcare reform act, aka "Obamacare." Attended by an overflow crowd of more than 2,000 people, according to reports: "Several times Giffords reminded the crowd to keep civility in the discussion and at one point asked some hecklers 'to be a little less rude.'"[93]

• FOURTEEN •

Shootings, Squabbles, and Much Slower Population Growth, 2010–2019

In front of the Oro Valley Town Hall stands a life-sized bronze sculpture of a bighorn sheep by Matthew Moutafis. Dedicated in 2001, the piece was paid for, in part, by development companies. Entitled "Pusch Ridge Majesty," the artwork represents a creature that vanished from the nearby steep, rocky slopes of the Santa Catalina Mountains around the year 2000 before being reintroduced 13 years later in a controversial program.

SHATTERING THE PEACE OF A CRISP January 8, 2011, morning, the seemingly never-ending sickening sound blasted out. The alarming noise resembled that of a hammer violently striking cement—"C-r-a-a-a-c-k! C-r-a-a-a-c-k! C-r-a-a-a-c-k!" More than 30 times the Glock 19 loudly fired, and as it did, numerous bodies fell with it. Once the mentally ill shooter was wrestled to the ground, a semblance of quiet returned to the chaotic north-side scene. Six people, however, lay dead and 13 more were seriously injured, including U.S. Congresswoman Gabrielle Giffords, who had been shot through the head.[1]

A few days later, U.S. President Barack Obama came to a grief-stricken community to console tens of thousands of people on the University of Arizona campus. He said of nine-year-old shooting victim Christina-Taylor Green: "I want to live up to her expectations. I want our democracy to be as good as Christina imagined it."[2]

Within hours of Giffords' admittance to University Medical Center (UMC), a makeshift shrine began to emerge on the hospital's front lawn. A few months later, 7,500 people attended a special spring training baseball game to help raise money for the Christina-Taylor Green Memorial Fund.

Serving on Gifford's staff, Ron Barber had been wounded in the January 8 melee. After her inevitable retirement, he went on to win a hotly contested race for the vacated congressional seat. Reflecting on the shooting's aftermath, he said of the gunman: "It's a sad commentary that the only way he gets [mental health] treatment is by killing six people and wounding 13 others."[3]

Despite this tragedy, the murder rate in Pima County actually dropped from a

Fourteen • Shootings, Squabbles, and Slower Population Growth, 2010–2019

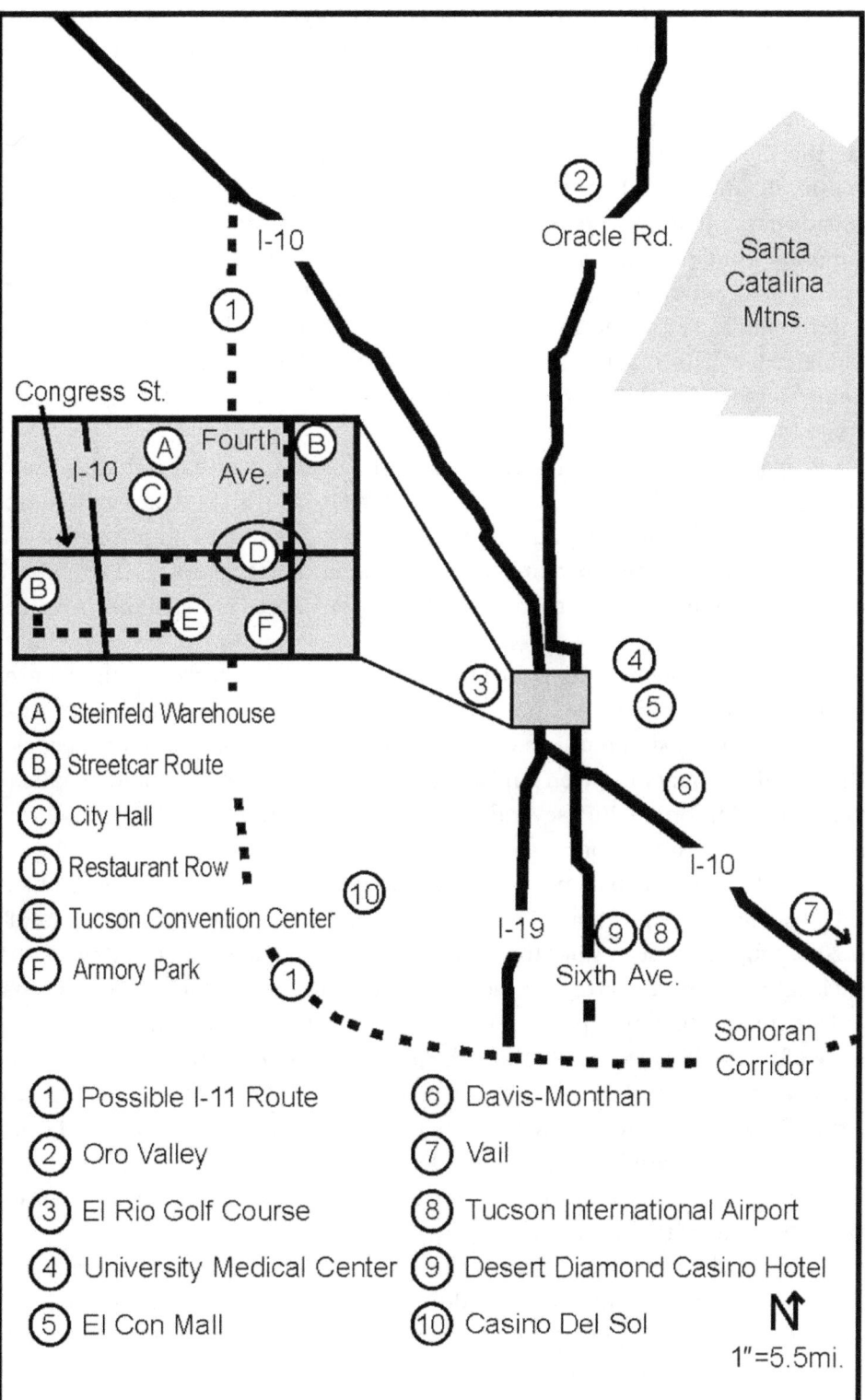

record high of 93 in 2010 to 56 five years later before rising again to 84 in 2017 then receding slightly.[4] The cause of many of these killings according to one local commentator was: "…what Tucson has is a domestic-violence killing problem, one that seems to be getting worse this year [2019] after a bad 2018."[5]

Among all the murders were a few horrific mass killings. In 2015 Christopher Carrillo shot his parents, brother, and 17-year-old niece before turning the gun on himself. Then in 2018, three people, including two teenagers, were killed in an eastside park. That same year, 41-year-old deputy U.S. Marshal Chase White was murdered while serving a search warrant. Thankfully, in 2012 TPD Sergeant Robert Carpenter miraculously survived a bullet to his head fired by an assailant. The longtime mystery behind the disappearance of two children—six-year-old Isabel Mercedes Celis in 2012 and 13-year-old Maribel Gonzalez two years later—were apparently solved in 2018 with kidnapping and murder charges filed against Christopher M. Clements.[6]

Property crime also remained high in the region. Annual statistics showed Tucson being one of the more unsafe cities in Arizona while the nearby suburban developments of Sahuarita and Oro Valley were at the other end of the list.[7] Larceny was a particular problem in Tucson, but the auto theft rate at least fell substantially, despite Mayor Jonathan Rothschild being car-jacked at his midtown home in 2017.[8]

Also during the decade, police officers in Pima County were killing a growing number of people in the line of duty. Officers with the Tucson Police Department (TPD) fatally shot four in a one-month stretch in 2011 and five more people in 2013. In Pima County between 2015 and 2021 a total of 51 people would be killed by police.[9] In addition, in 2015 several TPD officers were embarrassingly found to be involved with a prostitution ring.

The city's police department, once with more than 1,100 commissioned officers, had lost hundreds of positions through the years, reducing the number to below 800 by 2018, a figure not seen since the 1980s.[10] The financial fallout of the 2008 national and local economic downturn on the municipal budget was combined with substantially increased employee pension requirements that resulted in less general fund money for City Hall to spend. Thus, the public safety reductions were just one of several steps the city of Tucson was forced to adopt. To try to lessen these negative trends, Tucson voters were asked to increase the local sales tax by one-half cent in 2010 but refused. Despite that election defeat, after several years unpaid furlough days for city employees came to an end in 2011 as the local economy slowly began to stabilize following the recession.

Another shift took place in 2011 when Bob Walkup, mayor for 12 years, said he had accomplished what he wanted to do, especially downtown, and so chose not to run again. From their perspective, editors at the *Arizona Daily Star* remarked of Walkup: "[He] is an indisputably gracious and upbeat man, but his mayoral legacy will always be tied to the failure of Rio Nuevo."[11]

Municipal, Environmental, and Medical Happenings

That downtown improvement attempt remained mostly in limbo early in the decade, even after a state-appointed governing body took charge in 2010. For two years after that there was constant squabbling between the new board and the city council which was then followed by a period of increasing activity.

In revising the Rio Nuevo board, the Arizona Legislature had focused the new group's efforts on two projects—a downtown hotel and improvements to the Tucson Convention Center (TCC)—and each proceeded differently. The Tucson City Council in 2010 killed off, as fiscally unfeasible, a convention center hotel project that required massive public subsidies. In the summer of 2013, however, the Rio Nuevo board did approve almost $8 million to make at least some preliminary upgrades to the dilapidated TCC and followed it six years later with approval of $65 million more to implement improvements throughout the complex.[12]

During the decade, other downtown projects—either funded by Rio Nuevo, privately, or by a combination of public and private sources—were being implemented. These included Providence Service Corporation buying and renovating a property on Broadway Boulevard and Scott Avenue for its headquarters building, UniSource Energy Corporation, the parent company of Tucson Electric Power, constructing its new headquarters nearby, and a mixed-use, retail-office-residential development being erected at the corner of Broadway and Stone Avenue where Estevan Ochoa's house had once stood. Other projects were the Rialto Theater Foundation buying the historic building back from the Rio Nuevo entity in 2015, the El Rio Community Health Center renovating the former grand home of Levi Manning to use as offices, and a new Greyhound Bus terminal opening at Euclid Avenue and Broadway Boulevard. Multi-family housing also sprang up in the area along with several new hotels, including a 136-room AC Marriott, and more were planned. At the end of the decade, an outdoor wintertime ice skating rink even made an appearance.

There were some setbacks, of course. In 2016 nationally known celebrity chef, Chris Bianco, closed his downtown pizzeria after only two years in business. The long-existing original hotel next to the Convention Center was closed in 2012 and became a huge vacant eyesore. Plus an enormous hotel complex planned for land west of the TCC never materialized, and US Bank shuttered its downtown location in 2019.

Back on the positive side, businesspeople launched a monthly "2nd Saturday Downtown" outdoor event in 2010, and several small technology companies located their offices in the area. The historic Fox Theater was finally turning a profit by 2011, and some local retailers had even begun to open small shops downtown. Simultaneously, east Congress Street became a restaurant hub. Then in 2018, the Arizona Legislature extended the taxing authority for the Rio Nuevo district to 2035.

A few items of historic interest were also taking place in the area. After sitting vacant for several years, the more than 100-year-old, city-owned Steinfeld warehouse on west Sixth Street was renovated as were several privately owned warehouses on nearby Toole Avenue. While these structures were preserved and occupied, the Arizona Historical Society for a while shuttered the Sosa-Carrillo House next to the TCC in a cost-cutting move.

Far away from downtown, a 2017 fire heavily damaged the small chapel at Ted DeGrazia's foothills studio, but it was restored by 2019. Back in the central city, two community institutions—Santa Cruz Church on 22nd Street and the Safford School on 4th Avenue—celebrated centennials in 2019.

At City Hall several blocks away from that school, Democrat Jonathan Rothschild became mayor in 2011 and immediately had to address a controversy at the municipal zoo, somewhat reminiscent of the Sabu-the-elephant saga from 1970. In order to facilitate the arrival of a new group of breeding African elephants, the zoo's staff wanted to split up longtime favorites Connie and Shaba, a proposal decried as inhumane by protestors. In the end, both elephants went to the San Diego Zoo. Unfortunately, 45-year-old Connie died shortly after the move, but fortunately one of the elephants that had replaced her gave birth to a 245-pound baby girl, Nandi, in August 2014. Tragically, in 2018 one of the elephants that came to the zoo, 11-year-old Punga, died of a twisted gut.

With continuing tight financial conditions in the early years of his first term, Rothschild took an unprecedented step for a Tucson mayor by publicly advocating for new municipal incorporations in order to secure more state tax revenue for the region. Disregarding 60 years of vehement mayoral opposition to incorporations followed by Walkup's hands-off approach, Rothschild started pushing for more annexations plus new cities to be created. As he suggested shortly after taking office: "Incorporation is required for our economic and business survival."[13] Despite that belief, the second attempt to incorporate Vail, a 43-square-mile suburban community of 11,500 residents east of Tucson, was rejected by 56 percent of area voters in 2013.

Other topics confronting the Tucson City Council included money-losing golf courses and insufficient funds to open several public swimming pools in the summer of 2012. The first led to privatizing management of the courses early in 2014 and the second was aided by a private fundraising campaign. Continuing issues like these led prominent real estate businessman Hank Amos to place a 2015 full-page advertisement in the *Arizona Daily Star* that bemoaned what he believed was the continual decline of the city. "It is simply mind numbing how our community has degraded in so many ways," Amos observed, while also asking city voters to re-elect Rothschild but replace three Democratic incumbent council members with Republicans. That request was ignored, and the council remained an all–Democrat body.[14]

Facing ongoing fiscal problems because of the recession and other issues, the city government cut jobs, going from more than 6,000 employees in 2008 to 4,700 in 2016.[15] But some good news occurred in 2017 when voters approved raising the sales tax by one-half cent for a five-year period to pay for road maintenance work as well as public safety equipment. Later that year, city voters also approved a one-tenth percent increase in the sales tax to make improvements at the local zoo. Then in 2018, a $225 million bond package for park improvements was adopted by voters. What wasn't OK'd was the designation of Tucson as a "sanctuary city" for immigrants crossing the international border. In November 2019 the proposal was defeated by an almost 3–1 margin.

That same 2019 ballot was historic because Regina Romero, a three-term councilwoman, was elected mayor. She thus became the first woman, and only the second Mexican American, to hold the position. One of her initial acts, she said, would be to raise Tohono O'odham and Yaqui flags at City Hall to "pay respect to the place and the lands and the people that are from here."[16]

For the Pima County government, while progress was made on environmental and other issues, a big blow came at the ballot box in 2015. Voters rejected $815 million in bond funds in seven categories of improvements, leading conservative Republican supervisor Ally Miller to gleefully observe: "This is a victory [County Administrator] Chuck [Huckelberry] is not gonna be happy about."[17]

News from Pima County's second oldest city—South Tucson—was mostly about budget problems and voter discontent. The small enclave celebrated its 75th anniversary in 2015, and the same year its mayor was recalled and removed from office. Also that year, the private garbage collector contracted by the community stopped service because of unpaid bills, and the city of Tucson had to step in to help. Two years later, fire service became an issue when 14 firefighters resigned because of safety concerns. Upset with what was happening, South Tucson voters kicked four members off the town council in a 2018 recall election.

Further south, Sahuarita's population increased by almost one-third to 34,500 while on Tucson's north side, Marana just kept growing in size. By 2020, its population exceeded 52,000 people who were spread out across 122 square miles.

In nearby Oro Valley, the population increased to more than 47,000 by the end of the decade as officials wrestled with golf course issues, purchasing two privately owned courses that critics contended were big money losers. Then in 2018, four incumbents on the Oro Valley Town Council lost their re-election bids because, in the words of one of the victors, "residents [are] looking for a new direction for its Town Council."[18]

Believing wildfires in the rugged mountains near Oro Valley had improved the habitat for bighorn sheep and that new restrictions on hikers with dogs could be effective, early in the decade state officials planned to relocate up to 100 sheep into the Santa Catalina Mountains during a three-year period. To that idea, TucsonCitizen.com, which survived for a few years after the print edition's demise, commented: "The battle to save the sheep was lost decades ago. To transplant a herd of bighorn only to watch them struggle to survive and die is cruel and should be stopped before it's started."[19] That suggestion was ignored, and the reintroduction began in late 2013 with the release of 31 sheep, 16 of which were dead within four months along with three mountain lions shot for killing sheep. This was a grisly scorecard of death that resulted in intense public criticism of the program, but the releases of sheep and killing of mountain lions continued until 2016. At the end of the decade it was estimated there were up to 75 bighorn sheep in the Santa Catalina Mountains, and the herd was considered stabilized in size.[20]

Other outdoor news included the extended drought that gripped Tucson being labeled as "the worst and longest-lasting since historical records have been kept starting in the early 20th century," according to a 2015 analysis.[21] At the same time, local temperatures remained well above normal, with the second highest temperature of 116° being tied in 2017 and the five warmest years on record all being seen between 2014 and 2018.[22] As a result, at the end of the decade Tucson was designated as the third fastest-warming city in the United States.[23]

Concerning another long-term issue, after decades of talking about it, solar power seemed to be making at least some impact on the community. A large, two-square-mile array in Avra Valley west of Tucson was implemented early in the decade and was expected to supply energy to about 3,500 Tucson Electric Power (TEP) company residential customers. The vast majority of TEP's power at that time, though, still came from burning coal, but the utility did decide in 2013 to increase its use of cheaper natural gas. However, near the end of the decade, TEP was generating only 13 percent of its power from renewable—solar and wind—sources.[24]

In two other items related to the environment, annually more than 100,000 people were visiting the UA-operated Biosphere 2 near Oracle, and in 2011 the giant terrarium, along with a $20 million endowment, was donated to the university. By 2014 the region's air quality was in fairly good shape, but ozone levels remained a concern, with the American Lung Association giving Pima County either a "D" or "F" grade for three out of four years as 2020 approached.[25]

Meanwhile, implementation of Pima County's Sonoran Desert Conservation Plan that used open-space bonds and other sources of money to purchase property was continuing. By 2010 it could be written of that effort: "[It] has saved about 50,000 acres [78 square miles] of river-front land, oak woodlands, ranch lands and desert."[26] Six years later, when the Pima County Board of Supervisors unanimously adopted a Multi-Species Conservation Plan as part of the program, a representative of the real estate industry was impressed and remarked: "It really shows what happens when people sit down and really listen to each other."[27]

In medical news, early in the decade Pima County continued to heavily subsidize University Physicians Healthcare Hospital at Kino with $15 million a year, and there were no plans for those payments to stop.[28] But in 2015, after Banner Health of Phoenix acquired the University of Arizona Health Network, including Kino, the subsidies were reduced substantially, and a few years later, County Administrator Chuck Huckelberry called the privatization of Kino Hospital an "unqualified success."[29] With total hospital admissions in Pima County dropping by 10 percent in five years, other area hospitals were feeling financial strains, especially Carondelet's

St. Mary's and St. Joseph's. The ownership company of those hospitals was sold in 2015, and the new owners quickly laid off many employees.

In 2010 University Medical Center opened a new six-story wing, much of it devoted to children's care. Five years later, despite new owner Banner Health losing tens of millions of dollars a year in Tucson, the renamed Banner-University Medical Center Tucson hospital along Campbell Avenue began construction of an 11-story tower, a building that would open in early 2019. Several years before, Tucson Medical Center had begun work on a four-story addition, the first such project for the traditionally single-story facility. South of Tucson, in 2015 a 49-bed hospital opened in Green Valley, but within two years it was in bankruptcy and laying off dozens of workers.[30] On the other hand, Carondelet at the end of the decade was developing two suburban "microhospitals."

Remaining Poor but Optimistic with Some Changes

The local impacts of the 2008 national economic downturn had been severe on Tucson because of its heavy reliance on governmental employment, federal defense spending, tourism, and construction jobs. All of these were dramatically curtailed during and immediately after the recession and combined with the strength of the U.S. dollar versus the Mexican peso along with Tucson's failure to keep or attract many young entrepreneurs, the community's economy was in a poor position. These continuing financial difficulties were spotlighted by more attention being paid to the increasing number of poor people living in the region. A 2012 front-page revelation that Tucson was the nation's sixth poorest major metropolitan area caught many by surprise, and some people even tried to deny it.[31] What was especially shocking was that 38 percent of children inside the Tucson city limits lived in poverty.[32] At the end of 2014, a newspaper headline added to this gloomy situation: "Tucson ranked among America's neediest cities."[33] Another headline from early 2016 added: "Tucson is worst place in AZ to find a job, study says."[34] As the decade progressed, things improved somewhat, and by 2018 the poverty rate in the city of Tucson was around 22 percent and almost 28 percent for children.[35]

During the extended economic slowdown, Tucson lost approximately 35,000 jobs,[36] reportedly one of the highest numbers in the nation for a major city.[37] This decline was highlighted by the construction industry that totaled about 15,000 jobs in 2014, or approximately one half of its boom-time peak of 28,700.[38] One other long-time anchor of the local economy, tourism, was also declining, with tax collections down 23 percent between 2008 and 2013.[39] Based on downturns like these, job recovery in Pima County was extremely slow and one 2014 study pointed out the community was in the bottom ten nationally "for getting back to normal after the recession," and that trend would continue for a few more years.[40]

But near the end of decade, things finally began to pick up. Jobs in high-tech industries were increasing, and the 2016 announcement by Caterpillar, Inc. that they would move 600 high-paying jobs to downtown Tucson was called "the biggest [economic development] deal in 25-years."[41] Other additions to the job market included Vector Space Systems saying the same year they would open a local plant that could employ up to 500 within five years along with a few thousand more employees being hired by Raytheon after the company received large financial incentives from the state, county, and city governments. That was followed by an Amazon distribution center being announced in 2018 that would employ 1,500 people, and the same year TuSimple said they would hire 500 people to develop self-driving trucks.[42]

Other good economic news was received from the tourism and construction industries, both of which were rebounding following the recession. Around the same time, the high number of Tucson bankruptcies caused by the economic downturn fell from more than 8,000 annually in 2010 to less than half that number by 2015 before beginning to rise slowly again in 2017. In 2019 even the long-debated Rosemont Mine southeast of Tucson was given permission to proceed by the U.S. Corps of Engineers.[43]

All of this positive news eventually introduced the word "optimism" back into the local economic development outlook. After the Caterpillar and other upbeat job-creating news stories, one local real estate report proclaimed in 2017: "With these job announcements attitudes regarding the economic outlook of Tucson are now extremely positive, a near 180 from just a year ago."[44] But many of the new jobs in the community were at call centers, one of which was paying $10/hour plus a bonus to its new 2014 hires.[45] Across the decade, several of these firms opened, meaning that by 2019 there were thousands of local jobs in this sector, and a state minimum wage law passed by voters in 2016 would require a $12/hour salary by 2020.

There were some economic setbacks, of course. Vector Space Systems went temporarily out of business after only a few years but resumed operations before closing permanently, some call centers were laying people off at the end of the decade, and a new court ruling threw another legal roadblock in the path of the controversial Rosemont Mine. Plus, wages remained low, with local workers in 2017 earning on average 15 percent less than the national weekly average.[46] Early in the decade, Pima County's unemployment rate had topped 9 percent, but began a steady decline so that in 2019 it was 4.1 percent. Overall growth in employment, however, remained generally anemic throughout the decade.[47]

In response to this situation, numerous economic improvement plans and proposals were floated. As could be expected, protecting and enhancing employment opportunities at Davis-Monthan Air Force Base and Raytheon Missile Systems were on the top of several lists, as were attracting companies to relocate from California along with improving relations with Mexican businesses and shoppers. UA economist Marshall Vest had suggested in 2011: "It's important that we find a new industry to lead us in growth going forward,"[48] something that possibly the Caterpillar announcement partially addressed. Tucson's 2015 designation by the United Nations Educational, Scientific and Cultural Organization (UNESCO) as the first community in the United States to be a City of Gastronomy led a representative of the local tourism board to proclaim: "We should be proud, and we should be very excited about things like this."[49] The region's food traditions were then further celebrated with the 2020 publication of Carolyn Niethammer's award winning book—*A Desert Feast: Celebrating Tucson's Culinary Heritage*.

A bizarre attempt to attract jobs to Tucson came in 2017 after Amazon.com, Inc. announced it was looking to develop a second headquarters site in addition to Seattle, a development that could mean up to 50,000 high-paying jobs. Throwing its hat into the ring, the renamed Tucson economic development agency, Sun Corridor, sent Amazon founder Jeff Bezos a 21-foot-tall saguaro cactus, a move that was generally derided locally. Not surprisingly, Tucson was never seriously considered for the facility.[50]

Looking forward as the decade neared its conclusion, Bruce Wright, retiring University of Arizona associate vice-president for Tech Parks Arizona, commented in 2018: "I think people understand that we need to be an economy that's based on knowledge and invention and innovation. We can't be an economy that depends on population growth."[51] That seemed like sage advice since Pima County's total population had increased only by an average of less than 8,000 people a year during the entire decade to a little more than one million.

One economic development proposal did gather widespread support from a range of Tucson leaders. Continuing the community's generations-long tradition of prioritizing transportation above education, and echoing somewhat the "outer-loop" proposal from the defeated 1986 transportation sales tax election, the idea was to build a major roadway labeled the Sonoran Corridor Highway. It would be built in the vicinity of Sahuarita to link I-10 with I-19 and be a limited-access highway predicted to generate tens of billions of dollars of annual economic activity.[52] This new road would then tie in west of town to the proposed Interstate I-11, "a trade corridor connecting Las Vegas to Phoenix and running south to Mexico."[53] Projections for both these very long-term projects were that their implementation could lead to Tucson becoming a distribution, or "logistics," hub for products from south of the border, a development that would hopefully create several thousand jobs.[54] Despite that positive outlook, when $30 million of planning money for the Sonoran Corridor was included in the 2015 Pima County bond election, it was turned down by voters, greatly disappointing many local politicians.[55]

One other economic development possibility emerged in 2013 when the private, for-profit Grand Canyon University began looking for a second campus to complement its Phoenix facility. This project would potentially involve thousands of new, high-paying jobs, and talks with Tucson city officials soon focused on the municipally owned, money-losing westside El Rio Golf Course as a new campus location. That possibility infuriated a group of local residents who banded together under the name El Rio Coalition II that harkened back to the 1970 protests at the course. Based partially on that type of criticism, the idea of using the golf course was quickly dropped despite the vehement opposition of the Chamber of Commerce and many others, and Grand Canyon University soon decided to expand in the Phoenix area instead. In fact, no new campus was ever developed anywhere.

Along with the loss of many jobs during the economic downturn, there had been an estimated population loss of 50,000 in metropolitan Tucson. Figures in 2008 placed the population around 1,043,000, but by 2012, about 992,400 were believed to be residents. Thus, for only the second time in its American history, the community may have actually lost population over a period of time.[56] As one observer commented in 2015: "The Tucson area has been pretty much dead in the water since the recession."[57]

Even when these population declines eventually turned around, especially in the suburban areas, overall growth was extremely slow by historic measures.[58] Between 1977 and 2007, the area had grown at an annual rate of 2.4 percent.[59] But from 2008 until 2019, the annual growth in population at less than 0.8 percent was only one-third the traditional rate. Despite that, and the consistent over-estimating that had occurred ever since World War II, projections for Pima County in 2014 were still showing an ever-expanding population, with 1.4 million people predicted to live in the area by 2045. (A later projection reduced this number to 1.2 million.)[60]

While population growth was slow, the percentage of the county's population that was Hispanic rose rapidly, approaching 40 percent by 2020. At the same time, much of the limited new building development that was occurring took place in the suburban communities around Tucson, continuing the decades-long philosophy of "drive until you qualify" for a mortgage. The percentage of Pima County residents living inside the Tucson city limits, as a result, fell to 51 percent by 2020, way down from the 1960s figure of 80 percent.

One other fallout from the decline in population growth rate, combined with increased conservation measures, was a decreasing demand for water. According to Tucson Water in 2019: "Tucson uses the same amount of drinking water as it did 35 years ago."[61] That meant a large amount of the community's Central Arizona Project (CAP) allocation could be recharged into the ground in Avra Valley since it wasn't immediately needed for consumption. Thus, not only had Tucson Water met the state's "Safe-Yield" mandate of balancing natural supply with groundwater pumping many years before the 2025 legal deadline, but it had almost five years of stored recharged water available as an emergency backup.

As per capita water use steadily declined, long-term drought conditions continued, and the possibility of a "megadrought" was being contemplated.[62] Concurrently, the future supply of Colorado River water to the CAP canal remained an open question due to often lower rain and snow fall in the Rocky Mountains that were the major supply source for the CAP. To aid the effort to increase water in Lake Mead (a storage facility of CAP water), in 2016 the Tucson City Council began significantly reducing the annual amount of CAP water purchased by Tucson Water. In addition, because of the two factors—drought and uncertainty about the CAP—the prospects of drinking treated effluent water sometime in the future was raised once again in 2014, but in 2017 Tucson Water director Tim Thomure said of the idea: "At least from what we know today … this is decades out."[63]

What wasn't long-term was the threat to Tucson's groundwater from potential cancer-causing chemicals referred to as PFAS.[64] Contained in fire retardant products used by the U.S. Air Force as well as in other materials, in 2018 high levels of the chemicals were found in two wells just north of Davis-Monthan Air Force Base, and the wells were shut off. Then the chemicals were surprisingly detected in six wells in Marana, followed by wells already shut down north of the Air National Guard's base at Tucson International Airport. As the decade ended, who would pay to clean up the groundwater contamination was under debate.[65]

Traditional retailers and malls also faced serious challenges during the decade. Walmart was involved in a local controversy when, as part of the "demalling" of El Con Mall to become an outdoor complex of major retailers, the former Levy's building on its west end was demolished in 2012 to make way for a Walmart. The new 24-hour store was vigorously but unsuccessfully opposed by its residential neighbors. On the far northwest side, Tucson Premium Outlets opened in 2015 with 60 stores and many more planned, a development that immediately challenged Foothills Mall for customers and tenants. By the end of that year, Foothills Mall had defaulted on a $76 million loan, and in 2016 it was sold to buyers who sought "to tear down and refresh parts of the center to broaden its appeal beyond retail."[66] At Park Place mall on Broadway Boulevard, the Sears anchor store closed in 2018 and was replaced, in part, by a bowling and amusement business. Then at the end of that year, Tucson's original, and its last, Kmart store was scheduled to close after almost 50 years in business.

In other retail news, in ten years the number of Goodwill stores in Tucson had gone from four to 20; in 2012 Curacao opened a large southside electronics store catering to Spanish-speaking customers[67]; and Bookman's in 2017 moved out of its building on Grant Road in anticipation of a road widening project. The community also lost several longtime local businesses including Molina's Midway

Seriously wounded in a 2011 shooting when she was a U.S. Congresswoman representing Tucson and Pima County, Gabrielle Giffords received the Medal of Freedom from President Joe Biden in 2022 (Official White House photo by Adam Schultz, Wikimedia Commons).

Mexican food restaurant after 64 years, the 47-year-old Mother Hubbard's Café on Grant Road, the six-decade-old Clyde Wanslee Auto Sales at downtown's Five Points intersection, and Club 21 Mexican restaurant on Oracle Road after 73 years.

Overall, the Tucson economy had suffered a severe shock from the 2008 recession and had not bounced back quickly. Twelve years later in 2020, the community's per capita income remained low, at only about 88 percent of the national average. At least by 2016, the number of homeless people on the street was declining from around 2,350 in 2012 to less than 1,800 four years later, and the numbers continued to go down.[68]

Despite that decrease, widespread displeasure with the community's poverty and apparent declining economic outlook led to a variety of conclusions. For its part, the staff at the *Arizona Daily Star* summarized in 2011: "Here's what Tucson learned from the Great Recession: It was precarious to base our economy on building homes, shops and laundromats for a growing but relatively low-paid population."[69] From his perspective, Joe Snell from TREO (Tucson Regional Economic Opportunities), the region's lead economic development agency, observed in 2013: "The jobs we get are reflective of the [employee] talent we offer."[70]

Educational Issues

Along with all the various efforts and ideas to improve the local economy and enlarge the population, a few commentators called for more attention to be paid to education. At the end of 2013, Mayor Rothschild released an economic plan for the community based on five Ts: technology, trade, transportation, tourism, and teaching. "The linchpin to Rothschild's plan is education," was stated of the final T.[71] That seemed an especially important factor, since one local employer pointed out in 2014 about hiring in Tucson: "When you need people who are drug-free, have clean records, a good work history, good attendance, it's difficult."[72]

The reality of continual low funding for public education in Arizona was shown in a report from the U.S. Census Bureau that indicated Arizona per pupil spending in 2010 was higher than only two other states and was 26 percent below the national average.[73] Commenting on the low level of support for primary education, Calvin Baker, longtime superintendent of the Vail School District, observed in 2013: "The important truth is that [state] funding for both district schools and charter schools is shamefully inadequate.... It is a funding level that cheats our children, our future and our economic development."[74]

In other educational news, at the start of the decade Robert Shelton was president of the University of Arizona, but he resigned in 2011 after five years on the job in order to head the Fiesta Bowl football group in Phoenix.[75] Ann Weaver Hart from Temple University, the first woman UA president, succeeded Shelton in 2012, and within a few years claimed she had turned the institution around from one that was "beset by stale thinking, 'hocus-pocus' budgeting and insiders who spent more time trashing Arizona State University than planning for the UA's future."[76] Although paid $665,000 a year, in 2016 Hart agreed to also serve on the board of directors of the private DeVry University, a role that annually paid $70,000 plus $100,000 in stock. This decision quickly led to numerous people, including 21 members of the Arizona State Legislature, calling for Hart to resign her UA position. That was accomplished in June 2016 when she retained her presidential salary but became a faculty member, although in two years she never taught a class. Following that turmoil, cardiac surgeon and CEO of the Texas Medical Center in Houston, Robert C. Robbins, was employed by the university as president at an annual salary of almost one million dollars and said he planned "to remain at the UA for a decade or more."[77]

From 2010 to 2019, both enrollment and in-state tuition at the university continued to rise, the former reaching almost 36,000 full-time equivalent students by 2019 and the latter totaling close to $13,000 a school year. The steep price didn't deter thousands of students from moving into a cluster of expensive, high-rise, private luxury housing complexes built just west of the campus. In other UA news, by 2017 almost eight out of ten applicants were accepted to the UA, but only 61 percent graduated within six years, the lowest rate among 16 major universities.[78] More positively, between 2012 and 2017, Hispanic enrollment grew by close to 30 percent to 9,321, and in 2018 the UA received a "Hispanic Serving Designation" from the U.S. Department of Education. In news of another sort, gathering national attention was the 2017 recovery of the extremely valuable painting "Woman-Ochre" by Willem de Kooning. Stolen from the UA Art Museum in 1985, the somewhat damaged piece was found in a home in New Mexico.

Among other things happening on the campus was the 2011 selection of the UA by NASA to lead the OSIRIS-REx program, a "robotic space mission that will visit an asteroid and extract a sample that could provide clues to the origin of life on Earth."[79] When it was launched in September 2016 to begin a seven-year, billions-of-miles roundtrip journey, the spacecraft contained a plaque honoring Michael Drake, the late UA astronomer who had proposed the mission.

Because of the generosity of donor Agnese Nelms Haury, another renowned program at the university—the tree ring laboratory—in 2013 finally moved into a new building that replaced "temporary" space in the football stadium that had been used for 75 years. At about the same time, while federal budget reductions along with international competition had previously threatened some of Southern Arizona's historic ground-based astronomy facilities and the 26 telescopes on Kitt Peak, by 2015 new uses had been found for all the optical telescopes and in 2018 a visitor-related purpose for the iconic McMath-Pierce solar telescope was funded. Then, in 2019, a new telescope to study gamma rays was unveiled on Mount Hopkins south of Tucson.

The UA's Robert Shelton wasn't the only educator departing Tucson during the decade. In 2010 Elizabeth Celina-Fagen quit her job after only two years as superintendent of Tucson Unified School District (TUSD) to take a position in Colorado.

Her replacement, John Pedicone, retired after three school years and was followed by H.T. Sanchez, who was relieved of his duties in 2017 and replaced by Gabriel Truillo. Another educational leader, Robert Hill, superintendent of the Arizona State Schools for the Deaf and Blind, was put on leave in 2013 and reached a final financial termination settlement the next year. Roy Flores had been chancellor of Pima Community College (PCC) for nine years, but in 2012 he too was apparently forced out of his job after eight women made sexual harassment allegations against him, charges that had been ignored for a long time by the college's governing board. The following year, Lee Lambert became the new leader of Pima.

While repeating the serious administrative turnover it had experienced occasionally in the past, PCC was involved with other major issues as well. Because of the emerging views by many Americans of the critical value of being educated at a "name" school, along with changes in funding guidelines, student enrollment fell sharply at Pima from almost 21,300 in 2011 to 12,800 in 2019.[80] In addition to the problems with enrollment. the vast majority of students applying for admission to Pima weren't adequately prepared. "PCC's 2014 analysis," it was reported, "found that 87 percent of recent high school graduates coming through the door needed remedial help in [at least] one academic area—82 percent in math, 40 percent in reading and 36 percent in writing." The result of that reality? "Companies that want to grow and expand don't, because there are not enough qualified workers," concluded Tucson Chamber of Commerce president, Mike Varney in 2015.[81]

The reduction in enrollment at Pima, combined with the state of Arizona deciding to no longer fund community colleges, resulted in operating budget cuts by 2016 and a few tuition increases. By 2018 a Pima student paid $2,475 for a school year of 30 credits.

In 2013, for the second time in its 40-year history, the college was again placed on a two-year probation by the Higher Learning Commission that found a "culture of fear and retribution that pervaded the administration."[82] After that, it was put in an "on notice" category, but that designation finally ended in 2017.[83]

At the primary school level, a continued lack of adequate funding led to low teacher pay, increasing numbers of vacant teaching positions, and eventually a strike by classroom teachers. A 2015 study revealed that Tucson teachers were paid $16,000 per year less than the national average and were the lowest compensated among major Southwestern cities.[84] That same year, shortly before schools opened in Pima County, there were more than 210 vacant teacher positions that would have to be filled by long-term substitutes. As the inadequate funding situation continued across the state, in April 2018 Arizona public school teachers went on strike for one week. After Governor Doug Ducey signed a budget that included more money for education, teachers returned to the classroom but remained among the lowest paid in the nation. As one teacher in the Flowing Wells district commented of this situation in 2019: "[E]ducators must fight tooth and nail, every year, every day, of the [Arizona] legislative session, to make sure the students in public schools are not forgotten."[85]

Throughout the decade, enrollment in TUSD schools kept falling, and by 2018 fewer than 43,000 students were enrolled, a drop of 8,000 since 2011. Combined with the growth of suburban school districts, part of that loss was due to the expanding number of charter schools that reached a total of several dozen in Pima County by 2019. (The Arizona Department of Education lists 93 charter schools in Pima County in 2024.)[86] Responding to its drop in enrollment and ignoring widespread opposition, the TUSD school board closed about 20 out of around 100 total district schools during a period of several years. The district also began relying more heavily on the $64 million per year that it taxed property owners under the court-ordered desegregation program.

Another issue—Mexican American Studies (MAS)—also continued to roil TUSD during the decade. With Hispanic students by 2010 accounting for approximately 60 percent of district enrollment, but with their graduation rate remaining 11 percentage points lower than Anglo students, ethnic studies courses were one way TUSD used to try and close this gap.

Tom Horne, once the state superintendent of public instruction who was elected Arizona Attorney General in 2010, saw things completely differently, stating: "Public schools in the 21st century have no business dividing students by race."[87] Under a 2010 law Horne helped push through the Arizona legislature, the MAS program in TUSD was soon declared illegal by new State Superintendent of Public Instruction John Huppenthal, who later shockingly wrote on a blog: "Yes, MAS = KKK in a different color."[88] The TUSD board was thus faced with either sacrificing $14 million in annual state financial aid or canceling the MAS courses. Protesting the possibility of losing these classes, program supporters took over a TUSD board meeting in April 2011. Despite that protest, the TUSD board acquiesced to the state's will and cancelled the ethnic studies program.

That decision didn't halt the controversy, however, because of the district's still ongoing, decades-long, desegregation lawsuit. In 2013 a federal judge decided that the district had to "begin offering culturally relevant courses in the next school year."[89] Horne, naturally, objected to that decision, but a pilot program was established anyway and eventually received endorsement from the Arizona Department of Education. Also during the decade, the 2010 state law that had outlawed the original MAS program was challenged in court, and in 2017 a judge ruled: "Racism was behind an Arizona ban on ethnic studies that shuttered a popular Mexican American Studies program at Tucson Unified School District."[90] Thus, the law was thrown out.

While TUSD was losing students, several suburban districts grew rapidly. By 2018, there were more than 15,000 students in the Sunnyside district, 13,000 in Amphitheater, 12,500 in Vail, and 11,500 in Marana. Also during the decade, the new, traditional public high school Walden Grove opened in the Sahuarita district (2011) while Basis, a charter school, opened a high school in Oro Valley with an enrollment of around 300 students.

Some of Tucson's school districts occasionally asked their residents for budget overrides to increase their funding, but these requests were often denied. These rejections included seven consecutive failures in the Sunnyside district, including one in 2013 that led to the closure of two district schools and the elimination of dozens of teaching and other positions. Voter rejection in 2017 of either override or bond issues in three out of four districts, Flowing Wells being the lone exception, led a newspaper headline to conclude: "Phoenix embraces schools while Tucson says no."[91]

As local voters often turned thumbs down to more money for public education, in 2017 a city of Tucson election also overwhelmingly rejected a one-half cent sales tax increase to fund preschool vouchers. "The measure's defeat," summarized an article in the *Arizona Daily Star*, "was due in no small part to the vociferous campaign against the measure that united local Democrats, Republicans and groups like Americans for Prosperity—a right-wing political advocacy group funded by the Koch brothers."[92]

From "Like running in molasses" to Generally Good Times

While funding preschool vouchers lost out in 2017, much more community focus was on the future of Davis-Monthan Air Force Base. The general belief was that the A-10 combat airplane training mission carried on at DM for decades would eventually come to an end, and this assumption was accelerated in 2014 when the Obama administration proposed phasing out the plane during a five-year period. The date was later pushed back to 2022. This recommendation, of course, was met at first with strong negative reaction from DM supporters because of the estimated 3,000 jobs it would cost the community. In 2015, however, the idea of promoting a new mission at DM began gathering local momentum. The following year, Secretary of the Air Force, Deborah Lee James, called DM's future bright and added: "I think there's room for growth, in terms of missions [at DM]."[93]

To ensure military aviation's future in Tucson, some DM supporters had pushed having the new F-35 Joint Strike Fighter be considered for location in Tucson. Debatable Air Force noise approximations, though, pointed out the plane was almost twice as loud as the A-10s flying out of DM.[94] That reality, many midtown residents contended, would destroy their quality of life if the F-35 was based at DM, and in 2017 the Air Force decided, at least temporarily, not to base the plane in town.

It was a continuing decrease in the number of flights and passengers from Tucson International Airport (TIA) early in the decade that was causing concern there.[95] By 2015 the annual passenger numbers were around 3.2 million, a decrease of more than one million from seven years earlier. In an attempt to improve business, the airport began offering monetary incentives to airlines that introduced new domestic non-stop flights. Additionally, a resumption of flights to Mexico after an eight-year hiatus was anticipated. While a direct flight to New York City was started by American Airlines in 2016, and the same year flights by the Mexican airline Aeromar to

Hermosillo, Sonora, and points further south began, by 2017 both had ended. At least that year marked the 90th anniversary of airplane passenger service to Tucson. Low-cost Allegiant Air also began offering service to a few locations the same year, and by 2019 annual passenger counts were up to almost 3.8 million.

The long-term, local economic impacts following the 2008 national recession that affected TIA passenger counts also led to a sharp decline in home prices along with new home construction. By May 2014, the median home sales price was around $154,000, or 22 percent lower than the median in 2007 at the peak of the latest housing boom.[96] "It's like running in molasses," one real estate professional asserted of the local housing market in 2014.[97] Then things began to pick up, and by 2019 "[t]he average new house price [was] above $300,000 and a resale home [went] for around $220,000."[98]

Adding to the decline in home prices early in the decade was the huge number of vacant housing units, with a 2011 analysis showing that one in eight Tucson homes was empty.[99] Not surprisingly, new home construction remained quite sluggish at that point, with around 2,200 new home building permits issued annually, or about one-fifth of the boom-time highs. Along with increasing home prices, construction of new homes picked up somewhat later in the decade, with more than 3,000 single-family permits being issued in 2019. At that time the type of unit being built was changing somewhat, with high-end rentals becoming more popular.

As the overall housing market slowly began to turn around late in the decade, in part because outside investors were buying up large numbers of Tucson properties, the extremely high number of residential foreclosures seen previously finally started to slowly subside, and by 2016 it hit a 10-year low of less than 1,900. All of these shifts in the housing market resulted in housing affordability, once a Tucson selling point, continuing to be a problem for renters. The percentage of renter households burdened by their housing costs had risen sharply between 2000 and 2010 and remained around 50 percent through the next decade. Because of the generally low wages paid in town, this translated into Tucson being close to unaffordable for many people who rented their living units.[100]

Tucson's 21st-century economic bust, that in length had only been exceeded during the 1880s and the 1930s Great Depression, had impacts in many other areas as well as housing. Having been in Tucson for 26 years, Wingspan, a nonprofit organization serving the lesbian, gay, bisexual, transgender (LGBT) community, shut its doors in the summer of 2014, and some of its projects were assumed by the Southern Arizona AIDS Foundation. "After the recession we got hit hard," a Wingspan spokesman explained. "All of our major donors suffered from the recession. It has been downhill since 2009."[101] Another closure, this one caused by 2015 city of Tucson budget cuts along with evolving technology, was Access Tucson, the public television station that had once offered free airtime to almost anyone.

Local resorts were also seriously affected by the downturn with three—La Paloma, Starr Pass, and El Conquistador—at one time facing foreclosure.[102] Many hotels also went into bankruptcy. But while some tourist accommodations were experiencing monetary difficulties long after the recession, the Pascua Yaqui tribe was showing great confidence in its hospitality operations. In 2011 it debuted an eye-catching, 10-story, 215-room, $100 million Casino del Sol Resort, Spa and Conference Center on the far southwest side of town. In 2019 the tribe also opened a new 151-room, six-story hotel nearby. To staff all these facilities, the Yaquis focused on hiring their own, so 61 percent of employees were tribal members by 2016.

The Yaquis' success with their casinos was matched by the Tohono O'odham Nation. In 2017 the tribe, after a lengthy legal struggle, obtained state authorization to open a new casino in Glendale, Arizona, in Maricopa County. Together, the financial success of all these casino operations meant that by the second decade of the 21st century, Tucson's two Native American tribes had become major players in the local economy as well as frequent contributors to both charitable and community-service projects.

It wasn't financial abundance but rather a shortage of funds that was eventually affecting the Regional Transportation Authority (RTA) approved by Pima County voters in 2006. Because of lower than expected sales tax collections, caused in part by the weakened economy along with lower population growth than expected, estimates were made as early as 2010 that up to 25 percent of the approved RTA transportation projects may not be affordable.[103] RTA officials at first vigorously disputed that suggestion, but within a few years acknowledged there was a one-half billion dollar shortfall that would have to be covered from other sources.[104]

That pending problem didn't prevent the RTA in 2011 from proclaiming its first five years an amazing success story, including the unfinished modern streetcar line. The $200 million rail system was originally expected to be in operation by November 2011, then late 2013, but with great fanfare streetcars actually began running in July 2014 and were instantly popular. Estimates were, though, that operating the system would be a $4 million annual drain on the cash-strapped city of Tucson budget that was subsidizing the entire Sun Tran operation to the tune of almost $30 million a year.[105]

While RTA supporters publicly applauded the improvements financed by the transportation tax, critics pointed out the region's extremely slow growth rate was making some of the authority's traffic predictions obsolete. "Their view was we needed to prepare for another million people on the periphery," attorney Bill Risner said in 2011 of RTA backers. "My view [back in 2006] was ... that we should concentrate on the inside of the community. Turns out I was right. How's growth looking now?"[106]

It was deteriorating pavement conditions in both the city of Tucson and unincorporated Pima County, estimated to be a $2 billion problem, that had many other people's attention. One comic critic went so far as to write a 2013 Christmas-time poem entitled "A Tucson Carol: 'Jingle Bumps.'"[107] To address the car-rattling situation, Tucson voters in 2012 narrowly supported the issuance of bonds to pay for needed repairs on some city streets. At the end of the decade, for their constituents in unincorporated areas, Pima County officials adopted a 10-year, $220 million road maintenance package funded from property taxes.

Other transportation news included the latest in a long series of strikes by Sun Tran bus drivers, the one in 2010 lasting one week. Then in 2015 there was another strike that dragged on for 42-days, and the *Arizona Daily Star* declared in an editorial before it was resolved: "This strike is harming Tucsonans."[108]

In addition to bus strikes, another recurring theme throughout Tucson modern history was cars getting struck in "Lake Elmira" at the flooded Stone Avenue underpass downtown. It happened once again in 2016, but a possible solution was many years from being implemented.

For those on foot, 25 pedestrians in 2013 were killed on local streets, making it one of the deadliest years on record.[109] But the fatalities just kept climbing, reaching 39 killed on Tucson streets in 2019. Two of the victims were Anna Mentzer and her 7-year-old son Ethan, killed in daylight hours while walking in a marked crosswalk on Pima Street in 2017. At least in 2018, the Pima County Loop system of more than 100 miles of paved paths for pedestrians and bicyclists was finally completed. Because of amenities like that, in 2012, even as the Loop was still under development, *Outside* magazine ranked Tucson number one on its list of "Top 10 Bike Towns."[110]

Border Concerns

The first few years of the decade had seen a sharp decrease in illegal immigration into Southern Arizona as more crossers, including many women and children from Central America, chose to enter the U.S. through Texas instead. Apprehensions of border crossers in the Tucson sector, estimated to be about one-half the number of people actually crossing, fell from more than 600,000 in 2000 to about one-tenth that figure—63,400—by 2015 and remained in that range until 2019.[111] Despite the dramatic drop in the number of immigrant crossings into Arizona, there were continual loud public outcries about "doing something more about the border." Those pleas only intensified after Donald J. Trump was elected president in 2016 after promising to erect a "big beautiful wall" along the border that actually turned out in many places to be a tall fence with razor wire at its top. Opposition to the project came from environmentalists and others as well as reporters at the *Arizona Daily Star* who summarized: "The fence we already have has done most everything a fence can do."[112] Despite that opinion, President Trump's border barrier began being built late in the decade across miles of Southern Arizona desert land and in Nogales, Arizona.

The number of people crossing the border into Southern Arizona may have fallen dramatically at times, but fatalities among crossers still exceeded 150 every year between 2003 and 2013. Finally, in 2014 the number began to decline somewhat and would remain below 150 annually through the end of the decade.[113] At the same time, two Tucson churches—Southside Presbyterian and St. Francis in the Foothills United Methodist—again offered sanctuary to a few illegal immigrants who had lived in the United States for many years but were fearing arrest.

While the number of border crossers declined, the importation of illegal drugs was exploding. One account stated ominously: "The amount of fentanyl seized this year [2017] at Arizona's ports of entry on the Mexico border skyrocketed 600 percent over last year."[114] Gun smuggling into Mexico also saw no letup across the international boundary, but marijuana hauls into the U.S. dropped dramatically, in part probably because legal medical marijuana shops had sprung up across Arizona after a 2010 ballot-approved, voter initiative authorizing them.[115] At the same time, overdose deaths from drugs in Pima County rose dramatically. In 2010 there were just more than 200 of these fatalities, while in 2020 the number exceeded 400.[116]

Federal officials in the past may have occasionally deemed the border area "largely secured," but the continuing demands for increased security early in the decade were driven, in part, by the 2010 murder of Southern Arizona rancher Robert Krentz and the slaying later that year of U.S. Border Patrol agent Brian A. Terry.[117] Reacting to these shootings, as well as her mistaken belief that most illegal immigrants were actually drug runners, Arizona Governor Jan Brewer signed SB 1070 in April 2010. Her support for this bill, which was called "the toughest state law in the country designed to combat illegal immigration,"[118] helped Brewer easily win another term in office later that year. The U.S. Supreme Court eventually struck down much of the law but upheld a contentious part—"[a] requirement that police, while enforcing other laws, question people's immigration status if officers have reasonable suspicion they're in the country illegally."[119]

In 2015 alone, the cost to taxpayers to house illegal immigrants in Southern Arizona who had been apprehended but not yet deported was shown to be almost $275 million.[120] Statistics also showed that by 2019 about 35,000 undocumented people lived in Pima County.[121]

Charges of physical abuse of illegal immigrants by Border Patrol agents were also heard. Among these incidents, U.S. agent Lonnie Swartz in 2012 shot and killed 16-year-old José Antonio Elena Rodriguez who was in Nogales, Sonora, Mexico, one of seven shootings in the Tucson sector since 2010. In 2018, a jury acquitted Swartz of second-degree murder and, after a separate trial, of manslaughter. That same year, a Border Patrol agent was shot and wounded "by an unknown number of assailants" near Arivaca east of Nogales.

More than 330 National Guard troops were deployed to the border in 2018 by Arizona Governor Doug Ducey to "provide support for U.S. Customs and Border Patrol."[122] The Border Patrol also began arresting a few Americans who were attempting to provide aid to those who had crossed into the United States. Humanitarian activist Scott Warren in 2018 was arrested on felony charges of harboring illegal migrants along with conspiracy. Later that year, several other people "face[d] charges ranging from felony human smuggling in Ajo [Arizona] to misdemeanors for leaving food and water in the Cabeza Prieta National Wildlife Refuge" near Ajo.[123] In the end, four of them were found guilty and given probation, but their convictions were later overturned.[124] Four others pled guilty and each paid a $280 fine, while Warren, after two trials, was found not guilty.[125]

At the same time, some of those crossing, instead of risking their lives in the desert, were turning themselves into the Border Patrol at ports of entry and requesting asylum. By 2019 during the Trump administration, some of these people were being told to wait in Mexico. There were also more families with children crossing, and instead of Mexican nationals, many of the people were from Central America. Given the influx of immigrants, by the end of the decade the city of Tucson began temporarily housing dozens of these people for a night or two in a recreation center and other facilities before they moved on to various parts of the country. Also in 2019 the Pima County government got involved by leasing a former juvenile detention center to the Roman Catholic Church. The church had established the *Casa Alitas* (House of Wings) program in 2014 to assist people who were seeking asylum, and by the end of the decade it was helping about 1,000 immigrants a month.[126]

The number of Border Patrol agents in the Tucson sector had risen sharply early in the decade to more than 4,200 before falling, due to a shift in immigration patterns to Texas, to 3,600 in 2020. In 2011 only about five percent of the agents were women.[127] At that same time, the once all-male Tucson Fire Department had 34 female firefighters, or approximately the same percentage as the Border Patrol, but at least in 2015 Laura Baker became the department's highest-ranking woman ever when she became an assistant chief.

Win Some, Lose Some as Time Takes Its Toll

In outdoor activities, in 2012 the UA won the school's fourth NCAA baseball championship, and the team was welcomed home by 5,000 exuberant fans. Meanwhile, professional baseball, both major and minor, was being replaced at Kino Sports Complex by major league soccer teams training on the transformed fields. Summarizing the continual loss of sporting events in Tucson, sports columnist for the *Arizona Daily Star*, Greg Hansen, commented in 2014: "Over the last 15 years, sports in Tucson have suffered every conceivable indignity. We lost ... the Copper Bowl, the Diamondbacks, White Sox, Rockies, the LPGA, the Pro Bowlers Tour and pro baseball teams named Toros, Sidewinders and Padres."[128] On the other hand, three professional teams—Sugar Skulls (indoor football), Roadrunners (ice hockey), and FC Tucson (soccer)—made their debuts during the decade. Other final acts, however, came after 72 years with the 2016 end of dog racing at Tucson Greyhound Park and the 2019 shuttering of Golden Pin [Bowling] Lanes after 59 years. That same year, the El Tour de Tucson bicycle event ran into serious financial difficulties, resulting in a change in administration and a large donation from Banner-University Medicine in order to keep the event going. More on the positive side, the decade came to a close on a high note for young Marana auto racer, Alex Bowman, when he logged his first victory in the NASCAR Cup Series in July 2019.[129]

In 2012 UA student Brigetta Barrett won a silver medal in the high jump at the London Olympic Games while another UA student, Shirley Reilly, took home three medals, including one gold, from the Paralympic Games. Then in 2016, former UA swimmer Kevin Cordes won a gold medal as part of a 4×100 relay team. The UA football team was not as successful. Rich Rodriguez was hired in 2011 and led the team to a bowl victory his first year and a Pac-12 South Division title in 2014. But then things went downhill; he was fired in 2018 and replaced by Kevin Sumlin, the first African American to lead the program and a man who was called "a winner with character."[130] But Sumlin's first season ended with a 5–7 record and a one-point, home-game loss to archrival Arizona State University. After 16 years without a holiday season bowl game, at least the Nova Home Loans Arizona Bowl debuted in 2015 with Nevada defeating Colorado State 28–23 at Arizona Stadium before a crowd of 20,425.

Like the football program, men's basketball at the UA had a chaotic decade. The team won the Pac-12 championship five times but never advanced past the Elite Eight in the NCAA tournament. In 2010 the NCAA had placed sanctions on the UA basketball program for violations committed between 2006 and 2008 near the close of Lute Olson's regime. Also in 2010 the university's memorable run of 25 straight appearances in the NCAA basketball tournament came to an end before a new streak was begun.

It was off-court activity, however, that drew the most headlines for the men's basketball program. In September 2017, assistant coach Emanuel "Book" Richardson was arrested and charged by the federal government with bribery and fraud in his recruiting practices and he was later fired.[131] With the men's basketball team generating almost $22 million in revenue for the university athletic department, it wasn't surprising when administration officials rallied around head coach Sean Miller, even after unproven allegations of recruiting improprieties by him surfaced.[132] The women's UA basketball team, on the other hand, finished the decade on a high note. They capped a successful 2019 season by winning the Women's National Invitation Tournament (WNIT) championship before a joyous sellout home crowd of 14,644.

In other sport news, it was announced in June 2014 that Tucson's popular match play championship featuring the world's best golfers was leaving town for San Francisco and would be replaced by a senior men's tour stop. By that same year, Tucson's five municipal golf courses were losing money and owed the city's general fund $9 million. A few years later, some private courses were permanently closing, victims of a changing marketplace.[133] But the UA women's golf team, in heart pounding fashion, did win the 2018 NCAA golf championship.

Furthermore, campus athletes in general were doing considerably better academically than they had in the past, but both the football and basketball teams still ranked in the bottom one-third of the Pac-12 conference for graduation rates in

2013.¹³⁴ By the end of the decade, however, ten UA sport teams had perfect scores in the NCAA academic ranking system, and both football and men's basketball teams had improved considerably.

Among the cultural attractions premiering during the decade was the Oro Valley Meet Yourself Festival in 2015. Also several cultural organizations noted historic milestones: the UA Poetry Center marked 50 years (2010); Ballet Arizona, 25 seasons (2010); and the Tucson Corral of the Westerners, 60 years of celebrating Western history (2013). The Tucson Chamber Artists saw a decade of bringing professional chamber choir and orchestra to the community (2013), and the Tucson Chapter of the Model A Ford Club of America celebrated its 50th anniversary in 2014. In 2016 the Las Posadas Christmas-time procession featuring students from Carrillo K-5 Magnet School was held for the 80th time. The next year, both the Arizona Theater Company (50 years) and the YWCA (100 years) marked milestone anniversaries. Then in 2018, St. Luke's Home on Adams Street, having decades before transitioned from a tubercular sanitarium to a senior living center, celebrated its centennial.

In 2013 the Tucson Winter Chamber Music Festival was put on for the 20th time. Sponsored by the Arizona Friends of Chamber Music, the anniversary festival was the last held under the leadership of the group's longtime president Jean-Paul Bierny. Also retiring was maestro George Hanson, who stepped down in 2015 as conductor of the Tucson Symphony Orchestra after 19 seasons and was replaced by José Luis Gomez on the podium.

The state of Arizona marked its centennial in 2012. To commemorate the occasion in Tucson, events were held on the university campus as well as throughout downtown, including "A Special Chat with Noted Tucsonans of the Past" at the Fox Theater. This presentation included people portraying, among others, educator Morgan Maxwell, Sr., businesswoman Esther Tang, and Tohono O'odham chair, Josiah Moore.

Three books of local note were published in the decade. The massive *Gift of Angels* was the crowning achievement of author Bernard "Bunny" Fontana and photographer Edward McCain in documenting the artwork of the San Xavier Mission church. In *La Calle*, Lydia Otero analyzed the 1960s demise of much of downtown's historic barrio to make room for the Tucson Convention Center and other nearby government buildings. Then in 2019, John Warnock in *Tucson: A Drama in Time* traced the long history of the area in a series of chronological snippets.

Still continuing their work were some noteworthy Tucsonans including artist Barbara Grygutis who was winning commissions all across the country for her large metal sculptures. In 2010 UA professor Roger Angel received the prestigious Kavli Prize for his creative approach to making large telescope mirrors while folklorist Jim Griffith won a National Heritage Fellowship from the National Endowment of the Arts in 2011.

The decade also saw a few notable retirements. A rousing farewell was given in 2013 to Joe Cavaleri when, because of Parkinson's disease, he gave up his 34-year stint as the "Ooh Aah Man" at UA athletic events. Two years later, Clarence Dupnik stepped down after 25 years as Pima County Sheriff. Roman Catholic Bishop Gerald Kicanas also retired after serving 16 years and was replaced in 2017 by Edward Weisenburger.

Many Tucsonans, both famous and not famous, passed away during the decade. In 2010 pioneer retailing matriarch, Cele Peterson, died at the age of 101. Active until her death, it was said of her: "For more than 75 years [Peterson] served as Tucson's arbiter of fashion and grace."[135] Also passing away in 2010 was barber, bodybuilder, and World War II veteran Johnny Gibson. Educator, civil rights activist, and World War II internment camp enrollee Henry Oyama died at the age of 86 in 2013. Almost 60 service members with ties to Southern Arizona were killed in Iraq and Afghanistan since the wars began.

Among the former politicians who died between 2010 and 2019 were Mayor George Miller (2014), Governor Raúl Castro (2015), and Councilmember Chuck Ford (2019). Women who had impacted the community that passed away included Esther Tang (2015) and Betty Liggins (2019). Others voices that were silenced were archaeologist Jim Ayres (2015), civil-rights lawyer Ed Morgan (2017), former UA President Henry Koffler (2018), vacant-land investor Don Diamond (2019), and Dick Tomey (2019), the winningest football coach in UA history.

Eighty-five-year-old, retired UA anthropologist and Southwest historian, Bernard "Bunny" Fontana died in 2016. It was truthfully written of him as a tribute: "Fontana, a humble and humorous man, was generous with his time and research with other scholars, students, journalists and the public."[136]

• FIFTEEN •

Approaching Tucson's August 20, 2025, Semiquincentennial, 2020–2024

A small boulder just north of the Tucson Museum of Art bears a bilingual plaque that reads in part: "This native rock from Sentinel Peak [A Mountain] marks the location of the Bicentennial time capsule of the City of Tucson." Buried in December 1976 and to be opened on August 20, 2025, the concrete and steel capsule contains "documentary material from more than 100 local organizations including cultural, civic and historical groups."[1]

DEAD WITHIN ONE HOUR OF HER MARCH 2020 admittance to Tucson Medical Center (TMC), the 54-year-old woman with underlying health conditions became Pima County's first reported fatality from COVID-19.[2] By the time the worldwide pandemic had subsided almost three years later, more than 4,300 other county residents were claimed by the disease.[3] The first victim's sister had earlier observed about her loss to the virus: "Love your family... Don't wait. Tell them you love them."

From the beginning, the fallout from COVID cascaded like a rushing waterfall across the Tucson community. Intensive care units at local hospitals soon filled, and the "eerily quiet" one at TMC was described: "The only sounds are the beeps of machines and the shuffle of staff in protective gear entering and exiting rooms of people who lie sedated, eyes closed, with multiple tubes coming out of their mouths."[4] Schools quickly closed and turned to online instruction; University of Arizona (UA) and high school athletic seasons were called off; civic events from the Festival of Books to the Fourth Avenue Street Fair were cancelled; and Tucson's mayor, Democrat Regina Romero, on March 17 "declared a local emergency, ordering many businesses to close, limiting restaurants to drive-thru and takeout."[5] Then on March 30, the Arizona Governor, Republican Doug Ducey, issued a statewide "stay-at-home" order that would be in place until May 15.

Tucson International Airport saw an 80 percent drop in passengers as tourism and business travel evaporated. Unemployment skyrocketed, reaching almost 13 percent in April, as businesses either permanently closed, temporarily furloughed their employees, or turned to strictly online formats.

Tucson 2020 – 2024

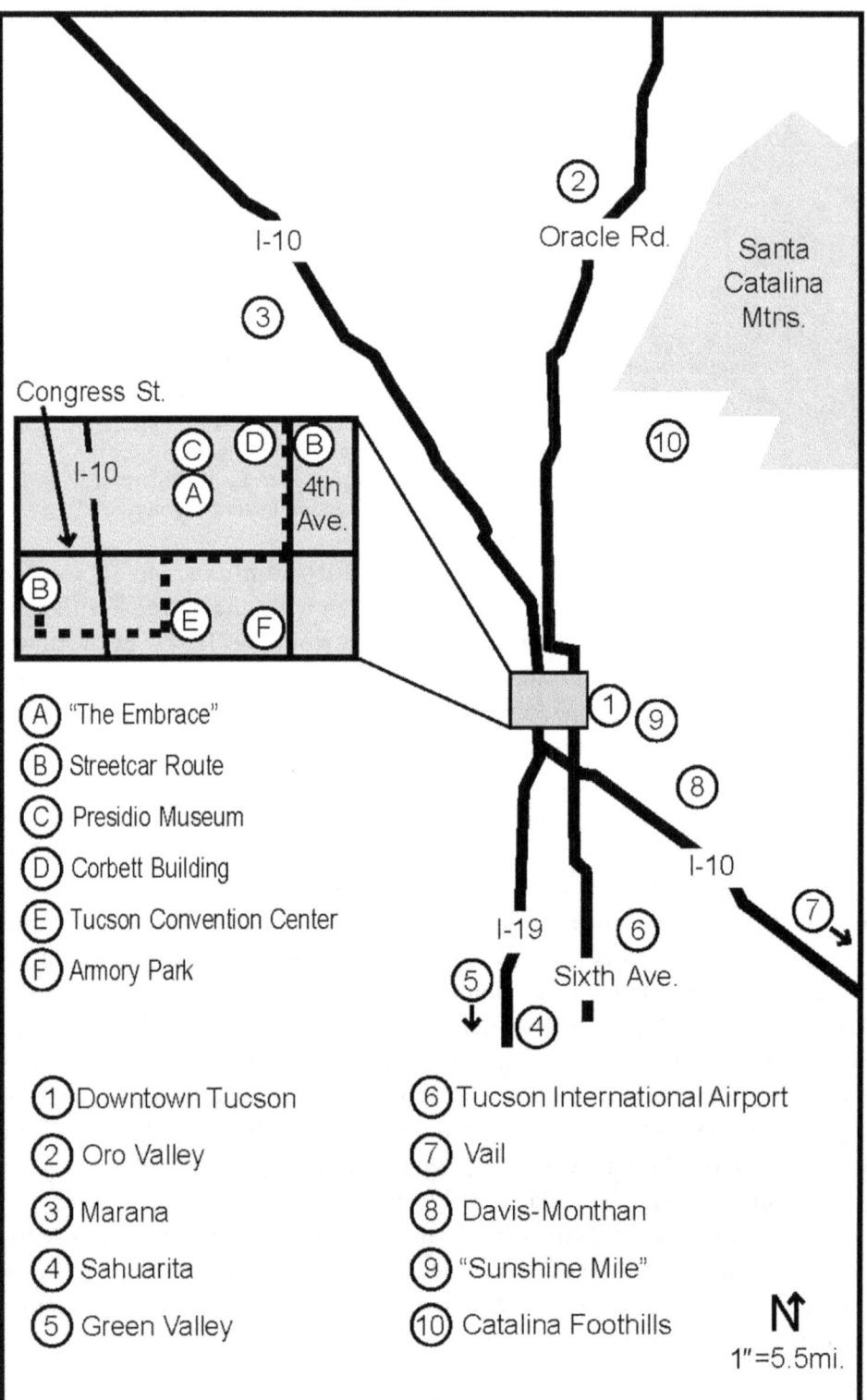

To combat the disease before a vaccine became available, and copying local strategies employed during the 1918 Spanish Flu epidemic, social distancing and mask wearing were mandated. But unlike the earlier effort, enforcement in 2020 was almost non-existent; instead public education about the disease was stressed.

By late May, some retailers and restaurants were reopening. Local COVID-19 deaths, concentrated among the elderly and those with preexisting medical conditions, had reached 235 by mid–June.[6] By the end of that month, Dr. Joe Gerald of the University of Arizona's College of Public Health observed: "Cases are increasing. Everything's trending [in] the wrong direction. Action is still warranted."[7] Responding to those trends, Governor Ducey ordered all theaters, bars and gyms closed again and pushed back the start of the new school year by two weeks.

Demonstrating the extent of the outbreak in Arizona, Mexican government officials and private citizens began taking unusual steps to discourage tourism from north of the border. With the state earning the dubious distinction of having a "status as one of the world's worst spots for the coronavirus outbreak," Pima County opened its first free testing site on July 13.[8]

The start of the new school year saw only a few UA classes being held in-person while most public school districts offered hybrid (in-person and online) instruction. Tucson Unified School District, however, remained with remote learning exclusively. With cases reaching "unprecedented levels" in Arizona by late November 2020, the city of Tucson and Pima County adopted somewhat different overnight curfews. A few people protested these actions, but it was reported in the *Arizona Daily Star*: "Pima County's hospitals are full and COVID-19 case counts keep reaching record highs."[9]

At the end of 2020, more than 1,000 people in Pima County had died of the disease, and almost all K-12 schools were planning to return to online only classes at the start of 2021.[10] But at least Pima County healthcare workers and the highly vulnerable residents of long-term care facilities had begun receiving vaccine injections as the first part of a multi-phase program to combat the disease.

The vaccine program accelerated in the new year to include many of the elderly along with essential workers and educators. Some problems, however, occurred for people wanting to be vaccinated who didn't have internet access in their homes. Around the same time, a Superior Court judge ruled against the county's curfew.

In early March 2021, with statewide case growth slowing, Governor Ducey relaxed some gathering restrictions. At the end of that month, even though the delta variant of the disease was making its appearance, the governor eliminated all restrictions "on businesses and public gatherings." In response, Tucson Mayor Romero insisted the city's mask mandate was still in effect as did Pima County Administrator Chuck Huckelberry.[11]

As April began, about 187,000 Pima County residents had received two COVID shots, meaning they were fully vaccinated, while almost another 1,300 local people had died of the disease in the first three months of the year alone.[12] By around that time, some Tucson stores were selling coronavirus shaped piñatas, "which means you can grab a baseball bat and whack the heck out of the spiky ball we've all come to hate."[13]

In May, masks started coming off as both case numbers dropped sharply and vaccine administration numbers rose. By August, though, cases were increasing again, so masks went back on at the University of Arizona and Pima Community College while the city of Tucson, followed by the UA, required its employees to be vaccinated or receive an exemption, moves opposed by the governor and then declared illegal by Arizona Attorney General Republican Mark Brnovich. A court, however, overturned his decision, and the vaccination mandate returned. At the same time, Pima County required its employees working with "vulnerable populations," i.e., healthcare workers and those at the county jail, to be vaccinated or face termination.[14]

By Thanksgiving 2021, Dr. Theresa Cullen, director of Pima County's health department, stated: "I believe we are looking at getting into a crisis situation," concerning the spread of COVID during holiday gatherings.[15] Fortunately, the delta variant of the disease hadn't proven as deadly as its predecessor, and as 2022 approached, the even less deadly but more contagious new variant, omicron, was appearing. Despite that, Pima County reinstated its mask mandate that would be in place for several months. In total, almost 2,200 county residents had lost their lives to the disease in 2021 while weekly case numbers for that year averaged more than 2,100.[16] Following through on its threat to fire unvaccinated employees, the county terminated 56 people in January 2022, the largest number from the jail. One of those let go explained his decision: "I am not anti-vaccine by any means. I'm just anti-mandate."[17]

The county's mask mandate was terminated again at the end of February 2022 as case numbers dropped once more, and the UA soon followed. After about 30 months of abnormality, by Labor Day life had returned to some semblance of the way things once were in Tucson. Even though there was a spike in cases in late November, the death count was low. Regardless, almost 1,000 residents lost their lives to COVID in 2022.[18] By April 2023, victory over the disease was finally declared as U.S. President Joe Biden "signed a bipartisan congressional resolution to bring it to a close after three years."[19] By then more than 4,300 Pima County residents had been claimed by COVID-19, while almost three-fourths of a million people had been fully vaccinated. The pandemic may have ended, but its impacts in Tucson would continue to reverberate.

Personal Loses and Honors Along with Medical Gains

After early 2020, among those who either died of COVID or other causes were a large number of notable Tucsonans. Musicians and music supporters lost included Desert Song Festival founder Jack Forsythe (2020), pianist Paula Fan (2020), bluesman George Howard (2023), and longtime president of the Arizona Friends of

Chamber Music, Jean-Paul Bierny (2023). Those who celebrated the community or wrote about it that died were Miracle on 31st Street promoter Ramon Gonzales (2020), multi-talented organizer and historian "Big Jim" Griffith (2021), author and world traveler Tom Miller (2022), La Fiesta de los Vaqueros rodeo general manager Gary Williams (2022), and the "Ooh Aah Man," Joe Cavaleri (2023).

Current and past politicians and government officials who passed away between 2020 and 2024 included compassionate Pima County Supervisor Richard Elias (2020), congenial former Tucson Mayor Bob Walkup (2021), long-serving Tucson City Manager and UA vice-president Joel Valdez (2022), retired consensus building Congressman Jim Kolbe (2022), and outspoken former county supervisor Ed Moore (2024). Among the prominent women dying were the eponym of the UA Poetry Center, Helen Schaefer (2022), educator and civil-rights advocate Laura Banks-Reed (2023), and journalist and UA vice-president Edith Auslander (2023).

Others lost included Punch Woods who had retired after successfully leading the Community Food Bank (2020), shoe salesman and hiker-extraordinaire Sid Hirsch (2020), and Hall-of-Fame UA basketball coach Lute Olson (2020). Educator and businessman Morgan Maxwell, Jr., died in 2020, and three years later, his lifelong friend from high school, Frank Borman, also passed away. Although he had gone go on to international fame as a NASA astronaut, Borman recalled of his hometown: "For me, Tucson High was a defining experience."[20]

Making news because of their retirements were UA softball coach Mike Candrea (2021), Tucson Pops conductor László Veres (2022), radio personality Bobby Rich (2023), and TV reporter Lupita Murillo (2024). Pima County Administrator Chuck Huckelberry retired in 2022 but did so only after being seriously injured when hit by a car while riding his bicycle downtown.

Among the numerous Tucsonans honored in the first few years of the decade were internationally known singer Linda Ronstadt along with community activist and historic preservationist Alva Torres. The former had the Tucson Convention Center Music Hall named after her while the latter's name was placed on the plaza in front of that building. Don Guerra of Barrio Bread was presented the James Beard Award for outstanding baker in 2022, and in 2024 local author Gary Paul Nabhan received the James Beard Media Award for writing *Agave Spirits: The Past, Present, and Future of Mezcals*. Also receiving national recognition was Marcia Rieke, a University of Arizona Regents professor, who in 2024 received the Gruber Foundation's Cosmology Prize for her "pioneering work on [the] astronomical instrumentation" of the James Webb space telescope.[21] Two other local women made history for much different reasons. On July 4, 2021, elementary school mathematics teacher Michelle Lesco won the women's title in the Nathan's Famous Hot Dog Eating Contest on Coney Island in Brooklyn, New York. Then in 2024, Sunnyside High School student Audrey Jimenez made history by winning the state wrestling championship in the 106-pound weight class, becoming "the first girl to win an Arizona state wrestling title against boys."[22]

Things were altering rapidly in the first few years of the decade due to social changes, COVID impacts, and many other reasons. Among the institutions affected were the area's hospitals that were put under huge financial strain during the pandemic because of an overall drop in total patient numbers with their staffs having to deal with COVID sufferers along with the simultaneous almost complete elimination of profitable elective surgeries. Most seriously impacted was the hospital in Green Valley that even a state $3.6 million subsidy couldn't save, and it closed in July 2022. Other suburban hospitals were opening around the same time with Northwest Healthcare establishing an 18-bed facility in Sahuarita in 2020, then premiering a 51-bed medical center in the southeast part of town in 2022. For its patients, Tucson Medical Center debuted a 60-bed hospital on the southeast side in 2024.

Local and statewide controversy swirled following the U.S. Supreme Court's 2022 abortion decision overturning *Roe v. Wade* (1973). With confusion reigning about what state law applied, a total ban or a 15-week measure, at first Planned Parenthood decided in July it would stop providing the procedure in Pima County but resumed offering abortions by the end of August.[23] That decision was upended in April 2024 when the Arizona Supreme Court decided the original 1864 territorial law banning almost all abortions was still in effect. Mayor Romero labeled the ruling "devastating."[24] Faced with intense public dissatisfaction following the court's decision, the Arizona legislature quickly repealed the territorial law, and it was signed by Arizona governor, Democrat Katie Hobbs.

Heated Housing Topics, Slow Population Growth, and a Lackluster Economy

Another controversial issue was how to deal with Tucson's homeless population. While their numbers had grown to more than 2,200 by 2023, that figure was similar in percentage of the total population as other Southwest cities.[25] The proliferation of a few large camps where people lived in tents occasionally caused conflicts with those residing nearby. In an infamous 2023 case, neighbors had 50 trees cut down on a vacant midtown city-owned lot that was used as a camp.[26] At an eastside site called "the Acres" that had once been used as a mountain bike trail park, dozens of people lived in tents, but in 2024 the city of Tucson was moving them out.[27]

While a few thousand people were without homes in Tucson, a much larger number were having a hard time paying their ever-increasing rent costs. "In 2020," one real estate spokesman pointed out, "Tucson was one of the nation's leaders in rent growth, and the city's multifamily vacancy rate was at its lowest level in 20 years."[28] Between 2020 and 2024, the fair market rent for a one bedroom apartment shot up almost 40 percent, from $720 per month to about $1,000.[29] The overall result was that "[s]ince the pandemic, Tucson rents have increased twice as fast as local workers' incomes."[30]

To combat the increasing unaffordability of many rental units, a number of projects and programs were implemented by local governments and non-profit organizations. The city of Tucson was converting some old motels into affordable living units along with building many new apartments. As Mayor Romero observed of these projects, "A private developer might say, 'It doesn't pencil out for us'…. Well, it pencils out for us as a city because we don't have to make a huge profit."[31]

In South Tucson, the Casa Maria soup kitchen bought two old motels, intending to convert them into affordable housing units. Some for-profit companies were also trying to provide this type of unit, including at a motel conversion on St. Mary's Road along with a new 77-unit complex on the southwest side and apartments for seniors downtown.

As rents zoomed up in the decade's early years, so did single-family home prices, driven in part by the pandemic-era extremely low interest rates. Despite the steep rise in prices, more than 4,300 permits were issued for new homes in 2020, and according to the Tucson Association of Realtors, the median sales price for a single-family home was $285,000. Three years later, the number of annual permits had fallen to 3,700, but median single-family home sales prices in July 2024 had spiked to $396,000.[32] By around that same time, however, these high prices were stabilizing and building permit numbers were increasing. Data from the National Association of Home Builders in early 2024 showed that the typical family in Pima County required 37 percent of their monthly income to be devoted to a mortgage payment, considerably higher than the recommended standard of 28–30 percent.[33]

The result of these large price increases was many homes were unaffordable to a quickly growing number of people. In 2021 almost 75 percent of "single-family homes sold in Tucson were affordable to a family earning the median income," but within two years that figure had dropped precipitously to 38 percent.[34] Thus Tucson was quickly losing the status of having been known for affordable homes and apartments.

The rapid rise in housing prices was apparently driven primarily by a lack of new supply, especially of rental units. At the same time, compared to its past, the Tucson region wasn't growing in population all that much. Between 2020, when Pima County's population was 1.04 million, and 2024, the entire region had grown by about 30,000 people, or 0.75 percent per year, to an estimated 1.07 million people. Much of this growth was taking place in suburban areas with Marana gaining 6,500 people for a total of almost 60,000, Oro Valley climbing by 2,000 to just under 50,000, Sahuarita adding 2,500 to show close to 37,000 residents, and unincorporated Vail housing 2,000 additional residents. For its part, the city of Tucson in those four years gained less than 7,000 new residents to reach 547,000 people, and this slow increase in population meant the prediction was made in 2023 that "Mesa [Arizona] should overtake Tucson as the second-most populous city in Arizona in about a decade."[35]

Another change for city residents was that the ethnic transition in the population seen in the previous few decades was continuing. The number of Hispanic

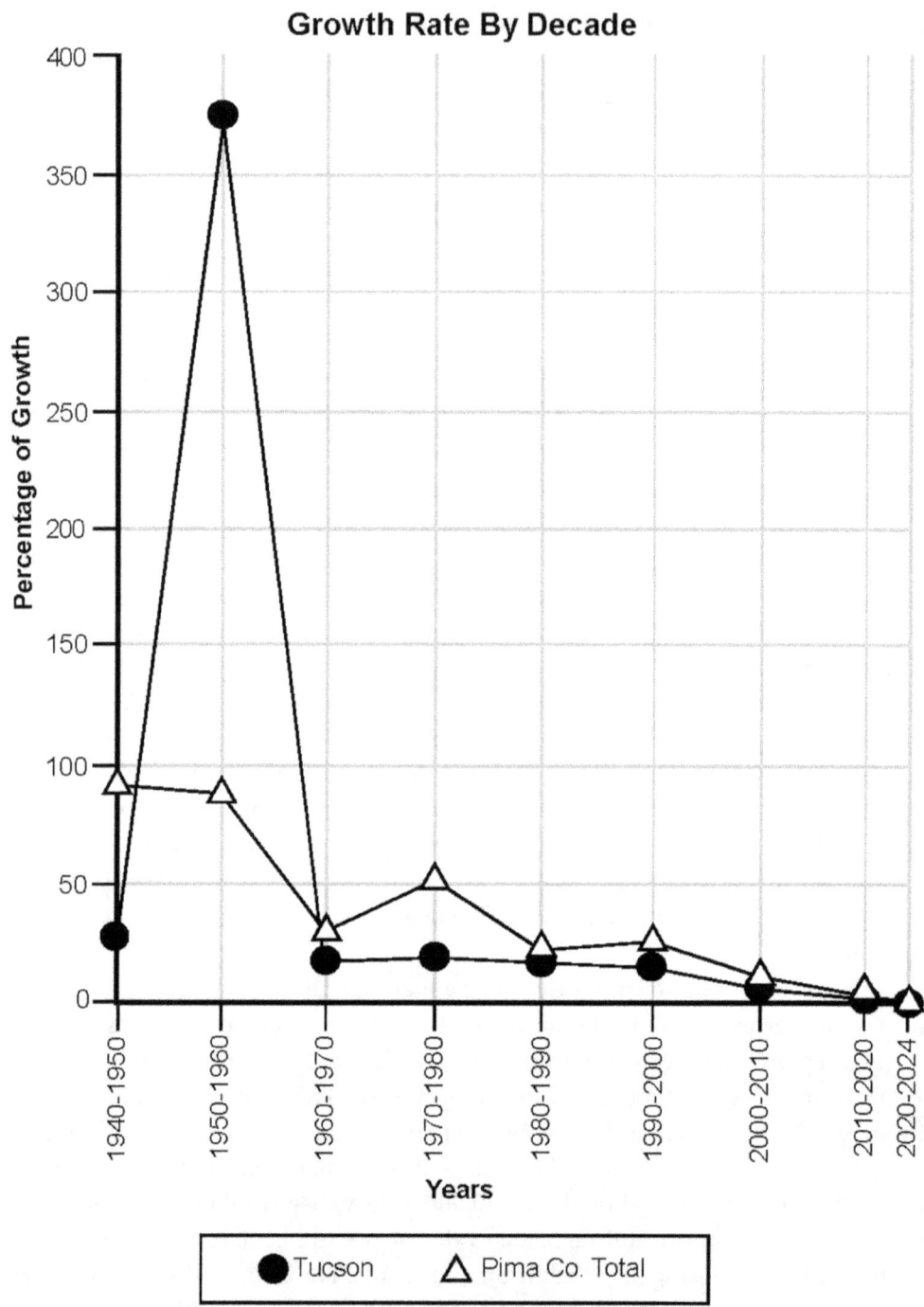

Source: Pima Association Of Governments; U.S. Census Bureau

people in the city of Tucson by 2024 was almost two percentage points greater than the White population, meaning that for the first time in around a century, Whites were not the largest population group inside the Tucson city limits. The Pima

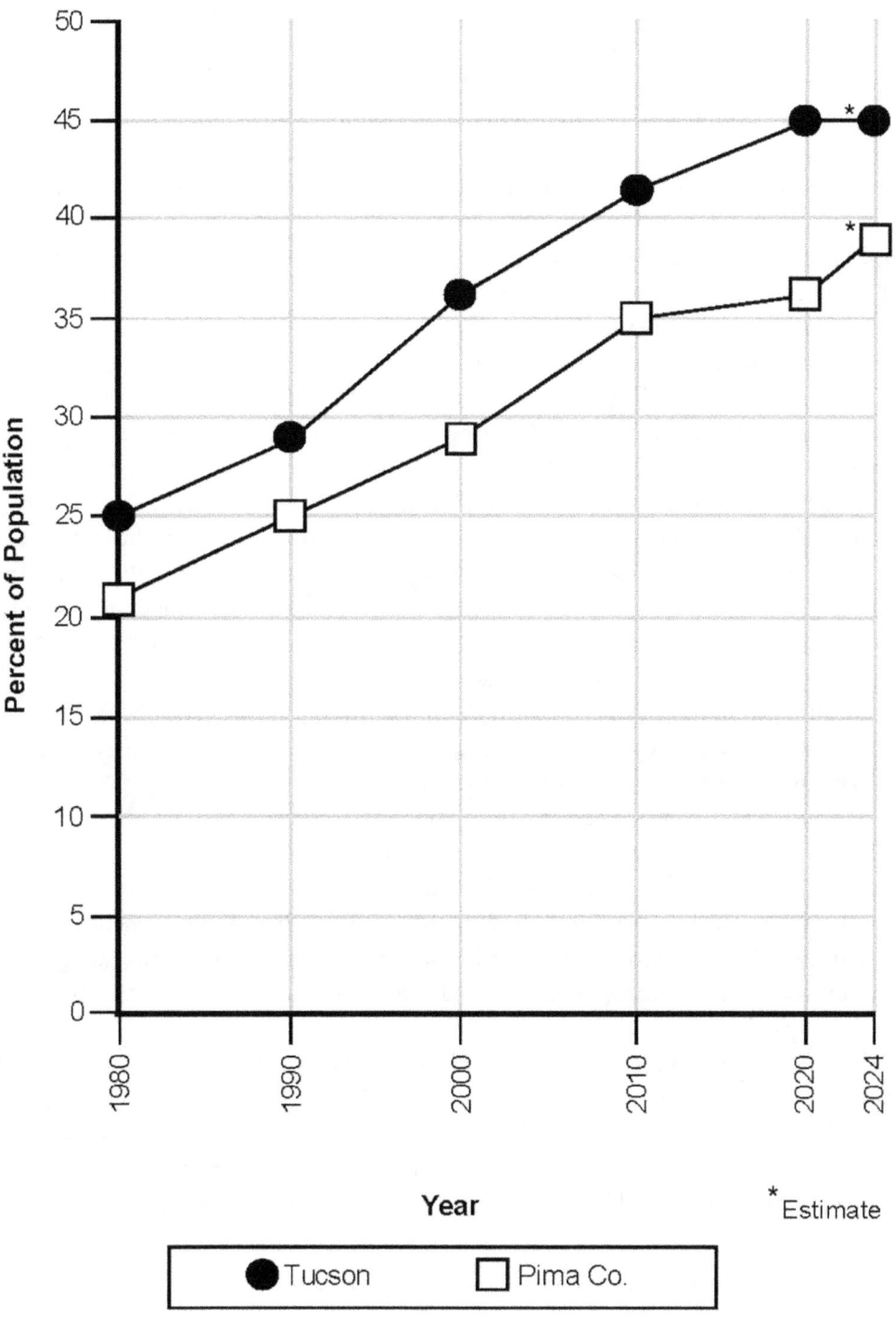

County population as a whole was 50 percent White, 38.5 percent Hispanic, 4.4 percent Black, and 3.3 percent Asian.

One reason for the continual slow population growth rate was that new jobs weren't being created all that quickly. Unsurprisingly, because of its heavy reliance on government, tourism, and service sector employment, Tucson lost almost 45,500 jobs in the early months of the COVID pandemic as these major economic sectors got hit extremely hard. That weakness continued through 2021 so it could be reported at the end of that year that "the Tucson area lags the entire state with just 78% of jobs lost during the pandemic recovered through October."[36] It wouldn't be until the end of 2022, around 30 months after the beginning of the COVID-19 era, that the region had recovered all its lost jobs and returned to a more normal slow rate of growth in job creation.[37]

Along with a gradual return of tourism and service sector employment by 2021, there were some new job opportunities including Amazon building a sorting center near the municipal airport, GEICO hiring 250 people to add to its already large local employee numbers, and a couple of lithium battery firms announcing they would either come to town or expand their existing operations. The 2022 Russian invasion of Ukraine specifically helped boost local employment at Raytheon to more than 12,000 people because the firm assembled missiles used in the conflict.[38] On the horizon was a new casino expected to open in 2026 on west Grant Road to be built by the Pascua Yaqui tribe. There was also the prospect of hundreds of jobs in the Santa Rita Mountains south of Tucson as Hudbay Minerals, Inc., proposed developing the multi-mine, long-term Copper World Complex. It was a controversial idea that supporters said would provide critically needed vital minerals but was opposed by many area people on environmental and scenic grounds.[39]

While the mine would create high-paying jobs, Tucson continued to be a generally low-wage community. The 2022 median household income in Tucson was $64,323, a figure only 86 percent of the national average and more than $15,000 lower than that for Phoenix.[40] At least by March 2024 the unemployment rate was an extremely low 2.8 percent. To aid the many people employed in low-paying jobs, Tucson voters in November 2021 approved a minimum wage initiative that required $15/hour pay by 2025.

Higher wages could certainly help lift some people out of poverty, and by 2022 the rate in Tucson was almost 20 percent and in Pima County 14.5 percent. These figures were somewhat lower than they had been a decade before but still extremely high by state and national standards. Many of these poor residents faced food insecurity, and the percentage of county households in that category was approaching 13 percent in 2020.[41]

Educational—Environmental—Entertainment Topics

While poverty, abortion procedures, proposed open pit mines, and homelessness were issues creating some controversy in Tucson in the post–COVID period, they couldn't compare with the 2023–24 financial turmoil at the University of Arizona. The sorry saga publicly began on November 6, 2023, when University president Robert C. Robbins informed the Arizona Board of Regents (ABOR) that a required reserve account budget would not meet its target. The shortfall, he estimated, would be $240 million, a situation labeled as a "financial crisis" by some ABOR members.[42] "We made a bet on spending money," Robbins explained to the regents. "We just overshot."[43]

The next day, Robbins told the university's Faculty Senate "draconian cuts" would be required to close the deficit. Sometime later he informed the same group that the Athletic Department had been loaned $87 million since the COVID pandemic began and hadn't paid any of it back. In staff shakeups, chief financial officer Lisa Rulney was replaced by ABOR executive director John Arnold, and athletic director Dave Heeke was let go.

By late January 2024, Governor Hobbs indicated she didn't trust the process University administrators were using to fix the budget problem. "This is no longer just about finances," she wrote. "This is about a lack of accountability, transparency, and at the end of the day, leadership."[44]

Around that time, the actual deficit was said to be $177 million, and Arnold was leading a budgetary cost-cutting effort that resulted in hundreds of faculty and staff member reductions.[45] Hobbs, however, remained dissatisfied with the UA, so on April 2, 2024, the *Arizona Daily Star* reported: "Robbins announces he will step down at the end of his contract on June 30, 2026, or sooner, if ABOR finds a replacement before then."[46] The Board did just that, quickly hiring University of Vermont president Suresh Garimella who took over in October 2024. Robbins, however, would continue to be paid approximately $1 million a year until the end of his contract while working "as a tenured faculty member at the university's Tucson College of Medicine."[47]

Former UA president John Schaefer wasn't impressed with the approach the Board of Regents took to replace Robbins. "There are no simple answers to the University's current problems," Schaefer wrote in May 2024, "but there are options that should be evaluated and discussed."[48]

Robbins' earlier handling of COVID-related issues on campus, that included across-the-board furloughs, pays cuts, and some layoffs, garnered him better reviews than his 2023–24 budgetary shortfall response. Following the peak COVID period, the fall 2021 university school year saw about two-thirds of classes held in-person, 75 percent of employees vaccinated against the disease, and a $50 million donation from R. Ken Coit to the College of Pharmacy. By the fall of 2023, on-campus enrollment exceeded 40,000 students and the following year had the most diverse freshman class in school history.

Rising housing costs along with higher annual tuition and fees of $13,900 for those from in-state and $42,300 from out-of-state would greet students when they arrived on campus in August 2024.[49] Those who chose to reside at Ari on Fourth

Avenue, a new gigantic private downtown housing project, would pay a minimum of $1,200 monthly for a bed in a two-bedroom apartment pod.

The approximately 400 Native American students from an Arizona tribe wouldn't pay any tuition or fees to attend the university, however, under a program announced in June 2022. Those students comprised about 3 percent of the undergraduate enrollment, while Hispanics were 26 percent, 6.5 percent were Black, 10 percent Asian, and the balance White.

As tuition and enrollment rose at the UA, things were somewhat different at Pima Community College (PCC). The number of students declined by almost 45 percent between 2013 and 2022 to 10,700 full-time equivalent students before rising to exceed 11,500 by 2023.[50] The school also saw an expansion of its highly regarded Aviation Technology Center as well as the opening a $35 million advanced manufacturing center in May 2023. Around that time, PCC Chancellor Lee Lambert announced he was leaving after 10 years to take a job in California.[51]

At the elementary and secondary education levels, there were a limited number of public protests about COVID restrictions. These included 150 people in September 2020 urging all public schools in the county be reopened for in-person instruction because "kids are depressed, disengaged, miss their friends, miss school sports and extracurricular activities."[52] After many districts returned to classroom instruction, some COVID cases occurred in their schools and their staff and students were quarantined. As a result, some of these districts temporarily went back to remote learning.[53] In April 2021, more than a year after the pandemic began, protestors complaining about the Vail district's mask mandate required the police to be summoned and forced the cancellation of a school board meeting.[54]

The pandemic also saw the flight of thousands of students from traditional public schools to charter and private schools or to in-home instruction that had less stringent COVID rules. By March 2021, almost 7,500 children had departed public schools for these options.[55] Once in-person classes began again in public schools, about one-half of these students returned.[56] But in 2022, when the state of Arizona began offering around $7,000 annual vouchers to all students to be used for any type of schooling, the flight from traditional public schools accelerated once again.

As a result of having lost nearly 3,350 students during COVID and its enrollment dropping to a total of around 42,000, the Tucson Unified School District (TUSD) let more than 60 teachers go for the 2021–22 term.[57] On a brighter note, after 44 years of legal wrangling, in July 2022 the district's desegregation lawsuit finally came to an end. Plus, in November 2023, district voters for the first time in 20 years approved a bond package, this one to spend $480 million to finance numerous capital improvements as well as security and safety measures.

Three other districts had either bond or operational overrides on the ballot at the same time, and they all passed, including a budget override in the Sunnyside district that broke a long string of failures. A lack of operational funds three years earlier had forced the district to cut 160 jobs. For its part, the Vail district opened Mica Mountain High School in 2020.

With several traditional public school districts experiencing declining enrollments during the COVID era, one way they had of balancing their budgets was to keep teacher pay low. A 2023 survey showed that Tucson's secondary school teachers, at $49,500 annually, were the lowest paid in 12 Southwest cities.[58] On a statewide basis, in 2024 Arizona continued to be next to the bottom in per-pupil speeding.[59]

While teacher's pay was a major problem, more public attention was focused on what was happening with Tucson's climate. The decade began with July 2020 being "the city's hottest month in the 125 years that records have been kept."[60] That startling statistic was then beaten the following month when the average daily high temperature was almost 106 blistering degrees. Overall, the four years from 2020 to 2023 all ranked in the top 11 warmest years on record, and heat-related deaths became a regularly reported statistic, claiming 126 local residents in 2023.[61]

Not only was the climate getting progressively warmer, but precipitation was also more extreme on both ends. In 2020 the least total annual rainfall—4.17 inches—in 125 years was seen. That amount was doubled in one month the following July when more than 8 inches of rain fell, making it the wettest month on record. The drought that had gripped Southern Arizona for decades was apparently subsiding by April 2024 with only small, scattered parts of Pima County having either exceptional or extreme drought conditions.[62]

Additional environmental news included Tucson Electric Power (TEP) providing 20 percent of its energy from renewable sources by 2023 with another seven percent coming from private, i.e., homeowner, solar systems. These figures exceeded TEP's legally mandated amount but dissatisfied the company's critics who thought they were too low.[63] The Santa Catalina Mountains in 2020 saw its Pusch Ridge sheep population hold steady at an estimated 100 while that same year lighting caused a major wildfire—Bighorn—that required people to once again evacuate the Summerhaven community on Mount Lemmon. Even though it exceeded the 2003 historic Aspen fire in size, this blaze didn't destroy any man-made structures. It did, however, bring about a lengthy closure of the popular Sabino Canyon Recreation Area due to the increased threat of flooding that could be caused by the loss of forest undergrowth to the fire.

After the flooding potential passed, the popular canyon reopened. Many traditional community activities also returned in 2021 after their COVID hiatus including 4th of July fireworks, the All Souls "Day of the Dead" procession, the weekend airshow at Davis-Monthan, the Fourth Avenue Winter Street Fair, and the Winterhaven festival of lights. Springtime in 2022 saw the rodeo parade and La Fiesta de los Vaqueros return as well as the Festival of Books and the Gem and Mineral Show. Two teams making the most of their return to play following the pandemic were the Pima Community College soccer squads. The men won the 2021 junior college national championship, and the women placed second.

On the UA campus, sports had some extreme highs and depressing lows. The Pac-12 played a pandemic-shortened football season in 2020, and Arizona's head coach Kevin Sumlin, after compiling a 9–20 record in three years, including a blowout 70–7 home loss to Arizona State University (ASU), was fired and replaced by Jedd Fisch. The team kept getting defeated until it beat the University of California–Berkeley in November 2021 to break an embarrassing 20-game losing streak. Then things turned around quickly, and by 2023 Arizona had a 9–3 record before beating Oklahoma in a bowl game, after which Fisch sauntered off to coach the University of Washington and was replaced by Brent Brennan, who signed a five-year, $17.5 million contract.

Also getting a substantial salary was new UA men's basketball coach Tommy Lloyd who inked a $15.5 million, five-year contract in 2021.[64] He had replaced Sean Miller whose teams in 12 years went 302–109 but didn't participate in the 2021 NCAA "March Madness" tournament because of previous serious infractions; Miller was fired in April 2021.

Women's basketball coach Adia Barnes was also paid well, signing an almost $6 million, 5-year contract in 2021. Her 2020–21 team rose higher than the men's program when, led by star player Aari McDonald, they got to the NCAA championship game but lost to Stanford, 54–53.

On the diamond, in 2023 the UA softball team failed to qualify for the NCAA tournament for the first time in 35 years, but they did qualify again in 2024. That same year, since the league was disbanding, the baseball team claimed what would prove to be the last of 65 Pac-12 league championship titles won by the UA in its almost five decades in the conference.

In other campus sports news, athletes were doing better in the classroom than in the past.[65] No UA team, however, won a NCAA championship between 2020 and 2024, but student Delaney Schnell did bring home a silver medal in 10-meter, synchronized diving from the 2021 Tokyo Olympics.

The two biggest campus sports news items, however, had nothing to do with game-day performance. First, starting with the pandemic, the athletic department was spending far more than it was earning, and that deficit was expected to substantially increase because of a 2025 NCAA-wide class action lawsuit settlement.[66] But instead of cutting the athletic budget, the decision was made that the department "will pay back its loans to the university in accordance with future net revenue instead of paying them back on a fixed schedule."[67] The second major sports item was that after 108 years, 46 of them with the UA as a member, the Pac-12 conference broke apart in 2024 with Arizona as well as ASU, Colorado, and Utah heading to the Big 12 conference.

In addition to the dismantling of the Pac-12 conference, during the first few years of the decade a few longtime local attractions and businesses closed, some temporarily, others permanently. Old Tucson shut down in the summer of 2020 but was back in business two years later. Tucson Greyhound Park, that hadn't seen live racing since 2016 but offered off-track betting, closed its doors for good in June 2022. That same year, a kitchen fire forced the shutdown of the well-liked Casa Molina restaurant on Speedway Boulevard that had been in business since the late 1940s. For financial and other reasons, both the 2024 and 2025 horse racing seasons at Rillito Downs were cancelled. Also closing was the Safari Club International's Wildlife Museum that shut its doors for the last time at the end of 2023. At the other end of the entertainment spectrum, in 2023 Tucson Meet Yourself celebrated 50 years of showcasing the community's diversity and that same year the whimsical Valley of the Moon marked its centennial. Then, in 2024, the Rogue Theater began its 20th season of producing thought-provoking performances while the Tucson Museum of Art commemorated its first 100 years with an exhibit entitled "Time Travelers: Foundations, Transformations, and Expansions at the Centennial."

Space—Fences—Crime

Travel of another sort was produced by the UA-led OSIRIS-REx space program. When its payload capsule touched down in the Utah desert on September 24, 2023, the mission had successfully navigated its seven-year lengthy route to the asteroid Bennu, obtained a sizable sample of rocks and dust, and returned. As the UA's Dante Lauretta, principal investigator of the mission, exclaimed after the spacecraft's initial 2020 contact with Bennu: "This is historic. This is amazing."[68]

But the truly amazing mission wasn't finished when the payload capsule returned to earth. In 2023 NASA had approved sending the spacecraft on an additional six year flight to study another asteroid, a follow-up effort headed by UA assistant professor Dani DellaGiustina. It was that type of space triumph that in 2022 maintained the 35-year streak of the UA being, "the nation's No. 1 school for astronomy and astrophysics research, according to data compiled by the National Science Foundation."[69]

For earth-bound aviation, at Tucson International Airport (TIA) by late 2023 most of the passenger traffic lost during the pandemic had returned.[70] At the same time, community leaders and Davis-Monthan Air Force Base (DM) supporters were breathing a sigh of relief as new missions began emerging to replace the base's slowly retiring A-10 attack aircraft. One of these was a special-operations wing that would fly a variety of military planes. "We're very optimistic about the future of D-M," proclaimed Linda Morales, chair of the base support group, DM50, in 2023.[71]

Like TIA, downtown Tucson had received a severe shock during the COVID era. The area lost two of its iconic restaurants—Suzana Davila's Café Poca Cosa and Janos Wilder's Downtown Kitchen & Cocktails.[72] Several downtown hotels opened, however, including one in 2023 when nine floors of Tucson's tallest building were converted into a hotel. Premiering in the area two years earlier was the memorial to Tucson's January 8, 2011, shooting victims entitled "The Embrace."

Early 2024 saw the completion of a decades-long, Rio Nuevo taxing-district-funded, $100 million program of improvements at the Tucson Convention Center. These included 233,000 square feet of new or upgraded meeting space, additional parking, and improvements to the grounds.

What hadn't happened downtown by the fall of 2024 was implementation of a long-planned, mixed-use project of retail, office, and residential spaces to be built above the Ronstadt Transit Center on Congress Street. Improvements needed to reopen the long-shuttered original convention center hotel also hadn't been made. But at least the historic 1930 Corbett lumberyard building on 6th Avenue was renovated and opened as a restaurant/bar featuring a few pickleball courts.

Another item reflecting local history was the 2020 listing on the National Register of Historic Places of Broadway Boulevard's "Sunshine Mile" of mid-century buildings from Euclid Avenue to Country Club Road. Four years later, the UA Farms on Campbell Avenue were also listed on the Register as were three Tucson Medical Center buildings.

In 2020 the Arizona Historical Society closed the eastside Fort Lowell Museum, but it reopened in 2023 after renovation and under the management of the Presidio Trust that additionally operated downtown's Presidio Museum. Also restored was Pima County's historic, mosaic-tiled third courthouse from 1929 with new uses including the Southern Arizona Heritage & Visitor Center as well as an impressive gem and mineral museum. The formerly segregated Dunbar School received a $1.1 million federal grant in 2022 to continue renovating the important structure on West Second Street. The next year, downtown's Sosa-Carrillo House was sold by the Historical Society to the Rio Nuevo taxing district to facilitate improvements to the adobe home believed to have built around 1880.

Some historic restaurants and other commercial establishments garnered special attention. Because of COVID, the El Casino ballroom marked its 75th anniversary one year late in 2023 and its manager observed: "That's why we hit 75, because the community is here for us. They are the heart and soul of El Casino."[73] Celebrating 50th anniversaries of being in business were Fourth Avenue's Antigone Books (2023), the multi-store Buffalo Exchange (2024), and the nonprofit artist group, WomanKraft (2024). Also that year, South Tucson's nationally famous Mi Nidito Mexican restaurant was sold by the Lopez family after 72 years of ownership.

Change was also coming to Tucson's shopping malls as the boost COVID gave to online shopping negatively impacted the large retail centers. The last Sears store in Tucson was located at Tucson Mall but shut its doors in 2020 and a few months later the Macy's at Park Place Mall also closed. Those were followed by J.C. Penney's pulling out of El Con Mall. In early 2023, a major project was begun to transfer Foothills Mall, renamed Uptown, from a shopping center to a "multi-use site with shops, restaurants, hotels and housing," the last being 157 apartment units.[74] The need for traditional shopping malls to rethink their business model was also demonstrated by the 2023 sale of Park Place at a foreclosure auction.

Also changing substantially was the federal government's handling of migrants seeking to enter the United States. During the administration of President Donald Trump, extensive construction on a border fence in Southern Arizona took place. At a 2020 re-election campaign stop in Tucson, Trump exclaimed of the fence: "You have a big chunk of it right here, and it's really worked. You have 200 miles, they tell me. 200 miles. 200 miles. I didn't even know you had that. That's a lot of mileage. You're not paying a damn cent for it either. All compliments of the federal government."[75]

The fence did stretch across much of Southern Arizona except in extremely difficult terrain and on the Tohono O'odham nation that did not allow construction along its 62 miles of border land. Tribal chair Verlon M. Jose in 2023 expressed the view to a U.S. Congressional subcommittee that "[w]hile migrants crossing the Tohono O'odham reservation are causing problems, those are overshadowed by problems from the construction of the border wall meant to stop them."[76]

Even before COVID arrived, the past federal practice of allowing asylum seekers following Border Patrol processing to enter the United States to await a judicial hearing had ended. It was under this policy that tens of thousands of people annually spent a day or two in Tucson before moving on to their final destination. But by January 2020, according to a federal official: "Catch and release has ended. Aliens will not be permitted to disappear into the U.S. before a court determines that they are entitled to relief or protection."[77]

With the arrival of COVID, people apprehended crossing the border were simply stopped from entering the United States entirely. One outcome of that policy shift was that migrants, often led by smugglers, sought to cross the border in more dangerous places. As a result, the number of those dying while attempting to cross rose to a ten-year high of 215 in 2020.[78]

After Joe Biden became president in January 2021, most of the construction on the border fence stopped, asylum seekers were once again processed in Tucson, and the number of people encountered along the international boundary in the Tucson Sector of the Border Patrol started rising sharply. For the federal fiscal year ending on September 30, 2021, around 191,000 total encounters had taken place, a ten-year high.[79] Overall, in May 2022 a monthly record number of 6,300 people required the services of Casa Alitas, the welcome center operated by the Catholic Church and funded by Pima County using federal money.[80]

In response to the growing number of crossers, with 252,000 encounters in the Tucson Sector during federal fiscal year 2022, Arizona Governor Doug Ducey in October of that year ordered two long gaps in the border fence filled with empty shipping containers.[81] By the time Katie Hobbs had replaced Ducey in January 2023, he had been forced by the federal government to begin removing the containers. A total of almost $164 million was spent on the temporary, unsuccessful project, labeled by Democrat Hobbs as a "political stunt."[82]

The containers were completely ineffective and migrants kept crossing the border in very high numbers, requiring the March 2023 opening of a second hospitality

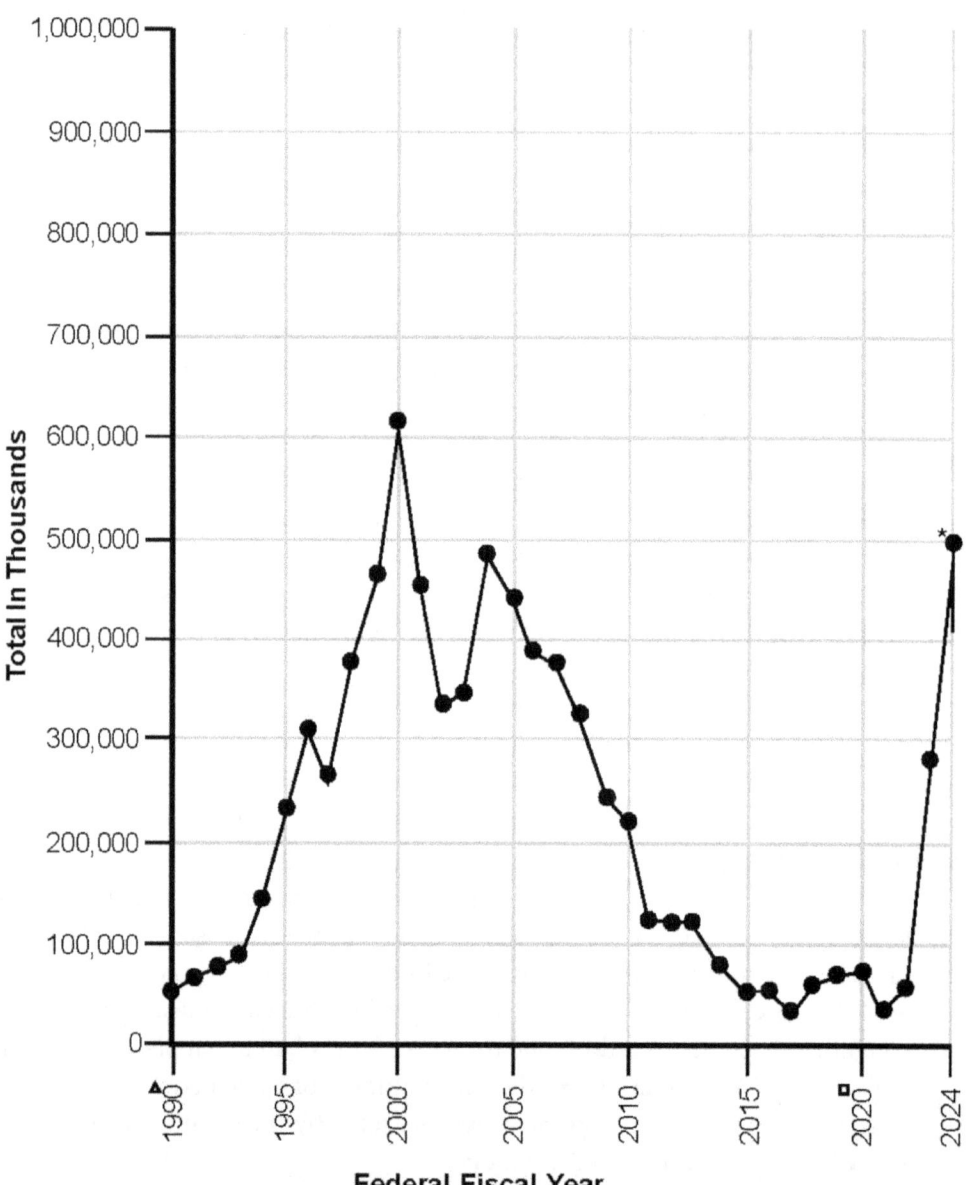

Border Patrol Tucson Sector Apprehensions/Encounters

▲ From Federal Fiscal Year 1990-2019
Figures For Border Apprehensions

▫ Federal Fiscal Year 2020-2024
Figures For Title 8 Border Encounters

*Estimate

Source: United States Border Patrol Apprehensions/Encounters By U.S. Fiscal Year

center in Tucson to supplement the services of the original Casa Alitas.[83] By May 2023, up to 1,600 people a night were being released in Tucson by the Border Patrol.[84] At the end of the 2023 federal fiscal year in September, 373,625 encounters had occurred in the Tucson Sector, meaning the number of encounters had almost doubled in a two year period.

The number of those encountered in the sector kept rising even further after that, peaking in December 2023 at more than 80,000 for the month. This was the highest number of any of the Border Patrol's nine sectors by the end of 2023, and Governor Hobbs ordered about one hundred Arizona National Guard troops to assist with border security operations. But in the twelve months ending in September 2024, the number of encounters had skyrocketed to almost 465,000, about one-fourth more than the previous federal fiscal year.[85] The vast increase led eastside Tucson Republican Congressman Juan Ciscomani to comment in February of 2024: "The numbers keep going up, things are getting worse, and people are suffering—they're dying crossing the desert. It's frustrating."[86]

Another thing that was going up was the amount of firearms and ammunition being smuggled into Mexico from the United States. Tens of thousands of rounds along with immense numbers of guns and gun parts were seized before being taken south of the border, meaning much more was probably getting through.

While politicians debated about what to do regarding the "border crisis," Tucson residents had joined others across the nation in protesting two events. The murder of George Floyd by a Minneapolis police officer in May 2020 led to well-attended, local peaceful demonstrations, with one on the UA campus attracting about 3,000 people. Plus, there were a few nights of downtown vandalism that resulted in an estimated $200,000 in property damage as well as dozens of arrests. Springtime in 2024 twice saw the creation of temporary protest campsites on the UA campus during the Hamas-Israel war in Gaza.

One much smaller protest followed the fatal shooting of Raymond Mattia, an unarmed 58-year-old man living on the Tohono O'odham reservation. Border Patrol officials claimed he was intoxicated, threw a machete in a sheath at their officers, then reached into his jacket before being shot ten times.[87] After no legal charges were filed against the involved officers, tribal chair Verlon Jose and vice-chair Carla L. Johnson called that decision "a travesty of justice" and added, "While politicians waste time debating walls and other ineffective and divisive ideas, our people are persecuted and, in this case, killed by federal agents. This must stop."[88] Eventually, Mattia's family filed a civil lawsuit seeking damages and more information about the case.

Other fatal shootings impacted the UA campus. In October 2022, University of Arizona professor Thomas Meixner, head of the Hydrology and Atmospheric Sciences Department, was gunned down in his office building by expelled student Murad Dervish.[89] The spring of 2024 saw sophomore student Erin Jones killed at an off-campus party where the shooting lasted more than six minutes and more than 80 rounds were fired.[90] Then in September, Pima Community College student Minhaj Jamshidi was shot and killed during a volleyball match on the UA campus.[91]

Despite those tragic individual cases, and Pima County Attorney Laura Conover observing in 2024 that the "community is just awash in firearms," in the early years of the decade homicides were actually falling in Pima County.[92] They went from a record high of 119 in 2021 to a total of 90 two years later. Among all those violent deaths were some mass killings with four people, including the shooter, dying in July 2021 and four more people in November of that same year. Another four people, including Pima County constable Deborah Martinez, died in a 2022 shooting and the next year a 12-year-old child murdered a man he was robbing before he himself was slain by gunfire from his victim's companion.

Also dying early in the decade were a few public safety officers. In October 2021, Drug Enforcement Administration (DEA) supervisory agent Michael Garbo was fatally shot as he tried to apprehend a drug smuggler aboard an Amtrak train stopped at the Tucson depot. In the summer of 2024, Rural Metro Fire cadet Cody Treatch "suffered a heat/dehydration-related emergency" while in training and passed away.[93] A few months earlier, as he rushed to assist on a service call, Tucson Police Department (TPD) officer Adam Buckner was killed in April 2024 by an inattentive motorist who "failed to yield."[94]

Officer Buckner's death was another blow to a department that continued to decrease in size. Police Chief Chris Magnus had warned in 2021 this trend would last as long as officer pay remained low. "When they're that far underpaid [13% below market value], there really doesn't seem to be much hope for the future," he observed.[95]

As a result of a staff that by 2023 was at only 830 officers, TPD stopped responding to many non-violent calls. After Magnus departed town for a job in Washington, D.C., new chief Chad Kasmar indicated he wanted more attention paid to traffic violations and pedestrian deaths. But both red-light running and those on foot crossing major streets seemingly everywhere had become common occurrences by then. As Kasmar commented in 2023: "We really need to think about as a community moving to a proudly funded police department."[96]

As homicides inside the Tucson city limits hit a record high in 2021 of 93, drug deaths from overdoses were also on the rise. Overdoses by 2021, many from fentanyl, accounted for almost 500 annual deaths in Pima County and two years later the number had reached 532.[97] Other crimes increasing within the Tucson city limits between 2020 and 2023 included aggravated assaults and burglaries, but sexual assaults and convenience store robberies both fell.[98]

Besides understaffing at TPD, many other city departments in 2021 had too few employees, including Parks & Recreation and the Public Safety Communications Department.[99] Another major topic confronting the Tucson City Council that year was the contentious issue of expanding the Reid Park Zoo. Following enormous public pressure, the council eventually decided to change the site of the expansion to a less controversial location. In 2020, the zoo had welcomed baby elephant Mapenzi (meaning Love), and in 2024 another one named Meru, after Mount Meru in Tanzania, was born.

Other news from City Hall included Juneteenth (June 19) being made an official city holiday in 2022. By 2023, only about ten percent of Mayor Romero's goal of planting one million trees by 2030 had been accomplished, but at least the federal government was temporarily chipping in a few million dollars to help the effort.[100]

In May 2023 Tucson voters soundly rejected an extension of the Tucson Electric Power (TEP) franchise that allowed the company to utilize public right-of-way for its infrastructure. One of the main causes of the defeat was a provision to increase every customer's electrical rates slightly to pay to underground a proposed high-voltage line near the UA campus.[101] Then in 2024, having served as city manager since 2015, Michael Ortega stepped down and was replaced by his chief deputy, Tim Thomure.

Also getting new administrative leadership was Pima County. After Chuck Huckelberry retired in 2022, he was replaced by his longtime assistant, Jan Lesher. The county jail was a contentious issue, with protestors pointing out the 10-year annual high of 10 deaths, several from fentanyl, that occurred there in 2021.[102] The idea of replacing the 50-year-old facility was examined but then dropped in favor of repairs.

Closer to downtown, South Tucson's election in 2022 brought Brian Flagg of the Casa Maria soup kitchen onto the city council. In the summer of 2024, the council decided to ask local voters if they wanted to extend home rule, a move that allowed the community "to establish their own spending limits, apart from what the state Constitution allows."[103]

In suburban news, having grown enormously in population since its founding, Oro Valley celebrated its 50th anniversary in 2024. One of the items commemorating the event was publication of the book *Oro Valley—The First Fifty Years* by James A. Williams. The author spoke to several former town officials and others about Oro Valley's five decades of sometimes tumultuous existence and concluded, "Battles over development, shopping centers, high density housing, parks, and related issues have ultimately led to a better community."[104]

Nearby Marana, as well as Sahuarita south of Tucson, just kept getting bigger. Those two places were incorporated municipalities, but in 2023 the southeast side residents of Vail turned down incorporation for the third time.

The Road Forward

The failure of both Vail and Green Valley as well as the Catalina foothills to ever incorporate has caused a long-term monetary drag on the municipalities of Pima County because of a state law that financially penalizes unincorporated areas.[105] But that wasn't the major reason why Tucson and some of its suburbs faced financial headwinds as the 21st century moved on. An economy based in large part on four components—government, military, housing, and tourism—had been shown both in 2008 and 2020 to be extremely vulnerable to major financial shocks.

In statistical terms, government jobs accounted for almost 20 percent of local employment, the highest percentage of any major economic sector. As Michael Guymon, president of the Tucson Metro Chamber of Commerce, observed of this fact in 2024: "[W]e're also still very much a government town and we don't really gain a whole lot of GDP [Gross Domestic Product] from government jobs. So, we still have some work to do to address the industry mix that exists here in Tucson."[106] Real estate legend Roy Drachman had made a somewhat similar comment in 1958 and 66 years later the concentration of Tucson's economy into a few major sectors was still a critical issue.

Some people looked at the proposed new I-11 highway project with a possible far westside route through Avra Valley as a way to encourage a more diverse Tucson economy. As the Arizona Department of Transportation (ADOT) wrote about I-11 in 2021: "[It] is envisioned as a multi-use corridor that would improve Arizona's access to regional and international markets while opening up new opportunities for enhanced travel, mobility, trade, commerce, job growth and economic competitiveness."[107] Many others, including a majority of the Pima County Board of Supervisors, vehemently disagreed, arguing the roadway would cause enormous environmental harm.

Meanwhile, with the Regional Transportation Authority's (RTA) 20-year funding program approaching its 2026 conclusion, the agency was expected to collect and spend about $500 million less than the original estimate of $2.1 billion. The shortfall was covered in large part by either delaying or redesigning several City of Tucson projects. The city was simultaneously locked into an ongoing battle with its suburban neighbors about whether to request county voter's approval to extend the one-half cent sales tax or not, but they ultimately decided to go along. Around the same time, the City Council scheduled a March 2025 election on a "Safe & Vibrant City" measure that would raise the sales tax by one-half cent to pay for improvements in several areas, including to hire additional police officers, firefighters, and 911 operators, but it failed miserably.[108]

The RTA had helped fund Sun Tran bus service, and with the advent of COVID fares on the system became free and would continue that way through 2024. But while the RTA contributed to SunTran, it didn't spend anything on roadway maintenance. Thus, Tucson voters in May 2022 approved a 10-year extension to a previously approved sales tax increase to "improve every city neighborhood street over the next decade."[109] For its part, in July 2023, Pima County planned to repair at least 100 miles of its roadways within 12 months and successfully achieved that goal.

While some progress was being made to upgrade the area's traditionally potholed streets, pedestrian and motorist deaths were climbing substantially. Between 2020 and 2023, the total number of people killed in motor-vehicle-related incidents went from 220 to 293.[110] Of this latter figure, 173 were in a motor vehicle, 43 were motorcycle riders, and 51 pedestrians. The previous year of 2022 had been especially horrible for pedestrian deaths, with 81 people being killed and many of them were found to have dangerous drugs in their systems. As Blake Olofson, traffic safety

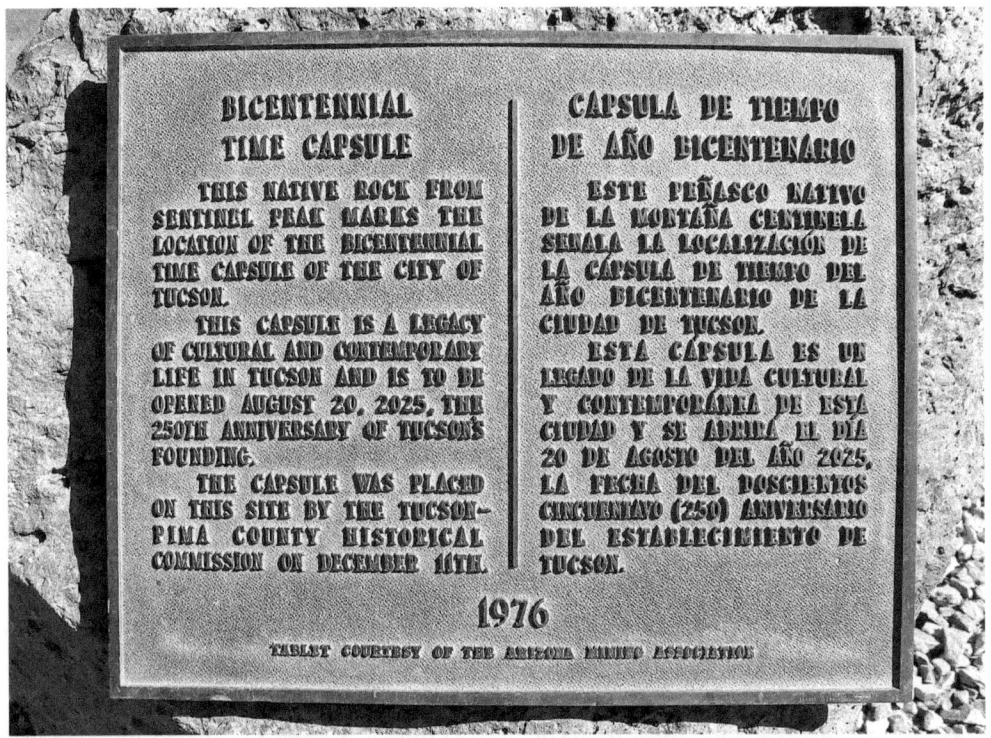

Buried in 1976, the Tucson time capsule was to be exhumed on August 20, 2025, to honor the 250 years, or semiquincentennial, since the location of the community was selected by Col. Hugo O'Conor (2024 photo by Tom Bergin).

engineer for the city of Tucson, summarized in 2024 of those killed on Tucson's streets: "[L]ast year, about 90% [of pedestrians killed] were at fault."[111]

Most of those pedestrians were unnamed victims of traffic accidents, but one received extensive media coverage. In January 2023, 63-year-old Lydia Reis, known as the "Umbrella Lady" because she wore vintage clothing and carried a large, colorful umbrella, was fatally struck down on Ina Road by a hit-and-run driver who was later arrested.

Pedestrian deaths and decades of demands by citizens for smoother roadways were among Tucson's major topics in 2024. Three main issues that Col. Hugo O'Conor in 1775 had addressed in selecting a site for a new presidio to be named San Agustín de Toixon, however, were availability of pasture and wood as well as a spot from which marauding Apaches could be confronted. Those concerns obviously no longer applied to Tucson almost 250 years later. But the primary issue O'Conor had listed still did—water.

After relying on pumping groundwater for most of its existence, Tucson in the 1990s turned to the Colorado River via the Central Arizona Project (CAP) canal as its new primary source. But by 2022, the long-term reliability of the CAP was being seriously questioned and cuts in the amount of water available to municipalities were possibilities.[112] The two major storage facilities for the river water were Lake

Mead, east of Las Vegas, Nevada, and Lake Powell further northeast. The former was only 33 percent full in July 2024 while the latter was at 42 percent.[113] Studies of future flows in the river varied, with some predicting further declines but one forecasting a possible small increase.[114]

By some accounts, because of lower demand, greater conservation, and the 1995 voter-authorized recharge basins in Avra Valley, the Tucson region was in a satisfactory position concerning future water supply. As Sharon Megdal, the University of Arizona director of the Water Resources Research Center, observed in June 2024: "[T]he Tucson area is doing quite well in water availability."[115]

But water pollution continued to present potential problems. Not only was the presence of PFAS in some groundwater wells an issue, but so was Hudbay's Copper World mining project, proposed to be implemented in the Santa Rita Mountains south of Tucson; it was seen by opponents as environmentally risky to downstream water supplies.

In the almost 250 years since the site of Tucson was selected, many things, excluding water supply issues, had changed. The 19th century vision that Tucson would always be the "metropolis of Arizona" as its largest community had long since faded away. More recently, the idea expressed early in the 21st century that implementation of the original Rio Nuevo westside museum complex would transform the community and "put Tucson on the map as one of America's great cities" had not been achieved. First the 1999 voter-approved project was thwarted by bureaucratic incompetence and then doomed by the state of Arizona's takeover of the downtown redevelopment process.

By 2024, those earlier dreams seemed to have all but vanished. Also seemingly gone was the decades-long focus on the need to promote rapid population growth as the best way to both better the community and secure its economic future. Instead, as one commentator concluded in 2024, Tucson was "a minor league city."[116] A critic of the community added: "I have lived and worked in big cities, small cities, corrupt cities, rich cities, impoverished cities, declining cities, and rising cities. Tucson tops all of them in provincialism, insularity, hubris, denial, and an aversion to prosperity."[117] On the other hand, to mark Earth Day 2024, Mayor Romero wrote that she and the city council were taking "action now so that Tucson continues to be [a] safe, thriving, sustainable and resilient desert city into the future."[118]

Residents of the city and its suburban communities in 2024 were apparently generally satisfied with their living situation and instead of obsessing on getting bigger were more interested in maintaining, protecting, and promoting the diversity of population, culture, and natural environment that made the area so attractive to many people. That, at least, was their local voting pattern in the 21st century. Tucson obviously had a long list of problems—education funding, poverty and low wages, crime, climate change, housing costs—but as its August 20, 2025, semiquincentennial rapidly approached, its citizens, in general, seemed satisfied with how things were going.

Chapter Notes

Preface

1. David Devine, *Tucson: A History of the Old Pueblo from the 1854 Gadsden Purchase*, McFarland, 2015, 1.
2. Ibid.
3. Quick Facts, United States Census Bureau, Pima County, Race and Hispanic Origin, 2023.
4. Devine, *Tucson*, 210.
5. Quick Facts, United States Census Bureau, Pima County, Population, 2023.
6. University of Arizona, MAP (Making Action Possible) Dashboard for Southern Arizona, "Workforce and Demographics," 2023, accessed August 29, 2024, https://mapazdashboard.arizona.edu/workforce-demographics/population-profile.
7. Tom Horne for Superintendent website, accessed June 20, 2024, https://electtomhorne.com/toms-plan.
8. John Schuster, "The Decline Continues: 'Star' Doesn't Benefit from 'Citizen' Closure," *Tucson Weekly*, October 14, 2010.
9. Devine, *Tucson*, 2, 4.

Chapter One

1. Henry F. Dobyns, *Spanish Colonial Tucson: A Demographic History*, University of Arizona Press, 1976.
2. Untitled, *Arizona Citizen*, August 21, 1875.
3. J.C. Martin, "The big shake," *Arizona Daily Star*, September 22, 1977.
4. "Pioneer's diary recalls 1887 quake in Tucson," translated from Spanish, *Arizona Daily Star*, June 3, 1970.
5. Both the *Arizona Daily Star* and the *Tucson Citizen* occasionally changed names and had weekly editions in their early years, plus the *Citizen* was even published in Florence, Arizona, in 1877 and 1878. For more information on the name changes, see Estelle Lutrell, "Newspapers and periodicals of Arizona 1859–1911."
6. "Local news," *Arizona Daily Citizen*, May 5, 1887.
7. "The hostiles," *Arizona Daily Citizen*, March 30, 1886.
8. "Geronimo's eloquence," *Arizona Weekly Star*, April 8, 1886.
9. "Geronimo," *Arizona Daily Citizen*, September 4, 1886.
10. "Unconditional surrender," *Arizona Weekly Star*, September 9, 1886.
11. Dawn Moore Santiago, "Wolf in sheep's clothing," 1. The original name of the bank had been Safford, Hudson & Company because former Arizona territorial governor, A.P.K. Safford, was an investor. In late 1881, however, he sold his shares and by January 1882 the bank was called Hudson & Company.
12. Ibid., 6.
13. Odie B. Faulk, ed., *Arizona's State Historical Society*, 2.
14. "Chinese cheap labor," *Arizona Daily Star*, July 20, 1879.
15. "The Chinese in Tucson," *Arizona Daily Star*, July 9, 1879.
16. C. Louise Boehringer, "Josephine Brawley Hughes—Crusader, State Builder," *Arizona Historical Review*, January 1930, 103.
17. Laws of the Territory of Arizona, 12th Legislative Assembly, 1883, 44; "Local Intelligence," *Weekly Citizen*, July 28, 1883.
18. "School Trustees," *Arizona Weekly Citizen*, August 9, 1884.
19. For more information on the Gadsden Purchase and the subsequent implementation of the railroad, see: David Devine, *Slavery, Scandal, and Steel Rails*.
20. The nation's first transcontinental railroad line would actually be built across the center of the country and finished in 1869. The southern route, including Tucson, came next, but wasn't completed until the 1880s.
21. John G. Bourke, *On the Border with Crook*, 77.
22. Journal of the Congress of the Confederate States of America, 1861–1865, January 13, 1862, 661.
23. Sidney DeLong to Estevan Ochoa, June 11, 1874.
24. Pima County Board of Supervisors' Records: 1865–1936, Minutes of the October 13, 1866, meeting.
25. Thomas E. Sheridan, "Peacock in the parlor," 251.
26. Stephen B. Weeks, *History of Public School Education in Arizona*, 33.

27. Elsie M. Dailey, "John Baptiste Salpointe," 27.
28. "The Tucson public schools," *Arizona Citizen*, June 19, 1875.
29. "Christmas in Tucson," *Arizona Weekly Citizen*, December 25, 1875.
30. Neil B. Carmony, transcriber and ed., *Whiskey, Six-Guns & Red-Light Ladies*, 28.
31. Gilbert J. Pedersen, "The townsite is now secure," 158.
32. Tucson Village Common Council, Minutes of the January 18, 1875, meeting.
33. Untitled, *Arizona Weekly Citizen*, June 19, 1875.
34. "The Fourth in Tucson," *Arizona Weekly Citizen*, July 10, 1875.
35. Carmony, *Whiskey, Six-Guns & Red-Light Ladies*, 55.
36. David Leighton, "Silverlake's namesake made a splash, powered flour mills," *Arizona Daily Star*, September 30, 2014.
37. Paul L. Allen, "Downtown gardens an entertainment center," *Tucson Citizen*, July 12, 2004.
38. "Village council," *Arizona Weekly Citizen*, February 12, 1876.
39. "General Phineas Banning and our territory," *Arizona Weekly Citizen*, February 17, 1877.
40. "Business of Tucson," *Arizona Weekly Citizen*, March 6, 1875.
41. Matt S. Meier, "Esteban Ochoa, Enterpriser," 18.
42. Tully, Ochoa & Co. advertisement, *Arizona Daily Star*, September 9, 1879.
43. "Arizona—As viewed by a Chicago Tribune correspondent," *Arizona Citizen*, May 12, 1877.
44. "Hymeneal," *Arizona Weekly Star*, November 8, 1877.
45. Reminiscences of Mrs. Juana Arvizo, 3.
46. Frank C. Lockwood, *Life in Old Tucson: 1854–1864*, 254. See also Lockwood, *Pioneer Portraits*, 86.
47. Untitled, *Arizona Weekly Star*, June 6, 1878. A military telegraph line reached Tucson in 1873 and a second line would accompany the 1880 arrival of the railroad. While individual telephones were in use as early as 1878, Tucson's first telephone exchange began operating in 1881.
48. "Reception," *Arizona Daily Star*, March 21, 1880.
49. "At the depot," *Arizona Weekly Star*, January 6, 1881.
50. "Hail to the Chief," *Weekly Arizona Citizen*, October 30, 1880.
51. "Tucson," *Arizona Weekly Star*, December 1, 1881.
52. "Accidentes," *El Fronterizo*, November 28, 1880.
53. Directory of the City of Tucson for the Year 1881, 58.
54. "The Electric Light," *Arizona Weekly Citizen*, August 11, 1883.
55. "Murder!" *Arizona Daily Star*, May 1, 1883.
56. C.L. Sonnichsen, *Tucson: The Life and Times of an American City*, 105.
57. Untitled, *Arizona Daily Citizen*, October 29, 1888.
58. Ida Myrtle Duffy, "Pioneer characters for whom some Tucson public schools have been named," 64.

Chapter Two

1. Gabriela Rico, "Apartments going up on 4th Ave.," *Arizona Daily Star*, November 5, 2023.
2. "C.C. Stephens," *Arizona Daily Citizen*, March 10, 1885.
3. The Howell Code, Adopted by the First Legislative Assembly of the Territory of Arizona, Prescott: Office of the *Arizona Miner*, 1865.
4. *Journals of the Ninth Legislative Assembly of the Territory of Arizona*, 78–79, 84–85.
5. George H. Kelly (compiler), *Legislative History of Arizona, 1864–1912*, 306.
6. "C.C. Stephens," *Arizona Daily Citizen*, March 10, 1885.
7. Kelly, *Legislative History of Arizona*, 315.
8. Untitled, *Arizona Daily Star*, November 28, 1886.
9. Untitled, *Arizona Daily Star*, October 6, 1891.
10. Rev. Howard Billman to Mrs. C.E. Walker, December 10, 1888.
11. Elsie P. Herndon, Personal Correspondence, June 1, 1900.
12. Sixty-Second Annual Report of the Commissioner of Indian Affairs to the Secretary of the Interior, 117.
13. Untitled, *Arizona Daily Citizen*, January 21, 1893; "The City Council," *Arizona Weekly Citizen*, April 8, 1893.
14. "A Tucson," *Arizona Daily Citizen*, July 5, 1892.
15. Reminiscences of Mose Drachman 1870–1935, 13.
16. J. Knox Corbett to his mother and father, March 4, 1881.
17. Corbett to his mother, dated June 12 but no year.
18. Main Street would later become Main Avenue.
19. Betty Blackburn, "New school honors city's first teacher," *Arizona Daily Star*, August 12, 1960.
20. Herbert Drachman, Personal Correspondence, no date.
21. "How Tucson is building up," *Arizona Daily Star*, February 26, 1896.
22. Armand Martin "Marty" Ronstadt, "Tucson's four Ronstadts."
23. "Old Tucson news and stories," dated March 9, 1927, and located in newspaper clipping file 550—Ronstadt, heading M. Ronstadt, Fred. Arizona Historical Society library, Tucson.
24. Kaye Lynn Briegel, "Alianza Hispano-Americana, 1894–1965."
25. "Arizona Lawmakers," *Arizona Republican*, March 4, 1891.
26. "The Constitution Convention," *Weekly Phoenix Herald*, September 24, 1891.

27. "The Constitutional Convention," *Weekly Phoenix Herald*, October 1, 1891.
28. Untitled, *Arizona Daily Star*, September 25, 1891.
29. Laws of Arizona, Twelve Legislative Session, No. 76, p. 137: *Cronly v. City of Tucson et. al.*, March 15, 1899, 56 Pacific Reporter, 876–878.
30. Untitled, *Arizona Daily Citizen*, November 16, 1900.
31. David T. Faust and Kenneth A. Randall, "Life at post: Fort Lowell, Arizona Territory 1873–1891."
32. Untitled, *Arizona Weekly Star*, November 16, 1899.
33. Untitled, *Arizona Daily Citizen*, March 10, 1900.
34. "The plaza and the people," *Arizona Daily Citizen*, June 1, 1900.
35. "Build a sewer system," *Arizona Daily Citizen*, September 21, 1900.
36. "Electric Lights," *Arizona Daily Star*, October 28, 1892.
37. Untitled, *Arizona Weekly Citizen*, September 16, 1893; Untitled, *Arizona Weekly Star*, July 21, 1898.
38. In the summer of 1899, the *Arizona Daily Citizen* of June 29 reported an attempt by "the janitor of the county jail" to solicit funds from Carnegie. The newspaper derided this effort, thinking it futile. By the fall of that same year, however, journalist G.W. Pittock was publicly being lauded for his similar efforts on behalf of the community. Thanks to William D. Kalt III for this information.
39. "The public library," *Arizona Weekly Star*, October 5, 1899; David Leighton, "Courtyard walkway once a road with literary links," *Arizona Daily Star*, July 8, 2014.
40. "Carnegie's gift," *Arizona Weekly Star*, November 16, 1899.
41. "Gen. Manning buys property," *Arizona Daily Citizen*, December 24, 1900.
42. "TUSD history—The first hundred years: Davis, Holladay and Drachman 1900-1910—Part 1."
43. Untitled, *Arizona Weekly Star*, August 31, 1899.
44. "Tucson's prospects," *Arizona Weekly Star*, October 5, 1899.
45. "Some big taxpayers," *Arizona Weekly Star*, December 14, 1899.
46. "'Curly' Neal new tycoon," *Black Heritage in Arizona*, 5.
47. "State pioneer taken in death," *Arizona Daily Star*, May 12, 1950.
48. "A charming resort," *Arizona Daily Citizen*, January 1, 1895.
49. "Tucson industries," *Arizona Weekly Star*, June 1, 1899.
50. "Minor miscellany," *Arizona Daily Citizen*, February 8, 1900.
51. "Tucson's growth," *Arizona Weekly Star*, March 9, 1899.
52. Untitled, *Arizona Weekly Star*, April 13, 1899.
53. Untitled, *Arizona Weekly Citizen*, September 2, 1893.
54. Untitled, *Arizona Weekly Citizen*, May 25, 1895.
55. "A Bicycle Collision," *Arizona Weekly Star*, August 29, 1895.
56. "It is a Locomobile," *Arizona Daily Star*, December 31, 1899.
57. Untitled, *Arizona Daily Citizen*, January 2, 1901.
58. Untitled, *Arizona Daily Citizen*, January 2, 1901.

Chapter Three

1. Tom Beal, "Pioneering botanical lab created on Tumamoc Hill," *Arizona Daily Star*, July 2, 2012.
2. Mount Lemmon was named after Sara Allen Plummer Lemmon, reportedly the "first white woman to ascend it."
3. Tucson City Council, Minutes of the June 22, 1908, meeting. Washington Park would later be renamed Armory Park.
4. Editorial, "Citizens express their dissatisfaction," *Arizona Daily Star*, July 30, 1908.
5. "Views pro and con of Tucson business folk," *Arizona Daily Star*, August 5, 1908.
6. *Ibid.*
7. "Railroad items," *Arizona Daily Star*, April 20, 1880.
8. William F. Greer, Donald W. Carson, ed., "Tucson—the early days"; Anonymous, "History of the Tucson Fire Department."
9. Ordinance No. 46, *Arizona Daily Star*, May 10, 1883.
10. William F. Greer, Donald W. Carson, ed., "Tucson—the early days."
11. City of Tucson, Ordinance Number 56.
12. In a chemical engine, "[t]he chemical was a combination of sulfuric acid [sometimes called oil of vitriol in those days] and sodium bicarbonate [generally known as baking soda]. When sulfuric acid is added to water containing dissolved sodium bicarbonate in a tank, the result is pressurized carbon dioxide, which forced the contents out of the tank and through the fire hoses." Lawrence G. Petrick, Jr., correspondence with the author.
13. "Great flow struck at the city waterworks," *Arizona Daily Citizen*, February 12, 1901.
14. City of Tucson, Ordinance 167.
15. "The sale of city lots—Much activity displayed," *Tucson Citizen*, March 2, 1903.
16. Robert S. Svob, "History of Intercollegiate Athletics at the University of Arizona (1897–1948)," 98.
17. "Athletics," *Arizona Daily Star*, September 20, 1908.
18. "Tucson Girls Win All Honors at Basket Ball," *Arizona Daily Star*, February 19, 1910; "Bisbee Boys Win Basket Ball Game," *The Bisbee Daily Review*, February 20, 1910.

19. City of Tucson, Ordinance 164.
20. William D. Kalt III, *High in Desert Skies: Early Arizona Aviation*, Printing Solutions, 2017, 19; "Eight-Cylinder BiPlane with Which Hamilton Broke the Record Arrived Today in Tucson," *Tucson Citizen*, February 16, 1910.
21. "Aviator Hamilton Makes a Splendid Flight and Gives Spectators a Thrill," *Tucson Citizen*, February 19, 1910.
22. "Gate Receipts Failed to Meet the Guarantee," *Tucson Citizen*, February 21, 1910.
23. Editorial, "Let us co-operate," *Arizona Daily Star*, April 8, 1903.
24. "Better fire protection special council session," *Tucson Citizen*, July 1, 1903.
25. "Water and fire," *Arizona Daily Star*, July 1, 1903.
26. "Autos must carry numbers," *Tucson Citizen*, September 6, 1905.
27. "Tucson City—Its present and future," *Arizona Daily Star*, September 8, 1907.
28. Bernard J. Wilson and Zaellotious A. Wilson, "From Maiden Lane to Gay Alley."
29. "Taps for red lights," *Tucson Citizen*, September 17, 1907.
30. Heney to Mayor and Tucson Common Council, December 11, 1907.
31. Untitled, *Arizona Weekly Citizen*, October 25, 1890.
32. "New administration now rules the city," *Tucson Citizen*, January 8, 1907.
33. "Opening speech of Mayor Heney to City Council," *Arizona Daily Star*, January 5, 1909.
34. Joss House was a common American term for a Chinese temple.
35. "Heavy loss is sustained in Chinatown fire," *Tucson Citizen*, March 5, 1909.
36. Tucson City Council, Minutes of the January 25, 1909, meeting.
37. "Will build 4 bungalows in North End," *Arizona Daily Star*, August 25, 1908.
38. "Mayor asks report on taps," *Tucson Citizen*, February 2, 1909.
39. Editorial, "Mayor Heney vs. non-partisan City Council," *Arizona Daily Star*, June 10, 1909.
40. "Mayor gives an interview," *Tucson Citizen*, June 21, 1909.
41. "Councilman Martin is Whitewashed," *Tucson Citizen*, July 7, 1909.
42. "Martin found not guilty of graft charges," *Arizona Daily Star*, July 8, 1909.
43. "Mass meeting tomorrow night" advertisement, *Tucson Citizen*, July 8, 1909.
44. "Heney repeats wail to many empty chairs," *Arizona Daily Star*, July 10, 1909.
45. Ibid.
46. "Large crowd present at public meeting," *Tucson Citizen*, July 10, 1909.
47. "Mayor Heney leads raid on Chinese gambling place," *Tucson Citizen*, July 26, 1909.
48. "Mayor in role of head sleuth conducts raid," *Arizona Daily Star*, July 27, 1909.
49. Editorial, "We believe in Tucson," *Tucson Citizen*, July 21, 1909.
50. "Many autos in Old Pueblo," *Tucson Citizen*, March 24, 1909.
51. "Work begun on Boulevard," *Tucson Citizen*, July 27, 1909.
52. "Pacheco is suspended; Wheeler in his place," *Tucson Citizen*, August 19, 1909.
53. "Tucson without chief of police; Pacheco is out," *Arizona Daily Star*, August 20, 1909.
54. Ibid.
55. "Council acquits Pacheco, wants mayor to resign; Heney promptly declines," *Tucson Citizen*, September 15, 1909.
56. "Council asks Heney to quit; clear Pacheco," *Arizona Daily Star*, September 16, 1909.
57. "Council takes step to remove mayor," *Tucson Citizen*, November 2, 1909.
58. Editorial, "The charges against the mayor," *Tucson Citizen*, November 2, 1909.
59. "What Heney has really done as Tucson's mayor," *Arizona Daily Star*, November 4, 1909.
60. Editorial, "Heney's record as mayor," *Tucson Citizen*, November 3, 1909.
61. "Mayor Heney deposed by the council while Tucson people wildly cheer him," *Tucson Citizen*, November 5, 1909.
62. Ibid.
63. "Heney deposed for disorderly conduct; Preston N. Jacobus is new mayor," *Arizona Daily Star*, November 5, 1909.
64. Ibid.
65. "Fist Fight in City Council Over Streets," *Arizona Daily Star*, November 8, 1910.
66. "Expulsion of Mayor Heney probable at tonight's meeting of City Council," *Tucson Citizen*, November 4, 1909.
67. "The Ignorant Vote," *Arizona Daily Star*, March 3, 1903.
68. "The Legislature Record of Friday," *Arizona Daily Star*, March 7, 1903.
69. "Brodie the Rough Rider," *Arizona Daily Star*, March 20, 1903.
70. Editorial, "Brodie Assassinates the Woman Suffrage Bill," *Arizona Daily Star*, March 20, 1903.
71. David R. Berman, *Reformers, Corporations, and the Electorate*, 54, 92.
72. Editorial, "Success of the new election law," *Tucson Citizen*, December 14, 1909. This territorial law's successor, adopted by the Arizona state legislature, wouldn't be repealed until 1972.
73. "Committees for Chamber," *Tucson Citizen*, March 24, 1908.
74. *Acts, Resolutions and Memorials of the Twenty-Fifth (1909) Legislative Assembly of the Territory of Arizona*, Chapter 67, 171.
75. "Emancipation Day observed in this city," *Arizona Daily Star*, June 21, 1910.
76. Untitled, *Tucson Citizen*, October 19, 1906.
77. Editorial, "Yesterday's Democratic victory," *Tucson Citizen*, December 14, 1909.
78. "Mayor Heney deposed by the Council while

Tucson people wildly cheer him," *Tucson Citizen*, November 5, 1909.

Chapter Four

1. "First arrest for speeding made to stick," *Arizona Daily Star*, February 1, 1911.
2. "Tucsonans to aid building of highway," *Arizona Daily Star*, February 11, 1912.
3. "Subway to open, many motorists will pass through," *Tucson Citizen*, June 14, 1916.
4. William D. Kalt III, "Sky sensations"; Kathy Klump, *The Vin Fiz Lands in Willcox*.
5. "Gradye Drown dies at 91, placed historic phone call," *Arizona Daily Star*, June 19, 1986.
6. "Indians to hunt Catalina exit of Colossal Cave," *Tucson Citizen*, December 13, 1917.
7. "Firefighters subdue blaze in forests," *Tucson Citizen*, June 17, 1910.
8. Editorial, *Tucson Citizen*, October 23, 1911.
9. "University to honor namer of Wildcats," *Arizona Daily Star*, October 24, 1964.
10. "Varsity giant 'A' now is complete," *Tucson Citizen*, March 6, 1916.
11. "Republican delegates from Pima County who opposed placing the judicial recall in Arizona's Constitution," *Tucson Citizen*, August 16, 1911. Besides Jácome, the other four delegates from Pima County were lawyers Samuel L. Kingan and William F. Cooper, railroader James C. White, and rancher George Pusch.
12. Editorial, "Adoption of the Constitution," *Arizona Daily Star*, February 8, 1911.
13. "Statehood or no statehood" advertisement, *Arizona Daily Star*, August 20, 1911.
14. "Tucsonians praise work of Cameron," *Tucson Citizen*, August 21, 1911.
15. "Good citizens to vote for Constitutional Amendment," *Arizona Daily Star*, December 10, 1911.
16. "University celebrates statehood," *Arizona Daily Star*, February 15, 1912.
17. Editorial, "The E.P.&S.W. a certainty," *Tucson Citizen*, August 1, 1911.
18. "Officials of railway holding company elated; thank citizens," *Tucson Citizen*, August 1, 1911.
19. "Elysian Grove Will Be Sold as City Lots," *Tucson Citizen*, July 24, 1911.
20. "The E.P. & S.W. a certainty" advertisement, *Tucson Citizen*, August 2, 1911.
21. Untitled, *Arizona Daily Star*, July 6, 1900.
22. "Mrs. Dr. Rose [sic] Boido Heads Suffragists," *Arizona Daily Star*, January 24, 1912. Dr. Rosa Boido would move to Phoenix in 1913. Five years later, she became the first Arizona physician to be tried, convicted, and imprisoned under an 1864 law for performing an abortion.
23. Mrs. L.C. Hughes, "Arizona State owes women the ballot," *Arizona Daily Star*, November 3, 1912.
24. "Parties Claim Heavy Vote in Pima County," *Tucson Citizen*, November 6, 1912.

25. "Steinfeld's Wine & Liquor Clearance Sale," *Tucson Citizen*, December 30, 1914.
26. National prohibition went into effect after ratification of the 19th amendment to the United States Constitution in 1920.
27. "The Crises in Tucson's Police Department," *Tucson Citizen*, January 29, 1917.
28. "Tucson school system best in Southwest," *Arizona Daily Star*, January 28, 1912.
29. *Acts, Resolutions and Memorials of the Regular Session First (1912) Legislature of the State of Arizona*, 382.
30. "Segregation of public schools was fought," *Arizona Daily Star*, May 5, 2011.
31. "Negro school to open doors next Monday," *Arizona Daily Star*, September 18, 1913.
32. Tucson City Council, Minutes of Meeting, March 21, 1910.
33. Editorial, "The water problem," *Tucson Citizen*, August 29, 1911.
34. Editorial, "Tucson in 1912," *Tucson Citizen*, January 2, 1912.
35. "Author buys property in Tucson," *Tucson Citizen*, February 3, 1912.
36. Harold Bell Wright, *Their Yesterdays*, 37.
37. "Harold Bell Wright who holds a world's record," *The American Magazine*.
38. C.L.G. Anderson, M.D., "Arizona as a health resort," 1.
39. Dick Hall, "Ointment of love," 112.
40. David Devine, *The St. Luke's in the Desert Story: A Century of Community Service*, Arizona Litho, 2018, 9.
41. Bradford Luckingham, "To Mask or Not to Mask: A Note on the 1918 Spanish Influenza in Tucson," *The Journal of Arizona History*, 192.
42. "Tucson Foils Flu Bug with Masks Today," *Arizona Daily Star*, November 23, 1918.
43. Homer Thiel, "We Have Been Here Before: A History of Epidemics in Southern Arizona," blog posting, April 8, 2020.
44. "O.E. Comstock, judge, printer, minister, dies," *Arizona Daily Star*, September 11, 1937.
45. "Von Petersdorff is disappointed by War Department," *Tucson Citizen*, September 15, 1917.
46. Leyla Cattan, "Former city architect, San Xavier mission restorer deserves recognition," J. C. Martin trans., *Arizona Daily Star*, February 21, 1988.
47. Patricia Peters Stephenson, *A Personal Journey through the West University Neighborhood;* "$75,000 suburban center is planned," *Tucson Citizen*, April 26, 1922.
48. Editorial, "Nineteen hundred twenty," *Tucson Citizen*, January 2, 1920.
49. "Noted author," *Tucson Citizen*, March 26, 1922.
50. "Homesteads in Tucson region are now 200," *Tucson Daily Citizen*, July 25, 1930.
51. James L. Sell and David Devine, "The novelist who shaped the city."
52. Editorial, "The growth of Tucson," *Tucson Citizen*, February 3, 1918.

53. "Census worries of Leach lead to Hot Lunch Club debate," *Tucson Citizen*, January 23, 1920.
54. Editorial, "Public spirit in Tucson," *Tucson Citizen*, January 25, 1920.
55. "Phoenix tries sharp trick," *Tucson Citizen*, May 13, 1920.
56. Editorial, "Weeping in Phoenix," *Tucson Citizen*, June 22, 1920.
57. Roy Drachman, interview by Don Bufkin, January 14, 1992, 1.
58. "Organization of Sunshine Climate Club completed and nationwide advertising campaign to follow," *Tucson Citizen*, September 24, 1922.
59. E.J. Whistler, "Tucson Sunshine," *Arizona Daily Star*, October 1, 1922.
60. Upon the 1924 completion of the new Tucson High School on the south side of Sixth Street, this building became Roskruge School, named after early surveyor, George Roskruge.
61. The H.K. McCann Company, *Situation Report and Advertising Recommendations for the Tucson Sunshine Climate Club*, 1.
62. *Ibid.*, 7.
63. Lawrence Tagg, *Harold Bell Wright—Storyteller to America*, 127.
64. *Long Ago Told: Legends of the Papago Indians*, vii.
65. Harold Bell Wright, *The Mine with the Iron Door*, 1.

Chapter Five

1. J.F. Weadock, "20,000 Greet Lindbergh at Tucson Field with biggest ovation in state's history," *Arizona Daily Star*, September 24, 1927.
2. "Four hundred greet Lindbergh at feast; Field is dedicated," *Tucson Citizen*, September 24, 1927.
3. "Aviator asks markings on 'Macauley [sic] Field' be made of crushed rock," *Arizona Daily Star*, January 23, 1919. While many sources list his name as Macauley, his real name was Macualay. See: William D. Kalt III, "Sky sensations: Early Arizona aviation tales," 89.
4. "Tucson air field first built by any U.S. city," *Tucson Citizen*, September 23, 1927.
5. "Fishburn to make first landing on new aviation field today in one of Barr's Flying Circus planes," *Tucson Citizen*, November 21, 1919.
6. Phoebe M. Bogan manuscripts, 1909–1926, S. 1, file 1.
7. Ophelia D. Hill (compiler) and Ella S. Swanson, ed., *Cemetery Records of the Binghampton Cemetery*.
8. W. Lane Rogers, "From Colonia Dublán to Binghampton," 34.
9. Edna Bingham Sabin, "Nephi Bingham and Elizabeth Dalkin Bingham."
10. 1926 Tucson City Directory.
11. Margaret Regan, "Remembering Rockfellow," *Tucson Weekly*, January 27, 2000.
12. El Conquistador dinner menu dated November 22, 1928.
13. "Pioneers given city land for new building," *Arizona Daily Star*, December 29, 1925. Also personal correspondence with William D. Kalt III dated February 14, 2008.
14. "City accords Centre and Wildcats royal reception upon arrival in Tucson," *Tucson Citizen*, December 29, 1921.
15. Paul L. Grimes, *The Pride of Arizona*.
16. "Mayor Rasmessen first to put signature to telegram to Cat poloists in East after title," *Tucson Citizen*, May 22, 1924.
17. "List of signers to polo team telegram is steadily growing; One now measures twelve feet," *Tucson Citizen*, May 25, 1924.
18. "Nora Sullivan Nugent," Plaza of the Pioneers information.
19. Bernice Cosulich, "Tucson's only policewoman finds they are not all bad," *Arizona Daily Star*, November 8, 1933.
20. *Ibid.*
21. *Ibid.*
22. "Subways, lights lose; Others carry," *Tucson Citizen*, May 16, 1920.
23. *Ibid.*
24. "55 Years in Tucson, sees Tucson lighted by candle, lamp, gas and electricity," *Arizona Daily Star*, December 23, 1927.
25. June Webb-Vignery, *Jacome's Department Store*, 56.
26. *Ibid.*, 62.
27. William Gin, interview by Ghislaine Martel, April 3, 1984.
28. "Tucson Badgers to clash with El Paso Tigers this afternoon," *Arizona Daily Star*, October 17, 1925.
29. Patrick Finley, "Ex-Badger a pioneer as state legislator, judge," *Arizona Daily Star*, July 1, 2011.
30. "Another step in progress of Tucson marks Rialto opening," *Tucson Citizen*, August 29, 1920.
31. "Tucson's great Fox Theater opens tomorrow night," *Tucson Daily Citizen*, April 10, 1930.
32. "Radio fan puts set in auto for vacation outing," *Tucson Citizen*, July 11, 1926.
33. Editorial, "The City Should Act," *Tucson Citizen*, January 16, 1929.
34. "The Desert Sanatorium and Institute of Research."
35. Mark Kimble, "An environmental battle that changed Tucson," *Tucson Citizen*, April 10, 2003.
36. "Automobile tourist spends $7 daily committee asserts," *Tucson Citizen*, March 28, 1922.
37. 1924 Tucson City Directory.
38. Myron M. Stearns, "That Bungalow Camp," *The Saturday Evening Post*, August 27, 1927, 37.
39. David Devine, "Dreaming of Autopia."
40. "Engineers are in city today placing signs," *Tucson Citizen*, April 17, 1922.
41. "Mansfield on highway list," *Arizona Daily Star*, January 24, 1929.
42. Editorial, "Good roads a profitable investment," *Tucson Citizen*, October 23, 1915.
43. Editorial, "Let's fly to the mountains," *Arizona Daily Star*, July 13, 1927.

44. Patrick Ettinger, "'We sometimes wonder what they will spring on us next,'" 168.
45. Clifford Alan Perkins, *Border Patrol*, 23.
46. Ettinger, "'We sometimes wonder what they will spring on us next,'" 180.
47. Editorial, "Exclusion in fact," *Tucson Citizen*, May 27, 1924.
48. Ettinger, "'We sometimes wonder what they will spring on us next,'" 180.
49. "Chinese Chamber of Commerce will build new home," *Tucson Citizen*, August 25, 1922.
50. "Negro voters of Old Pueblo will organize," *Tucson Citizen*, August 4, 1922.
51. George Herbert Smalley, "What Prohibition did to Arizona," *Sunset*, January 1916, 27.
52. For a discussion of prohibition law enforcement in this interim period, see: Harry David Ware, "Alcohol, temperance and Prohibition in Arizona," 308–330.
53. "City onslaught on bootleggers is renewed by Ford," *Tucson Citizen*, December 17, 1921.
54. Yndia Smalley Moore, interview by Phyllis Reed, April 21, 1983, 50.
55. "Clothing enterprise pays off for Tucsonan," *Arizona Daily Star*, Oct. 9, 1981.
56. "The mud flats of Snob Hollow," *Tucson Citizen*, July 18, 1919.
57. Eleazar D. Herreras, interview by Lyn Papanikolas, March 9 and 11, 1983, 41.
58. Carmen Duarte, "Local architect spruced up historic Tucson," *Arizona Catholic Lifetime*, February 17, 1980, 8.
59. Eleazar D. Herreras, interview by Lyn Papanikolas, March 9 and 11, 1983, 10.
60. "Menzies to have factory building," *Arizona Daily Star*, May 6, 1928.
61. "Stocks rally at opening of N.Y. Market," *Tucson Citizen*, October 30, 1929.

Chapter Six

1. "Jobless man ends his life by shooting," *Tucson Daily Citizen*, December 19, 1930.
2. Eleazar D. Herreras interview by Lyn Papanikolas, March 9 and 11, 1983, 9.
3. "Historic Fort Lowell being re-created from debris of many thrilling decades," *Tucson Daily Citizen*, May 28, 1931.
4. Marlys Bush Thurber, Linda L. Mayro, Frank P. Behlau, and R. Brooks Jeffery, *Survey of Joesler/Murphey Structures in Tucson and Environs*, 4.
5. Thomas E. Sheridan, *Arizona.... A History*, 254.
6. Abraham Hoffman, *Unwanted Mexican Americans in the Great Depression*, 123.
7. *Ibid*., 122.
8. Joe Burchell, "Transient problems are not new," *Arizona Daily Star*, October 27, 1984.
9. Melvin Hoefle interview by Linda C. Swedberg, April 8, 1983, 16.
10. Lucille Budd Juliani interview by John Bret-Harte, August 12, 1990, 18.
11. "General 'clean-up' of city launched by new council to give unemployed work," *Tucson Daily Citizen*, January 6, 1931.
12. J.C. Martin, "Clothing enterprise pays off for Tucsonan," *Arizona Daily Star*, October 9, 1981.
13. Elgie Batteau interview by Annie Sykes, 1988, 12.
14. *Ibid*.
15. Richard Salvatierra, "Racial discrimination ends, but scars still show," *Tucson Citizen*, September 8, 2003.
16. *Ibid*.
17. *Ibid*.
18. Paul L. Allen, "Esther Tang's local roots stay deep, strong," *Tucson Citizen*, November 27, 1998.
19. For a discussion of prohibition law enforcement during this interim period, see: Harry David Ware, "Alcohol, temperance and Prohibition in Arizona," 308–330.
20. *Ibid*., 327.
21. "Repeal voted as delegates consume beer," *Phoenix Gazette*, September 5, 1933.
22. George E. Webb, *Tree Rings and Telescopes: The Scientific Career of A.E. Douglass*, 158.
23. Lynn D. Baker, *Tucson Water History: A Reference Book*, 13–5.
24. Jim Turner, "A nice place to visit: A brief history of Sabino Canyon," 16–17.
25. Bonnie Henry, "Local projects have withstood touch of time—and water," *Arizona Daily Star*, July 4, 1991.
26. Sharon E. Hunt, *Vail and Colossal Cave Mountain Park*.
27. E. Lendell Cockrum (compiler), *Cavemen of Colossal Cave*, 12.
28. "First rodeo parade put on with budget of $20," *Arizona Daily Star*, February 17, 1957.
29. "Will Rogers pleases large audience here and raises $2,000 for polo trip fund," *Tucson Daily Citizen*, May 9, 1931.
30. "Local men given preference in Broadway subway work," *Tucson Daily Citizen*, December 11, 1930.
31. Roy Drachman oral interview, April 3, 1980, 5.
32. John A. Haney and Cirino G. Scavone, "Cars stop here," 53.
33. "Swim subway to get to wedding," *Arizona Daily Star*, July 27, 1936.
34. Howard Welty, "Subway ferry proposed as city is asked to name lake," *Arizona Daily Star*, August 16, 1936.
35. John Jennings, "How 'Lake Elmira' story got launched," *Tucson Citizen*, August 29, 1994.
36. David Devine, "Dreaming of Autopia: Southern Arizona auto courts of the 1920s and 30s," 175.
37. *Ibid*., 176.
38. Lucille Budd Juliani interview by John Bret-Harte, August 12, 1990, 31.
39. Roy Drachman interview by Don Bufkin, January 14, 1992, 40.
40. Patricia Stephenson and Alex Jay Kimmelman, *Tom Marshall's Tucson*, 84.

41. "Doctors disagree in Marshall case," *Tucson Daily Citizen*, September 16, 1931.
42. "Aged woman given liberty as trial ends," *Tucson Daily Citizen*, September 24, 1931.
43. "Late News," *Tucson Daily Citizen*, June 29, 1931.
44. Stan Benjamin, "Without a shot fired: The 1934 capture of the Dillinger Gang in Tucson," 210.
45. *Ibid.*
46. David Devine, "Struggle for survival: The South Tucson Story," 5–6.
47. "South Tucson Council fails to show up at fire meeting," *Arizona Daily Star*, May 5, 1937.
48. Editorial, "South Tucson's new gadgets," *Arizona Daily Star*, June 6, 1937.
49. Robert White, "Sudeten Tucson writhes in contemplated coups d'etat," *Arizona Daily Star*, November 30, 1938.
50. "Majority votes to incorporate in South Tucson," *Arizona Daily Star*, March 28, 1939.
51. Editorial, "Hold on a minute," *Arizona Daily Star*, December 14, 1935.
52. Editorial, "Tucson's water supply assured," *Tucson Daily Citizen*, November 11, 1930.
53. "City officials tell senate committee Tucson wants San Xavier surplus water," *Tucson Daily Citizen*, April 20, 1931.
54. Bernard L. Fontana. *Of Earth and Little Rain: The Papago Indians*," 87.
55. David W. Lazaroff. *Sabino Canyon: The Life of a Southwestern Oasis*, 95.
56. "County and city unanimous in support of Sabino Dam," *Arizona Daily Star*, September 11, 1936.

Chapter Seven

1. Joshua R. Pahigian, *Spring Training Handbook*, 247.
2. Editorial, "Behind Tucson's growth," *Arizona Daily Star*, October 1, 1940.
3. *Ibid.*
4. Oliver Drachman interview by Lyn Papanikolas, April 19, 1983, 23.
5. "Assassin bug invasions threatening Old Tucson," *The Weekly Arizonan*, May 25, 1860.
6. W. Ward Marsh, "One moment, please!," *The Cleveland Plain Dealer*, October 31, 1940.
7. Don Schellie, "How press agent got taste of the Old West," *Tucson Daily Citizen*, January 9, 1970.
8. Ladislas Segoe and Andre M. Faure, *Aviation and Airports*, 23.
9. Alva Torres interview in *They Opened Their Hearts*, 14.
10. "Humor, seriousness mix in Tucson's celebration," *Arizona Daily Star*, August 15, 1945.
11. William E. Bigglestone, *Tucsonans Who Died in Military Service During World War II*.
12. Jeré Franco, "Beyond reservation boundaries: Native American laborers in World War II," 247.
13. Johnny Gibson interview by Richard Kimball, September 29, 1988, 32.
14. "Many new naval officers training at Tucson Center," *Arizona Daily Star*, February 22, 1943.
15. "Brave sons of China are flying cadets at Marana," *Arizona Daily Star*, February 22, 1943.
16. George H. Pittman, "History," *The (Flagstaff) Sun*, November 3, 1985.
17. Bonnie Henry, "Davis-Monthan Air Force Base," *Arizona Daily Star*, May 20, 1987.
18. William W. Hodgman, Jr., to his mother, September 10, 1943.
19. Pvt. Frank G. Lopez to Dear Sirs, August 10, 1944.
20. Julie A. Campbell, "Madres Y Esposas: Tucson's Spanish-American Mothers and Wives Association," 163.
21. David Devine, "From warehouse to re-use: The story of the northside of Tucson's downtown, Part 2: 1940–1995," 71.
22. "Pima County responds to scrap appeal," *Arizona Daily Star*, February 22, 1943.
23. Ruben Moreno interview in *They Opened Their Hearts*, 54.
24. Estella Jácome interview by Caryl J. Taylor, March 21, 1990, 23.
25. "Large crowd at dedication of neon flag," *Tucson Daily Citizen*, July 9, 1942; See also: David Devine, "From Warehouse to re-use," 70.
26. Ada P. McCormick, "An open letter" advertisement, *Arizona Daily Star*, January 18, 1942.
27. "Former principal dead at age of 84," *Tucson Citizen*, March 21, 1987.
28. *The Population of Tucson and Its Environs*, March 1943, 1.
29. Editorial, "Save us from our friends," *Arizona Daily Star*, March 11, 1944.
30. "Official statement by the co-chairman, at the meeting of the Tucson Committee for Inter-Racial Understanding," March 22, 1944. The statement about Indians not being able to vote refers to a 1928 Arizona Supreme Court decision that denied the vote to Native Americans, a ruling that was finally overturned in 1948.
31. Pearlie Mae Purdie interview in *They Opened Their Hearts*, 37.
32. Ruben Moreno, *They Opened Their Hearts*, 54.
33. Henry "Hank" Oyama interview in *They Opened Their Hearts*, 59.
34. In 1999, the prison camp site, which had become a recreational area, was named in honor of Hirabayashi.
35. "Flag is raised at high school," *Tucson Daily Citizen*, May 8, 1945.
36. "Letter from home" newsletter, August 17, 1945.
37. "Humor, seriousness mix in Tucson's celebration," *Arizona Daily Star*, August 15, 1945.
38. William D. Kalt III, *Tucson Was a Railroad Town*, 292.
39. "'Old Tucson' nearly beyond repair stage," *Tucson Daily Citizen*, December 21, 1945.

40. Linwood C. Thompson, "The motion picture history of southern Arizona and Old Tucson (1912–1983)."
41. Michael F. Wendland, *The Arizona Project*, 174.
42. Gilbert Ronstadt oral interview, 1980, 6.
43. Helen Urech Shaffer interview in *They Opened Their Hearts*, 21.
44. Erskine Caldwell, *With All My Might*, 208–211.
45. Maria I. Vigil, "El Casino ballroom: Same set, different cast," *Tucson Citizen*, June 7, 1980.
46. Bill Veeck with Ed Linn, *Veeck—As in Wreck*, 177–178.
47. "Remembrance of springs past—Larry Doby," *Arizona Daily Star*, March 1, 1992. See also: David Devine, "Less than accommodating," *Tucson Weekly*, February 12, 2009.
48. Roy Drachman, "Wartime changes," *Tucson Citizen*, April 9, 1998.
49. W.R. Harrod, "Deputy Sheriff John Anderson falls to death in Sabino rescue attempt," *Arizona Daily Star*, August 10, 1948.
50. Jim Hart, "Rescued youth tells of fall," *Arizona Daily Star*, August 10, 1948.
51. "Jacome's celebrating 50th anniversary this weekend," *Arizona Daily Star*, March 16, 1946.
52. "Cool, cool water," *The Magazine Tucson*, December 1948, 45.
53. "Village adopts 5 ordinances in initial session," *Arizona Daily Star*, May 23, 1947.
54. "Abandon 'Old Main'? Not yet, says Prexy, Herreras says unsafe," *Arizona Daily Star*, June 25, 1938.
55. Editorial, "Old Main and its architecture," *Arizona Daily Star*, July 22, 1938.
56. Ibid.
57. Editorial, "Old Main and its passing," *Arizona Daily Star*, June 26, 1938.
58. J.M. Creighton to D.E. Creighton, July 27, 1938.
59. "Students: 'Tear down Old Main,'" *Arizona Wildcat*, March 5, 1948.
60. "Regents to mull student union site question," *Arizona Wildcat*, May 14, 1948.
61. Minutes of a Meeting of the Board of Regents of the University and State Colleges of Arizona, May 25, 1948.
62. Abe Chanin, *They Fought Like Wildcats*, 153.
63. Donald W. Carson and James W. Johnson, *Mo—The Life and Times of Morris K. Udall*, 47.
64. William T. Healy, *The History of Tucson Country Club*, 4.
65. Bonnie Henry, "Brook recalls Tucson Jewish Center's 'salad days,'" *Arizona Daily Star*, April 18, 1993.
66. Micheline Keating, "History of Tucson—4th installment," *The Magazine Tucson*, April 1949, 31.
67. Frank E. Russell interview by the author, April 6, 2008.
68. Ibid.

Chapter Eight

1. Flowers and Bullets mission statement, accessed April 10, 2024, https://www.flowersandbullets.com/mission.
2. Vic Thornton, "Work begun on Hughes plant," *Arizona Daily Star*, February 3, 1951.
3. Editorial, "Our greatest windfall," *Tucson Daily Citizen*, February 5, 1951.
4. Roy P. Drachman, *From Cowtown to Desert Metropolis: Ninety Years of Arizona Memories*, 180.
5. "Getting new plant here wasn't easy," *Tucson Daily Citizen*, February 3, 1951.
6. Drachman, *From Cowtown to Desert Metropolis*, 182–183.
7. Editorial, "Our greatest windfall."
8. Ibid.
9. "This woman kept a secret," *Tucson Daily Citizen*, February 3, 1951.
10. Lester N. Inskeep, "New Pima Solon given labor job," *Arizona Daily Star*, October 22, 1953.
11. Ellsworth Moe, "'John Spring School' will be Dunbar's new name on July 1," *Arizona Daily Star*, May 16, 1951.
12. "Trial in Tucson," *Time*.
13. "Race bars still high in Tucson," *Arizona Daily Star*, January 22, 1957.
14. "Accommodations for all on equal basis backed," *Arizona Daily Star*, November 12, 1958.
15. "Papagos defeat new Constitution," *Arizona Daily Star*, May 18, 1958.
16. Mark Turner, "'We just wanted to get married,' so they fought the state to do it," *Arizona Daily Star*, December 28, 1984.
17. Mrs. David Tang, "With deep humility, I thank Tucson," letter to the editor, *Tucson Citizen*, January 10, 1956.
18. Cecil James, "Methods vary; Border Patrol gets same results as in 1926," *Arizona Daily Star*, September 8, 1957.
19. "Drivers go on strike," *Arizona Daily Star*, October 21, 1955.
20. Roger O'Mara, "Tucson bus strike settled," *Arizona Daily Star*, December 3, 1955.
21. "Tucson gets millions of tourist dollars," *Arizona Daily Star*, July 26, 1953.
22. Vince Davis, "Plan initiated to bring new business here," *Arizona Daily Star*, May 14, 1953.
23. Tucson Chamber of Commerce, "Come to the growing Southwest—to Tucson for Industry and 'A Way of Life,'" 1952.
24. Bert M. Fireman, "Air coolers turned state around," *Tucson Daily Citizen*, April 20, 1973.
25. Vince Davis, "Douglas Aircraft launches branch facility in Tucson," *Arizona Daily Star*, May 21, 1954.
26. Roger O'Mara, "Accusations fly in City Council," *Arizona Daily Star*, March 5, 1957.
27. "Issue of airport zoning is aired," *Arizona Daily Star*, September 17, 1958.
28. John Fahr, "345 children attend newest city school," *Arizona Daily Star*, December 8, 1953.

29. "Colonel fearful about perils in zoning at base," *Arizona Daily Star*, October 25, 1956.
30. "Tucson called Arizona top target for H-bomb," *Arizona Daily Star*, June 4, 1957.
31. Dale Parris, "Bomb blast could blot out city," *Arizona Daily Star*, October 12, 1958.
32. "45,000 Tucsonans 'dead or injured' in imaginary hydrogen bomb raid," *Arizona Daily Star*, April 19, 1959.
33. "Satellite due over city at 10:20 p.m.," *Tucson Daily Citizen*, October 7, 1957.
34. William E. Bigglestone, *Tucson's Korean War Dead*.
35. "Flight training at Marana Air Base to end June 30," *Arizona Daily Star*, May 3, 1957; "Graduation set for Marana's last trainees," *Arizona Daily Star*, June 14, 1957.
36. "Volunteer aid in harvesting cotton asked," *Arizona Daily Star*, October 23, 1953.
37. "Drachman urges master planning," *Arizona Daily Star*, July 12, 1958.
38. Roy P. Drachman, letter to the Sports Forum, *Arizona Daily Star*, October 22, 1957.
39. Roger O'Mara, "City sales tax, bond issues approved by landslide majority," *Arizona Daily Star*, August 6, 1958.
40. "S. Arizona water use 'alarming,'" *Arizona Daily Star*, April 4, 1959.
41. "CC denies any water scarcity," *Arizona Daily Star*, July 8, 1959.
42. "M'Farland would bring Colo. water into state without waiting for government's assistance," *Arizona Daily Star*, July 8, 1955.
43. "Mayor sees expansion of city," *Arizona Daily Star*, April 21, 1956.
44. For more information on population and economic growth in Phoenix see: Bradford Luckingham, "Urban development in Arizona: The rise of Phoenix."
45. "S. Tucson urged to join city," *Arizona Daily Star*, March 16, 1956.
46. David Devine, "Struggle for survival: The South Tucson story," 17.
47. "Annex plan criticized by assn.," *Arizona Daily Star*, January 22, 1959.
48. Roger O'Mara, "City annexes 20-sq.-mile area," *Arizona Daily Star*, March 27, 1959.
49. Roger O'Mara, "Building boom Tucson's top story," *Arizona Daily Star*, December 31, 1956.
50. "2,000 persons on hand as new Penney's opens," *Arizona Daily Star*, September 20, 1957.
51. Dick Prouty, "Firemen rescue 7 in blaze," *Arizona Daily Star*, November 30, 1956.
52. Henry Arline, "Oro Valley project outlined," *Arizona Daily Star*, August 3, 1958.
53. Don Hummel, "City officials seek solution to downtown traffic problems," *Arizona Daily Star*, January 25, 1957.
54. "Slum area clearance advocated," *Arizona Daily Star*, March 7, 1957.
55. "City survey of culture ordered," *Arizona Daily Star*, September 29, 1954.
56. Ibid.
57. "Freeway motel plan opposed," *Arizona Daily Star*, October 1, 1955.
58. Hal Marshall, "Bonanno case is continued to Jan. 17," *Arizona Daily Star*, December 17, 1954.
59. Geraldine Sullivan, "Herreras.... Southwest beauty reborn," *Tucson Citizen*, May 24, 1973.
60. "Tucson pioneer Ronstadt dies," *Arizona Daily Star*, December 14, 1954.
61. "Death claims Monte Mansfield," *Tucson Citizen*, December 19, 1959.
62. "Record snow falls in Tucson; 3 Scouts lost in mountains," *Tucson Daily Citizen*, November 17, 1958. See also: Cathy Hufault, *Death Clouds on Mount Baldy*.
63. Roy Nickerson, "Painter seeks 'open spaces,'" *Arizona Daily Star*, April 18, 1957.
64. "Rules for operating your TV set," *Arizona Daily Star*, January 11, 1953.
65. Bonnie Henry, "Ex-city slickers hatched idea," *Arizona Daily Star*, June 22, 1988.
66. "History of the Desert Museum," 1.
67. Bonnie Henry, "Yes indeed, Buddy Holly played here," *Arizona Daily Star*, August 26, 1987.
68. Raymond Carlson, "Tucson—the New Pueblo," *Arizona Highways*, February 1958, 1.
69. L.W. Casaday, "Tucson—boom city in a booming state," *Arizona Highways*, February 1958, 36.

Chapter Nine

1. Don Moser, "The Pied Piper of Tucson," *Life*, 23.
2. Ibid., 24.
3. "City's 1960 crime rate shows 19 pct. increase," *Arizona Daily Star*, January 12, 1961.
4. "Cosa Nostra puts mark on Tucson," *Arizona Daily Star*, April 25, 1969.
5. "2 named in Pfeffer case," *Arizona Daily Star*, December 4, 1969.
6. Don Robinson, "Area crime commission created by joint panel," *Arizona Daily Star*, February 19, 1969.
7. "Governor signs loyalty oath, anti-red bill," *Arizona Daily Star*, March 31, 1961.
8. Joseph E. Bryson, *Legality of Loyalty Oath and Non-Oath Requirements for Public School Teachers*, 2.
9. David Devine, "Barbara Elfbrandt: She protected constitutional freedoms by standing up against a Red Scare-motivated law," *Tucson Weekly*, December 24, 2009.
10. "Star salutes the outstanding Tucson women of 1966," *Arizona Daily Star*, January 1, 1967.
11. "Billy Lane Lauffer," *Wikipedia*; Mark Kimble, "After 39 years, Tucson honoring war hero Lauffer," *Tucson Citizen*, May 19, 2005.
12. King spoke in Tucson in 1959 and 1962. See: David Leighton, "MLK Jr., raised his voice to the rafters in Tucson in '50s, '60s," *Arizona Daily Star*, April 3, 2017.
13. "71 percent of city cafes don't discriminate," *Arizona Daily Star*, June 9, 1960.

14. Don Carson, "Bill lifting racial bans draws fire," *Arizona Daily Star*, July 23, 1960; Don Carson, "Action on accommodation law is put aside for four months," *Arizona Daily Star*, August 2, 1960.
15. "Public accommodations ordinance is approved," *Arizona Daily Star*, June 26, 1964.
16. Judy Donovan, "Harvill denies bias charge," *Arizona Daily Star*, October 3, 1967.
17. "President signs measure giving Yaquis a home," *Arizona Daily Star*, October 9, 1964.
18. Margaret Kuehlthau, "First family expected to move into New Pascua Pueblo March 1," *Tucson Citizen*, February 10, 1967.
19. "Chavez plans to unionize area farm work," *Arizona Daily Star*, December 5, 1969.
20. Ron Radcliff, "Police 'walkout' over," *Arizona Daily Star*, August 10, 1969.
21. Kimberly Matas and Carmen Duarte, "50 years ago, gas explosion killed 7, leaving city in shock," *Arizona Daily Star*, March 29, 2013.
22. Pete Cowgill, "Tucson smog problem cited by UA professor," *Arizona Daily Star*, August 17, 1960.
23. Pete Cowgill, "Broadway underpass is opened to public," *Arizona Daily Star*, October 5, 1963.
24. Barbara Sears, "Hot debate expected on expressway plan," *Arizona Daily Star*, January 9, 1968.
25. "Old Pueblo is sinking in spots," *Arizona Daily Star*, April 14, 1960.
26. "Central Ariz. project is 'vital' to Tucson," *Arizona Daily Star*, May 25, 1963. Phoenix is located in Maricopa County.
27. "City waste water use studied," *Arizona Daily Star*, June 27, 1963; "Effluent report slated," *Arizona Daily Star*, August 24, 1963; "City hopes to reuse its water," *Arizona Daily Star*, June 19, 1965.
28. "New lake is waiting for water," *Arizona Daily Star*, March 15, 1964.
29. Pete Cowgill, "Golder Lake project just a big mudhole," *Arizona Daily Star*, January 29, 1968.
30. Dave Brinegar, "Skiing on Mount Lemmon becomes big business," *Arizona Daily Star*, March 12, 1965.
31. Bob Thomas, "Margaret Sanger hailed as woman of century," *Arizona Daily Star*, March 23, 1965.
32. John Riddick, "Mrs. Sanger Sees No Control of Birth Boom," *Tucson Daily Citizen*, October 30, 1964.
33. "Abortion Clinic Hit in Nogales," *Tucson Daily Citizen*, November 1, 1968; Gene Lindsey, "Tucson Doctor Abortion Link," *Arizona Daily Star*, November 23, 1968.
34. Lester N. Inskeep, "Longtime legislator is popular," *Arizona Daily Star*, September 2, 1962.
35. Melissa Amdur, *Linda Ronstadt*, 36.
36. Al Bradshaw, Jr., "85,000 see hero of space ride," *Arizona Daily Star*, January 11, 1966.
37. Ken Burton, "Pima bond plan defeated badly," *Arizona Daily Star*, March 12, 1969.
38. Bettina O'Neil Lyons, "The Pioneer Hotel: The Steinfeld family builds a Tucson landmark"; Genevieve Doyle, "$6 Million Expansion Planned for Pioneer," *Arizona Daily Star*, February 6, 1963.
39. Don Robinson, "City approves ordinance regulating cable-TV," *Arizona Daily Star*, July 19, 1966.
40. "Tucson's taxes near top for Western cities," *Arizona Daily Star*, June 25, 1969.
41. "Annexation claims draw new opponent," *Arizona Daily Star*, September 29, 1964.
42. "County attorney warns Miss Marteny, council," *Arizona Daily Star*, March 24, 1962.
43. "Cele Peterson opening Casas Adobes branch," *Arizona Daily Star*, November 7, 1963.
44. Jerry Few, "Theater runs its last film," *Arizona Daily Star*, June 19, 1963.
45. Don Carson, "Urban renewal called key to city's future," *Arizona Daily Star*, January 1, 1960.
46. Eleazar Herreras, interview by Lyn Papanikolas, March 9 and 11, 1983, 57.
47. E.C. Rutherford, "Urban renewal plan debated," *Arizona Daily Star*, May 26, 1961.
48. Dean Fairchild, "6 bond, tax issues defeated," *Arizona Daily Star*, June 27, 1962.
49. Don Robinson, "Tucson voters approve urban plan," *Arizona Daily Star*, March 2, 1966.
50. "Renewal area landowners protest city's appraisals," *Arizona Daily Star*, June 14, 1967.
51. Don Robinson, "Officials hail City Hall tower," *Arizona Daily Star*, October 24, 1967.
52. "City Council officially establishes Committee for Historical Sites," *Arizona Daily Star*, April 13, 1965.
53. Bill Moore, "Benton ired by Old Pueblo," *Arizona Daily Star*, October 12, 1962.
54. Editorial, "'The ugliest street in the U.S.,'" *Arizona Daily Star*, January 11, 1962; Michael Rougier, photographer, and Loudon Wainwright, author, "Blight blossoms on the American highway," *Life*.
55. Corky Simpson, "UA has earned its position as groundbreaker in hiring of minority coaches," *Tucson Citizen*, October 31, 2003.
56. John Riddick, "Dr. Douglass, astronomer, tree-ring scientist, dies," *Tucson Daily Citizen*, March 20, 1962.
57. "Arizonans put most in schools," *Arizona Daily Star*, May 3, 1969; "Arizona slips in school aid ranking," *Arizona Daily Star*, July 11, 1969.
58. Genevieve Doyle, "Retiring principal banks heavily on today's youth," *Arizona Daily Star*, February 15, 1968.
59. Pete Cowgill, "Kitt Peak eyes 150-inch 'scope," *Arizona Daily Star*, July 30, 1967.
60. "Tucson apathy cited in survey," *Arizona Daily Star*, April 22, 1966.
61. Al Rudis, "Health is key to new growth," *Arizona Daily Star*, May 5, 1966.
62. Dean Fairchild, "Lew Davis calls for more jobs," *Arizona Daily Star*, January 8, 1963.
63. Harvey Kitchel, "Researcher into Tucson's economy says tourism is over-emphasized," *Arizona Daily Star*, June 6, 1968.

64. "Cash in till irks TIDB," *Arizona Daily Star*, April 6, 1961.
65. Editorial, "Tucson's high wage scale," *Arizona Daily Star*, October 5, 1967.
66. Art Ehrenstrom, "30¢ 'siren song' infuriates unions," *Arizona Daily Star*, February 22, 1969.
67. Ibid.

Chapter Ten

1. Richard Saltus, "250 invade El Rio for picnic, tour," *Arizona Daily Star*, August 16, 1970.
2. "Seven protesters at El Rio seized," *Arizona Daily Star*, September 20, 1970.
3. Bob Svejcara, "Study forecasts 1.5 million Tucsonans by 2012," *Arizona Daily Star*, May 1, 1979.
4. Editorial, "Tucson's growth is good growth," *Arizona Daily Star*, July 18, 1979.
5. Richard Gilman, "Cactus power spreads its roots," *Arizona Daily Star*, June 9, 1974.
6. Ken Burton, "Businessmen jump into politics; Target? Asta," *Arizona Daily Star*, June 13, 1976.
7. Bob Lowe and Clark Hallas, "Pima capped rezoning blitz with 9,810 acres in '79," *Arizona Daily Star*, August 6, 1980.
8. Diane Johnsen, "Water rates raised to expand system," *Arizona Daily Star*, January 12, 1977.
9. David Hatfield, "Water lift fee is turned off," *Arizona Daily Star*, August 7, 1976.
10. Editorial, "Starting over," *Arizona Daily Star*, March 5, 1977.
11. "Corbett's activities detailed in column," *Tucson Daily Citizen*, March 23, 1970; Richard Saltus, "Corbett silent about 'gossip,'" *Arizona Daily Star*, March 24, 1970.
12. "Incorporation foes now in favor of it," *Arizona Daily Star*, March 25, 1977.
13. The name means "a jungle, a tangle or a thicket" in Spanish according to the Marana, Arizona, website.
14. The actual boundaries of Murphy's proposal were the Saguaro National Monument on the east, Gates Pass to the west, north to the "upper reaches" of the Catalina Foothills, and "just north of Sahuarita" on the south.
15. Lewis Murphy, "Ex-Mayor Murphy, on incorporation: 'I told you so,'" *Tucson Citizen*, October 15, 1997.
16. Bob Svejcara, "New twist added to 'metro' idea," *Arizona Daily Star*, December 16, 1975.
17. Bob Svejcara, "Planners and public to meet on Tucson's growth," *Arizona Daily Star*, October 18, 1973.
18. "Governments urged to set policy to guide area in future growth," *Arizona Daily Star*, March 8, 1975.
19. Tom Turner, "The CPP: A quiet funeral," *Arizona Daily Star*, December 3, 1978.
20. Bill Turner, "Uproar over planned growth now dying down," *Arizona Daily Star*, October 19, 1975.
21. Wade Cavanaugh, "Police rebuff determined applicant," *Arizona Daily Star*, November 16, 1971.
22. Beverly Medlyn, "'First step' stirs call for more Hispanics at UA," *Arizona Daily Star*, April 21, 1978.
23. "New law makes Yaquis an official tribe," *Arizona Daily Star*, September 19, 1978.
24. "Discrimination at Tucson Country Club charged by Jews," *Arizona Daily Star*, July 30, 1971.
25. "Gay Lib holds first Tucson meeting," *Arizona Daily Star*, July 26, 1971.
26. "Youths get probation in June killing," *Arizona Daily Star*, October 21, 1976; Rhonda Bodfield, "Gay bashing not down, activists say," *Tucson Citizen*, August 18, 1994.
27. "Illegal alien influx rising, agents say," *Arizona Daily Star*, January 25, 1974.
28. "Arraignments set today for UA gym disturbance," *Arizona Daily Star*, March 3, 1970.
29. Kerry Hibbs and Elizabeth Maggio, "Refugees' economic drain feared here," *Arizona Daily Star*, May 1, 1975.
30. J.C. Martin, "Opening the doors," *Arizona Daily Star*, April 14, 1977.
31. These figures are for total students. Eventually numbers would be given for full-time equivalent students.
32. Beverly Medlyn, "Tang urges PCC board to quit," *Arizona Daily Star*, May 24, 1978.
33. Dave O'Hern, "District One race data criticized," *Arizona Daily Star*, February 20, 1970.
34. David Carter and Edith Sayre Auslander, "Nine Tucson schools ordered desegregated," *Arizona Daily Star*, June 6, 1978.
35. Adolfo Quezada, "Chicano leaders still wielding power but with softer stick," *Arizona Daily Star*, June 15, 1975.
36. "School spending tops U.S. rate," *Arizona Daily Star*, January 27, 1970.
37. "Arizona cheapest in school funding, NEA official says," *Arizona Daily Star*, September 9, 1979.
38. Judy Donovan, "Arizona response is wide-ranging," *Arizona Daily Star*, January 23, 1973.
39. Sheryl Kornman, "Abortions Are Routine at Air Base," *Tucson Daily Citizen*, January 28, 1971.
40. "Nixon Curbs Abortions at U.S. Military Bases," *Arizona Daily Star*, April 4, 1971.
41. Sheryl Kornman, "Tucson abortion cases increase," *Tucson Daily Citizen*, April 26, 1972.
42. Douglas Kreutz, "Judge Strikes Down State Abortion Law," *Tucson Daily Citizen*, September 29, 1972.
43. Clark Hallas, "'A miracle a month' goal of heart doctor," *Arizona Daily Star*, September 17, 1979.
44. Tom Turner, "Harold Steinfeld's mark left on city of Tucson," *Arizona Daily Star*, December 21, 1979.
45. Joel Nilsson, "Jury rules Taylor set Pioneer blaze," *Arizona Daily Star*, March 22, 1972.
46. Taylor later filed a civil lawsuit that sought "money from Tucson and Pima County for wrong-

ful imprisonment and prosecutorial misconduct" but as of September 2024, a trial date was still pending. See: Charles Borla, "Trial seeking damages in hotel fire case canceled," *Arizona Daily Star*, June 21, 2024.

47. "Murders mark Tucson as drug-smuggling capital," *Arizona Daily Star*, April 1, 1977.

48. John Tabor, "Burglaries put city atop U.S. crime list," *Arizona Daily Star*, October 29, 1978.

49. "First in the nation?," *Arizona Daily Star*, February 1, 1973.

50. "Tucsonan Bonanno is Mob's western kingpin," *Arizona Daily Star*, March 27, 1977. See also: Michael F. Wendland, *The Arizona Project: how a team of investigative reporters got revenge on deadline*.

51. "Police, firemen return," *Arizona Daily Star*, September 29, 1975.

52. Richard Hall, "School to stay open despite D-M peril," *Arizona Daily Star*, October 11, 1972.

53. Al Bradshaw, Jr., "D-M closure effects weighed," *Arizona Daily Star*, February 13, 1973.

54. Betty Beard, "Debate flares on D-M's worth to Tucson area," *Arizona Daily Star*, March 16, 1973.

55. "Building curb urged in D-M flight path," *Arizona Daily Star*, August 11, 1975.

56. Michael D. Lopez, "1967-style crash will not recur, D-M says," *Arizona Daily Star*, December 21, 1977.

57. "Appellate Court asked to stop Sunnyside suit," *Arizona Daily Star*, June 26, 1971.

58. Editorial, "Tucson can be proud," *Arizona Daily Star*, November 7, 1972.

59. Editorial, "'Ma' can't be replaced," *Arizona Daily Star*, July 14, 1972.

60. Jacqi Tully, "Desert influences artists' works," *Arizona Daily Star*, April 8, 1979.

61. Ed Severson, "The Ooh Aah Man," *Arizona Daily Star*, November 1, 1979.

62. John Rawlinson, "Death for zoo elephant favored by commission," *Arizona Daily Star*, November 20, 1970.

63. Jason Eberhart-Phillips, "Schaefer rebuffs panel, backs big-time UA sports," *Arizona Daily Star*, November 25, 1978.

64. "Art center changes debated," *Arizona Daily Star*, December 23, 1971.

65. P.J. Stewart, "Million dollar museum complex officially opens today," *Arizona Daily Star*, May 4, 1975.

66. Art Ehrenstrom, "Civic center called key to Tucson's convention growth," *Arizona Daily Star*, September 2, 1970.

67. "Rising costs blanket increase in action at community center," *Arizona Daily Star*, January 26, 1975.

68. Don Robinson, "La Placita—the end of a dream?" *Arizona Daily Star*, February 27, 1977.

69. "Downtown property taxes cut by 20 percent," *Arizona Daily Star*, December 29, 1971.

70. Stephen B. Sherretta, "2 closure's downtown 'not all bad,'" *Arizona Daily Star*, November 9, 1979.

71. Carol Stengel, "'Fun' housing being planned for downtown," *Arizona Daily Star*, January 5, 1977.

72. "Council creates bodies for downtown development," *Arizona Daily Star*, January 16, 1979.

73. "City needs historic zoning law to protect barrio, Murphy says," *Arizona Daily Star*, January 7, 1972.

74. Originally called the Fremont House, the structure was later renamed in honor of José Maria Sosa III, Jesusita and Leopoldo Carrillo, and Elizabeth Frémont. Because Frémont's association with the home was minor, it is now referred to as the Sosa-Carrillo House.

75. Located on Main Avenue south of the Tucson Convention Center, people burn candles and leave paper messages at *El Tiradito*, the Wishing Shrine, a site that recalls an illicit love affair.

76. "Condemned Joesler home drops its walls after news of its adoption," *Arizona Daily Star*, December 2, 1978.

77. W.J. Delong to Mayor James N. Corbett, Jr., "Official Anniversary Date of Tucson," February 8, 1971.

78. James E. Officer to Mayor Corbett, October 5, 1971.

79. Henry F. Dobyns to The Mayor, City of Tucson, February 5, 1972.

80. "Firm accused of violations on radiation," *Arizona Daily Star*, April 4, 1979.

81. "Tritium talk gives expert tough time," *Arizona Daily Star*, May 4, 1979.

82. "'77 is a lucky number only for heat record buffs," *Arizona Daily Star*, September 3, 1977.

83. "The toughest hunt in Arizona," *Arizona Daily Star*, December 8, 1974; Edward J. Sylvester, "…Catalina State Park awaits completion," *Arizona Daily Star*, August 12, 1977.

84. "Golder Dam a flood threat, officials fear," *Arizona Daily Star*, February 2, 1979.

85. Tom Turner, "Tucson's basin can supply water for 375 years," *Arizona Daily Star*, June 12, 1970; "CAP water could slow depletion," *Arizona Daily Star*, August 15, 1975.

86. "Water official calls CAP essential to area's need," *Arizona Daily Star*, September 23, 1977.

87. Ben MacNitt, "Supervisors dubious of CAP's merits," *Arizona Daily Star*, November 9, 1973; "Six politicians lend support to local group fighting CAP," *Arizona Daily Star*, May 20, 1975.

88. An acre-foot of water is approximately 326,000 gallons, enough to supply about four households for one year.

89. Elaine Nathanson, "Butterfield route's foes planning march and rally," *Arizona Daily Star*, September 23, 1971.

90. Gerry Reeves, "Major employers press board for action on roads," *Arizona Daily Star*, August 3, 1978.

91. Editorial, "Drying up Lake Elmira," *Arizona Daily Star*, August 31, 1974.

92. Stephen B. Sherretta, Bobbie Jo Buel and

Bob Svejcara, "'80s gazers see a record for Tucson economy," *Arizona Daily Star*, December 2, 1979.
93. Art Ehrenstrom, "Motorola buys 196 acres for plant north of city," *Arizona Daily Star*, June 26, 1970.
94. Bill Bank, "Tucson in '79 comin' up roses," *Arizona Daily Star*, December 3, 1978.
95. Carol Stengel, "Tucsonans vent anger over DATE," *Arizona Daily Star*, March 29, 1977.
96. Valley National Bank would become Bank One in 1992 and it became Chase in 2004.
97. Sherry Stern, "Businessmen doubt TV special will turn off tourist tap...," *Arizona Daily Star*, February 24, 1977.
98. Jeff Smith, "But we only meant to help...," *Arizona Daily Star*, June 30, 1974.
99. Bill Bank, "5 more firms have eyes on location here," *Arizona Daily Star*, June 29, 1979.

Chapter Eleven

1. Cindy Hubert, "Southsiders jam forum on polluted water," *Arizona Daily Star*, June 4, 1985.
2. Jane Kay, "Solvent in wells sparks inquiry, health meeting," *Arizona Daily Star*, May 15, 1981.
3. Ernie Heltsley, "Hughes sues city, airport in TCE dumping," *Arizona Daily Star*, November 21, 1986. The National Cancer Institute in 2023 stated: "Prolonged or repeated exposure of trichloroethylene causes kidney cancer. Some evidence suggests that it may be associated with an increased risks of non-Hodgkin lymphoma and possibly, liver cancer."
4. Jane Kay, "Neglect of TCE issue compelled Star to investigate," *Arizona Daily Star*, May 19, 1985.
5. Steve Meissner, "Tucson will get big CAP pipeline," *Arizona Daily Star*, November 13, 1981.
6. "Judges tap Tucson water as best in North America," *Arizona Daily Star*, June 15, 1987.
7. In response to a 2023 e-mail inquiring about the current status of the plant off Ajo Road, a Tucson Water representative responded: "I'm not familiar with the history of Tucson. What is the address of the treatment plant in question?"
8. Steve Meissner, "Plan to build 3 dams would increase groundwater," *Arizona Daily Star*, August 26, 1981.
9. Tom Beal, "Some will leave, but most will live with it," *Arizona Daily Star*, October 4, 1983.
10. While often referred to as the Rillito River, its official name is Rillito Creek.
11. Judith Ratliff, "County lining up a linear park along Rillito," *Arizona Daily Star*, March 30, 1985.
12. Steve Williams, "State's first 'great urban park' opens," *Arizona Daily Star*, May 26, 1983.
13. "Former principal dead at age of 84," *Tucson Citizen*, March 21, 1987.
14. Robert Ramsey, "Sunday evening to lose its forum in April," *Arizona Daily Star*, February 11, 1984.

15. Mary Powers, "The intricate search for Quasar 0055 + 004," *Arizona Daily Star*, January 11, 1981.
16. Cindy Hubert, "UA at cutting edge in design, building of giant telescopes," *Arizona Daily Star*, July 13, 1984.
17. Jackie Rothenberg, "Titan silo is first ICBM museum," *Arizona Daily Star*, May 6, 1986.
18. Richard Ducote, "Backers of Tucson Air plan decry lack of local support," *Arizona Daily Star*, July 28, 1989.
19. Keith Bagwell, "Air pollution problems hit home," *Arizona Daily Star*, May 8, 1988.
20. Bernard L. Fontana, "Tucson's 'Emergence Place,'" *Arizona Daily Star*, March 12, 1989.
21. Richard Ducote, "Neighborhoods are big roadblock, land-use chairman says," *Arizona Daily Star*, January 31, 1988.
22. Joe Watt, "Get ready for growth," *Arizona Daily Star*, February 11, 1983.
23. Don Robinson, "Former city architect learned value of education by working for dad," *Arizona Daily Star*, April 1, 1986.
24. Edward Abbey, "Already big enough," letter to the editor, *Arizona Daily Star*, December 30, 1986.
25. David L. Teibel, "Blacks seek audit, claim police bias," *Arizona Daily Star*, December 9, 1980.
26. Lourdes Medrano Leslie, "Slogans aside, Hispanics say it wasn't their decade," *Arizona Daily Star*, December 25, 1989.
27. Bob Svejcara, "UA lacks strong minority hiring," *Arizona Daily Star*, May 3, 1983.
28. Carmen Ramos Chandler, "Discrimination a fact in Tucson, poll shows," *Arizona Daily Star*, June 22, 1986.
29. Susan Knight, "Official English group says TUSD used public funds to aid opponents," *Arizona Daily Star*, March 16, 1988.
30. Lourdes Medrano Leslie, "Slogans aside, Hispanics say it wasn't their decade."
31. Edmund Lawler, "Patrol chief retiring from 'unrealistic' task of controlling the border," *Arizona Daily Star*, December 27, 1982.
32. Joe Burchell, "City, Yaquis talk, plans are laid, but Old Pascua's blight goes on," *Arizona Daily Star*, April 20, 1980.
33. Ernie Heltsley, "$100 million project awaits Papago lease," *Arizona Daily Star*, May 17, 1983.
34. Joe Burchell, "Businessmen's group offers to aid city, county with plans for growth," *Arizona Daily Star*, January 5, 1980.
35. Bob Svejcara, "Area's population could triple by 2012," *Arizona Daily Star*, November 12, 1980.
36. Felipe Garcia, "Tucson 30 is formed to bring growth here," *Arizona Daily Star*, June 8, 1983.
37. Debbie Kornmiller, "Study expects huge AiResearch impact," *Arizona Daily Star*, March 12, 1983.
38. Roderick Gary, Chris Limberis, and Bob Svejcara, "'That shoots the economy,'" *Arizona Daily Star*, June 30, 1988.
39. Richard Ducote, "Job cutback at IBM will

slow growth, but can be absorbed, UA experts say," *Arizona Daily Star*, July 13, 1988.
40. "U.S. spent $12 billion in Arizona in fiscal '88; state ranks 19th," *Arizona Daily Star*, March 31, 1989.
41. Bob Christman, "Tourism state's gold, says Kolbe," *Arizona Daily Star*, May 16, 1989.
42. Steve Meissner, "Booming statistics hide state's underemployment," *Arizona Daily Star*, December 23, 1984.
43. "Ariz. living standards found low," *Arizona Daily Star*, October 11, 1988.
44. Stephen B. Sherretta, "Low wages mean high growth for Arizona, says forecast," *Arizona Daily Star*, October 17, 1980.
45. In 2009, the federal definition of homelessness was changed, reducing the number of people who were considered homeless.
46. Carmen Ramos Chandler, "Homeless set up 'Murphyville' outside old county courthouse," *Arizona Daily Star*, March 25, 1986.
47. Chris Limberis, "Brian Flagg: An advocate at home with the homeless," *Arizona Daily Star*, May 5, 1986.
48. John Rawlinson, "It'll be 'business as usual' as Murphy era nears end," *Arizona Daily Star*, March 5, 1987.
49. Steve Meissner, "Murphy revives city-county government consolidation," *Arizona Daily Star*, August 4, 1983.
50. John Rawlinson, "Forced-annexation era is finished, Volgy says," *Arizona Daily Star*, October 26, 1988.
51. Joe Burchell, "TCC is proposed site of high-rise hotel," *Arizona Daily Star*, April 18, 1987.
52. Joe Burchell, "Plans for downtown aren't the first," *Arizona Daily Star*, December 21, 1980.
53. The business name was derived from the first letter of co-owner Ed Irving's first name and co-owner Bob Greenberg's last name to form a new word—eegee's.
54. Tom Beal, "Elections mean status quo on growth," *Arizona Daily Star*, September 13, 1987.
55. Margo Hernandez, "Oro Valley settles suit to allow controversial shopping center," *Arizona Daily Star*, September 23, 1988.
56. Editorial, "Mission San Xavier," *Arizona Daily Star*, February 12, 1989.
57. Lisa Robinson, "Ronstadt widens horizons," *Arizona Daily Star*, January 2, 1983.
58. "Ceremony, sentiment mark railroad's centennial," *Arizona Daily Star*, March 21, 1980.
59. J.C. Martin, "'Los Tucsonenses,'" *Arizona Daily Star*, August 24, 1986.
60. Rev. Charles W. Polzer, S.J., "Distorted past," letter to the editor, *Arizona Daily Star*, July 15, 1981.
61. Convicted of murdering Vicki Lynn Hoskinson, Frank Jarvis Atwood was executed in 2022.
62. John Rawlinson, "Big 'prime-time' rapist reward to be offered," *Arizona Daily Star*, July 3, 1986.

63. The painting was found in New Mexico in 2017. After restoration, it went back on display at the University of Arizona Art Museum in 2022 and is valued at more than $100 million.
64. Ernie Heltsley, "Bonanno story," *Arizona Daily Star*, May 15, 1983.
65. Tom Beal, "Neely says crime 'out of control' here," *Arizona Daily Star*, May 27, 1981.
66. Douglas Kreutz, "County dedicates jail to replace 'semidungeon,'" *Arizona Daily Star*, February 5, 1987.
67. Cindy Hubert, "Snowstorm of cocaine hitting city," *Arizona Daily Star*, June 17, 1984.
68. Margo Hernandez, "5 men found slain; police suspect drug link," *Arizona Daily Star*, March 28, 1989.
69. C.T. Revere, "Killing of 5 called a hint of the future," *Arizona Daily Star*, March 29, 1989.
70. Officer Down Memorial Page, "Detective Willis Henry 'Bill' Gravel," accessed August 9, 2024.
71. Bob Christman, "Copper Bowl I called lacking in luster," *Arizona Daily Star*, December 28, 1989.
72. Robert S. Cauthorn, "Photography's new Center," *Arizona Daily Star*, February 5, 1989.
73. Jerre Johnston, "Provincial attitude," letter to the editor, *Arizona Daily Star*, July 19, 1981.
74. Chip Warren, "Scobee's death was a 'personal loss' for UA, Koffler tells shuttle mourners," *Arizona Daily Star*, January 31, 1986.
75. Bob Christman, "UA's wave of the future may be an Apple for the student," *Arizona Daily Star*, April 5, 1984.
76. Susan M. Knight, "PCC chief seeks end to probation," *Arizona Daily Star*, August 22, 1989.
77. Susan M. Knight, "PCC gives Navarrette $96,233 settlement," *Arizona Daily Star*, April 28, 1989.
78. Editorial, "Fantastic free offer," *Arizona Daily Star*, January 13, 1984.
79. Cindy Hubert, "Tucsonan critical with city's second confirmed AIDS case," *Arizona Daily Star*, May 19, 1983.
80. Bob Womack, "Tucson gays step up efforts to cope with AIDS spiral," *Arizona Daily Star*, May 22, 1985.
81. Jackie Rothenberg, "Report faults Arizona on care of mentally ill," *Arizona Daily Star*, March 19, 1986.
82. Carmen Duarte, "Study says Arizona spends the least on care for mentally ill," *Arizona Daily Star*, September 14, 1988.
83. Carmen Duarte and Bob Christman, "Disincorporation drive 'dead,' Yetman says," *Arizona Daily Star*, February 6, 1985.
84. John DeWitt, "Voters sent message to Tucson movers, shakers," *Arizona Daily Star*, September 15, 1984.
85. John DeWitt, "Dewhirst, Moore and Morrison look like winners," *Arizona Daily Star*, November 7, 1984.
86. Dan Huff, "Ed Moore," *Arizona Daily Star*, November 9, 1986.

87. Chris Limberis, "Yetman asks secession from Northern Arizona," *Arizona Daily Star*, May 29, 1987.
88. Richard Ducote, "Catalyst Energy, parent of Alamito, agrees to buyout," *Arizona Daily Star*, July 22, 1988.
89. Richard Ducote, "3 top execs leaving Alamito in major management change," *Arizona Daily Star*, March 14, 1989.
90. Richard Ducote, "TEP spinoff of Alamito called harmful," *Arizona Daily Star*, May 10, 1989.
91. In January 1989, the share price was $50, but fell to just above $30 by early July. A slight rebound then took the price to $32, which was when Greve sold his shares.
92. Richard Ducote, "2 state utilities take beating on Wall Street" *Arizona Daily Star*, November 22, 1989.

Chapter Twelve

1. David Pittman, "Tucson gets high on Cats, say experts—and rest of us," *Tucson Citizen*, April 2, 1997.
2. Carlos David Mogollon, "Sport complex group's goal," *Tucson Citizen*, January 11, 1995.
3. Dave Petruska, "Gem in the desert," *Tucson Citizen*, February 26, 1998.
4. "Major sport graduation rate lags," *Tucson Citizen*, March 27, 1991.
5. Michael R. Graham, "For UA faithful, Rose Bowl is so close they can smell it," *Tucson Citizen*, December 5, 1998.
6. Chuck Graham, "Tucson gets its own 'Pastorela,'" *Tucson Citizen*, December 12, 1996.
7. Nicole Greason, "Louis Bernal recalled as artist who fed the soul," *Tucson Citizen*, August 19, 1993.
8. "Tucson: King for a day," *Tucson Citizen*, February 26, 1999.
9. Michael R. Graham, "He eats his way into hearts of S. Tucson," *Tucson Citizen*, February 26, 1999.
10. Gabrielle Fimbres, "Old Pueblo patriarch," *Tucson Citizen*, November 18, 1999.
11. Roy P. Drachman, "Light rail for Tucson would be impractical, costly," *Tucson Citizen*, August 29, 1995.
12. C.T. Revere, "Mo leaves legacy of integrity," *Tucson Citizen*, December 14, 1998.
13. Emily Kaiser, "Eleazar Herreras, designer of St. Augustine's, dies at 95," *Tucson Citizen*, May 12, 1992.
14. A.J. Flick, "A movie you can't refuse," *Tucson Citizen*, July 13, 1999.
15. David L. Teibel, "Tucson 12th in crime rate," *Tucson Citizen*, August 13, 1991.
16. David L. Teibel, "Drug murders surge here," *Tucson Citizen*, June 4, 1990.
17. Stuart Faxon, "Dr. Sydney E. Salmon, 1936–1999," *Sombrero*.
18. Blake Morlock, "Outlook bleak for Kino's survival, report says," *Tucson Citizen*, October 23, 1999.
19. Mark Kimble, "Kolbe may stake his job on opposition to gay ban," *Tucson Citizen*, July 22, 1993.
20. Linda Witt, "TPD's Burkett blazed the way as pioneer female cop," *Tucson Citizen*, February 3, 1999.
21. Norma Coile, "Hedtke: 'I've done my best,'" *Tucson Citizen*, November 10, 1993.
22. Linda Witt, "Minority recruiting still tough for police," *Tucson Citizen*, August 8, 1998.
23. Matt Stewart, "Anti-Semitism on the rise here," *Tucson Citizen*, February 19, 1996.
24. Gabriela C. Rico and Joseph Garcia, "UA move called historic," *Tucson Citizen*, April 2, 1991.
25. United States Census, QuickFacts, Pima County, Arizona, July 1, 2023; United States Census, QuickFacts, Tucson city, Arizona, July 1, 2023.
26. "Migrant Deaths in Southern Arizona," University of Arizona, April 2021, 7.
27. Pima County Medical Examiner, "Undocumented Border Crosser Remains by Calendar Year," 2023. As of October 2, there had been 126 deaths in 2024.
28. Pamela Hartman, "Losing battle on the border," *Tucson Citizen*, February 3, 1995.
29. Editorial, "'Sonora' would be more at home on another planet," *Tucson Citizen*, September 28, 1990.
30. Eddie North-Hager, "Old Pueblo's palette," *Tucson Citizen*, July 28, 1999.
31. Paul L. Allen, "'Must-see' historic park proposed," *Tucson Citizen*, July 29, 1991.
32. Jack Johnson, "Rio Nuevo would boost culture, ex–Flandrau director says," *Tucson Citizen*, October 11, 1999.
33. Paul L. Allen, "Rio Nuevo work could start in 90 days," *Tucson Citizen*, December 15, 1999.
34. Salomón R. Baldenegro, "Latinos part of local history, not just spectators," *Tucson Citizen*, August 23, 2006.
35. Tucson Water's annual CAP allocation by that time was 136,000 acre-feet with another 8,200 acre-feet pending reallocation.
36. Editorial, "Reservoir for CAP storage must be built," *Tucson Citizen*, June 6, 1995.
37. Jerry Juliani, "Should Tucson keep out CAP? Proposition 200 is vitally needed," *Tucson Citizen*, September 25, 1995.
38. Rhonda Bodfield, "Facts are still murky on possible CAP lake," *Tucson Citizen*, October 27, 1995.
39. Michael Lafleur, "Walkup says city's water war is over," *Tucson Citizen*, November 12, 1999.
40. "Gutierrez: Running his hometown," *Tucson Citizen*, November 25, 1996.
41. Christina O. Valdez, "City grows by 16½ square miles," *Tucson Citizen*, August 22, 1995.
42. George Miller, "Bill to kill 1961 incorporation limit is trap for many," *Tucson Citizen*, March 16, 1999.

43. Rhonda Bodfield, "Roszak to resign, claiming 'developers run this town,'" *Tucson Citizen*, July 4, 1996.
44. Alan Lurie, "Oro Valley's unfair impact fees hurt home buyers," *Tucson Citizen*, March 1, 1995.
45. David Pittman, "Boom times in Sahuarita," *Tucson Citizen*, March 15, 1999.
46. Jennifer Katleman, "Bronson: Win a victory over developers," *Tucson Citizen*, November 6, 1996.
47. David Pittman, "Graytide," *Tucson Citizen*, October 25, 1999.
48. Blake Morlock, "Canoa failure marks new era—Astronomers, residents knock $900M plan," *Tucson Citizen*, January 13, 1999.
49. Joyesha Chesnick and Blake Morlock, "Getting a grip on growth," *Tucson Citizen*, April 19, 1999.
50. William G. Clemens, "American dream fading," *Tucson Citizen*, March 13, 1995.
51. United States Census, QuickFacts, Tucson city, Arizona, July 1, 2022.
52. Mitch Tobin, "Tucson may swell to 1.7 million by 2050," *Tucson Citizen*, December 7, 1999.
53. Rhonda Bodfield, "Growth debate back on; annexation fuels the fire," *Tucson Citizen*, May 7, 1994.
54. Editorial, "Tucson economy is not as as [sic] bad as it looks lately," *Tucson Citizen*, November 30, 1991.
55. "Arizona job growth 'staggering,'" *Tucson Citizen*, May 9, 1997.
56. Kathleen Allen, "Tucson next Silicon Valley?" *Tucson Citizen*, July 27, 1992.
57. William G. Clemens, "Microsoft picks Tucson site," *Tucson Citizen*, September 27, 1995.
58. William G. Clemens, "'Bragging rights' to Microsoft lost," *Tucson Citizen*, February 20, 1997.
59. Norma Coile, "UA students rally 'round the troops," *Tucson Citizen*, January 25, 1991.
60. Ann-Eve Pedersen, "Subsidy plans for Hughes released," *Tucson Citizen*, August 3, 1993.
61. Editorial, "Everyone needs chance to talk in D-M debate," *Tucson Citizen*, August 25, 1990.
62. Kathleen Allen, "Trade pact: boon to Tucson," *Tucson Citizen*, August 12, 1992.
63. Jonathan J. Higuera, "Fallout of NAFTA still being debated," *Tucson Citizen*, March 22, 1999.
64. David Pittman, "Let's cooperate, Tucsonans say," *Tucson Citizen*, October 1, 1992.
65. "For entrepreneurs, Tucson's hot," *Tucson Citizen*, October 26, 1995.
66. Heather Newman, "Poverty level unacceptable, mayor says," *Tucson Citizen*, January 7, 1994.
67. M. Scot Skinner, "Hike to $7 an hour soundly trounced," *Arizona Daily Star*, November 5, 1997.
68. Todd M. Hardy, "Crackdown on street people—'Compassion fatigue' hits home," *Tucson Citizen*, December 15, 1998.
69. Linda Witt, "UA has 'eyes' on Mars—Images of red planet breathtaking," *Tucson Citizen*, July 5, 1997.
70. David Pittman, "Canyon Ranch giving UA $10M," *Tucson Citizen*, October 1, 1997.
71. Francine Knowles, "School finance woes called threat to economy here," *Tucson Citizen*, March 22, 1990.
72. George F. Garcia, "TUSD: Good, getting better," *Tucson Citizen*, April 27, 1992.
73. Mary Bustamante, "Mexican American studies program requested for TUSD," *Tucson Citizen*, November 13, 1996.
74. Marisa Samuelson, "Fewer Hispanics drop out here," *Tucson Citizen*, February 9, 1998.
75. Marisa Samuelson, "Marketplace of schools—Charter school alternative generates praise, fear," *Tucson Citizen*, March 11, 1999.
76. William G. Clemens, "Pygmy owl gives wing to debate on growth," *Tucson Citizen*, July 21, 1995.
77. Blake Morlock, "Groups seek to preserve desert area," *Tucson Citizen*, May 16, 1998.
78. Ibid.
79. "Biosphere gets oxygen," *Tucson Citizen*, January 13, 1993.
80. Joel E. Cohen and David Tilman, "Biosphere 2 and biodiversity: The lessons so far," *Science*.
81. Stephanie Innes, "Tucsonans upbeat, like life here," *Tucson Citizen*, January 1, 1998.
82. Robert D. Kaplan, "Travels into America's future," *The Atlantic Monthly*, 56–57.

Chapter Thirteen

1. Billie Stanton, "RTA: The road ahead—Please, let's not mess up our hard-won RTA plan," *Tucson Citizen*, May 22, 2006.
2. "We hit 1 million today," *Arizona Daily Star*, November 12, 2006.
3. Garry Duffy, C.T. Revere, and Larry Copenhaver, "Focus shifts to light rail," *Tucson Citizen*, May 22, 2002.
4. The PAG transportation board was made up of a representative of Pima County government, the county's five municipalities and two Native American tribes plus one member representing the Arizona Transportation Board, who in 2006 was Schorr.
5. Garry Duffy, "'Great people mover'—or joke on Tucson?" *Tucson Citizen*, April 24, 2006.
6. Garry Duffy, "Bad roads cost us $400 yearly, says new study," *Tucson Citizen*, June 2, 2005.
7. Michael Lafleur, "Walk through the past," *Tucson Citizen*, February 27, 2001.
8. Teya Vitu, "Rainbow Bridge: Over the top or bold concept?" *Tucson Citizen*, February 20, 2006.
9. Editorial, "Downtown's time is now," *Tucson Citizen*, May 19, 2007.
10. Editorial, "Let's Call It 'Rio Never,'" *Tucson Citizen*, May 31, 2008.
11. Editorial, "First-class hotel downtown is a high priority," *Tucson Citizen*, May 4, 2006.
12. Tom Stauffer, "Wilder to open downtown restaurant," *Tucson Citizen*, April 4, 2009.
13. Tom Stauffer, "Long waits for burger

customers at In-N-Out's first store in Tucson," *Tucson Citizen*, April 25, 2007.

14. Lorrie Cohen, "Values soaring in housing boom," *Tucson Citizen*, January 26, 2000.

15. David Pittman, "New, resale home prices up 12 percent over last year," *Tucson Citizen*, December 23, 2004.

16. Eric Sagara, "New-home fees may add $2,000 to prices," *Tucson Citizen*, March 3, 2007.

17. Teya Vitu, "Housing to cool off in '06, UA expert predicts," *Tucson Citizen*, December 10, 2005.

18. Mark Kimble, "Future shock: Phoenix growth outlook mind-boggling," *Tucson Citizen*, June 12, 2003.

19. Irwin M. Goldberg, "Oro Valley tops in high-end sales," *Tucson Citizen*, September 23, 2002.

20. Teya Vitu and Stephen Ohlemacher, "Arizona becomes fastest-growing state," *Tucson Citizen*, December 22, 2006.

21. Josh Brodesky, "Housing starts down to 132; foreclosure sales drop slightly," *Arizona Daily Star*, December 19, 2009.

22. B. Poole, "Even better local economy forecast for 2008," *Tucson Citizen*, December 9, 2006.

23. B. Poole, "Expect a lean 2009, then slow recovery," *Tucson Citizen*, December 13, 2008.

24. Polly Higgins and Lorrie Cohen, "City losing out on film dollars," *Tucson Citizen*, February 7, 2002.

25. Shella Calamba, "Shrinking industry," *Tucson Citizen*, November 9, 2002.

26. B. Poole, "Discouraging words: Local ranching fades," *Tucson Citizen*, May 29, 2007.

27. Oscar Abeyta, "Ariz. atop copper market despite lull," *Tucson Citizen*, July 27, 2001.

28. Tim Steller, "City a vital link in drug trade," *Arizona Daily Star*, December 9, 2001.

29. Teya Vitu, "Slim-Fast shuts down, lays off 71 employees," *Tucson Citizen*, December 29, 2004.

30. Teya Vitu, "Do Not Call not affecting call centers," *Tucson Citizen*, February 25, 2004; Teya Vitu, "Call centers create most new jobs here," *Tucson Citizen*, October 8, 2004.

31. David Pittman, "Bioscience park a tech boost?" *Tucson Citizen*, June 21, 2006.

32. Tech Park Arizona, accessed January 19, 2024, https://techparks.arizona.edu/the-bridges.

33. Sheryl Kornman and Brad Branan, "Tucson has highest poverty rate," *Tucson Citizen*, August 30, 2006.

34. University of Arizona MAP Dashboard, "Poverty Rate," accessed January 19, 2024, https://mapazdashboard.arizona.edu/health-social-well-being/poverty-rate.

35. "Tucsonans lag farther behind in wages," *Tucson Citizen*, January 10, 2000.

36. Dave Petruska, "300,000 in S. Ariz. relying on charity for daily needs," *Tucson Citizen*, November 14, 2001.

37. Blake Morlock, "Spiral often starts with missed paycheck," *Tucson Citizen*, January 14, 2004. After this time, the federal definition of homelessness changed, resulting in a significant drop in total numbers.

38. Oscar Abeyta, "Growth in wages here lags," *Tucson Citizen*, March 12, 2002.

39. Irwin M. Goldberg and Teya Vitu, "Whatever the right formula is, Tucson hasn't found it," *Tucson Citizen*, January 20, 2003.

40. Renée Schafer Horton, "Business leaders clamor for literacy," *Tucson Citizen*, November 14, 2007.

41. Dan Sorenson, "Recovery signs start to appear in Tucson," *Tucson Citizen*, May 17, 2009.

42. Editorial, "Phoenix values education more than Tucson," *Arizona Daily Star*, November 5, 2009.

43. Renée Schafer Horton, "UA's Shelton weathers stormy second year," *Tucson Citizen*, June 27, 2008.

44. Mary Bustamante, "Enrollment dwindles at TUSD over past four years," *Tucson Citizen*, November 8, 2003.

45. Konstantinos Kalaitzidis, "New tech ed classes to draw 17,000 students," *Tucson Citizen*, August 6, 2007.

46. "Tucson 'hate speech' gets on TV," *Tucson Citizen*, April 14, 2006.

47. Editorial, "Horne needs to leave TUSD ethnic-studies program alone," *Tucson Citizen*, November 26, 2007.

48. Mary Bustamante and Ryn Gargulinski, "Government leaders debate Raza Studies," *Tucson Citizen*, June 13, 2008.

49. Arizona State Legislature, HB 2281 (2010).

50. Luke Turf, "Desert aid camp opens," *Tucson Citizen*, June 1, 2004.

51. Susan Carroll, "Ashcroft: U.S. gaining control along line," *Tucson Citizen*, May 7, 2001.

52. Sheryl Kornman, "Changing of the guard," *Tucson Citizen*, January 28, 2005.

53. Mary Bustamante, "Bilingual ed support—Prop. 203 forum draws emotional crowds," *Tucson Citizen*, October 19, 2000. Many schools gained exemptions from the law and for those that did participate, test data reported by the National Education Policy Center in 2005 showed: "Proposition 203 has not resulted in increased achievement."

54. Sheryl Kornman, "Proposition 200 wins easily but may never become law," *Tucson Citizen*, November 3, 2004. The law's requirement that proof of citizenship be shown when registering to vote was modified by the U.S. Supreme Court in 2013.

55. David L. Teibel and David J. Cieslak, "Stabbing of gay man at 4th Ave. restaurant a hate crime, police say," *Tucson Citizen*, February 8, 2000.

56. David J. Cieslak, "Marching against hate—Stabbing victim surprise speaker to 1,500 at rally," *Tucson Citizen*, February 14, 2000.

57. A.J. Flick, "Trial starts in gay man's slaying," *Tucson Citizen*, January 14, 2005.

58. Tim Steller and Rhonda Bodfield, "Elite club is hit with civil-rights complaints," *Arizona Daily Star*, December 6, 2009.

59. Salomón Baldenegro, "Mexican American effort at UA a great success," *Tucson Citizen*, May 14, 2002.
60. Blake Morlock, "UA Hispanics: ¿Donde están?" *Tucson Citizen*, October 3, 2003.
61. Editorial, "ChiSox headed to Glendale? A stinking deal," *Tucson Citizen*, November 17, 2006.
62. Anthony Gimino, "Mowatt miracle," *Tucson Citizen*, June 7, 2007.
63. Irene Hsiao, "UA athletes' graduation rate below the nation's," *Tucson Citizen*, September 30, 2002.
64. David J. Cieslak and Eric Weslander, "Toll: 12 hurt, 17 arrested, cars torched," *Tucson Citizen*, April 3, 2001.
65. Irene Hsiao, "Bell tolls for three," *Tucson Citizen*, November 5, 2002.
66. Carli Brosseau, "TPD: Gang activity up; added officers to help," *Tucson Citizen*, April 17, 2008.
67. *Ibid.*
68. Larry Lopez and Roger Tamietti, "Public safety price: PRO—Police, fire agencies must be a high priority," *Tucson Citizen*, October 4, 2009.
69. University Physicians Incorporated (UPI) was established in 1985 and 20 years later its name became University Physicians Healthcare (UPH). In 2011, all of its "entities" were called the University of Arizona Health Network.
70. Anne T. Denogean, "Kino thinks BIG," *Tucson Citizen*, July 7, 2005.
71. Michael Lafleur, "Sahuarita mayor ousted, then resigns," *Tucson Citizen*, August 11, 2000.
72. Blake Morlock, "Tortolita's township bid looking dead," *Tucson Citizen*, July 8, 2000.
73. Blake Morlock, "One metro governing body key city idea," *Tucson Citizen*, February 1, 2003.
74. B. Poole, "Hunt is on for more sources of water," *Tucson Citizen*, July 3, 2008.
75. Peter Backus, "Pima County bond election Question 1: Open spaces $174.3 million—PRO," *Tucson Citizen*, April 5, 2004.
76. Blake Morlock, "Desert plan seeks backing," *Tucson Citizen*, March 23, 2001.
77. Chuck Huckelberry, "Desert protection key to our future," *Tucson Citizen*, April 23, 2001.
78. B. Poole, "Sabino a total washout," *Tucson Citizen*, August 5, 2006.
79. Mary Ellen Barnes, *Forged by Fire*, 152.
80. "Casa de los Niños worker's caring 'makes all the kids feel safe,'" *Arizona Daily Star*, July 11, 2009. Two-year-old Ben Maré Packard died of croup in 2002.
81. "Walkup: D-M will avoid closure," *Tucson Citizen*, December 21, 2002.
82. Lorrie Cohen, "'Optics Valley': Fighting to keep the title," *Tucson Citizen*, April 6, 2000.
83. Editorial, "UA feats in space dazzle all the world," *Tucson Citizen*, January 19, 2005.
84. Alan Fischer, "Smith: Tucson's own 'rock star' of science," *Tucson Citizen*, May 22, 2008.
85. B. Poole, "Sun sets on UA-led Phoenix Mars Lander," *Tucson Citizen*, November 11, 2008.
86. "Tucson responds," *Tucson Citizen*, September 11, 2001.
87. A.J. Flick and Blake Morlock, "Antiwar protestors close Congress Street," *Tucson Citizen*, March 21, 2003.
88. David Pittman, "City votes 7-0 to keep peak's A in patriotic colors," *Tucson Citizen*, April 8, 2003.
89. Mike Eckel, "A-10 pilots trained at D-M are 'cops on beat' in Afghanistan," *Tucson Citizen*, November 28, 2002.
90. Sandra Valdez Gerdes, "Rockwell of the O'odham," *Tucson Citizen*, May 18, 2004.
91. C.J. Karamargin, "Drachman on growth," *Tucson Citizen*, January 19, 2001.
92. Paul L. Allen, "Sun sets on a don," *Tucson Citizen*, May 13, 2002.
93. Stephanie Innes, "Overflow crowd greets Giffords on health care," *Arizona Daily Star*, September 2, 2009.

Chapter Fourteen

1. Those killed were Christina-Taylor Green, Dorothy Morris, Judge John Roll, Phyllis Schneck, Dorwan Stoddard, and Gabe Zimmerman.
2. Rhonda Bodfield and Becky Pallack, "'What matters is not wealth, or status, or power or fame, but how well we have loved,'" *Arizona Daily Star*, January 13, 2011.
3. Stephanie Innes, "Barber: Treatment could have prevented crimes," *Arizona Daily Star*, November 9, 2012.
4. "Homicide Deaths 2011-2020," Pima County Office of the Medical Examiner—Annual report 2020, 12.
5. Tim Stellar, "Tucson's murder problem is rooted in domestic violence," *Arizona Daily Star*, March 20, 2019.
6. Clements was convicted in 2022 for the murder of Maribel Gonzalez and of Isabel Celis in 2024.
7. "2019 Crime in the United States," Federal Bureau of Investigation, 2019, accessed February 10, 2024, https://ucr.fbi.gov/crime-in-the-u.s/2019/crime-in-the-u.s.-2019/tables/table-8/table-8-state-cuts/arizona.xls.
8. University of Arizona MAP Dashboard, "Quality of Place—Public Safety," accessed February 10, 2023, https://mapazdashboard.arizona.edu/quality-place/public-safety; Norma Coile, "Rothschild carjacked at gunpoint at his home," *Arizona Daily Star*, February 19, 2017.
9. Julia Jackman and Allan N. Williams, "Gun Violence in Arizona: Data to Inform Prevention Policies," Arizona Public Health Association, March 2023, 48.
10. Joe Ferguson, "City, police try to halt dire exodus of officers," *Arizona Daily Star*, March 11, 2018.
11. Editorial, "Walkup's legacy will be morass that is Rio Nuevo, like it or not," *Arizona Daily Star*, February 25, 2011.

12. Justin Sayers, "Rio Nuevo OKs $65M plan for upgrades of TCC venues," *Arizona Daily Star*, August 27, 2019.

13. Rhonda Bodfield, "Mayor: County areas must be annexed for economic survival," *Arizona Daily Star*, February 15, 2012.

14. Hank Amos, "Dear Tucsonans," advertisement, *Arizona Daily Star*, November 2, 2015.

15. Patrick McNamara, "City looks for ways to balance future budgets," *Arizona Daily Star*, January 21, 2016.

16. The first Mexican American mayor was Estevan Ochoa in 1875. Justin Sayers, "Romero declares readiness to begin 'historic journey' as Tucson mayor," *Arizona Daily Star*, December 3, 2019.

17. "All seven bonds trailing, leaving backers 'stunned,'" *Arizona Daily Star*, November 4, 2015.

18. Logan Burtch-Buus, "Challengers Sweep in Oro Valley," *Tucson Weekly*, August 28, 2018.

19. Editorial, "Bighorn, people don't mix; reintroducing herd is a bad idea," *Arizona Daily Star*, August 19, 2013.

20. "Sheep take a leap in Catalinas survey," *Arizona Daily Star*, October 2, 2019.

21. Tony Davis, "Study: Worst SW drought in 1,000 years is coming," *Arizona Daily Star*, February 13, 2015.

22. Mikayla Mace, "Tucson's 2018 weather year 4th-hottest, eased drought," *Arizona Daily Star*, January 1, 2019.

23. Tony Davis and Andrew Howard, "Not cool: Tucson 3rd on list of fastest-warming U.S. cities," *Arizona Daily Star*, April 24, 2019.

24. Tucson Electric Power, "2019 Preliminary Integrated Resource Plan," July 1, 2019, 31.

25. Tony Davis and Ayurella Horn-Muller, "As temperatures rise here, so do concerns over health risks tied to higher ozone levels," *Arizona Daily Star*, May 19, 2019.

26. Tony Davis, "County, on short end in quest to save land, may get no more," *Arizona Daily Star*, October 24, 2010.

27. Murphy Woodhouse, "Supes OK agreement for conservation plan," *Arizona Daily Star*, September 7, 2016.

28. In 2011 the name of the hospital complex was changed once again, this time to UA Medical Center—South Campus.

29. Chuck Huckelberry, "County, Banner partnership a unqualified success," Under the Dome, unknown date.

30. David Wichner, "Hospital in Green Valley lays off dozens, changes name after exiting bankruptcy," *Arizona Daily Star*, August 2, 2018.

31. Khara Persad, "Census: Tucson sixth-poorest large city," *Arizona Daily Star*, September 26, 2012. See also: Julia Grace Smith and Lane Kenworthy, *Poverty in Tucson*.

32. Census Bureau statistics from 2014 indicated this number falling to below 34 percent. See: Yoohyun Jung, "Census finds fewer Tucson kids in poverty," *Arizona Daily Star*, September 19, 2014.

33. Howard Fischer, "Tucson ranked among America's neediest cities," *Arizona Daily Star*, December 10, 2014.

34. Howard Fischer, "Tucson is worst place in AZ to find a job, study says," *Arizona Daily Star*, January 5, 2016.

35. "City of Tucson Poverty and Urban Stress," 2020, 1.

36. Dale Quinn, "Signs of a recovery in Tucson," *Arizona Daily Star*, December 10, 2011.

37. "Where the recovery isn't happening," *Arizona Daily Star*, October 5, 2014.

38. Bureau of Labor Statistics, "Databases, tables & calculators by subject," Tucson, Arizona Construction.

39. Becky Pallack, "Tourism struggles to gain ground," *Arizona Daily Star*, June 30, 2013; and "Tucson tourism demand tops growth projections," *Arizona Daily Star*, August 24, 2014.

40. Carli Brosseau, "High-pay jobs not in Tucson forecast," *Arizona Daily Star*, November 12, 2013; Howard Fischer, "Study: Tucson, other Ariz. cities lag in recovery," *Arizona Daily Star*, August 2, 2014.

41. Gabriela Rico, "Caterpillar 'biggest deal in 25 years,'" *Arizona Daily Star*, May 4, 2016.

42. In early 2024, TuSimple ceased operations in Tucson and the city government sought to recoup $110,000 in incentive money it had provided the firm.

43. Tony Davis, "Corps gives Rosemont Mine final permit for construction," *Arizona Daily Star*, March 9, 2019.

44. Gabriela Rico, "Tucson area is expected to add 7,100 jobs, spurring investment," *Arizona Daily Star*, February 12, 2017.

45. "Agero looking to hire 200 at call center here," *Arizona Daily Star*, May 15, 2014.

46. Howard Fischer, "Wage increases for AZ workers lagging behind rest of U.S.," *Arizona Daily Star*, February 3, 2018.

47. David Wichner, "Growth barely perceptible in Tucson as hangover lingers from federal cuts," *Arizona Daily Star*, June 5, 2014; George Hammond, "The economy of Tucson is improving, but gains are slow," *Arizona Daily Star*, March 22, 2016; "Tucson economy: MAP Dashboard—Tucson lags peer cities for job growth, despite some improvement," *Arizona Daily Star*, April 28, 2019.

48. Dale Quinn, "S. AZ consensus: We need science-based jobs," *Arizona Daily Star*, April 3, 2011.

49. Andi Berlin, "Int'l honor: UNESCO designates Tucson as City of Gastronomy," *Arizona Daily Star*, December 12, 2015.

50. David Wichner, "Tucson sending saguaro to Bezos in bid to get HQ," *Arizona Daily Star*, September 14, 2017. In the end, a site in Arlington, Virginia, was selected.

51. David Wichner, "Wright, who turned UA Tech Park into 'powerhouse,' to call it quits," *Arizona Daily Star*, September 23, 2018.

52. Patrick McNamara, "Report says new

corridor worth billions," *Arizona Daily Star*, October 14, 2015.

53. Gabriela Rico, "Proposed Interstate 11 gains support from leaders," *Arizona Daily Star*, August 30, 2013.

54. Gabriela Rico, "S. Ariz. scrambling for Sonora business," *Arizona Daily Star*, September 23, 2012.

55. Despite that defeat, the Arizona Department of Transportation in 2021 selected a corridor route for the project and in the fall of 2024 was scheduled to hold public meetings as it began a new planning phase for the corridor. This phase was scheduled to be completed with a public hearing in the summer of 2026.

56. It was only between 1884 and 1896 that the community had previously declined in population.

57. Howard Fischer, "Arizona cities lag as outlying areas gain population," *Arizona Daily Star*, May 21, 2015.

58. "Coming and going, births and deaths," *Arizona Daily Star*, March 27, 2014; Howard Fischer, "Phoenix suburbs lead in population growth estimates," *Arizona Daily Star*, May 22, 2014.

59. Tim Stellar, "If our economy ignites, population will grow," *Arizona Daily Star*, December 16, 2015.

60. Emily Bregel, "Buy land now for affordable housing later, Tucson told," *Arizona Daily Star*, August 18, 2014; 2022 medium range projections by the Arizona Commerce Authority were that approximately 1.22 million people would live in Pima County in 2045.

61. "Water Matters," Tucson Water, March 2019.

62. Tony Davis, "S. Ariz. closer to an epic drought," *Arizona Daily Star*, August 31, 2014.

63. Tony Davis, "Pilot project could treat wastewater for drinking in as soon as three years," *Arizona Daily Star*, August 3, 2014; and "By end of 2017, 'toilet to tap' water could be legal in Arizona, officials say," *Arizona Daily Star*, January 26, 2017.

64. "PFAS are man-made chemicals that have been used in industry and consumer products worldwide since the 1940s… While it is difficult to show that substances directly cause health conditions in humans, scientific studies have shown that exposure to some PFAS in the environment may be linked to harmful health effects in humans and animals." Agency for Toxic Substances and Disease Registry, accessed October 3, 2024, https://www.atsdr.cdc.gov/pfas/health-effects/overview.html.

65. Lawsuits seeking financial compensation for remediation were filed by the cities of Marana and Tucson against the manufacturers of the chemicals while in September 2024 the town of Marana filed suit against the federal government.

66. Gabriela Rico, "Local investors buy Foothills Mall, plan major redo," *Arizona Daily Star*, December 21, 2016.

67. In 2024, the store moved to the Tucson Mall.

68. Emily Bregel, "Count shows dip in city's homeless population," *Arizona Daily Star*, June 4, 2016. In 2019, 1,372 people were identified as homeless.

69. "Building Science City," *Arizona Daily Star*, April 3, 2011.

70. David Wichner, "Regional challenge: Building talent to fill the jobs we want," *Arizona Daily Star*, April 28, 2013.

71. Darren DaRonco, "Mayor's new economic plan swaps old 5 C's for new 5 T's," *Arizona Daily Star*, December 14, 2013.

72. Tim Steller, "If only raising wages were as simple as Obama says," *Arizona Daily Star*, February 2, 2014.

73. Howard Fischer, "AZ near bottom in per-pupil spending," *Arizona Daily Star*, June 23, 2012.

74. Calvin Baker, "Charter, district schools are all woefully underfunded by state," *Arizona Daily Star*, December 18, 2013.

75. In 2014 Shelton returned to Tucson as head of the Research Corporation for Science Advancement.

76. Carol Ann Alaimo, "I turned around a declining UA, Hart said in '14," *Arizona Daily Star*, September 5, 2015.

77. Carol Ann Alaimo, "$988K pay package for UA's new president," *Arizona Daily Star*, April 4, 2017. In reality, Robbins would complete just over seven years as UA President.

78. Mikayla Mace and Yoohyun Jung, "To catch peers, UA looks at tightening admissions," *Arizona Daily Star*, December 3, 2017.

79. Tom Beal and Becky Pallack, "UA wins $800M NASA contract," *Arizona Daily Star*, May 26, 2011.

80. These figures are full-time equivalent student numbers. Full-time equivalent is defined by the University of Arizona as: "A measure used to assess enrollment by assuming that all students are studying of a full-time basis."

81. Alexis Huicochea and Carol Ann Alaimo, "PCC: 87% from local schools not prepared for college," *Arizona Daily Star*, May 17, 2015.

82. Kimberly Matas, "'Culture of fear' is found at PCC," *Arizona Daily Star*, March 17, 2013.

83. Yoohyun Jung and Carol Ann Alaimo, "PCC's sanctions lifted 4 years later," *Arizona Daily Star*, March 10, 2017.

84. Alexis Huicochea, "Teacher pay here is $16K lower than across U.S.," *Arizona Daily Star*, October 15, 2015.

85. Jan Autenreith, "No, the Ariz. School funding shortage isn't fixed," *Arizona Daily Star*, May 21, 2019.

86. Arizona Department of Education, accessed August 24, 2024, https://www.ade.az.gov/charterschools/search.

87. Carmen Duarte, "Legality of ethnic studies law debated," *Arizona Daily Star*, March 23, 2011.

88. Tim Steller, "On blogs, Huppenthal reveals his inner ugliness," *Arizona Daily Star*, June 25, 2014.

89. Alexis Huicochea, "Judge orders TUSD to teach about culture," *Arizona Daily Star*, February 7, 2013.

90. Astrid Galvan, "Judge: Racism fueled AZ ethnic-studies ban," *Arizona Daily Star,* August 23, 2017.

91. Tim Steller, "Phoenix embraces schools while Tucson says no," *Arizona Daily Star*, November 12, 2017.

92. Hank Stephenson and Ava Garcia, "Voters reject tax to support scholarships for preschool," *Arizona Daily Star*, November 8, 2017. In 2021, the Pima County Board of Supervisors approved funding support for 1,365 children to attend "high quality" preschools.

93. Emily Bregel, "AF secretary: D-M's future may be found beyond A-10s," *Arizona Daily Star*, March 10, 2016.

94. David Wichner, "A-10 retirement plan raises stakes for D-M noise critics," *Arizona Daily Star*, June 29, 2014; Correction July 2, 2014.

95. David Wichner, "Air-control tower project ready for takeoff," *Arizona Daily Star*, January 28, 2014. In federal fiscal year 2008, TIA had approximately 4.4 million passengers, but that number had fallen 25 percent to 3.3 million by fiscal year 2013 and continued to slowly decline after that before starting to rebound in 2016. See: "Tucson International Airport: 10 years of passenger statistics."

96. "Tucson market overview," *Zillow.*

97. Emily Bregel, "Real estate market 'like running in molasses,'" *Arizona Daily Star*, January 24, 2014.

98. Gabriela Rico, "Home Values in Tucson up 10.3%—nation's 2nd highest rate," *Arizona Daily Star*, December 8, 2019.

99. Rob O'Dell, "Our home-vacancy problem," *Arizona Daily Star*, October 30, 2011.

100. University of Arizona MAP Dashboard, "Health & Social Well-Being—Housing Cost Burden," accessed March 2, 2014, https://mapazdashboard.arizona.edu/health-social-well-being/housing-cost-burden.

101. Carmen Duarte, "Wingspan to close, hopes its services live on," *Arizona Daily Star*, June 28, 2014.

102. Dale Quinn, "Bankrupt La Paloma keeps going," *Arizona Daily Star*, November 19, 2010; Dale Quinn, "Lenders battle over Marriott Starr Pass," *Arizona Daily Star*, February 5, 2012; Carli Brosseau, "Another Tucson resort in default," *Arizona Daily Star*, September 29, 2012.

103. Rob O'Dell and Andrea Kelly, "RTA crisis may wipe out 25 percent of projects," *Arizona Daily Star*, July 18, 2010.

104. Murphy Woodhouse, "RTA 'on-schedule, within budget,' state audit says," *Arizona Daily Star*, May 8, 2017.

105. Becky Pallack, "1st-yr. streetcar subsidy is $4 million," *Arizona Daily Star*, October 9, 2012; Becky Pallack and Patrick McNamara, "Tax hike may be only way to fund Sun Tran," *Arizona Daily Star*, August 30, 2015.

106. Dave Devine, "Under construction," *Tucson Weekly*, May 19, 2011.

107. Roger Allen, Letter to the Editor, "A Tucson carol: 'Jingle Bumps,'" *Arizona Daily Star*, December 13, 2013. The entire jingle is:

Bumpety bump bump
Bumpety bump bump
Over the streets we go.
Bumpety bump bump
Bumpety bump bump
Driving where potholes grow.
Tucson—the Old Pueblo—is a jolly place to be
Our vehicles jingle happily—but that's not so for me!
Bumpety bump bump
Let's go have some tea!

108. Editorial, "Strike must end for the good of Tucson," *Arizona Daily Star*, September 4, 2015.

109. Becky Pallack and Kim Matas, "Pedestrian deaths at record level across area," *Arizona Daily Star*, October 27, 2013; Alison Dorf, "Pedestrian fatalities haunt city," *Arizona Daily Star*, May 11, 2014.

110. "Tucson is No. 1 bike town in U.S., says Outside magazine," *Arizona Daily Star*, July 19, 2012.

111. "By the numbers," *Arizona Daily Star*, June 30, 2014; Perla Trevizo, "More border crossers fled or returned to Mexico in 2013 vs. 2012," *Arizona Daily Star*, September 21, 2014; United States Border Patrol—Southwest Border Sectors (Tucson)—"Total Illegal Alien Apprehensions By Fiscal Year," 1960 to 2020, accessed August 16, 2024, https://www.cbp.gov/sites/default/files/assets/documents/2021-Aug/US59B8~1.PDF.

112. "Trump's Wall: redundant, impractical," *Arizona Daily Star* special section, July 10, 2016, 2.

113. Perla Trevizo and Luis F. Carrasco, "Border crossers' survival rate up," *Arizona Daily Star*, September 28, 2014; "Border deaths," *Arizona Daily Star*; "Migrant Deaths in Southern Arizona, Recovered Undocumented Border Crosser Remains Investigated by the Pima County Office of the Medical Examiner, 1990-2020," April 2021, 7.

114. Jessica Suriano, "Fentanyl seizures skyrockets at border in Arizona," *Arizona Daily Star*, November 26, 2017. See also: Prerana Sannappanavar, "Record fentanyl seizure made along Arizona-Mexican border," *Arizona Daily Star*, August 3, 2024.

115. "Border officers in Nogales seize record-setting load of pot," *Arizona Daily Star*, November 20, 2013.

116. Pima County Overdose Fatality Review Annual Report 2019, Pima County Health Department, 1.

117. Seven people suspected of being involved with Terry's shooting were eventually convicted, but in 2024 one had his conviction overturned by an appeals court.

118. Howard Fischer, "Brewer signs sweeping immigration measure," *Arizona Daily Star*, April 24, 2010.

119. Brady McCombs, "Fed moves will limit SB 1070 enforcement," *Arizona Daily Star*, June 26, 2012.

120. Curt Prendergast, "Border detentions here cost taxpayers $2 billion since '07," *Arizona Daily Star*, May 21, 2017.

121. Luis F. Carrasco, "Half under executive act eligible for relief," *Arizona Daily Star*, January 16, 2015.
122. Howard Fischer and Bob Christie, "Ducey, noting added arrests at border, assigns 338 soldiers," *Arizona Daily Star*, April 10, 2018.
123. Curt Prendergast, "Border status quo being threatened by prosecutions of aid volunteers," *Arizona Daily Star*, October 21, 2018.
124. Nicole Ludden, "Federal charges against four No More Deaths volunteers are dropped," Cronkite News, February 21, 2019.
125. Henry Brean, "Border aid volunteer Warren found not guilty of harboring," *Arizona Daily Star*, November 21, 2019; Curt Prendergast, "Border aid case ends as feds drop last complaint," *Arizona Daily Star*, February 28, 2020.
126. Chuck Huckelberry, "Asylum Seeker Processing at Casa Alitas at the Juvenile Justice Center," Memorandum to Pima County Board of Supervisors, December 30, 2019.
127. Brenna Goth, "Ranks of women low in Border Patrol," *Arizona Daily Star*, December 25, 2011.
128. Greg Hansen, "Bye match play, hello champions," *Arizona Daily Star*, June 10, 2014.
129. In 2024, Bowman also won the NASCAR Cup Series race held in downtown Chicago.
130. Michael Lev, "Sumlin: A winner with character," *Arizona Daily Star*, January 15, 2018.
131. Richardson would eventually plead guilty to one count of bribery and was given a 3-month sentence.
132. Bruce Pascoe and Caitlin Schmidt, "'Outraged' Miller returns, will lead Cats rest of season," *Arizona Daily Star*, March 2, 2018.
133. Darren DaRonco, "Turnaround bid by city golf coming up short," *Arizona Daily Star*, December 6, 2014.
134. Jon Gold, "Arizona football shows increase in graduation rate," *Arizona Daily Star*, October 25, 2013. The Pac-10 became the Pac-12 on July 1, 2011, with the addition of the universities of Colorado and Utah.
135. Bonnie Henry, "Tucson fashion icon since '30s dies," *Arizona Daily Star*, May 7, 2010.
136. Emily Bregel and Ernesto Portillo, Jr., "Renowned Southwestern historian, anthropologist Fontana dies at 85," *Arizona Daily Star*, April 3, 2016.

Chapter Fifteen

1. "History in the hole," *Tucson Citizen*, December 4, 1976. Another time capsule to be opened on August 20, 2025, was placed in Tucson City Hall in January 2000.
2. Jasmine Demers, "Pima County reports its 1st COVID-19 death," *Arizona Daily Star*, March 24, 2020, and "Family: Tucson's first fatal COVID-19 case 'wasn't just a statistic…. She was everything,'" *Arizona Daily Star*, March 26, 2020. The Centers for Disease Control and Prevention (CDC) states "COVID-19 (coronavirus disease 2019) is a disease caused by a virus named SARS-CoV-2. It can be very contagious and spreads quickly…. COVID-19 most often causes respiratory symptoms that can feel much like a cold, the flu, or pneumonia. COVID-19 may attack more than your lungs and respiratory system. Other parts of your body may also be affected by the disease."
3. "Weekly look at COVID-19 in Arizona," *Arizona Daily Star*, April 1, 2023.
4. Stephanie Innes, "TMC's staff wages silent battle to save virus patients inside intensive-care ward," *Arizona Daily Star*, July 12, 2020.
5. Justin Sayers and Cathalena Burch, "Romero orders closure of bars, eateries," *Arizona Daily Star*, March 18, 2020.
6. "2,519 new cases of coronavirus mark another daily AZ record," *Arizona Daily Star*, June 19, 2020.
7. Alex Devoid, "Health officials from Pima mull how to enforce mask-wearing inside businesses," *Arizona Daily Star*, June 28, 2020.
8. Justin Sayers, "County set to open free COVID-19 testing site on Monday," *Arizona Daily Star*, July 10, 2020.
9. Patty Machelor and Alex Devoid, "As feared, Tucson's hospitals say they're maxed out," *Arizona Daily Star*, December 13, 2020.
10. "COVID-19 in Arizona," *Arizona Daily Star*, January 1, 2021.
11. Howard Fischer, "Ducey says virus is under control, takes away limits," *Arizona Daily Star*, March 26, 2021; Nicole Ludden and Howard Fischer, "Pima County will continue to mandate use of masks," *Arizona Daily Star*, March 31, 2021.
12. "COVID-19 in Arizona," *Arizona Daily Star*, April 1, 2021.
13. Gloria Knott, "COVID-shaped piñatas a hit at party stores, *Arizona Daily Star*, April 24, 2021.
14. Howard Fischer, "Brnovich says mandatory shots for city workers is illegal," *Arizona Daily Star*, September 8, 2021; Nicole Ludden, "Unvaccinated city workers face Dec. 1 termination," and "Certain county workers required to get shots," *Arizona Daily Star*, October 20, 2021.
15. Alex Devoid, "COVID in county 'a crisis situation,'" *Arizona Daily Star*, November 24, 2021.
16. "COVID-19 in Arizona," *Arizona Daily Star*, January 4, 2022; Alex Devoid and Patty Machelor, "COVID-19 cases have doubled in Pima County," *Arizona Daily Star*, January 6, 2022.
17. Nicole Ludden, "56 county employees fired," *Arizona Daily Star*, January 12, 2022.
18. "Weekly look at COVID-19 in Arizona," *Arizona Daily Star*, January 7, 2023.
19. The Associated Press and Zeke Miller, "Biden ends COVID national emergency after Congress acts," April 10, 2023.
20. "Apollo astronaut Frank Borman dies at 95," *Arizona Daily Star*, November 11, 2023.
21. Henry Brean, "UA professor wins award for space telescope work," *Arizona Daily Star*, May 16, 2024.

22. Richard Obert, "Jimenez 1st girl to win boys division," *Arizona Daily Star*, February 19, 2024.

23. Bob Christie, "Planned Parenthood won't resume abortions," *Arizona Daily Star*, July 13, 2022; Patty Machelor, "Clinics resume abortions in Tucson," *Arizona Daily Star*, August 30, 2022.

24. Prerana Sannappanavar, "Political reaction to Arizona abortion ruling swift," *Arizona Daily Star*, April 10, 2024.

25. Nicole Ludden, "Solutions evasive as Tucson grapples with homeless camps," *Arizona Daily Star*, July 2, 2023; Hanna Love and Tracy Hadden Loh, *Homelessness in U.S. cities and downtowns: The perception, the reality, and how to address both*, Brookings, December 7, 2023.

26. Nicole Ludden, "Neighbor group behind chopping over 50 trees," *Arizona Daily Star*, September 25, 2023.

27. Charles Borla, "Portion of Tucson's biggest homeless camp gets a clear-out notice," *Arizona Daily Star*, May 16, 2024.

28. Gabriela Rico, "Apartment occupancy, sales continue to soar," *Arizona Daily Star*, June 9, 2021.

29. Gabriela Rico, "Rents in Tucson start to stabilize," *Arizona Daily Star*, February 3, 2023; RentData.org, accessed August 30, 2024, https://www.rentdata.org/tucson-az-msa/2024.

30. Gabriela Rico, "Rent costs rise with remote workers," *Arizona Daily Star*, March 10, 2024.

31. Gabriela Rico, "Affordable rental housing project underway," *Arizona Daily Star*, November 26, 2023.

32. Tucson Association of Realtors, "Monthly Indicators," December 2020 and "Market Activity and Pricing," June 2024.

33. Gabriela Rico, "Home prices in Tucson level off," *Arizona Daily Star*, May 12, 2024; National Association of Home Builders, "Cost of Housing Index," First Quarter, 2024.

34. Tucson economy: MAP Dashboard, "Housing affordability," *Arizona Daily Star*, June 27, 2021, and August 26, 2024. This increasing housing affordability was also a national occurrence.

35. Ronald J. Hansen, "Tucson on pace to drop to Arizona's third-biggest city," *Arizona Daily Star*, November 7, 2023.

36. David Wichner, "AZ recovery on pause as COVID resurges," *Arizona Daily Star*, December 4, 2021.

37. Tucson economy: MAP Dashboard, "Growth rate in total non-farm employment (2023)," *Arizona Daily Star*, March 31, 2024.

38. David Wichner, "Raytheon awarded $1.2B contract," *Arizona Daily Star*, September 14, 2024.

39. Tony Davis, "Hudbay changes mining plans," *Arizona Daily Star*, June 12, 2022.

40. Tucson economy: MAP Dashboard, "Median household income (2022)," *Arizona Daily Star*, July 28, 2024.

41. Beatriz Del Campo-Carmona, "High levels of Food Insecurity in Tucson, Arizona MSA" University of Arizona MAP Dashboard, January 31, 2023, https://mapazdashboard.arizona.edu/food-insecurity-tucson-ranks-high.

42. Ellie Wolfe, "University of Arizona cuts budget amid 'financial crisis,'" *Arizona Daily Star*, November 7, 2023.

43. Ellie Wolfe, "Recapping the UA money crisis so far," *Arizona Daily Star*, April 7, 2024.

44. Ibid.

45. By September 2024, the projected deficit for the end of the 2024/25 fiscal year was $65 million. See: Helen Rummel, "Budget: UA still $65M in the red," *Arizona Daily Star*, September 9, 2024 and Ellie Wolfe, "Departing UA president to be paid through June 2026," *Arizona Daily Star*, September 12, 2024.

46. Ibid.

47. Ellie Wolfe, "Regents approve Robbins' new contract," *Arizona Daily Star*, September 27, 2024.

48. John P. Schaefer, "Address the University of Arizona's real issues," *Arizona Daily Star*, May 8, 2024.

49. University of Arizona, Scholarships and Financial Aid, 2024–25 Cost of Attendance for Incoming First Year and Transfer, https://financialaid.arizona.edu/cost/incoming.

50. Earlier cited Pima Community College enrollment figures were total students.

51. In June 2024, Dr. Jeffrey Nasse from Broward College in Florida was named the new chancellor.

52. Danyelle Khmara, "Protestors want kids back in school on full-time basis," *Arizona Daily Star*, September 10, 2020.

53. Danyelle Khmara, "Sahuarita closes high schools, citing COVID-19 increases, staffing issues," *Arizona Daily Star*, December 4, 2020, and "No in-person classes after break at most Tucson-area schools," December 15, 2020.

54. Danyelle Khmara and Clara Migoya, "Protestors force school board to cancel meeting," *Arizona Daily Star*, April 29, 2021.

55. Danyelle Khmara, "Charters swell as local school districts see enrollment slide," *Arizona Daily Star*, March 7, 2021.

56. Danyelle Khmara, "Half who left public schools here last year have returned," *Arizona Daily Star*, September 5, 2021.

57. Danyelle Khmara, "TUSD cutting over 60 teachers," *Arizona Daily Star*, April 16, 2021.

58. Tucson economy: MAP Dashboard, "Median annual wage for secondary school teachers (2022)," *Arizona Daily Star*, October 29, 2023.

59. Nick Sullivan, "AZ near bottom in per pupil spending," *Arizona Daily Star*, May 2, 2024.

60. Tony Davis, "July scorches its way into the record books as hottest month ever recorded in Tucson," *Arizona Daily Star*, August 9, 2020. The current record is July 2023 besting the former hottest month by two degrees to an average temperature of 94.2^0.

61. "Heat-related includes deaths where environmental heat exposure is either the primary cause of death (heat-caused) or a significant contributing

factor to the death (heat-contributing)." This figure does not include undocumented border crossers. Pima County Medical Examiner Data Dashboards & Reports, "2023 Heat Related Deaths."

62. Arizona State Climate Office, "Arizona Long-Term Drought" map, April 2024, https://www.azwater.gov/drought/drought-status.

63. In the summer of 2024, the Tucson City Council employed a consultant firm to explore the possibility of acquiring the utility company. See: Isabelle Marceles, "Tucson prepares as TEP contract nears end," *Arizona Daily Star*, July 31, 2024.

64. Brian J. Pedersen, "Tommy Lloyd's contract details released by Arizona," *Arizona Desert Swarm*, April 15, 2021. After his first UA team went 33-4, Lloyd was given a $1 million annual raise, then in 2024 his yearly pay was boosted to $5.25 million with some of the money coming from donors.

65. Bruce Pascoe, "Wildcats tie school APR mark," *Arizona Daily Star*, May 3, 2023.

66. The *House v. NCAA* case deals with athlete Name, Image, and Likeness issues and, if court approved, is expected to cost major universities in excess of $21 million a year plus up to $10 million annually for additional athletic scholarships.

67. Bruce Pascoe, "UA has plan to tackle athletics shortfall," *Arizona Daily Star*, June 21, 2024.

68. Henry Brean, "UA-led space mission makes history with stop on asteroid," *Arizona Daily Star*, October 21, 2020.

69. Henry Brean, "UA still No. 1 in nation in astronomy," *Arizona Daily Star*, December 23, 2022.

70. Tucson International Airport, Ten Years of Passenger Statistics, Tucson Airport Authority website, accessed May 30, 2024, https://s20532.pcdn.co/files/Ten-Years-Fiscal-History.pdf.

71. David Wichner, "New special ops wing planned for Tucson's Davis-Monthan base," *Arizona Daily Star*, April 21, 2023.

72. In September 2023, Wilder would return to the area with Studio Janos, a private dining/cooking school endeavor.

73. Cathalena E. Burch, "At 75, El Casino Ballroom is Tucson Latino community's heartbeat," *Arizona Daily Star*, September 7, 2023.

74. Gabriela Rico, "Apartments going up at Foothills Mall site," *Arizona Daily Star*, March 9, 2024.

75. Rev transcript of Donald Trump's October 19, 2020 Tucson speech, accessed June 6, 2024, https://www.rev.com/blog/transcripts/donald-trump-rally-transcript-tucson-arizona-october-19.

76. Alexandria Cullen, "Tohono O'odham leader: Wall a problem," *Arizona Daily Star*, October 21, 2023.

77. Curt Prendergast, "Asylum seekers anxiously wait at Sonora port of entry," *Arizona Daily Star*, January 12, 2020.

78. Pima County Office of the Medical Examiner, "Undocumented Border Crosser Remains by Calendar Year," accessed June 3, 2024.

79. United States Border Patrol, Southwest Land Border Encounters, Tucson Sector, accessed June 3, 2024, https://www.cbp.gov/newsroom/stats/nationwide-encounters. Because encounters are single events, an individual seeking to cross the border multiple times that is apprehended by the Border Patrol would account for several encounters.

80. Danyelle Khmara, "Migrant encounters on rise at Arizona-Mexico border," *Arizona Daily Star*, June 18, 2022. In 2023, the total number of those assisted went up to 195,000.

81. The federal fiscal year goes from October 1 to September 30.

82. Anita Snow, "Shipping container border wall is mostly dismantled," *Arizona Daily Star*, January 8, 2023; Howard Fischer, "End of case adds to cost of containers," *Arizona Daily Star*, August 29, 2023.

83. In 2024, the operation of the second service center was turned over to AMI Expeditionary Healthcare, a for-profit group. See: Emily Bregel, "Casa Alitas narrows scope of help," *Arizona Daily Star*, July 16, 2024.

84. Nicole Ludden, "Tucson shelters avoid street releases—so far," *Arizona Daily Star*, May 20, 2023.

85. United States Border Patrol, Southwest Land Border Encounters, Tucson Sector, accessed October 12, 2024, https://www.cbp.gov/newsroom/stats/southwest-land-border-encounters-by-component. In June 2024, the Biden administration introduced new asylum procedures that were intended to drop the number of encounters significantly and initially they appeared to be working successfully.

86. Julian Resendiz, "'It's gotten worse': Lawmakers tour border as daily migrant encounters shoot up again," *Border Report*, February 8, 2024.

87. Tim Steller, "Tohono O'odham man killed by Border Patrol was intoxicated," *Arizona Daily Star*, June 24, 2023.

88. Emily Bregel, "Tribal leaders decry no charges," *Arizona Daily Star*, October 14, 2023.

89. Dervish was convicted of the murder in May 2024.

90. Erika Wurst, "Tucson police plead for tips in killing of UA student," *Arizona Daily Star*, May 15, 2024. In June 2024, four teenagers were arrested and charged with the murder.

91. Prerana Sannappanavar, "Man killed in shooting on UA campus," *Arizona Daily Star*, September 24, 2024.

92. Prerana Sannappanavar, "Some gun crimes now have added charges," *Arizona Daily Star*, October 7, 2024.

93. Erika Wurst, "Rural Metro cadet dies of heat/dehydration, chief says," *Arizona Daily Star*, August 26, 2024.

94. Charles Borla, "Tucson police officer killed responding to call," *Arizona Daily Star*, April 2, 2024.

95. Caitlin Schmidt, "TPD chief: Officers will keep leaving if pay doesn't improve," *Arizona Daily Star*, February 14, 2021. According to ZipRecruiter, by September 2024, TPD officer pay was similar to that in Oro Valley but lower than that in Marana and at the Pima County Sheriff's Department.

96. Caitlin Schmidt and Jamie Donnelly, "In Tucson: Drug use, traffic deaths up; homicides down," *Arizona Daily Star*, February 5, 2023.

97. Patty Machelor, "Progress shown in fentanyl cases," *Arizona Daily Star*, February 28, 2022; Pima County Medical examiner, Data Dashboard and Reports, "Overview of Overdose Deaths," accessed June 6, 2024.

98. Tucson Police Data & Analysis, accessed June 5, 2024, https://policeanalysis.tucsonaz.gov/pages/reported-crimes.

99. Sam Kmack, "City is battling staff shortages," *Arizona Daily Star*, October 4, 2021.

100. Alli Burgess, "1 million trees plan gaining support," *Arizona Daily Star*, February 7, 2023; Charles Borla, "Feds to spread $5.4 million in Tucson to plant trees," *Arizona Daily Star*, September 16, 2023.

101. David Wichner and Nicole Ludden, "TEP, Tucson pressing on after Prop. 412 flop," *Arizona Daily Star*, May 18, 2023.

102. Nicole Ludden, "Fentanyl is killing inmates in Pima jail," *Arizona Daily Star*, February 27, 2022.

103. Blake Morlock, "Oro Valley votes on $151 million budget, South Tucson seeks 'home rule,'" *TucsonSentinel.com*, June 3, 2024; Minutes of South Tucson City Council, June 18, 2024.

104. James A. Williams, *Oro Valley—The First Fifty Years*, publisher not identified, 2023.

105. John Hudak, "Stop Giving Your $$ to PHX!" *Tucson Lifestyle*, April 8, 2022.

106. David Wichner, "Tucson posts healthy gains despite obstacles," *Arizona Daily Star*, April 28, 2024.

107. Arizona Department of Transportation (ADOT), "ADOT and FHWA publish Interstate 11 Record of Decision," November 16, 2021.

108. Charles Borla, "Tucson voters to decide on higher city sales tax," *Arizona Daily Star*, September 13, 2024.

109. Nicole Ludden, "Voters OK half-cent sales tax for roads," *Arizona Daily Star*, May 19, 2022.

110. Pima County Medical Examiner, "Motor Vehicle-Related Deaths," updated on May 2, 2024.

111. Erika Wurst, "Tucson still deadly for pedestrians," *Arizona Daily Star*, April 14, 2024.

112. Central Arizona Project and Arizona Department of Water Resources, "Colorado River Shortage—2022 Fact Sheet," accessed August 17, 2024, https://www.azwater.gov/sites/default/files/media/ADWR-CAP-FactSheet-CoRiverShortage-081321.pdf.

113. U.S. Bureau of Reclamation, Lower Colorado Water Supply Report, July 22, 2024, https://www.usbr.gov/lc/region/g4000/weekly.pdf.

114. Tony Davis, "Study: Higher future flows likely on Colorado," *Arizona Daily Star*, May 12, 2024.

115. Analeise Mayor, "Tucson sees economic gains, housing challenges," *Arizona Daily Star*, June 6, 2024.

116. Tim Steller, "The principal hurts in Roadrunners deal," *Arizona Daily Star*, June 2, 2024.

117. Craig J. Cantoni, "As the U of A goes, so goes Tucson," *Arizona Daily Star*, April 22, 2024.

118. Regina Romero, "Tucson is building resilience in changing climate," *Arizona Daily Star*, April 21, 2024.

Bibliography

Acts, Resolutions and Memorials of the Regular Session First Legislature of the State of Arizona. Phoenix: The McNeil Company, printers, 1912.

Acts, Resolutions and Memorials of the Twenty-Fifth Legislative Assembly of the Territory of Arizona. Phoenix: Press of Phoenix Printing Company, 1909.

Amdur, Melissa. *Linda Ronstadt.* New York: Chelsea House Publishers, 1993.

Anderson, C.L.G., M.D. "Arizona as a Health Resort." Read at the second meeting of the Washington County Medical Society, Hagerstown, Maryland, April 9, 1890.

Arizona Department of Transportation (ADOT). "ADOT and FHWA Publish Interstate 11 Record of Decision," November 16, 2021.

Arizona State Climate Office. "Arizona Long-Term Drought," map, April 2024.

Arizona State Legislature. HB 2281, Forty-Ninth Legislature, Second Regular Session (2010).

"'Arizona'—The Wild Old West Lives Again in Columbia's Great Screen Classic." *Arizona Highways,* vol. XVI (September 1940): 4–9, 31.

Arvizo, Mrs. Juana. Interview by Maggie Brady, interpreter, and Mrs. George F. Kitt, 1928. Bio file, Arizona Historical Society library, Tucson.

"Assassin Bug Invasions Threatening Old Tucson," *The Weekly Arizonan,* dated May 25, 1860. Arizona Historical Society library, Tucson. The date is fictitious since the newspaper was only published during the filming of the movie *Arizona.*

Baker, Lynn D. *Tucson Water History: A Reference Book.* Tucson: L.D. Baker, vol. 1, 2000.

Barnes, Mary Ellen. *Forged by Fire: The Devastation and Renewal of a Mountain Community.* Tucson: Vireo House, 2005.

Batteau, Elgie. Interview by Annie Sykes, 1988. *Dunbar School: Shared Memories of a Special Past.* Arizona Historical Society library, Tucson.

Benjamin, Stan. "Without a Shot Fired: The 1934 Capture of the Dillinger Gang in Tucson." *The Smoke Signal* 80 (December 2005): 197–216.

Berman, David R. *Reformers, Corporations, and the Electorate: An Analysis of Arizona's Age of Reform.* Niwot, CO: University Press of Colorado, 1992.

Bigglestone, William E. *Tucsonans Who Died in Military Service During World War II.* Tucson: Self-published, 1994.

Bigglestone, William E. *Tucson's Korean War Dead.* Tucson: Self-published, 2000.

Billman, Rev. Howard, to Mrs. C.E. Walker. Tucson Indian Training School Records, MS 809, Arizona Historical Society library, Tucson.

Boehringer, C. Louise. "Josephine Brawley Hughes-Crusader, State Builder," *Arizona Historical Review,* January 1930, 98–107.

Bogan, Phoebe M., Manuscripts, 1909–1926. MS 0081, Arizona Historical Society library, Tucson.

"Border Deaths." *Arizona Daily Star* website, accessed August 19, 2014, http://tucson.com/online/databases.

Bourke, John G. *On the Border with Crook.* New York: Charles Scribner's Sons, 1891.

Briegel, Kaye Lynn. "Alianza Hispano-Americana, 1894–1965: A Mexican American Fraternal Insurance Society." Ph.D. dissertation, University of Southern California, 1974.

Bryson, Joseph E. *Legality of Loyalty Oath and Non-Oath Requirements for Public School Teachers.* Boone, NC: Appalachian State Teachers College, 1963.

Bureau of Labor Statistics. "Databases, Tables & Calculators by Subject." Tucson, Arizona Construction, accessed June 28, 2014. http://data.bls.gov; search "databases, tables & calculators Tucson construction" and go to U.S. Bureau of Labor Statistics—databases & tables.

Caldwell, Erskine. *With All My Might.* Atlanta: Peachtree Publishers, 1987.

Campbell, Julie A. "Madres Y Esposas: Tucson's Spanish-American Mothers and Wives Association." *The Journal of Arizona History,* 31 (Summer 1990): 161–182.

Carlson, Raymond. "Tucson—the New Pueblo." *Arizona Highways,* vol. XXXIV, no. 2 (February 1958): 1.

Carmony, Neil B., transcriber and ed. *Whiskey, Six-Guns & Red-Light Ladies: George Hand's Saloon Diary, Tucson, 1875–1878.* Silver City, NM: High-Lonesome Books, 1994.

Carson, Donald W., and James W. Johnson. *Mo—The Life and Times of Morris K. Udall.* Tucson: University of Arizona Press, 2001.

Casaday, L.W. "Tucson—boom city in a booming state." *Arizona Highways,* vol. XXXIV, no. 2 (February 1958): 30–36.

Centers for Disease Control and Prevention

(CDC). "About COVID-19," at https://www.cdc.gov/covid/about/index.html.

Central Arizona Project and Arizona Department of Water Resources. "Colorado River Shortage–2022 Fact Sheet."

Chanin, Abe. *They Fought Like Wildcats.* Tucson: Midbar Press, 1979.

Cockrum, E. Lendell, compiler. *Cavemen of Colossal Cave.* Tucson: Self-published, 2000.

Cohen, Joel E., and David Tilman. "Biosphere 2 and Biodiversity: The Lessons So Far." *Science* 274 (November 1996): 1150–1151.

"Cool, Cool Water." *The Magazine Tucson*, vol. 1, no. 9 (December 1948): 44–45.

Corbett, J. Knox. Letters to his family. Corbett family papers, MS 174, Arizona Historical Society library, Tucson.

Creighton, J.M., to D.E. Creighton. Letter dated July 27, 1938. Robert Humphrey Forbes Papers 1869–1966, MS 261, Arizona Historical Society library, Tucson.

Cronly v. City of Tucson et. al., March 15, 1899, 56 Pacific Reporter, 876–878.

"'Curly' Neal New Tycoon." *Black Heritage in Arizona* 2 (February 1976): 1, 3–5, 7.

Dailey, Elsie M. "John Baptiste Salpointe: First Roman Catholic Bishop of Arizona." *Arizoniana—The Journal of Arizona History* IV (Spring 1963), 23–30.

DeLong, Sidney. DeLong-Ochoa letters, MS 543, Arizona Historical Society library, Tucson.

Delong, W.J. Memorandum to Mayor James N. Corbett, Jr., "Official Anniversary Date of Tucson," February 8, 1971. Arizona Historical Society, Places-Arizona-Tucson-celebrations-birthday observations [ephemera file].

"The Desert Sanatorium and Institute of Research." Tucson: The Desert Sanatorium, 1929. University of Arizona Special Collections Library.

Devine, David. "Dreaming of Autopia: Southern Arizona Auto Courts of the 1920s and 30s." *The Smoke Signal* 68 (Fall 1997): 161–188.

Devine, David. "From Warehouse to Re-Use: The Story of the Northside of Tucson's Downtown, Part 2:1940–1995." *The Smoke Signal* 64A (Winter 1996): 69–84.

Devine, David. *The St. Luke's in the Desert Story: A Century of Community Service.* Tucson: AZ Litho, 2018.

Devine, David. *Slavery, Scandal, and Steel Rails: The 1854 Gadsden Purchase and the Building of the Second Transcontinental Railroad Across Arizona and New Mexico Twenty-Five Years Later.* Lincoln, NE: iUniverse, 2004.

Devine, David. "Struggle for Survival: The South Tucson Story." *The Smoke Signal* 71 (Summer 2000): 1–24.

Devine, David. *Tucson: A History of the Old Pueblo from the 1854 Gadsden Purchase.* Jefferson, NC: McFarland, 2015.

Dobyns, Henry F. Letter to "The Mayor," City of Tucson, February 5, 1972. Arizona Historical Society, Places-Arizona-Tucson-celebrations-birthday observations [ephemera file].

Dobyns, Henry F. *Spanish Colonial Tucson: A Demographic History.* Tucson: University of Arizona Press, 1976.

Don, Harold. Interview by Ruben Moreno, January 9, 1994. AV 0553–12, transcript, Arizona Historical Society library, Tucson.

Drachman, Herbert. Samuel Drachman papers 1867–1934. MS 0216, Arizona Historical Society library, Tucson.

Drachman, Mose. "Reminiscences of Mose Drachman 1870–1935." Mose Drachman papers, MS 226, Arizona Historical Society library, Tucson.

Drachman, Oliver. Interview by Lyn Papanikolas, April 19, 1983. AV 0368–05, transcript. Arizona Historical Society library, Tucson.

Drachman, Roy P. *From Cowtown to Desert Metropolis: Ninety Years of Arizona Memories.* San Francisco: Whitewing Press, 1999.

Drachman, Roy P. Interview by Don Bufkin, January 14, 1992. AV 0505–18, transcript. Arizona Historical Society library, Tucson.

Drachman, Roy P. Unknown interviewer, April 3, 1980. AV 0406–06, transcript. Arizona Historical Society library, Tucson.

Duarte, Carmen. "Local architect spruced up historic Tucson." *Arizona Catholic Lifetime* (February 17, 1980): 8–9. Herreras bio file, Arizona Historical Society library, Tucson.

Duffy, Ida Myrtle. "Pioneer Characters for Whom Some Tucson Public Schools Have Been Named." Master's thesis, University of Arizona, 1941.

El Conquistador Hotel dinner menu dated November 22, 1928. El Conquistador ephemera file, Arizona Historical Society library, Tucson.

Ettinger, Patrick. "'We sometimes wonder what they will spring on us next': Immigrants and Border Enforcement in the American West, 1882–1930." *The Western Historical Quarterly* 37 (Summer 2006): 159–181.

Faulk, Odie B., ed. *Arizona's State Historical Society: Its History and Leaders, and Its Service to the Public.* Tucson: Arizona Pioneers' Historical Society, 1966.

Faust, David T., and Kenneth A. Randall. "Life at Post: Fort Lowell, Arizona Territory 1873–1891." *The Smoke Signal* 74 (Spring 2002): 61–100.

Faxon, Stuart. "Dr. Sydney E. Salmon, 1936–1999." *Sombrero*, Pima County Medical Society (November 1999): 9, 26.

Federal Bureau of Investigation. 2019 Crime in the United States—Arizona, accessed February 10, 2024, https://ucr.fbi.gov/crime-in-the-u.s/2019/crime-in-the-u.s.-2019/tables/table-8/table-8-state-cuts/arizona.xls.

Fierman, Floyd S. "The Drachmans of Arizona." *American Jewish Archives* XVI (November 1964): 135–160.

Flowers and Bullets Mission statement, accessed April 10, 2024, https://www.flowersandbullets.com/mission.

Fontana, Bernard L. *Of Earth and Little Rain: The*

Papago Indians. Tucson: University of Arizona Press, 1989.

Franco, Jeré. "Beyond Reservation Boundaries: Native American Laborers in World War II." *Journal of the Southwest* 36 (Autumn 1994): 242-254.

Gart, Jason Howard. "Electronics and Aerospace Industry in Cold War Arizona, 1945-68: Motorola, Hughes Aircraft, Goodyear Aircraft." Ph.D. dissertation, Arizona State University, 2006.

Geronimo, S.M. Barrett, ed. *Geronimo: His Own Story.* New York: E.P. Dutton & Co., 1970.

Gibson, Johnny. Interview by Richard Kimball, September 29, 1988. AV 0438-02, transcript. Arizona Historical Society library, Tucson.

Gin, William. Interview by Ghislaine Martel, April 3, 1984. AV 0001-08, transcript. Arizona Historical Society library, Tucson.

Greer, William F., and Donald W. Carson, ed. "Tucson—the Early Days." *Tucson Fire Department, 1881-1981,* Tucson (1981). University of Arizona Special Collections Library.

Grimes, Paul L. *The Pride of Arizona: A History of the University of Arizona Band 1885-1985.* Tucson: Arizona Lithographers, 1985.

Hall, Dick. "Ointment of Love." *The Journal of Arizona History* 19 (Summer 1978): 111-130.

Haney, John A., and Cirino G. Scavone. "Cars Stop Here." *The Smoke Signal* 23 (Spring 1971): 45-64.

"Harold Bell Wright Who Holds a World's Record." *The American Magazine,* vol. LXXXV (February 1918), 8.

Healy, William T. *The History of Tucson Country Club.* Tucson: Tucson Country Club, 1990. Pima County Library.

Heney, Ben. Letter to Mayor and Common Council, City of Tucson, December 11, 1907. Tucson City Clerk's office.

Herndon, Elsie P. Herndon Papers, MS 1038, Arizona Historical Society library, Tucson.

Herreras, Eleazar D. Interview by Lyn Papanikolas, March 9 and 11, 1983. AV 0368-07, transcript. Arizona Historical Society library, Tucson.

Hill, Ophelia D., compiler, and Ella S. Swanson, ed. *Cemetery Records of the Binghampton Cemetery,* Tucson (1996), Arizona Historical Society library, Tucson.

"History of the Desert Museum." Tucson: Arizona-Sonora Desert Museum, 2001. University of Arizona Special Collections Library.

"History of the Tucson Fire Department." Tucson (1965?). University of Arizona Special Collections Library.

Hodgman, William W., Jr. Letter to his mother dated September 10, 1943. William H. Hodgman Jr., papers 1942-1958, MS 357, Arizona Historical Society library, Tucson.

Hoefle, Melvin. Interview by Linda C. Swedberg, April 8, 1983. AV 0368-08, transcript. Arizona Historical Society library, Tucson.

Hoffman, Abraham. *Unwanted Mexican Americans in the Great Depression: Repatriation Pressures 1929-1939.* Tucson: University of Arizona Press, 1974.

Howell Code, Adopted by the First Legislative Assembly of the Territory of Arizona, Prescott: Office of the *Arizona Miner,* 1865.

Huckelberry, Chuck. "Asylum Seeker Processing at Casa Alitas at the Juvenile Justice Center." Memorandum to Pima County Board of Supervisors, December 30, 2019.

Huckelberry, Chuck. "County, Banner partnership an unqualified success." Under the Dome, unknown date.

Hudak, John. "Stop Giving Your $$ to PHX!" *Tucson Lifestyle,* April 8, 2022.

Hufault, Cathy. *Death Clouds on Mount Baldy: Tucson's Lost Tragedy.* Vail, AZ: Arizona Mountain Publications, 2011.

Hunt, Sharon E. *Vail and Colossal Cave Mountain Park.* Charleston, SC: Arcadia Publishing, 2007.

Jackman, Julia, and Allan N. Williams. "Gun Violence in Arizona: Data to Inform Prevention Policies," Arizona Public Health Association, March 2023, 48.

Jácome, Estella. Interview by Caryl J. Taylor, March 21, 1990. AV 0458, transcript. Arizona Historical Society library, Tucson.

Journal of the Congress of the Confederate States of America (1861-1865), Library of Congress, January 13, 1862.

Journals of the Ninth (1877) *Legislative Assembly of the Territory of Arizona.* Publisher unknown.

Juliani, Lucille Budd. Interview by John Bret-Harte, August 12, 1990. AV 0485, transcript. Arizona Historical Society library, Tucson.

Kalt, William D. III. *High in Desert Skies: Early Arizona Aviation.* Tempe, AZ: Printing Solutions, 2017.

Kalt, William D. III. "Sky Sensations: Early Arizona Aviation Tales." *The Smoke Signal* 94 (February 2014): 69-92.

Kalt, William D. III. *Tucson Was a Railroad Town.* Mountlake Terrace, WA: VTD Rail Publishing, 2007.

Kalt, William D., III, and David Devine. "Tucson's Wondrous Railroad Depot: A History of the Toole Avenue Train Station." *The Smoke Signal* 88-89 (December 2010): 217-264.

Kaplan, Robert D. "Travels into America's Future." *The Atlantic Monthly,* vol. 282, issue 1 (July 1998): 47-68.

Karaim, Reed. "Tucson—Finding History in the Sunbelt Southwest." *Preservation,* vol. 65, no. 1 (Winter 2013): 62.

Keating, Micheline. "History of Tucson—4th Installment." *The Magazine Tucson,* vol. 2, no. 4 (April 1949): 30-31, 56.

Kelly, George H., compiler. *Legislative History of Arizona 1864-1912.* Phoenix: The Manufacturing Stationers, Inc., 1926.

Klump, Kathy. *The Vin Fiz Lands in Willcox: The Story of Cal Rodgers and the First Transcontinental Flight.* Willcox, AZ: Sulphur Springs Valley Historical Society, 2011.

"Lauffer, Billy Lane." *Wikipedia*, accessed August 19, 2014, http://www.en.wikipedia.org/wike/Billy_Lane_Lauffer.

Laws of the Territory of Arizona, Twelfth Legislative Assembly. Prescott, Arizona: *Daily and Weekly Arizona Miner*, 1883.

Lazaroff, David W. *Sabino Canyon: The Life of a Southwestern Oasis*. Tucson: University of Arizona Press, 1993.

Lesher, Jan. "Hudbay Copper World Project Update." Memorandum to the Pima County Board of Supervisors, January 30, 2024.

"Letter from Home" file. Arizona Historical Society library, Tucson.

Lindbergh, Charles A. *Autobiography of Values*. New York: Harcourt Brace Jovanovich, 1977.

Lockwood, Frank C. *Life in Old Tucson: 1854–1864*. Los Angeles: Ward Ritchie Press, 1943.

Lockwood, Frank C. *Pioneer Portraits*. Tucson: University of Arizona Press, 1968.

Long Ago Told: Legends of the Papago Indians. New York: D. Appleton and Company, 1929.

Lopez, Pvt. Frank G., Dear Sirs. Letter dated August 10, 1944, "Letter from Home" file, Arizona Historical Society library, Tucson.

Love, Hanna, and Tracy Hadden Loh. "Homelessness in U.S. cities and downtowns: The perception, the reality, and how to address both." Brookings, December 7, 2023, accessed August 29, 2024, https://www.brookings.edu/articles/homelessness-in-us-cities-and-downtowns.

Luckingham, Bradford. "To Mask or Not to Mask: A Note on the 1918 Spanish Influenza in Tucson." *The Journal of Arizona History*, 25 (Summer 1984): 191–204.

Luckingham, Bradford. "Urban Development in Arizona: The Rise of Phoenix." *The Journal of Arizona History* 22 (Summer 1981): 197–234.

Lutrell, Estelle. "Newspapers and Periodicals of Arizona 1859–1911." *University of Arizona Bulletin*, vol. XX, no. 3 (July 1949).

Lyons, Bettina O'Neil. "The Pioneer Hotel: The Steinfeld Family Builds a Tucson Landmark." *The Journal of Arizona History* 49 (Autumn 2008): 205–232.

"Marana History." Town of Marana website, accessed May 3, 2013, http://www.marana.com/index.aspx?NID=69.

McClintock, James H. *Arizona: Prehistoric—Aboriginal—Pioneer—Modern, Vol. II*. Chicago: S.J. Clarke Publishing Company, 1916.

Meier, Matt S. "Esteban Ochoa, Enterpriser." *Journal of the West* XXV (January 1986): 15–21.

Miller, Darlis A. "Civilians and Military Supply in the Southwest." *The Journal of Arizona History* 23 (Summer 1982): 115–138.

Moore, Yndia Smalley. Interview by Phyllis Reid, April 21, 1983. AV 0368-15, transcript. Arizona Historical Society library, Tucson.

Moser, Don. "The Pied Piper of Tucson." *Life* (March 4, 1966): 18–24, 80.

National Association of Home Builders, "Cost of Housing Index," First Quarter, 2024.

Officer, James E. Letter to Mayor Corbett, October 5, 1971. Arizona Historical Society, Places-Arizona-Tucson-celebrations-birthday observations [ephemera file].

"Official Statement by the Co-Chairman, at the meeting of the Tucson Committee for Inter-Racial Understanding," March 22, 1944. Tucson Committee for Inter-Racial Understanding, Records 1943–1945, MS 904, box 1, file 2. Arizona Historical Society library, Tucson.

Pahigian, Joshua R. *Spring Training Handbook*. Jefferson, NC: McFarland, 2005.

Pedersen, Gilbert J. "'The Townsite Is Now Secure': Tucson Incorporates, 1871." *The Journal of Arizona History* 11 (Autumn 1970): 151–174.

Perkins, Clifford Alan. *Border Patrol*. El Paso: Texas Western Press, University of Texas at El Paso, 1978.

Petrick, Lawrence G., Jr. Deputy Director, Department of Occupational Health & Safety, International Association of Fire Fighters, Correspondence with the author, August 11, 2014.

Pima County Board of Supervisors' Records: 1865–1936. Pima County Collection, MS 0183, box 1, Arizona Historical Society library, Tucson.

Pima County Health Department. "Pima County Overdose Fatality Review Annual Report 2019," 1.

Pima County Medical Examiner. Data Dashboard and Reports, "Heat-Related Deaths."

Pima County Medical Examiner. Data Dashboard and Reports, "Overview of Overdose Deaths," accessed June 6, 2024.

Pima County Medical Examiner. "Motor Vehicle-Related Deaths," updated on May 2, 2024.

Pima County Office of the Medical Examiner. Annual report 2020. "Homicide Deaths 2011-2020," 12.

Pima County Office of the Medical Examiner. "Undocumented Border Crosser Remains by Calendar Year," accessed June 3, 2024.

Plaza of the Pioneers Information. Arizona Historical Society library, Tucson.

The Population of Tucson and Its Environs. Report prepared for the Tucson Planning and Zoning Commission. Tucson: Tucson Regional Plan, Inc. March 1943.

Regan, Margaret. "Remembering Rockfellow." *Tucson Weekly* (January 27, 2000).

RentData.org. Tucson Fair Market Rent, FY 2024, Tucson, AZ MSA Rental Data.

Resendiz, Julian. "'It's gotten worse': Lawmakers tour border as daily migrant encounters shoot up again," *Border Report*, February 8, 2024.

Rev transcript of Donald Trump's 2020 Tucson speech, accessed June 6, 2024, https://www.rev.com/blog/transcripts/donald-trump-rally-transcript-tucson-arizona-october-19.

Rogers, W. Lane. "From Colonia Dublán to Binghampton: The Mormon Odyssey of Frederick, Nancy, and Amanda Williams." *The Journal of Arizona History* 35 (Spring 1994): 19–46.

Ronstadt, Armand Martin "Marty." "Tucson's

Four Ronstadt's: Fred–Dick–Emilia–Pepe." *The Smoke Signal* 93 (May 2013): 49–68.

Ronstadt, Gilbert. Unknown interviewer, 1980. AV 0389–02, transcript. Arizona Historical Society library, Tucson.

Rougier, Michael, photographer, and Loudon Wainwright, author. "Blight Blossoms on American Highways," *Life* (July 24, 1970): 26–34.

Russell, Frank E. Interview by David Devine. April 6, 2008.

Sabin, Edna Bingham. "Nephi Bingham and Elizabeth Dalkin Bingham." Narrative at "Erastus to You," accessed June 21, 2014, http://leongoodman.tripod.com.

Santiago, Dawn Moore. "Wolf in Sheep's Clothing: The Saga of Safford, Hudson & Company Bankers." Paper presented at the Arizona Historical Convention, Prescott, Arizona (March 1999).

Segoe, Ladislas, Planning Consultant, and Andre M. Faure, Resident Planner. *Aviation and Airports*. A component of the Tucson Regional Plan. Tucson: City of Tucson, 1942.

Sell, James L. and David Devine. "The Novelist Who Shaped the City." *Tucson Weekly* (November 9, 2000).

Session Laws of the Nineteenth Legislative Assembly of the Territory of Arizona. "An Act Providing for Certain City Elections." No. 76, p. 137, Unknown Printer, 1897.

Sheridan, Thomas E. *Arizona.... A History*. Tucson: University of Arizona Press, 1995.

Sheridan, Thomas E. "Peacock in the Parlor: Frontier Tucson's Mexican Elite." *The Journal of Arizona History* 25 (Autumn 1984): 245–264.

Situation Report and Advertising Recommendations for the Tucson Sunshine Climate Club. Los Angeles: H.K. McCann Company, 1922. Arizona Historical Society library, Tucson.

Sixty-Second Annual Report of the Commissioner of Indian Affairs to the Secretary of the Interior. Washington, D.C.: Government Printing Office, 1893.

Smalley, George Herbert. "What Prohibition Did to Arizona." *Sunset* 36 (January 1916): 26–27.

Smith, Julia Grace and Lane Kenworthy. *Poverty in Tucson*. Report to Members of the City of Tucson Mayor's Commission on Poverty, August 25, 2014.

Sonnichsen, C.L. *Tucson: The Life and Times of an American City*. Norman: University of Oklahoma Press, 1982.

Stearns, Myron M. "That Bungalow Camp." *The Saturday Evening Post* (August 27, 1927): 35,37,145–146.

Stephenson, Patricia and Alex Jay Kimmelman. *Tom Marshall's Tucson*. Tucson: Print Expressions Inc., 1996.

Stephenson, Patricia Peters. *A Personal Journey through the West University Neighborhood*. Tucson: Self-published, 1990.

Svob, Robert S. "History of Intercollegiate Athletics at the University of Arizona (1897–1948)," 1950, University of Arizona, Special Collections Library.

Tagg, Lawrence. *Harold Bell Wright—Storyteller to America*. Tucson: Westernlore Press, 1986.

Tech Park Arizona, accessed January 19, 2024, https://techparks.arizona.edu/the-bridges.

They Opened Their Hearts: Tucson Elders Tell World War II Stories to Tucson Youth. Tucson: Voices: Community Stories Past & Present, Inc., 2005.

Thiel, Homer. "We Have Been Here Before: A History of Epidemics in Southern Arizona," blog posting, April 8, 2020, https://desert.com/epidemic/.

Thompson, Linwood C. "The Motion Picture History of Southern Arizona and Old Tucson (1912–1983)." Master's thesis, Brigham Young University, December 1984.

Thurber, Marlys Bush, Linda L. Mayro, Frank P. Behlau, and R. Brooks Jeffery. *Survey of Joesler/Murphey Structures in Tucson and Environs*. Tucson: Tucson-Pima County Historical Commission, September 1992.

Tom Horne for Superintendent website, accessed June 20, 2024, https://electtomhorne.com/toms-plan.

"Trial in Tucson." *Time*, October 8, 1951, 84.

Tucson Association of Realtors. "Monthly Indicators," December 2020 and "Market Activity and Pricing," June 2024.

Tucson Chamber of Commerce. "Come to the Growing Southwest—to Tucson for Industry and 'A Way of Life.'" 1952. University of Arizona Special Collections Library.

Tucson City Council. Minutes of Meeting, March 21, 1910.

Tucson City Directory for 1881 (San Francisco: H.S. Crocker & Co.); 1924 (Tucson: Acme Printing Company); 1926 (Tucson: Acme Printing Company).

Tucson, City of. "City of Tucson Poverty and Urban Stress," April 2020, 1.

Tucson, City of. Ordinance 56 (adopted January 28, 1887).

Tucson, City of. Ordinance 164 (adopted February 2, 1903).

Tucson, City of. Ordinance 167 (adopted April 6, 1903).

Tucson Electric Power. "2019 Preliminary Integrated Resource Plan," July 1, 2019, 31.

"Tucson International Airport: 10 Years of Passenger Statistics." Tucson Airport Authority website, accessed August 19, 2014, www.flytucson.com/tucson-airport-authority/media-center/statistics; at the bottom of the page select "10 year passenger statistics."

Tucson International Airport, Ten Years of Passenger Statistics. Tucson Airport Authority website, accessed August 6, 2024, https://s20532.pcdn.co/files/Ten-Years-Fiscal-History.pdf.

"Tucson Market Overview." Zillow website, accessed August 19, 2014, www.zillow.com/tucson-az/home-values.

Tucson Police Data and Analysis, accessed June 5, 2024, https://policeanalysis.tucsonaz.gov/pages/reported-crimes.

"Tucson Police." City of Tucson website, accessed August 19, 2014, http://budget.tucsonaz.gov/budget/prior-year-budgets.

Tucson, Village and City of. Minutes of 1875, 1901, 1902, 1907, 1908, 1909 meetings of the Common Council. Tucson City Clerk's office.

Tucson Water, "Water Matters," March 2019.

Turner, Jim. "A Nice Place to Visit: A Brief History of Sabino Canyon." *The Smoke Signal* 81 (December 2006): 1–24.

"TUSD History—The First Hundred Years: Davis, Holladay and Drachman 1900–1910—Part 1," Tucson Unified School District website, accessed March 11, 2014, http://www.tusd1.org; search "History."

United States Border Patrol. Nationwide Encounters, accessed June 3, 2024, https://www.cbp.gov/newsroom/stats/nationwide-encounters.

United States Border Patrol. Southwest Border Sectors (Tucson)—Total Illegal Alien Apprehensions by Fiscal Year, https://www.cbp.gov/sites/default/files/assets/documents/2021-Aug/US59B8~1.PDF.

United States Border Patrol. Southwest Land Border Encounters (By Component), accessed June 4, 2024, and October 12, 2024, https://www.cbp.gov/newsroom/stats/southwest-land-border-encounters-by-component.

United States Bureau of Reclamation. Lower Colorado Water Supply Report, July 22, 2024.

United States Census. QuickFacts, Pima County, Arizona, July 1, 2023.

United States Census. QuickFacts, Tucson City, Arizona, July 1, 2022, and July 1, 2023.

University and State Colleges of Arizona. Minutes of a Meeting of the Board of Regents, May 25, 1948.

University of Arizona. "Cost of Attendance for Incoming First Year and Transfer," Scholarships and Financial Aid, 2024–25.

University of Arizona. "Migrant Deaths in Southern Arizona." Binational Migration Institute, April 2021, 7.

University of Arizona MAP (Making Action Possible) Dashboard. https://mapazdashboard.arizona.edu.

Van Orden, Jay, and Mary Ellen Barnes. "When No One Had a Camera: An Artist-Participant Paints the Tully & Ochoa Wagon Train Fight." *The Journal of Arizona History* 54 (Autumn 2013): 319–336.

Veeck, Bill, with Ed Linn. *Veeck—As in Wreck.* New York: G.P. Putnam's Sons, 1962.

Ware, Harry David. "Alcohol, Temperance and Prohibition in Arizona." Ph.D. dissertation, Arizona State University, 1995.

Webb, George E. *Tree Rings and Telescopes: The Scientific Career of A.E. Douglass.* Tucson: University of Arizona Press, 1983.

Webb-Vignery, June. *Jacome's Department Store: Business and Culture in Tucson, Arizona 1896–1980.* New York: Garland Publishing, 1996.

Weeks, Stephen B. *History of Public School Education in Arizona.* Washington, D.C.: Government Printing Office, Bulletin No. 17, 1918. Arizona Historical Society library, Tucson.

Wendland, Michael F. *The Arizona Project: How a Team of Investigative Reporters Got Revenge on Deadline.* Kansas City: Sheed Andrews and McMeel, 1977.

Wendland, Michael F. *The Arizona Project.* Mesa, AZ: Blue Sky Press, Revised 1988.

White, Sgt. George E., to Dear Sirs. Letter dated August 14, 1944, "Letter from Home" file, Arizona Historical Society library, Tucson.

Williams, James A. *Oro Valley—The First Fifty Years,* publisher not identified, 2023.

Wilson, Bernard J. and Zaellotious A. Wilson. "From Maiden Lane to Gay Alley: Prostitutes and Prostitution in Tucson, 1880–1912." *The Journal of Arizona History,* 55 (Summer 2014): 167–186.

Wright, Harold B. *The Mine with the Iron Door.* New York: D. Appleton and Company, 1923.

Wright, Harold B. *Their Yesterdays.* Chicago: The Book Supply Company, 1912.

Newspapers

Arizona Desert Swarm (Tucson)
Arizona Republic (Phoenix)
Arizona Weekly Citizen, Arizona Daily Citizen, Arizona Citizen, Tucson Daily Citizen, and *Tucson Citizen* (Tucson)
Arizona Weekly Star and *Arizona Daily Star* (Tucson)
Arizona Wildcat (Tucson)
The Associated Press (New York City)
The Bisbee Daily Review
The Cleveland Plain Dealer
Cronkite News (Phoenix)
El Fronterizo (Tucson)
Phoenix Gazette
The Sun (Flagstaff, Arizona)
Tucson Weekly
TucsonSentinel.com
Weekly Phoenix Herald

Index

Numbers in ***bold italics*** indicate pages with illustrations

"A" Mountain 55, 91, 221, 228, 247, 275
A-7D Corsairs 161
A-10 161, 245, 247, 266, 289, 317*n*89, 320*n*93
Abbey, Edward 182, 312*n*24
Abendano, Gabriel 207
abortion 1, 139, 159, 284, 309*n*33, 310*n*39–42, 322*n*23–24; banned 20, 280; convicted 96, 303*n*22
Abrams, Herbert 248
Abusida, Dawud 240
Access Tucson 267
"the Acres" 281
Adams, Ansel 157, 195
Aeromar 267
Aerospace Maintenance and Regeneration Center (boneyard) 107
affordable living units 85, 281, 319*n*60
Afghanistan war 232, 247, 274, 317*n*89
Aguirre, Pedro 25
AIDS 175, 196–197, 207, 209, 241, 248, 267, 313*n*79–80
air conditioning 95, 119
air pollution/quality 136–137, 170, 181, 256, 312*n*19
air shows 139, 244, 287
aircraft accidents 104, 120, 136, 161–162, 179, 247
aircraft companies *see* Bombardier, Inc.; Consolidated Vultee Aircraft Corporation; Douglas Aircraft; Grand Central Aircraft; Hughes Aircraft; Learjet; Lockheed
aircraft noise 120, 162
AiResearch Manufacturing Company 185, 312*n*37
airfields *see* Davis-Monthan; Gilpin Airport; Marana Basic Flying School; Ryan Field; Tucson International (Municipal) Airport
airport security 162
Ajo, Arizona 42, 271
Alamito Company 199, 314*n*88–90; *see also* Tucson Electric Power (TEP)
Albuquerque, New Mexico 114, 178
Alianza Hispano-Americana 26, 81, 145, 300*n*24
All Souls "Day of the Dead" procession 287
Allegiant Air 267
Allen, John B. 14
AlphaGraphics 190
Amazon, Inc. 258–259, 284
American Airlines 219, 266
American Atomics Corporation 169
The American Magazine 61
Americans for Prosperity 266
Amlee, Richard 152, 157
Amos, Hank 254, 318*n*14
Amphitheater proposed city 123
Amphitheater School District 89, 123, 133, 147, 196, 222–223, 234, 265
Anderson, Elmer 85
Anderson, John 110, 307*n*49
Angel, Roger 179, ***180***, 273
annexation: before 1960 for Tucson 65, 97–98, 122–123, 129; since 1960 for Tucson 141–142, 188, 199, 254; 309*n*41; 313*n*50; 315*n*53; suburban communities 191, 215–216
annual rainfall 56, 171, 287
anti-war protests 134, 157, 293
Antigone Books 290
Apaches 7, 297
aquarium 211, 227–228
architect *see* Creighton, J.M.; Herreras, Eleazar; Holmes & Holmes; Jaastad, Henry O.; Joesler, Josias; Place, Roy; Rockfellow, Annie Graham; Trost, Henry
Ari on 4th Avenue 20
Arizona (MOVIE) 103
Arizona Air National Guard 162, 180, 245, 261
Arizona Attorney General 227, 236, 265, 278
Arizona ballot measures: casinos 237; immigrant related 183; other 58, 270; prohibition 81, 90
Arizona Bank 168
Arizona Board of Regents 91, 112, 146, 195, 221, 285, 307*n*61
Arizona Cancer Center 197, 207
Arizona Canning 232
Arizona capital city 20, 22, 49, 66, 148
Arizona Citizen 5; *see also Tucson Citizen*; *Weekly Citizen*
Arizona Corporation Commission 202
Arizona Daily Star 7, 27, 38, 49, 56, 59, 79, 106, 146, 162; Chinese 8, 23, 103; education 146, 234, 266; growth 26, 41–42, 98, 100, 123, 148, 151, 173, 225, 262; politics 43, 45–50, 152, 252; South Tucson 97–98; transportation 80, 269; University of Arizona 22, 112, 194, 285; water 28, 41, 94, 173, 175
Arizona Department of Transportation 189, 296
Arizona Diamondbacks 202, 238, 271
Arizona Friends of Chamber Music 273, 278
Arizona governors *see* Babbit, Bruce; Brewer, Jan; Brodie, Alexander; Castro, Raúl;

Index

Ducey, Doug; Fannin, Paul; Hobbs, Katie; Napolitano, Janet; Safford, A.P.K.; Symington, Fife; Zulich, C. Meyer
Arizona Highways 129
Arizona Historical Society (Society of Arizona Pioneers) 8, 145, 167, 192–193, 211, 227, 254, 290
Arizona Hut 88
Arizona Inn 88, 127
Arizona International Campus (AIC) 221
Arizona International Film Festival 237
Arizona Land Title and Trust Company 124
Arizona Motel (Tourist Court) 85, 94
Arizona National Guard 270, 293
Arizona School(s) for the Deaf and Blind 88, 196
Arizona-Sonora Desert Museum 2, 128, 166, 214, 237
Arizona state government 134, 154, 162, 233, 263
Arizona State Legislature 98, 154, 188, 302n72, 316n49; civil rights 118, 134; education 233–234, 263; Rio Nuevo 229, 253
Arizona State Museum 87, 157, 203, 227–228
Arizona state representatives *see* Cajero, Bernardo; Cajero, Carmen; Giffords, Gabrielle; Higuera, Jesus "Chuy"; Hutcheson, Etta Mae "Ma Hutch"; Kromko, John; Maynard, Ethel; Stephens, C.C.
Arizona State University (College) 112, 119, 145, 165, 263, 272, 288
Arizona statehood 27, 52, 55–57, 60, 138, 228, 303n16
Arizona Supreme Court 27, 133, 153, 183, 187, 280, 306n30
Arizona Territorial Legislature 9, 12, 15, 20, 27, 50, 59, 139
Arizona Territory 8–9, 17, 50
Arizona Theater Company 189, 273
Arizona (Tucson) Opera Company 166
Arizona Water Commission 170
Arizona Women's Christian Temperance Union (WCTU) 9, 59
Arizona's Women's Suffrage Association 27–28

Armory Park 28, 168, 178, 187, 301n3; *see also* Military Plaza; Washington Park
Arnold, John 285
art exhibits 203
Arthur, Jean 102
Ashcroft, John 236
Asian 222, 284, 286
Aspen fire 244, 247, 287
Asta, Ron 137, 151, 155, 188
astronomy 122, 147, 162, 179, 232, 245, 263, 289
asylum 271, 291, 323n85
The Atlantic Monthly 224
Atwood, Julius 63
Auslander, Edith 279
author *see* Abbey, Edward; Barnes, Will C.; Caldwell, Erskine; Carmony, Neil; Drachman, Roy; Fontana, Bernard "Bunny"; Granger, Byrd; Kalt, William D. III; Kelland, Clarence B.; Kingsolver, Barbara; Lautman, Mark; Martin, Patricia Preciado; Miller, Tom; Nabhan, Gary Paul; Niethammer, Carolyn; Officer, Jim; Otero, Lydia; Sheridan, Tom; Sonnichsen, C.L.; Warnock, John; Williams, James A.; Wright, Harold Bell
auto courts 77–78, 85, 94, 108
Automatic Teller Machines (ATMs) 174
automobile 33, 40, 47–48, 52, 77–79, 105, 181, 205; regulations 41, 74, 136–137; thefts 206, 240
average daily high temperature 287
Aviation Parkway 181, 189, 212
Avra Valley 161, 214–215, 242, 256, 260, 296, 298
Ayres, Jim 3, 246, 274
AZPM 232

B-24 104
B-47 119
Babbit, Bruce 178, 196, **197**
Baja Arizona 199
Baker, Calvin 262, 319n74
Baker, Laura 271
Baldenegro, Salomón 149, 156, 222, 237, 314n34, 317n59
Ballet Arizona 273
balloon-borne astronomy 232
bank robbery 193
Bankhead Highway 79
bankruptcies 167, 239, 257, 268
Banks-Reed, Laura 279
Banner Health 225, 256–257, 271

Barber, Ron 250
Barleycorn, Kevin 207
Barnes, Adia 288
Barnes, Will C. 139
Barnes, William H. 27
Barraza, Maclovio 212
Barrett, Brigetta 272
baseball major league teams *see* Arizona Diamondbacks; Chicago White Sox; Cleveland Indians; Colorado Rockies; Doby, Larry; Hi Corbett field; Leon, Eddie; Little League; NCAA championships; Tucson Electric Park; Tucson Padres; Tucson Sidewinders; Tucson Toros; Veeck, Bill
Basis school 265
basketball 40, 157, 195, 200, 239, 272–273; *see also* NCAA championships
Bass, Ed 223
Bates, Michael 200
Batiste, Fred 112
Batiste, Joe 112
Batteau, Elgie 89
Bayless, Charles 202
beans 87, 91
Bear Canyon 37
"Beat the Peak" 171
Beaudry, Bob 215
Bee, Tim 247, 249
Beigel, Allan 220
Beillard, Jerôme 207, **209**
Bell, Edward H. 161
Bennu asteroid 289
Ben's Bells Project 244
Benson, Arizona 18, 57, 78
Benton, Thomas Hart 145
Berger Memorial Fountain 65
Bernal, Louis 203
Bezos, Jeff 259
Bianco, Chris 253
bicentennial, Tucson 169, 275
bicycles 33, 240, 271
Biden, President Joe 278, 291, 323n85
Bierny, Jean-Paul 273, 279
Big 12 Conference 288
"bigger is better" philosophy 3, 67, 182
Bighorn fire 287
bighorn sheep 170, 250, 255–256
billboards 188, 242
Billman, Howard 22
Bingham, Elizabeth Dalkin 72
Bingham, Floyd 72
Bingham, Nephi 72
Binghampton 69, 72, 304n8
bingo 133, 166, 184–185, 210
biosphere 2 223–224, 256, 315n80

Blacks 11, 50, 81, 89, 140, 162; discrimination against 50, 59, 76, 89, 105–106, 110, 113, 117, 134, 155, 183; population 183, 208, 284, 286
Blaser, John 207
Boido, Dr. Rosa Goodrich 58, 303n22
Boleyn, D.J. "Jack" 44
Bombardier, Inc. 219
bombings 133, 206
Bonanno, Joe 108, 127, 133, 160, 193–194, 206, 229, 249
Bonanno, Salvatore 108
bonds 104, 141, 243, 256; school 147, 222; transportation 79–80, 126, 269; water 27, 65, 75
Bonillas, Ignacio 13, 16
Bookman's 191, 261
Booth, Ruth 166
bootleggers 59, 81
Border Conference 146
border crosser fatalities 183, 209, 235, 269–270; see also desert crossing deaths
border encounters 80, 118, 156, 184, 208, 235–236, *292*, 323n79, 323n84
border fence/wall 291; see also shipping containers
Border Patrol 81, 118, 208–209, 236, 270–271, 291–293; see also U.S. Border Patrol
border security 184, 293
Borderlands Theater Company 203
Borman, Frank **140**, 279
Bowman, Alex 272
Boy Scouts 127–128; see also Early, Mike; Greenberg, David; LaNoue, Michael
Boyd, J. Homer 114
Brennan, Brent 288
Brewer, Jan 270
Brichta, Augustus 24
Bricklayers, Masons and Plasters' Union 126
Brierly, Jack 127
Brnovich, Mark 278
Broadway (Boulevard) 66, 79, 93, 137, 172, 212, 227; originally Camp Street 15, 34
Brodie, Alexander 49–50
Bronson, Sharon 217
Brown, C.B. 78
Brown, Tom 147, 185, 248
Buckner, Adam 294
Buffalo Exchange 290
Bufkin, Don 206
Building and Land Committee 38, 48
Bullock, Wynn 157
Bullock fire 244
Burkett, Linda 208

Burr, Waldon 160
Burr-Brown Research Corporation 147, 185–186, 232
bus companies see Greyhound Bus; Old Pueblo Transit; Sun Tran; Tucson (Rapid) Transit
Bush, Pres. George W. 247, 249
Butterfield Route/Parkway 137, 172
Byailis, Refugia 25

Cabeza Prieta National Wildlife Refuge 271
cable TV 153, 188
cactus ferruginous pygmy owl 223, 243
"cactus power" political movement 151–152, 155, 171
Café Poca Cosa 289
Cajero, Bernardo 196
Cajero, Carmen 162, 196, **197**
Caldwell, Erskine 109
call centers 186, 219, 232, 258
Callahan, Harry 157
Calvillo, Ernest 194
Cameron, Ralph 55–56
Camp Dreamland 78
Camp Grant massacre 7, 8
Camp Lowell 13, 28; see also Fort Lowell
campaign finance 188
Campbell, Carolyn 223, **243**
Campbell Avenue Penetration Route 137; see also I-710; Kino Boulevard/Parkway
campgrounds 78
camps 62, 91, 93, 107, 280, 293
Cañada del Oro 71, 138, 170
Candrea, Mike 279
Canoa Ranch 217–218
Canyon Ranch 221
Carmony, Neil 204
Carnegie, Andrew 30
Carnegie Library 28, 38, 141, 210
Carondelet 256–257
Carpenter, Robert 252
Carr, Bill 128
Carrillo, Christopher 252
Carrillo, Leopoldo 14, 311n74
Carrillo, Raymond 103
Carrillo, Stephen 103
Carrillo's Gardens 14, 34, 40; see also Elysian Grove
Carter, Pres. Jimmy 162
Caruthers, Ed 146
Casa Alitas 271, 291–292
Casa Maria Free Kitchen 187, 281, 295
Casa Molina 289
Casas Adobes 143, 216, 241–242
casino 131, 205, 237, 268, 284; see also Casino del Sol;

Casino of the Sun; Desert Diamond Casino
Casino del Sol 237, 268
Casino of the Sun 131, 210, 237
Castillo, Joe 161
Castro, Raúl 139, 162, 274
Catalina foothills 1, 215
Catalina foothills proposed city 216
Catalina Foothills School District 158, 222
Catalina Park 36; see also Northside Park
Catalina State Park 170, 178, 217
Cataudella, Sean Kelly 247
catch and release program 291
Caterpillar Inc. 257–258
Catholic Church 12, 16–17, 239, 271, 291
cattle ranching 231
Cauthorn, Robert 151–152
Cavaleri, Joe 164, 273, 279
CBS 174
Celina-Fagen, Elizabeth 263
Celis, Isabel Mercedes 252, 317n6
census: in 19th century 7, 10; in 20th century 24, 66–67, 85, 98, 142, 208, 218; in 21st century 1, 225, 237
Center for Creative Photography 157, 195
Central Arizona Project (CAP) 2, 154, 177, 215, 242; allocation 138, 171, 260, 297; ballot initiatives 214–215; problems with 213–214, 242; recharge basins 2, 177, 214–215, 260, 298
Chamber of Commerce 38, 92, 147, 154–156, 221; on economy 119, 148, 260, 264, 296; on growth 66, 220; on transportation 172, 181; on water 99, 122, 152, 171; see also Tucson Metro Chamber of Commerce
Chana, Leonard 248
charter schools 222, 234, 262, 265, 286
"Chatter" publication 104
Chavez, Cesar 135, 235, 246
chemical fire engine 39, 44, 301n12
Chicago Tribune 16
Chicago White Sox 202, 238
children, murdered and missing see Celis, Isabel Mercedes; Fritz, Cathy; Fritz, Gretchen; Fritz, Wendy; Galez, Esther "Lizette"; Gonzalez, Maribel; Grajeda, Karen; Green, Christina-Taylor; Hoskinson, Vicki Lynn; Perry, Michael;

Pickett, Zosha Lee; Rowe, Alleen
Chinatown 8, 59; petition 23
Chinese 46–47, 60, 103, 169; business/social organizations 44, 81, 118, 156, 238, 302n34; discrimination against 8, 23, 58, 89–90; grocers 25, 32, 68, 75; immigration 23, 80–81, 118
Chinese Exclusion Act 23, 80
Church of Jesus Christ of Latter Day Saints 72; *see also* Mormons
Cinco de Mayo 203
Ciscomani, Juan 293
Citi Cards 200
Civilian Conservation Corps (CCC) 90, *91*, 92
Claassen, Susan 166
Clapton, Eric 164
Clarke, Ray 246
Clements, Christopher M. 252, 317n6
Cleveland Indians 100, 109, 200
Click, Jim 151, 204, 215
climate 18, 38, 52, 60, 64, 67, 108, 147; temperature 287; and tuberculosis 62
Clinton, Pres. Bill 203–204, *205*, 244
Club 21 262
Club Filarmonico Tucsonense 26
Clyde Wanslee Auto Sales 262
Coalition for Sonoran Desert Protection 223, 243
Cody, William F. "Buffalo Bill" 32
Coffman, Justin 213
Colonia Solana subdivision 66
Colorado River 11, 16, 98, 107, 122, 213, 260, 297
Colorado Rockies 100, 200, 238
Colossal Cave 54, *91*
Columbia University 224
Committee on Tolerance 117
Communism 133
Community Food Bank 187, 246, 279
comprehensive planning process (CPP) 154–155
comprehensive regional planning program 106
computers 190, 196
Comstock, Oliver 61–64
Confederate States of America 10–11, 14, 55
Congress Street 25–26, 41, 74, 168; as boundary 39, 57, 125, 143; businesses along 75, 77, 124; 143–144, 160, 253; Rio Nuevo 189, 211, 228; the Wedge 25–26

Congress Street School 24, 31
Congressional organic act 50
Congressional representatives, House *see* Barber, Ron; Cameron, Ralph; Ciscomani, Juan; Giffords, Gabrielle; Greenway, Isabella; Grijalva, Raúl; Kolbe, Jim; Pastor, Ed; Udall, Morris "Mo"; Udall, Stewart
Congressional representatives, Senate *see* DeConcini, Dennis; Kelly, Mark
Connie the elephant 254
Consolidated Bank 82
Consolidated Vultee Aircraft Corporation 104, 107, 119
construction jobs 136, 231, 257
contained growth 154
Continental Ranch (Peppertree Ranch) 193
cooling 95, 119
Copeland, Dr. Jack C. 159, 198
Copeland, Harold 208
copper mines 15, 121, 135, 220, 258, 284, 298; *see also* mining
Copper World Complex 284, 298
Corbett, Hiram S. "Hi" 67, 103, 109, 126
Corbett, J. Knox 24–25, 28, 47, 56, 125, 166
Corbett, Jim 152, 169
Corbett Lumberyard 25, 46; building 92, 290
Cordes, Kevin 272
Cordova House 145, 167
Coronado National Forest 36
Cosa Nostra 131, 133, 308n4; *see also* Mafia
Costie, Candy 195
cotton farming 121, 231
Cottonwood Properties 186, 188; *see also* Mehl, David; Mehl, George
COVID-19 275, 277–278, 280, 284–287, 290–291, 321n2
Cramer, Martha 208
Creighton, J.M. 112
crime rate 131, 160, 194, 206, 240, 252, 294
crimes 193, 206–207, 239, 294, 324n98; *see also* children, murdered and missing; multiple murders; murders
Crocker, Charles 9, 16
Cronly, Andrew 27, 301n29
Crook, George 6
Cross, Cheri 152
Crouch, Molly 104
Cruz, Juan 207
Cullen, Dr. Theresa 278
Cummings, Bryon 87
Curacao 261, 319n67

curfews 277
"Curving Arches" sculpture 195

Daniels, Hayzel B. 76
Davidson, Alexander 72
Davidson School 72
Davila, Suzana 289
Davis, James 81
Davis, Jefferson 10–11
Davis, Lew 134, 144
Davis, Samuel H. 69
Davis, William C. 31
Davis-Monthan Air Force Base (DM) 69, 71, 107, 159, 188, 261, 287; and A-10 245, 247, 266; accidents 104, 136, 161; economic impact 102, 186, 220, 244, 258, 289; noise 119, 136, 244–245; relocation proposals 120, 161; World War II 103–104; zoning restrictions around 120, 136, 161, 180
DeConcini, Dennis 162, 194
DeConcini, Evo 124, 127, 133, 194, 229
Deep Throat MOVIE 160
DeGrazia, Ted 127, 178, 254
de Kooning, Willem 193, 263
DellaGiustina, Dani 289
DeLong, W. J. 169
Depression 74, 85, 87, 90–91, 267
Dervish, Murad 293
desegregation lawsuit against TUSD 158, 265, 286
Desert Botanical Laboratory 36
desert crossing deaths 183, 209, 235, 291, 320n113; *see also* border crossing fatalities
Desert Diamond Casino 210
Desert Springs 217
Development Authority for Tucson's Economy (DATE) 148, 173
DeVry University 263
Diamond, Don 217, 274
DiCarlo, George 195
Dick, Benton 42–43
Dillinger, John 96, 306n44
disincorporation efforts 14, 198; *see also* South Tucson; Village of Tucson
DM50 289
Doakes, Elmira 94; *see also* "Lake Elmira"
Doakes, Jack 94
Doby, Larry 109, *110*
Dobyns, Henry 169, 311n79
dogs 13, 33, 182, 255
domestic violence 59, 205, 252
Douglas, Lewis W. 88

Douglas Aircraft 119
Douglass, Andrew Ellicott 65, 91, 146
Dove Mountain resort 238
downtown arts district 189
Downtown Business Association 211
downtown high-rises 57, 82, 123, 145, 168, 189
Downtown Kitchen & Cocktails 289
"Downtown Saturday Night" 211
Drachman, Emanuel 40, 57, 77
Drachman, Herbert 25
Drachman, Mose 24, 40, 49, 300n15
Drachman, Oliver 104, 107, 113, *116*, 126, 147, 206
Drachman, Roy 95, *116*, 197, 204, 248; on economy 110, 121, 147, 296; on growth 67, 182; Hughes Aircraft 114; on planning 185; profession 100, 113, 124; on sports 73, 121, 202; on transportation 93, 126; on urban renewal 114, 167
Drake, Michael 263
"drive until you qualify" philosophy 155, 260
drought: 19th century 6; 20th century 122, 127, 170; 21st century 242, 256, 260, 287, 323n62
Drown, Gradye 54
drug deaths 270, 294
Ducey, Doug 264, 270, 275, 277, 291, 321n11
Dunbar, Paul Laurence 59
Dunbar School 59, 89, 105, 117, 210, 290; *see also* John Spring School
Dupnik, Clarence 274
Dusenberry, Katie 151, 198

Eagle Flour Mill 32
Early, Mike 127; *see also* Boy Scouts
earthquake 5, 7, 149
"Easy Company" 120
Eckstrom, Dan 142, 198
"eco-raiders" 151
economic downturn: 19th century 5, 7, 24; 20th century 144; 21st century 228, 232, 241, 245, 252, 257–258, 260; *see also* Depression
economic/industrial development 148, 186, 219, 222, 258–259, 262
economic/industrial development individuals *see* Drachman, Roy;

Gonzales, Robert; Snell, Joe; Stephenson, William
economic/industrial development organizations *see* Development Authority for Tucson's Economy; Greater Tucson Economic Council; Regional Economic Redevelopment Corporation; Sunshine Climate Club; Tucson Boosters Club; Tucson Economic Development Corporation; Tucson Industrial Development Board; Tucson Industrial Development Enterprises Corporation; Tucson Regional Economic Opportunities 30
economic sectors 3, 187, 284
education funding 2, 158, 233–234, 262, 264, 266
educational qualifications for voting 49–50
eegee's 190, 313n53
Eggle, Kris 235
1891 Constitutional Convention 27
18th amendment 81
88-Crime 161
Eisenhower, Pres. Dwight D. 127
El Casino Ballroom 109, 203, 244, 290, 323n73
El Cine Plaza Theater 143, 160; *see also* Paramount; Rialto Theatre
El Con ("Elcon") Mall 143, 166, 174, 212, 230, 261, 290
El Conquistador Hotel 72–73, 117, 124, 143
El Dorado Hospital 159, 241
El Encanto Estates 66, 100, 111
El Mosquito newspaper 81
El Paso, Texas 57, 71, 76, 114, 238
El Paso & Southwestern Railroad 57, 89
El Presidio San Agustín del Tucson 1, 228, 290, 297; *see also* presidio
El Rio Coalition 149, 259
El Rio Community Health Center 253
El Rio Golf Course 149, 154, 259
El Tiradito (The Wishing Shrine) 168, 172, 311n75
El Tour de Tucson 200, 271
El Tucsonense newspaper 81
electric light company 19, 30, 99
elephants 165, 254, 294; *see also* Connie; Mapenzi; Meru; Nandi; Sabu; Shaba

Elfbrandt, Barbara 133
Elfbrandt, Vernon 133
Elias, Richard 279
Elliott, Sean 195
Elliott, William 23
Elysian Grove 40–41, 50, 54, 57–58; *see also* Carrillo's Gardens
"The Embrace" 289
"English-only ballot initiative" 183
Enke, Fred 146, 188
enrollment: greater than 30,000 2, 195, 221, 234, 263, 285; Pima Community College 157, 196, 222, 264, 286; school districts other than TUSD 265; Tucson Unified School District 50, 147, 196, 234, 265, 286; University of Arizona below 30,000 34, 40, 54, 73, 90, 122, 146, 157
Equal Suffrage Club 58
Estes, William, Jr. 217
ethnic population 1, 208, 260, 282, 284
ethnic studies 3, 235, 265, 320n90

F-4 Phantom 136, 161
F-16 180
F-35 Joint Strike Fighter 245, 266
fair market rent 280
Fan, Paula 278
Fannin, Paul 145
FC Tucson 271
Federal Emergency Relief Administration (FERA) 90–91
federal fiscal year 291, 293
Felix, Clarissa 162
Fenner, Dr. Hiram 33, 47, 60
fentanyl 270, 294–295
Festival of Books 238, 275, 287
Fiedler, Arthur 167
Fife, John 184, 235
filmmaking 102, 108, 139, 178, 206, 231
financial subsidy 219, 280
Finch, Leo 114
fire: business 41, 44, 63, 96–97, 114, 124, 203, 254, 289; forest 54, 244, 247, 287; Pioneer Hotel 159–160; threats of 38–39, 42
fire regulations 39, 41
fire station 38–39, 44, **45**, 169
firearms and ammunition, smuggled 293–294
Fireman, Bert 119
fireworks 13, 169, 287
First Christian Church 156

First Magnus Financial Corporation 232
Fisch, Jedd 288
Fish, Maria Wakefield 9
Fish/Stevens House 145
Fitzgerald, John 152
Flagg, Brian 187, 295
Flandrau planetarium 162, 211, 227
flight from traditional public schools 286
flooding 99, 137, 172, 212–213, 287
floodplains 170
Flores, Roy 234, 264
Flowing Wells Irrigation District 142
Flowing Wells proposed city 123
Flowing Wells School District 91, 120, 122–123, 158, 264, 266
Floyd, George 293
Fontana, Bernard "Bunny" 168, 181, *191*, 192, 273–274, 312*n*20
football *34*, 40, 73, 7, 121, 165, 194, 271, 288; Tucson bowl games 195, 238, 272; UA bowl games 2, 72, 202
Foothills Mall 190, 212, 261, 290
Ford, Chuck 162, 189, 274
Ford, Doris 183
foreclosures 227, 231, 267
forest fires 54, 244, 247, 287; *see also* Aspen fire; Bighorn fire; Bullock fire
Forsythe, Jack 278
Fort Bowie 6
Fort Lowell 28, 87, 128, 145; *see also* Camp Lowell
Fort Lowell Museum 290
Fourth Avenue 36, 47, 52, 75, 92, 227; riot 239
Fourth Avenue Street Fair 166, 275, 287
Fox Theater 77, 168, 189, 228, 253
Franco, Lorcuzo 25
Frank Borman Planetarium 140
Frazer, Robert 25
"Freehaven" proposed city 123
Fremont House 145, 168, 311*n*74; *see also* Sosa, Carrillo, Frémont House
Frey, Betty 204
Frey, William 158
Frias, Herminia 237
Fritz, Cathy 193
Fritz, Gretchen 131
Fritz, Wendy 131
Fulmer, Nat 48–49

Gabrielli, David 207
Gadsden Purchase 1, 4, 10, 128
Galaz, Esther "Lizette" 207
gambling, non–Indian 13–14, 32, 46–47, 82, 97, 129, 205
garbage 125, 181, 242, 255
Garbo, Michael 294
Garcia, George 222
Garcia, Margot 152
Garcia, Roy 153, 198
Garcia-Dugan, Margaret 235
Garimella, Suresh 285
Gaslight Theater 166
gasoline shortage 104, 174
Gay Alley 42–43, 47; *see also* prostitution
gays/homosexuals 156, 182, 207, 236
Gaza 293
Geary Act 23
GEICO 232, 284
Gem and Mineral Show 128, 237, 287
General Instruments Corporation 185
General Motors Corporation 185, 219
Gerald, Dr. Joe 277
Geronimo 6
Gibson, Johnny 103, 274
Giffords, Gabrielle 249–250, ***261***
Gila River 10, 199
Gilkinson, William 155
Gilpin Airport 120–121
Golden Pin [Bowling] Lanes 271
Golder, Lloyd III 138, 170
Golder Dam 138, 149, 170
golf courses 73, 149, 166, 186, 188, 238, 254–255, 272; Randolph 73, 91; *see also* El Rio Golf Course; Tucson County Club
golf tournaments 109, 179, 238
Gomez, José Luis 273
Gonzales, Ramon 279
Gonzalez, Maribel 252
Goodwill stores 261
government consolidation 142, 154, 188, 242
Goyette, C. Edgar 116
graduation rates 202, 265, 272
Graham, Timothy 240
Grajeda, Karen 207
Grand Canyon University 259–260
Grand Central Aircraft 119
Granger, Byrd 139
Graves, Randall 194
Greater Tucson Economic Council (GTEC) 233
Green, Christina-Taylor 250, 317*n*1

Green, Bishop Francis J. 159
Green Valley 1–2, 141, 190–191, 217, 220, 295; failed incorporation elections 153, 192, 215, 241; hospital 257, 280
Greenberg, David 127; *see also* Boy Scouts
Greenway, Isabella 88
Greve, Einar 199, 314*n*91
Greyhound Bus 253
Griffith, "Big Jim" 203, 273, 279
Grijalva, Adelita 158
Grijalva, Raquel 158
Grijalva, Raúl 149, 158, 183, 199, 217, 249
Groundwater Management Act 177
Grygutis, Barbara 164, ***165***, 189, 273
Guerra, Don 279
Guerrero, Lalo 203, ***204***, 248
gun smuggling 270, 293
Gutierrez, Luis 215, 242
Guymon, Michael 296

Hallas, Chuck 194
Hamilton, Charles 40–41
Hand, George 13–14, 204
Hansen, Greg 271
Hanson, George 273
Hardesty, Patrick 240
Harold Bell Wright Estates 52
Harris, John 72
Harrison, Pattie 164
Hart, Ann Weaver 262
Harvill, Richard 121, 134, 157
Haury, Agnese Nelms 263
Hayes, Pres. Rutherford B. 17
Headricks, Barry 161
Heakin, Richard J. 156
Hearst, William Randolph 54
heat-related deaths 287, 322*n*61
Hedtke, Elaine S. 208
Heeke, Dave 285
Heifetz, Jascha 77
Hein, Mike 228, 242
Heineman, Mrs. Simon 77
Heney, George Benjamin "Ben" ***43***, 44–49, 51
Herndon, Elsie P. 23
Herreras, Andres 64
Herreras, Eleazar 64, 82, ***83***, 85, 127, 167, 206; building inspector 87, 111, 127; viewpoints 143, 182
Herring, William 50
Hi Corbett field 100, 109, 139, 200
high schools by district: Amphitheater 89, 147, 223, 234; Basis 265; Catalina Foothills 158, 222; Catholic 234; Flowing Wells 122, Marana 158, 196; Sahuarita

147, 222, 265; Sunnyside 122, 196; Tanque Verde 234; Tucson High School 67, 76–77, 89, 112; Tucson Unified other than Tucson High 76–77, 122, 147; Vail 234, 287; *see also* Tucson High School
Higuera, Jesus "Chuy" 205
Hill, Robert 264
Himmel Park 91, 141, 145, 156, 244
Hirabayashi, Gordon 107, 306*n*34
Hirsch, Sid 279
Hispanic 82, 89, 183, 203; enrollment 222, 237, 263, 265, 286; population 1, 208, 260, 282, **283**, 284
Hispanic Chamber of Commerce 183
historic preservation 143, 168, 210, 227; *see also* San Xavier del Bac Mission church
Historical Sites Committee 125, 145, 309*n*52
Hite, Erik 240
Hobbs, Katie 280, 285, 291, 293
hockey 202, 271; *see also* Roadrunners
Hodgman, William 104
Hoefle, Melvin 87
Hoff, Charles 31
Hoff, Gus 28–30
Holbrook, Andrew 18
Holden, William 102
Holladay, Leonidas 31
Holmes & Holmes 44
Holub, Hugh 199
Home Depot 230
home ownership 218
home prices 216, 230–231, 267, 281
home rule 111, 295
home vacancy 267, 280
homeless 186, 221, 233, 262, 280, 313*n*45, 319*n*68
homicides 206, 239, 294; *see also* children, murdered and missing; multiple murders; murders
Hooton, James 152
Horne, Tom 3, 235, 265
horse and dog racing tracks 40, 165, 237, 271, 288
Hoskinson, Vicki Lynn 193, 313*n*61
Hospital Corporation of America 197
hospitality center 291
Hotel Congress 96
hotels 32, 78, 117, 134, 253, 268, 289
house, average new price 216, 230–231, 267

housing affordability 218, 267, 280–281
housing permits 99, 191, 231, 267, 281; *see also* single family housing permits
Howard, George 278
Hubble Space Telescope 179, 221, 245
Huckelberry, Chuck 164, 178; county administrator 217, 223, 241, 243, 255–256, 277, 279, 295
Hudbay Minerals, Inc. 284, 298
Hudbay's Copper World 298
Hudson, Charles 6
Hudson & Company bank 7, 8, 299*n*11
Huerta, Dolores 235
Huff, Sam Williams 247
Hughes, Howard 116
Hughes, Josephine Brawley 9, 27, 58
Hughes, Lewis C. 8, 23, 27
Hughes, Sam 14, 24
Hughes Aircraft 114, 116, 148, 175, 185–186, 215, 219; *see also* Raytheon
Humane Borders 235
Hummel, Don 117, 120, 122–123, 125–126, 141, 143–144
Humphery, Leticia Felix 162
Huppenthal, John 265
Hutcheson, Etta Mae "Ma Hutch" 117, 139, 163, **164**

I-10 126, 137, 143, 172, 181, 212, 259
I-11 259, 296
I-19 137, 229, 237, 259
I-710 172; *see also* Campbell Avenue Penetration Route; Kino Boulevard/Parkway
Iaeger, L.J.F., Jr. 38
IBM 173, 186, 200, 221, 232
illegal drugs 160, 240, 270, 296
immigration 23, 80–81, 118, 183–184, 235–236, 247, 269–271; *see also* BORDER CROSSING FATALITIES; border security; desert crossing deaths; Mexican deportations; sanctuary movement; S.B. 1070; U.S. Border Patrol
impact fees 152, 155, 216, 230
in-home instruction 286
In-N-Out Burger 230
incorporations, successful: Marana 153, Oro Valley 153, South Tucson 96–98, Sahuarita 216, Village of Tucson 13
incorporations, unsuccessful: Amphitheater 123; Casas

Adobes 216, 241–242; Catalina foothills 216, 295; Flowing Wells 123; "Freehaven" 123; Green Valley 2, 153, 191–192, 215, 241, 295; "Rincon Village" 111; "Santa Catalina" 111; Tortolita 216, 241–242; Vail 3, 215, 254, 295
Indian gaming 210, 237; *see also* bingo; Casino del Sol; Casino of the Sun; Desert Diamond Casino
Indian Wars 5, 7–8
inflatable dams 177
Invisible Theater 166
Iraq war 219, 232, 247, 274
Ironwood National Monument 244

Jaastad, Henry O. 82, 96, 98, 111
Jack the dog 44
Jacobus, Preston 49
Jácome, Alex 126, 189
Jácome, Carlos C. 26, 56, 75, 110
Jácome, Estella 105
Jacome Department Store 75, 110, 124, 188; *see also* La Bonanza
jail 96, 194, 278, 295
James Beard award 279
James Webb space telescope 279
Jamshidi, Minhaj 293
Jarvis, Francesca 139
J.C. Penney department store 75, 124, 143, 189, 229, 290
Jensen, Robert 234
Jews 89, 106, 113, 236, 247
Jimenez, Audrey 279
Joesler, Josias 71, 169
John Spring School 117; *see also* Dunbar School
Johnson, Carla L. 292
Johnson, Pres. Lyndon B. 134
Joint Technological Education District 234
Jones, Erin 293
Jones, John 227
Jordan, Mary Ann 118
Jose, Verlon M. 290, 293
Joyner, Conrad 198
Juan-Saunders, Vivian 237
Julia Keen School 114, 120, 136, 161
Juliani, Harry O. 86, 97–98
Juliani, Jerry 214
Juliani, Lucille 86, 95, 248
Juneteenth 50, 166, 295
Junior Chamber of Commerce 108

Kalt, William D. III 246
Kasmar, Chad 294

Katzenstein, William 41
Kautenburger, Lambert 142
KCNA radio 109
KDTU television 178
Keating, Charles H. 193
Keene, James 242
Kelland, Clarence B. 102
Kelly, Mark 249
Kennedy, Doug 152
Kennedy, Pres. John F. 127, 134
Kicanas, Bishop Gerald 5, 239, 274
King, Martin Luther, Jr. 134, 183
Kingsolver, Barbara 204, 246
Kino, Eusebio Francisco 193
Kino Boulevard/Parkway 172, 193, 232; see also Campbell Avenue Penetration Route; I-710
Kino Hospital 159, 197–198, 202, 207, 240–241, 256; see also Banner Health
Kipnis, Sam 97
Kirpnick, Alexander 209
Kitt, Katherine 68
Kitt Peak 122, 147, 162, 245, 263
Kivel, Joseph 124
Kmart 174, 261
Koffler, Henry 195, 221, 274
Kolb Road 123, 172
Kolbe, Jim 179, 186, **205**, 207, 220, 249, 279
KOPO television 128
Korean War 120–121
Krentz, Robert 270
Kromko, John 181, 217, 241
KTUC radio 77
KXCI radio 178

La Bonanza 75; see also Jacome Department Store
La Encantada shopping center 230
La Entrada housing project 168
La Fiesta de los Vaqueros 92, 279, 287; see also Tucson Rodeo
La Paloma resort (Westin) 186, 206, 267
La Placita development 167, 210
labor actions 135, 160, 173, 264; bus driver strikes 118–119, 135, 227, 269
Lago del Oro 138
"Lake Elmira" 94, 99, 137, 172–173, 212, 269
Lake Mead 260, 298
Lambert, Lee 264, 286
Lamm, Louis 120
land subsidence 138, 171, 177
Landau, Martin 206

Lang, Alan 205
LaNoue, Michael 127; see also Boy Scouts
Las Posadas 91, 273
Las Vegas, Nevada 237, 246, 259
Lauffer, Billy 133
Lauretta, Dante 289
Leach, R.B. 66
League of Women Voters 170
Learjet 173, 186, 219
Leatherwood, R.N. 9
Lee, Lorraine 237, **248**
Leon, Eddie 146
Lesco, Michelle 279
Lesher, Jan 295
Letcher, Mike 242
"Letter from Home" 104, 107
Levin, Alex 14, 33
Levin's Gardens 9, **10**, 14, 18
Levitz, Sam 110, 174, 248
Levy, David 179
Levy's Department Store 124, 143
Lewis, Deanna 182
libraries 141, 153, 157, 181, 196, 210; Carnegie 28, 30–31, 38, 188, 210, 301n38
Life magazine 131, 145
Liggins, Betty 274
Likins, Peter 221, 228, 234
Lindbergh, Charles 69
Lindsey, Ben 194
Lininger, Schuyler 152
literacy programs 204, 233
lithium battery firms 284
Little League 195
Lloyd, Tommy 288, 323n64
local sales tax 122, 141, 252, 266, 268; for transportation 182, 227, 254–255, 259, 296
Lockheed 220
Locomotive #1673 145, 244
Loft Theater 203, 206, 237
Loomis, Paul 225
Loop pedestrian/bicycle trail 178, 269
Lopez, Humberto 185
lost jobs 108, 121, 147, 254, 284, 287; in construction 231, 257; in manufacturing 219–220, 232
lotteries 46
Lowe, Bob 194
Lucky Wishbone 190
Lupino, Art 121
Lurie, Alan 223, 243

Macy's 290
Mafia 133, 249; see also Cosa Nostra
Magnus, Chris 294
Maiden Lane 13, 31, 42; see also prostitution

Main Avenue (Street) 8, 24, 39, 300n18
major economic sectors 3, 85, 187, 284, 296
Manning, Levi H. 31, 71, 82, 253
Mansfeld, Jacob 8, 22, 52
Mansfield, Eleanor 117
Mansfield (Mansfeld), Monte 52, 73, 98, 103, 113, **116**, 127; transportation involvement 79, 93, 126
manufacturing 147, 174, 185–186, 188, 219–220, 232, 286; promote 119, 148
Mapenzi the elephant 294
maquiladoras 148
Marana 153, 231, 241, 243, 261, 265, 295, 310n13; annexations 191, 215–216; population 1, 255, 281
Marana Basic Flying School/Air Base 103, 121
Marana School District 133, 158, 196
mariachi festival 166, 203, 237
Maricopa County 20, 138, 145, 238, 268
marijuana 160, 209, 232, 270
Marks, Jack 159
Marshall, Louise 65, 95
Marshall, Tom 65, 95
Martin, George **29**, 30
Martin, Jack 52
Martin, John B. 46
Martin, Patricia Preciado 192, 246
Martinez, Deborah 294
mask mandate 63, 277–278, 286
Mason, Tony 194
Mattia, Raymond 293
Maxwell, Morgan, Jr. 113, **140**, **163**, 279
Maxwell, Morgan, Sr. 105–106, 117, 146, 162, **163**, 178, 273; see also Dunbar School; John Spring School
Maynard, Ethel 140
McCain, Edward 273
McCartney, Linda 164, 206
McCormick, Ada P. 105
McCormick, J. Bryan 112
McCulloch Corporation 186, 220
McDonald, Aari 288
McDonough, Sharon 236
McGaffic, Cheryl 225
McGinnis, Lew 193
McKale, James Fred "Pop" 146
McKinnon, Ellen 208
McLoughlin, Emmett 155
McMath-Pierce solar telescope 263
median household income 262, 281, 284

Meeks, Joe 54
Megdal, Sharon 298
Mehl, David 186, 188; *see also* Cottonwood Properties
Mehl, George 186, 188; *see also* Cottonwood Properties
Meixner, Thomas 293
mental health 197, 240, 250
Mentzer, Anna 269
menudo 102
Menzies, Edward 104
Mercer, James 54
Meru the elephant 294
Mesa, Arizona 281
"Metropolis of Arizona" 18, 22, 33, 66, 298
Metropolitan Water District 214
Mexican American Studies (MAS) 3, 222, 235, 265, 315n73; *see also* Tucson Unified School District (TUSD)
Mexican food/restaurants 67, 178, 204, 232, 261–262, 290
Meyer, Charles 14
Meyer, J. Karl 148
Meyer Street 23, 81, 167
Mi Nidito 204
Mica Mountain High School 287
Microsoft 219
Midvale Farms (Park) 188, 190
migrants: in 20th century 80–81, 184, 209; in 21st century 235–236, 255, 270–271, 290–291
Mikelatis, Isabel Baffert 104
military aircraft 104, 120, 162, 179, 224, 247, 289
military casualties *see* Berger Memorial Fountain; Carrillo, Raymond; Carrillo, Stephen; Cataudella, Sean Kelly; Huff, Sam Williams; Lauffer, Billy; Moreno, Manuel; Olson, Patrick B.; Time, Tina
Military Plaza 28-31, 38; *see also* Armory Park, Washington Park
Miller, Ally 255
Miller, George 214, 216, 219, 274
Miller, Sean 239, 272, 288
Miller, Tom 279
minimum wage 220–221, 258, 284
mining 42, 54, 220, 231, 298; general industry 7, 32, 135, 173, 185, 219; *see also* copper mines
Miranda, Richard 242
Mission Gardens 227–228
Mission Road 181
Mission San Agustín and Convento 211, 227–228; *see also* San Augustín del Tucson Mission and Convento
MLK Apartments 134
MLK holiday 183
Model A Ford Club of America 273
Model Cities program 153
Molina's Midway 261
Monroe, Barbara 225
Monthan, Oscar 69
Moore, Ed 198, 217, 279
Moore, James P. 82
Moore, Josiah 210, *211*, 273
Moore, Yndia Smalley 82, 206
Morales, Linda 289
Moreno, Carlos 213
Moreno, Manuel 121
Moreno, Bishop Manuel D. 183, 239
Moreno, Ruben 105–106
Morgan, Ed 274
Mormons 71–72, 157; *see also* Church of Jesus Christ of Latter Day Saints
Morrow, Robert 117, 146
Mother Hubbard's Café 262
motorist deaths 296
Motorola 173
Mount Graham 179
Mount Hopkins 147, 162, 179, 218, 245, 263; *see also* Whipple observatory
Mount Lemmon 36, 139, 179, 206, 244, 247, 287, 301n2; highway 79–80, 107; *see also* forest fires; Summerhaven
Mountain Oyster Club 202
movie theaters 77, 143, 160, 166, 190, 203, 212, 230; closures 143, 203, 238; *see also* Fox Theater; Loft Theater; Rialto Theatre
Mowatt, Taryne 238
multiple murders 131, 194, 207, 225, 240, 252, 294
Municipal Utilities Management Authority (MUM) 154
murder rate 250, 294
murders 7, 18–19, 194, 235, 240, 252, 293–294, 311n47, 317n5; in 19th century 23; in 20th century 41, 131, 156, 193, 206–207; in 21st century 239, 253, 270; *see also* children, murdered and missing; multiple murders
Murillo, Lupita 279
Murphey, John W. 71–73, 87, 99
Murphy, Lew 152, 154, 161, 168, 178, 181, 183, 187–188
Murphyville 187
Myerson's White House Department Store 168

NAACP 134, 158
Nabhan, Gary Paul 279
NAFTA 220
Nakai, R. Carlos 246
Nandi the elephant 254
Napolitano, Janet **246**
NASA 245, 263, 289
Nasse, Jeffrey 322n51
National Association of Home Builders 281
national championship 287; *see also* NCAA championships
National Organization for Women 205
Native American 7, 156, 181, 184, 224, 237, 268, 286; discrimination against 89, 106; school 23; *see also* Apaches; Pascua Yaqui; Pascua Yaqui pueblo (village); Tohono O'odham (Papago); Yaqui Indians
natural rate of growth 2
Navarrette, Diego A. 196
NCAA academic ranking 202, 273, 288
NCAA championships 165 195, 200, 238, 271–272, 288; *see also* baseball; basketball; golf; softball
Neal, Annie Box 32
Neal, William 32
Neely, Stephen 194, 313n65
Neighborhood Coalition of Greater Tucson 198
Neighborhood Protection Amendment 181
Nelson, Clifford 71
neon signs 85, 94, 105, 121, 126
Niemann, Joseph 114
Niethammer, Carolyn 259
NIMBYs 218
9/11 236
Nixon, Pres. Richard 159
Nogales, Arizona 95, 209, 269
Nogales, Sonora 104, 139, 148, 270
Noland, Dr. Patricia 175
Norteño event 203
North Tucson Business Association 126
Northside Park 44, 47; *see also* Catalina Park
Northwest Healthcare 280
Northwest Medical Center 197
Northwest Medical Center Oro Valley 241
Nova Home Loans Arizona Bowl 272
nuclear attack 120
nuclear energy 169–170

nudity 133, 160
Nugent, Nora 73–74

Obama, Pres. Barack 250
observatories 65, 122, 147, 179, 196, 218, 245; *see also* Kitt Peak; Mount Graham; Mount Hopkins; Mount Lemmon; Steward Observatory; Whipple Observatory
Ochoa, Estevan 9, 12, 16, *17*, 19, 24, 192; *see also* Tully & Ochoa
Ochoa, Estevan, II 16, *17*
Ochoa, Juana 16
Ochoa, Lorena 238
Ochoa, Peter 192
Ochoa, Stephen 127
Ochoa Elementary School 5
Ochoa Street 5
O'Conor, Don Hugo 5, 297
Officer, Jim 169, 192
oil embargo 166
Old Main 22, 65, 111–113, 168
Old Pueblo Club 202
Old Pueblo Mexican Orchestra 91
Old Pueblo motto 47, 68
Old Pueblo Transit 118, 172
Old Tucson movie studio 108, 203, 288
Olofson, Blake 296
Olson, Lute 194, 239, 272, 279
Olson, Patrick B. 219
Olympians *see* Barrett, Brigetta; Bates, Michael; Batiste, Joe; Candrea, Mike; Caruthers, Ed; Cordes, Kevin; Costie, Candy; DiCarlo, George; Reilly, Shirley; Ruiz, Tracie; Schnell, Delaney; Strug, Kerri; Van Dyken, Amy
O'Neill, Kevin 239
O'Neill, Pauline Schindler 28
Opera House 46, 65
Operation Desert Storm 219
"Optics Valley" 245
Oracle, Arizona 32, 79, 223, 256
"Oracle Road Landing Ground for Airplanes" 69
Organized Charities 63–64
O'Rielly, "Buck" 185
O'Rielly, Frank 74, 113
O'Rielly's Auto 74
Oro Valley 1, 231, 243, 250, 252, 295; annexations 191, 215–216; early years 124, 153; growth 153, 217, 241, 255, 281
Oro Valley Acres 124
Oro Valley businesses 185–186, 241
Oro Valley Meet Yourself Festival 273

Ortega, Michael 295
Osburn, Kelsey 248
OSIRIS-REx space program 263, 289
Otero, Lydia 273
overdose deaths 270, 294
Overland Auto Company 65
Oyama, Henry 107, 118, 274
ozone 256

Pac–10 and Pac-12 conference 2, 165, 202, 272, 288, 321n134
Pacheco, Manuel 208, 221
Pacheco, Nabor 47, 50
Pacific Fruit Express 121
Pack, Arthur 128, 166
Packard, Ben Maré 244, 317n80
The Palms restaurant 73–74
Pantano, Arizona 18
Paramount 143; *see also* Cine Plaza Theater; Rialto Theatre
Park (Place) Mall 174, 212, 261, 290
Parker, O.C. 63
Pascua Yaqui 135, 156, 210, 237, 268, 284
Pascua Yaqui pueblo (village) *109*, 122, 131, 135, 184
Pastime Park 69, 96
Pastor, Ed 206
Pathfinder space craft 221
Patronato San Xavier 168, 192
Pat's drive-in 190
pedestrian deaths 42, 127, 269, 294, 296–297
pedestrians 269
Pedicone, John 264
pedophile priests 239
Pellon, Pedro C. 26
Penney, J. C. 124
per capita income 262, 284
per pupil spending 146, 262, 264, 287
Perkins, Clifford 80
Perry, Michael 193
Pershing, John J. 65
Peterson, Cele (née Fruitman) *88*, 228, 274; business 82, 109, 124, 143, 168
Peterson, Thomas H. 89
Peterson, Tom, Jr. 167
PFAS 261, 298, 319n64
Pfeffer, Newton 133
Pfeuffer, Roger 234–235
Phelps, Harlow 120
Phoenix, Arizona 31, 54, 63, 78–79, 114, 178, 199, 233, 238, 259–260; education spending 234, 266; income comparison with Tucson 148, 284; population 66–67, 123, 218–219; statehood 27
Phoenix Gazette 90
Phoenix Project 245, *246*

Pickett, Zosha Lee 193
Pickwick Inn 134
Pierce, President Franklin 10
Pima Association of Governments (PAG) 172, 225, 227, 315n4
Pima Community College 158, 183, 196, 222, 234, 278, 286–287, 293; board turmoil 157, 264; founding 146, 157; tuition 264; *see also* Flores, Roy; Jensen, Robert; Nasse, Jeffrey; Navarrette, Diego A.; Tang, Esther
Pima County Board of Supervisors 13, 202, 213, 246; controversy 142, 161, 217; environment 78, 136, 223, 256; growth and development projects 125, 151, 155, 170, 186, 218; incorporation attempts 97–98, 111, 123, 153; Kino Hospital 159, 198, 241; minority issues 50, 235; transportation 172, 181, 296; *see also* impact fees; Kino Hospital; Pima County Supervisors
Pima County courthouse 145, 168
Pima County fair 92
Pima County government 154, 255, 271
Pima County jail 96, 278, 295
Pima County Salvage Committee 105
Pima County Sheriff's Department 160, 183, 208, 274
Pima County Supervisors *see* Asta, Ron; Boyd, J. Homer; Bronson, Sharon; Castillo, Joe; Dusenberry, Katie; Eckstrom, Dan; Grijalva, Raúl; Joyner, Conrad; Kautenburger, Lambert; Moore, Ed; Ochoa, Estevan; Ronstadt, Joseph; Walker, E.S. "Bud"; Yetman, David
piñatas 278
Pioneer Hotel 82, 110, 117, 127, 133, 139, 141, 159; *see also* Steinfeld, Harold; Steinfeld, Margaret; Taylor, Lewis
Pittock, G.W. 30
Place, Roy 77, 92
Planned Parenthood 139, 159, 280
Poitier, Sidney 139
Polk, Shawntinice 248
Pollack, Elliott 218
polo 73, 92, 146
Polzer, Charles 193
Pooley, Don 238

population 57, 66, 113, 148, 155, 171, 230–231, 268, **282**, 284, 298; communities other than Tucson 153, 216, 241, 255, 281, 295; Pima County less than 500,000 6–7, 129; Pima County more than 500,000 2, 149, 185, 199, 218, 225, 259–260; Tucson less than 50,000 6–7, 17, 32, 36, 66, 100; Tucson more than 50,000 41–43, 60, 67, 98, 106, 122–123, 129, 142, 218, 281
population growth rate 2, 148–149, 260, 281–**282**
population projections: between 50,000 and one million for Pima County and Tucson 41–43, 67, 98, 106, 142, 149; greater than one million for Pima County 185, 218, 230, 260
pornography 143, 160
Poston, Charles D. 8–9
poverty 3, 68, 183–184, 227, 262, 284; children 220, 257; rate 187, 233
precipitation 5, 99, 170, 177–178, 260, 287
preschool vouchers 266, 320n92
Prescott, Arizona 20, 22, 49
presidential visits *see* Bush, George W.; Clinton, Bill; Eisenhower, Dwight D.; Hayes, Rutherford B.; Obama, Barack; Trump, Donald J.
presidio 1, 77, 297; *see also* El Presidio San Agustín del Tucson
Presidio museum 228, 290
Presidio Trust 290
"Prime Time" rapist 193
private schools 110, 286
prohibition 27, 59, 81–82, 90, 303n26
property crime 160, 252
prostitution 42–43, 160, 252; *see also* Gay Alley; Maiden Lane
Providence Service Corporation 253
public safety officers slain *see* Abendano, Gabriel; Anderson, John; Barleycorn, Kevin; Bell, Edward H.; Blaser, John; Boleyn, D. J. "Jack"; Brierly, Jack; Buckner, Adam; Calvillo, Ernest; Cruz, Juan; Eggle, Kris; Elliott, William; Gabrielli, David; Garbo, Michael; Graham, Timothy; Gravell,

Willis Henry "Bill"; Graves, Randall; Hardesty, Patrick; Headricks, Barry; Hite, Erik; Holbrook, Andrew; Katzenstein, William; Kirpnick, Alexander; Meeks, Joe; Mercer, James; Nelson, Clifford; Rebel, Ed; Ross, Jeffery; Smith, James; Terry, Brian D.; Valenzuela, John; Walker, John
Public Works Administration (PWA) 90–91
"Pueblo Plaza" 113
Pulitzer Prize 194
Purdie, Pearlie Mae 106
Pusch Ridge sheep population 250, 255–256

racial discrimination 89, 105, 107, 113, 118, 208; African Americans before 1950 50, 106, 110, 112; African Americans following 1950 117, 134, 157; Chinese 8, 59, 89; Mexican Americans 135, 183, 265; *see also* school segregation; segregation
racial makeup 1, 208, 284, 286
radiation 169
radio 77, 96, 279; *see also* KCNA; KTUC; KXCI
Rainbow Bridge 228
Randolph, Epes 73
Randolph Park 91, 109, 139, 141
rape 133, 193
rationing 104–105
Raytheon 200, 219, 232, 258, 284; *see also* Hughes Aircraft
Razo, Carlos 213
Readers Digest 138
Reagan, Pres. Ronald 184
Reaves, Alamo "Bitsy" 182
Rebel, Ed 194
recall elections 152, 205; communities other than Tucson 216, 241, 255; school districts 196, 222
recharge 2, 177, 214–215, 242, 260, 298
reclaimed sewage water 138, 243, 261
recycling 242
red-light running 294
Reed, Lonnie B. 108
Regional Transportation Authority (RTA) 225, 227, 268, 296
Reid Park Zoo 139, 165, 254–255, 294
Reilly, Shirley 272
Reis, Lydia 297
renewable–solar and wind–sources 256, 287

resale home price 218, 230, 267
Research Corporation 147, 195, 319n75
restaurant chefs *see* Bianco, Chris; Davila, Suzana; Wilder, Janos
restaurant establishments *see* Café Poca Cosa; eegee's; El Güero Canelo; Lucky Wishbone; Mexican food restaurants; Mi Nidito; The Palms; Pat's; Tack Room
Revelle, James 95
reversible lane 137, 172, 182, 213, 227; *see also* suicide lane
rezoning request 126, 151, 173, 198, 218
Rialto Theatre 77, 143, 160, 228, 253; *see also* Cine Plaza Theater; Paramount
Rich, Bobby 279
Richardson, Emanuel "Book" 272, 321n131
Rieke, Marcia 279
Rillito Creek (River) 72, 178, 224, 312n10
Rillito horse track 165, 289
Rillito-Pantano Parkway 137, 172, 181, 198
"Rincon Village" proposed city 111
Rio Nuevo project 168, 189, 211, 227–229, 252–253, 289–290, 298
Risner, Bill 128, **129**, 137, 227, 242, 268
Rita Ranch 188
road maintenance 254, 269; *see also* street maintenance
Roadrunners hockey team 271
Robbins, Robert C. 263, 285, 319n77
Rockfellow, Annie Graham 72
Rocking K 217
rodeo parade 139, 178, 203, 287; *see also* La Fiesta de los Vaqueros; Tucson Rodeo
Rodgers, Calbraith 54
Rodriguez, José Antonio Elena 270
Rodriguez, Rich 272
Roe v. Wade 159, 280
Rogers, Robin 225
Rogers, Will 92
Romero, Regina 255, 275, 277, 280–281, 295, 298
Ronstadt, Fred 5, 26, 28, 36, 56, 67, 127, 192
Ronstadt, Gilbert 108
Ronstadt, Joseph (Jose Maria) 26
Ronstadt, Linda 140, 164, 203, 246, 279
Ronstadt, Peter 194

Ronstadt Transit Center 213, 290
Roosevelt, Pres. Franklin D. 88, 90
Roosevelt, Pres. Theodore 36
Rose Bowl game 2, 202
Rosemont Mine 220, 258
Ross, Jeffery 194
Rothschild, Jonathan 252, 254, 262
Rowe, Alleen 131
Ruiz, Tracie 195
Rulney, Lisa 285
Russell, Frank E. 113
Ryan Field 103

Sabino Canyon 36, 54, **55**; 91, 99, 110, 244, 287
Sabino Springs 217
Sabu the elephant 165, 254
Safari Club International's Wildlife Museum 289
"Safe-Yield" 177, 260
Safford, A.P.K. 12–13, 15, 299n11
Safford School 64, 254
Saguaro National Monument (Park) 91, 139, 224
Sahuarita 1, 107, 231, 252, 255, 259, 280, 295; development 192, 216, 241, 281
Sahuarita School District 147, 222, 234, 265
St. Augustine Cathedral/Church 5, 16, 32, 118
St. Francis in the Foothills United Methodist Church 270
St. Joseph's Hospital 145, 257
St. Luke's in the Desert 63, 273
St. Martin's Center 187
St. Mary's Hospital 17, **62**, 257
Salazar, Altagracia 16, **17**
sales tax 141, 259; Pima County 182, 227, 268; State of Arizona 211, 229; Tucson 122, 140, 252, 254–255, 266, 296
Salmon, Dr. Sydney 207
saloon 14, 50, 59, 81
Salvatierra, Richard 89
Samaniego, Mariano 26
Samaniego House 145
San Augustín del Tucson Mission and Convento 181; see also Mission San Agustín and Convento
San Augustine School 42
San Manuel, Arizona 121, 220
San Xavier del Bac Mission church 15, 23, 60, 128, 170, 184, 273; rehabilitation 87, 168, 192, 206, 210
San Xavier festival 203
San Xavier Hotel 41

San Xavier Indian agency/reservation 15, 156, 184
Sanchez, H.T. 264
"sanctuary city" 255
sanctuary movement 184, 235, 270
Sanger, Margaret 139
sanitariums 62–63, 273
Santa Catalina Mountains 54, 61, 68, 71, 80, 99, 151, 287; part of federal agency 36
"Santa Catalina" proposed city 111
Santa Cruz Church 254
Santa Cruz River 4, 9, 14, 99
Santa Rita Hotel 38, 109, 185
Santa Rita Mountains 127, 284, 298
Sapphire Lounge 229
SB 1070 270
Schaefer, Helen 279
Schaefer, John P. 157, 166, 195, 199, 202, 285
Schecklebrooke 149, 190, 217
Schmid, Charles "Smitty" 131
Schnell, Delaney 288
school budget overrides 196, 222, 234, 266, 286
School District #1 trustees 9, 58–59, 158
school funding 158, 233, 262, 264, 310n37
school segregation 50, 59, 117, 158, 265, 286; see also racial discrimination; segregation
school superintendents other than TUSD see Baker, Calvin; Billman, Howard; Hill, Robert; Isquierdo, Manuel
school superintendents, TUSD see Celina-Fagen, Elizabeth; Garcia, George; Lee, Thomas; Morrow, Robert; Pedicone, John; Pfeuffer, Roger; Sanchez, H.T.; Truillo, Gabriel
Schorr, Eleanor 197
Schorr, S.L. 144, 197, 225
Science magazine 224
Scobee, Francis R. "Dick" 195
Scottsdale, Arizona 218, 231
sculptures see "Curving Arches"; "Sonora"; "The Tree of Life"
Sears 143, 186, 219, 261, 290
2nd Saturday Downtown 253
segregation 50, 59, 76, 113, 117, 134, 158; see also racial discrimination; school segregation
self-service gas stations 141, 190
Semien, Valerie 166
semiquincentennial **297**, 298

service sector employment 219, 231, 284
sewers, administration of 28–30, 36, 154
Shaba the elephant 254
Shaffer, Helen Urech 108
Shantz, Homer L. 92
Shelton, Robert 234, 262, 319n75
Sheraton El Conquistador 186, 267
Sheridan, Tom 192, 204
Sherman, William T. 17
shipping containers 291; see also border fence/wall
shopping centers 138, 142, 144, 295; malls 124, 143, 166, 174, 290; strip centers 65, 113, 124, 143, 229
Sierra Club 138
Sigworth, Heather 159
Silver Lake 14, 57
Simmons, Cicero 59; see also school segregation
single-family home prices 230–231, 267, 281
single-family housing permits 191, 231, 267, 281; see also housing permits
Siskind, Aaron 157
Slack, Charles 38
slavery 10, 166
Slim Fast 232
Smalley, George Herbert 81–82
Smith, Bradford 162
Smith, James 194
Smith, Peter 221, **246**
smugglers 209, 291
Snell, Joe 262
"Snob Hollow" 82
snow 108, 127, 170, 260
Snow, Craig 248
soccer 271, 287
softball 200, 238, 288; see also NCAA championships
solar energy 256, 287
"Solid Five" (Six) 45–47
Sommer, Frederick 157
Sonnichsen, C.L. 192
Sonora, Mexico 13, 19, 104, 139, 148, 266, 270
"Sonora" sculpture 210
Sonoran Corridor Highway 259
Sonoran Desert Conservation Plan 223, 243, 256
Sorenstam, Annika 238
Sosa, Carrillo, Frémont House 254, 290, 311n74; see also Fremont House
Sound of Music MOVIE 131
South Tucson 85, 123, 186, 203–204, 207, 216, 280, 295;

city council 97, 142, 242, 255, 294; incorporation 97–98; problems 142, 153, 198, 255; proposals to disincorporate 97, 198; *see also* disincorporation efforts; incorporations
Southern Arizona AIDS Foundation 207, 267
Southern Arizona Heritage & Visitor Center 290
Southern Arizona Hiking Club 166
Southern Arizona Homebuilders Association (SAHBA) 154, 216; positions on growth 171, 181, 223, 225, 230, 243
Southern Arizona Sports Development Corporation 200
Southern Pacific Railroad 5, 20, 25, 40, 42, 89, 128, 142, 210; before 1900 8–9, 15–17; 1900 to 1950 32, 58, 75, 85, 107; following 1950 125, 135, 145, 156, 190, 219; *see also* Ochoa, Estevan; Southern Pacific train station
Southern Pacific train station 9, 17, 26, 38, 41, 75, 120; replace/remodel 42, 105, 210, 229; *see also* Southern Pacific Railroad
Southside Presbyterian Church 184, 270
Southwest Air 71
Southwest Center for Biological Diversity 223
Southwest Gas Corporation 170
Spanish-American Independent Club of South Tucson 97
Spanish-American Mothers and Wives Association 104
Spanish Influenza epidemic 1, 63
Speedway (Boulevard) 52, 60, 127, 145, 149, 182; prior to 1950 39, 47, 65, 68
Spirit of St. Louis 69
sprawl 65, 68, 113, 149, 190, 196, 205, 218, 230; objections to 2, 151, 174, 234; prior to 1980 106, 131, 171, 174
Springerville generating plant 170, 199
Sputnik 120
Starr Pass resort 267
state sales tax receipts 211, 229
statehood 27, 52, 55–57, 60, 138, 228
"stay-at-home" order 275
Steinfeld, Albert 30, 40, 42, 50, 75, **76**, 96; views on change 32, 38, 67
Steinfeld, Harold **76**, 82, 113, 124, 126, 128, 141, 159; *see also* Pioneer Hotel
Steinfeld, Margaret 159
Steinfeld warehouse 42, 253
Steinfeld's Department Store 42, 57, 59, 88, 124, 128, 159, 168
Stephens, C.C. 20, 22
Stephenson, William 222
Steward, Lavinia 65
Steward Observatory 65, 196
Stone Avenue 25–26, 39, 73, 125; subway 75, 93–94, 99, 137, 173, 212, 269; *see also* "Lake Elmira"
street maintenance 227, 296; *see also* road maintenance
streetcar system 26, 31, 36, 227, 268
Strug, Kerri 200
Suarez, Felipa, Mrs. 135
subways: on Broadway 92–93, 137, 212; on Fourth Avenue 52, 75, 227; on Sixth Avenue 75, 92; on Stone Avenue 75, 93–94; *see also* "Lake Elmira"
suffrage 1, 9, 27, 49–50, 56, 58–59
Sugar Skulls 271
suicide lane 137, 227; *see also* reversible lane
Sullivan, Jim 166
Sullivan, John L. 111
Sullivan, Patrick 74
Sumlin, Kevin 272, 288
summer monsoon 5, 30, 94, 99, 173, 212
Summerhaven 206, 244, 287; *see also* Mount Lemmon
Summers, Richard 125
Sun City Vistoso (Rancho Vistoso) 190–191, 217
Sun Corridor 259
Sun Tran 172, 182, 227, 269
Sunday Evening Forum 178
Sung Kei 25
Sunnyside Junior High School 162
Sunnyside School District 158, 234, 266, 286; schools 65, 122, 133, 162, 196, 265
Sunshine Climate Club 67–68, 100, 113, 119, 147
"Sunshine Mile" 290
Supreme Cleaners 136
Symington, Fife 209, 213

Tack Room 190, 238
Taft, Pres. William Howard 55–57
Tang, Esther (née Don) 89, 118, 157, 204, **205**, 273–274; *see also* Pima Community College
Tanque Verde falls 178
Tanque Verde School District 196, 222, 234
Target 230
taxes 3, 202, 225, 230; on businesses 14, 97; on property 122, 167, 269; *see also* sales tax
Taylor, Louis 159–160, 310*n*46; *see also* Pioneer Hotel
teacher pay 264, 287
technology 80, 212, 232, 234, 253, 262, 267
telegraph 16, 300*n*47
telephone 114, 138, 161, 190, 300*n*47; prior to 1950 16, 31, 54, 67
television 128, 174, 190, 232, 267; *see also* ACCESS TUCSON; AZPM; KDTU; KOPO
temperance 9, 59
temperature 77, 95, 181, 256, 287, 322*n*60
Temple Emanu-El (original) 192
Temple of Music and Art 77, 167, 188–189
Tena, Maria Luisa 244
tennis 40
"Tentville" 62, 68
Territorial Legislature 9, 12, 15, 20, 27, 50, 59, 139
Terry, Brian D. 270, 320*n*117
testing site for COVID-19 277
Texas Instruments 232
Thomure, Tim 261, 295
time capsule 275, **297**, 321*n*1
Time magazine 117
Time, Tina 247
Titan missile 136, 179; museum 179
Title IX 156
Tohono O'odham (Papago) 23, 68, 156, 185, 203, 255, 293; gaming 184, 210, 237, 268; nation/reservation 60, 99, 118, 209, 291; *see also* Desert Diamond Casino; Johnson, Cara L.; Jose, Verlon M.; Juan-Saunders, Vivian; Moore, Josiah; San Xavier del Bac Mission church
Tombstone, Arizona 17–18, 198
Tomey, Dick 274
Toole, James 8, 14
tornado 170
Torres, Alva 102, 104, 279
Tortolita 216, 241–242
tourism 174, 187, 231, 258–259, 262, 277, 284, 295; facilities 99, 110, 186; promotion of 67, 119, 147, 154; statistics 119, 186,

220, 232, 257, 275; *see also* Sunshine Climate Club
track and field 40
traditional public schools 222, 286–287
traffic violations 74, 294
transit centers 213, 290
transportation elections 79, 126, 181–182, 198, 212, 225, 227, 259; *see also* Regional Transportation Authority (RTA)
transportation plans 137, 172, 182, 227, 259
Treatch, Cody 294
"The Tree of Life" sculpture 225
tree planting 295
Tree Ring Research lab 90, 263
Triano, Gary 206
trichloroethylene (TCE) 175, 177, 215, 312n3
Trost, Henry 31
truck bypass 125–126
Truillo, Gabriel 264
Truman, Pres. Harry S. 107
Trump, Pres. Donald J. 269, 271, 291
tuberculosis 60–61, **62**, 63, 68
Tucson (Rapid) Transit 118, 135
Tucson AIDS Project 196, 248
"Tucson Air" 180
Tucson Airport Authority 116, 215
Tucson Area Transportation Planning Agency 137
Tucson Arizona Boys Chorus 128
Tucson Artists' Coalition 189
Tucson Association of Realtors 281
Tucson Audubon Society 171, 224
Tucson Boosters Club 46
Tucson Botanical Gardens 139
Tucson Chamber Artists 273
Tucson Children's Museum 28, 210
Tucson Citizen 41, 57, 65, 73, 82, 84, 200, 206, 216, 245; border issues 81; on economy 77–78, 114, 218–219; on politics 45, 50; on prohibition 59; on projects 54, 79–80, 210, 228–229; out of business 249; sports-related 238–239; on water 60, 214; *see also Arizona Citizen*; *Weekly Citizen*
Tucson City (Village) Council members *see* Amlee, Richard; Cauthorn, Robert; Cross, Cheri; Ford, Chuck; Garcia, Margot; Hooton, James; Kennedy, Doug; Lininger, Schuyler; Linner, Marvin; Martin, John B.; McLoughlin, Emmett; Ochoa, Stephen; Phelps, Harlow; Summers, Richard; Weymann, Barbara
Tucson city charter 77, 141
Tucson City Council 14, 36, 42, 44, 50, 64, 120, 137, 154, 162, 187, 190–191, 247, 294, 298; annexation/incorporation 123, 142, 154, 242, 254; civil/human rights 134; committees 125, 157, 165, 169; downtown 28, 31, 60, 126, 141, 144–145, 168, 188–189, 227, 229, 253; economy 148, 296; employees 161, 215; fire 38–39, 41, 44; growth 151–152, 155, 185; impeachment 45–49; legislation 40–41, 43, 88, 230, 246; morality issues 13, 42–43, 160; transportation 33, 40–41, 94, 172, 181–182; water 28, 60, 97, 111, 151, 171, 177, 213–214, 242, 260; *see also* Central Arizona Project; Rio Nuevo; Tucson Village Council; urban renewal programs
Tucson City Hall 31, 36, 38, 44, 145, 187, 255
Tucson Commission on the Status of Women 157
Tucson Committee for Interracial Understanding 106
Tucson Convention Center (TCC) 167, 189, 229, 247, 253, 273, 279, 290; arena 229; hotel 253, 290
Tucson Corral of the Westerners 273
Tucson Country Club 113, 156, 236
Tucson Economic Development Corporation 173–174, 185, 222
Tucson Electric Park 238, 247; *see also* baseball
Tucson Electric Power (TEP) 183, 199, 202, 253, 256, 287, 295; *see also* Alamito Company; Tucson Gas, Electric Light and Power Company
Tucson Electric Power share price 202, 314n91
Tucson Festival Society 128, 166
Tucson Fire Department 157, 182, 236, 271; prior to 1910 18, 38–39, 41, 44, **45**, 48; *see also* fire station
Tucson Firefighters Association 207, 240
Tucson Folk Festival 202
Tucson founding location 5, 169, **297**
Tucson Gas, Electric Light and Power Company 99, 169; *see also* electric light companies; Tucson Electric Power (TEP)
Tucson Gem & Mineral Show 128, 178, 237, 287
Tucson General Hospital 207
Tucson Gila Monsters 202
Tucson Golf and Country Club 73
Tucson Greyhound Park 108, 271, 288
Tucson High School 67, 76–77, 107, 196, 279, 304n60; athletes 112, 135; marching band 92, 137, 145; racial issues 89, 135, 235
Tucson Indian School 22–23, 42, 146
Tucson Industrial Development Board 147
Tucson Industrial Development Enterprises Corporation (TIDE) 148
Tucson International (Municipal) Airport 114, 157, 161, 245, 261, 267, 320n95; passengers 180, 266, 275, 289; prior to 1940 71, 102; zoning around 136, 162; *see also* Arizona Air National Guard
Tucson Mall 188, 190, 212, 290
Tucson mayors *see* Allen, John B.; Corbett, Jim; Davis, Lew; Heney, George Benjamin "Ben"; Hoff, Gus; Hummel, Don; Jaastad, Henry O.; Jacobus, Preston; Leatherwood, R.N.; Manning, Levi H.; Miller, George; Murphy, Lew; Niemann, Joseph; Ochoa, Estevan; Parker, O.C.; Romero, Regina; Rothschild, Jonathan; Slack, Charles; Toole, James; Volgy, Tom; Walkup, Bob
Tucson Medical Center (TMC) 77, 257, 275, 280, 290
Tucson Meet Yourself 203, 289
Tucson Metro Chamber of Commerce 296; *see also* Chamber of Commerce
Tucson Mountain Park 78, 177
Tucson Museum of Art (Tucson Art Center) 141, 167, 203, 229, 244, 275, 289
Tucson Padres 238, 271
Tucson Pastorela 203

Tucson Poetry Festival 238
Tucson Police Department (TPD) 96–97, 133, 160, 239, 252; minority/women officers 108, 155, 183, 208; officers 23, 41, 153, 161, 194, 207, 240, 294; staffing levels 74, 155, 160, 240, 252, 252, 294
Tucson Police Officers Association 240
Tucson Pops Orchestra 237, 279
Tucson Premium Outlets 261
Tucson Regional Economic Opportunities (TREO) 233, 262
Tucson Rodeo 92, 139, 178, 203, 287; *see also* La Fiesta de los Vaqueros
Tucson Sash, Door & Mill Company 25
Tucson School District One 58, 74, 133, 146–147, 162; school segregation/integration 59, 89, 117, 158; schools 31, 72, 120, 161; *see also* Dunbar School; high schools; John Spring School; Julia Keen School; Tucson High School; Tucson Unified School District
Tucson Sector of U.S. Border Patrol 118, 156, 184, 208–209, 236, 270–271, 291–293
Tucson Sidewinders 238, 271
"Tucson Sunshine" the song 67
Tucson Symphony Orchestra 97, 166, 224, 237, 273
Tucson Tomorrow 185
Tucson Toros 139, 200, 271
Tucson Unified School District (TUSD) 3, 169, 210, 222, 263, 277; desegregation efforts and lawsuit 158, 265, 286; enrollment 50, 147, 196, 234, 265, 286; school closures 114, 235, 265; *see also* high schools, Mexican American Studies (MAS); Tucson High School; Tucson School District One
Tucson Village Council 13, 169; *see also* Tucson City Council
Tucson Water 91, 97, 151–152, 171, 175, 261, 312*n*7; Central Arizona Project (CAP) 177, 213–214, 242, 260, 314*n*35; *see also* Central Arizona Project (CAP); PFAS; reclaimed sewage water; trichloroethylene (TCE)
Tucson Weekly 189
Tucson Zoo Commission 165
tuition and fees 285; *see also* Pima Community College; University of Arizona tuition

Tully, Pinckney Randolph 10–11, 16–17, 19
Tully & Ochoa 11, 15–16, 18–19
TuSimple 258, 318*n*42
20th century 19–20, 32–34, 36, 52, 166, 205, 256
21st amendment 90
21st century 3, 20, 224, 239, 242, 265, 267–268, 295, 298

UA Art Museum 263, 313*n*63
UA Farms 290
UA Tech Park 200; 221; 232
UA Tech Park at the Bridges 232
Udall, Morris "Mo" 113, 138, 162, *164*, 179, 197, 206
Udall, Stewart 113, 138
Ukraine 284
Umbrella Lady 297
Umeh, McCollins "MC" 248
underground high-voltage line 295
"underwater" mortgages 231
undocumented people 80–81, 118, 156, 183–184, 194, 208–209, 235–236, 269–270
unemployment rate 148, 218, 231, 258, 275, 284
UNESCO City of Gastronomy 258–259
Union on 6th 20
Union Pacific Railroad 219
U.S. Air Force 114, 136, 162, 177, 244–245, 261, 266
U.S. Army Corps of Engineers 258
U.S. Border Patrol 81, 118, 208–209, 236, 270–271, 291–293; *see also* Border Patrol
U.S. Customs and Border Patrol 270
U.S. Defense (War) Department 94, 186, 232
U.S. Department of Health, Education and Welfare (HEW) 158
U.S. Environmental Protection Agency 175
U.S. Geological Survey 171
U.S. Highway 80 78, 94
U.S. Immigration Service 80
University Medical Center (UMC) 159, 225, 227, 250, 257; heart transplants 159, 198; and Kino Hospital 207, 241, 256; *see also* Copeland, Dr. Jack C.; Kino Hospital; multiple murders
University of Arizona 76, 85, 103, 183, 186, 219, 240, 247, 250, 289, 293; athletics other than football 34, 146, 200, 239, 271; campus buildings 22, 90, 111–112, 168, 195, 197; during pandemics 63, 275, 277–278, 288; football 2, *34*, 40, 54, 73, 121, 165, 194–195, 202, 238, 248, 272, 288; founding 20, 22; minority relations 112, 134, 156–157, 183, 236–237, 262–263, 286; observatories 65, 122, 162, 179, 245; *see also* baseball; basketball; Center for Creative Photography; football; Mount Graham; softball; Steward Observatory
University of Arizona Athletic Department 112, 194, 272, 285, 288
University of Arizona band 73, 146
University of Arizona Bio Park 232
University of Arizona enrollment: between 1 and 10,000 22, 34, 40, 54, 73, 90; between 10,000 and 30,000 122, 146, 157; more than 30,000 2, 195, 234, 263, 285
University of Arizona enrollment cap 195, 221, 234
University of Arizona Health Network 256, 317*n*69
University of Arizona medical school 145–146
University of Arizona Poetry Center 273
University of Arizona presidents *see* Hart, Ann Weaver; Harvill, Richard; Koffler, Henry; Likins, Peter; McCormick, J. Bryan; Pacheco, Manuel; Robbins, Robert C.; Schaefer, John P.; Shantz, Homer L.; Shelton, Robert; Wilde, Arthur H.
University of Arizona Press 139
University of Arizona school colors 34, 40, 195
University of Arizona Science Center (Universe of Discovery) 211, 227–228
University of Arizona scientists *see* Angel, Roger; DellaGiustina, Dani; Douglass, Andrew Ellicott; Drake, Michael; Lauretta, Dante; Smith, Bradford; Smith, Peter
University of Arizona tuition 34, 195, 221, 234, 263, 285–286
University Physicians Incorporated 241, 317*n*69
"Up with People" 203
urban renewal programs 59–60, 125, 143–146, 167, 172

US Bank 253
USO 105

vaccine 277–278
Vail, Banning 54
Vail community 1–3, 215, 231, 254, 281, 295
Vail School District 196, 222, 234, 262, 265, 286–287
Valdez, Joel 215, 279
Valenzuela, John 207
Valley of the Moon 128, 289
vandalism 151, 239, 293
Van Dyken, Amy 200
Van Harlingen, James 82–83, 85
Van Hulse, Camil 166
Van Loan, Jack 157
Varga, John 152
variant of COVID-19 277–278
Varney, Mike 264
Vector Space Systems 258
Veeck, Bill 109; *see also* Cleveland Indians
Velasco, Carlos 26
Ventana Canyon resort (Loews) 186
Veres, László 237, 279
Vest, Marshall 186, 230, 258
Veterans Hospital 96
victims 48, 62, 68, 196, 269, 297; of murder 247, 289
Vietnam War 133–134, 157
Villa, Pancho 193
Village of Tucson 13, 169; *see also* disincorporation efforts; incorporations
Villegas, Shirley 242
Vito, Martha 167
Volgy, Tom 182, 188
von Petersdorff, Charles F. 64
voter initiative and other petitions 11, 23, 38, 42, 73, 78, 94, 134; incorporation 14, 97–98, 111, 123; Old Main 112; prohibition 81, 90; water 177, 214
voting 2, 138, 227, 298; regulations 9, 27, 58, 236; snafu 215
Vyas, Manoj 217

wages 219, 227; high 32, 117, 135, 148, 220; low 174, 187, 218, 233, 258, 267, 284
Waila Festival 203
Walden Grove High School 265
Walgreen's 229
Walker, E.S. "Bud" 198
Walker, John 161
Walker, Milo "Swede" 96
Walkup, Bob 215, 225, 236, 242, 244, 246, 252, 279
Wall Street Journal 148
Walmart 190, 261

Walsh, James 127
warmest years 256, 287
Warnock, John 273
Warren, Scott 270–271
Washington Park 38, 44, 57, 301n3; *see also* Armory Park; Military Plaza
water 54, 58, 72, 78, 94–95, 97, 170, 184; availability 3, 5, 39, 99, 174, 260, 297–298; Central Arizona Project 2, 98, 138, 154, 171, 213–215, 242, 260; conservation 60, 171; emergency 235, 271; quality 175, 177, 261, 298; rates 151–152; system expansion 27–28, 36, 40–41, 65, 75, 111, 122; *see also* Central Arizona Project (CAP); land subsidence; PFAS; reclaimed sewage water; "Safe-Yield"; trichloroethylene (TCE); water pollution
Water Consumer Protection Act 2, 214
water pollution 175, 177, 215, 261, 298, 319n64; *see also* trichloroethylene (TCE); PFAS
Water Resources Research Center 298
weather 5, 11, 110, 170
Webster, Calvin 134
the Wedge 25–26, 41–42
Weekly Citizen 9, 33; *see also* *Arizona Citizen*; *Tucson Citizen*
Weisenburger, Bishop Edward 274
Weiser Lock 186, 232
Welp, Theodore M. 199
West University Neighborhood Association 191
Western Athletic Conference 146
westside museum complex 189, 211, 228, 298
Weymann, Barbara 151–152
Wheatley, W.T. 44
Wheeler, Harry 47
Whipple Observatory 179, 218; *see also* Mount Hopkins
Whipple, Fred Lawrence 179
White, Chase 252
White House Department Store 168
whites: in 19th century 7, 11; in 20th century 46, 50, 59, 89, 105, 109; in 21st century 208, 282, 284, 286
Whitwell Hospital or "Sanatorium for Diseases of the Lungs and Throat" 44, 63
Wilbur the Wildcat 121
Wildcats 54, 73, 165

Wilde, Arthur H. 54
Wilder, Janos 229, 289, 323n72
Williams, Gary 279
Williams, James A. 295
Williams, Willie 146
Williams Addition 66
Williams Centre 193
Wilson, Tom 215
Wilson, Pres. Woodrow 60
Wingspan 267
Winslow, Bob 112
Winterhaven festival of lights 166, 287
Wishing Shrine *see* El Tiradito
"Woman-Ochre" painting 263
WomanKraft 290
women 34, 52, 74, 103–104, 131, 169, 200, 274; 19th century 7, 9, 13, 27; 1900 to 1950 40, 43, 46, 49–50, 58–59, 63, 89, 95; 1950 to 1999 117, 133, 139, 155–157, 159, 182–183, 205, 208; 21st century 236, 247, 264, 269, 271–272, 279
Women's Christian Temperance Union 9, 27, 59
women's suffrage *see* suffrage
Woods, Charles "Punch" 246, 279
Works Progress Administration (WPA) 90–91
World War I 64, 85, 88
World War II 103, 106, 110, 113, 119
Wright, Bruce 259
Wright, Harold Bell 52, 60, **61**, 63–65, 68, 77

Yaqui Indians 71, 91, 255; gaming 184, 210, 237, 268, 284; reservation/tribal status 131, 135, 156, 184; village **109**, 122, 184; *see also* Casino del Sol; Casino of the Sun; Frias, Herminia; Pascua Yaqui pueblo (village)
Yetman, David 155, 198–199
Yocum, Harrison 139
"Youth on Their Own" 244
Yunt, Bud 95
Yunt, John 94
Yunt, Ruth 94
YWCA 273

Zeller, Olive 96
Zimmerman, Tony 206
zoning 136, 161, 180; city of Tucson 111, 120, 126, 168; Pima County 111, 128, 151, 173, 198, 218
Zuckerman, Enid 221; *see also* Canyon Ranch
Zuckerman, Mel 221; *see also* Canyon Ranch

www.ingramcontent.com/pod-product-compliance
Lightning Source LLC
Chambersburg PA
CBHW060335010526
44117CB00017B/2834